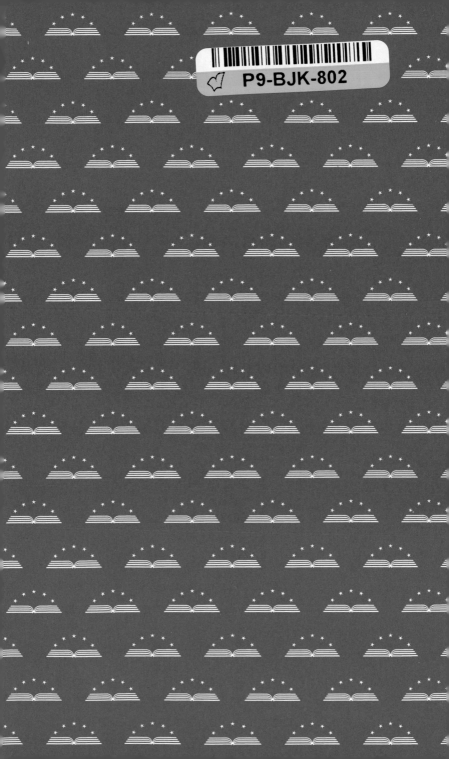

John Adams

JOHN ADAMS

REVOLUTIONARY WRITINGS
1755–1775

Gordon Wood, editor

THE LIBRARY OF AMERICA

The paper used in this publication meets the
minimum requirements of the American National Standard for
Information Sciences-Permanence of Paper for Printed
Library Materials, ANSI Z39.48—1984

Distributed to the trade in the United States
by Penguin Group (USA) Inc.
and in Canada by Penguin Books Canada Ltd.

Library of Congress Control Number: 2010930470
ISBN: 978-1-59853-089-6

First Printing
The Library of America—213

Manufactured in the United States of America

John Adams: Revolutionary Writings 1755–1775
is kept in print in honor of

JAMES GRANT

a dear and observant friend

with a gift
to the Guardians of American Letters Fund,
established by The Library of America
to ensure that every volume in the series
will be permanently available.

John Adams: Revolutionary Writings 1755–1775
is published with support from

THE ANDREW W. MELLON FOUNDATION

and

THE BODMAN FOUNDATION

Contents

LAWYER AND PATRIOT
1755–1774

To Nathan Webb

Dear sir   Worcester Octr: 12th: I believe, 1755

All that part of Creation that lies within our observation is liable to Change. Even mighty States and kingdoms, are not exempted. If we look into History we shall find some nations rising from contemptible beginnings, and spreading their influence, 'till the whole Globe is subjected to their sway. When they have reach'd the summit of Grandeur, some minute and unsuspected Cause commonly effects their Ruin, and the Empire of the world is transferr'd to some other place. Immortal Rome was at first but an insignificant Village, inhabited only by a few abandoned Ruffins, but by degrees it rose to a stupendous Height, and excell'd in Arts and Arms all the Nations that præceeded it. But the demolition of Carthage (what one should think would have establish'd it in supream dominion) by removing all danger, suffer'd it to sink into debauchery, and made it att length an easy prey to Barbarians.—England Immediately, upon this began to increase (the particular, and minute causes of which I am not Historian enough to trace) in Power and magnificence, and is now the greatest Nation upon the globe.—Soon after the Reformation a few people came over into this new world for Concience sake. Perhaps this (apparently) trivial incident, may transfer the great seat of Empire into America. It looks likely to me. For if we can remove the turbulent Gallicks, our People according to the exactest Computations, will in another Century, become more numerous than England itself. Should this be the Case, since we have (I may say) all the naval Stores of the Nation in our hands, it will be easy to obtain the mastery of the seas, and then the united force of all Europe, will not be able to subdue us. The only way to keep us from setting up for ourselves, is to disunite Us. Divide et impera. Keep us in distinct Colonies, and then, some great men, in each Colony, desiring the Monarchy of the Whole, they will destroy each others influence and keep the Country in Equilibrio.

Be not surprised that I am turn'd Politician. This whole

3

town is immers'd in Politicks. The interests of Nations, and all the dira of War, make the subject of every Conversation. I set and hear, and after having been led thro' a maze of sage observations, I some times retire, and by laying things together, form some reflections pleasing to myself. The produce of one of these reveries, You have read above. Different employment and different objects may have drawn your thoughts other ways. I shall think myself happy if in your turn, you communicate your Lucubrations to me. I wrote you, some time since, and have waited, with impatience, for an answer, but have been disappointed. I hope that Lady at Barnstable, has not made you forget your Friends. Friendship, I take it, is one of the distinguishing Glorys of man. And the Creature that is insensible of its Charms, tho he may wear the shape, of Man, is unworthy of the Character. In this, perhaps, we bear a nearer resemblance of unbodied intelligences than any thing else. From this I expect to receive the Cheif happiness of my future life, and am sorry that fortune has thrown me at such a distance from those of my Friends who have the highest place in my affections. But thus it is; and I must submit. But I hope e'er long to return and live in that happy familiarity, that has from earliest infancy subsisted between yourself, and affectionate Friend,

John Adams

Quincy April 22 1807. Nathan Webb was the Son of the late Deacon Jonathan Webb of Quincy and the Grandson of Benjamin Webb of the same place. The Father and Grandfather were intimate Friends of my Father and Grandfather, and the Grandson was my Playfellow at the Grammar School in Braintree, and my Contemporary at Colledge. He had Wit, humour and good Nature, equal to his Understanding And Judgment which were very good. He died young, and I attended him in his last Sickness, with equal Grief and assiduity, and watched with him a Night or two before his death. He left this Letter and some others in possession of his Father, who left it with his whole Estate to his Nephew, Captain Jonathan Webb, now of this Town living in the old Seat of the Family, who about a fortnight ago was kind enough to send it to me, after it had

lain fifty one years and an half among the Papers of the Family
in Oblivion. It was written soon after I took my first degree at
Colledge, and some days before I was twenty years old.
Nathan was named after his Unkle Nathan Webb the Minister
of Uxbridge, who married my Fathers Sister.

John Adams

From the Diary:
February 11–March 29, 1756

11 WEDNESDAY.

Serene Weather, but somewhat cool. I am constantly forming, but never executing good resolutions. I take great Pleasure, in viewing and examining the magnificent Prospects of
Nature, that lie before us in this Town. If I cast my Eyes one
Way, I am entertained with the Savage and unsightly appearance of naked woods and leafless Forests. In another place a
chain of broken and irregular mountains, throws my mind into
a pleasing kind of astonishment. But if I turn my self round, I
perceive a wide extensive Tract before me, made up of Woods,
and meadows, wandring streams, and barren Planes, covered
in various places by herds of grazing Cattle, and terminated by
the distant View of the Town.

February 11, 1756

16 MONDAY.

A most beautiful morning. We have the most moderate
Winter that ever was known in this country. For a long time
together we have had serene and temperate Weather and all
the Roads perfectly settled and smooth like Summer.—The
Church of Rome has made it an Article of Faith that no man
can be saved out of their Church, and all other religious Sects
approach to this dreadfull opinion in proportion to their Ignorance, and the Influence of ignorant or wicked Priests. Still
reading the Independent Whigg. Oh! that I could wear out of
my mind every mean and base affectation, conquer my natural

Pride and Self Conceit, expect no more defference from my fellows than I deserve, acquire that meekness, and humility, which are the sure marks and Characters of a great and generous Soul, and subdue every unworthy Passion and treat all men as I wish to be treated by all. How happy should I then be, in the favour and good will of all honest men, and the sure prospect of a happy immortality!

February 16, 1756

18 WEDNESDAY.

A charming morning. My Classmate Gardner drank Tea with me. Spent an Hour in the beginning of the evening at Major Gardiners, where it was thought that the design of Christianity was not to make men good Riddle Solvers or good mystery mongers, but good men, good majestrates and good Subjects, good Husbands and good Wives, good Parents and good Children, good masters and good servants. The following Question may be answered some time or other—viz. Where do we find a præcept in the Gospell, requiring Ecclesiastical Synods, Convocations, Councils, Decrees, Creeds, Confessions, Oaths, Subscriptions and whole Cartloads of other trumpery, that we find Religion incumbered with in these Days?

February 18, 1756

19 THURSDAY.

No man is intirely free from weakness and imperfection in this life. Men of the most exalted Genius and active minds, are generally perfect slaves to the Love of Fame. They sometimes descend to as mean tricks and artifices, in pursuit of Honour or Reputation, as the Miser descends to, in pursuit of Gold. The greatest men have been the most envious, malicious, and revengeful. The miser toils by night and Day, fasts and watches, till he emaciates his Body, to fatten his purse and increase his coffers. The ambitious man rolls and tumbles in his bed, a stranger to refreshing sleep and repose thro anxiety about a preferment he has in view. The Phylosopher sweats and labours at his Book, and ruminates in his closet, till his bearded and grim Countenance exhibit the effigies of pale Want and Care, and Death, in quest of hard Words, solemn nonsense, and ridiculous grimace. The gay Gentleman rambles over half the Globe, Buys one Thing and Steals another, murders one man, and disables another, and gets his own limbs and head broke, for a few transitory flashes of happiness. Is this perfection, or downright madness and distraction?—A cold day.

February 19, 1756

22 SUNDAY.

Suppos a nation in some distant Region, should take the Bible for their only law Book, and every member should regulate his conduct by the precepts there exhibited. Every member would be obliged in Concience to temperance and frugality and industry, to justice and kindness and Charity towards his fellow men, and to Piety and Love, and reverence towards almighty God. In this Commonwealth, no man would impair his health by Gluttony, drunkenness, or Lust—no man would sacrifice his most precious time to cards, or any other trifling and mean amusement—no man would steal or lie or any way defraud his neighbour, but would live in peace and good will with all men—no man would blaspheme his maker or prophane his Worship, but a rational and manly, a sincere and unaffected Piety and devotion, would reign in all hearts. What a Eutopa, what a Paradise would this region be. Heard Thayer all Day. He preach'd well.

Spent the Evening at Coll. Chandlers, with Putnam, Gardiner, Thayer, the Dr. and his Lady, in Conversation, upon the present scituation of publick affairs, with a few observations concerning Heroes and great Commanders. Alexander, Charles 12th., Cromwel.

February 22, 1756

2 TUESDAY.

A snow fall last night, half leg deep. Began this afternoon, my 3rd. quarter. The great and almighty Author of nature, who at first established those rules which regulate the World, can as easily Suspend those Laws whenever his providence sees sufficient reason for such suspension. This can be no objection, then, to the miracles of J C. Altho' some very thoughtfull, and contemplative men among the heathen, attained a strong persuasion of the great Principles of Religion, yet the far greater number having little time for speculation, gradually sunk in to the grossest Opinions and the grossest Practices. These therefore could not be made to embrace the true religion, till their attention was roused by some astonishing and miraculous appearances. The reasonings of Phylosophers having nothing surprizing in them, could not overcome the force of Prejudice, Custom, Passion, and Bigotry. But when wise and virtuous men, commisioned from heaven, by miracles awakened mens attention to their Reasonings the force of Truth made its way, with ease to their minds.

March 2, 1756

3 WEDNESDAY.

Fair Weather. Natural Phylosophy is the Art of deducing the generall laws and properties of material substances, from a series of analogous observations. The manner of reasoning in this art is not strictly demonstrative, and by Consequence the knowledge hence acquired, not absolutely Scientifical, because the facts that we reason upon, are perceived by Sence and not by the internal Action of the mind Contemplating its Ideas. But these Facts being presumed true in the form of Axioms, subsequent reasonings about them may be in the strictest sence, scientifical. This Art informs us, in what manner bodies will influence us and each other in given Circumstances, and so teaches us, to avoid the noxious and imbrace the beneficial qualities of matter. By this Art too, many curious Engines have been constructed to facilitate Business, to avert impending Calamities, and to procure desired advantages.

March 3, 1756

15 MONDAY.

I sometimes, in my sprightly moments, consider my self, in my great Chair at School, as some Dictator at the head of a commonwealth. In this little State I can discover all the great Genius's, all the surprizing actions and revolutions of the great World in miniature. I have severall renowned Generalls but 3 feet high, and several deep-projecting Politicians in peticoats. I have others catching and dissecting Flies, accumulating remarkable pebbles, cockle shells &c., with as ardent Curiosity as any Virtuoso in the royal society. Some rattle and Thunder out A, B, C, with as much Fire and impetuosity, as Alexander fought, and very often sit down and cry as heartily, upon being out spelt, as Cesar did, when at Alexanders sepulchre he recollected that the Macedonian Hero had conquered the World before his Age. At one Table sits Mr. Insipid foppling and fluttering, spinning his whirligig, or playing with his fingers as gaily and wittily as any frenchified coxcomb brandishes his Cane or rattles his snuff box. At another sitts the polemical Divine, plodding and wrangling in his mind about Adam's fall in which we sinned all as his primmer has it. In short my little school like the great World, is made up of Kings, Politicians, Divines, L.D., Fops, Buffoons, Fidlers, Sychophants, Fools, Coxcombs, chimney sweepers, and every other Character drawn in History or seen in the World. Is it not then the highest Pleasure my Friend to preside in this little World, to bestow the proper applause upon virtuous and generous Actions, to blame and punish every vicious and contracted Trick, to wear out of the tender mind every thing that is mean and little, and fire the new born soul with a noble ardor and Emulation. The World affords no greater Pleasure. Let others waste the bloom of Life, at the Card or biliard Table, among rakes and fools, and when their minds are sufficiently fretted with losses, and inflamed by Wine, ramble through the Streets, assaulting innocent People, breaking Windows or debauching young Girls. I envy not their exalted happiness. I had rather sit in school and consider which of my pupils will turn out in his future Life, a Hero, and which a rake, which a phylosopher, and which a parasite, than change breasts with them, tho possest of 20 lac'd wast coats and £1000 a year. Methinks I hear you say, this is odd talk for J. Adams. I'll tell you, then the Ocasion of it. About 4 months since a poor Girl in this neighbourhood walking by the meeting H upon some Ocasion, in the evening, met a fine Gentleman with laced hat and wast coat, and a sword who sollicited her to turn aside with him into the horse Stable. The Girl relucted a little, upon which he gave her 3 Guineas, and wished he might be damned if he did not have her in 3 months. Into the horse Stable they went. The 3 Guineas proved 3 farthings—and the Girl proves with Child, without a Friend upon Earth that will own her, or knowing the father of her 3 farthing Bastard.

March 15, 1756

---

29 MONDAY.

A little hail and rain fell to Day. We find our Selves capable of comprehending many Things, of acquiring considerable Degrees of Knowledge by our slender and contracted Faculties. Now may we not suppose our minds strengthened, and Capacities dilated, so as fully to comprehend this Globe of Earth, with its numerous appendages? May we not suppose them further enlarged to take in the Solar System, in all its relations? Nay why may we not go further and suppose them increased to comprehend the Whole created Universe, with all its inhabitants, their various Relations, Dependencies, Duties and necessities. If this is supposeable, then a Being of such great Capacity, indowed with sufficient Power, would be an accomplished Judge of all rational Beings . . . would be fit to dispense rewards to Virtue and Punishments to Vice.

March 29, 1756

CHOOSING A PROFESSION

To Charles Cushing

My Friend   Worcester April 1. 1756

I had the Pleasure, a few Days since, of receiving your favour of February 4th. I am obliged to you for your advice, and for the manly and rational Reflections with which you inforced it. I think I have deliberately weighed the subject and had almost determined as you advise. Upon the Stage of Life, we have each of us a part, a laborious and difficult Part, to Act, but we are all capable of acting our Parts, however difficult, to the best advantage. Upon common Theatres indeed the applause of the Audience is of more importance to the Actors than their own approbation. But upon the Stage of Life, while Concience Clapps, let the World hiss! On the contrary if Conscience disapproves, the loudest applauses of the World are of little Value. While our own minds commend, we may calmly despise all the Frowns, all the Censure, all the Malignity of men.

> Should the whole Frame of Nature round us break
> In ruin and Confusion hurld
> We unconcern'd might hear the mighty crack
> And stand unhurt amidst a falling World.

We have indeed the liberty of Chusing what Character we shall sustain in this great and important Drama. But to chuse rightly, we should consider in what Character we can do the most service to our fellow men, as well as to our selves. The Man who lives wholly to himself is of less worth than the Cattle in his Barn. Let us look upon a Lawyer: In the beginning of Life we see him, fumbling and raking amidst the rubbish of Writs, indightments, Pleas, ejectments, enfiefed, illatebration and a 1000 other lignum Vitæ words that have neither harmony nor meaning. When he getts into Business, he often foments more quarrells than he composes, and inriches himself at the expence of impoverishing others more honest and deserving than himself. Besides the noise and bustle of Courts, and the labour of inquiring into and pleading dry and difficult Cases, have very few Charms in my Eyes. The study of Law is indeed an Avenue to the more important offices of the state, and the happiness of human Society is an object worth the pursuit of any man. But the Acquisition of these important offices depends upon so many Circumstances of Birth and fortune, not to mention Capacity, which I have not, that I can have no hopes of Being Usefull that way.

The Physician If he has real Skill and Ingenuity, as things go now, will have no employment. And if he has not skill and Ingenuity, will kill rather than Cure. I have not mentioned the infinite toil and Labour of his Occupation.

The Divine has a Thousand Obstacles to encounter. He has his own and his Peoples Prejudices to Combat—the capricious

Humours and Fancies of the Vulgar to submit to—Poverty to struggle with—the charge of Heresy to bear—systematical Divinity, alias systematical vexation of spirit to study and sift. But on the other hand He has more Leisure to inform his mind, to subdue his Passions—fewer Temptations to intemperance and injustice, tho' more to trimming and Hypocrisy—an opportunity of diffusing Truth and Virtue among his People. Upon the Whole I think if he relies on his own understanding more than the decrees of Councils, or the sentiments of Fathers, if he resolutely discharges the Duties of his Station, according to the Dictates of his mind, if he spends his Time in the improvement of his Head in Knowledge and his heart in Virtue, instead of sauntering about the streets, he will be able to do more good to his fellow men and make better provision for his own future Happiness in this Profession, than in any other.

However I am as yet very contented in the place of a School Master. I shall not therefore very suddenly become a Preacher. When I do I hope to live a year or two in the same neighbourhood with you. Had indulgent Heaven thrown me into the neighbourhood of a Dalton, or some other such kind Friend of my former acquaintance, I think little had been wanting to compleat my satisfaction. It is late in the evening, and my Candle, my pen, and more than all, my inclination, calls upon me to subscribe my self your Sincere Friend & Servt.,

J.A.

P.S. There is a story about Town that I am an *Orminian*.

Pray write me, every opportunity, and be so kind as to omit 1/2 dozen wafers in your next. The last was barr'd and barricadoed with so many Seals, that I was out of all patience before I could come to the Treasure.

From the Diary: April 24–August 15, 1756

23 SATURDAY.
A cloudy morn. All my Time seems to roll away unnoticed. I long to study sometimes, but have no opportunity. I long to

be a master of Greek and Latin. I long to prosecute the mathematical and philosophical Sciences. I long to know a little of
Ethicks and moral Philosophy. But I have no Books, no Time,
no Friends. I must therefore be contented to live and die an
ignorant, obscure fellow. A showery Day.

April 24, 1756

30 SATURDAY.

A rainy Day. If we consider a little of this our Globe we find
an endless Variety of Substances, mutually connected with and
dependent on Each other. In the Wilderness we see an amazing profusion of vegetables, which afford Sustenance and covering to the wild Beasts. The cultivated Planes and Meadows
produce grass for Cattle, and Herbs for the service of man.
The milk and the Flesh of other Animals, afford a delicious
provision for mankind. A great Part of the human Species are
obliged to provide food and nourishment for other helpless
and improvident Animals. Vegetables sustain some Animals.
These animals are devoured by others, and these others are
continually cultivating and improving the vegetable Species.
Thus nature, upon our Earth, is in a continual Rotation. If we
rise higher, we find the sun and moon to a very great degree
influencing us. Tides are produced in the ocean, Clouds in the
Atmosphere, all nature is made to flourish and look gay by
these enlivening and invigorating Luminaries. Yea Life and
Chearfulness is diffused to all the other Planets, as well as ours,
upon the sprightly Sunbeams. No doubt There is as great a
multitude and variety of Bodies upon each Planet in proportion to its magnitude, as there is upon ours. These Bodies are
connected with and influenced by each other. Thus we see
the amazing harmony of our Solar System. The minutest Particle in one of Saturns Sattelites, may have some influence
upon the most distant Regions of the System. The Stupendous
Plan of operation was projected by him who rules the universe,
and a part assigned to every particle of matter to act, in this
great and complicated Drama. The Creator looked into the remotest Futurity, and saw his great Designs accomplished by
this inextricable, this mysterious Complication of Causes. But
to rise still higher this Solar System is but one, very small wheel

in the great the astonishing Machine of the World. Those
Starrs that twinkle in the Heavens have each of them a Choir
of Planets, Comets, and Satellites dancing round them, playing mutually on each other, and all together playing on the
other Systems that lie around them. Our System, considered as
one body hanging on its Center of Gravity, may affect and be
affected by all the other Systems, within the Compass of Creation. Thus it is highly probable every Particle of matter, influences, and is influenced by every other Particle in the whole
collective Universe. A stormy Day.

May 1, 1756

11 TUESDAY.

A pleasant day. The first Day of Court. Nature and Truth or
rather Truth and right are invariably the same in all Times and
in all Places. And Reason, pure unbiassed Reason perceives
them alike in all Times and in all Places. But Passion, Prejudice, Interest, Custom and Fancy are infinitely precarious. If
therefore we suffer our Understandings to be blinded or perverted by any of these, the Chance is that of millions to one,
that we shall embrace error. And hence arises that endless Variety of Opinions entertained by Mankind.—The Weather and
the Season are beyond expression delightful. The Fields are
coverd with a bright and lively Verdure. The Trees are all in
bloom, and the atmosphere is filled with a ravishing Fragrance.
The Air is soft and yielding and the Setting sun Sprinkled his
departing Rays over the Face of Nature, and enlivened all the
Land skips around me. The Trees put forth their Leaves and
the Birds fill the Spray. Supd at Gardiners.

May 11, 1756

16 MONDAY.

The Elephant and the Lion, when their Strength is directed
and applyd by Man, can exert a prodigious Force. But their
Strength, great and surprizing as it is, can produce no great Effects, when applyed by no higher Ingenuity than their own.
But Man, allthough the Powers of his Body are but small and
contemptible, by the Exercise of his Reason can invent En-

gines and Instruments, to take advantage of the Powers in Nature, and accomplish the most astonishing Designs. He can rear the Valley into a lofty mountain, and reduce the mountain to a humble Vale. He can rend the Rocks and level the proudest Trees. At his Pleasure the Forest is cleard and Palaces rise. When He pleases, the soaring Eagle is precipitated to Earth, and the light footed Roe is stop'd in his Career. He can cultivate and assist Nature in her own Productions. By pruning the Tree, and manuring the Land, he makes the former produce larger and fairer Fruit, and the latter bring forth better and greater Plenty of Grain. He can form a Communication between remotest Regions, for the benefit of Trade and Commerce, over the yielding and fluctuating Element of water. The Telescope has settled the Regions of Heaven, and the Microscope has brought up to View innumerable millions of Animals that Escape the observation of our naked sight.

May 17, 1756

---

27 FRYDAY.

Dined at the Majors. A pleasant Day.—If we examine critically the little Prospect that lies around us at one view we behold an almost infinite Variety of substances. Over our heads the sun blazes in divine Effulgence, the Clouds tinged with various Colors by the refracted Sunbeams exhibit most beautiful appearances in the Atmosphere, the cultivated Planes and meadows are attired in a delightful Verdure and variegated with the gay enamell of Flowers and Roses. On one hand we see an extensive Forest, a whole Kingdom of Vegetables of the noblest Kind. Upon the Hills we discern Flocks of Grazing Cattle, and on the other hand a City rises up to View, with its Spires among the Clouds. All these and many more objects encounter our Eyes in the Prospect of one Horizon, perhaps 2, or 3 miles in diameter. Now every Animal that we see in this Prospect, Men and Beasts, are endued with most curiously organized Bodies. They consist of Bones, and Blood, and muscles, and nerves, and ligaments and Tendons, and Chile and a million other things, all exactly fitted for the purposes of Life and motion, and Action. Every Plant has almost as complex and curious a structure, as animals, and the minutest Twigg is supported, and supplied with Juices and Life, by organs and Filaments proper to draw this Nutrition of the Earth. It would be endless to consider minutely every Substance or Species of Substances that falls under our Eyes in this one Prospect. Now let us for a minute Consider how many million such Prospects there are upon this single Planet, all of which contain as great and some a much Greater Variety of animals and Vegetables. When we have been sufficiently astonished at this incomprehensible multitude of substances, let us rise in our Thoughts and consider, how many Planets and Sattellites and Comets there are in this one solar system, each of which has as many such Prospects upon its surface as our Earth. Such a View as this may suffice to show us our Ignorance. But if we rise still higher in our Thoughts, and consider that stupendous Army of fixt Starrs that is hung up in the immense Space, as so many Suns, each placed in Center of his respective system and diffusing his inlivening and invigorating Influences to his whole Choir of Planets, Comets and sattellites, and that each of this unnumbered multitude has as much superficies, and as many Prospects as our Earth, we find our selves lost and swallowed up in this incomprehensible I had almost said infinite Magnificence of Nature. Our Imaginations after a few feignt Efforts, sink down into a profound Admiration of what they cannot comprehend. God whose almighty Fiat first produced this amazing Universe, had the whole Plan in View from all Eternity, intimately and perfectly knew the Nature and all the Properties of all these his Creatures. He looked forward through all Duration and perfectly knew all the Effects, all the events and Revolutions, that could possibly, and would actually take place, Throughout Eternity.

May 28, 1756

———————

28 SATURDAY.

Drank Tea at Mr. Putnams.—What is the proper Business of Mankind in this Life? We come into the World naked and destitute of all the Conveniences and necessaries of Life. And if we were not provided for, and nourished by our Parents or others should inevitably perish as soon as born. We increase in strength of Body and mind by slow and insensible Degrees.

1/3 of our Time is consumed in sleep, and 3/4 of the remainder, is spent in procuring a mere animal sustenance. And if we live to the Age of three score and Ten and then set down to make an estimate in our minds of the Happiness we have enjoyed and the Misery we have suffered, We shall find I am apt to think, that the overballance of Happiness is quite inconsiderable. We shall find that we have been through the greatest Part of our Lives pursuing Shadows, and empty but glittering Phantoms rather than substances. We shall find that we have applied our whole Vigour, all our Faculties, in the Pursuit of Honour, or Wealth, or Learning or some other such delusive Trifle, instead of the real and everlasting Excellences of Piety and Virtue. Habits of Contemplating the Deity and his transcendent Excellences, and correspondent Habits of complacency in and Dependence upon him, Habits of Reverence and Gratitude, to God, and Habits of Love and Compassion to our fellow men and Habits of Temperance, Recollection and self Government will afford us a real and substantial Pleasure. We may then exult in a Conciousness of the Favour of God, and the Prospect of everlasting Felicity.

May 29, 1756

---

2 WEDNESDAY.

Went to Spencer in the afternoon.—When we come into the World, our minds are destitute of all Sorts of Ideas. Our senses inform us of various Qualities in the substances around us. As we grow up our Acquaintance with Things enlarges and spreads. Colours are painted in our minds through our Eyes. All the various Modulations of Sounds, enter by our Ears. Fragrance and Fœtor, are perceived by the Smell, Extention and Bulk by the Touch. These Ideas that enter simple and uncompounded thro our Senses are called simple Ideas, because they are absolutely one and indivisible. Thus the Whiteness of Snow can not be divided or seperated into 2 or more Whitenesses. The same may be said of all other Colours. It is indeed in our Power to mix and compound Colours into new and more beautiful Appearances, than any that are to be found in Nature. So We can combine various Sounds into one melodious Tune. In Short we can modify and dispose the Simple Ideas of

Sensation, into whatever shape we please. But these Ideas can enter our minds no other Way but thro the senses. A man born blind will never gain one Idea of Light or Colour. One born deaf will never get an Idea of sound.

June 2, 1756

14 MONDAY.

Drank Tea at Mr. Putnams. Spent the Evening at the Majors, with Esqrs. Chandler of Woodstock and Brewer of Worcester.—He is not a wise man and is unfit to fill any important Station in Society, that has left one Passion in his Soul unsubdued. The Love of Glory will make a General sacrifice the Interest of his Nation, to his own Fame. Avarice exposes some to Corruption and all to a Thousand meannesses and villanies destructive to Society. Love has deposed lawful Kings, and aggrandiz'd unlawful, ill deserving Courtiers. Envy is more Studious of eclipsing the Lustre of other men by indirect Strategems, than of brightening its own Lustre by great and meritorious Actions. These Passions should be bound fast and brought under the Yoke. Untamed they are lawless Bulls, they roar and bluster, defy all Controul, and some times murder their proper owner. But properly inured to Obedience, they take their Places under the Yoke without Noise and labour vigorously in their masters Service. From a sense of the Government of God, and a Regard to the Laws established by his Providence, should all our Actions for ourselves or for other men, primarily originate. And This master Passion in a good mans soul, like the larger Fishes of Prey will swallow up and destroy all the rest.

June 14, 1756

15 TUESDAY.

Consider, for one minute, the Changes produced in this Country, within the Space of 200 years. Then, the whole Continent was one continued dismall Wilderness, the haunt of Wolves and Bears and more savage men. Now, the Forests are removed, the Land coverd with fields of Corn, orchards bending with fruit, and the magnificent Habitations of rational and civilized People. Then our Rivers flowed through gloomy deserts and offensive Swamps. Now the same Rivers glide smoothly on through rich Countries fraught with every delightful Object, and through Meadows painted with the most beautyful scenery of Nature, and of Art. The narrow Hutts of the Indians have been removed and in their room have arisen fair and lofty Edifices, large and well compacted Cities.

June 15, 1756

---

21 WEDNESDAY.

Kept School.—I am now entering on another Year, and I am resolved not to neglect my Time as I did last Year. I am resolved to rise with the Sun and to study the Scriptures, on Thurdsday, Fryday, Saturday, and Sunday mornings, and to study some Latin author the other 3 mornings. Noons and Nights I intend to read English Authors. This is my fixt Determination, and I will set down every neglect and every compliance with this Resolution. May I blush whenever I suffer one hour to pass unimproved. I will rouse up my mind, and fix my Attention. I will stand collected within my self and think upon what I read and what I see. I will strive with all my soul to be something more than Persons who have had less Advantages than myself.

July 21, 1756

---

25 SUNDAY.

Rose 1/2 after 6.—Good Sense, some say, is enough to regulate our Conduct, to dictate Thoughts and Actions which are proper upon certain Occasions. This they say will soften and refine the Motions of our Limbs into an easy and agreable Air altho the Dancing Master never was applied to, and this will suggest good Answers, good Observations and good Expressions to us better than refined Breeding. Good sense will make us remember that others have as good a right to think for themselves and to speak their own Opinions as I have, that another mans making a silly Speech, does not warrant my ill nature and Pride in grasping the Opportunity to ridicule him, and show my Witt. A puffy, vain, conceited Conversation, never fails to bring a Man into Contempt, altho his natural Endowments be ever so great, and his Application and Industry ever so intense. No Accomplishments, no Virtues are a sufficient Attonement for Vanity, and a haughty overbearing Temper in Conversation. And such is the Humour of the World the greater a mans Parts and the nobler his Virtues in other Respects, the more Derision and Ridicule does this one Vice and Folly throw him into. Good sense is generally attended with a very lively sense and delight in Applause. The Love of Fame in such men is generally much stronger than in other People, and this Passion it must be confessed is apt to betray men into impertinent Exertions of their Talents, sometimes into censorious Remarks upon others, often into little meannesses to sound the opinions of others and oftenest of all into a childish Affectation of Wit and Gaiety. I must own my self to have been, to a very heinous Degree, guilty in this Respect. When in Company with Persons much superior to my self in Years and Place, I have talked to shew my Learning. I have been too bold with great men, which Boldness will no doubt be called Self Conceit. I have made ill natured Remarks upon the Intellectuals, manners, Practice &c. of other People. I have foolishly aimed at Wit and Spirit, at making a shining Figure in gay Company, but instead of shining briter I only clouded the few Rays that before rendered me visible. Such has been my unhappy Fate.—I now resolve for the future, never to say an ill naturd Thing, concerning Ministers or the ministerial Profession, never to say an envious Thing concerning Governors, Judges, Ministers, Clerics, Sheriffs, Lawyers, or any other honorable or Lucrative offices or officers, never to affect Wit upon laced Wastecoats or large Estates or their Professors, never to shew my own Importance or Superiority, by remarking the Foibles, Vices, or Inferiority of others. But I now resolve as far as lies in me, to take Notice chiefly of the amiable Qualities of other People, to put the most favourable Construction upon the Weaknesses, Bigotry, and Errors of others, &c. and to labour more for an inoffensive and amiable than for a shining and invidious Character.—Heard Crawford in the morning, and Harding in the afternoon.

July 25, 1756

31 SATURDAY.

A rainy forenoon. Dined at Mr. Paines. A fair afternoon. The Nature and Essence of the material World is not less conceal'd from our knowledge than the Nature and Essence of God. We see our selves surrounded on all sides with a vast expanse of Heavens, and we feel our selves astonished at the Grandeur, the blazing Pomp of those Starrs with which it is adorned. The Birds fly over our Heads and our fellow animals Labour and sport around us, the Trees wave and murmur in the Winds, the Clouds float and shine on high, the surging billows rise in the Sea, and Ships break through the Tempest. Here rises a spacious City, and yonder is spread out an extensive Plain. These Objects are so common and familiar, that we think our selves fully Acquainted with them; but these are only Effects and Properties, the substance from whence they flow is hid from us in impenetrable Obscurity.

God is said to be self existent, and that therefore he may have existed from Eternity, and throughout Immensity. God exists by an absolute Necessity in his own Nature. That is, it implies a Contradiction to suppose him not to exist. To ask what this Necessity is, is as if you should ask what the Necessity of the Equality between twice 2 and 4, is. Twice 2 are necessarily in their own nature equal to 4, not only here but in every Point of Space, not only now, but in every Point of Duration. In the same manner God necessarily exists not only here but throughout unlimited Space, not only now but throughout all Duration, past, and future.

We observe, in the animate and in the inanimate Creation, a surprizing Diversity, and a surprizing Uniformity. Of inanimate Substances, there is a great variety, from the Pebble in the Streets, quite up to the Vegetables in the Forrest. Of animals there is no less a Variety of Species from the Animalculs that escape our naked sight, quite through the intermediate Kinds up to Elephants, Horses, men. Yet notwithstanding this Variety, there is, from the highest Species of animals upon this Globe which is generally thought to be Man, a regular and uniform Subordination of one Tribe to another down to the apparently insignificant animalcules in pepper Water, and the same Subordination continues quite through the Vegetable

Kingdom. And it is worth observing that each Species regularly and uniformly preserve all their essential and peculiar properties, without partaking of the peculiar Properties of others. We dont see Chickens hatched with fins to swim, nor Fishes spawned with wings to fly. We dont see a Colt folded with Claws like a Bird, nor men with the Cloathing or Armour which his Reason renders him capable of procuring for himself. Every Species has its distinguishing Properties, and every Individual that is born has all those Properties without any of the distinguishing Properties of another Species. What now can preserve this prodigious Variety of Species's and this inflexible Uniformity among the Individuals, but the continual and vigilant Providence of God.

July 31, 1756

---

14 SATURDAY.

I seem to have lost sight of the Object that I resolved to pursue. Dreams and slumbers, sloth and negligence, will be the ruin of my schemes. However I seem to be awake now. Why cant I keep awake? I have wrote Scripture pretty industriously this morning.—Why am I so unreasonable, as to expect Happiness, and a solid undisturbed Contentment amidst all the Disorders, and the continual Rotations of worldly Affairs? Stability is no where to be found in that Part of the Universe that lies within our observation. The natural and the moral World, are continually changing. The Planets, with all their Appendages, strike out their amazing Circles round the Sun. Upon the Earth, one Day is serene, and clear, no cloud intercepts the kind influence of the Sun, and all Nature seems to flourish and look gay. But these delightfull scenes soon vanish, and are succeeded by the gloom and Darkness of the Night. And before the morning Appears, the Clouds gather, the Winds rise, Lightnings glare, and Thunders bellow through the vast of Heaven. Man is sometimes flushed with Joy and transported with the full Fury of sensual Pleasure, and the next Hour, lies groaning under the bitter Pangs of Disappointments and adverse Fortune. Thus God has told us, by the general Constitution of the World, by the Nature of all terrestrial Enjoyments, and by the Constitution of our own Bodies, that

This World was not designed for a lasting and a happy State, but rather for a State of moral Discipline, that we might have a fair Opportunity and continual Excitements to labour after a cheerful Resignation to all the Events of Providence, after Habits of Virtue, Self Government, and Piety. And this Temper of mind is in our Power to acquire, and this alone can secure us against all the Adversities of Fortune, against all the Malice of men, against all the Opperations of Nature. A World in Flames, and a whole System tumbling in Ruins to the Center, has nothing terrifying in it to a man whose Security is builded on the adamantine Basis of good Conscience and confirmed Piety. If I could but conform my Life and Conversation to my Speculations, I should be happy.—Have I hardiness enough to contend with omnipotence? Or have I cunning enough to elude infinite Wisdom, or Ingratitude enough to Spurn at infinite Goodness? The Scituation that I am in, and the Advantages that I enjoy, are thought to be the best for me by him who alone is a competent Judge of Fitness and Propriety. Shall I then complain? Oh Madness, Pride, Impiety.

August 14, 1756

---

15 SUNDAY.

If one Man or Being, out of pure Generosity, and without any Expectation of Returns, is about to confer any Favour or Emolument upon Another, he has a right and is at Liberty to choose in what manner, and by what means, to confer it. He may convey the Favour by his own Hand or by the Hand of his Servant, and the Obligation to Gratitude is equally strong upon the benefited Being. The mode of bestowing does not diminish the kindness, provided the Commodity or good is brought to us equally perfect and without our Expence. But on the other Hand, If our Being is the original Cause of Pain, Sorrow or Suffering to another, voluntarily and without provocation, it is injurious to that other, whatever means he might employ and whatever Circumstances the Conveyance of the Injury might be attended with. Thus we are equally obliged to the Supream Being for the Information he has given us of our Duty, whether by the Constitution of our Minds and Bodies or by a supernatural Revelation. For an instance of the latter let us take original sin. Some say that Adams sin was enough to damn the whole human Race, without any actual Crimes committed by any of them. Now this Guilt is brought upon them not by their own rashness and Indiscretion, not by their own Wickedness and Vice, but by the Supream Being. This Guilt brought upon us is a real Injury and Misfortune because it renders us worse than not to be, and therefore making us guilty upon account of Adams Delegation, or Representing all of us, is not in the least diminishing the Injury and Injustice but only changing the mode of conveyance.

August 15, 1756

PROVIDENCE AND HISTORY

To Richard Cranch

My Friend   August 29th 1756

I am set down with a Design of writing to you.—But the narrow Sphere I move in, and the lonely unsociable Life I lead, can furnish a Letter with little more than Complaints of my hard fortune. I am condemnd to keep School two Years longer. This I sometimes consider as a very grievous Calamity and almost sink under the Weight of Woe.—But shall I dare to complain and to murmur against Providence for this little Punishment, when my very Existence, all the Pleasure I enjoy now, and all the Advantages I have of preparing for hereafter, are Expression of Benevolence that I never did and never could deserve? Shall I Censure the Conduct of that Being who has poured around me, a great Profusion, of those good Things that I really want, because he has kept from me other Things that might be improper and fatal to me if I had them. That Being has furnished my Body with several senses, and the world around it with objects suitable to gratify them. He has made me an erect Figure, and has placed in the most advantageous Part of my Body, the sense of Sight. And He has hung up in the Heavens over my Head and Spread out in the Fields of Nature around me those glorious Shows and appearances

with which my Eyes and my Imagination are extremely delighted. I am pleasd with the beautiful Appearance of the
Flower, and still more pleased with the Prospect of Forrests
and of Meadows, of verdant Feilds and Mountains covered
with Flocks, but I am thrown into a kind of Transport when I
behold the amazing Concave of Heaven sprinkled and glittering with Starrs. That Being has bestowed upon some of the
Vegetable species a fragrance that can almost as agreably entertain our sense of smell. He has so wonderfully constituted the
Air we live in, that by giving it a particular Kind of Vibration,
it produces in us as intense sensations of Pleasure as the organs
of our Bodies can bear in all the varieties of Harmony and
Concord. But all the Provision that he has made for the Gratification of my senses, tho very engaging Instances of Kindness,
are much inferiour to the Provisions for the Gratification of my
nobler Powers of Intelligence and Reason. He has given me
Reason to find out the Truth, and the real Design of my Existence here, and has made all Endeavours to promote that Design, agreable to my mind, and attended with a conscious
Pleasure and Complacency. On the Contrary, he has made a
different Course of Life, a Course of Impiety and Injustice, of
Malevolence and Intemperance, appear shocking and deformed to my first Reflection. He has made my Mind capable
of receiving an infinite Variety of Ideas from those numerous
material Objects with which we are environed. And of retaining, compounding and arranging the vigourous Impressions
which we receive from these into all the Varieties of Picture
and of Figure. By inquiring into the Scituation, Produce,
Manufactures &c. of our own, and by travailing into, or reading about other Countries, I can gain distinct Ideas of almost
every Thing upon this Earth at present, and by looking into
history I can settle in my mind a clear and a Comprehensive
View of the Earth at its Creation, of its various Changes and
Revolutions, of its progressive Improvement, sudden Depopu-
lation by a Deluge, and its graduall Repeopling, of the Growth
of several Kingdoms and Empires, of their Wealth and Commerce, their Wars and Politicks, of the Characters of their principal Leading Men, of their Grandeur and Power their Virtues
and Vices, of their insensible Decays at first, and of their swift
Destruction at last. In fine we can attend the Earth from its

Nativity, thro all the various Turns of Fortune, through all its successive Changes, thro all the Events that happen on its surface, and all the successive Generations of Mankind, to the final Conflagration, when the whole Earth with its appendages shall be consumed by the furious Element of Fire. And after our minds are furnishd with this ample store of Ideas, far from feeling burdend or overloaded, our thots are more free, and active, and clear than before, and we are capable of spreading our acquaintance with Things much further. Far from being satiated with Knowledge our Curiosity is only improved and increasd, our Thoughts rove beyond the visible diurnal sphere, range thro the immeasurable Regions of the Universe, and loose them selves amongst a Labyrinth of Worlds, and not contented with knowing what is, they run forward into Futurity, and search for new Employment there. Then they can never stop! The wide, the boundless Prospect lies before them! Here alone they find Objects adequate to their Desires. Shall I now presume to complain of my hard Fate, when such ample Provision has been made to gratify all my senses, and all the Faculties of my soul? God forbid. I am happy and I will remain so, while Health is indulgd to me, in Spight of all the other Adverse Circumstances that Fortune can place me in. I expect to be joked upon, for writing in this serious manner, when it shall be known what a Resolution I have lately taken. I have engagd with Mr. Putnam to study Law with him, 2 years, and to keep the school at the same time. It will be hard work, but the more difficult and dangerous the Enterprize, a brighter Crown of Lawrell is bestowed on the Conqueror. However I am not without Apprehensions concerning the success of this Resolution. But I am under much fewer Apprehensions than I was when I thought of preaching. The frightful Engines of Ecclesiastical Councils, of diabolical Malice and Calvinistical good nature never failed to terrify me exceedingly whenever I thought of Preaching. But the Point is now determined, and I shall have Liberty to think for myself without molesting others or being molested myself. Write to me the first Opportunity, and tell me freely whether you approve my Conduct. Please to present my tenderest Regards to our two Friends at Boston, and suffer me to subscribe myself your sincere Friend,

John Adams

RESOLVING TO STUDY LAW

To Charles Cushing

My Friend   Worcester, Oct. 19th 1756

I look upon myself obliged to give you the reasons that induced me to resolve upon the study and profession of the law, because you were so kind as to advise me to a different profession. When yours came to hand I had thoughts of preaching, but the longer I lived, and the more experience I had of that order of men, and of the real design of their institution, the more objections I found in my own mind to that course of life. I have the pleasure to be acquainted with a young gentleman of a fine genius, cultivated with indefatigable study, of a generous and noble disposition, and of the strictest virtue, a gentleman who deserves the countenance of the greatest men and the charge of the best parish in the Province. But with all these accomplishments, he is despised by some, ridiculed by others, and detested by more, only because he is suspected of Arminianism. And I have the pain to know more than one, who has a sleepy stupid soul, who has spent more of his waking hours in darning his stockings, smoking his pipe, or playing with his fingers than in reading, conversation or reflection, cry'd up as promising young men, pious and orthodox youths and admirable Preachers. As far as I can observe, people are not disposed to inquire for piety, integrity, good sense or learning in a young preacher, but for stupidity (for so I must call the pretended sanctity of some absolute dunces), irresistible grace and original sin. I have not in one expression exceeded the limits of truth, tho' you think I am warm. Could you advise me, then, who you know have not the highest opinion of what is called Orthodoxy, to engage in a profession like this.* But I have other reasons too numerous to explain fully. This you will think is enough. What I said to you in my last, against the practitioners in the law, I cannot recollect. It is not unlikely my expressions were unguarded, as I am apt to speak and write

---

*After I had wrote so far I received yours for which I return my thanks and pray the continuance of your favors.

too much at random. But my present sentiments are that some of those practitioners adorn and others disgrace, both the law that they profess and the country they inhabit. The students in the law are very numerous and some of them, youths of which no country, no age, would need to be ashamed—and if I can gain the honor of treading in the rear and silently admiring the noble air and gallant atchievements of the foremost rank, I shall think myself worthy of a louder triumph, than if I had headed the whole army of orthodox preachers.

The difficulties and discouragements I am under are a full match for all the resolution I am master of. But I comfort myself with this consideration. The more danger the greater glory. The general who at the head of a small army, encounters a more numerous and formidable enemy, is applauded if he strove for the victory and made a skillful retreat, although his army is routed and a considerable extent of territory lost. But if he gains a small advantage over the enemy, he saves the interest of his country, and returns, amidst the acclamations of the people bearing the triumphal laurel to the capitol. (I am in a very bellicose temper of mind to night, all my figures are taken from war.) I have cast myself wholly upon fortune, what her ladyship will be pleased to do with me I can't say. But wherever she shall lead me, or whatever she shall do with me, she cannot abate the sincerity with which I trust I shall always be your friend,

John Adams

From the Diary:
October 25, 1758–Summer 1759

WEDNESDAY.

Went in the morning to Mr. Gridleys, and asked the favour of his Advice what Steps to take for an Introduction to the Practice of Law in this County. He answered "get sworn."

Ego. But in order to that, sir, as I have no Patron, in this County.

G. I will recommend you to the Court. Mark the Day the

Court adjourns to in order to make up Judgments. Come to Town that Day, and in the mean Time I will speak to the Bar for the Bar must be consulted, because the Court always inquires, if it be with Consent of the Bar.

Then Mr. Gridley inquired what Method of Study I had pursued, what Latin Books I read, what Greek, what French. What I had read upon Rhetorick. Then he took his Common Place Book and gave me Ld. Hales Advice to a Student of the Common Law, and when I had read that, he gave me Ld. C J Reeves Advice to his Nephew, in the Study of the common Law. Then He gave me a Letter from Dr. Dickins, Regius Professor of Law at the University of Cambridge, to him, pointing out a Method of Studying the civil Law. Then he turned to a Letter He wrote himself to Judge Lightfoot, Judge of the Admiralty in Rhode Island, directing to a Method of Studying the Admiralty Law. Then Mr. Gridley run a Comparison between the Business and studies of a Lawyer or Gentleman of the Bar, in England, and that of one here. A Lawyer in this Country must study common Law and civil Law, and natural Law, and Admiralty Law, and must do the duty of a Counsellor, a Lawyer, an Attorney, a sollicitor, and even of a scrivener, so that the Difficulties of the Profession are much greater here than in England.

The Difficulties that attend the study may discourage some, but they never discouraged me. Here is conscious superiority.

I have a few Pieces of Advice to give you Mr. Adams. One is to pursue the Study of the Law rather than the Gain of it. Pursue the Gain of it enough to keep out of the Briars, but give your main Attention to the study of it.

The next is, not to marry early. For an early Marriage will obstruct your Improvement, and in the next Place, twill involve you in Expence.

Another Thing is not to keep much Company. For the application of a Man who aims to be a lawyer must be incessant. His Attention to his Books must be constant, which is inconsistent with keeping much Company.

In the study of Law the common Law be sure deserves your first and last Attention, and He has conquered all the Difficulties of this Law, who is Master of the Institutes. You must conquer the Institutes. The Road of Science is much easier, now, than it was when I sett out. I began with Co. Litt. and broke thro.

I asked his Advice about studying Greek. He answered it is a matter of meer Curiosity.—After this long and familiar Conversation we went to Court. Attended all Day and in the Evening I went to ask Mr. Thatchers Concurrence with the Bar. Drank Tea and spent the whole Evening, upon original sin, Origin of Evil, the Plan of the Universe, and at last, upon Law. He says He is sorry that he neglected to keep a common Place Book when he began to study Law, and he is half a mind to begin now. Thatcher thinks, this County is full.

October 25, 1758

MONDAY.

Went to Town. Went to Mr. Gridleys office, but he had not returned to Town from Brookline. Went again. Not returned. Attended Court till after 12 and began to grow uneasy expecting that Quincy would be sworn and I have no Patron, when Mr. Gridly made his Appearance, and on sight of me, whispered to Mr. Prat, Dana, Kent, Thatcher &c. about me. Mr. Prat said no Body knew me. Yes, says Gridley, I have tried him, he is a very sensible Fellow.—At last He rose up and bowed to his right Hand and said "Mr. Quincy," when Quincy rose up, then bowed to me, "Mr. Adams," when I walked out. "May it please your Honours, I have 2 young Gentlemen Mr. Q. and Mr. Adams to present for the Oath of an Attorney. Of Mr. Q. it is sufficient for me to say he has lived 3 Years with Mr. Prat. Of Mr. Adams, as he is unknown to your Honours, It is necessary to say that he has lived between 2 and 3 Years with Mr. Put of Worcester, has a good Character from him, and all others who know him, and that he was with me the other day several Hours, and I take it he is qualified to study the Law by his scholarship and that he has made a very considerable, a very great Proficiency in the Principles of the Law, and therefore that the Clients Interest may be safely intrusted in his Hands. I therefore recommend him with the Consent of the Bar to your Honors for the Oath." Then Mr. Prat said 2 or 3 Words and the Clerk was ordered to swear us. After the Oath Mr. Gridley took me by the Hand, wished me much Joy and recommended me to the Bar. I shook Hands with the Bar, and received their Congratulations, and invited them over to Stones to drink some Punch. Where the most of us resorted, and had a very chearful [   ].

November 6?, 1758

What are the Proofs, the Characteristicks of Genius?—Answer Invention of new Systems or Combinations of old Ideas.

The Man, who has a faculty of inventing and combining into one Machine, or System, for the Execution of some Purpose and Accomplishment of some End, a great Number and Variety of Wheels, Levers, Pullies, Ropes &c. has a great Mechanical Genius. And the Proofs of his Genius, (unless it happen by mere luck) will be proportionably to the Number, and Variety of Movements, the Nice Connection of them, and the Efficacy of the entire Machine to answer its End. The last, I think at present, ought to be considered in [   ] any Genius. For altho Genius may be shewn in the Invention of a complicated Machine, which may be useless, or too expensive, for the End proposed, yet one of the most difficult Points is to contrive the Machine in such a manner, as to shorten, facilitate, and cheapen, any Manufacture &c. For to this End a Man will be obliged to revolve in his Mind perhaps an hundred Machines, which are possible but too unwieldy or expensive, and to select from all of them, one, which will answer the Purposes mentioned.

2. The Man who has a Faculty of feigning and combining into one regular, correct, consistent Plan or Story, a great Number and Variety of Characters, Actions, Events &c. has a great poetical Genius. And the Proofs of his Genius are in Proportion to the Variety, Consistency and Number of his Characters, Actions and Events; and to the nice Connection and Dependence of these upon each other thro a whole Poem. And these Proofs have been given in a surprizing degree by Milton and Shakespear, Homer, Virgil &c. Milton has feigned the Characters of Arch Angells and Devills, of Sin, Death, &c., out of his own creative Imagination and has adjusted, with great Sagacity, every Action and Event in his whole Poem to these Characters.

3. The Man, who has a Faculty of inventing Experiments and reasoning on them [   ] of Starting new Experiments from that Reasoning, and on these Experiments forming new Reasonings till he reduces all his Experiments, all his Phenomena, to general Laws and Rules, and combines those Rules to an orderly and regular Dependance on each other, thro the whole System, has a great Phylosophic Genius.

4. The Man who has a Faculty of considering all the faculties and Properties of human Nature, as the Senses, Passions, Reason, Imagination and faith, and of classing all these into order, into Rules, for the Conduct of private Life, has a great Genius in Morality.

5. He who has a Faculty of combining all these into Rules, for the Government of Society, to procure Peace, Plenty, Liberty, has a great political Genius.

Thus Order, Method, System, Connection, Plan, or whatever you call it, is the greatest Proof of Genius, next to Invention of new Wheels, Characters, Experiments, Rules, Laws, which is perhaps the first and greatest. Q. Does not the Word Invention express both these faculties, of inventing Wheels &c. and putting them in order.

Q. May not Genius be shewn in aranging a Mans Diet, Exercise, Sleep, Reading, Reflection, Writing &c. in the best order and Proportion, for His Improvement in Knowledge?

Autumn 1758

SATURDAY.

How a whole Family is put into a Broil sometimes by a Trifle. My P. and M. disagreed in Opinion about boarding Judah, that Difference occasioned passionate Expressions, those Expressions made Dolly and Judah snivell, Peter observed and mentioned it, I faulted him for it, which made him mad and all was breaking into a flame, when I quitted the Room, and took up Tully to compose myself. My P. continued cool and pleasant a good while, but had his Temper roused at last, tho he uttered not a rash Word, but resolutely asserted his Right to govern. My Mamma was determined to know what my P. charged a Week for the Girls Board. P. said he had not determined what to charge but would have her say what it was worth. She absolutely refused to say. But "I will know if I live and breath. I can read yet. Why dont you tell me, what you charge? You do it on purpose to teaze me. You are mighty arch this morning. I wont have all the Towns Poor brought here, stark naked, for me to clothe for nothing. I wont be a slave to other folks folk for nothing."—And after the 2 Girls cryed.— "I must not speak a Word to your Girls, Wenches, Drabbs. I'le kick both their fathers, presently. You want to put your Girls over me, to make me a slave to your Wenches." Thus when the Passions of Anger and Resentment are roused one Word will inflame them into Rage.

This was properly a conjugal Spat. A Spat between Husband and Wife. I might have made more critical observations on the Course and Progress of human Passions if I had steadily observed the faces, Eyes, Actions and Expressions of both Husband and Wife this morning.

M. seems to have no Scheme and Design in her Mind to persuade P. to resign his Trust of Selectman. But when she feels the Trouble and Difficulties that attend it she fretts, squibs, scolds, rages, raves. None of her Speeches seem the Effect of any Design to get rid of the Trouble, but only natural Expressions of the Pain and Uneasiness, which that Trouble occasions. Cool Reasoning upon the Point with my Father, would soon bring her to his mind or him to hers.

Let me from this remark distinctly the Different Effects of Reason and Rage. Reason, Design, Scheme, governs pretty constantly in Puts House, but, Passion, Accident, Freak, Humour, govern in this House. Put knows what he wants, and knows the Proper means to procure it, and how to employ them. He employs, Reason, Ridicule, Contempt, to work upon his Wife.

December 30, 1758

WEDNESDAY.

Drank Tea at Coll. Quincies. Spent the Evening there, and the next morning. In the afternoon, rode out to German Town.

H Q or O. Suppose you was in your Study, engaged in the Investigation of some Point of Law, or Philosophy, and your

Wife should interrupt you accidentally and break the Thread of your Thoughts, so that you never could recover it?

Ego. No man, but a crooked Richard, would blame his Wife, for such an accidental Interruption. And No Woman, but a Xantippe, would insist upon her Husbands Company, after he had given her his Reasons for desiring to be alone.

O. Should you like to spend your Evenings, at Home in reading and conversing with your Wife, rather than to spend them abroad in Taverns or with other Company?

Ego. Should prefer the Company of an agreable Wife, to any other Company for the most Part, not always. I should not like to be imprisoned at home.

O. Suppose you had been abroad, and came home fatigued and perplexed, with Business, or came out of your Study, wearied and perplexed with Study, and your Wife should meet you with an unpleasant, or an inattentive face, how should you feel?

I would flee my Country, or she should.

O. How shall a Pair avoid falling into Passion or out of humour, upon some Occasions, and treating each other unkindly.

Ego. By resolving against it. Forbid angry words &c.? Every Person knows that all are liable to mistakes, and Errors, and if the Husband finds his Wife in one he should [   ] reasonably and convince her of it, instead of being angry, and so on the Contrary. But if it happens, that both get out of humour and an angry dispute ensues, yet both will be sorry when their anger subsides, and mutually forgive and ask forgiveness, and love each other the better for it, for the future.

O. thinks more than most of her Sex. She is always thinking or Reading. She sits and looks steadily, one way, very often, several minutes together in thought. E. looks pert, sprightly, gay, but thinks and reads much less than O.

[   ] expos'd himself to Ridicule, by affectation, by Pretensions to Strength of mind and Resolution, to depth and Penetration. Pretensions to Wisdom and Virtue, superiour to all the World, will not be supported by Words only. If I tell a man I am wiser and better than he or any other man, he will either despize, or hate, or pity me, or perhaps all 3.—I have not conversed enough with the World, to behave rightly. I talk to

Paine about Greek, that makes him laugh. I talk to Sam Quincy about Resolution, and being a great Man, and study and improving Time, which makes him laugh. I talk to Ned, about the Folly of affecting to be a Heretick, which makes him mad. I talk to Hannah and Easther about the folly of Love, about despizing it, about being above it, pretend to be insensible of tender Passions, which makes them laugh. I talk to Mr. Wibirt about the Decline of Learning, tell him, I know no young fellow who promises to make a figure, cast Sneers on Dr. Marsh for not knowing the Value of old Greek and Roman Authors, ask "when will a Genius rise, that will shave his Beard, or let it grow rather and sink himself in a Cell, in order to make a figure." I talk to Parson Smith about despizing gay Dress, grand Buildings, great Estates, fame, &c. and being contented with what will satisfy the real Wants of Nature.

All This is Affectation and Ostentation. 'Tis Affectation of Learning, and Virtue and Wisdom, which I have not, and it is a weak fondness to shew all that I have, and to be thot to have more than I have.

Besides this I have insensibly fallen into a Habit of affecting Wit and Humour, of Shrugging my Shoulders, and moving and distorting the Muscles of my face. My Motions are stiff and uneasy, ungraceful, and my attention is unsteady and irregular.

These are Reflections on myself that I make. They are faults, Defects, Fopperies and follies, and Disadvantages. Can I mend these faults and supply these Defects?

O. makes Observations on Actions, Characters, Events, in Popes Homer, Milton, Popes Poems, any Plays, Romances &c. that she reads and asks Questions about them in Company. What do you think of Helen? What do you think of Hector &c. What Character do you like best? Did you wish the Plot had not been discovered in Venice preserved? These are Questions that prove a thinking Mind. E. asks none such.

Thus in a Wild Campaign, a dissipating Party of Pleasure, observations and Improvement may be made. Some Foppery, and folly and Vice, may be discerned in ones self, and Motives, and Methods may be collected to subdue it. Some Virtue, or agreable Quality may be observed in ones self and improved and cherished, or in another and transplanted into ones self.

O. Tho O. knows and can practice the Art of pleasing, yet she fails, sometimes. She lets us see a face of Ridicule, and Spying, sometimes, inadvertently, tho she looks familiarly, and pleasantly for the most part. She is apparently frank, but really reserved, seemingly pleased, and almost charmed, when she is really laughing with Contempt. Her face and Hart have no Correspondence.

Hannah checks Parson Wibirt with Irony.—It was very sawcy to disturb you, very sawcy Im sure &c.

I am very thankful for these Checks. Good Treatment makes me think I am admired, beloved, and my own Vanity will be indulged in me. So I dismiss my Gard and grow weak, silly, vain, conceited, ostentatious. But a Check, a frown, a sneer, a Sarcasm rouses my Spirits, makes me more careful and considerate. It may in short be made a Question, whether good Treatment or bad is the best for me, i.e. wether Smiles, kind Words, respectful Actions, dont betray me into Weaknesses and Littlenesses, that frowns, Satirical Speeches and contemptuous Behaviour, make me avoid.

January 1759

The other night, the Choice of Hercules came into my mind, and left Impressions there which I hope will never be effaced nor long unheeded. I thought of writing a Fable, on the same Plan, but accommodated, by omitting some Circumstances and inserting others, to my own Case.

Let Virtue address me—"Which, dear Youth, will you prefer? a Life of Effeminacy, Indolence and obscurity, or a Life of Industry, Temperance, and Honour? Take my Advice, rise and mount your Horse, by the Mornings dawn, and shake away amidst the great and beautiful scenes of Nature, that appear at that Time of the day, all the Crudities that are left in your stomach, and all the obstructions that are left in your Brains. Then return to your Study, and bend your whole soul to the Institutes of the Law, and the Reports of Cases, that have been adjudged by the Rules, in the Institutes. Let no trifling Diversion or amuzement or Company decoy you from your Books, i.e. let no Girl, no Gun, no Cards, no flutes, no Violins, no

Dress, no Tobacco, no Laziness, decoy you from your Books.
(By the Way, Laziness, Languor, Inattention, are my Bane, am
too lazy to rise early and make a fire, and when my fire is made,
at 10 o'clock my Passion for knowledge, fame, fortune or any
good, is too languid, to make me apply with Spirit to my
Books. And by Reason of my Inattention my mind is liable to
be called off from Law, by a Girl, a Pipe, a Poem, a Love Letter, a Spectator, a Play, &c.) But, keep your Law Book or some
Point of Law in your mind at least 6 Hours in a day. (I grow
too minute and lengthy.) Labour to get distinct Ideas of Law,
Right, Wrong, Justice, Equity. Search for them in your own
mind, in Roman, grecian, french, English Treatises of natural,
civil, common, Statute Law. Aim at an exact Knowledge of the
Nature, End, and Means of Government. Compare the different forms of it with each other and each of them with their Effects on public and private Happiness. Study Seneca, Cicero,
and all other good moral Writers. Study Montesque, Bolin-
broke, [   ], &c. and all other good, civil Writers, &c."

Prat. There is not a Page in Flavels Works without several
sentences of Latin. Yet the common People admire him. They
admire his Latin as much as his English, and understand it as
well. [   ] preached the best sermon that ever I heard. It was
plain common sense. But other sermons have no sense at all.
They take the Parts of them out of their Concordances and
connect them together Hed and Tail.

How greatly elevated, above common People, and above
Divines is this Lawyer. Is not this Vanity, littleness of mind?

What am I doing? Shall I sleep away my whole 70 Years. No
by every Thing I swear I will renounce the Contemplative, and
betake myself to an active roving Life by Sea or Land, or else I
will attempt some uncommon unexpected Enterprize in Law.
Let me lay the Plan and arouse Spirit enough to push boldly. I
swear I will push myself into Business. I will watch my Opportunity, to speak in Court, and will strike with surprize—
surprize Bench, Bar, Jury, Auditors and all. Activity, Boldness,
Forwardness, will draw attention. Ile not lean, with my Elbows
on the Table, forever like Read, Swift, Fitch, Skinner, Story,
&c. But I'le not forego the Pleasure of ranging the Woods,

Climbing Cliffs, walking in fields, Meadows, by Rivers, Lakes, &c., and confine my self to a Chamber for nothing. Ile have some Boon, in Return, Exchange, fame, fortune, or something.

Here are 2 nights, and one day and an half, spent in a softening, enervating, dissipating, series of hustling, pratling, Poetry, Love, Courtship, Marriage. During all this Time, I was seduced into the Course of unmanly Pleasures, that Vice describes to Hercules, forgetful of the glorious Promises of Fame, Immortality, and a good Conscience, which Virtue, makes to the same Hero, as Rewards of a hardy, toilsome, watchful Life, in the service of Man kind. I could reflect with more satisfaction on an equal space of Time spent in a painful Research of the Principles of Law, or a resolute attempt of the Powers of Eloquence.

But where is my Attention? Is it fixed from sunrise to midnight, on grecian, roman, gallic, british Law, History, Virtue, Eloquence? I dont see clearly The objects, that I am after. They are often out of Sight. Moats, Attoms, feathers, are blown into my Eyes, and blind me. Who can see distinctly the Course he is to take, and the objects that he pursues, when in the midst of a whirl Wind of dust, straws, attoms and feathers.

January 1759

WORCESTER FEB. 11. 1759.

I have been in this Town a Week this night. How much have I improved my Health by Exercise, or my mind by Study or Conversation, in this Space? I have exercised little, eat and drank and slept intemperately. Have inquired a little, of Mr. Putnam and of Abel Willard, concerning some Points of Practice in Law. But dining once at Coll. Chandlers, once at Mr. Pains, once at the Doctors, drinking Tea once at Mr. Paines, once at the Drs. and spending one Evening at the Drs., one at Gardiners and several at Putnams in Company has wasted insensibly the greatest and best Part of my time since I have been in Town. Oh how I have fulfilled the vain Boast I made to Dr. Webb, of reading 12 Hours a day! What a fine scene of study is this office! a fine Collection of Law, oratory, History, and Phy-

losophy. But I must not stay. I must return to Braintree. I must
attend a long Superiour Court at Boston. How shall I pursue
my Plan of Study?

Bob Paine acted a scene that happened on the Common
when the Troops were reviewed by the Governor. People
crouded very near to the Troops, till a highland serjeant of a
gigantic size, and accoutred with a Variety of Instruments of
Cruelty and Death, stalked out with his vast Halbert to drive
them back. He brandished his Halbert and smote it on the
Ground and cryed with a broad, Roaring Voice, Sta ban, i.e.
Stand back. Sta ba. His size, armour, Phyz and Voice, frighted
People so that they presd backwards and almost trampled
on one another. But in the highest of his fury, he sprung on-
ward, and shrieked out Sta, but then saw some Ladies before
him, which softened him. At once, he drops his Halbert,
takes off his Bonnet, and makes a very complaisant Bow, pray
Ladies, please to stand a little back, you will see a great deal
better.
    Pain lifts up his Eyes and Hands to Heaven and cryes, of all
Instruments of Defence, good Heavens, give me Beauty. It
could soften the ferocity of your highland serjeant.
    Paine and Dr. Wendel took Katy Quincy and Polly Jackson,
and led them into a retired Room and there laughed, and
screamed, and kissed and hussled. They came out glowing like
furnaces.

MARCH 14. 1759.
    Reputation ought to be the perpetual subject of my
Thoughts, and Aim of my Behaviour. How shall I gain a Reputation! How shall I Spread an Opinion of myself as a Lawyer
of distinguished Genius, Learning, and Virtue. Shall I make
frequent Visits in the Neighbourhood and converse familiarly
with Men, Women and Children in their own Style, on the
common Tittletattle of the Town, and the ordinary Concerns
of a family, and so take every fair opportunity of shewing my
Knowledge in the Law? But this will require much Thought,
and Time, and a very particular Knowledge of the Province
Law, and common Matters, of which I know much less than I

do of the Roman Law. This would take up too much Thought and Time and Province Law.

Shall I endeavour to renew my Acquaintance with those young Gentlemen in Boston who were at Colledge with me and to extend my Acquaintance among Merchants, Shop keepers, Tradesmen, &c. and mingle with the Crowd upon Change, and trapes the Town house floor, with one and another, in order to get a Character in Town. But this too will be a lingering method and will require more Art and Address, and Patience too than I am Master of.

Shall I, by making Remarks, and proposing Questions to the Lawyers att the Bar, endeavour to get a great Character for Understanding and Learning with them. But this is slow and tedious, and will be ineffectual, for Envy, Jealousy, and self Intrest, will not suffer them to give a young fellow a free generous Character, especially me. Neither of these Projects will bear Examination, will avail.

Shall I look out for a Cause to Speak to, and exert all the Soul and all the Body I own, to cut a flash, strike amazement, to catch the Vulgar? In short shall I walk a lingering, heavy Pace or shall I take one bold determined Leap into the Midst of some Cash and Business? That is the Question. A bold Push, a resolute attempt, a determined Enterprize, or a slow, silent, imperceptible creeping. Shall I creep or fly.

I feel vexed, fretted, chafed, the Thought of no Business mortifies, stings me. I feel angry, vexed with my Uncle Field, &c. But Let me banish these Fears. Let me assume a Fortitude, a Greatness of Mind.

In such a gradual ascent to fame and fortune, and Business, the Pleasure that they give will be imperceptible, but by a bold, sudden rise, I shall feel all the Joys of each at once. Have I Genius and Resolution and Health enough for such an attchievement?

> Oh but a Wit can study in the Streets
> and raise his mind above the Mob he meets.

Who can study in Boston Streets. I am unable to observe the various Objects, that I meet, with sufficient Precision. My Eyes are so diverted with Chimney Sweeps, Carriers of Wood,

Merchants, Ladies, Priests, Carts, Horses, Oxen, Coaches, Market men and Women, Soldiers, Sailors, and my Ears with the Rattle Gabble of them all that I cant think long enough in the Street upon any one Thing to start and pursue a Thought. I cant raise my mind above this mob Croud of Men, Women, Beasts and Carriages, to think steadily. My Attention is sollicited every moment by some new object of sight, or some new sound. A Coach, Cart, a Lady or a Priest, may at any Time, by breaking a Couplet, disconcert a whole Page of excellent Thoughts.

What is meant by a nodding Beam, and pig of Lead. He means that his Attention is necessary to preserve his Life and Limbs, as he walks the streets, for Sheets of Lead may fall from the Roofs of Houses. I know of no nodding Beam, except at the Hay Market.

Monday, March 19, 1759

The Principle in Nature is Imitation, Association of Ideas, and contrasting Habits. How naturally we imitate, without Design or with, Modes of thinking, Speaking, Acting, that please us! Thus we conform gradually to the Manners and Customs of our own family, Neighbourhood, Town, Province, Nation &c. At Worcester, I learned several Turns of Mind of Putnam, and at Boston I find my self imitating Otis, &c.—But Q, Who will learn the Art soonest, and most perfectly, he who reads without a Design of extracting Beauties or he who reads with? The last undoubtedly. Design attends, and observes nicely, and critically. I learned with Design to imitate Put's Sneer, his sly look, and his look of Contempt. This look may serve good Ends in Life, may procure Respect.

To form a style, therefore, read constantly the best Authors. Get a Habit of clear Thinking and strength and Propriety and Harmony of Expression. This one Principle of Imitation would lead me thro the whole human System. A Faculty acquired accidentally, without any Endeavours or forsight of the Effect. He read for Amuzement, not to learn to write.

Let me recollect, and con over, all the Phenomena of Imitation that I may take advantage of this Principle in my own make, that I may learn easier and sooner.

c. early April 1759

The Difference between a whole Day and a divided scattered Day.

Q. Can any Man take a Book in his hand, in the Morning, and confine his Thoughts to that till Night. Is not such a Uniformity tiresome? Is not Variety more agreable, and profitable too? Read one Book one Hour, then think an Hour, then Exercise an Hour, then read another Book an Hour, then dine, smoke, walk, cutt Wood, read another Hour loud, then think, &c. and thus spend the whole day in perpetual Variations, from Reading to thinking, Exercise, Company, &c. But what is to be acquired by this Wavering Life, but a Habit of Levity, and Impatience of Thought?

I never spent a whole Day upon one Book in my Life.

What is the Reason that I cant remove all Papers and Books from my Table, take one Volume into my Hands, and read it, and then reflect upon it, till night, without wishing for my Pen and Ink to write a Letter, or taking down any other Book, or thinking of the Girls? Because I cant command my attention. My Thoughts are roving from Girls to friends, from friends to Court, to Worcester, to Piscataquay, Newbury, and then to Greece and Rome, then to France, from Poetry to oratory, and Law, and Oh, a rambling, Imagination. Could I fix my attention, and keep off every fluttering thought that attempts to intrude upon the present subject, I could read a Book all Day. Wisdom, curse on it, will come soon or late.

I have to smooth and harmonise my Mind, teach every Thought within its Bounds, to roll, and keep the equal Measure of the Soul.

Spring 1759

Now let me collect my Thoughts, which have been long scattered, among Girls, father, Mother, Grandmother, Brothers, Matrimony, Husling, Chatt, Provisions, Cloathing, fewel, servants for a family, and apply them, with steady Resolution and an aspiring Spirit, to the Prosecution of my studies. Now Let me form the great Habits of Thinking, Writing, Speaking. Let my whole Courtship be applyed to win the Applause and Ad-

miration of Gridley, Prat, Otis, Thatcher &c. Let Love and
Vanity be extinguished and the great Passions of Ambition,
Patriotism, break out and burn. Let little objects be neglected
and forgot, and great ones engross, arouse and exalt my soul.

The Mind must be aroused, or it will slumber. To make and
[   ] in his Mind a Contempt of Cowardice, and an Admiration of Bravery.

I found a Passion growing in my heart and a consequent
Habit of thinking, forming and strengthening in my Mind,
that would have eat out every seed of ambition, in the first,
and every wise Design or Plan in the last.

Spring 1759

P W is crooked, his Head bends forwards, his shoulders are
round and his Body is writhed, and bended, his head and half
his Body, have a list one Way, the other half declines the other
Way, and his lower Parts from his Middle, incline another Way.
His features are as coarse and crooked as his Limbs. His Nose
is a large roman Nose with a prodigious Bunch Protuberance,
upon the Upper Part of it. His Mouth is large, and irregular,
his Teeth black and foul, and craggy. His Lips [   ] to command, when he speakes, they dont move easily and limberly
pliant. His lips are stiff, rigid, not pliant and supple. His Eyes
are a little squinted, his Visage is long, and lank, his Complexion wan, his Cheeks are fallen, his Chin is long, large, and lean.
These are the Features, these the Limbs, and this the Figure of
the worthy Mr. Wibirt.

But his Air, and Gesture, is still more extraordinary. When
he stands, He stands, bended, in and out before and behind
and to both Right and left; he tosses his Head on one side.
When he prays at home, he raises one Knee upon the Chair,
and throws one Hand over the back of it. With the other he
scratches his Neck, pulls the Hair of his Wigg, strokes his
Beard, rubbs his Eyes, and Lips.

When he Walks, he heaves away, and swaggs on one side,
and steps almost twice as far with one foot, as with the
other.

When he sitts, he sometimes lolls on the arms of his Chair,
sometimes on the Table. He entwines his leggs round the

Leggs of his Chair, lays hold of the Iron Rod of the stand with one Hand. Sometimes throws him self, over the back of his Chair, and scratches his Hed, Vibrates the foretop of his Wigg, thrusts his Hand up under his Wigg, &c.

When he speakes, he cocks and rolls his Eyes, shakes his Head, and jerks his Body about.

Thus clumsy, careless, slovenly, and lazy is this sensible Man.

It is surprizing to me that the Delicacy of his Mind has not corrected these Indecent, as well as ungraceful Instances of Behaviour. He has Wit, and he has Fancy, and he has Judgment. He is a Genius. But he has no Industry, no Delicacy, no Politeness. Tho' he seems to have a sort of Civility, and Cleverness in his Manners. A civil, clever Man. He observes that in Dana which I have observed—a cleverness, a good Humored look.

Spring 1759

Why have I not Genius to start some new Thought. Some thing that will surprize the World. New, grand, wild, yet regular Thought that may raise me at once to fame.

Where is my Soul? where are my Thoughts.

When shall I start some new Thought, make some new Discovery, that shall surprize the World with its Novelty and Grandeur?

Spring 1759

Is it not absurd to study all Arts but that of Living in the World, and all sciences but that of Mankind? Popularity is the Way to gain and figure.

The Arts of Gain are necessary. You may get more by studying Town meeting, and Training Days, than you can by reading Justinian and all his voluminous and heavy Commentators.

Mix with the Croud in a Tavern, in the Meeting House or the Training Field, and grow popular by your agreable assistance in the Tittle tattle of the Hour, never think of the deep hidden Principles of natural, civil, or common Law, for thoughts like these will give you a gloomy Countenance and a stiff Behaviour.

Spring 1759

It would be an agreable and useful speculation to inquire into that Faculty which we call Imagination. Define it, enquire the Good Ends it answers in the human system, and the Evils it sometimes produces.

What is the Use of Imagination? It is the Repository of Knowledge. By this faculty, are retained all the Ideas of visible objects, all the observations we have made in the Course of Life on Men and Things, our selves &c.

I am conscious that I have the faculty of Imagination, that I can at Pleasure review in my Thoughts, the Ideas and Assemblages of Ideas that have been before in my Mind. Can revive the scenes, Diversions, sports of Childhood, Youth. Can recall my youthful Rambles, to the farms, frolicks, Dalliances, my lonely Walks thro the Groves, and swamps, and fields, and Meadows at Worcester. Can imagine my self with the wildest Tribe of Indians in America in their Hunting, their Warrs, their tedious Marches, thro wild swamps and Mountains. Can fly by this faculty to the Moon, Planets, fixed Starrs, unnumbered Worlds. Can cross the Atlantic and fancy my self in Westminster Hall, hearing Causes in the Courts of Justice, or the Debates in the Houses of Commons or Lords.—As all our knowledge is acquired by Experience, i.e. by sensation or Reflection, this faculty is necessary to retain the Ideas we receive and the observations we make, and to recall them, for our Use, as Occasion requires.

I am conscious too, that this faculty is very active and stirring. It is constantly in Action unless interrupted by the Presence of external Objects, by Reading, or restrained by Attention. It hates Restraint, it runs backward to past scenes &c. or forward to the future. It flyes into the Air, dives in the sea, rambles to foreign Countries, or makes excursions to foreign planetary starry Worlds. These are but Hints, irregular observations, not digested into order.

But what are the Defects of this faculty? What are the

Errors, Vices, Habits, it may betray us into, if not curbed? What is the Danger.

I must know all the Ends of this faculty, and all its Phenomena, before I can know all its Defects. Its Phenomena are infinitely various, in different Men, and its Ends are different. Therefore its Defects must be almost infinitely various. But all its Defects may be reduced to general Laws.

The Sphere of Imagination includes both Actuality and Possibility, not only what is but what may be.

One Use of Imagination, is to facilitate the Acquisition and Communication of Knowledge. How does it facilitate the Acquisition. It lays up, It retains, the Ideas of Things and the Observations we make upon them. By reviving past scenes, or creating new, it suggests Thoughts and inquiries. Starts Hints and doubts, and furnishes Reason with Materials in our retired Hours. In the Hours of solitude, Imagination recalls the Ideas of Things, Men, Actions, Characters, and Reason reduces them to order, and forms Inferences and Deductions from them.

How does it help to communicate? Why by recalling our Knowledge, and by comparing abstract Notions with sensible Images—by Metaphor, allusion &c.

Another End of Imagination, may be personal Pleasure and Entertainment. We take Pleasure in viewing the Works of Nature, and the Productions of Art, as Painting, Statuary, Poetry, oratory &c., but are not these rather objects and Pleasures of sense than of Imagination?

We take Pleasure in recollecting the Sports, Diversions, Business, scenes of Nature &c. that we have seen in our past Lives. We take Pleasure in fancying our selves in Places, among Objects, Persons, Pleasures, when we are not; and a still greater Pleasure in the Prospect which Imagination constantly gives us of future Pleasure, Business, Wealth, fame &c.

This Prospect of futurity, which Imagination gilds and brightens, is the greatest Spur to Industry and Application. The scholars spur to study. The Commanders spur to Activity and Courage. The Statesmans Spur to the Invention and Execution of Plans of Politicks. The Lovers Spur to assiduity, and &c.

Spring 1759

Consider what figure is fittest for you to make. Consider what Profession you have chosen? The Law. What Rule and Method must I observe to make a figure to be useful, and respectable in that Station. Ask this Question upon every Occasion, of what Use to the Lawyer? of what use at the Bar— [   ] perfection of Knowledge in Theory or Expertness in Practice, or Eloquence at Bar? Let my Views concenter, and terminate in one focus, in one Point, a great, useful, virtuous Lawyer. With this View I might plan a system of study for seven Years to come, that should take in most Parts of Science and Literature. I might study Mathematics, and Poetry and Rhetorick and Logick, as auxiliary Sciences and Arts, but my principal Attention should be directed at british Law, and roman and Grecian Antiquities.

Summer 1759

Parson Smith has no small share of Priest Craft.—He conceals his own Wealth, from his Parish, that they may not be hindered by knowing it from sending him Presents.—He talks very familiarly with the People, Men and Women of his Parish, to gain their affection.—He is a crafty designing Man.—He watches Peoples Looks and Behaviour.—He laughs at Parson Wibirts careless Air and Behaviour—his Walk across the Room, his long step and his Clapping his naked sides and Breasts with his Hands before the Girls.—He made just Remarks on the Character of Mr. Maccarty.—his Conceit, his orthodoxy, his Ignorance &c. and I caught him, several times, looking earnestly at my face.—He is not one of the heedless, inattentive Crew, that take no Notice of Mens Behaviour and Conversation and form no Judgment of their Characters.

Polly and Nabby are Wits. Ned will not take Account of all of every Colour that spring from the Quincys. Easthers Simile.

A Man of fond Passions. Cranch was fond of his Friend, fond of his Girl, and would have been fond of his Wife and Children. Tender and fond. Loving and compassionate. H.Q. is of the same Character, fond of her Brother, fond of herself and tenderly pitiful. Q, are fondness and Wit compatible? Parson Smiths Girls have not this fondness, nor this Tenderness.

Fondling and Indulgence. They are the faulty Effects of good Nature. Good nature is H's universal Character. She will be a fond, tender Wife, and a fond indulgent Mother. Cranch is endeavoring to amend this Defect, to correct this fault in his Character, he affects an Asperity, to the Children, to his old Friends. His former Complaisance is vanished.—Do real Fondness, and Frankness, always go together. They met in C. and they met in H.—Fondness and Candour, and Frankness. Frankness, and Simplicity. Fondness is doting Love. Candor is a Disposition to palliate faults and Mistakes, to put the best Construction upon Words and Actions, and to forgive Injuries. Simplicity is a direct, open, artless, undisguised, Behaviour.

Are S Gils either Frank or fond, or even candid.—Not fond, not frank, not candid.

Summer 1759

———————————

Secondat says, that a Man, in the State of Nature i.e. unimproved by Education or Experience, would feel Nothing but his own Impotence and would tremble at the motion of a Leaf, and fly from every Shadow.

But Q.—What proof can be given of this Assertion? What Reason is there to think that Timidity, rather than Confidence or Presumption, would hold the Ascendancy in him? Is it not as reasonable to think he would be too bold, as too timorous, and engage oak Trees, unwieldy Rocks, or wild Beasts, [   ] as that he would fly from every Shadow? The scarcity of Phenomena, make it impossible to decide. There never was more than one or two Men found, at full Age, who had grown up with the Beasts in the Woods and never seen a human Creature, and they were not very critically observed. What does he mean by a Man in a State of Nature? Suppose a Child, confined in a Room, and supplied with Necessaries, by some secret invisible avenue, till 20 years old, without ever seeing a human Creature. That Man would be in a State of Nature, i.e. unimproved by Experience and human Conversation. Suppose a Man of the same Age and size let into this poor fellows Cell. What would be the Effect of the Meeting. Would the savage be frightened, or pleased. Surprized he would be, but agreably, or disagreably. Would his fears make him fly, or his Curiosity examine, or his Presumption assault the new object?

In a total Inexperience and Ignorance, how would human Passions operate? I cant say. A Child, at its first Entrance upon the World, discovers no signs of Terror or Surprize at the new scenes and objects, that lie around it, and if the Child is not terrified, why should the Man be. The Child is pleased as soon as its Eyes are first opened with bright and luminous objects, not frightened. It will smile not cry. Suppose then a whole Army of Persons, trained up in this manner in single seperate Cells, brought together, would they mutually dred and fly each other, or be pleased with the sight of each other, and by consequence allured gradually to a more intimate Acquaintance or would they fall together by the Ears for the Mastery as two Herds of strange Cattle do? Would the State of Nature be a State of War or Peace? Two might meet, and be pleased with each others looks, and fall to play, like two Lambs. Two others might meet, and one might apply his Hands to the others Body and hurt him, and then both fall afighting like 2 Dogs. So that both Friendship and Squabbles might be the Consequences of the first Congress. But Passions work so differently in different men especially when several of them are complicated together, and several, as Surprize, Joy, fear, Curiosity would in this Case be combined, that we cant judge what the Consequences would be in such an imaginary Congress.

Hobbes thinks, that Men like Cattle, if in a state of Nature, would mutually desire and strive for the Mastery, and I think Secondat's Argument from the Complexity of the Idea of Dominion, is not a Refutation of Hobbes's Hypothesis, for Cattle fight for Dominion, and Men in the State of Nature may be supposed to have as clear an Idea of Dominion as the Cattle have. The Laws received in a State of Nature i.e. before the Establishment of society, are the Laws of Nature. How can man be considered out of Society, before the Establishment of Society. We put possible imaginable Cases, and then ask what would be the Effect. The Species cant subsist, without Society, but an Individual may, as the wild Man found in a forrest, or a Child bred alone in a Cell out of all Human sight. Now suppose 1000 such Individuals should exist at once and all be collected and turned loose together in the same forrest. What would succeed. Some squabbles, wild [   ], and some plays, [   ], Copulation would soon succeed.

[   ] Lust of Dominion could not at first produce a War of all against all. They would not feel any such Desire of ruling and subduing. They would soon feel hunger and thirst, and desire of Copulation and Calf, and would endeavour to supply these Wants and gratify these Desires, but would not yet conceive the Thought and Wish of governing all the Rest. Peace, Nourishment, Copulation, and Society. Recur to this by all means, when I get into a thotless dissipated [   ], set down and write my self into [   ] thinking.

Law is human Reason. It governs all the Inhabitants of the Earth; the political and civil Laws of each Nation should be only the particular Cases, in which human Reason is applied.

Let me attend to the Principle of Government. The Laws of Britain, should be adapted to the Principle of the british Government, to the Climate of Britain, to the Soil, to its situation, as an Island, and its Extent, to the manner of living of the Natives as Merchants, Manufacturers and Husbandmen, to the Religion of the Inhabitants.

Summer 1759

———————

Have been out of Humour, this Evening, more than I have been for some Weeks if not Months. Reflection, thinking on a Girl, ill Health, Want of Business, &c., wrought me by insensible degrees into a peevish Mood. I felt reduced to Necessities, needy, poor, pennyless, empty Pockets. I have given away at least 10s. this day. Thus decayed Merchants must preserve the Appearances of Affluence. But Poverty is infinitely less deplorable to me than a nervous Languor of the Body. If I have good Digestion and Spirits, I can bear with an easy Mind an empty Purse.

But I have been stupid, to the last Degree, in neglecting to spred my Acquaintance. I have neglected Parson Robbins, Parson Tafte, and Parson Smith too. I have neglected Dr. Tufts and Esqr. Niles, Eben Miller, Dr. Miller, and Edmund Quincy. Dr. Millers &c., Mr. Allins, Mr. Borlands, Mrs. Apthorps, Edd. Quincies. I should aim at an Acquaintance. Not to spend much Time at their Houses but to get their good Word. And behave with Spirit too. I have hitherto behaved with too much Reserve to some and with too stiff a face and air, and with a face and Air and Tone of Voice of pale Timidity. I should look bold, speak with more Spirit. Should talk Divinity with P Tafte, and gain his Love or else extort his Admiration, or both. Make him love and admire. I ought to hire, or wheedle or allure two or 3 in every Town, to trumpet my Character abroad. But I have no Trumpets in Weighmouth, none in Skadin, none in Milton. Oh! what have I been about? I lay no schemes to raise my Character. I lay no schemes to draw Business. I lay no Schemes to extend my Acquaintance, with young fellows nor young Girls, with Men of figure, Character nor fortune. Am content to live unknown, poor, with the lowest of all our species for Company. This is the Tenor of my Conduct.

Summer 1759

FAME AND CICERO

To Jonathan Sewall

FEB.   1760

I am very willing to join with you, in renouncing the Reasoning of some of our last Letters.

There is but little Pleasure, which Reason can approve to be received from the Noisy applause, and servile Homage that is paid to any Officer from the Lictor to the Dictator, or from the sexton of a Parish to the sovereign of a Kingdom: And Reason will despize equally, a blind undistinguishing Adoration of what the World calls fame. She is neither a Goddess to be loved, nor a Demon to be feared, but an unsubstantial Phantom existing only in Imagination.

But with all this Contempt, give me Leave to reserve (for I am sure that Reason will warrant) a strong affection for the honest Approbation of the wise and the good both in the present, and in all future Generations. Mistake not this for an Expectation of the Life to come, in the Poets Creed.—Far otherwise. I expect to be totally forgotten within 70 Years from the present Hour unless the Insertion of my Name in the Colledge Catalogue, should luckily preserve it longer.—When Heaven designs an extraordinary Character, one that shall distinguish his Path thro' the World by any great Effects, it never fails to furnish the proper Means and Opportunities; but the common Herd of Mankind, who are to be born and eat and sleep and die, and be forgotten, is thrown into the World as it were at Random, without any visible Preparation of Accommodations.—Yet tho I have very few Hopes, I am not ashamed to own that a Prospect of an Immortality in the Memories of all the Worthy, to the End of Time would be a high Gratification to my Wishes.

But to Return, Tully, therefore, had but few Advantages, in the Estimation of Reason more than We have, for a happy Life.—He had greater Political Objects to tempt his Ambition, he had better Opportunities to force the Hozanna's of his Countrymen, but these are not Advantages for Happiness. On the Contrary, the Passions which these Objects were designed to gratify, were so many stings for ever smarting in his Mind, which at last goaded him into that Excess of Vanity and Pusillanimity, for which he has been as often blamed, as ever he was praised for his Genius and his Virtues. Tis true, he had Abler Masters and more Opportunities for instructive Conversation, in a City, so fruitful of great Men. But in other Respects the rational sources of Pleasure, have been much enlarged since his Day.

In the Acquisition of Knowledge, without which it would be a Punishment to live, we have much greater Advantages (whatever some ingenious Men may say) than he had or could have. For the Improvements in Navigation, and the surprizing Augmentation of Commerce, by spreading civilized Nations round the Globe, and sending Men of Letters into all Countries, have multiplied the Means of Information concerning the Planet we inhabit; and the Invention of the Art of Printing, has perpetuated and cheapened the Means of every Kind of Knowledge, beyond what could have been immagined in his Day.

Europe has been, ever since his Death, the Constant Theatre of surprizing Characters, Actions, Events, Revolutions, which have been preservd in a sufficient Plenty of Memorials, to constitute a series of Political Knowledge of a greater Variety of Characters, more important Events, and more complicated Circumstances; and of Consequence better adapted for an Agreable Entertainment to the Mind, than any, that the World had ever known in his Times; and perhaps there never was before, nor has been since his Day, a Period, abounding with greater Heroes and Politicians, or with more surprizing Actions and Events, than that in which we live.

In Metaphysicks, Mr. Locke, directed by my Lord Bacon, has steered his Course into the unenlightened Regions of the human Mind, and like Columbus has discoverd a new World. A World whose soil is deep and strong producing Rank and unwholsome Weeds as well as wholsome fruits and flowers; a World that is incumbered with unprofitable Brambles, as well as stored with useful Trees; and infested with motly Savages; as well as capable of furnishing civilized Inhabitants; he has shewn us by what Cultivation, these Weeds may be Extirmined and the fruits raised; the Brambles removed as well as the Trees grubbed; the savages destroyd, as well as the civil People increased. Here is another Hemisphere of Science therefore abounding with Pleasure and with Profit too, of which Cicero had but very few and we have many Advantages for learning.

But in Mathematicks, and what is founded on them, Astronomy and Phylosophy, the Modern Discoveries have done Honour to the human Understanding. Here is the true sphere of Modern Genius.—What a noble Prospect of the Universe have these Men opened before us. Here I see Millions of Worlds and systems of Worlds, swarming with Inhabitants, all engaged in the same Active Investigation of the great System of Universal and eternal Truth, and overflowing with Felicity.

And while I am ravished with such Contemplations as these, it imports me little on what Ground I tread or in what Age I live.

The Intention of the Testator to be collected from the Words, is to be observd in the Construction of a Will—and where any Title to Lands or Goods, or any other Act is devisd to any one, without any mention of something previous or concomitant, without which the Act or Title is not valid, in such Case the Thing previous or concomitant shall by Implication be devised too, e.g.

A Man devises Lands and Tenements to A.B., the said A.B. paying £100 out of the same Lands to B.C.—Here are no Words of Inheritance or of Freehold you see, yet since The Testator plainly intended, that £100 should be paid to B.C. out of the Land, it must be presumed that he knew the Rule of Law which entitles a Devisee of Lands encumbered with a Charge, to a Fee simple, and therefore a fee simple shall pass by Implication. So also

A Man devisd Lands and Tenements to A.B. in Trust for C.D. and his Heirs. Here are no Words of Inheritance, yet as he has established a Trust that may last forever, he shall be presumed to have intended a Fee simple in his Devise, and the Devisee shall hold the Tenements to himself and his own Heirs for ever, by Implication, altho the Cestuy que Trust should die Heirless tomorrow. Now

En mesure le manner. The Testator intended plainly that his Negro should have his Liberty, and a Legacy. Therefore the Law will presume that he intended his Executor should do all that, without which he could have neither. That this Indemnification was not in the Testators mind, cannot be proved from the Will, any more than it could be proved in the 1st Case above that the Testator did not know a Fee simple would pass a Will without the Word Heirs; nor than in the 2d Case, that the Devise of a Trust that might continue for ever would convey a fee simple without the like Words.

I take it therefore, that the Executor of this Will is by Implication obligd to give Bonds to the The Town Treasurer, and in his Refusal is a wrong doer, and I cant think he ought to be allowed to take advantage of his own Wrong so much as to alledge this Want of an Indemnification, to evade an Action of the Case brot for the Legacy, by the Negro himself.

But why may not the Negro bring a special Action of the Case vs. Executor setting forth the Will, the Devise of Freedom, and a Legacy, and then the Necessity of Indemnification by the Province Law, and then a Refusal to indemnify and of Consequence to set free, and to pay the Legacy.

Perhaps the Negro is free at common Law by the Devise.

Now the Province Law seems to have been made, only to oblige the Master to maintain his manumitted servant, not to declare a Manumission in the Masters lifetime or at his Death, void. Should a Master give his Negro his freedom under his Hand and seal, without giving Bond to the Town, and should afterwards repent and endeavour to recall the Negro into servitude, would not that Instrument be sufficient discharge vs. the Master?

P.S. I felt your Reproof, very sensibly, for being ceremonious. I must beg Pardon in a style that I threatend you with as a Punishment, a few letters ago, Μηδ' ἐχθαιρε φίλον σὸν ἁμαρτάδος εινεκα μικρης.

However, it is not Ceremony, so much as Poverty.

From the Diary:
May 26, 1760–February 9, 1761

MONDAY MAY 26TH 1760.

Spent the Evening at Mr. Edd. Quincy's, with Mr. Wibird, and my Cozen Zab. Mr. Quincy told a remarkable Instance of Mr. Ben. Franklin's Activity, and Resolution, to improve the Productions of his own Country, for from that source it must have sprang, or else from an unheard of Stretch of Benevolence to a stranger. Mr. Franklin, happening upon a Visit to his Germantown Friends, to be at Mr. Wibirts Meeting, was asked, after Meeting in the afternoon, to drink Tea, at Mr. Quincys. The Conversation turned upon the Qualities of American soils, and the Different Commodities raised in these Provinces. Among the rest, Mr. Franklin mentioned, that the Rhenish Grape Vines had been introduced, into Pensylvania, and that some had been lately planted in Phyladelphia, and succeeded very well. Mr. Quincy said, upon it, I wish I could get some into my Garden. I doubt not they would do very well in this Province. Mr. Franklin replied, Sir if I can supply you with some of the Cuttings, I shall be glad to. Quincy thanked him and said, I dont know but some time or other I shall presume to trouble you. And so the Conversation passed off. Within a few Weeks Mr. Quincy was surprised with a Letter from some of Franklins friends in Boston, that a Bundle of these Rhenish slips were ready for him. These came by Water. Well, soon afterwards he had another Message that another Parcell of slips were left for him by the Post. The next Time Mr. Franklin was in Boston Mr. Quincy waited on him to thank him for his slips, but I am sorry Sir to give you so much Trouble. Oh Sir, says Franklin the Trouble is nothing Sir, to me, if the Vines do but succeed in your Province. However I was obliged to take more Pains than I expected when I saw you. I had been told, that the Vines were in the City but I found none and was obliged to send up to a Village 70 miles from the City for them. Thus he took the Trouble to hunt over the City, and not finding Vines there, he sends 70 miles into the Country, and then sends one Bundle by Water, and least they should miscarry another by Land, to a Gentleman whom he owed nothing, and was but little acquainted with, purely for the sake of Doing Good in the World by Propagating the Rhenish Wines thro these Provinces. And Mr. Quincy has some of them now growing in his Garden. This is an Instance too of his amazing Capacity for Business. His Memory and Resolution. Amidst so much Business as Counsellor, Post Master, Printer, so many private studies, and so many Publick Avocations too, to remember such a transient Hint and exert himself, so in answer to it, is surprising.

JUNE 5TH. THURDSDAY.

Arose late. Feel disordered. 8 o'Clock, 3 1/2 Hours after Sun rise, is a sluggard's rising Time. Tis a stupid Waste of so much Time. Tis getting an Habit hard to conquer, and Tis very hurtful to ones Health. 3 1/2, 1/7 of the 24, is thus spiritlessly dozed away. God grant me an Attention to remark, and a Resolution to pursue every Opportunity, for the Improvement of my Mind, and to save, with the Parsimony of a Miser, every moment of my Time.

June 5, 1760

MONDAY. JUNE 16TH.

Arose before the sun. Now I am ignorant of my Future Fortune, what Business, what Reputation, I may get, which is now far from my Expectations. How many Actions shall I secure this Day? What new Client shall I have? I found at Evening, I had secured 6 Actions, but not one new Client, that I know of.

June 16, 1760

NOVR. 14TH. 1760.

Another Year is now gone and upon Recollection, I find I have executed none of my Plans of study. I cannot Satisfy my self that I am much more knowing either from Books, or Men, from this Chamber, or the World, than I was at least a Year ago, when I wrote the foregoing Letter to Sewal. Most of my Time has been spent in Rambling and Dissipation. Riding, and Walking, Smoking Pipes and Spending Evenings, consume a vast Proportion of my Time, and the Cares and Anxieties of Business, damp my Ardor and scatter my attention. But I must stay more at home—and commit more to Writing. A Pen is certainly an excellent Instrument, to fix a Mans Attention and to inflame his Ambition. I am therefore beginning a new literary Year, with the 26th. of my life.

1760. DECR. 2D.

Spent the Evening at Coll. Q.'s with Captn. Freeman. About the middle of the Evening Dr. Lincoln and his Lady came in. The Dr. gave us an ample Confirmation of our Opinion of his Brutality and Rusticity. He treated his Wife, as no drunken Cobler, or Clothier would have done, before Company. Her father never gave such Looks and Answers to one of his slaves in my Hearing. And he contradicted he Squibd, shrugged, scouled, laughd at the Coll. in such a Manner as the Coll. would have called Boorish, ungentlemanly, unpolite, ridiculous, in any other Man. More of the Clown, is not in the World. A hoggish, ill bred, uncivil, haughty, Coxcomb, as ever I saw. His Wit is forced and affected, his Manners to his father, Wife, and to Company are brutally rustic, he is ostentatious of his Talent at Disputation, forever giving an History, like my

Uncle Hottentot, of some Wrangle he has had with this and
that Divine. Affects to be thought an Heretic. Disputes against
the Eternity of Hell, torments &c. His treatment of his Wife
amazed me. Miss Q. asked the Dr. a Question. Miss Lincoln
seeing the Dr. engaged with me, gave her Mother an Answer,
which however was not satisfactory. Miss Q. repeats it. "Dr.
you did not hear my Question."—"Yes I did, replies the Dr.,
and the Answer to it, my Wife is so pert, she must put in her
Oar, or she must blabb, before I could speak." And then
shrugged And affected a laugh, to cow her as he used to, the
freshmen and sophymores at Colledge.—She sunk into silence
and shame and Grief, as I thought.—After supper, she says
"Oh my dear, do let my father see that Letter we read on the
road." Bela answers, like the great Mogul, like Nero or
Caligula, "he shant."—Why, Dr., do let me have it! do!—He
turns his face about as stern as the Devil, sour as Vinegar. "I
wont."—Why sir says she, what makes you answer me so
sternly, shant and wont?—Because I wont, says he. Then the
poor Girl, between shame and Grief and Resentment and
Contempt, at last, strives to turn it off with a Laugh.—"I wish
I had it. Ide shew it, I know."—Bela really acts the Part of the
Tamer of the Shrew in Shakespear. Thus a kind Look, an
obliging Air, a civil Answer, is a boon that she cant obtain from
her Husband. Farmers, Tradesmen, Soldiers, Sailors, People of
no fortune, Figure, Education, are really more civil, obliging,
kind, to their Wives than he is.—She always is under Restraint
before me. She never dares shew her endearing Airs, nor any
fondness for him.

There is every Year, some new and astonishing scene of
Vice, laid open to the Consideration of the Public. Parson Potters Affair, with Mrs. Winchester, and other Women, is hardly
forgotten. A Minister, famous for Learning, oratory, orthodoxy, Piety and Gravity, discovered to have the most debauched and polluted of Minds, to have pursued a series of
wanton Intrigues, with one Woman and another, to have got
his Maid with Child and all that.—Lately Deacon Savils Affair
has become public. An old Man 77 Years of Age, a Deacon,
whose chief Ambition has always been Prayer, and religious

Conversation, and sacerdotal Company, discovered to have been the most salacious, rampant, Stallion, in the Universe—rambling all the Town over, lodging with this and that Boy and Attempting at least the Crime of Buggery.

Thursday, December 18, 1760

1760. DECR. 18.

Justice Dyer says there is more Occasion for Justices than for Lawyers. Lawyers live upon the sins of the People. If all Men were just, and honest, and pious, and Religious &c. there would be no need of Lawyers. But Justices are necessary to keep men just and honest and pious, and religious.—Oh sagacity!

But, it may be said with equal Truth, that all Magistrates, and all civil officers, and all civil Government, is founded and maintained by the sins of the People. All armies would be needless if Men were universally virtuous. Most manufacturers and Tradesmen would be needless. Nay, some of the natural Passions and sentiments of human Minds, would be needless upon that supposition. Resentment, e.g. which has for its object, Wrong and Injury. No man upon that supposition would ever give another, a just Provocation. And no just Resentment could take Place without a just Provocation. Thus, our natural Resentments are founded on the sins of the People, as much as the Profession of the Law, or that of Arms, or that of Divinity. In short Vice and folly are so interwoven in all human Affairs that they could not possibly be wholly separated from them without tearing and rending the whole system of human Nature, and state. Nothing would remain as it is.

JANY. 2ND. 1760 FRYDAY.

The Representatives in their Address to the Governor, have told him that "Great Britain is the leading and most respectable Power in the whole World."—Let us examine this.—Is she the Leading Power, either in War or Negociation?—In War? She has no Army, not more than 50 or 60 thousand Men, whereas France has a standing Army, of 250,000 men in Camp and in Garrison. And their officers are as gallant and skillful, their Gunners and Engineers, the most accomplished of any in

Europe. Their Navy indeed is now inconsiderable, And our Navy alone has given us the Advantage. But our Navy alone will not make us the leading Power. How we can be called the Leading Power I cant see. Holland, Spain, Portugal, Denmark, and all Italy has refused to follow us, and Austria, Russia, Sweeden, and indeed almost all the states of Germany, the Prince of Hesse excepted, have followed France. The only Power, independent Power that has consented to follow us is Prussia, and indeed upon Recollection it seems to me we followed Prussia too, rather than the Contrary.—Thus we are the Leading Power without Followers.

And, if we are not the leading Power, in War, we never have been the Leading Power in Negociation.—It is a common Place observation that the French have regained by Treaty, all the Advantages, which we had gained by Arms. Now whether this arose from the superior Dexterity of the french Plenipotentiaries, or from the universal Complaisance of the other Plenipotentiaries of Europe to France and frenchmen, it equally proves that England is not the leading Power, in Councils.

How are we the most respectable?—The most respected, I am sure, we are not!—else how came all Europe to remain Neuters, or else take Arms against us—how came foreigners, from all Countries, to resort to France, to learn their Policy, Military Discipline, fortification, Manufactures, Language, Letters, Science, Politeness &c. so much more than to England? How comes the french Language to be studied and spoken as a polite Accomplishment, all over Europe, and how comes all Negociations to be held in french.

And if we consider every Thing, The Religion, Government, Freedom, Navy, Merchandize, Army, Manufactures, Policy, Arts, Sciences, Numbers of Inhabitants and their Virtues, it seems to me, that England falls short in more and more important Particulars, than it exceeds the Kingdom of France.

To determine the Character of "Leading and respectable," as Dr. Savil does, from a few Victories and successes, by which Rules he makes Charles 12th to have been in his day, the leading and most respectable Power, and Oliver Cromwell in his, and the K. of Prussia in this, is most ignorant and silly.

In short, "Leading and Respectable," is not to be determined, either by the Prince, the Policy, the Army, Navy, Arts,

Science, Commerce, nor by any other national Advantage, taken singly and abstracted from the rest. But that Power is to be denominated so, whose Aggregate, of component Parts, is most.

January 2, 1761

1761 MONDAY. FEBY. 9TH.

This morning, as I lay abed, I recollected my last Weeks Work. I find I was extreamly diligent, constantly in my Chamber, Spent no Evenings abroad, not more than one at the Drs. Have taken no Walks, never on Horseback the whole Week, excepting once, which was on Tuesday, when I went to Boston. Yet how has this Retirement, and solitude been spent? In too much Rambling and Straggling from one Book to another, from the Corpus Juris Canonici, to Bolingbroke, from him to Pope, from him to Addison, from him to Yoricks sermons, &c. In fine, the whole Week, and all my Diligence has been lost, for want of observing De Wits Maxim, "one Thing at once." This Reflection raised a Determination to re-assume the Corpus Juris, or Rather Lancelots Institutes, read nothing else, and think of nothing else—till sometime.

DEFINING GENIUS

To Samuel Quincy

Dr. Sir   April 22d. 1761

Since you claim a Promise I will perform as well as I can. The Letter so long talked of, is but a Mouse though the offspring of a pregnant Mountain. However, if amidst the cares of business, the gay diversions of the Town, the sweet refreshments of private study, and the joyful expectations of approaching Wedlock, you can steal a moment to read a letter from an old Country-friend, I shall chearfully transcribe it, such as it is, without the least alteration, or the least labor to connect this preamble to the subsequent Purview.

The Review of an old Letter from you upon original

Composition and original Genius, has raised a war in my mind. "Scraps of Verse, sayings of Philosophers," the received opinion of the World, and my own reflections upon all, have thrown my imagination into a Turmoil, like the reign of Rumour in Milton, or the jarring elements in Ovid, Where

> "Nulli sua forma manebat
> Obstabatque alliis aliud."

a picture of which I am determined to draw.

Most writers have represented Genius as a rare Phenomenon, a Phœnix. Bolingbroke says, "God mingles sometimes among the societies of Men, a few and but a few, of Those on whom he is graciously pleased to bestow a larger portion of the ætherial spirit, than in the ordinary Course of his Providence he bestows on the Sons of Men." Mr. Pope will tell you, that this "vivida vis animi, is to be found in very few, and that the utmost stretch of study, learning, and industry, can never attain to This." Dr. Cheyne shall distinguish between his Quick-thinkers, and Slow-thinkers, and insinuate that the former are extreamly scarce.

We have a becoming Reverence for the authority of these Writers, and of many Others of the same Opinion—but we may be allowed to fear that the vanity of the human heart, had too great a share in determining these Writers that Opinion.

The same vanity which gave rise to that strange religious Dogma, that God elected a precious few (of which few however every Man who believes the doctrine is always One) to Life eternal without regard to any foreseen Virtue, and reprobated all the Rest, without regard to any foreseen Vice—A doctrine which, with serious gravity, represents the world, as under the government of Humour and Caprice, and which Hottentots and Mohawks would reject with horror.

If the orthodox doctrine of Genius is not so detestable as that of unconditional Election, it is not much less invidious, nor much less hurtful. One represents eternal life, as an unattainable Thing without the special favor of the Father—and even with that attainable by very few, one of a Tribe or two of a Nation, and so tends to discourage the practice of virtue. The other represents the talents to excell as extreamly scarce, indulged by Nature to very few, and unattainable by all the

Rest, and therefore tends to discourage Industry. You and I shall never be persuaded or frightened either by Popes or Councils, Poets or Enthusiasts, to believe that the world of nature, learning and grace is governed by such arbitrary Will or inflexible fatality. We have much higher Notions of the efficacy of human endeavours in all Cases.

It is not improbable (as some Men are taller, stronger, fairer &c., than Others) that some may be by the Constitution of their bodies more sensible than others, so some may be said to be born with greater geniuses than others—and the middle point between that of the most perfect organization and the least perfect, in an healthy Child, that is not an Idiot nor a Monster, is the point of Common Sense. It is therefore likely, there are as many who have more than Common Sense, and so may be in different degrees denominated great geniuses, as there are who have less, and these surely will not by Mr. Pope, my Lord Bolingbroke, or Dr. Cheyne, be thought extreamly few.—The falacy seems to lie here. We define Genius to be the innate Capacity, and then vouchsafe this flattering Title only to Those few, who have been directed, by their birth, education and lucky accidents, to distinguish themselves in arts and sciences, or in the execution of what the World calls great Affairs, instead of planting Corn, freighting Oysters, and killing Deer, the worthy employments in which most great Geniuses are engaged—for in truth according to that definition the world swarms with Them.

Go down to the Market-place, and enquire of the first Butcher you see, about his birth, education and the fortunes of his Life, and in the course of his rude history, you will find as many instances of Invention (Mr. Pope's Criterion of genius) as you will find in the works of most of the celebrated Poets. Go on board an Oyster-boat, and converse with the Skipper, he will relate as many instances of invention, and intrepidity too, as you will find in the lives of many British Admirals, who shine in history as the ornaments of their Country. Enquire of a Gunner in Braintree-bay, or of an Hunter upon the Frontiers of this Province, and you will hear of as many artful devices to take their Game, as you will read in the lives of Cæsar, or Charles or Frederick. And as genius is more common, it seems to me it is much more powerful than is generally thought. For this mighty favour of Nature, of which the Poets and Orators, Philosophers and Legislators of the world, have been in all ages so proud and which has been represented as sufficient of itself to the formation of all those Characters—is so far otherwise, that if you pick out your great Men, from Greek or Roman, and from English history, and suppose them born and bred in Eskimeaux or Caffraria, Patagonia or Lapland, no Man would imagine that any great effects from their genius would have appeared.

Mr. Pope tells us, that De la Motte confesses, in whatever age Homer had lived, he must have been the greatest Poet of his Nation—but in my humble opinion, Mr. Waller was nearer the truth when he said, that in certain Circumstances,

> "The Conqueror of the world had been,
> But the first Wrestler on the Green."

The gods sell all Things to Industry, and Invention among the Rest. The Sequel upon Industry, you may possibly have sometime or other, but remember it is not promised by,

J. A.

From the Diary: August 1–October 18, 1761

The English Constitution is founded, tis bottomed And grounded on the Knowledge and good sense of the People. The very Ground of our Liberties, is the freedom of Elections. Every Man has in Politicks as well as Religion, a Right to think and speak and Act for himself. No man either King or Subject, Clergyman or Layman has any Right to dictate to me the Person I shall choose for my Legislator and Ruler. I must judge for myself, but how can I judge, how can any Man judge, unless his Mind has been opened and enlarged by Reading. A Man who can read, will find in his Bible, in the common sermon Books that common People have by them and even in the Almanack and News Papers, Rules and observations, that will enlarge his Range of Thought, and enable him the better to judge who has and who has not that Integrity of Heart, and that Compass of Knowledge and Understanding, which form the Statesman.

August 1, 1761

Among the numberless Imperfections of human Nature and society, there is none that deserves to be more lamented, because there is none that is the source of greater Evils, than the Tendency of great Parts and Genius, to imprudent sallies and a Wrong Biass. If We move back, thro the History of all ages and Nations, we shall find, that all the Tumults, Insurrections, and Revolutions, that have disturbed the Peace of society, and spilled oceans of Blood, have arisen from the giddy Rashness and Extravagance of the sublimest Minds. But in those Governments where the People have much Power, tho the best that can be found, the Danger from such spirits is the greatest of all. That unquenchable Thirst of superiority, and Power which, in such Governments, inkindles the Lust of Popularity, often precipitates Persons of the Character I describe, into the wildest Projects and Adventures, to set the World aware of their Parts and Persons, without attending to the Calamities that must ensue. Popular orators are generally opposite to the present Administration, blaming public Measures, and despizing or detesting Persons in Power, whether wise or foolish, wicked or upright, with all their Wit, and Knowledge, merely to make themselves the Idols of a slavish, timid People, who are always jealous and invidious of Power and therefore devoted to those that expose, ridicule or condemn it. Eloquence that may be employed wisely to persuade, is often employed wickedly to seduce, from the Eloquence of Greece and Rome down to the rude speeches of our American Town Meeting. I have more charity, than to believe, that these orators really intend an Injury to their Country; but so subtle are our Hearts in deceiving ourselves, we are so apt to think our own Parts so able and capable and necessary to the public, that we shall richly repair, by our Capacity in public station any Mischiefs we occasion in our Way to them. There is perhaps a sincere Patriotism in the Hearts of all such Persons; but it must be confessed, that the most refined Patriotism to which human Nature can be wrought, has in it an alloy of Ambition, of Pride and avarice that debases the Composition, and produces mischievous Effects.

As unhappy and blamable as such Persons are, the general Method in Use among Persons in Power of treating such spirits, is neither less unhappy, or blamable or hurtful. Such Minds, with a wise and delicate Management, may be made the ornaments and Blessings: but by an unskilfull and rough Usage, will be rendered desperate and therefore the Worst Blemishes and Plagues of their Country.

I therefore who am setting up for the Monitor of all future Legislators, a Character for which by my great Age, Experience, Sense and Learning I am well qualified, hereby advise the orator, to guard himself and his Country, against the Danger to which his Passions expose both, and the Man in Power, instead of thwarting, and insulting and over bearing a Person who perhaps is full as wise and good as he, to [   ] and cool and soften by a mild obliging Behaviour, and a just Attention to the [   ].

October 18, 1761

AN ORDER FOR KISSES

To Abigail Smith

Miss Adorable   Octr. 4th. 1762

By the same Token that the Bearer hereof *satt up* with you last night I hereby order you to give him, as many Kisses, and as many Hours of your Company after 9 O'Clock as he shall please to Demand and charge them to my Account: This Order, or Requisition call it which you will is in Consideration of a similar order Upon Aurelia for the like favour, and I presume I have good Right to draw upon you for the Kisses as I have given two or three Millions at least, when one has been received, and of Consequence the Account between us is immensely in favour of yours,   John Adams

"THE STEEL AND THE MAGNET"

To Abigail Smith

Dear Madam   Braintree Feby. 14th. 1763
   Accidents are often more Friendly to us, than our own
Prudence.—I intended to have been at Weymouth Yesterday,
but a storm prevented.—Cruel, Yet perhaps blessed storm!—
Cruel for detaining me from so much friendly, social Company, and perhaps blessed to you, or me or both, for keeping
me at *my Distance*. For every experimental Phylosopher
knows, that the steel and the Magnet or the Glass and feather
will not fly together with more Celerity, than somebody And
somebody, when brought within the striking Distance—and,
Itches, Aches, Agues, and Repentance might be the Consequences of a Contact in present Circumstances. Even the Divines pronounce casuistically, I hear, "unfit to be touched
these three Weeks."
   I mount this moment for that noisy, dirty Town of Boston,
where Parade, Pomp, Nonsense, Frippery, Folly, Foppery,
Luxury, Polliticks, and the soul-Confounding Wrangles of the
Law will give me the Higher Relish for Spirit, Taste and Sense,
at Weymouth, next Sunday.
   My Duty, where owing! My Love to Mr. Cranch And Lady,
tell them I love them, I love them better than any Mortals who
have no other Title to my Love than Friendship gives, and that
I hope he is in perfect Health and she in all the Qualms that
necessarily attend Pregnancy, and in all other Respects very
happy.
   Your—(all the rest is inexpressible)   John Adams

"Humphrey Ploughjogger" No. I

Lofing Sun   Bostun, the thurd of March 1763
Thes fue Lins cums to let you no, that I am very wel at prisent,
thank God for it, hoping that you and the family are so too. I
haf bin here this fortnite and it is fiftene yeres you no sins I was
here laste, and ther is grate alterashons both in the plase and
peple, the grate men dus nothin but quaril with one anuther
and put peces in the nues paper aginst one anuther, and sum
sayes one is rite, and others sayes tuther is rite and they dont
know why or wherefor, there is not hafe such bad work
amumgst us when we are a goin to ordane a minstur as there is
amungst these grate Fokes, and they say there is a going to be
a standin armey to be kept in pay all pece time and I am glad of
it Ime sure for then muney will be plenty and we can sell off
our sauce and meat, but some other peple says we shall be
force to pay um and that wil be bad on tuther hand becaus we
haf pade taksis enuf alredy amungst us, and they say we are
despretly in det now but howsomever we dont pay near upon
it so much as bostun folks and thats som cumfurt but I hop
our depetys will be so wise as to take care we shant pay no more
for that, the Bostun peple are grone dedly proud for I see
seven or eight chirch minsturs tuther day and they had ruffles
on and grate ty wigs with matter a bushel of hair on um that
cums haf way down there baks, but I dont wonder they go so
fin for there is a parcel of peple in Lundun that chuses um as
they say and pays um, but our m– – – – – thinks themselfs
well off if they can get a toe shirt to go to Leckshun in, but
that is not their sorts for if they ant well pade they cant help it
and they ort to be for the bible says the laburrer is wurthy of
his hier and they that prech the Gospel should live by the
Gospel, but Ime dredful afrade that now there is so many of
these minsturs here that they will try to bring in popiree
among us and then the pritandur will come and we shal all be
made slaves on. I have bote your juse harp and intend to come
home next week and tell your mother so. so no more at prisent
but that I am Your lofeing father   Humphry Ploughjogger

Boston Evening-Post, March 14, 1763

"Humphrey Ploughjogger" No. II

To the Publishers of the BOSTON EVENING-POST.
Plese to put this following, in your next Print.
I arnt book larnt enuff, to rite so polytly, as the great gentlefolks, that rite in the News-Papers, about Pollyticks. I think it
is pitty, they should know how to rite so well, saving they
made a better use ont. And that they might do, if they would
rite about something else. They do say we are a matter a million of muney in det. If so be the matter be so, I dont see but
the Cunstibles must dragg two thirds on us to goal, for our
land and housen and creeturs wont pay tacksis, without ther is
muney to sell them for. And I am shure ther arnt haff a million
of muney amongst us. And now the war is done, we cant bring
in any more amungst us.—In the war time I could sell my fatt
ocksen, and sheep, and every thing I could raise on my place,
for a pretty good round price in muney. So that the war did me
some good, 'tho' I lost by it two of my sons, as stout young
fellows as ever took a man by the sholders. But now I cant sell
any thing, because nobody has no muney hardly. And they do
say that amost all the muney folks can rake and scrape, is sent
away by water to buy Corn and Hemp and such like, besides
that that is sent to buy fine cloths. As to finery gentlefolks may
do what they ples, for we cant make um so fine here as they
bring um from Lunnun. But I know we can raise as good In-
gean corn here as they can in Virginny, and as good Wheet as
they can in Connetticut, and folks say we could raise as good
Hemp, as they raise in any part of the world. And if so be, this
be true we might raise anuff amongst us, to send to Lunnun to
pay for our fine cloths; for they do say, it fetches a nation price,
and they want abundance of it ther, about their shipping, but
no body amungst us knows how to raise it.
    What I'me ater is, to get some great larnt gentleman, who
has been to Old Ingland, and knows how they raise Hemp
there, and can read books about it, and understand um, to
print in your News, some direckshon, about it, that we may go
to trying, for we cant afford to run venters, by working, may
be, a month and then have nothing come of it for want of
working right.—I'le affirm it, a little short piece in the print,

no bigger than these few lines I send you at this present riting, if it did but tell us how to raise Hemp, how to fitt our land and feed, how and when to sow it, how to gather the crop and when, and how to dress it, and suck like would do a thousand pounds worth of good.

Seems to me folks must have a queer kind of souls to love to study, to fling dirt and play hide and seek in the News, better to walk or ride about the country, in good weather, and study like King Solomon, the Herbs from the Cedar of Lebanon to the Hysop in the wall. I'le avouch it I've took more delight in looking upon a bunch of leeves, or blossoms, or sprigs of grass for two hours together, to see how nice and pretty it is made, than I ever did last winter, or spring in reeding any of them scolding pieces in the News, and yet tho' I want bro't up to College I love to reed.

I wonder why folks will rite so as they do in the News, they make amost all the world hate um for it. whereas I'le say it they could make every body love um if they would rite about farming, and teech country folks how to pay their rates by rasing hemp and such like. For it would be strange, if we in a land of light were not as good as Heathens, and I've seen it in a sermon book, that they worshipt, even arter he was dead, that man that taut um how to use Grapes, and tother too that taut um how to sow corn and such like. Thes Pagans were fools to worship um, tho it shows that they lov'd and honour'd the man that did um good, which we Chrischans dont always do, tho I hope most of us should.—Sum of our ministers say that none of thes heathens are sav'd, which I cant hardly beleeve.

I do say that our great knowing rich men cant answer it to a good conshence, if they dont take sum panes and spend sum muney too, to learn us little ignorant poor folks how to pay our rates, and get a living, dont they remember the parable of the Talents!—besides we have work'd hard and lost our sons and brothers in the war, to defend them in hole skins, and got so far in det that we cant pay saving they contrive sum way for us.—I wonder whether they ever sit alone and medetate.—If they did their bowels would yerne toward us.—I sit up sumtimes till 12 a Clock at night thinking about myself and Naibours our land and stock and rates, and about the war, and about my too poor dear sons, one of um died of a camp fevur, and tother was skalp'd by the Ingeans, till my hart is redy to burst and my eyes run over. I'm shure if I had as much larning, books and time to spaer from my labor, with my poor abillitys, thof I say it, I could find out 20 ways of teeching mankind things they want to know, and helping um pay their dets and live comfortable.

Good Mr. Elliot did rite sumthing once about farming, but not enuff about Hemp.—I see his book tother day, poor man he's ded now, but our loss in his gain.—I red a good deel in his book, and like it extrordinary well. I wish I had one of um. I suppose I could get one for haff a dollur. I think I'le leeve off tacking the News papers for haff a yeer, and bye one, and in haff a yeer I hope the News will get cleer again of so much wicked langage, and ripping and rending of one grate man agenst another! There's sundry leeves at the end ont, put out by a fine man, folks say I know him, I've seen him ride by my house, and thof I durst not speek to him yet I'm a fool for it, for they say he's a nice good-natur'd free Gentleman, yet I love him for the pains he has took to make folks ditch their meadows, and sow Wheet and Hemp and such like.

I do say it would be a nice thing if we could raise enuff Hemp to pay our rates, and bye a little rum and shuger, which we cant well do without, and a little Tea, which our Wifes wont let us have any peace without.

I've been as long as a sarmon amost, so I wont rite no more at present. Sumbody put a lettur of mine into the print tother day that I was asham'd to see there, so I wanted to let the world know I could if I try'd both spell and word a lettur, abundance better than that was, and I have told um sum things they would do well to think on, when they go to bed and when they get up, if their Wifes dont pester um too much. So I remain yours to sarve.

Humphrey Ploughjogger

P.S. Seems to me if grate Men dont leeve off writing Polly-ticks, breaking Heads, boxing Ears, ringing Noses and kicking Breeches, we shall by and by want a world of Hemp more for our own consumshon.

Boston Evening-Post, June 20, 1763

"U" No. I

Messieurs Edes & Gill,
Please to give the following a Place in your next.
Among the Votaries of Science, and the numerous Competitors for literary Fame, Choice and Judgment, about the Utility of their Studies, and the Interest of the human Race, have been remarkably neglected. Mathematicians have exerted, an obstinate Industry, and the utmost Subtilty of Wit, in demonstrating, little Niceties, among the Relations of Lines and Numbers, of Surfaces and Solids; and in searching for other Demonstrations, which, there is not the least Probability, will ever be found. Great Advantages of Genius, Learning, Wealth, and Leisure, have been improved by Philosophers, in examining and describing to the World, the Formation of Shells and Pebbles, of Reptiles and Insects, in which Mankind has no more Concern, than it would have in sage Conjectures about the Weight of the Indian's Elephant and Tortoise. Many Pens have been employed, and much Mischief and Malevolence occasioned, by Controversies concerning Predestination.—The original of Evil.—And other abstruse Subjects, which, having been to no good Purpose, under learned Examination, for so many Centuries, may by this Time, be well enough concluded unfathomable by the humane Line.

But Agriculture, the nursing Mother of every Art and Science, every Trade and Profession in Society, has been most imprudently, and ungratefully despised. It has been too much so, till of late in Europe; but much more so in America; and perhaps not the least so, in the Massachusetts-Bay.

With Advantages of Soil and Climate, which few Countries under Heaven can pretend to rival; we have never raised our own Bread.—Capable as we are, of making many wholsome and delicious Liquors, at a small Expence, we send abroad annually, at a very great Expence, for others that are less wholsome agreable and delicate.—When it is in our Power, without any Difficulty, to raise many other Commodities, in sufficient Plenty, not only for our own Consumption, but for Exportation, we send all the Globe over, Yearly to import such Commodities for our own Use!

All these Facts are indisputably true: But Things cannot long continue in the same Course. Many Sources of our Wealth are dried away; and unless we seek for Resources, from Improvements in our Agriculture, and an Augmentation of our Commerce, by such Means, we must forego the Pleasure of Delicacies, and Ornaments, if not the Comfort of real Necessaries, both in Diet and Apparel.

The Intention of this Paper then, is to intreat my worthy Countrymen, who have any Advantages, of Leisure, Education, or Fortune, to amuse themselves, at convenient Opportunities, with the study, and the Practice too, of Husbandry. Nor let any who have Ability, to think and act, tho' in narrow Circumstances, be discouraged, from exerting the Talents that have been given them, in the same Way.

> *Haud facile emergunt, quorum Virtutibus Obstat*
> *Res angusta Domi,*

With all its Truth and Pathos, has been the occasion of greater Evil, by Soothing the Pride and Indolence of Genius; than it ever was of Good, by prompting the rich and powerful, to seek the solitary Haunts of Merit, and to amplify her Sphere. In making Experiments, upon Soils and Manures, Grains and Grasses, Trees and Bushes; and in your Enquiries into the Course of Nature in producing them: You will find as much Employment for your Ingenuity, and as high a Gratification to a good Taste, as in any Business or Amusement you can choose to pursue. I said as high a Gratification to a good Taste; for, believe me, the finest Productions of the Poet or the Painter, the Statuary, or the Architect; when they stand in Competition with the great and beautiful Works of Nature, in the Animal and Vegetable Kingdoms; must be pronounced mean, and despicable Baubles—In such Inquiries as these, the Mathematician, the Philosopher, the Chymist and the Poet, may all improve their favourite Sciences to the Advancement of their Health, the Increase of their Fortunes, and the Benefit of their Country.

If I might descend, without Presumption, to Particulars, I would recommend such Enquiries to Divines and Physicians, more than to any other Orders. For, without enquiring into the Truth of the Observation, that the Lawyers among us, are the most curious in Husbandry, which, if true, is unnatural and accidental,—Divines, having more Leisure, and better Opportunities for Study than any Men, will find, in that Science, an agreeable Relaxation from the arduous Labours of their Profession, an useful Exercise for the Preservation of their Health, a Means of supplying their Families with many Necessaries that might otherwise cost them dear, and an excellent Example of Ingenuity and Industry, removing many Temptations of Vice and Folly, to the People under their Charge.—Besides, their Acquaintance with the Sciences subservient to Husbandry, will give them great Advantages, and in the Prosecution of such studies, they will find their Sentiments raised, their Ideas of divine Attributes display'd in the Scenes of Nature, improved, and their Adoration of the great Creator, and his Providence exalted.—Physicians have many Advantages, not only of the World in general, but of other liberal Professions—The Principles of those Sciences, which subserve more immediately their peculiar Occupation, are at the same Time the Foundations of all real, and rational Improvements in Husbandry. Necessitated as they are to much Travel and frequent Conversations, with many sorts of People, they might, for their own mere Diversion, remark the Appearances of Nature, and store their Minds with many useful observations, which they might disperse among their Patients, without the least Loss of Time, or Interruption to the Duties of their Profession.

These Reflections have been occasion'd, by a late Piece in the *Evening-Post*, signed *Humphrey Ploughjogger.*—Who was the Writer of that Piece, what were his Intentions, whether to do good or to do Evil, for what Reasons he chose that Manner of Conveyance to the Public, or whether the whole was written to introduce the Postscript,

> And "to shew by one Satyric Touch
> No Country wanted Hemp so much"

I am not at Leisure to inquire. And indeed, since Mr. *J.* with his noble and ignoble Trumpeters, has propagated an universal Jealousy, of every Writer in your Paper, I shall leave the important Questions, whether this Publication springs from Benevolence or Vanity, a public Spirit or seditious Views, a Love of

Money, or Desire of Fame, to the sage Discussion of Mr. *J* and his adherents.

My professed Design, as well as that of Mr. *Ploughjogger*, is not only innocent but important. There is no Subject less understood, or less considered, by Men in general even of the learned Orders, than the Theory of Agriculture. And the Writer, who should direct with Success, the Attention of inquisitive Minds, to that Branch of Learning, whether he intended to befriend the Public, or to blow it into Flames, would certainly be the occasion of much publick Utility. The particular Subject which, that Writer has chosen to recommend to the Consideration of the Province, promises, more fairly than any other, private Profit to the Farmer, and the Merchant, public Benefit to this Province, and perhaps to the Provinces in general, as well as to Great-Britain, (the Parent and Protector of them all) whose Society of Arts &c. have discovered their kind Concern for us, as well as their wise Provision for their native Country, among many other Instances, by offering Encouragement for raising this Commodity, in New-England. It has been said that "a thousand Weight to an Acre is an ordinary Crop of Hemp," that "several Hundred Thousand Pounds worth of foreign Hemp, is yearly expended, in New-England," that "Hemp may be raised, on drained Lands;" and that "if we can raise more than to supply our own Occasions, we may send it home." It has been said too, by another good Authority, "that an Acre of Land well tilled, will produce a Ton Weight, and that a Ton of it is worth Sixty Pounds of Lawful Money."

It is not without Reason then, that I embrace with Pleasure, the Opportunity of seconding Mr. *Ploughjogger*, in his Attempt, to recommend, to the Labours of the Farmer, the Enquiries of the Curious, and the Encouragement of Statesmen, a subject so important to this Province, to New-England in general, to Great-Britain herself, to the present Age, and to future Generations.

Hemp, is a Plant of great Importance, in the Arts and Manufactories, as it furnishes a great Variety of Threads, Cloths, and Cordage. It bears the nearest Resemblance to Flax, in its Nature, the manner of its Cultivation, and the Purposes to which it serves. It must be annually sown afresh. It arises, in a little space of Time, into a tall, slender, shrub, with an hollow Stem. It bears a small round seed, filled with a solid Pulp. Its Bark is a Tissue of Fibres, joined together with a soft substance, which easily rots it.—There are two Kinds of it, male, and female, the former only bears the seed, and from that seed arises both male and female. The seed should be sown in the Month of May, in a warm Sandy rich soil. They begin to gather it about the first of *August*, the Female being soonest ripe. The Proofs of its Ripeness are an Alteration of the Colour of its Leaves to Yellow, and its Stalks to White. It must be pulled up by the Roots and then bound in Bundles. The Male should stand Eight or Ten Days in the Air, that the Seed may ripen, which they afterwards get out, by cutting off, the Heads, and threshing them. It must then, be watered, by laying it, about a Week, in a Pond, in order to rot the Bark. I said, a Pond, tho' a Brook would be better if it did not give the Water an unwholsome Quality. After it is taken out, and dry'd, the woody Part of the Stem, must be broken from the Bark which covers it, by Crushing it, in an Instrument, called a Brake, beginning at the Roots. After it has been sufficiently broken, the small shivers, must be swingled out, as we swingle Flax. When this is done it must be beaten on a Block, or in a Trough with an Hammer, or with Beetles, till it becomes soft and pliable. When it has been well beaten it must be huckled, or passed thro' a toothed Instrument, like the Clothier's Comb, to seperate the shorter Tow, from that which is fit to be spun.

This is a very short Answer to Mr. *Ploughjogger's* Enquiries, extracted from Writers, upon this excellent Plant; But if he or any other Person has a Curiosity to see a more particular Account of it (and give me Leave to tell him and them there is not an Herb, from the Cedar to the Hyssop, that may be studied to more Advantage) let them consult the Præceptor, Nature delineated, Chamber's Dictionary, and above all the Compleat Body of Husbandry.

And that I may add no more, Let the World in general consider, that the Earth, the Air, and Seas, are to furnish all Animals with Food and Raiment: That mere Animal Strength, which is common to Beasts and Men, is not sufficient to avail us, of any considerable Part of the bountiful Provision of Nature: That our Understandings, as well as our Limbs and

Senses, must be employed in this service. And let the Few, who have been distinguished by greater Intellectual Abilities, than Mankind in general, consider that Nature intended them for Leaders of Industry. Let them be cautious, how they suffer their Talents to sleep or rust, on one Hand; and of certain Airs of Wisdom and Superiority, on the other, by which some Gentlemen of real Sense, Learning and public Spirit, giving offence to the common People have in some Measure defeated their own benevolent Intentions. Let them not be too sparing of their Application or Expence, lest, failing of visible Profit and Success, they expose themselves to ridicule, and rational, useful Husbandry itself, to Disgrace, among the common People.—The Example of the few, if skilfully and judiciously set, will soon be admir'd and followed. For human Nature is not so stupid, or so abandoned as many worthy Men imagine, nor the common People if their peculiar Customs and Modes of Thinking are a little studied, so ungrateful or intractible, but that their Labours may be conducted by the Genius and Experience of a Few, to very great and useful Purposes.

U.

Boston Gazette, July 18, 1763

"U" No. II

To the Printers.

Man, is distinguished from other Animals, his Fellow-Inhabitants of this Planet, by a Capacity of acquiring Knowledge and Civility, more than by any Excellency, corporeal, or mental, with which, mere Nature, has furnished his Species.—His erect Figure, and sublime Countenance, would give him but little Elevation above the Bear, or the Tyger: nay, notwithstanding those Advantages, he would hold an inferior Rank in the Scale of Being, and would have a worse Prospect of Happiness, than those Creatures; were it not for the Capacity, of uniting with others, and availing himself of Arts and Inventions, in social Life. As he comes originally from the Hands of his Creator, Self Love, or Self-Preservation, is the only Spring, that moves within him.—He might crop the Leaves, or Berries, with which his Creator had surrounded him, to satisfy his Hunger—He might sip at the Lake or Rivulet, to slake his Thrist—He might screen himself, behind a Rock or Mountain, from the bleakest of the Winds—or he might fly from the Jaws of voracious Beasts, to preserve himself from immediate Destruction.—But would such an Existence be worth preserving? Would not the first Precipice, or the first Beast of Prey, that could put a Period to the Wants, the Frights and Horrors, of such a wretched Being, be a friendly Object, and a real Blessing?

When we take one Remove from this forlorn Condition, and find the Species propagated, the Banks of Clams, and Oysters, discovered, the Bow and Arrow, invented, and the Skins of Beasts, or the Bark of Trees, employed for Covering: altho' the human Creature has a little less Anxiety and Misery than before; yet each Individual is independent of all others: There is no Intercourse of Friendship: no Communication of Food or Cloathing: no Conversation or Connection, unless the Conjunction of Sexes, prompted by Instinct, like that of Hares and Foxes, may be called so: The Ties of Parent, Son, and Brother, are of little Obligation: The Relations of Master and Servant, the Distinction of Magistrate and Subject, are totally unknown: Each Individual is his own Sovereign, accountable to no other upon Earth, and punishable by none.—In this Savage State, Courage, Hardiness, Activity and Strength, the Virtues of their Brother Brutes, are the only Excellencies, to which Men can aspire. The Man who can run with the most Celerity, or send the Arrow with the greatest Force, is the best qualified to procure a Subsistence. Hence to chase a Deer over the most rugged Mountain; or to pierce him at the greatest Distance, will be held, of all Accomplishments, in the highest Estimation. Emulations and Competitions for Superiority, in such Qualities, will soon commence: and any Action which may be taken for an Insult, will be considered, as a Pretension to such Superiority; it will raise Resentment in Proportion, and Shame and Grief will prompt the Savage to claim Satisfaction, or to take Revenge. To request the Interposition of a third Person, to arbitrate, between the contending Parties, would be considered, as an implicit Acknowledgment of Deficiency, in

those Qualifications, without which, none in such a barbarous
Condition, would choose to live. Each one then, must be this
own Avenger. The offended Parties must fall to fighting. Their
Teeth, their Nails, their Feet or Fists, or perhaps the first
Clubb or Stone that can be grasped, must decide the Contest,
by finishing the Life of one. The Father, the Brother, or the
Friend, begins then to espouse the Cause of the deceased; not
indeed so much from any Love he bore him living, or from any
Grief he suffers for him, dead, as from a Principle of Bravery
and Honour, to shew himself able and willing to encounter the
Man who had just before vanquished another.—Hence arises
the Idea of an Avenger of Blood: and thus the Notions of Revenge, and the Appetite for it, grow apace. Every one must
avenge his own Wrongs, when living, or else loose his Reputation: and his near Relation must avenge them for him, after he
is dead, or forfeit his.—Indeed Nature has implanted in the
human Heart, a Disposition to resent an Injury, when offered:
And this Disposition is so strong, that even the Horse, treading by Accident on a gouty Toe, or a Brick-batt falling on
the Shoulders, in the first Twinges of Pain, seem to excite the
angry Passions, and we feel an Inclination to kill the Horse and
to break the Brick-batt. Consideration, however, that the Horse
and Brick were without Design, will cool us; whereas the
Thought that any Mischief has been done, on Purpose to
abuse, raises Revenge in all its Strength and Terrors: and the
Man feels the sweetest, highest Gratification, when he inflicts
the Punishment himself.—From this Source arises the ardent
Desire in Men to judge for themselves, when and to what Degree they are injured, and to carve out their own Remedies, for
themselves.—From the same Source arises that obstinate Disposition in barbarous Nations to continue barbarous; and the
extreme Difficulty of introducing Civility and Christianity
among them. For the great Distinction between Savage Nations and polite ones, lies in this, that among the former, every
Individual is his own Judge and his own Executioner; but
among the latter, all Pretensions to Judgment and Punishment,
are resigned to Tribunals erected by the Public: a Resignation
which Savages are not without infinite Difficulty, perswaded to
make, as it is of a Right and Priviledge, extremely dear and tender to uncultivated Nature.

To exterminate, from among Mankind, such revengeful Sentiments and Tempers, is one of the highest and most important Strains, of civil and humane Policy: Yet the Qualities which contribute most, to inspire and support them, may, under certain Regulations, be indulged and encouraged. Wrestling, Running, Leaping, Lifting, and other Exercises of Strength, Hardiness, Courage and Activity, may be promoted, among private Soldiers, common Sailors, Labourers, Manufacturers and Husbandmen, among whom they are most wanted, provided sufficient Precautions are taken, that no romantic cavalier-like Principles of Honor intermix with them, and render a Resignation of the Right of judging and the Power of executing, to the Public, shameful. But whenever such Notions spread, so inimical to the Peace of Society, that Boxing, Clubbs, Swords or Fire-Arms, are resorted to, for deciding every Quarrel, about a Girl, a Game at Cards, or any little Accident, that Wine, or Folly, or Jealoussy, may suspect to be an Affront; the whole Power of the Government should be exerted to suppress them.

If a Time should ever come, when such Notions shall prevail in this Province to a Degree, that no Priviledges shall be able to exempt Men from Indignities and personal Attacks; not the Priviledge of a Councellor, not the Priviledge of an House of Representatives of "speaking freely in that Assembly, without Impeachment or Question in any Court or Place," out of the General Court; when whole armed Mobs shall assault a Member of the House—when violent Attacks shall be made upon Counsellors—when no Place shall be sacred, not the very Walls of Legislation,—when no Personages shall over awe, not the whole General Court, added to all the other Gentlemen on Change—when the broad Noon-Day shall be chosen to display before the World such high, heroic Sentiments of Gallantry and Spirit—when such Assailants shall live unexpelled from the Legislature—when slight Censures and no Punishments shall be inflicted,—there will really be Danger of our becoming universally, ferocious, barbarous and brutal, worse than our Gothic Ancestors, before the Christian Æra.

The Doctrine that the Person assaulted "should act with Spirit," "should defend himself, by drawing his Sword, and killing, or by wringing Noses and Boxing it out, with the Offender," is the Tenet of a Coxcomb, and the Sentiment of a Brute.—The Fowl upon the Dung-Hill, to be sure, feels a most gallant and heroic Spirit, at the Crowing of another, and instantly spreads his Cloak, and prepares for Combat.—The Bulls Wrath inkindles into a noble Rage, and the Stallions immortal Spirit, can never forgive the Pawings, Neighings, and Defiances, of his Rival. But are Cocks, and Bulls and Horses, the proper Exemplars for the Imitation of Men, especially of Men of Sense, and even of the highest Personages in the Government!

Such Ideas of Gallantry, have been said to be derived from the Army. But it was injuriously said, because not truly. For every Gentleman, every Man of Sense and Breeding in the Army, has a more delicate and manly Way of thinking; and from his Heart despises all such little, narrow, sordid Notions. It is true, that a Competition, and a mutual Affectation of Contempt, is apt to arise among the lower, more ignorant and despicable, of every Rank and Order in Society. This Sort of Men, (and some few such there are in every Profession) among Divines, Lawyers, Physicians, as well as Husbandmen, Manufacturers and Labourers, are prone from a certain Littleness of Mind, to imagine that their Labours alone, are of any Consequence in the World, and to affect, a Contempt for all others. It is not unlikely then, that the lowest and most despised Sort of Soldiers may have expressed a Contempt for all other Orders of Mankind, may have indulged a Disrespect to every Personage in a Civil Character, and have acted upon such Principles of Revenge, Rusticity, Barbarity and Brutality, as have been above described. And indeed it has been observed by the great Montesquieu, that "From a Manner of Thinking that prevails among Mankind (the most ignorant and despicable of Mankind, he means) they set an higher Value upon Courage than Timourousness, on Activity than Prudence, on Strength than Counsel. Hence the Army will ever despise a Senate, and respect their own Officers; they will naturally slight the Orders sent them by a Body of Men, whom they look upon as Cowards; and therefore unworthy to command them."—This Respect to their own Officers, which produces a Contempt, of Senates and Counsels, and of all Laws, Orders, and Constitutions, but those of the Army, and their Superiour Officers, tho' it may have prevailed among some Soldiers of the illiberal Character, above described, is far from being universal. It is not found in one Gentleman of Sense and Breeding in the whole service. All of this Character know, that the Common Law of England, is Superiour to all other Laws Martial or Common, in every English Government; and has often asserted triumphantly, its own Preheminence against the insults and Encroachments of a giddy and unruly Soldiery. They know too, that Civil Officers in England hold a great Superiority to Military Officers; and that a frightful Despotism would be the speedy Consequence of the least Alteration in these Particulars.—And knowing this, these Gentlemen who have so often exposed their Lives in Defence of the Religion, the Liberties and Rights of Men and Englishmen, would feel the utmost Indignation at the Doctrine which should make the Civil Power give Place to the Military; which should make a Respect to their superior Officers destroy or diminish their Obedience to Civil Magistrates, or which should give any Man a Right, in Conscience, Honor, or even in Punctilio and Delicacy, to neglect the Institutions of the Public, and seek their own Remedy, for Wrongs and Injuries of any Kind.

U.

Boston Gazette, August 1, 1763

"U" No. III

To the PRINTERS.

My worthy and ingenious friend, Mr. *J*, having strutted and foamed his hour upon the stage and acquired as well as deserved a good reputation as a man of sense and learning, some time since made his exit, and now is heard no more.

Soon after Mr. *J*s departure, your present correspondent made his appearance; but has not yet executed his intended plan.—Mr. *J* inlisted himself under the banners of a *faction*, and employed his *agreable* pen, in the propagation of the principles and prejudices of a *party*: and for this purpose he found himself obliged to exalt some characters and depress others,

equally beyond the truth—The greatest and best of all mankind, deserve less admiration; and even the worst and vilest deserve more candour, than the world in general is willing to
allow them.—The favourites of parties, altho' they have always
some virtues, have always many imperfections. Many of the
ablest tongues and pens, have in every age been employ'd in
the foolish, deluded, and pernicious flattery of one set of partisans; and in furious, prostitute invectives against another: But
such kinds of oratory never had any charms for me.—And if I
must do one or the other, I would quarrel with both parties,
and with every individual of each, before I would subjugate
my understanding, or prostitute my tongue or pen to either.

To divert mens minds from subjects of vain curiosity or unprofitable science, to the useful as well as entertaining speculations of agriculture,—To eradicate the Gothic and pernicious
principles of *private revenge*, that have been lately spread among
my countrymen, to the debasement of their character, and to
the frequent violation of the public peace,—and to recommend a careful attention to political *measures*, and a candid
manner of reasoning about them; instead of abusive *insolence*,
or uncharitable *imputations* upon *men* and characters, has,
since I first undertook the employment of entertaining the
Public, been my constant and invariable point of view. The difficulty or impracticability of succeeding in my enterprize, has
often been objected to me, by my friends: but even this has
not wholly disheartened me—I own it would be easier to de-
populate a province, or subvert a monarchy; to transplant a nation, or enkindle a new war; and that I should have a fairer
prospect of success, in such designs as those: But my consolation is this, that if I am unable by my writings to effect any
good purpose I never will subserve a bad one. If engagements
to a *party*, are necessary to make a fortune, I had rather make
none at all, and spend the remainder of my days like my
favourite author, that ancient and immortal husbandman,
philosopher, politician and general, *Xenophon*, in his retreat;
considering kings and princes as shepherds, and their people
and subjects like flocks and herds, or as mere objects of contemplation and parts of a curious machine in which I had no
interest; than to wound my own mind by engaging in any *party*,
and spreading prejudices, vices or follies.—Notwithstanding

this, I remember the *Monkish* maxim, *fac officium taliter qualiter, sed sta benè cum priore.* And it is impossible to *stand well* with the Abbot, without *fighting* for his cause thro' *fas* and *nefas.*

Please to insert the foregoing and following, which is the last Deviation I purpose to make from my principal and favourite Views of writing on *Husbandry* and *Mechanic* Arts.

U.

There is nothing in the science of human nature, more curious, or that deserves a critical attention from every order of men, so much, as that principle, which moral writers have distinguished by the name of *self-deceit.* This principle is the spurious offspring of *self-love*; and is perhaps the source of far the greatest, and worst part of the vices and calamities among mankind.

The most abandoned minds are ingenious in contriving excuses for their crimes, from constraint, necessity, the strength, or suddenness of temptation, or the violence of passion; which serves to soften the remordings of their own consciences, and to render them by degrees, insensible equally to the charms of virtue, and the turpitude of vice. What multitudes, in older countries, discover, even while they are suffering deservedly the most infamous and terrible of civil punishments a tranquility, and even a magnanimity, like that, which we may suppose in a real patriot, dying to preserve his country!—Happy would it be for the world, if the fruits of this pernicious principle were confined to such profligates. But if we look abroad, shall we not see the most modest, sensible and virtuous of the common people, almost every hour of their lives, warped and blinded, by the same disposition to flatter and deceive themselves! When they think themselves injured, by any foible or vice in others, is not this injury always seen thro' the magnifying end of the perspective: When reminded of any such imperfection in themselves, by which their neighbours or fellow citizens are sufferers, is not the perspective instantly reversed? Insensible of the beams in our own eyes, are we not quick in discerning motes in those of others?—Nay however melancholy it may be, and how humbling soever to the pride of the human heart, even the few favourites of nature, who have received from her clearer understandings, and more happy tempers than other men; who seem designed under providence to be the great conductors of the art and science, the war and peace, the laws and religion of this lower world, are often seduced by this unhappy disposition in their minds, to their own destruction, and the injury, nay often to the utter desolation of millions of their fellow-men.—Since truth and virtue, as the means of present and future happiness, are confessed to be the only objects that deserve to be pursued; to what imperfection in our nature or unaccountable folly in our conduct, excepting this of which we have been speaking, can mankind impute the multiply'd diversity of opinions, customs, laws and religions, that have prevailed, and is still triumphant, in direct opposition to both? From what other source can such fierce disputations arise concerning the two things which seem the most consonant to the entire frame of human nature?—Indeed it must be confessed, and it ought to be with much contrition lamented, that those eyes which have been given us to see, are willingly suffered by us to be obscured; and those consciences, which by the commission of God almighty have a rightful authority over us, to be deposed by prejudices, appetites and passions, which ought to hold a much inferior rank in the intellectual and moral system. —Such swarms of passions, avarice and ambition, servility and adulation, hopes, fears, jealousies, envy, revenge, malice and cruelty are continually buzzing in the world, and we are so extremely prone to mistake the impulses of these for the dictates of our consciences; that the greatest genius, united to the best disposition, will find it hard to hearken to the voice of reason, or even to be certain of the purity of his own intentions.

From this true but deplorable condition of mankind, it happens that no improvements in science or literature, no reformation in religion or morals, nor any rectification of *mistaken measures* in government can be made, without opposition from numbers, who, flattering themselves that their own intentions are pure (how sinister soever they may be in fact,) will reproach impure designs to others; or fearing a detriment to their interest, or a mortification to their passions from the innovation, will even think it lawful directly and knowingly to falsify the *motives* and *characters* of the innovators.

Vain ambition and other vicious motives, were charged by

the sacred congregation, upon *Gallilæi*, as the causes of his hypothesis concerning the motion of the earth, and charged so
often and with so many terms, as to render the old man at last
suspicious, if not satisfy'd that the charge was true: tho' he had
been led to this hypothesis by the light of a great genius, and
deep researches into Astronomy.—Sedition, rebellion, ped-
antry, desire of fame, turbulence and malice, were always reproached to the great reformers, who delivered us from the
worst chains that were ever forged by Monks or Devils, for the
human mind.—*Zozimus* and *Julian* could easily discover, or
invent annecdotes, to dishonour the conversion of *Constantine*, and his establishment of christianity, in the empire.

For these reasons, we can never be secure in a resignation of
our understandings, or in confiding *enormous power*, either to
the *Bramble* or the *Cedar*; no, nor to *any mortal*, however
great or good: And for the same reasons, we should always be
upon our guard against the epithets and reflections of writers
and declaimers, whose constant art it is to falsify and blacken
the characters and measures they are determined to discredit.

These reflections have been occasioned by the late controversies in our News-Papers, about certain measures in the political world.—Controversies that have this, in common with
others of much greater figure and importance; and indeed
with all others (in which numbers have been concerned) from
the first invention of letters to the present hour: that more
pains have been employed in charging "desire of popularity,
restless turbulence of spirit, ambitious views, envy, revenge,
malice, and jealousy," on one side: and servility, adulation, tyranny, principles of arbitrary power, lust of dominion, avarice,
desires of civil or military commissions on the other; or in
fewer words, in attempts to blacken and discredit the motives
of the disputants on both sides; than in rational enquiries into
the merits of the cause, the truth and rectitude of the measures
contested.

Let not writers nor statesmen deceive themselves. The
springs of their own conduct and opinions are not always so
clear and pure, nor are those of their antagonists in politics,
always so polluted and corrupted as they believe, and would
have the world believe too. Mere readers, and private persons,
can see virtues and talents on each side: and to their sorrow

they have not yet seen any side altogether free from atrocious vices, extreme ignorance, and most lamentable folly.—Nor will mere readers and private persons be less excuseable, if they should suffer themselves to be imposed on by others, who first impose upon themselves.—Every step in the public administration of government, concerns us *nearly.* Life and fortune, our own, and those of our posterity, are not *trifles* to be neglected or *totally entrusted* to other hands: And these, in the vicissitudes of human things, may be rendered in a few years, either totally uncertain, or as secure as fixed Laws and the *British* constitution *well administered* can make them, in consequence of *measures* that seem at present but *trifles,* and to many scarcely worth attention. Let us not be bubbled then out of our reverence and obedience to Government, on one hand; nor out of our right to think and act *for ourselves,* in our own departments, on the other. The steady management of a good government is the most anxious arduous and hazardous vocation on this side the grave: Let us not encumber those, therefore, who have *spirit* enough to embark in such an enterprize, with any kind of opposition, that the preservation or perfection of our mild, our happy, our most excellent constitution, does not *soberly* demand.

But on the other hand, as we know that ignorance, vanity, excessive *ambition* and venality, will in spight of all human precautions creep into government, and will ever be aspiring at *extravagant* and *unconstitutional* emoluments to *individuals*; let us never relax our attention, or our resolution to keep these unhappy imperfections in human nature, out of which material, frail as it is, all our rulers *must be* compounded, under a strict *inspection,* and a just *controul.*—We *Electors* have an important *constitutional* power placed in our hands: We have a check upon two branches of the legislature, as each branch has upon the other two; the power I mean of electing, at stated periods, *one* branch, which branch has the power of electing another. It becomes necessary to every subject then, to be in some degree a *statesman*: and to examine and judge for *himself* of the *tendency* of political *principles* and *measures.* Let us examine them with a *sober,* a *manly,* a *British,* and a *Christian* spirit. Let us neglect all *party* virulence and advert to *facts.* Let us believe no man to be *infallible* or *impeccable* in government, any more than in religion: take no man's word against evidence, nor *implicitly* adopt the sentiments of others, who may be deceived themselves, or may be *interested* in deceiving us.

U.

Draft of an Essay on Power

All Men would be Tyrants if they could.

My Brother J and my self have been very liberal of our Promises to the Publick and very Sparing of Performance: but I shall take the Liberty to suspend the Execution of my Plan of Essays upon Agriculture, and entertain my Readers with an Explanation in some greater Detail of the moral and political Principles, contained in my former Essay upon Self Decipt.— "Self Deceit is perhaps the source of far the greatest and worst Part of the Vices and Calamities among Man kind."— The Love of Pleasure and Aversion to Pain, our affections for all Things that have Power either in Reality or in our own Imaginations only to give us the former, and our Hatred of all Things that communicate the later, our Senses, our Appetites, our Passions, and all our Habits and Prejudices, nay even our very Virtues and useful Qualities, our Piety towards God and our Benevolence to Mankind, The Reverence for our Parents and Affection to our Children, our Desires of Fame and aspirations after Independence, have all of them in their Turns a Tendency, unless more cautiously watched than the Condition of Humanity will allow, to deceive us into Error.—This is the great and important and melancholy Truth that is conveyd to us by the old Maxim, that I have chosen for the Motto of this Paper, that all Men would be Tyrants if they could.—The Meaning of that Maxim is not so uncharitable, as to suppose that all the sons of Adam, are so many abandond Knaves regardless of all Morality and Right, who would violate their Consciences, and oppress, mangle, burn, butcher and destroy their fellow Men, in direct opposition to their Judgments. It means, in my opinion no more than this plain simple observation upon human Nature which every Man, who has ever read a Treatise upon Morality, or conversd with the World or endeavord to estimate the comparative strength of the different springs of Action in his own Mind, must have often made, vist. that the selfish Passions, are stronger than the social, and that the former would always prevail over the latter in any Man, left to the natural Emotions of his own Mind, unrestrained and uncheckd by other Power extrinsic to himself.—i.e. that any Man, the best, the wisest, the brightest you can find, would after all external awe, and Influence should be taken away i.e. after he should be intrusted with sufficient Power, would soon be brought to think, by the strong Effervescence of his selfish Passions against the weaker Efforts of his social in opposition to them, that he was more important, more deserving, knowing and [   ] than he is, that he deserves more respect and Reverence Wealth and Power than he has, and that he was doing but his Duty in Punishing with great Cruelty those who should esteem him no higher and shew him no more Reverence and give him no more Money or Power than he deservd.

This which is no new Discovery, but has been many thousands of Years considered by thinking Men, seems to have given rise to the wisest and best of Governments which seems to be calculated on Purpose, to controul and counteract the Ruinous Tendency of this Imperfection in our Natures.

Power is a Thing of infinite Danger and Delicacy, and was never yet confided to any Man or any Body of Men without turning their Heads.—Was there ever, in any Nation or Country, since the fall, a standing Army that was not carefully watched and contrould by the State so as to keep them impotent, that did not, ravish, plunder, Massacre and ruin, and at last inextricably inslave the People,—Was there ever a Clergy, that have gained, by their Natural Ascendancy over private Consciences, any important Power in the State, that did not restlessly aspire by every Art, by Flattery and Intrigues, by Bribery and Corruption, by wresting from the People the Means of Knowledge, and by inspiring misterious and awful apprehensions of themselves by Promises of Heaven and by Threats of Damnation, to establish themselves in oppulence,

Indolence and Magnificence, at the Expence of the Toil, and Industry, the Limbs, the Liberties and Lives of all the rest of Mankind.

Aware of this usurping and encroaching Nature of Power, our Constitution, has laid for its Basis, this Principle that, all such unnatural Powers, as those of Arms and those of Confessions and Absolution for sin, should always bow to the civil orders that Constitute the State.—Nor is this the only Precaution she has taken. She has been as sensible of the Danger from civil as from military or casuistical Power, and has wisely provided against all.

No simple Form of Government, can possibly secure Men against the Violences of Power. Simple Monarchy will soon mould itself into Despotism, Aristocracy will soon commence an Oligarchy, and Democracy, will soon degenerate into an Anarchy, such an Anarchy that every Man will do what is right in his own Eyes, and no Mans life or Property or Reputation or Liberty will be secure and every one of these will soon mould itself into a system of subordination of all the moral Virtues, and Intellectual Abilities, all the Powers of Wealth, Beauty, Wit, and Science, to the wanton Pleasures, the capricious Will, and the execrable Cruelty of one or a very few.

c. August 29, 1763

This last Paragraph has been the Creed of my whole Life and is now March 27 1807 as much approved as it was when it was written by John Adams.

"Humphrey Ploughjogger" No. III

To the Publishers of the BOSTON EVENING-POST.
Plese to print this in your next,
Humphry Ploughjogger.

It is a pleasant Thing to see ones Works in print.—When I see the news, with my letter int about Hemp, I do say it made me feel as glad, as a glass full of West India rum, sweetened with loaf shugar, would.—But yet, even then I want so presumptious, as to hope hardly, that such a fine ellokent gentleman, as Mr. *U.* would stoop to take so much notice of me.—He is a noble, high flown riter, like Mr. Harvey, amost. I've red Mr. Harvey's meditations, our minister lent it to me.—But tho' I will own Mr. *U.* is a wonderful, lofty, sublyme riter, yet I cant join with him, in a good many things. I hope his honor, wont be offended, if I tell him what they be.

1st. I dont like his advice to leeve off studying the decrees, and original sin.—for tho I cant hardly beleeve, that heathens and infants are all lost, for Adams first transgreshon, yet them doctrines are great misterees, that we ought to pry into, as far as the word can guide us.—I do declare I would not leeve off reeding Mr. Willard, Mr. Edwards, and Mr. Taylor, and Dr. Whitby about them points, for all my knowledge in farming, added to Mr. *U*'s knowledge too.

2dly. Next comes one thing that I do like, that is the line of latin. I love to see, now and then, some latin, in the books I reed. I amost think I understand it sumtimes, especially when I see it in Mr. Flavels works, it comes in so natural.—I ask our ministur to conster it to me, and our schoolmaster sumtimes. But I find they dont understand every thing, they get plunged, now and then. I got our school-master to conster that line in Mr. *U*'s piece. He made bungling work ont, but as well as I cou'd pick out it ment "that a man could not swim above water, that had poverty pulling him downwards at his heels."—This is a queer picture, it made me laff, tho I tho't it was hardhearted too for poverty to keep pulling a man down under water that try'd to keep up.—And I dont know, since my ritings have been taken so much notice off, but I should have been a great larnt man if it had not been for this cruel jade poverty, that has allways been striving mite and main to drown me.—Nevertheless it put me in mind of a rogue's trick, I used to play when I was a boy.—I used to catch a grate pout, and put a wyth in his gills, and then put him in the water.—He would swim and struggle about the top of the water, but could not dive down deep. Now seems to me, we mite as well conster that latin thus. "The pout can't dive to the bottom that has a wyth in his gills."—Poverty can be signify'd by a wyth in his gills, keeping the pout at the top of the water, as well as by an old rinkled hagg at a man's heels, pulling him under. But conster it which way you will there is a deel of sense int.— Seems to me there's more sense in sum of these latin skraps, that I get our larnt men to conster, than in so much Inglish any where.—I wonder how tis! I allways rite best about what I dont understand.—Ive rit a deel about this latin, and it sounds very well too, seems to me, considering.

3dly. Next comes one thing that I cant bare, i.e. advising ministurs to study farming and work at it too.—Our ministurs are wordly-minded enuff, aready, and they dont give themselves haff enuff to reeding and study now—I'm sure, many of um dont make so good sarmons, as I could with my poor abilities, thof I say't.—But if they should take to farming they would not reed at all hardly.—they would not reed their bibles enuff, I'm afeard, and they would leeve off reeding of Mr. Dodridge's works, and Mr. Harvey's, and Sandyman's and such like wonderful works, and would do nothing but grind sarmons, in that sarmon-mill a Concordance.—Their duty is to provide food and cloathing for our souls not our bodies, to feed the spiritual sheep and lambs, not to spend time in taking care of the herds and flocks of the field—to sow the seed of the word, and pray for the preparation of the spiritual soil in mans hart to receeve it, not to till the carnal ground.—I do avouch it, this tho't of Mr. U's is worse than poperee, and I had rather ministurs should be as lazey as they do say monks are in other countries and unmarried like them, that they mite give themselves wholly to reeding and study and prayer, than have um careful about farming.

4thly. But I do like his advice to doctors wonderful well. I wonder how Mr. U. could think of all them sensible remarks he made about the doctors. They mite do a world of good by taking his advice. Yet I'm afeard they wont, for if they should they would cure or prevent a grate many destempurs, that now fetch um good fees,—Yet I do raly beleeve they would do more good to mens health, by making um drink good, cleer, well-made, well-kept cydur, and good currunt wine, and cherry wine, and such like, insteed of rum and brandy and wine made of haff rum and haff cydur, as they do now, than they can by all their pills and drops and rubub. And yet I beleeve they do a grate deel of good with these things, too.—

Mr. U. does but just mention Lawyers, and indeed I dont
know what bisness he had to mention them at all when riting
about farming, or any thing else that is good, unless theyre
grown better than they were when I was a young man. My
great grandfather was one of Oliver Cromwell's men, and I've
heard it, in our family by tradishon, that good, pious, larnt Mr.
Hugh Peters us'd to say, it would never be good times, till the
nation got rid of 150.—Sumbody asked what he ment by 150?
—He said three L's.—and when he was asked what he ment by
three L's? he said, the Lords, the Levites and the Lawyers.—
About 30 years ago, when I us'd to go to court sumtimes, I
used to be of Mr. Peters's mind amost about Lawyers, sumtimes.—But they do say, Lawyers are grown much better
now, and stand up stoutly for liberty.—Indeed I've heard my
grandfather say, his father told him, there was abundance of
lawyers, that bawled out for liberty, and fought for it too, in his
day, tho most of um went over o' t'other side to that calf the
holy martir.

5thly. The next thing I dont altogether like.—Mr. U seems
to run quite out of his way, to pick a quarrel with Mr. J.—I
cant devise what his reason was.—I guess several things.—
Sumtimes I think he has studied oratary, and oratary, our ministur says, is the art of gaining attenshon. And he mite think
there was no way of gaining attenshon so shure, as to make
fokes think him a party-man. For he would get the attenshon
of one haff the world thro love, and of tother thro hatred.—
Sumtimes I think he made a pass at Mr. J. to let fokes know his
reason for signing himself U.—But upon the whole, I beleeve
it most likely Mr. U. has been a deputy for sum town, and
been made a justice by the Governor and then was dropt by his
town, and so forsooth tho't his town was angry with him for
taking a favour from the Governor, and now is turning about
to tother side in order to get in again.—But I beleeve he is out
in his pollyticks, for country fokes love to have their deputys in
good understanding with the Governor, and I guess Mr. U's
town turn'd him out for sumthing else.—Nevertheless I dont
know but Mr. U is rite to quarrel a little, for there is sumthing
in man that delites in fighting.—When I was a boy, I used to
love to see boys box it, and cocks fight, and rams too.—I see
two rams fight once, they would run back two or three rod,

and then run head to head, till one of them split the skull rite in two, and down he dropp'd, as dead as a herring.—This was a dredful cruel fight, yet I do say, I lov'd to see it.—And they do say, that in other countries, grate gentelfokes keep dogs, and bares, and bulls, a purpose to see um fight. Now just so our grate fokes do seem to love to see newspaper fighting among us, deerly. And Mr. U. by fighting a little this way, might hope to make fokes take more notice about our fine plant Hemp.—So that his quarrelling may do sum good.—But if he rites again I hope he'll go farther—For I've alter'd my mind since I rit my tother letter, and I amost think, he and I may rite, in a good natur'd way, to all itarnity, about any thing to do good, and our works will never be read twice.—But there is one sartain way of making fokes reed and study our works as larnt men do latin books, and that is by drawing plaguy, black, ugly pictures of sum grate men, as the Governor, Lt. Governor, sum Counsellors or Judges, or of Bluster and Whackum, and Gamuts and Chaplains.—Let us pick out sum rite down clever man, no matter what side he is of, and tell a parcel of rouzing lies about him, and our ritings will be got by heart, and by this meens we may slide into mens minds sum knolledge about hemp.—My mind is alter'd by what I since see in good Mr. Flavell's works, that "man is more wrathful than grateful."

6thly. I dont know what bissness he had to suspect me of bad designs in what I rote.—I'le take my corporal oath, I never went to meeting of a sabbath day, nor never followed a corps to the grave in my life, with less mallice in my heart, and less designs of doing hurt, than I had when I rote that lettur, let U, or J, or he, or they suspect or beleeve what they will.

But I dont never know when to stop, hardly, matter comes in to my noddle so fast.—I've read abundance in my day, but I did not begin to read a grate deel till I was matter of 35, and I cant larn to spell nicely. But since I married this second wife, that is a young woman, I dont love to go to bed so soon as she does, so I reed and rite a world now, and I do spell better and better.

I've rambled about so long that I've no room hardly to say any thing about hemp, and I'm resolved I wont never rite a piece without sum stroke or other about hemp.—Mr. U has

convinced me more than ever of the worth ont, and I'm resolved to sow an acre or two out next May, and if I make it do
pritty well I'le send you an account ont, for I do desine to reed
and rite and study and work about hemp, till I get it into
fashon.—Our deputy tells me that a ropemaker told him, the
best hemp he uses all the year round, grows in this country. I
wish I knew where it grows.—When I go to Boston I'le ask
the ropemakers what town it is raised in, and then rite a lettur
(not to be printed tho) to sumbody in that town, and ask him
a few more questions about it, for Mr. U hant made every
thing quite cleer to me.—I want to know whether they sow it
in rows, and so plough amongst it, or whether they sprinkle it
over all the land.—Whether they plough the land at first deep
or shallow.—And how they brake and swingle and hatchel it.—
It is such grate long trade I cant devise how they handle it.
And I want to know whether they use such brakes and swingle
boards and knives as we do about flax.—As for beeting with
beetles or hammers I dont understand that very well.

They do say, they raise abundance ont, at Phyladelphy. I
wish sum of our rich men would send there and hire a man
that knows about it, and could do the labour to come here and
teech us.—He would find his account int, and prove himself a
grate paytrot.—But sum how or other I will find out how to
manage it, if I spend a month in a year every year about it.—
For it is a thing of grate value.—One thing I know, if we'd
rais'd a little more ont for 20 years past, and made a proper use
ont, I'll be hang'd with the first hemp I can raise, if we should
have had so big rates to pay.

So no more at present, Cousin Fleets, from your lofing
kinsman

Humphry Ploughjogger

Boston Evening-Post, September 5, 1763

SMALLPOX INOCULATION

John Adams to Abigail Smith

My dear Diana   Saturday Evening Eight O'Clock
    For many Years past, I have not felt more serenely than I do
this Evening. My Head is clear, and my Heart is at ease. Business of every Kind, I have banished from my Thoughts. My
Room is prepared for a Seven Days' Retirement, and my Plan
is digested for 4 or 5 Weeks. My Brother retreats with me, to
our preparatory Hospital, and is determined to keep me Company, through the Small Pox. Your Unkle, by his agreable Account of the Dr. and your Brother, their Strength, their Spirits,
and their happy Prospects, but especially, by the Favour he left
me from you, has contributed very much to the Felicity of my
present Frame of Mind. For, I assure you Sincerely, that, (as
Nothing which I before expected from the Distemper gave me
more Concern, than the Thought of a six Weeks Separation
from my Diana) my Departure from your House this Morning
made an Impression upon me that was severely painfull. I
thought I left you, in Tears and Anxiety—And was very glad to
hear by your Letter, that your Fears were abated. For my own
Part, I believe no Man ever undertook to prepare himself for
the Small Pox, with fewer [   ] than I have at present. I have
considered thoughrououghly, the Diet and Medicine prescribed me, and am fully satisfyed that no durable Evil can result from Either, and any other Fear from the small Pox or it's
Appurtenances, in the modern Way of Inoculation I never had
in my Life.—Thanks for my Balm. Present my Duty and Gratitude to Pappa for his kind offer of Tom. Next Fryday, for certain, with suitable Submission, We take our Departure for
Boston. To Captn. Cunninghams We go—And I have not the
least doubt of a pleasant 3 Weeks, notwithstanding the Distemper.—Dr. Savil has no Antimony—So I must beg your
Care that John Jenks makes the Pills and sends them by the
Bearer. I enclose the Drs. Directions. We shall want about 10 I
suppose for my Brother and me. Other Things we have of Savil.
    Good Night, my Dear, I'm a going to Bed!

Sunday Morning 1/2 After 10.—The People all gone to Meeting, but my Self, and Companion, who are enjoying a Pipe in great Tranquility, after the operation of our Ipichac. Did you ever see two Persons in one Room Iphichacuana'd together? (I hope I have not Spelled that ineffable Word amiss!) I assure you they make merry Diversion. We took turns to be sick and to laugh. When my Companion was sick I laughed at him, and when I was sick he laughed at me. Once however and once only we were both sick together, and then all Laughter and good Humour deserted the Room. Upon my Word we both felt very sober.—But all is now easy and agreable, We have had our Breakfast of Pottage without salt, or Spice or Butter, as the Drs. would have it, and are seated to our Pipes and our Books, as happily as Mortals, preparing for the small Pox, can desire.

5 o clock afternoon.—Deacon Palmer has been here and drank Tea with me. His Children are to go with us to Cunninghams. He gives a charming Account of the Dr. and your Brother, whom he saw Yesterday. Billy has two Eruptions for certain, how many more are to come is unknown—But is as easy and more [   ] (the Deacon says) than he ever saw him in his Life.

Monday. Ten O'Clock.—Papa was so kind as to call and leave your Favor of April the Eighth—For which I heartily thank you. Every Letter I receive from you, as it is an Additional Evidence of your Kindness to me, and as it gives me fresh Spirits and great Pleasure, confers an Additional Obligation upon me. I thank you for your kind and judicious Advice. The Deacon made me the offer Yesterday, which, for the very Reasons you have mentioned, I totally declined. I told you before We had taken our Vomits and last Night We took the Pills you gave me, and we want more. Lent We have kept ever since I left you, as rigidly as two Carmelites. And you may rely upon it, I shall strictly pursue the Drs. Directions, without the least Deviation. Both the Physick and the Abstinence, have hitherto agreed extreamly well with me, for I have not felt freer from all Kinds of Pain and Uneasiness, I have not enjoyed a clearer Head, or a brisker flow of Spirits, these seven Years, than I do this day.

My Garden, and My Farm, (if I may call what I have by that Name) give me now and then a little Regret, as I must leave them in more Disorder than I could wish. But the dear Partner of all my Joys and sorrows, in whose Affections, and Friendship I glory, more than in all other Emoluments under Heaven, comes into my Mind very often and makes me sigh. No other Consideration I assure you, has given me, since I began my Preparation, or will give me I believe, till I return from Boston any Degree of Uneasiness.

Papa informs me that Mr. Ayers goes to Town, tomorrow Morning. Will you be so kind as to write the Dr., that I shall come into Town on Fryday, that I depend on Dr. Perkins and no other. And that I beg he would write me whether Miss Le Febure can take in my Brother and me in Case of Need. For My Unkle writes me, I must bring a Bed, as his are all engaged, it seems. I have written him, this Moment, that I can not carry one, and that he must procure one for me, or I must look out Elsewhere. I shall have an Answer from him to night and if he cannot get a Bed, I will go to Mrs. Le Febures if she can take us.

Should be glad if Tom might be sent over, Fryday Morning. My Love and Duty where owing. Pray continue to write me, by every opportunity, for, next to Conversation, Correspondence, with you is the greatest Pleasure in the World to yr.

John Adams

P.S. My Love to Mr. and Mrs. Cranch. Thank 'em for their kind Remembrance of me, and my Blessing to my Daughter Betcy.

April 7, 1764

RECEIVING GOOD WISHES

To Abigail Smith

Wednesday Eveng.
This is the last Opportunity I shall have to write you from Braintree for some Weeks. You may expect to hear from me, as

soon after my Arrival at Boston as possible. Have had a peaceable, pleasant Day upon the whole. My Brother and I have the Wishes, the good Wishes of all the good People who come to the House. They admire our Fortitude, and wish us well thro, even some, who would heartily rejoice to hear that both of Us were dead of the small Pox provided no others could be raised up in our stead to be a Terror to evil Doers, and a Praise and Encouragement to such as they mortally hate, those that do well.

But I have attained such an Elevation in Phylosophy as to be rendered very little, the better or worse, more chearful or surly, for the good or ill Wishes or Speeches of such Animals, as those.

Amusement engages the most of my Attention. I mean that as I am necessitated to spend three or four Weeks in an Absolute Vacation of Business and study, I may not amuse myself, with such silly Trifles as Cards and Baubles altogether, but may make the very Expletives of Time, the very Diverters from Thinking, while I am under the small Pox of some Use or Pleasure, to me, after I get well. For this Purpose beg Papa, to lend me, all the Volumes of Swifts Examiner and send them over by Tom to yr   John Adams

Love and Duty where, and in Proportion as, it is due.

April 11, 1764

OBSERVING HUMAN NATURE

To Abigail Smith

Dr. Diana   Thurdsdy. 5. Oclock. 1764

I have Thoughts of sending you a Nest of Letters like a nest of Basketts; tho I suspect the latter would be a more genteel and acceptable Present to a Lady. But in my present Circumstances I can much better afford the former than the latter. For, my own Discretion as well as the Prescriptions of the Faculty, prohibit any close Application of Mind to Books or Business—Amusement, Amusement is the only study that I follow. Now Letter-Writing is, to me, the most agreable

Amusement: and Writing to you the most entertaining and Agreable of all Letter-Writing. So that a Nest of an hundred, would cost me Nothing at all.—What say you my Dear? Are you not much obliged to me, for making you the cheapest of all possible Presents?

Shall I continue to write you, so much, and so often after I get to Town? Shall I send you, an History of the whole Voyage? Shall I draw You the Characters of all, who visit me? Shall I describe to you all the Conversations I have? I am about to make my Appearance on a new Theatre, new to me. I have never been much conversant in scenes, where Drs., Nurses, Watchers, &c. make the Principal Actors. It will be a Curiosity to me. Will it be so to you? I was always pleased to see human Nature in a Variety of shapes. And if I should be much alone, and feel in tolerable Spirits, it will be a Diversion to commit my Observations to Writing.

I believe I could furnish a Cabinet of Letters upon these subjects which would be exceeded in Curiosity, by nothing, but by a sett describing the Characters, Diversions, Meals, Wit, Drollery, Jokes, Smutt, and Stories of the Guests at a Tavern in Plymouth where I lodge, when at that Court—which could be equalled by nothing excepting a minute History of Close stools and Chamber Potts, and of the Operation of Pills, Potions and Powders, in the Preparation for the small Pox.

Heaven forgive me for suffering my Imagination to straggle into a Region of Ideas so nauseous And abominable: and suffer me to return to my Project of writing you a Journal. You would have a great Variety of Characters—Lawyers, Physicians (no Divines I believe), a Number of Tradesmen, Country Colonells, Ladies, Girls, Nurses, Watchers, Children, Barbers &c. &c. &c. But among all These, there is but one whose Character I would give much to know better than I do at present. In a Word I am an old Fellow, and have seen so many Characters in my Day, that I am almost weary of Observing them.—Yet I doubt whether I understand human Nature or the World very well or not?

There is not much Satisfaction in the study of Mankind to a benevolent Mind. It is a new Moon, Nineteen Twentyeths of it opaque and unenlightened.

Intimacy with the most of People, will bring you acquainted with Vices and Errors, and Follies enough to make you despize them. Nay Intimacy with the most celebrated will very much diminish our Reverence and Admiration.

What say you now my dear shall I go on with my Design of Writing Characters?—Answer as you please, there is one Character, that whether I draw it on Paper or not, I cannot avoid thinking on every Hour, and considering sometimes together and sometimes asunder, the Excellencies and Defects in it. It is almost the only one that has encreased, for many Years together, in Proportion to Acquaintance and Intimacy, in the Esteem, Love and Admiration of your

John Adams
April 12, 1764

UNDERGOING INOCULATION

To Abigail Smith

My dearest

We arrived at Captn. Cunninghams, about Twelve O'Clock and sent our Compliments to Dr. Perkins. The Courrier returned with Answer that the Dr. was determined to inoculate no more without a Preparation preevious to Inoculation. That We should have written to him and have received Directions from him, and Medicine, before We came into Town. I was surprized and chagrined. I wrote, instantly, a Letter to him, and informed him we had been under a Preparation of his prescribing, and that I presumed Dr. Tufts had informed him, that We depended on him, in Preference to any other Gentleman. The Dr. came, immediately with Dr. Warren, in a Chaise—And after an Apology, for his not Recollecting—(I am obliged to break off my Narration, in order to swallow a Porringer of Hasty Pudding and Milk. I have done my Dinner)—for not recollecting what Dr. Tufts had told him, Dr. Perkins demanded my left Arm and Dr. Warren my Brothers. They took their Launcetts and with their Points divided the

skin for about a Quarter of an Inch and just suffering the
Blood to appear, buried a Thread about a Quarter of an Inch
long in the Channell. A little Lint was then laid over the
scratch and a Piece of a Ragg pressed on, and then a Bandage
bound over all—my Coat and waistcoat put on, and I was bid
to go where and do what I pleased. (Dont you think the Dr.
has a good Deal of Confidence in my Discretion, thus to leave
me to it?)

The Doctors have left us Pills red and black to take Night
and Morning. But they looked very sagaciously and impor-
tantly at us, and ordered my Brother, larger Doses than me, on
Account of the Difference in our Constitutions. Dr. Perkins is
a short, thick sett, dark Complexioned, Yet pale Faced, Man,
(Pale faced I say, which I was glad to see, because I have a
great Regard for a Pale Face, in any Gentleman of Physick, Divinity or Law. It indicates search and study). Gives himself the
alert, chearful Air and Behaviour of a Physician, not forgeting
the solemn, important and wise. Warren is a pretty, tall, Genteel, fair faced young Gentleman. Not quite so much Assurance in his Address, as Perkins, (perhaps because Perkins was
present) Yet shewing fully that he knows the Utility thereof,
and that he will soon, practice it in full Perfection.

The Doctors, having finished the Operation and left Us,
their Directions and Medicines, took their Departure in infinite Haste, depend on't.

I have one Request to make, which is that you would be
very careful in making Tom, Smoke all the Letters from me,
very faithfully, before you, or any of the Family reads them.
For, altho I shall never fail to smoke them myself before seal-
ing, Yet I fear the Air of this House will be too much infected,
soon, to be absolutely without Danger, and I would not you
should take the Distemper, by Letter from me, for Millions. I
write at a Desk far removed from any sick Room, and shall use
all the Care I can, but too much cannot be used.

I have written thus far, and it is 45 Minutes Past one O
Clock and no more.

My Love to all. My hearty Thanks to Mamma for her kind
Wishes. My Regards as due to Pappa, and should request his
Prayers, which are always becoming, and especially at such
Times, when We are undertaking any Thing of Consequence

as the small Pox, undoubtedly, tho, I have not the Least Apprehension att all of what is called Danger.

I am as ever Yr.   John Adams
                                                         April 13, 1764

"IS MAN A RATIONAL CREATURE"

To Abigail Smith

                                        Tuesday 17th. April 1764

Yours of April 15th. this moment received. I thank You for it—and for your offer of Milk, but We have Milk in vast Abundance, and every Thing else that we want except Company.

You cant imagine how finely my Brother and I live. We have, as much Bread and as much new pure Milk, as much Pudding, and Rice, and indeed as much of every Thing of the farinaceous Kind as We please—and the Medicine We take is not att all nauseous, or painfull.

And our Felicity is the greater, as five Persons in the same Room, under the Care of Lord And Church, are starved and medicamented with the utmost severity. No Bread, No Pudding, No Milk is permitted them, i.e. no pure and simple Milk, (they are allowed a Mixture of Half Milk and Half Water) and every other Day they are tortured with Powders that make them as sick as Death and as weak as Water. All this may be necessary for them for what I know, as Lord is professedly against any Preparation previous to Inoculation. In which opinion I own I was fully agreed with him, till lately. But Experience has convinced me of my Mistake, and I have felt and now feel every Hour, the Advantage and the Wisdom of the contrary Doctrine.

Dr. Tufts and your Brother have been here to see Us this Morning. They are charmingly well and chearfull, tho they are lean and weak.

Messrs. Quincy's Samuel and Josiah, have the Distemper very lightly. I asked Dr. Perkins how they had it. The Dr. answerd in the style of the Faculty "Oh Lord sir; infinitely light!" It is extreamly pleasing, says he, wherever we go We see every

Body passing thro this tremendous Distemper, in the lightest, easiest manner, conceivable.

The Dr. meaned, those who have the Distemper by Inoculation in the new Method, for those who have it in the natural Way, are Objects of as much Horror, as ever. There is a poor Man, in this Neighbourhood, one Bass, now labouring with it, in the natural Way. He is in a good Way of Recovery, but is the most shocking sight, that can be seen. They say he is no more like a Man than he is like an Hog or an Horse—swelled to three times his size, black as bacon, blind as a stone. I had when I was first inoculated a great Curiosity to go and see him; but the Dr. said I had better not go out, and my Friends thought it would give me a disagreable Turn. My Unkle brought up one Vinal who has just recoverd of it in the natural Way to see Us, and show Us. His face is torn all to Pieces, and is as rugged as Braintree Commons.

This Contrast is forever before the Eyes of the whole Town, Yet it is said there are 500 Persons, who continue to stand it out, in spight of Experience, the Expostulations of the Clergy, both in private and from the Desk, the unwearied Persuasions of the select Men, and the perpetual Clamour and astonishment of the People, and to expose themselves to this Distemper in the natural Way!—Is Man a rational Creature think You?—Conscience, forsooth and scruples are the Cause.—I should think my self, a deliberate self Murderer, I mean that I incurred all the Guilt of deliberate self Murther, if I should only stay in this Town and run the Chance of having it in the natural Way.

Mr. Wheat is broke out, and is now at the Card Table to amuze himself. He will not be able to get above a score or two. Badger has been pretty lazy and lolling, and achy about the Head and Knees and Back, for a Day or two, and the Messengers appear upon him, that foretell the compleat Appearance of the Pox in about 24. Hours.

Thus We see others, Under the symptoms, and all the Pains that attend the Distemper, under the present Management, every Hour, and are neither dismayed nor in the least disconcerted, or dispirited. But are every one of Us wishing that his Turn might come next, that it might be over, and we about our Business, and I return to my Farm, my Garden, but above

all, to my Diana who is the best of all Friends, And the Richest
of all Blessings to her own   Lysander

How shall I express my Gratitude to your Mamma and your
self, for your Kind Care and Concern for me. Am extreamly
obliged for the Milk, and the Apples. But would not have you
trouble yourselves any more for We have a sufficient, a plentiful supply, of those, and every other good Thing that is permitted Us. Balm is a Commodity in very great Demand and
very scarce, here, and there is a great Number of Us to drink
of its inspiring Infusion, so that my Unkle, Aunt, and all the
Patients under their Roof would be obligd, as well as myself, if
you could send me some more.

I received Your agreable Favour by Hannes, this Morning,
and had but just finished My Answer to it, when I received the
other, by Tom.

I never receive a Line from you without a Revivification of
Spirits, and a joyful Heart. I long to hear that—something you
promissed to tell me, in your next. What can that Thing be?
thought I. My busy fancy will be speculating and conjecturing
about it, night and day, I suppose, till your next Letter shall
unriddle the Mystery. You are a wanton, malicious, what shall
I call you for putting me in this Puzzle and Teaze for a day or
two, when you might have informd me in a Minute.

You had best reconsider and retract that bold speech of
yours I assure You. For I assure you there is another Character,
besides that of Critick, in which, if you never did, you always
hereafter shall fear me, or I will know the Reason why.

Oh. Now I think on't I am determined very soon to write
you, an Account in minute Detail of the many Faults I have
observed in you. You remember I gave you an Hint that I had
observed some, in one of my former Letters. You'l be surprized, when you come to find the Number of them.

By the Way I have heard since I came to Town an Insinuation to your Disadvantage, which I will inform you of, as soon
as you have unravelled Your Enigma.

We have very litle News, and very little Conversation in
Town about any Thing, but the Adulterated Callomel that
kill'd a Patient at the Castle, as they say. The Town divides into
Parties about it, and Each Party endeavours to throw the

Blame, as usual, where his Interest, or Affections, prompt him to wish it might go.

Where the Blame will center, or where the Quarrell will terminate, I am not able to foresee.

The Persons talked of are Dr. Gelston, Mr. Wm. Greenleaf, the Apothecary who married Sally Quincy, and the Serjeant, French a Braintree man, who is said to have caried the Druggs from the Apothecary to the Physician. But I think the Serjeant is not much suspected. After all, whether any Body att all is to blame, is with me a dispute.

Make my Compliments to all the formall, give my Duty to all the honourable, and my Love to all the Friendly, whether at Germantown, Weymouth or Elsewhere, that enquire after me, and believe me to be with unalterable Affection Yr.   J. Adams

40 minutes after one O.Clock Tuesday April 17th. 1764

"OUR TURN COMES NEXT"

To Abigail Smith

Dr. Diana   April 18. Wednesday 2 O Clock

Three of our Company, have now the Small Pox upon them, Wheat, Badger, and Elderkin. We have seen them for two or Three days each, wading thro Head Acks, Back Acks, Knee Achs, Gagging and Fever, to their present state of an indisputable Eruption, chearful Spirits, coming Appetites and increasing strength. Huntington begins to complain and look languid.—Our Turn comes next.

We have compleated five days, and entered two Hours on the sixth, since Innoculation, and have as yet felt no Pains, nor Languors from Pox or Medicine, worth mentioning. Indeed what the others have suffered is a mere Trifle. They arise every day with the Rest, having slept as soundly as the rest, eat and drink with the Rest, walk about the Chamber and chat with the rest, excepting that they love lolling and tumbling on the Bed rather more than the rest, and are somewhat less sociable and more frettful, groan a little oftener and wish more to see the Dr.   But as soon as the Pock is out, these Pains depart, their Spirits rise, Tongues run, and they eat, drink, laugh and sport like Prisoners released.

Sylvia wants the Pen and I'm weary of it so I will use it no more than to subscribe the Name of   Lysander

                                                              April 18, 1764

"A SHORT SHIVERING FIT"

To Abigail Smith

                                                Boston April 26th. 1764

Many have been the particular Reasons against my Writing for several days past, but one general Reason has prevailed with me more than any other Thing, and that was, an Absolute Fear to send a Paper from this House, so much infected as it is, to any Person lyable to take the Distemper but especially to you. I am infected myself, and every Room in the House, has infected People in it, so that there is real Danger, in Writing.

However I will write now, and thank you for yours of Yesterday. Mr. Ayers told you the Truth. I was comfortable, and have never been otherwise. I believe, None of the Race of Adam, ever passed the small Pox, with fewer Pains, Achs, Qualms, or with less smart than I have done. I had no Pain in my Back, none in my side, none in my Head. None in my Bones or Limbs, no reching or vomiting or sickness. A short shivering Fit, and a succeeding hot glowing Fit, a Want of Appetite, and a general Languor, were all the symptoms that ushered into the World, all the small Pox, that I can boast of, which are about Eight or Ten, (for I have not yet counted them exactly) two of which only are in my Face, the rest scattered at Random over my Limbs and Body. They fill very finely and regularly, and I am as well, tho not so strong, as ever I was in my Life. My Appetite has returned, and is quick enough and I am returning gradually to my former Method of Living.

Very nearly the same may be said of my Brother excepting that, he looks leaner than I, and that he had more sickness and Head Ach about the Time of the Eruption than I.

Such We have Reason to be thankful has been our Felicity.

And that of Deacon Palmers Children has been, nearly the same. But others in the same House have not been so happy—pretty high Fevers, and severe Pains, and a pretty Plentiful Eruption has been the Portion of Three at last of our Companions. I join with you sincerely in your Lamentation that you were not inoculated. I wish to God the Dr. would sett up an Hospital at Germantown, and inoculate you. I will come and nurse you, nay I will go with you to the Castle or to Point Shirley, or any where and attend you. You say rightly safety there is not, and I say, safety there never will be. And Parents must be lost in Avarice or Blindness, who restrain their Children.

I believe there will be Efforts to introduce Inoculation at Germantown, by Drs. Lord and Church.

However, be carefull of taking the Infection unawares. For all the Mountains of Peru or Mexico I would not, that this Letter or any other Instrument should convey the Infection to you at unawares.

I hope soon to see you, mean time write as often as possible to yrs.,   John Adams

P.S. Dont conclude from any Thing I have written that I think Inoculation a light matter.—A long and total Abstinence from every Thing in Nature that has any Taste, Two heavy Vomits, one heavy Cathartick, four and twenty Mercurial and Antimonial Pills, and Three Weeks close Confinement to an House, are, according to my Estimation of Things, no small matters.—However, who would not chearfully submit to them rather than pass his whole Life in continual Fears, in subjection, under Bondage.

Sylvia and Myra send Compliments.

A CATALOGUE OF IMPERFECTIONS

To Abigail Smith

Boston May 7th. 1764
I promised you, Sometime agone, a Catalogue of your Faults, Imperfections, Defects, or whatever you please to call

them. I feel at present, pretty much at Leisure, and in a very suitable Frame of Mind to perform my Promise. But I must caution you, before I proceed to recollect yourself, and instead of being vexed or fretted or thrown into a Passion, to resolve upon a Reformation—for this is my sincere Aim, in laying before you, this Picture of yourself.

In the first Place, then, give me leave to say, you have been extreamly negligent, in attending so little to Cards. You have very litle Inclination, to that noble and elegant Diversion, and whenever you have taken an Hand you have held it but aukwardly and played it, with a very uncourtly, and indifferent, Air. Now I have Confidence enough in your good sense, to rely upon it, you will for the future endeavour to make a better Figure in this elegant and necessary Accomplishment.

Another Thing, which ought to be mentioned, and by all means amended, is, the Effect of a Country Life and Education, I mean, a certain Modesty, sensibility, Bashfulness, call it by which of these Names you will, that enkindles Blushes forsooth at every Violation of Decency, in Company, and lays a most insupportable Constraint on the freedom of Behaviour. Thanks to the late Refinements of modern manners, Hypocrisy, superstition, and Formality have lost all Reputation in the World and the utmost sublimation of Politeness and Gentility lies, in Ease, and Freedom, or in other Words in a natural Air and Behaviour, and in expressing a satisfaction at whatever is suggested and prompted by Nature, which the aforesaid Violations of Decency, most certainly are.

In the Third Place, you could never yet be prevail'd on to learn to sing. This I take very soberly to be an Imperfection of the most moment of any. An Ear for Musick would be a source of much Pleasure, and a Voice and skill, would be a private solitary Amusement, of great Value when no other could be had. You must have remarked an Example of this in Mrs. Cranch, who must in all probability have been deafened to Death with the Cries of her Betcy, if she had not drowned them in Musick of her own.

In the Fourth Place you very often hang your Head like a Bulrush. You do not sit, erected as you ought, by which Means, it happens that you appear too short for a Beauty, and the Company looses the sweet smiles of that Countenance and the bright sparkles of those Eyes.—This Fault is the Effect and Consequence of another, still more inexcusable in a Lady. I mean an Habit of Reading, Writing and Thinking. But both the Cause and the Effect ought to be repented and amended as soon as possible.

Another Fault, which seems to have been obstinately persisted in, after frequent Remonstrances, Advices and Admonitions of your Friends, is that of sitting with the Leggs across. This ruins the figure and the Air, this injures the Health. And springs I fear from the former source vizt. too much Thinking.—These Things ought not to be!

A sixth Imperfection is that of Walking, with the Toes bending inward. This Imperfection is commonly called Parrottoed, I think, I know not for what Reason. But it gives an Idea, the reverse of a bold and noble Air, the Reverse of the stately strutt, and the sublime Deportment.

Thus have I given a faithful Portraiture of all the Spotts, I have hitherto discerned in this Luminary. Have not regarded Order, but have painted them as they arose in my Memory. Near Three Weeks have I conned and studied for more, but more are not to be discovered. All the rest is bright and luminous.

Having finished the Picture I finish my Letter, lest while I am recounting Faults, I should commit the greatest in a Letter, that of tedious and excessive Length. There's a prettily turned Conclusion for You! from yr.   Lysander

"I SEE NOTHING BUT FAULTS"

To Abigail Smith

My dear Diana   Septr. 30th. 1764

I have this Evening been to see the Girl.—What Girl? Pray, what Right have you to go after Girls?—Why, my Dear, the Girl I mentioned to you, Miss Alice Brackett. But Miss has hitherto acted in the Character of an House-Keeper, and her noble aspiring Spirit had rather rise to be a Wife than descend to be a Maid.

To be serious, however, she says her Uncle, whose House she keeps cannot possibly spare her, these two Months, if then, and she has no Thoughts of leaving him till the Spring, when she intends for Boston to become a Mantua Maker.

So that We are still to seek. Girls enough from fourteen to four and Twenty, are mentioned to me, but the Character of every Mothers Daughter of them is as yet problematical to me. Hannah Crane (pray dont you want to have her, my Dear) has sent several Messages to my Mother, that she will live with you as cheap, as any Girl in the Country. She is stout and able and for what I know willing, but I fear not honest, for which Reason I presume you will think of her no more.

Another Girl, one Rachael Marsh, has been recommended to me as a clever Girl, and a neat one, and one that wants a Place. She was bred in the Family of one of our substantial Farmers and it is likely understands Country Business, But whether she would answer your Purposes, so well as another, I am somewhat in Doubt.

I have heard of a Number of younger Girls of Fourteen and thereabout, but these I suppose you would not choose.

It must therefore be left with you to make Enquiry, and determine for yourself. If you could hear of a suitable Person at Mistick or Newtown, on many Accounts she would be preferable to one, nearer home.

So much for Maids—now for the Man. I shall leave orders for Brackett, to go to Town, Wednesday or Thursday with an Horse Cart. You will get ready by that Time and ship aboard, as many Things as you think proper.

It happens very unfortunately that my Business calls me away at this Juncture for two Weeks together, so that I can take no Care at all about Help or Furniture or any Thing else. But Necessity has no Law.

Tomorrow Morning I embark for Plymouth—with a disordered stomach, a pale Face, an Aching Head and an Anxious Heart. And What Company shall I find there? Why a Number of bauling Lawyers, drunken Squires, and impertinent and stingy Clients. If you realize this, my Dear, since you have agreed to run fortunes with me, you will submit with less Reluctance to any little Disappointments and Anxieties you may meet in the Conduct of your own Affairs.

I have a great Mind to keep a Register of all the stories, Squibbs, Gibes, and Compliments, I shall hear thro the whole Week. If I should I could entertain you with as much Wit, Humour, smut, Filth, Delicacy, Modesty and Decency, tho not with so exact Mimickry, as a certain Gentleman did the other Evening. Do you wonder, my Dear, why that Gentleman does not succeed in Business, when his whole study and Attention has so manifestly been engaged in the nobler Arts of smutt, Double Ententre, and Mimickry of Dutchmen and Negroes? I have heard that Imitators, tho they imitate well, Master Pieces in elegant and valuable Arts, are a servile Cattle. And that Mimicks are the lowest Species of Imitators, and I should think that Mimicks of Dutchmen and Negroes were the most sordid of Mimicks. If so, to what a Depth of the Profound have we plunged that Gentlemans Character. Pardon me, my dear, you know that Candour is my Characteristick—as it is undoubtedly of all the Ladies who are entertained with that Gents Conversation.

Oh my dear Girl, I thank Heaven that another Fortnight will restore you to me—after so long a separation. My soul and Body have both been thrown into Disorder, by your Absence, and a Month or two more would make me the most insufferable Cynick, in the World. I see nothing but Faults, Follies, Frailties and Defects in any Body, lately. People have lost all their good Properties or I my Justice, or Discernment.

But you who have always softened and warmed my Heart, shall restore my Benevolence as well as my Health and Tranquility of mind. You shall polish and refine my sentiments of Life and Manners, banish all the unsocial and ill natured Particles in my Composition, and form me to that happy Temper, that can reconcile a quick Discernment with a perfect Candour.

Believe me, now & ever yr. faithful   Lysander

P.S. My Duty to my worthy Aunt. Oh! I forget myself. My Prophetick Imagination has rap'd me into future Times. I mean, make my Compliments to Mrs. Smith. And tell Betcy I wont expose her Midnight Walks to her Mamma, if she will be a good Girl.

Since the enclosed was written my Mother has informed me, that Molly Nash and her Mother too asked her to get a Place for Molly with me. She is a pretty, neat, Girl, and I believe has been well bred. Her Mother is a very clever Woman. The Girl is about 17.

But my Mother says that Judah will do very well for your service this Winter. She is able to do a good deal of Business. And my mother farther says that she shall have no Occasion for her this Winter and that you may take her if you please and return her in the Spring, when it is likely she will have Occasion again for some Help and you will it is likely want some better Help.

This last Project is the most saving one. And Parcimony is a virtue that you and I must study. However I will submit to any Expence, for your Ease and Conveniency that I can possibly afford.

All these Things I mention to you, that you may weigh them [   ] and I shall acquiesce with Pleasure in your Determination.

A Dissertation on the Canon
and the Feudal Law No. I

To the Printers.

"IGNORANCE and inconsideration are the two great causes of the ruin of mankind." This is an observation of Dr. *Tillotson*, with relation to the interest of his fellow-men, in a future and immortal state: But it is of equal truth and importance, if applied to the happiness of men in society, on this side the grave. In the earliest ages of the world, *absolute monarchy* seems to have been the universal form of government. Kings, and a few of their great counsellors and captains, exercised a cruel tyranny over the people who held a rank in the scale of intelligence, in those days, but little higher than the camels and elephants, that carried them and their engines to war.

BY what causes it was bro't to pass, that the people in the middle ages, became more *intelligent* in general, would not perhaps be possible in these days to discover: But the fact is certain; and wherever a general knowledge and sensibility have prevail'd among the *people*, arbitrary government, and every kind of oppression, have lessened and disappeared in proportion. Man has certainly an exalted soul! and the same principle in humane nature, that aspiring noble principle, founded in benevolence, and cherished by knowledge, I mean the love of power, which has been so often the cause of *slavery*, has, whenever freedom has existed, been the cause of *freedom*. If it is this principle, that has always prompted the princes and nobles of the earth, by every species of fraud and violence, to shake off, all the *limitations* of their power; it is the same that has always stimulated the common people to aspire at independency, and to endeavor at confining the power of the great within the limits of *equity* and *reason*.

THE poor people, it is true, have been much less successful than the great. They have seldom found either leisure or opportunity to form an union and exert their strength—ignorant as they were of arts and letters, they have seldom been able to frame and support a regular opposition. This, however, has been known, by the great, to be the temper of mankind, and they have accordingly laboured, in all ages, to wrest from the populace, as they are contemptuously called, the knowledge of their rights and wrongs, and the power to assert the former or redress the latter. I say RIGHTS, for such they have, undoubtedly, antecedent to all earthly government—*Rights* that cannot be repealed or restrained by human laws—*Rights* derived from the great legislator of the universe.

SINCE the promulgation of christianity, the two greatest systems of tyranny, that have sprung from this original, are the *cannon* and the *feudal* law. The desire of dominion, that great principle by which we have attempted to account for so much good, and so much evil, is, when *properly restrained*, a very useful and noble movement in the human mind: But when such restraints are taken off, it becomes an incroaching, grasping, restless and ungovernable power. Numberless have been the systems of iniquity, contrived by the great, for the gratification of this passion in themselves: but in none of them were they ever more successful, than in the invention and establishment of the *cannon* and the *feudal* law.

BY the *former* of these, the most refined, sublime, extensive, and astonishing constitution of policy, that ever was conceived by the mind of man, was framed by the *Romish* clergy for the aggrandisement of their own order. All the epithets I have here given to the Romish policy are just: and will be allowed to be so, when it is considered, that they even persuaded mankind to believe, faithfully and undoubtingly, that GOD almighty had intrusted *them* with the keys of heaven; whose gates *they* might open and close at pleasure—with a power of dispensation over all the rules and obligations of morality—with authority to licence all sorts of sins and crimes—with a power of deposing princes, and absolving subjects from allegiance—with a power of procuring or withholding the rain of heaven and the beams of the sun—with the management of earthquakes, pestilence and famine. Nay with the mysterious, awful, incomprehensible power of creating out of bread and wine, the flesh and blood of God himself. All these opinions, they were enabled to spread and rivet among the people, by reducing their minds to a state of sordid ignorance and staring timidity; and by infusing into them a *religious* horror of letters and knowledge. Thus was human nature chained fast for ages, in a cruel, shameful and deplorable servitude, to him and his subordinate tyrants, who, it was foretold, would exalt himself above all that was called God, and that was worshipped.

IN the latter, we find another system similar in many respects, to the former: which, altho' it was originally formed perhaps, for the necessary defence of a *barbarous* people, against the inroads and invasions of her neighbouring nations; yet, for the same purposes of tyranny, cruelty and lust, which had dictated the *cannon* law, it was soon adopted by almost all the princes of Europe, and wrought into the constitutions of their *government*. It was originally, a code of laws, for a vast army, in a perpetual encampment. The general was invested with the sovereign propriety of all the lands within the territory. Of *him*, as his servants and vassals, the first rank of his great officers held the lands: and in the same manner, the other subordinate officers held of *them*: and all ranks and degrees held their lands, by a variety of *duties* and *services*, all tending to bind the chains the faster, on *every* order of mankind. In this manner, the common people were held together, in herds and clans, in a state of *servile* dependance on their lords; bound, even by the tenure of their lands to follow them, whenever they commanded, to their wars; and in a state of total ignorance of every thing divine and human, excepting the use of arms, and the culture of their lands.

BUT, another event still more calamitous to human liberty, was a wicked confederacy, between the *two systems* of tyranny above described. It seems to have been even *stipulated* between them, that the *temporal* grandees should contribute every thing in their power to maintain the ascendency of the *priesthood*; and that the spiritual grandees, in their turn, should employ that ascendency over the *consciences* of the *people*, in impressing on their minds, a *blind, implicit* obedience to civil magistracy.

THUS, as long as this confederacy lasted, and the people were held in ignorance; Liberty, and with her, Knowledge, and Virtue too, seem to have deserted the earth; and one age of darkness, succeeded another, till GOD, in his benign providence, raised up the champions, who began and conducted the *reformation*. From the time of the reformation, to the first settlement of *America*, knowledge gradually spread in Europe, but especially in *England*; and in proportion as *that* increased and spread among the people, *ecclesiastical* and *civil* tyranny, which I use as synonimous expressions, for the *cannon* and *feudal* laws, seem to have lost their strength and weight. The people grew more and more sensible of the wrong that was done them, by these systems; more and more impatient under it; and determined at all hazards to rid themselves of it; till, at last, under the *execrable* race of the *Steuarts*, the struggle between the people and the confederacy aforesaid of temporal and spiritual tyranny, became formidable, violent and bloody.

IT was this great struggle, that peopled America. It was not religion *alone*, as is commonly supposed; but it was a love of *universal Liberty*, and an hatred, a dread, an horror of the infernal confederacy, before described, that projected, conducted, and accomplished the settlement of America.

IT was a resolution formed, by a sensible people, I mean the *Puritans*, almost in despair. They had become intelligent in general, and many of them learned. For this fact I have the testimony of archbishop *King* himself, who observed of that people, that they were more intelligent, and better read than even the members of the church whom he censures warmly for that reason. This people had been so vexed, and tortured by the powers of those days, for no other crime than their knowledge, and their freedom of enquiry and examination, and they had so much reason to despair of deliverance from those miseries, on that side the ocean; that they at last resolved to fly to the *wilderness* for refuge, from the temporal and spiritual principalities and powers, and plagues, and scourges, of their *native* country.

AFTER their arrival here, they began their settlements, and formed their plan both of ecclesiastical and civil government, in *direct opposition* to the *cannon* and the *feudal* systems. The leading men among them, both of the clergy and the laity, were men of sense and learning: To many of them, the historians, orators, poets and philosophers of *Greece* and *Rome* were quite familiar: and some of them have left libraries that are still in being, consisting chiefly of volumes, in which the wisdom of the most enlightned ages and nations is deposited, written however in languages, which their great grandsons, *tho' edu-cated in European Universities*, can scarcely read.

Boston Gazette, August 12, 1765

A Dissertation on the Canon and the Feudal Law No. II

Thus accomplished were many of the first Planters of these Colonies. It may be thought polite and fashionable, by many modern fine Gentlemen perhaps, to deride the Characters of these Persons, as enthusiastical, superstitious and republican: But such ridicule is founded in nothing but foppery and affectation, and is grosly injurious and false. Religious to some degree of enthusiasm it may be admitted they were; but this can be no peculiar derogation from their character, because it was at that time almost the universal character, not only of England, but of Christendom. Had this however, been otherwise, their enthusiasm, considering the principles in which it was founded, and the ends to which it was directed, far from being a reproach to them, was greatly to their honour: for I believe it will be found universally true, that no great enterprize, for the honour or happiness of mankind, was ever achieved, without a large mixture of that noble infirmity. Whatever imperfections may be justly ascribed to them, which however are as few, as any mortals have discovered their judgment in framing their policy, was founded in wise, humane and benevolent principles; It was founded in revelation, and in reason too; It was consistent with the principles, of the best, and greatest, and wisest legislators of antiquity. Tyranny in every form, shape, and appearance was their disdain, and abhorrence; no fear of punishment, not even of *Death* itself, in exquisite tortures, had been sufficient to conquer, that steady, manly, pertenacious spirit, with which they had opposed the tyrants of those days, in church and state. They were very far from being enemies to monarchy; and they knew as well as any men, the just regard and honour that is due to the character of a dispenser of the misteries of the gospel of Grace: But they saw clearly, that popular powers must be placed, as a guard, a countroul, a ballance, to the powers of the monarch, and the priest, in every government, or else it would soon become the man of sin, the whore of Babylon, the mystery of iniquity, a great and detestable system of fraud, violence, and usurpation. Their greatest concern seems to have been to establish a government of the church more consistent with the scriptures, and a government of the state more agreable to the dignity of humane nature, than any they had seen in Europe: and to transmit such a government down to their posterity, with the means of securing and preserving it, for ever. To render the popular power in their new government, as great and wise, as their principles and theory, i. e. as human nature and the christian religion require it should be, they endeavored to remove from it, as many of the feudal inequalities and dependencies, as could be spared, consistently with the preservation of a mild limited monarchy. And in this they discovered the depth of their wisdom, and the warmth of their friendship to human nature. But the first place is due to religion. They saw clearly, that of all the nonsense and delusion which had ever passed thro' the mind of man, none had ever been more extravagant than the notions of absolutions, indelible characters, uninterrupted successions, and the rest of those phantastical ideas, derived from the canon law, which had thrown such a glare of mystery, sanctity, reverence and right reverence, eminence and holiness, around the idea of a priest, as no mortal could deserve, and as always must from the constitution of human nature, be dangerous in society. For this reason, they demolished the whole system of Diocesan episcopacy and deriding, as all reasonable and impartial men must do, the ridiculous fancies of sanctified effluvia from episcopal fingers, they established sacerdotal ordination, on the foundation of the bible and common sense. This conduct at once imposed an obligation on the whole body of the clergy, to industry, virtue, piety and learning, and rendered that whole body infinitely more independent on the civil powers, in all respects than they could be where they were formed into a scale of subordination, from a pope down to priests and fryars and confessors, necessarily and essentially a sordid, stupid, wretched herd; or than they could be in any other country, where an archbishop held the place of an universal bishop, and the vicars and curates that of the ignorant, dependent, miserable rabble aforesaid; and infinitely more sensible and learned than they could be in either. This subject has been seen in the same light, by many illustrious patriots, who have lived in America, since the days of our fore fathers, and who have adored their memory for the same reason. And methinks there has not appeared in New England a stronger veneration for their memory, a more penetrating insight into the grounds and principles and spirit of their policy, nor a more earnest desire of perpetuating the blessings of it to posterity, than that fine institution of the late chief justice Dudley, of a lecture against popery, and on the validity of presbyterian ordination. This was certainly intended by that wise and excellent man, as an eternal memento of the wisdom and goodness of the very principles that settled America. But I must again return to the feudal law.

The adventurers so often mentioned, had an utter contempt of all that dark ribaldry of hereditary indefeasible right—the Lord's anointed—and the divine miraculous original of government, with which the priesthood had inveloped the feudal monarch in clouds and mysteries, and from whence they had deduced the most mischievous of all doctrines, that of passive obedience and non resistance. They knew that government was a plain, simple, intelligible thing founded in nature and reason and quite comprehensible by common sense. They detested all the base services, and servile dependencies of the feudal system. They knew that no such unworthy dependences took place in the ancient seats of liberty, the republic of Greece and Rome: and they tho't all such slavish subordinations were equally inconsistent with the constitution of human nature and that religious liberty, with which Jesus had made them free. This was certainly the opinion they had formed, and they were far from being singular or extravagant in thinking so. Many celebrated modern writers, in Europe, have espoused the same sentiments. Lord Kaim's, a Scottish writer of great reputation, whose authority in this case ought to have the more weight, as his countrymen have not the most worthy ideas of liberty, speaking of the feudal law, says, "A constitution so contradictory to all the principles which govern mankind, can never be brought about, one should imagine, but by foreign conquest or native usurpations." Brit. Ant. P. 2. Rousseau speaking of the same system, calls it "That most iniquitous and absurd form of government by which human nature was so shamefully degraded." Social Compact, Page 164. It would be easy to multiply authorities, but it must be needless, because as the original of this form of government was among savages, as the spirit of it is military and despotic, every writer, who would allow the people to have any right to life or property, or freedom, more than the beasts of the field, and who was not hired or inlisted under arbitrary lawless power, has been always willing to admit the feudal system to be inconsistent with liberty and the rights of mankind.

Boston Gazette, August 19, 1765

A Dissertation on the Canon and the Feudal Law No. III

To have holden their lands, allodially, or for every man to have been the sovereign lord and proprietor of the ground he occupied, would have constituted a government, too nearly like a commonwealth. They were contented therefore to hold their lands of their King, as their sovereign Lord, and to him they were willing to render homage: but to no mesne and subordinate Lords, nor were they willing to submit to any of the baser services. In all this, they were so strenuous, that they have even transmitted to their posterity, a very general contempt and detestation of holdings by quit rents: As they have also an hereditary ardor for liberty and thirst for knowledge.

They were convinced by their knowledge of human nature derived from history and their own experience, that nothing could preserve their posterity from the encroachments of the two systems of tyranny, in opposition to which, as has been observed already, they erected their government in church and state, but knowledge diffused generally thro' the whole body of the people. Their civil and religious principles, therefore, conspired to prompt them to use every measure, and take every precaution in their power, to propagate and perpetuate

knowledge. For this purpose they laid, very early the foundations of colleges, and invested them with ample priviledges
and emoluments; and it is remarkable, that they have left
among their posterity, so universal an affection and veneration
for those seminaries, and for liberal education, that the meanest of the people contribute chearfully to the support and
maintenance of them every year, and that nothing is more generally popular than projections for the honour, reputation and
advantage of those seats of learning. But the wisdom and
benevolence of our fathers rested not here. They made an early
provision by law, that every town consisting of so many families, should be always furnished with a grammar school. They
made it a crime for such a town to be destitute of a grammar
school master, for a few months, and subjected it to an heavy
penalty. So that the education of all ranks of people was made
the care and expence of the public in a manner, that I believe
has been unknown to any other people ancient or modern.

The consequences of these establishments we see and feel
every day. A native of America who cannot read and write is as
rare an appearance, as a Jacobite or a Roman Catholic, i. e. as
rare as a Comet or an Earthquake. It has been observed, that
we are all of us, lawyers, divines, politicians and philosophers.
And I have good authorities to say that all candid foreigners
who have passed thro' this country, and conversed freely with
all sorts of people here, will allow, that they have never seen so
much knowledge and civility among the common people in any
part of the world. It is true, there has been among us a party
for some years, consisting chiefly not of the descendants of the
first settlers of this country but of high churchmen and high
statesmen, imported since, who affect to censure this provision
for the education of our youth as a needless expence, and an
imposition upon the rich in favour of the poor—and as an institution productive of idleness and vain speculation among
the people, whose time and attention it is said ought to be devoted to labour, and not to public affairs or to examination
into the conduct of their superiours. And certain officers of the
crown, and certain other missionaries of ignorance, foppery,
servility and slavery, have been most inclined to countenance
and increase the same party. Be it remembred, however, that
liberty must at all hazards be supported. We have a right to it,

derived from our Maker. But if we had not, our fathers have earned, and bought it for us, at the expence of their ease, their estates, their pleasure, and their blood. And liberty cannot be preserved without a general knowledge among the people, who have a right from the frame of their nature, to knowledge, as their great Creator who does nothing in vain, has given them understandings, and a desire to know—but besides this they have a right, an indisputable, unalienable, indefeasible divine right to that most dreaded, and envied kind of knowledge, I mean of the characters and conduct of their rulers. Rulers are no more than attorneys, agents and trustees for the people; and if the cause, the interest and trust is insidiously betray'd, or wantonly trifled away, the people have a right to revoke the authority, that they themselves have deputed, and to constitute abler and better agents, attorneys and trustees. And the preservation of the means of knowledge, among the lowest ranks, is of more importance to the public, than all the property of all the rich men in the country. It is even of more consequence to the rich themselves, and to their posterity. The only question is whether it is a public emolument? and if it is, the rich ought undoubtedly to contribute in the same proportion, as to all other public burdens, i. e. in proportion to their wealth which is secured by public expences. But none of the means of information are more sacred, or have been cherished with more tenderness and care by the settlers of America, than the Press. Care has been taken, that the art of printing should be encouraged, and that it should be easy and cheap and safe for any person to communicate his thoughts to the public. And you, Messieurs Printers, whatever the tyrants of the earth may say of your paper, have done important service to your country, by your readiness and freedom in publishing the speculations of the curious. The stale, impudent insinuations of slander and sedition, with which the gormandizers of power have endeavor'd to discredit your paper, are so much the more to your honour; for the jaws of power are always opened to devour, and her arm is always stretched out if possible to destroy, the freedom of thinking, speaking and writing. And if the public interest, liberty and happiness have been in danger, from the ambition or avarice of any great man or number of great men, whatever may be their politeness, address, learning, ingenuity and in other respects integrity and humanity, you have done yourselves honour and your country service, by publishing and pointing out that avarice and ambition. These views are so much the more dangerous and pernicious, for the virtues with which they may be accompanied in the same character, and with so much the more watchful jealousy to be guarded against.

"Curse on such virtues, they've undone their country."

Be not intimidated therefore, by any terrors, from publishing with the utmost freedom, whatever can be warranted by the laws of your country; nor suffer yourselves to be wheedled out of your liberty, by any pretences of politeness, delicacy or decency. These as they are often used, are but three different names, for hypocrisy, chicanery and cowardice. Much less I presume will you be discouraged by any pretences, that malignant's on this side the water will *represent* your paper as factious and seditious, or that the Great on the other side the water will take offence at them. This Dread of *representation*, has had for a long time in this province effects very similar to what the physicians call an hydropho, or dread of water. It has made us delirious. And we have rushed headlong into the water, till we are almost drowned, out of simple or phrensical fear of it. Believe me, the character of this country has suffered more in Britain, by the pusillanimity with which we have borne many insults and indignities from the creatures of power at home, and the creatures of those creatures here, than it ever did or ever will by the freedom and spirit that has been or will be discovered in writing, or action. Believe me my countrymen, they have imbibed an opinion on the other side the water, that we are an ignorant, a timid and a stupid people, nay their tools on this side have often the impudence to dispute your bravery. But I hope in God the time is near at hand, when they will be fully convinced of your understanding, integrity and courage. But can any thing be more ridiculous, were it not too provoking to be laughed at, than to pretend that offence should be taken at home for writings here? Pray let them look at home. Is not the human understanding exhausted there? Are not reason, imagination, wit, passion, senses and all, tortured to find out satyr and invective against the characters of the vile and futile fellows who sometimes get into place and power? The most exceptionable paper that ever I saw here, is perfect prudence and modesty, in comparison of multitudes of their applauded writings. Yet the high regard they have for the freedom of the Press, indulges all. I must and will repeat it, your Paper deserves the patronage of every friend to his country. And whether the defamers of it are arrayed in robes of scarlet or sable, whether they lurk and skulk in an insurance office, whether they assume the venerable character of a Priest, the sly one of a scrivener, or the dirty, infamous, abandoned one of an informer, they are all the creatures and tools of the lust of domination.

The true source of our sufferings, has been our timidity.

Boston Gazette, September 30, 1765

Instructions to Braintree's Representative Concerning the Stamp Act

We hear from Braintree that the Freeholders and other Inhabitants of that Town, legally assembled on Tuesday the Twenty fourth of September last, unanimously voted, that Instructions should be given their Representative, for his Conduct in General Assembly, on this great Occasion—The Substance of these Instructions is as follows:

To EBENEZER THAYER, Esq.

SIR,
"In all the Calamities which have ever befallen this Country, we have never felt so great a Concern, or such alarming Apprehensions, as on this Occasion.—Such is our Loyalty to the King, our Veneration for both Houses of Parliament, and our Affection for all our Fellow subjects in Britain, that Measures, which discover any Unkindness in that Country towards Us, are the more sensibly and intimately felt. And we can no longer forbear complaining, that many of the Measures of the late Ministry, and some of the late Acts of Parliament, have a Tendency, in our Apprehension, to divest us of our most

essential Rights and Liberties.—We shall confine ourselves, however, chiefly to the Act of Parliament, commonly called the Stamp-Act, by which a very burthensome, and in our Opinion, unconstitutional Tax, is to be laid upon us all; and we subjected to numerous and enormous Penalties, to be prosecuted, sued for, and recovered, at the Option of an Informer, in a Court of Admiralty without a Jury.

We have called this a burthensome Tax, because the Duties are so numerous and so high, and the Embarrassments to Business in this infant, sparsely-settled Country, so great, that it would be totally impossible for the People to subsist under it, if we had no Controversy at all about the Right and Authority of imposing it. Considering the present Scarcity of Money, we have Reason to think, the Execution of that Act for a short Space of Time would drein the Country of its Cash, strip Multitudes of all their Property, and reduce them to absolute Beggary. And what the Consequence would be to the Peace of the Province, from so sudden a Shock and such a convulsive Change, in the whole Course of our Business and Subsistence, we tremble to consider.—We further apprehend this Tax to be unconstitutional: We have always understood it to be a grand and fundamental Principle of the Constitution, that no Freeman should be subjected to any Tax, to which he has not given his own Consent, in Person or by Proxy. And the Maxims of the Law as we have constantly received them, are to the same Effect, that no Freeman can be separated from his Property, but by his own Act or Fault. We take it clearly, therefore, to be inconsistent with the Spirit of the Common Law, and of the essential fundamental Principles of the British Constitution, that we should be subjected to any Tax, imposed by the British Parliament: because we are not represented in that Assembly in any Sense, unless it be by a Fiction of Law, as insensible in Theory as it would be injurious in Practice, if such a Taxation should be grounded on it.

But the most grievous Innovation of all, is the alarming Extension of the Power of Courts of Admiralty. In these Courts, one Judge presides alone! No Juries have any Concern there! —The Law, and the Fact, are both to be decided by the same single Judge, whose Commission is only during Pleasure, and with whom, as we are told, the most mischievous of all Customs has become established, that of taking Commissions on all Condemnations; so that he is under a pecuniary Temptation always against the Subject. Now, if the Wisdom of the Mother Country has thought the Independency of the Judges, so essential to an impartial Administration of Justice, as to render them independent of every Power on Earth, independent of the King, the Lords, the Commons, the People, nay independent, in Hope and Expectation, of the Heir apparent, by continuing their Commissions after a Demise of the Crown; What Justice and Impartiality are we, at 3000 Miles distance from the Fountain to expect from such a Judge of Admiralty? We have all along thought the Acts of Trade in this Respect a Grievance: but the Stamp-Act has opened a vast Number of Sources of new Crimes, which may be committed by any Man, and cannot, but be committed by Multitudes, and prodigious Penalties are annexed, and all these are to be tried by such a Judge of such a Court!—What can be wanting, after this, but a weak or wicked Man for a Judge, to render Us the most sordid and forlorn of Slaves? We mean the Slaves of *a Slave* of the Servants of a Minister of State:—We cannot help asserting therefore, that this Part of the Act will make an essential Change in the Constitution of Juries, and is directly repugnant to the Great Charter itself. For by that Charter "No Amerciament shall be assessed, but by the Oath of honest and lawful Men of the Vicinage."—And "No Freeman shall be taken, or imprisoned, or disseized of his Freehold, or Liberties, or free Customs, nor passed upon, nor condemned, but by lawful Judgment of his Peers, or by the Law of the Land."—So that this Act will "make such a Distinction, and create such a Difference between" the Subjects in Great-Britain, and those in America as we could not have expected from the Guardians of Liberty in "Both."

As these, Sir, are our Sentiments of that Act, We, the Freeholders and other Inhabitants, legally assembled for this Purpose, must enjoin it upon you, to comply with no Measures or Proposals for countenancing the same, or assisting in the Execution of it, but by all lawful Means, consistent with our Allegiance to the King, and Relation to Great Britain, to oppose the Execution of it, till we can hear the Success of the Cries and Petitions of America for Relief.

We further recommend the most clear and explicit Assertion and Vindication of our Rights and Liberties, to be entered on the Public Records; that the World may know, in the present and all future Generations, that we have a clear Knowledge and a just Sense of them, and, with Submission to Divine Providence, that we never can be Slaves.

Nor can we think it adviseable to agree to any Steps for the Protection of stamped Papers, or Stamp-Officers.—Good and wholsome Laws we have already, for the Preservation of the Peace: And we apprehend there is no further Danger of Tumult and Disorder,—to which we have a well-grounded Aversion; and that any extraordinary and expensive Exertions, would tend to exasperate the People and endanger the public Tranquility, rather than the contrary.—Indeed we cannot too often inculcate upon you our Desires, that all extraordinary Grants and expensive Measures, may, upon all Occasions, as much as possible be avoided.—The Public Money, of this Country, is the Toil and Labour of the People, who are under many uncommon Difficulties and Distresses, at this Time: So that all reasonable Frugality ought to be observed. And we would recommend particularly, the strictest Care, and the utmost Firmness to prevent all unconstitutional Draughts upon the Public Treasury.

Boston Gazette, October 10, 1765

"Humphrey Ploughjogger" No. IV

Messieurs EDES & GILL,   Monday, October 14, 1765

I han't rit nothing to be printed a great while: but I can't sleep a nights, one wink hardly, of late. I hear so much talk about the stamp act and the governor's speech, that it seems as if 'twould make me crazy. The governor has painted a dreadful picture of the times after the first of November—I hate the thoughts of the first of November. I hope twill be a great storm, and black and gloomy weather, as our faces and hearts will all be. Tis worse than all the fifth of Novembers that ever was. The Pope never did half so much mischief, as that stamp act will do, if the world stands as long as the Pope has done. However, seems to me the governor has represented the times worse than they will be. For in the first place they do say, that thieves and robbers and rioters, ay and lyars too, and all sorts of rogues, may be punish'd as well after the stamp act takes place as before. And as to suing poor folks for money, that does no body no good but the lawyers. But as to trade and shipping and such like, it seems to me we had better be without the most of that than with it—for it only makes rum and such things cheap, and so makes folks drink toddy and flip instead of cyder, when they an't half so good and holsome—and it mades makes us all beaus, and dresses us up fine. We got into a way on't o late,—our young men buy them blue surtouts, with fine yellow buttons, and boughton broad cloth coats jackets and breeches—and our young women wear callicoes, chinces and laces, and other nicknacks to make them fine. But the naughty jacks and trollops must leave off such vanity, and go to nitting and spinning. I always used to keep a comely boughten coat to go to meeting in, but I'le vow I'le never put it on again after first November, if the stamp act takes place; I'le cut up the hide of my fat Ox that I'm fatting for my winter's beef first, and make a coat of that, with the hair on. I'm sure I could be edified as much with the sermon, as if I had on a royal robe, and be as warm in it too. I've read somewhere that the folks in old England before Cæsar went there, wore such skins of beasts, and yet loved liberty, and knew how to keep it too. I don't believe our young folks would love to dance together at husking frolicks, and to kiss one another a bit the less, if they wore woolen shirts and shifts of their own making, than they do now in their fine ones. I do say, I won't buy one shilling worth of any thing that comes from old England, till the stamp act is appeal'd, nor I won't let any of my sons and daughters; I'de rather the Spittlefield weavers should pull down all the houses in old England, and knock the brains out of all the wicked great men there, than this country should loose their liberty. Our fore fathers came over here for liberty of conscience, and we have been nothing better than servants to 'em all along this 100 years, and got just enough to keep soul and body together, and buy their goods to keep us from freezing to death, and we won't be their negroes. Providence never designed us for negroes, I know, for if it had it wou'd have given us black hides, and thick lips, and flat noses, and short woolly hair, which it han't done, and therefore never intended us for slaves. This I know is good a sillogissim as any at colledge, I say we are as handsome as old England folks, and so should be as free.

So I don't like the governor's speech very well, any more than I did tother speech that he made, where he has not done fairly by me. I'me sure I wrote abundance, about Hemp before he said a word about it. Mr. U and I wrote a good many papers, and us'd many arguments for it, and told the way of managing ont, a year or two before the governor said a word about it. Ay, and a great many folks were stirred up to try it, by our writings too, and I believe raly Mr. U and I ought to have the honor and glory and profit ont too—of bringing ont into fashion. I dont see why it would not be reasonable for our Deputies to make Mr. U and I a grant or two for our extraordinary services, as they do sometimes to other great men that dont deserve it half so much.

HUMPHRY PLOUGHJOGGER
Boston Gazette, October 14, 1765

A Dissertation on the Canon and the Feudal Law No. IV

We have been afraid to think. We have felt a reluctance to examining into the grounds of our privileges, and the extent in which we have an indisputable right to demand them against all the power and authority, on earth. And many who have not scrupled to examine for themselves, have yet for certain prudent reasons been cautious, and diffident of declaring the result of their enquiries.

The cause of this timidity is perhaps hereditary and to be traced back in history, as far as the cruel treatment the first settlers of this country received, before their embarkation for America, from the government at Home. Every body knows how dangerous it was to speak or write in favour of any thing in those days, but the triumphant system of religion and politicks. And our fathers were particularly, the objects of the persecutions and proscriptions of the times. It is not unlikely therefore, that, although they were inflexibly steady in refusing their positive assent to any thing against their principles, they might have contracted habits of reserve, and a cautious diffidence of asserting their opinions publickly. These habits they probably brought with them to America, and have transmitted down to us. Or, we may possibly account for this appearance, by the great affection and veneration, Americans have always entertained for the country from whence they sprang—or by the quiet temper for which they have been remarkable, no country having been less disposed to discontent than this—or by a sense they have, that it is their duty to acquiesce, under the administration of government, even when in many smaller matters gravaminous to them, and until the essentials of the great compact are destroy'd or invaded. These peculiar causes might operate upon them; but without these we all know, that human nature itself, from indolence, modesty, humanity or fear, has always too much reluctance to a manly assertion of its rights. Hence perhaps it has happened that nine tenths of the species, are groaning and gasping in misery and servitude.

But whatever the cause has been, the fact is certain, we have been excessively cautious of giving offence by complaining of grievances. And it is as certain that American governors, and their friends and all the crown officers have avail'd themselves of this disposition in the people. They have prevailed on us to consent to many things, which were grosly injurious to us, and to surrender many others with voluntary tameness, to which we had the clearest right. Have we not been treated formerly, with abominable insolence, by officers of the navy? I mean no insinuation against any gentleman now on this station, having heard no complaint of any one of them to his dishonor. Have not some generals, from England, treated us like servants, nay more like slaves than like Britons? Have we not been under the most ignominious contribution, the most abject submission, the most supercilious insults of some custom house officers? Have we not been trifled with, browbeaten, and trampled on, by former governors, in a manner which no king of England since James the second has dared to indulge towards his subjects? Have we not raised up one family, in them placed an unlimitted confidence, and been soothed and battered and intimidated by their influence, into a great part of this infamous tameness and submission? "These are serious and alarming questions, and deserve a dispassionate consideration."

This disposition has been the great wheel and the mainspring in the American machine of court politicks. We have been told that "the word 'Rights' is an offensive expression." That "the King his ministry and parliament will not endure to hear Americans talk of their Rights." That "Britain is the mother and we the children, that a filial duty and submission is due from us to her," and that "we ought to doubt our own judgment, and presume that she is right, even when she seems to us to shake the foundations of government." That "Britain is immensely rich and great and powerful, has fleets and armies at her command, which have been the dread and terror of the universe, and that she will force her own judgment into execution, right or wrong." But let me intreat you Sir to pause and consider. Do you consider your self as a missionary of loyalty or of rebellion? Are you not representing your King his ministry and parliament as tyrants, imperious, unrelenting tyrants by such reasoning as this? Is not this representing your most gracious sovereign, as endeavouring to destroy the foundations of his own throne? Are you not putting language into the royal mouth, which if fairly pursued will shew him to have no right to the crown on his own sacred head? Are you not representing every member of parliament as renouncing the transactions at Runningmede, and as repealing in effect the bill of rights, when the Lords and Commons asserted and vindicated the rights of the people and their own rights, and insisted on the King's assent to that assertion and vindication? Do you not represent them as forgetting that the prince of Orange, was created King William by the People, on purpose that their rights might be eternal and inviolable? Is there not something extremely fallacious, in the common-place images of mother country and children colonies? Are we the children of Great-Britain, any more than the cities of London, Exeter and Bath? Are we not brethren and fellow subjects, with those in Britain, only under a somewhat different method of legislation, and a totally different method of taxation? But admitting we are children; have not children a right to complain when their parents are attempting to break their limbs, to administer poison, or to sell them to enemies for slaves? Let me intreat you to consider, will the mother, be pleased, when you represent her as deaf to the cries of her children? When you compare her to the infamous miscreant, who lately stood on the gallows for starving her child? When you resemble her to Lady Macbeth in Shakespear, (I cannot think of it without horror)

> Who "had given suck, and knew
> How tender 'twas to love the Babe that milk'd her."
>   But yet, who could
> "Even while 'twas smiling in her Face,
> Have pluck'd her Nipple from the boneless Gums,
> And dash'd the Brains out."

Let us banish forever from our minds, my countrymen, all such unworthy ideas of the King, his ministry and parliament. Let us not suppose, that all are become luxurious effeminate and unreasonable, on the other side the water, as many designing persons would insinuate. Let us presume, what is in fact true, that the spirit of liberty, is as ardent as ever among the body of the nation, though a few individuals may be corrupted. Let us take it for granted, that the same great spirit, which once gave Cæsar so warm a reception; which denounced hostilities against John 'till Magna Charta was signed; which severed the head of Charles the first from his body, and drove James the second from his kingdom; the same great spirit (may heaven preserve it till the earth shall be no more) which first seated the great grand father of his present most gracious Majesty, on the throne of Britain, is still alive and active and warm in England; and that the same spirit in America, instead of provoking the inhabitants of that country, will endear us to them for ever and secure their good will.

This spirit however without knowledge, would be little better than a brutal rage. Let us tenderly and kindly cherish, therefore the means of knowledge. Let us dare to read, think, speak and write. Let every order and degree among the people rouse their attention and animate their resolution. Let them all become attentive to the grounds and principles of government, ecclesiastical and civil. Let us study the law of nature;

search into the spirit of the British constitution; read the histories of ancient ages; contemplate the great examples of Greece and Rome; set before us, the conduct of our own British ancestors, who have defended for us, the inherent rights of mankind, against foreign and domestic tyrants and usurpers, against arbitrary kings and cruel priests, in short against the gates of earth and hell. Let us read and recollect and impress upon our souls, the views and ends, of our own more immediate forefathers, in exchanging their native country for a dreary, inhospitable wilderness. Let us examine into the nature of that power and the cruelty of that oppression which drove them from their homes. Recollect their amazing fortitude, their bitter sufferings! The hunger, the nakedness, the cold, which they patiently endured! The severe labours of clearing their grounds, building their houses, raising their provisions amidst dangers from wild beasts and savage men, before they had time or money or materials for commerce! Recollect the civil and religious principles and hopes and expectations, which constantly supported and carried them through all hardships, and patience and resignation! Let us recollect it was liberty! The hope of liberty for themselves and us and ours, which conquered all discouragements, dangers and trials! In such researches as these let us all in our several departments chearfully engage! But especially the proper patrons and supporters of law, learning and religion.

Let the pulpit resound with the doctrines and sentiments of religious liberty. Let us hear the danger of thraldom to our consciences, from ignorance, extream poverty and dependance, in short from civil and political slavery. Let us see delineated before us, the true map of man. Let us hear the dignity of his nature, and the noble rank he holds among the works of God! that consenting to slavery is a sacriligious breach of trust, as offensive in the sight of God, as it is derogatory from our own honor or interest or happiness; and that God almighty has promulgated from heaven, liberty, peace, and good-will to man!

Let the Bar proclaim, "the laws, the rights, the generous plan of power," delivered down from remote antiquity; inform the world of the mighty struggles, and numberless sacrifices, made by our ancestors, in defence of freedom. Let it be known, that British liberties are not the grants of princes or parliaments, but original rights, conditions of original contracts, coequal with prerogative and coeval with government. —That many of our rights are inherent and essential, agreed on as maxims and establish'd as preliminaries, even before a parliament existed. Let them search for the foundations of British laws and government in the frame of human nature, in the constitution of the intellectual and moral world. There let us see, that truth, liberty, justice and benevolence, are its everlasting basis; and if these could be removed, the superstructure is overthrown of course.

Let the colleges join their harmony, in the same delightful concern. Let every declamation turn upon the beauty of liberty and virtue, and the deformity, turpitude and malignity of slavery and vice. Let the public disputations become researches into the grounds and nature and ends of government, and the means of preserving the good and demolishing the evil. Let the dialogues and all the exercises, become the instruments of impressing on the tender mind, and of spreading and distributing, far and wide, the ideas of right and the sensations of freedom.

In a word, let every sluice of knowledge be open'd and set a flowing. The encroachments upon liberty, in the reigns of the first James and the first Charles, by turning the general attention of learned men to government, are said to have produced the greatest number of consummate statesmen, which has ever been seen in any age, or nation. Your Clarendons, Southamptons, Seldens, Hampdens, Faulklands, Sidneys, Locks, Harringtons, are all said to have owed their eminence in political knowledge, to the tyrannies of those reigns. The prospect, now before us, in America, ought in the same manner to engage the attention of every man of learning to matters of power and of right, that we may be neither led nor driven blindfolded to irretrievable destruction. Nothing less than this seems to have been meditated for us, by somebody or other in Great-Britain. There seems to be a direct and formal design on foot, to enslave all America. This however must be done by degrees. The first step that is intended seems to be an entire subversion of the whole system of our Fathers, by an introduction of the cannon and feudal law, into America. The cannon and feudal systems tho' greatly mutilated in England, are not yet de-stroy'd. Like the temples and palaces, in which the great con-trivers of them, once worship'd and inhabited, they exist in ruins; and much of the domineering spirit of them still re-mains. The designs and labours of a certain society, to intro-duce the former of them into America, have been well exposed to the public by a writer of great abilities, and the further at-tempts to the same purpose that may be made by that society, or by the ministry or parliament, I leave to the conjectures of the thoughtful. But it seems very manifest from the S– – –p A–t itself, that a design is form'd to strip us in a great measure of the means of knowledge, by loading the Press, the Colleges, and even an Almanack and a News-Paper, with restraints and duties; and to introduce the inequalities and dependances of the feudal system, by taking from the poorer sort of people all their little subsistance, and conferring it on a set of stamp officers, distributors and their deputies. But I must proceed no further at present. The sequel, whenever I shall find health and leisure to pursue it, will be a "disquisition of the policy of the stamp act." In the mean time however let me add, These are not the vapours of a melancholly mind, nor the effusions of envy, disappointed ambition, nor of a spirit of opposition to government: but the emanations of an heart that burns, for its country's welfare. No one of any feeling, born and educated in this once happy country, can consider the numerous distresses, the gross indignities, the barbarous ignorance, the haughty usurpations, that we have reason to fear are meditating for our-selves, our children, our neighbours, in short for all our countrymen and all their posterity, without the utmost agonies of heart, and many tears.

Boston Gazette, October 21, 1765

From the Diary:
December 18, 1765–January 2, 1766

BRAINTREE DECR. 18TH. 1765. WEDNESDAY.

How great is my Loss, in neglecting to keep a regular Journal, through the last Spring, Summer, and Fall. In the Course of my Business, as a Surveyor of High-Ways, as one of the Committee, for dividing, planning, and selling the North-Commons, in the Course of my two great Journeys to Pounalborough and Marthas Vineyard, and in several smaller Journeys to Plymouth, Taunton and Boston, I had many fine Opportunities and Materials for Speculation.—The Year 1765 has been the most remarkable Year of my Life. That enormous Engine, fabricated by the british Parliament, for battering down all the Rights and Liberties of America, I mean the Stamp Act, has raised and spread, thro the whole Continent, a Spirit that will be recorded to our Honour, with all future Generations. In every Colony, from Georgia to New Hampshire inclusively, the Stamp Distributors and Inspectors have been compelled, by the unconquerable Rage of the People, to renounce their offices. Such and so universal has been the Resentment of the People, that every Man who has dared to speak in favour of the Stamps, or to soften the detestation in which they are held, how great soever his Abilities and Virtues had been esteemed before, or whatever his fortune, Connections and Influence had been, has been seen to sink into universal Contempt and Ignominy.

The People, even to the lowest Ranks, have become more attentive to their Liberties, more inquisitive about them, and more determined to defend them, than they were ever before known or had occasion to be. Innumerable have been the Monuments of Wit, Humour, Sense, Learning, Spirit, Patriotism, and Heroism, erected in the several Colonies and Provinces, in the Course of this Year. Our Presses have groaned, our Pulpits have thundered, our Legislatures have resolved, our Towns have voted, The Crown Officers have every where trembled, and all their little Tools and Creatures, been afraid to Speak and ashamed to be seen.

This Spirit however has not yet been sufficient to banish, from Persons in Authority, that Timidity, which they have discovered from the Beginning. The executive Courts have not yet dared to adjudge the Stamp-Act void nor to proceed with Business as usual, tho it should seem that Necessity alone would be sufficient to justify Business, at present, tho the Act should be allowed to be obligatory. The Stamps are in the Castle. Mr. Oliver has no Commission. The Governor has no Authority to distribute, or even to unpack the Bales, the Act has never been proclaimed nor read in the Province; Yet the Probate office is shut, the Custom House is shut, the Courts of Justice are shut, and all Business seems at a Stand. Yesterday and the day before, the two last days of Service for January Term, only one Man asked me for a Writ, and he was soon determined to waive his Request. I have not drawn a Writ since 1st. Novr.

How long We are to remain in this languid Condition, this passive Obedience to the Stamp Act, is not certain. But such a Pause cannot be lasting. Debtors grow insolent. Creditors grow angry. And it is to be expected that the Public offices will very soon be forced open, unless such favourable Accounts should be received from England, as to draw away the Fears of the Great, or unless a greater Dread of the Multitude should drive away the Fear of Censure from G. Britain.

It is my Opinion that by this Inactivity we discover Cowardice, and too much Respect to the Act. This Rest appears to be by Implication at least an Acknowledgement of the Authority of Parliament to tax Us. And if this Authority is once acknowledged and established, the Ruin of America will become inevitable.

This long Interval of Indolence and Idleness will make a large Chasm in my affairs if it should not reduce me to Distress and incapacitate me to answer the Demands upon me. But I must endeavour in some degree to compensate the Disadvantage, by posting my Books, reducing my Accounts into better order, and by diminishing my Expences, but above all by improving the Leisure of this Winter, in a diligent Application to my Studies. I find that Idleness lies between Business and Study, i.e. The Transision from the Hurry of a multiplicity of Business, to the Tranquility that is necessary for intense Study, is not easy. There must be a Vacation, an Interval between them, for the Mind to recollect itself.

The Bar seem to me to behave like a Flock of shot Pidgeons. They seem to be stopped, the Net seems to be thrown over them, and they have scarcely Courage left to flounce and to flutter. So sudden an Interruption in my Career, is very unfortunate for me. I was but just getting into my Geers, just getting under Sail, and an Embargo is laid upon the Ship. Thirty Years of my Life are passed in Preparation for Business. I have had Poverty to struggle with—Envy and Jealousy and Malice of Enemies to encounter—no Friends, or but few to assist me, so that I have groped in dark Obscurity, till of late, and had but just become known, and gained a small degree of Reputation, when this execrable Project was set on foot for my Ruin as well as that of America in General, and of Great Britain.

———————

1765. DECEMBER. 23D. MONDAY.

Went to Boston. After Dinner rambled after Messrs. Gridley and Otis but could find neither. Went into Mr. Dudleys, Mr. Dana's, Mr. Otis's office, and then to Mr. Adams's and went with him to the Monday night Clubb. There I found Otis, Cushing Wells, Pemberton, Gray, Austin, two Waldo's, Inches, Dr. Parker—And spent the Evening very agreably, indeed. Politicians all at this Clubb. We had many curious Anecdotes, about Governors, Councillors, Representatives, Demagogues, Merchants &c. The Behaviour of these Gentlemen is very familiar and friendly to each other, and very polite and complaisant to Strangers. Gray has a very tender Mind, is extreamly timid —he says when he meets a Man of the other Side he talks against him, when he meets a Man of our Side he opposes him, so that he fears, he shall be thought against every Body, and so every Body will be against him. But he hopes to prepare the Way for his Escape at next May from an Employment, that neither his Abilities, nor Circumstances nor turn of Mind, are fit for.

Cushing is steady and constant, and busy in the Interest of Liberty and the Opposition, is famed for Secrisy, and his Talent at procuring Intelligence.

Adams is zealous, ardent and keen in the Cause, is always for

Softness, and Delicacy, and Prudence where they will do, but is stanch and stiff and strict and rigid and inflexible, in the Cause.

Otis is fiery and fev'rous. His Imagination flames, his Passions blaze. He is liable to great Inequalities of Temper—sometimes in Despondency, sometimes in a Rage. The Rashnesses and Imprudences, into which his Excess of Zeal have formerly transported him, have made him Enemies, whose malicious watch over him, occasion more Caution, and more Cunning and more inexplicable Passages in his Conduct than formerly. And perhaps Views at the Chair, or the Board, or possibly more expanded Views, beyond the Atlantic, may mingle now with his Patriotism.

The Il Penseroso, however, is discernible on the Faces of all four.

Adams I believe has the most thourough Understanding of Liberty, and her Resources, in the Temper and Character of the People, tho not in the Law and Constitution, as well as the most habitual, radical Love of it, of any of them—as well as the most correct, genteel and artful Pen. He is a Man of refined Policy, stedfast Integrity, exquisite Humanity, genteel Erudition, obliging, engaging Manners, real as well as professed Piety, and a universal good Character, unless it should be admitted that he is too attentive to the Public and not enough so, to himself and his family.

The Gentlemen were warm to have the Courts opened. Gridley had advised to wait for a Judicial Opinion of the Judges. I was for requesting of the Governor that the general Court might assemble at the Time to which they stood prorogued—and if the Town should think fit to request the Extrajudicial Opinion of the Judges. I was for petitioning the Governor and Council to determine the Question first as Supreme ordinary. Gridley will be absent, and so shall I. But I think the apparent Impatience of the Town must produce some spirited Measures, perhaps more spirited than prudent.

DECR. 29TH. 1765. SUNDAY.

Heard Parson Wibird. Hear O Heavens and give Ear O Earth, "I have nourished and brought up Children and they have rebelled against me."—I began to suspect a Tory Sermon on the Times from this Text. But the Preacher confined himself to Spirituals. But I expect, if the Tories should become the strongest, We shall hear many Sermons against the Ingratitude, Injustice, Disloyalty, Treason, Rebellion, Impiety, and ill Policy of refusing Obedience to the Stamp-Act. The Church Clergy to be sure will be very eloquent. The Church People are, many of them, Favourers of the stamp Act, at present. Major Miller, forsooth, is very fearful, that they will be *stomachful* at Home and angry and resentful. Mr. Vesey insists upon it that, We ought to pay our Proportion of the public Burdens. Mr. Cleverly is fully convinced that they i.e. the Parliament have a Right to tax Us. He thinks it is wrong to go on with Business. We had better stop, and wait till Spring, till we hear from home. He says We put the best face upon it, that Letters have been received in Boston, from the greatest Merchants in the Nation, blaming our Proceedings, and that the Merchants dont second us. Letters from old Mr. Lane, and from Mr. Dubert. He says that Things go on here exactly as they did in the Reign of K C 1st. that blessed St and Martyr.

Thus, that unaccountable Man goes about sowing his pernicious Seeds of Mischief, instilling wrong Principles in Church and State into the People, striving to divide and disunite them, and to excite fears to damp their Spirits and lower their Courage.

Etter is another of the poisonous Talkers, but not equally so. Cleverly and Vesey are Slaves in Principle. They are devout religious Slaves—and a religious Bigot is the worst of Men.

Cleverly converses of late at Mr. Lloyds with some of the Seekers of Appointments from the Crown—some of the Dozen in the Town of Boston, who ought as Hanncock says to be beheaded, or with some of those, who converse with the Governor, who ought as Tom Boylstone says to be sent Home with all the other Governors on the Continent, with Chains about their Necks.

———————

1765. DECR. 30TH. MONDAY.

We are now concluding the Year 1765, tomorrow is the last day, of a Year in which America has shewn such Magnanimity and Spirit, as never before appeared, in any Country for such a Tract of Country. And Wednesday will open upon Us a new Year 1766, which I hope will procure Us, innumerable Testimonies from Europe in our favour and Applause, and which we all hope will produce the greatest and most extensive Joy ever felt in America, on the Repeal both of the stamp Act and sugar Act, at least of the former.

Q. Who is it, that has harrangued the Grand Juries in every County, and endeavoured to scatter Party Principles in Politicks? Who has made it his constant Endeavour to discountenance the Odium in which Informers are held? Who has taken Occasion in fine spun, spick and span, spruce, nice, pretty, easy warbling Declamations to Grand Inquests to render the Characters of Informers, honourable and respectable? Who has frequently expressed his Apprehensions, that the form of Government in England was become too popular. Who is it, that has said in public Speeches, that the most compleat Monarchy in Europe was the Government of France? Who is it, that so often enlarges on the Excellency of the Government of Queen Elizabeth, and insists upon it so often, that the Constitution, about the Time of her Reign and under her Administration, was nearest the Point of Perfection? Who is it that has always given his opinion in Favour of Prerogative and Revenue, in every Case in which they have been brought into Question, without one Exception? Who is it that has endeavoured to biass simple Juries, by an Argument as warm and vehement, as those of the Bar, in a Case where the Province was contending vs. a Custom-House-Officer? And what were the other Means employed in that Cause vs. the Resolutions of the General Assembly? Who has monopolized almost all the Power, of the Government, to himself and his family, and who has been endeavouring to procure more, both on this side and the other side the Atlantic?

Read Shakespears Life of K. Henry 8th. Spent the Evening with the Company of Singers at Moses Adams's.

ANNO DOMINI 1766
1766. JANUARY 1ST. WEDNESDAY.

Severe cold, and a Prospect of Snow.

We are now upon the Beginning of a Year of greater Expectation than any, that has passed before it. This Year brings Ruin or Salvation to the British Colonies. The Eyes of all America, are fixed on the B Parliament. In short Britain and America are staring at each other.—And they will probably stare more and more for sometime.

At Home all day. Mr. Joshua Hayward Jur. dined with me. Town Politicks, the Subject. Dr. Tufts here in the Afternoon, American Politicks the Subject. Read, in the Evening a Letter from Mr. Du berdt our present Agent to Ld. Dartmouth, in which he considers three Questions. 1st. Whether in Equity or Policy America ought to refund any Part of the Expence of driving away the French in the last War? 2d. Whether it is necessary for the Defence of the B Plantations, to keep up an Army there? 3d. Whether, in Equity, the Parliament can tax Us? Each of which he discusses like a Man of Sense, Integrity and Humanity, well informed in the Nature of his Subject. In his Examination of the last Question he goes upon the Principle of the Ipswich Instructions, vizt. that the first Settlers of America, were driven by Oppression from the Realm, and so dismembered from the Dominions, till at last they offered to make a Contract with the Nation, or the Crown, and to become subject to the Crown upon certain Conditions, which Contract, Subordination and Conditions were wrought into their Charters, which give them a Right to tax themselves. This is a Principle which has been advanced long ago. I remember in the Tryal of the Cause at Worcester between Governor Hopkins of Rhode Island and Mr. Ward one of the Witnesses swore that he heard Governor Hopkins, some Years before, in a Banter with Coll. Amy, advancing that We were under no subjection to the British Parliament, that our Forefathers came from Leyden &c.—and indeed it appears from Hutchinsons History, and the Massachusetts Records, that the Colonies were considered formerly both here and at Home, as Allies rather than Subjects. The first Settlement certainly was not a national Act, i.e. not an Act of the People nor the Parliament.

Nor was it a national Expence. Neither the People of England, nor their Representatives contributed any thing towards it. Nor was the Settlement made on a Territory belonging to the People nor the Crown of England.

Q. How far can the Concern the Council at Plymouth had, in the first Settlement, be considered as a national Act? How far can the Discoveries made by the Cabots, be considered as an Acquisition of Territory to the Nation or the Crown?—and Q. whether the Council at Plymouth or the Voyages of the Cabots, or of Sir Walter Rawleigh &c. were any Expence to the Nation?

In the Paper there are also, Remarks on the Proceedings of Parliament relating to the stamp Act taken from the London Magazine Septr. 1765. This remarker says, as a great Number of new Offences, new Penalties, and new offices and officers, are by this Act created, We cannot wonder at its being extreamly disgustful to our Fellow Subjects in America. The patient and long suffering People of this Country would scarcely have born it at once—they were brought to it by Degrees—and they will be more inconvenient in America than they can be in England.

The Remarker says further, that the design of one Clause in the Stamp Act, seems to be, that there shall be no such Thing as a practising Lawyer in the Country, the Case of the Saxons. This design he says ludicrously, by compelling every man to manage and plead his own Cause, would prevent many delays and Perversions of Justice, and so be an Advantage to the People of America. But he seriously doubts whether the Tax will pay the Officers. People will trust to Honour, like Gamesters and Stockjobbers. He says he will not enter into the Question, whether the Americans are right or wrong in the Opinion they have been indulged in ever since their Establishment, that they could not be subjected to any Taxes, but such as should be imposed by their own respective Assemblies. He thinks a Land Tax the most just and convenient of any—an Extension of the British Land Tax to the American Dominions. But this would have occasioned a new Assessment of the improved Value of the Lands in England as well as here, which probably prevented the Scheme of a Land tax, for he hopes, no

View of extending the corruptive Power of the Ministers of the Crown had any Effect.

It is said at N. York, that private Letters inform, the great Men are exceedingly irritated at the Tumults in America, and are determined to inforce the Act. This irritable Race, however, will have good Luck to inforce it. They will find it a more obstinate War, than the Conquest of Canada and Louisiana.

1766. JANY. 2D. THURSDAY.

A great Storm of Snow last night. Weather tempestuous all Day. Waddled thro the Snow, driving my Cattle to water at Dr. Savils. A fine Piece of glowing Exercise.—Brother spent the Evening here in chearful Chat.

At Phyladelphia, the Heart and Hand fire Company has expelled Mr. Hewes the Stamp Man for that Colony. The Freemen of Talbot County in Maryland have erected a Jibbet before the Door of the Court House 20 feet High, and have hanged on it, the Effigies of a Stamp Informer in Chains, in Terrorem, till the Stamp Act shall be repealed, and have resolved unanimously to hold in Utter Contempt and Abhorrence every Stamp Officer, and every Favourer of the Stamp Act, and to have no Communication with any such Person, not even to speak to him, unless to upbraid him with his Baseness. —So tryumphant is the Spirit of Liberty, every where.—Such an Union was never before known in America. In the Wars that have been with the french and Indians, a Union could never be effected.—I pitty my unhappy fellow Subjects in Quebeck and Hallifax, for the great Misfortune that has befallen them. Quebec consists chiefly of French Men who with a few English and awed by an Army—tho it seems the Discontent there is so great that the Gazette is drop'd. Hallifax consists of a sett of Fugitives and Vagabonds, who are also kept in fear by a Fleet and an Army. But can no Punishment be devised for Barbadoes and Port Royal in Jamaica? For their base Desertion of the Cause of Liberty? Their tame Surrender of the Rights of Britons? Their mean, timid Resignation to slavery? Meeching, sordid, stupid Creatures, below Contempt, below Pity. They deserve to be made Slaves to their own

Negroes. But they live under the scortching Sun, which melts them, dissipates their Spirits and relaxes their Nerves. Yet their Negroes seem to have more of the Spirit of Liberty, than they. I think we sometimes read of Insurrections among their Negroes. I could wish that some of their Blacks had been appointed Distributors and Inspectors &c. over their Masters. This would have but a little aggravated the Indignity.

"Clarendon" to "William Pym" No. I

SIR,

The revolution which one century has produced in your opinions and principles, is not quite so surprizing to me, as it seems to be to many others. You know, very well, I had always a jealousy, that your humanity was counterfeited, your ardor for liberty canker'd with simulation, and your integrity problematical at least.

I confess however, that so sudden a transition from licentiousness to despotism, so entire a transformation, from a fiery, furious declaimer against power, to an abject hireling of corruption; tho' it furnishes a clue to the labyrinth of your politicks in 1641, gives me many very painful reflections on the frailty, inconstancy and depravity of the human race. These reflections nevertheless are greatly molified by the satisfaction I feel in finding your old friend and coadjutor Mr. Hampden, unalter'd and unalterable in the glorious cause of liberty and law. His inflexibility, has confirmed the great esteem my Lord Fau'kland and I, always had of his wisdom, magnanimity and virtue: and we are both of us at present as well convinced of his excellency as a subject and citizen, as we were formerly of his amiable accomplishments in private life. But your apostacy has confirmed our belief of what was formerly suspected, viz. your subornation of witnesses, your perjuries, briberies, and cruelties; and that tho' your cunning was exquisite enough to conceal your crimes from the public scrutiny, your heart was desperately wicked and depraved.

Can any thing less abominable have prompted you to commence an enemy to liberty? an enemy to human nature? Can you recollect the complaints and clamours, which were founded with such industry, and supported by such a profusion of learning in law and history, and such invincible reasoning by yourself and your friends; against the star chamber, and high commission; and yet remain an advocate for the newly formed courts of admiralty in America? Can you recall to your memory, the everlasting changes which were rung, by yourself and your party, against ship-money, and the other projects of that disgraceful reign; and on the consent of the subject, as indispensably necessary, to all taxations, aids, reliefs, tallages, subsidies, duties, &c. and yet contend for a taxation of more than Five Million subjects, not only without their consent expressed, or implied, but directly against their most explicit, and determined declarations, and remonstrances?

You of all mankind should have been the last, to be hired by a minister to defend or excuse such taxes and such courts.— Taxes, more injurious and ruinous, than Danegeld of old, which our countryman Speed says, "emptied the land of all the coyn, the kingdom of her glory, the commons of their content, and the Sovereign of his wanted respects and observance"— Courts, which seem to have been framed in imitation of an ancient jurisdiction, at the bare mention of which I have often seen your eyes lighten, I mean *the court of the masters of the King's forfeitures.* I cannot omit so fair an opportunity of repeating the history and unfolding the powers of that court, as it seems to have been the very antitipe of the new courts of admiralty in America, and to have been created and erected with the same powers and for the same purposes. It was in the reign of King Henry the seventh that a British parliament was found to be so timid, or ignorant or corrupt, as to pass an act, that "justices of assize, as well as justices of peace, without any finding or presentment of twelve men, upon a bare information for the King, should have full power and authority, to hear and determine by their discretions, all offences against the form, ordinance and effect of certain penal statutes. This unconstitutional act was passed, in the eleventh year of that reign, and thus the commons were found, to sacrifice that sacred pillar, that fundamental law, that everlasting monument of liberty the great charter, in complaisance to the ravenous avarice of that monarch. In pursuance of this act, Sir Richard Empson and Edmund Dudley, were made justices throughout England, and *"masters of the King's forfeitures.* The old sage Coke says that act was against and in the face of that fundamental law, Magna Charta, and that it is incredible what oppressions and exactions, were committed by Empson and Dudley, upon this unjust and injurious act shaking that fundamental law." And that in the first year of the reign of King Henry the eighth the parliament recited that unconstitutional act, and declared it void." And those two vile oppressors fell a sacrifice to the righteous indignation of an injured and exasperated nation. And he closes with an admonition, that the fearful end of these two oppressors, should deter others from committing the like, and admonish parliaments, that instead of this ordinary and precious tryal per pares, et per legem terræ, they bring not in absolute and partial tryals by discretion.

Give me leave, now, to ask you Mr. Pym, what are the powers of the new courts of admiralty in America? Are the tryals in these courts per pares, or per legem terræ? Is there any grand jury there to find presentments or indictments? Is there any pettit jury to try the fact guilty or not? Is the tryal per legem terræ, or by the institutes, digests, and codes and novells, of the Roman law? Is there not a judge appointed or to be appointed over all America? Is not this a much more expensive jurisdiction than that of Empson and Dudley as justices over all England? Will you say that no Empsons and Dudleys will be sent to America?—Perhaps not.—But are not the jurisdiction and power, given to the judges greater than that to those oppressors? Besides, how can you prove that no Empsons will be sent there? Pray let me know, are not the forfeitures to be shared by the governors and the informers? Are we not to prophecy the future by the experience of the past? And have not many governors been seen in America, whose avarice, was at least as ravenous as that of Henry the seventh? Have not many of their tools, been as hungry, restless, insolent and unrelenting as Empson and Dudley in proportion to their power? Besides, are not the Americans at such a distance from their King, and the august council of the mother country, and at the same time so poor, as to render all redress of such insolence and rapacity impracticable?

If you reconsider the nature of these new American taxations, the temper and manners of the people in that country, their religious and civil principles; and if you recollect the real constitution of Great-Britain, and the nature of the new courts of admiralty, you will not wonder at the spirit that has appeared in that country. Their resistance is founded in much better principles, and aims at much better ends, than I fear yours did in Charles's reign, tho' I own you was much nearer the truth and right of the cause then, than now.—And you know, if you had lived in America, and had not been much changed, you would have been the first, to have taken arms against such a law, if no other kind of opposition would do. You would have torn up the foundations, and demolished the whole fabrick of the government, rather than have submitted; and would have suffered democracy, aristocracy, monarchy, anarchy, any thing or nothing to have arisen in its place.

You may perhaps wonder to hear such language as the foregoing from me, as I was always in an opposite faction, to yours, while we lived on earth. I will confess to you, that I am in many respects altered, since my departure from the body, my principles in government were always the same, founded in law, liberty, justice, goodness and truth: But in the application of those principles I must confess, my veneration for certain churchmen, and my aspiring ambitious temper sometimes deceived me and led me astray. This was a source of remorse, at times, thro' my life, and since my seperation, and the sublimation of my faculties, and the purification of my temper, the detestation of some parts of my conduct has been greatly increased. But as these are subjects of very great importance, I shall make them the materials of a correspondence with you for some time to come.

CLARENDON

Boston Gazette, January 13, 1766

From the Diary: January 16, 1766

THURDSDAY. JANY. 16TH. 1766.

Dined at Mr. Nick Boylstones, with the two Mr. Boylstones, two Mr. Smiths, Mr. Hallowel and the Ladies. An elegant Dinner indeed! Went over the House to view the Furniture, which alone cost a thousand Pounds sterling. A Seat it is for a noble Man, a Prince. The Turkey Carpets, the painted Hangings, the Marble Tables, the rich Beds with crimson Damask Curtains and Counterpins, the beautiful Chimny Clock, the Spacious Garden, are the most magnificent of any Thing I have ever seen.

The Conversation of the two Boylstones and Hallowell is a Curiosity. Hotspurs all.—Tantivi.—Nick. is a warm Friend of

the Lieutenant Governor, and inclining towards the Governor.
Tom a firebrand against both. Tom is a perfect Viper—a Fiend
—a Jew—a Devil—but is orthodox in Politicks however. Hallowell tells stories about Otis and drops Hints about Adams,
&c., and about Mr. Dudley Atkins of Newbury. Otis told him,
he says, that the Parliament had a Right to tax the Colonies
and he was a d——d fool who deny'd it, and that this People
never would be quiet till we had a Council from Home, till our
Charter was taken away, and till we had regular Troops quartered upon Us.

He says he saw Adams under the Tree of Liberty, when the
Effigies hung there and asked him who they were and what.
He said he did not know, he could not tell. He wanted to
enquire.

"Clarendon" to "William Pym" No. II

SIR,
You and I have changed Sides. As I told you in my last, I can
account for your Tergiversation, only on the Supposition of
the Insincerity, Baseness and Depravity of your Heart. For my
own Part, as the Change in me is not so great, neither is it so
unaccountable. My Education was, in the Law, the Grounds of
which were so riveted in me, that no Temptation could induce
me, knowingly, to swerve from them. The Sentiments, however, which I had imbibed in the Course of my Education,
from the Sages of the Law, were greatly confirmed in me, by
an Accident that happened to me, in my Youth. This is an
Anecdote, relative to my Father and me, which I presume you
must have heard—A Scene, which will remain with indelible
impressions on my Soul, throughout my Duration. I was upon
that Circuit, which led me down to my native Country, and on
a Visit to my aged Father; who gave me an Invitation to take a
Walk with him, in the Field. I see the good old Gentleman,
even at this Distance of Time, and in his venerable Countenance, that parental Affection to me, that Zeal for the Law, that
fervent Love of his Country, that exalted Piety to God and
Good will to all Mankind, which constituted his real Character.

My Son says he, I am very old, and this will probably be the last Time I shall ever see your Face. Your Welfare is near my Heart. The Reputation you have in your Profession, for Learning, Probity, Skill and Eloquence, will in all Probability, call you to manage the great Concerns of this Nation in Parliament, and to council your King in some of the greatest Offices of State. Let me warn you, against that Ambition, which I have often observed in Men of your Profession, which will sacrifice all, to their own Advancement. And I charge you, on a Father's Blessing, never to forget this Nation, nor to suffer the Hope of Honors or Profits; nor the Fear of Menaces or Punishments from the Crown, to seduce you from the Law, the Constitution, and the real Welfare and Freedom of this People.— And—these Words were scarcely pronounced, before his Zeal and Concern were too great for his Strength, and he fell upon the Ground before me,—never to rise more! His Words sank deep into my Heart, and no Temptation, no Bias, or Prejudice, could ever obliterate them. And you Mr. Pym, are one Witness for me, that, altho' I was always of the Royal Party, and for avoiding Violence and Confusion, I never defended what could be proved to be real Infringements on the Constitution, while I sat in Parliament with you I was as heartily for rectifying those Abuses, and for procuring still further Security of Freedom, as any of you. And after the Restoration, when the Nations were rushing into a Delirium with Loyalty, I was obliged, in Order to preserve even the Appearance of the Constitution, to make a Stand. And afterwards, in the Reign of my infamous and detestable, tho' Royal Son in Law James the Second, I chose to go into Banishment, rather than renounce the Religion and Liberties of my Country.

I have made these Observations to excuse my Conduct in those Reigns, in some Degree; tho' I must confess there were many Parts of it, which admit of no Excuse at all. I suffered myself to be blindly attached to the King, and some of his spiritual and temporal Minions, particularly Laud and Stafford, in some Instances, and to connive at their villainous Projects, against my Principles in Religion and Government, and against the dying Precepts of my Father:—Besides my Intimacy with that Sort of Company, had gradually wrought into me, too great a Reverence for kingly and priestly Power, and too much

Contempt of the Body of the People; as well as too much Virulence against many worthy Patriots of your Side the Question; with whom, if I had co-operated, instead of assisting the
Court, perhaps all the Confusions and Bloodshed which followed might have been prevented, and all the Nation's Grievances redressed.

These Reflections were a Sourse of Remorse, at Times, thro'
my Life: And since my Departure from the Earth, I have re-
volved these Things so often, and seen my Errors so clearly,
that were I to write an History of your Opposition now, I
should not entitle it a Rebellion; nay I should scarcely call the
Protectorate of Cromwell, an Usurpation.

With such Principles as these, and divested as I am of all
Views and Motives of Ambition, as well as all Attachment to
any Party, you may depend upon it, the Conduct of *Barbados,*
has given me great Uneasiness. That Island, was settled in the
Oliverian Times, by certain Fugitives of the Royal Party, who
were zealous Advocates for passive Obedience: And I suppose
a Remnant of the servile Spirit of their Ancestors, and of that
ruinous Doctrine, has prevailed on them to submit. I own it as
a severe Mortification to me, to reflect that I ever acted in
Concert with a People with such Sentiments, a People who
were capable of so mean, and meaching a Desertion of the
Cause both of Liberty and Humanity.* But the gallant Struggle in *St. Christopher's,* and on the Continent of NORTH
AMERICA, is founded in Principles so indisputable, in the
Moral Law; in the revealed Law of God; in the true Constitution of Britain; and in the most apparent Welfare of the British
Nation, as well as of the whole Body of the People in America;
that it rejoices my very Soul. When I see that worthy People,
even in the Reign of a wise and good King fetterd, chained,
and sacrificed, by a few abandoned Villains, whose Lust of
Gain and Power, would at any Time fasten them in the Interest of France or Rome or Hell, my Resentment and Indignation are unutterable.

If ever an Infant Country deserved to be cherished, it is
America: If ever any People merited Honor and Happiness,

*Nova Scotia, Quebec, Pensacola, &c. are more excuseable on account of
their Weakness and other peculiar Circumstances.

they are her Inhabitants. They are a People, whom no Character can flatter or transmit in any Expressions, equal to their Merit and Virtue. With the high Sentiments of Romans, in the most prosperous and virtuous Times of that Common Wealth, they have the tender Feelings of Humanity, and the noble Benevolence of Christians. They have the most habitual, radical Sense of Liberty, and the highest Reverence for Vertue. They are descended from a Race of Heroes, who, placing their Confidence in Providence alone, set the Seas and Skies, Monsters and Savages, Tyrants and Devils, at Defiance for the Sake of Religion and Liberty.

And the present Generation have shewn themselves worthy of their Ancestors. Those cruel Engines, fabricated by a British Minister, for battering down all their Rights and Privileges; instead of breaking their Courage, and causing Despondency, as might have been expected in their Situation, have raised and spread thro' the whole Continent, a Spirit, that will be recorded to their Honor with all future Ages. In every Colony from Georgia to New-Hampshire, inclusively, the Executioners of their Condemnation, have been compelled by the unconquerable and irresistable Vengeance of the People to renounce their Offices. Such and so universal has been the Resentment, that every Man, who has dared to speak in Favour of them, or to soften the Detestation in which they are held, how great soever his Character had been before, or whatever were his Fortune, Connections and Influence; has been seen to sink into universal Contempt and Ignominy. The People, even to the lowest Ranks, have become more attentive to their Liberties, more inquisitive about them, and more determined to defend them, than they were ever before known, or had Occasion to be; innumerable have been the Monuments of Wit, Humour, Sense, Learning, Spirit, Patriotism and Heroism, erected in the several Provinces in the Course of this Year. Their Counties, Towns, and even private Clubs and Sodalities, have voted and determined; their Merchants have agreed to sacrifice even their Bread to the Cause of Liberty; their Legislatures have Resolved; the united Colonies have Remonstrated; the Presses have every where groaned; and the Pulpits have thundered: And such of the Crown Officers as have wished to see them enslaved, have every where trembled, and all their little Tools and Creatures been afraid to speak, and ashamed to be seen. Yet this is the People, Mr. Pym, on whom you are contributing for paltry Hire, to rivet and confirm, everlasting Oppression.

CLARENDON

Boston Gazette, January 20, 1766

"Clarendon" to "William Pym" No. III

Sir,

You are pleased to charge the Colonists with ignorance of the British constitution—But let me tell you there is not even a *Son of Liberty* among them who has not manifested a deeper knowledge of it, and a warmer attachment to it, than appears in any of your late writings. They know the true constitution and all the resources of liberty in it, as well as in the law of nature which is one principal foundation of it, and in the temper and character of the people, much better than you, if we judge by your late most impudent pieces, or than your patron and master, if we judge by his late conduct.

The people in America have discovered the most accurate judgment about the real constitution, I say, by their whole behaviour, excepting the excesses of a few, who took advantage of the general enthusiasm, to perpetrate their ill designs: tho' there has been great enquiry, and some apparent puzzle among them about a formal, logical, technical definition of it. Some have defined it to be the practice of parliament; others, the judgments and precedents of the King's courts; but either of these definitions would make it a constitution of wind and weather, because, the parliaments have sometimes voted the King absolute and the judges have sometimes adjudg'd him to be so. Some have call'd it custom, but this is as fluctuating and variable as the other. Some have call'd it the most perfect combination of human powers in society, which finite wisdom has yet contrived and reduced to practice, for the preservation of liberty and the production of happiness. This is rather a character of the constitution, and a just observation concerning it, than a regular definition of it; and leaves us still to dispute what it is. Some have said that the whole body of the laws; others that King, Lords, and Commons, make the constitution. There has also been much inquiry and dispute about the essentials and fundamentals of the constitution, and many definitions and descriptions have been attempted: But there seems to be nothing satisfactory to a rational mind, in any of these definitions: Yet I cannot say, that I am at any loss about any man's meaning when he speaks of the British constitution, or of the essentials and fundamentals of it.

What do we mean when we talk of the constitution of the human body? What by a strong and robust, or a weak and feeble constitution? Do we not mean certain contextures of the nerves, fibres and muscles, or certain qualities of the blood and juices, as fizy, or watery, phlegmatic or fiery, acid or alkaline? We can never judge of any constitution without considering the *end* of it; and no judgment can be formed of the human constitution, without considering it as productive of *life* or *health* or *strength*. The physician shall tell one man that certain kinds of exercise, or diet, or medicine, are not adapted to his constitution, that is, not compatible with his *health*, which he would readily agree are the most productive of *health* in another. The patient's habit abounds with acid, and acrimonious juices: Will the doctor order vinegar, lemmon juice, barberries and cramberries, to work a cure? These would be unconstitutional remedies; calculated to increase the evil, which arose from the want of a balance, between the acid and alkaline ingredients, in his composition. If the patient's nerves are over-braced, will the doctor advise to jesuits bark? There is a certain quantity of exercise, diet, and medicine, best adapted to every man's constitution, will keep him in the best health and spirits, and contribute the most to the prolongation of his life. These determinate quantities are not perhaps known to him, or any other person: but here lies the proper province of the physician to study his constitution and give him the best advice what and how much he may eat and drink; when and how long he shall sleep; how far he may walk or ride in a day; what air and weather he may improve for this purpose; when he shall take physick, and of what sort it shall be; in order to preserve and perfect his *health*, and prolong his *life*. But there are certain other parts of the body, which the *physician* can in no case have any *authority* to *destroy* or *deprave*; which may properly be called *stamina vitæ*, or *essentials* and *fundamentals of the constitution.* Parts, without which life itself cannot be preserved a moment. Annihilate the heart, lungs, brain, animal spirits, blood; any one of these, and life will depart at once. These may be strictly called fundamentals, of the human constitution: Tho' the limbs may be all amputated, the eyes put out, and many other mutilations practiced to impair the strength, activity and other attributes of the man; and yet the essentials to life may remain, unimpaired many years.

Similar observations may be made with equal propriety concerning every kind of machinery. A clock has also a constitution, that is a certain combination of weights, wheels and levers, calculated for a certain use and end, the mensuration of time. Now the constitution of a clock, does not imply such a perfect constructure of movement as shall never go too fast or too slow, as shall never gain nor lose a second of time, in a year or century. This is the proper business of Quare, Tomlinson, and Graham, to execute the workmanship like artists, and come as near to perfection, i.e. as near to a perfect mensuration of time, as the human eye and finger will allow. But yet there are certain parts of a clock, without which, it will not go at all, and you can have from it no better account of the time of day, than from the ore of gold, silver brass and iron, out of which it was wrought. These parts therefore are the essentials and fundamentals of a clock.

Let us now enquire whether the same reasoning is not applicable in all its parts to government. For government is a frame, a scheme, a system, a combination of powers, for a certain end, viz the good of the whole community. The public good, the salus populi is the professed end of all government, the most despotic, as well as the most free. I shall enter into no examination which kind of government, whether either of the forms of the schools, or any mixture of them is the best calculated for this end. This is the proper inquiry of the founders of Empires. I shall take for granted, what I am sure no Briton will controvert, viz. that Liberty is essential to the public good, the salus populi. And here lies the difference between the British constitution, and other forms of government, viz. that Liberty is its end, its use, its designation, drift and scope, as much as grinding corn is the use of a mill, the transportation of burdens the end of a ship, the mensuration of time the scope of a watch, or life and health the designation of the human body.

Were I to define the British constitution, therefore, I should say, it is a limited monarchy, or a mixture of the three forms of government commonly known in the schools, reserving as much of the monarchial splendor, the aristocratical independency, and the democratical freedom, as are necessary, that each of these powers may have a controul both in legislation and execution, over the other two, for the preservation of the subjects liberty.

According to this definition, the first grand division of constitutional powers is, into those of legislation and those of execution. In the power of legislation, the King, Lords, Commons, and People, are to be considered as essential and fundamental parts of the constitution. I distinguish between the house of commons, and the people who depute them, because there is in nature and fact a real difference; and these last have as important a department in the constitution as the former, I mean the power of election. The constitution is not grounded on "the enormous faith of millions made for one." It stands not on the supposition that kings are the favourites of heaven; that their power is more divine than the power of the people, and unlimited but by their own will and discretion. It is not built on the doctrine that a few nobles or rich commons have a right to inherit the earth, and all the blessings and pleasures of it: and that the multitude, the million, the populace, the vulgar, the mob, the herd and the rabble, as the great always delight to call them, have no rights at all, and were made only for their use, to be robbed and butchered at their pleasure. No, it stands upon this principle, that the meanest and lowest of the people, are, by the unalterable indefeasible laws of God and nature, as well intitled to the benefit of the air to breathe, light to see, food to eat, and clothes to wear, as the nobles or the king. All men are born equal: and the drift of the British constitution is to preserve as much of this equality, as is compatible with the people's security against foreign invasions and domestic usurpation. It is upon these fundamental principles, that popular power was placed as essential in the constitution of the legislature; and the constitution would be as compleat without a kingly as without a popular power. This popular power however, when the numbers grew large, became impracticable to be exercised by the universal and immediate suffrage of the people: and this impracticability has introduced from the feudal system, an expedient which we call a representation. This expedient is only an equivalent for the suffrage of the whole people, in the common management of public concerns. It is in reality nothing more than this, the people chuse attornies to vote for them in the great council of the nation, reserving always the fundamentals of the government, reserving also a right to give their attornies instructions how to vote, and a right, at certain stated intervals of choosing a new, discarding an old attorney, and choosing a wiser and a better. And it is this reservation, of fundamentals, of the right of giving instructions, and of new elections, which creates a popular check, upon the whole government which alone secures the constitution from becoming an aristocracy, or a mixture of monarchy and aristocracy only.

The other grand division of power, is that of execution. And here the King is by the constitution, supreme executor of the laws, and is always present in person or by his judges, in his courts, distributing justice among the people. But the executive branch of the constitution, as far as respects the administration of justice, has in it a mixture of popular power too. The judges answer to questions of law: but no further. Were they to answer to questions of fact as well as law, being few they might be easily corrupted; being commonly rich and great, they might learn to despise the common people, and forget the feelings of humanity: and then the subjects liberty and security would be lost. But by the British constitution, *ad questionem facti respondent juratores*, the jurors answer to the question of fact. In this manner the subject is guarded, in the execution of the laws. The people choose a grand jury to make enquiry and presentment of crimes. Twelve of these must agree in finding the Bill. And the petit jury must try the same fact over again, and find the person guilty before he can be punished. Innocence therefore, is so well protected in this wise constitution, that no man can be punished till twenty four of his Neighbours have said upon oath, that he is guilty. So it is also in the tryal of causes between party and party: No man's property or liberty can be taken from him, till twelve men in his Neighbourhood, have said upon oath, that by laws of his own making it ought to be taken away, i.e. that the facts are such as to fall within such laws.

Thus it seems to appear that two branches of popular power, voting for members of the house of commons, and tryals by juries, the one in the legislative and the other in the executive part of the constitution are as essential and fundamental, to the great end of it, the preservation of the subject's liberty, to preserve the balance and mixture of the government, and to prevent its running into an oligarchy or aristocracy; as the lords and commons are to prevent its becoming an absolute monarchy. These two popular powers therefore are the heart and lungs, the main spring, and the center wheel, and without them, the body must die; the watch must run down; the government must become arbitrary, and this our law books have settled to be the death of the laws and constitution. In these two powers consist wholly, the liberty and security of the people: They have no other fortification against wanton, cruel power: no other indemnification against being ridden like horses, fleeced like sheep, worked like cattle, and fed and cloathed like swine and hounds: No other defence against fines, imprisonments, whipping posts, gibbets, bastenadoes and racks. This is that constitution which has prevailed in Britain from an immense antiquity: It prevailed, and the House of Commons and tryals by juries made a part of it, in Saxon times, as may be abundantly proved by many monuments still remaining in the Saxon language: That constitution which had been for so long a time the envy and admiration of surrounding nations: which has been, no less than five and fifty times, since the Norman conquest, attacked in parliament, and attempted to be altered, but without success; which has been so often defended by the people of England, at the expence of oceans of their blood, and which, co operating with the invincible spirit of liberty, inspired by it into the people, has never yet failed to work the ruin of the authors of all settled attempts to destroy it.

What a fine reflection and consolation is it for a man to reflect that he can be subjected to no laws, which he does not make himself, or constitute some of his friends to make for him: his father, brother, neighbour, friend, a man of his own rank, nearly of his own education, fortune, habits, passions, prejudices, one whose life and fortune and liberty are to be affected like those of his constituents, by the laws he shall consent to for himself and them. What a satisfaction is it to reflect, that he can lie under the imputation of no guilt, be subjected to no punishment, lose none of his property, or the necessaries, conveniencies or ornaments of life, which indulgent providence has showered around him: but by the judgment of his peers, his equals, his neighbours, men who know him, and to whom he is known; who have no end to serve by punishing him; who wish to find him innocent, if charged with a crime; and are indifferent, on which side the truth lies, if he disputes with his neighbour.

Your writings, Mr. Pym, have lately furnished abundant Proofs, that the infernal regions, have taken from you, all your shame, sense, conscience and humanity: otherwise I would appeal to them who has discovered the most ignorance of the British constitution; you who are for exploding the whole system of popular power, with regard to the Americans, or they who are determined to stand by it, in both its branches, with their lives and fortunes?

CLARENDON

Boston Gazette, January 27, 1766

From the Diary: March 17–December 24, 1766

MONDAY MARCH 17TH. 1766.

Rain. A Piece in Even Post March 10th. Remarks and Observations on Hutch's History. The Writer seems concerned least his Country men should incur the Censure of hissing from the stage all Merit of their own Growth.

But Q. Allowing Mr. Hutchinsons great Merit, what Disposition has his Country men discovered to hiss it from the Stage? Has not his Merit been sounded very high by his Country men?—for 20 Years? Have not his Countrymen loved, admired, revered, rewarded, nay almost adored him? Have not 99 in an 100 of them really thought him, the greatest and best Man in America? Has not the Perpetual Language of many Members of both Houses, and of a Majority of his Brother Councillors been, that Mr. Hutchinson is a great Man, a pious, a wise, a learnd, a good Man, an eminent Saint, a Phylosopher &c., the greatest Man in the Province, the greatest on the Continent? Nay has not the Affection and Admiration of his Countrymen, arisen so high, as often to style him, the greatest and best Man in the World? that they never saw nor heard, nor read of such a Man?—a Sort of Apotheosis like that of Alexander and that of Cæsar while they lived?

As to Rewards, have they not admitted him to the highest Honours, and Profits, in the Province? Have they not assisted him chearfully in raising himself and his family to allmost all the Honours and Profits—to the Exclusion of much better Men? Have they not rewarded him so far, as to form invincible Combinations to involve every Man of any Learning and Ingenuity, in generall Detestation, Obloquy, and Ruin, who has been so unfortunate as to think him rather too craving?

DECR. 24TH.

Who are to be understood by the better Sort of People? There is in the Sight of God and indeed in the Consideration of a sincere Xtian or even of a good Philosopher, no Difference between one Man and another, but what real Merit creates. And I mean, by real Merit, that I may be as well understood as my Adversary, nothing more nor less than the Compound Ratio of Virtue and Knowledge. Now if the Gentleman means by the better sort of People, only such as are possessed of this real Merit, this Composition of Virtue and Ability, I am content to join Issue with him but who shall sit as judge between Us?—If a Whig shall be Judge, he will decide in favour of one set of Persons, if a Tory, he will give sentence for another; but if a Jacobite, he will be for a third.

But that I may be as little tedious as possible, I will take the Gentlemans own Difinition, and will understand those of every Rank of plain, good understanding, who by an uniform steady behaviour, testify their thorough sense of the Blessings of good Government, who without Affectation evince an habitual Regard for Peace, order, Justice and Civility, towards all Mankind. But I find myself again in the same Difficulty. And the Q. recurs, who shall be judge. Phylanthrop confidently denys that the better Sort according to this Deffinition, are either alarmed or offended at any Behaviour of the Governor. I as possitively affirm, that the better sort thro the Province both in Boston and in the other seaport and Country Towns (I use Phylanthrops Language so will not answer for Accuracy of Writing or Grammar) are both alarmed and offended, at many Instances of the Governors Behaviour. I dont intend to submit this Question between Us to be decided by the Governor, nor by Philanthrop, nor any other of his Creatures, rich, nor poor, titled or untitled, powerful or impotent: Nor do I desire he should submit it to me, or any of my Particular Friends, Patrons or Connections.—No I appeal to the Public, to the Province, as Judges between Us, who are the better sort, in Phylanthrops sense of the Word. Let the whole Body of the Province then judge.—Well they have judged and by the happy Constitution of our Government, they must every Year determine who they esteem the better sort. The whole Body of the People, in every Yearly Election, depute a Number of Persons to represent them, and by their suffrages they declare such Persons to be the better sort of People among them, in their Estimation. This representative Body are in their Turn every Year, to chuse 28 out of the whole Province for Councillors, and by such Election, no doubt determine such to be of the very best sort, in their Understandings.

Thus far, It seems to me, I have proceeded on safe Ground, and may fairly conclude that the honourable his Majestys Council, and the honourable the House of Representatives, the Public, the Body of the People being Judges, are of the better sort of People in Phylanthrops own sense of the Words. I might go further here, and insist upon it, that the present Council, purifyed as it is, by the Governors Cathartic Negative, even his Excellency being Judge, consists entirely of the better sort of People. Otherwise, it is not to be supposed, at least by our scribler, that he would have approved of those Gentlemen. Let Us then enquire, whether his Majestys

Council, and the honourable House have not exhibited abundant Proofs, that they are almost unanimously alarmed and offended at the Behaviour of the Governor.

The Council, in their Answer to the Governors Speech to both Houses in May, have expressed as much Resentment against his Behaviour as can well be conveyed by Words, 'tho the Decorum and Dignity of the Board is preserved. They have flatly charged the Governor with bringing an unjust Accusation against the Province.

The honourable House in their Answers, which were adopted almost unanimously, tho they have been on their Guard, that no unwarrantable Expressions might escape them at that critical Conjuncture, have expressed as much just Indignation and disdain of his unworthy treatment of them, as was ever expressed by a british House of Commons, against a Tyrant on the Throne.

Answer to Governor's Speech last Session, in which the honourable House, 48 vs. 24 voted, with great Grief, and Concern and Alarm and Offence its Resentment, that the Governors Behaviour had been the sole Cause why Compensation was not made to the sufferers. This I should think was a Proof Instar omnium, that those 48 had taken alarm and offence.

Further, the House proceeded last session to the daring Enterprise of removing Mr. Jackson from the Agency, the Governors darling Friend and endearing Confederate, on whom the Governor had so set his Heart as to employ the most exceptionable Influence in order to get him chosen. This Removal was voted by 81 out of 87 in the House and unanimously in the Council, and the World believes, that Apprehensions of the Governors ill Intentions, and of the Danger to the Province from that Confederacy, influenced a Great Part of both Houses to vote for the Dissolution of it.

To proceed a little further, the House are so allarmed and offended, at the Author of some late Misinformations and Misrepresentations to his Majesty, who appears beyond reasonable Doubt from Ld. Shelbournes Letter to be the Governor himself, that they have almost unanimously voted Letters to be sent to Ld. Shelbourne himself, and to their Agent, Mr.

Debert, in order to remove those slanders and aspersions, in which their sense of the Ingratitude, Haughtiness and Cruelty of the Governor is expressed in very strong Terms.

But I will not confine my self to the two Houses of Assembly.

I ask whether those Gentlemen who have the Honour of his Majestys Commissions in his Revenue, are to be esteemed the better Sort of People, or not? If they are, I would ask again, have not the Customhouse Officers in General from the surveyor General downwards taken Offence at the Governor's Behaviour. I say in general—I would not be understood universally. I except a C– –k–e and a Paxton. These at least one of them, have always declared they would worship the sun while he was above the Horison, tho he should be covered all over with Clouds.

I ask further whether the Officers of his Majestys Navy, who have been occasionally on this station, will be allowed to be the better sort of People. If they should, is it not notorious that Govr. Bernards Conduct has been very disagreable and disgustful to them?

Where shall I go for better sort of People? The Judges of the superiour Court, move in so sublime an orbit—They tread in such exalted steps—That I dare not approach their Persons, so I cannot say what their sentiments of the Governors Conduct may be. They will not indulge themselves in speaking openly against any Person in Authority, so I believe they reserve their Opinion, till the Matter shall come judicially before them. Many of the Judges of the Inferiour Courts in many of the Counties, I can affirm, from Knowledge, because I have heard it from their own Mouths, have taken Alarm and offence, att all the Governors Negatives last May, at both his Speeches to the Assembly in May and June, at the Expression quoted in the Address of the Lords, and especially at his overbearing, threatning, wheedling Arts to get Mr. Jackson chosen Agent, and at his foolish Dismission of Military officers from Colonels down to little Ensigns—but most of all at his restless, impatient, uncontroulable, insatiable Machinations, by all Means, humane, inhumane, and diabolical, from his first Arrival in this Government to this moment, to enrich himself.

Thus I believe that it appears to all who consider the Matter, that almost all the People, whether better or worse, are of one Mind about the Governor and absolutely hate him and despize him—let Phylanthrop say what he will. And indeed I have very good Reasons to think that Phylanthrop lyed when he said that the better sort had taken no Offence, and absolutely endeavoured to impose a palpable falshood upon the Public.

December 24, 1766

"Humphrey Ploughjogger" to "Philanthrop"

Messieurs EDES & GILL,
    Please to insert the following.
      To the learned PHILANTHROP.
In your first Treatise, I find these Words, "Whatever tends to
create in the Minds of the People, a Contempt of the Persons
of those who hold the highest Offices in the State, tends to induce in the Minds of the People a Belief that Subordination is
not necessary, and is no essential Part of Government." Now if
I understand the Meaning of your high-flown Words, for the
Gizzard of me, I can't see the Truth of them. Should any one
say, and in Print too, that the Steeple of Dr. Sewall's Meeting-
House, was old, and decayed, and rotten, as it was the last
Time I see it, and in Danger of falling on the Heads of the
People in the Street, would this tend to induce in the Minds of
the People, a Belief that a Steeple was not necessary to a Meeting-House, and that any Meeting House, might as well be
turned topsy-turvey, and the Steeple stuck down into the
Earth, instead of being erected into the Air? Again, suppose
the Sweep of my Cyder-Mill was cracked and shivered, so that
it had not Strength to grind an Apple, or to turn the Rolls, if
one of my Neighbours should tell me of this, would this tend
to create in me a Belief, that a Sweep was no necessary Part of
a Cyder-Mill, and that the Sweep might as well be placed
where the Rolls are, or where the Hopper is, or the Trough, as
where we commonly put it? Once more, I have a Mare that is
old, and lean, and hipped, and stifled, and spavined, and heavy,
and botty, and has lost her Mane and Tail, and both her Ears,
by the naughty Boys. Now if I should put this Jade into a
Horse Cart, and lead her through the Town in the Sight of all
the People, I believe they would one and all, despise my old
Beast, and laugh at her too, and if any of them came near her,
and she should kick 'em and bite 'em, they would hate her
too; but would all this their Contempt and Laughter and Hatred, tend to induce in their Minds a Belief that a Horse was
not necessary to draw a Horse Cart, and that a Cart might as
well be put before a Horse, as a Horse before a Cart?

This now seems to be a strong Rashosination, so do you answer my Questions directly, not find Fault with my Pointing and Spelling as you served Mr. X, who our School-Master tells me is a Man of better Sense than you are, and Spells and Points better too, notwithstanding your Braggadocio airs.

So I remain your's to sarve,

H. PLOUGHJOGGER

P.S. I'm so well known in the larned World, that I tho't it not worth while to write my Name out at length, but you may print it so if you pleas.

Boston Gazette, January 5, 1767

"Governor Winthrop to Governor Bradford" No. I

Messi'rs EDES and GILL
Please to insert the following.
GOVERNOR WINTHROP to GOVERNOR BRADFORD

We have often congratulated each other, with high satisfaction, on the glory we secured in both worlds, by our favourite enterprize of planting America. We were Englishmen. We were citizens of the world. We were christians. The history of nations and of mankind was familiar to us; and we considered the species chiefly in relation to the system of great nature, and her all-perfect author. In consequence of such contemplations as these, it was the unwearied endeavour of our lives, to establish a society, on English, humane, and christian principles. This, (altho' we are never unwilling to acknowledge that the age in which we lived, the education we received, and the scorn and persecution we endured, had tinctured our minds with prejudices unworthy of our general principles and real designs,) we are conscious was our noble aim. We succeeded to the astonishment of all mankind, and our posterity, in spite of all the terrors, and temptations which have from first to last surrounded them, and endangered their very being, have been supremely happy. But what shall we say to the principles, maxims, and schemes, which have been adopted, warmly defended, and zealously propagated in America, since our departure out of it? adopted I say, and propagated, more by the descendents of some of our worthiest friends, than by any others? You and I, have been happier, in this respect, than most of our contemporaries. If our posterity, have not, without interruption maintained the principal ascendency in public affairs, they have always been virtuous and worthy, and have never departed from the principles of the Englishman, the citizen of the world, and the christian. You very well remember, the grief, we felt, for many years together, at the gradual growth and prevalence of principles opposite to ours; nor have you forgotten our mutual joy, at the very unexpected resurrection of a spirit, which contributed so much to the restoration of that temper and those maxims, which we have all along wished and pray'd might be established in America. Calamities are the caarsticks and catharticks of the body politick. They arouse the soul. They restore original virtues. They reduce a constitution back to its first principles. And to all appearance, the iron sceptre of tyranny, which was so lately extended over all America; and which threatned to exterminate all, for which it was worth while to exist upon earth; terrified the inhabitants into a resolution and an ardor for the noble foundations of their ancestors.

But how soon is this ardor extinguished! In the course of a few months, they have cooled down, into such a tame, torpid state of indolence and inattention; that the missionaries of slavery, are suffered to preach their abominable doctrines, not only with impunity, but without indignation and without contempt. What will be the consequence, if that, (I will not say contemptible but abominable) writer Philanthrop, is allowed, to continue his wicked labours? I say, allowed, tho' I would not have him restrained by any thing, but the cool contempt and dispassionate abhorrence of his countrymen; because the country whose interiour character is so depraved as to be endangered from within by such a writer, is abandoned and lost. We are fully perswaded that New-England is in no danger from him; unless his endeavours should excite her enemies abroad, of whom she has many and extreamly inveterate and malicious; and enable them, in concert with others within her own bosom, whose rancour is no less malignant and venemous, to do her a mischief. With pleasure I see that gentlemen are taking measures to administer the antidote, with the poison.

As the sober principles of civil and ecclesiastical tyranny are so gravely inculcated, by this writer, as his artifices are so insidious, and his mis-affirmations so numerous, and egregious, you will excuse me if I should again trouble you with a letter upon these subjects, from your assured and immutable friend,

WINTHROP

Boston Gazette, January 26, 1767

From the Diary: March 1767–January 30, 1768

SATURDAY MARCH 1767.

Went with Captn. Thayer to visit Robert Peacock and his poor distressed Family. We found them, in one Chamber, which serves them for Kitchen, Cellar, dining Room, Parlour, and Bedchamber. Two Beds, in one of which lay Peacock, where he told us he had lain for 7 Weeks, without going out of it farther than the Fire. He had a little Child in his Arms. Another Bed stood on one side of the Chamber where lay 3 other Children. The Mother only was up, by a fire, made of a few Chips, not larger than my Hand. The Chamber excessive cold and dirty.

These are the Conveniences and ornaments of a Life of Poverty. These the Comforts of the Poor. This is Want. This is Poverty! These the Comforts of the needy. The Bliss of the Necessitous.

We found upon Enquiry, that the Woman and her two oldest Children had been warned out of Boston. But the Man had not, and 3 Children had been born since.

Upon this Discovery we waited on Coll. Jackson, the first Select Man of Boston, and acquainted him with the facts and that we must be excused from any Expence for their Support.

When I was in that Chamber of Distress I felt the Meltings of Commiseration. This Office of Overseer of the Poor leads a Man into scenes of Distress, and is a continual Exercise of the benevolent Principles in his Mind. His Compassion is constantly excited, and his Benevolence encreased.

MAY, 1767. SATURDAY NIGHT.

At Howlands in Plymouth. Returned this day from Barnstable. The Case of Cotton and Nye at Sandwich is remarkable. Cotton has been driving his Interest. This driving of an Interest, seldom succeeds. Jones of Weston, by driving his, drove it all away.—Where two Persons in a Town get into such a Quarrell, both must be very unhappy—Reproaching each other to their faces, relating facts concerning each other, to their Neighbours. These Relations are denied, repeated, misrepresented, additional and fictitious Circumstances put to them, Passions inflamed. Malice, Hatred, Envy, Pride fear, Rage, Despair, all take their Turns.

Father and son, Uncle and Nephew, Neighbour and Neighbour, Friend and Friend are all set together by the Ears. My Clients have been the Sufferers in both these Representative Causes. The Court was fixed in the Sandwich Case. Cotton is not only a Tory but a Relation of some of the Judges, Cushing particularly. Cushing married a Cotton, Sister of Jno. Cotton, the Register of Deeds at Plymouth. Cushing was very bitter, he was not for my arguing to the Jury the Question whether the Words were Actionable or not. He interrupted me—stopped me short, snapd me up.—"Keep to the Evidence—keep to the Point—dont ramble all over the World to ecclesiastical Councils—dont misrepresent the Evidence." This was his impartial Language. Oliver began his Speech to the Jury with—"A Disposition to slander and Defamation, is the most cursed Temper that ever the World was plagued with and I believe it is the Cause of the greatest Part of the Calamities that Mankind labour under." This was the fair, candid, impartial Judge. They adjudged solemnly, that I should not dispute to the Jury, whether the Words were actionable or not.

May 16, 1767

1768. JANUARY 30TH. SATURDAY NIGHT.

To what Object, are my Views directed? What is the End and Purpose of my Studies, Journeys, Labours of all Kinds of Body and Mind, of Tongue and Pen? Am I grasping at Money, or Scheming for Power? Am I planning the Illustration of my Family or the Welfare of my Country? These are great Questions. In Truth, I am tossed about so much, from Post to Pillar, that I have not Leisure and Tranquillity enough, to consider distinctly my own Views, Objects and Feelings.—I am mostly intent at present, upon collecting a Library, and I find, that a great deal of Thought, and Care, as well as Money, are necessary to assemble an ample and well chosen Assortment of Books.—But when this is done, it is only a means, an Instrument. When ever I shall have compleated my Library, my End will not be answered. Fame, Fortune, Power say some, are the Ends intended by a Library. The Service of God, Country, Clients, Fellow Men, say others. Which of these lie nearest my Heart? Self Love but serves the virtuous Mind to wake as the small Pebble stirs the Peacefull Lake, The Center Moved, a Circle straight succeeds, another still and still another spreads. Friend, Parent, Neighbour, first it does embrace, our Country next and next all human Race.

I am certain however, that the Course I pursue will neither lead me to Fame, Fortune, Power Nor to the Service of my Friends, Clients or Country. What Plan of Reading or Reflection, or Business can be pursued by a Man, who is now at Pownalborough, then at Marthas Vineyard, next at Boston, then at Taunton, presently at Barnstable, then at Concord, now at Salem, then at Cambridge, and afterwards at Worcester. Now at Sessions, then at Pleas, now in Admiralty, now at Superiour Court, then in the Gallery of the House. What a Dissipation must this be? Is it possible to pursue a regular Train of Thinking in this desultory Life?—By no Means.—It is a Life of *Here and every where*, to use the Expression, that is applyed to Othello, by Desdemona's Father. Here and there and every where, a rambling, roving, vagrant, vagabond Life. A wandering Life. At Meins Book store, at Bowes's Shop, at Danas House, at Fitches, Otis's office, and the Clerks office, in the Court Chamber, in the Gallery, at my own Fire, I am thinking on the same Plan.

"Sui Juris"

Who is this uncircumcised Philistine, that he should defy the Armies of the living God?

David.

Not many Years ago, were transmitted to the Public, thro' the Channel of the Boston-Gazette, a few desultory Essays, on the Spirit of the Canon and Feudal Law: in some of which were expressed Apprehensions of the future Mischiefs, that might be caused in America by the Efforts and Exertions of those expiring and detested systems. That those apprehensions were too well founded, Time has, already, sufficiently shewn: and we have now, perhaps, stronger Reasons to fear, a still further Increase of those Mischiefs, than we had then. It is therefore the opinion of many Persons, who wish well to the Religion, the Learning, the Liberty and Happiness of this injured and insulted Country, that a Reassumption of that inexhaustible Subject, would not be improper, at the present Juncture. And it is, without any further Apology, proposed, to continue a Series of Dissertations upon that and similar Subjects, for some Months, if not Years to come. It is claimed as an incontestible Right to pursue our own Plan, Method and Style: and, if in the Course of our Lucubrations, we should depart from the Rules, of established Logicians and Rhetoricians, if we should sometimes in Haste throw our Thoughts together in rude Heaps, if a few Blunders and Solecisms should escape us, or if we should now and then mis-spell and mis-point, we shall not think it worth our While to engage in any Contention, concerning such Matters, with the little Scribblers, and paltry Critics, whose Ambition never aspired, and whose Capacity never attained to greater Objects. Our Labours will be interrupted whenever the Paroxisms of the Gout or the Spleen, the Fits of Dulness or Lazyness, or the Avocations of Business or Amusement shall make an Interruption expedient. These Reservations have been thought proper to be made for our own Ease and Advantage. And we now take the Freedom to inform the Reader, that the Champion, who has lately, with so much Heroism chal-

lenged America, to contest with him the Right of Diocæsan
Episcopacy, first roused us, from our long Lethargy, and determined us, once more to try our Fortune in the Field.

But to renounce Metaphor and speak soberly: The Appeal
to the Public in favour of an American Episcopate, is so flagrant an Attempt to introduce the Canon Law, or at least some
of the worst Fruits of it, into these Colonies, hitherto un-
stained with such Pollution, uninfected with such Poison, that
every Friend of America ought to take the Alarm. Power, in
any Form, and under any Limitations, when directed only by
human Wisdom and Benevolence, is dangerous: but the most
terrible of all Power, that can be entrusted to Man, is spiritual.
Because our natural Apprehensions of a Deity, Providence and
future State, are so strong, and our natural Disposition to Enthusiasm and Superstition, so prevalent, that an Order of Men
entrusted with the sacred Rites of Religion, will always obtain
an Ascendency over our Consciences: and will therefore be
able to perswade us, (by us I mean the Body of the People)
that to distinguish between the Cause of God and the Clergy,
is Impiety; to speak or write freely of the Clergy, is Blasphemy;
and to oppose the Exorbitancy of their Wealth and Power, is
Sacriledge, and that any of these Crimes will expose us, to eternal Misery.

And whenever Conscience is on the Side of the Canon Law,
all is lost. We become capable of believing any Thing that a
Priest shall prescribe. We become capable of believing, even
Dr. Chandler's fundamental Aphorisms, viz. that Christianity
cannot exist without an uninterrupted Succession of Diocæsan
Bishops, and that those who deny the Succession to have been
uninterrupted, must prove it to have been broken: which very
curious and important Doctrines will be considered more at
large hereafter. Mean Time, I am, and ever will be

SUI JURIS

Boston Gazette, May 23, 1768

Instructions to Boston's Representatives

To the Hon. JAMES OTIS, *and* THOMAS CUSHING, *Esq'rs; Mr.*
SAMUEL ADAMS, *and* JOHN HANCOCK, *Esqr.*;
GENTLEMEN,

After the repeal of the late American Stamp Act, we were
happy in the pleasing prospect of a restoration of that tranquility and unanimity among ourselves, and that harmony and
affection between our parent country and us, which had generally subsisted before that detestable Act. But with the utmost
grief and concern, we find that we flatter'd ourselves too soon,
and that the root of bitterness is yet alive.—The principle on
which that Act was founded continues in full force, and a revenue is still demanded from America.

We have the mortification to observe one Act of Parliament
after another passed for the express purpose of raising a revenue from us; to see our money continually collecting from us
without our consent, by an authority in the constitution of
which we have no share, and over which we have no kind of influence or controul; to see the little circulating cash that remained among us for the support of our trade, from time to
time transmitted to a distant country, never to return, or what
in our estimation is worse, if possible, appropriated to the
maintenance of swarms of Officers and Pensioners in idleness
and luxury, whose example has a tendency to corrupt our
morals, and whose arbitrary dispositions will trample on our
rights.

Under all these misfortunes and afflictions, however, it is
our fixed resolution to maintain our loyalty and duty to our
most gracious Sovereign, a reverence and due subordination
to the British Parliament as the supreme legislative in all cases
of necessity, for the preservation of the whole empire, and our
cordial and sincere affection for our parent country; and to use
our utmost endeavours for the preservation of peace and order
among ourselves: Waiting with anxious expectation, for a favorable answer to the petitions and sollicitations of this continent,
for relief. At the same time, it is our unalterable resolution, at
all times, to assert and vindicate our dear and invaluable rights
and liberties, at the utmost hazard of our lives and fortunes;

and we have a full and rational confidence that no designs formed against them will ever prosper.

That such designs have been formed and are still in being, we have reason to apprehend. A multitude of Place men and Pensioners, and an enormous train of Underlings and Dependants, all novel in this country, we have seen already: Their imperious tempers, their rash inconsiderate and weak behaviour, are well known.

In this situation of affairs, several armed vessels, and among the rest, his Majesty's ship of war the Romney, have appeared in our harbour; and the last, as we believe, by the express application of the Board of Commissioners, with design to overawe and terrify the inhabitants of this town into base compliances and unlimitted submission, has been anchored within a cable's length of the wharves.

But passing over other irregularities, we are assured, that the last alarming act of that ship, viz. the violent, and in our opinion illegal seizure of a vessel lying at a wharf, the cutting of her fasts and removing her with an armed force in hostile manner, under the protection of the King's ship, without any probable cause of seizure that we know of, or indeed any cause that has yet been made known; no libel or prosecution whatever having yet been instituted against her, was by the express order, or request in writing of the Board of Commissioners to the commander of that ship.

In addition to all this, we are continually alarmed with rumours and reports of new revenue Acts to be passed, new importations of Officers and Pensioners to suck the life-blood of the body politick, while it is streaming from the veins: fresh arrival of ships of war to be a still severer restraint upon our trade; and the arrival of a military force to dragoon us into passive obedience: orders and requisitions transmitted to New-York, Halifax and to England, for regiments and troops to preserve the public peace.

Under the distresses arising from this state of things, with the highest confidence in your integrity, abilities and fortitude, you will exert yourselves, Gentlemen, on this occasion, that nothing be left undone that may conduce to our relief; and in particular we recommend it to your consideration and discretion, in the first place, to endeavour that impresses of all kinds may if possible be prevented. There is an act of parliament in being, which has never been repealed, for the encouragement of the trade to America. We mean by the 6th Ann. Chap. xxxvii. Sect. 9. it is enacted, "That no mariner, or other person who shall serve on board, or be retained to serve on board, any privateer, or trading ship or vessel that shall be employed in any part of *America*, nor any mariner, or other person, being on shore in any part thereof, shall be liable to be impressed, or taken away by any officer or officers of or belonging to any of her Majesty's ships of war, impowered by the lord high admiral, or any other person whatsoever, unless such mariner shall have before deserted from such ship of war belonging to her Majesty, at any time after the fourteenth day of February 1707, upon pain that any officer or officers so impressing or taken away, or causing to be impressed or taken away, any mariner or other person, contrary to the tenor and true meaning of this act, shall forfeit to the master, or owner or owners of any such ship or vessel, *Twenty Pounds* for every man he or they shall so impress or take, to be recovered with full costs of suit in any court within any part of her Majesty's dominions." So that any impresses of any mariner, from any vessel whatever, appears to be in direct violation of an act of parliament. In the next place, 'tis our desire that you inquire and use your endeavors to promote a parliamentary enquiry for the authors and propagators of such alarming rumours and reports as we have mentioned before; and whether the Commissioners or any other persons whatever have really wrote or solicited for troops to be sent here from New-York, Halifax, England or elsewhere, and for what end; and that you forward, if you think it expedient, in the House of Representatives, resolutions, that every such person who shall solicit or promote the importation of troops at this time, is an enemy to this town and province, and a disturber of the peace and good order of both

Then the Meeting was dissolved.

Boston Gazette, June 20, 1768

From the Diary:
August 13, 1769–July 12, 1770

AUG. 13. SUNDAY.

At Mr. Quincys. Here is Solitude and Retirement. Still, calm, and serene, cool, tranquil, and peaceful. The Cell of the Hermit. Out at one Window, you see Mount Wollaston, the first Seat of our Ancestors, and beyond that Stony field Hill, covered over with Corn and fruits.

At the other Window, an Orchard and beyond that the large Marsh called the broad Meadows. From the East Window of the opposite Chamber you see a fine Plain, covered with Corn and beyond that the whole Harbour and all the Islands. From the End Window of the East Chamber, you may see with a prospective Glass, every Ship, Sloop, Schooner, and Brigantine, that comes in, or goes out.

Heard Mr. Wibirt, Upon Resignation and Patience under Afflictions, in Imitation of the ancient Prophets and Apostles, a Sermon calculated for my Uncles family, whose Funeral was attended last Week. In the afternoon Elizabeth Adams the Widow of Micajah Adams lately deceased was baptized, and received into full Communion with the Church. She never knew that she was not baptized in her Infancy till since her Husbands Decease, when her Aunt came from Lynn and informed her. Mr. Wibirt prayed, that the Loss of her Husband might be sanctified to her, this she bore with some firmness, but when he came to pray that the Loss might be made up to her little fatherless Children, the Tears could no longer be restrained. Then the Congregation sang an Hymn upon Submission under Afflictions to the Tune of the funeral Thought. The whole together was a moving Scene, and left scarcely a dry Eye in the House. After Meeting I went to Coll. Quincys to wait on Mr. Fisk of Salem 79 Year Old.

This Mr. Fisk and his Sister Madam Marsh, the former born in the very Month of the Revolution under Sir Edmund Andros, and the latter 10 Years before that, made a very venerable Appearance.

August 13, 1769

MONDAY AUGUST 14.

Dined with 350 Sons of Liberty at Robinsons, the Sign of Liberty Tree in Dorchester. We had two Tables laid in the open Field by the Barn, with between 300 and 400 Plates, and an Arning of Sail Cloth overhead, and should have spent a most agreable Day had not the Rain made some Abatement in our Pleasures. Mr. Dickinson the Farmers Brother, and Mr. Reed the Secretary of New Jersey were there, both cool, reserved and guarded all day. After Dinner was over and the Toasts drank we were diverted with Mr. Balch's Mimickry. He gave Us, the Lawyers Head, and the Hunting of a Bitch fox. We had also the Liberty Song—that by the Farmer, and that by Dr. Church, and the whole Company joined in the Chorus. This is cultivating the Sensations of Freedom. There was a large Collection of good Company. Otis and Adams are politick, in promoting these Festivals, for they tinge the Minds of the People, they impregnate them with the sentiments of Liberty. They render the People fond of their Leaders in the Cause, and averse and bitter against all opposers.

To the Honour of the Sons, I did not see one Person intoxicated, or near it.

Between 4 and 5 O clock, the Carriages were all got ready and the Company rode off in Procession, Mr. Hancock first in his Charriot and another Charriot bringing up the Rear. I took my Leave of the Gentlemen and turned off for Taunton, oated at Doty's and arrived, long after Dark, at Noices. There I put up. I should have been at Taunton if I had not turned back in the Morning from Roxbury—but I felt as if I ought not to loose this feast, as if it was my Duty to be there. I am not able to conjecture, of what Consequence it was whether I was there or not.

Jealousies arise from little Causes, and many might suspect, that I was not hearty in the Cause, if I had been absent whereas none of them are more sincere, and stedfast than I am.

August 14, 1769

SEPT. 3D. SUNDAY.

Heard Dr. Cooper in the forenoon, Mr. Champion of Connecticutt in the Afternoon and Mr. Pemberton in the Evening at the Charity Lecture. Spent the Remainder of the Evening and supped with Mr. Otis, in Company with Mr. Adams, Mr. Wm. Davis, and Mr. Jno. Gill. The Evening spent in preparing for the Next Days Newspaper—a curious Employment. Cooking up Paragraphs, Articles, Occurences, &c.—working the political Engine! Otis talks all. He grows the most talkative Man alive. No other Gentleman in Company can find a Space to put in a Word—as Dr. Swift expressed it, he leaves no Elbow Room. There is much Sense, Knowledge, Spirit and Humour in his Conversation. But he grows narrative, like an old Man. Abounds with Stories.

September 3, 1769

MONDAY.

Spent the Evening at Dr. Peckers, with the Clubb. Mr. Otis introduced a Stranger, a Gentleman from Georgia, recommended to him by the late Speaker of the House in that Province. Otis indulged himself in all his Airs. Attacked the Aldermen, Inches and Pemberton, for not calling a Town meeting to consider the Letters of the Governor, General, Commodore, Commissioners, Collector, Comptroller &c.—charged them with Timidity, Haughtiness, Arbitrary Dispositions, and Insolence of Office. But not the least Attention did he shew to his Friend the Georgian.—No Questions concerning his Province, their Measures against the Revenue Acts, their Growth, Manufactures, Husbandry, Commerce—No general Conversation, concerning the Continental Opposition—Nothing, but one continued Scene of bullying, bantering, reproaching and ridiculing the Select Men.—Airs and Vapours about his Moderatorship, and Membership, and Cushings Speakership.—There is no Politeness nor Delicacy, no Learning nor Ingenuity, no Taste or Sense in this Kind of Conversation.

September 4, 1769

1770 JANUARY 16.

At my Office all Day.

Last Evening at Dr. Peckers with the Clubb.—Otis is in

Confusion yet. He looses himself. He rambles and wanders like a Ship without an Helm. Attempted to tell a Story which took up almost all the Evening. The Story may at any Time be told in 3 minutes with all the Graces it is capable of, but he took an Hour. I fear he is not in his perfect Mind. The Nervous, Concise, and pithy were his Character, till lately. Now the verbose, roundabout and rambling, and long winded. He once said He hoped he should never see T.H. in Heaven. Dan. Waldo took offence at it, and made a serious Affair of it, said Otis very often bordered upon Prophaneness, if he was not strictly profane. Otis said, if he did see H. there he hoped it would be behind the Door.—In my fathers House are many Mansions, some more and some less honourable.

In one Word, Otis will spoil the Clubb. He talkes so much and takes up so much of our Time, and fills it with Trash, Obsceneness, Profaneness, Nonsense and Distraction, that We have no time left for rational Amusements or Enquiries.

He mentioned his Wife—said she was a good Wife, too good for him—but she was a tory, an high Tory. She gave him such Curtain Lectures, &c.

In short, I never saw such an Object of Admiration, Reverence, Contempt and Compassion all at once as this. I fear, I tremble, I mourn for the Man, and for his Country. Many others mourne over him with Tears in their Eyes.

1770. MONDAY FEBY. 26. OR THEREABOUTS.

Rode from Weymouth. Stoppd at my House, Veseys Blacksmith shop, my Brothers, my Mothers, and Robinsons.

These 5 Stops took up the day. When I came into Town, I saw a vast Collection of People, near Liberty Tree—enquired and found the funeral of the Child, lately kill'd by Richardson was to be attended. Went into Mr. Rowes, and warmed me, and then went out with him to the Funeral, a vast Number of Boys walked before the Coffin, a vast Number of Women and Men after it, and a Number of Carriages. My Eyes never beheld such a funeral. The Procession extended further than can be well imagined.

This Shewes, there are many more Lives to spend if wanted in the Service of their Country.

It Shews, too that the Faction is not yet expiring—that the Ardor of the People is not to be quelled by the Slaughter of one Child and the Wounding of another.

At Clubb this Evening, Mr. Scott and Mr. Cushing gave us a most alarming Account of O. He has been this afternoon raving Mad—raving vs. Father, Wife, Brother, Sister, Friend &c.

JUNE 26.

Last of Service; very little Business this Court. The Bar and the Clerks universally complain of the Scarcity of Business. So little was perhaps never known, at July Term. The Cause must be the Non Importation agreement, and the Declension of Trade. So that the Lawyers loose as much by this Patriotic Measure as the Merchants, and Tradesmen.

Stephens the Connecticutt Hemp Man was at my Office, with Mr. Counsellor Powell and Mr. Kent. Stephens says that the whole Colony of Connecticutt has given more implicit Observance to a Letter from the Select Men of Boston than to their Bibles for some Years. And that in Consequence of it, the Country is vastly happier, than it was, for every Family has become a little manufactory House, and they raise and make within themselves, many Things, for which they used to run in debt to the Merchants and Traders. So that No Body is hurt but Boston, and the Maritime Towns.—I wish there was a Tax of 5s. st. on every Button, from England. It would be vastly for the good of this Country, &c. As to all the Bustle and Bombast about Tea, it has been begun by about 1/2 doz. Hollands Tea Smugglers, who could not find so much Profit in their Trade, since the Nine Pence was taken off in England.—Thus He. Some Sense and some Nonsense!

June 26, 1770

JUNE 27. WEDNESDAY MORN.

Very fine—likely to be hot—at my Office early. The only Way to compose myself and collect my Thoughts is to set down at my Table, place my Diary before me, and take my Pen into my Hand. This Apparatus takes off my Attention from other

Objects. Pen, Ink and Paper and a sitting Posture, are great Helps to Attention and thinking.

Took an Airing in the Chaise with my Brother Sam. Adams, who returned and dined with me. He says he never looked forward in his Life, never planned, laid a scheme, or formed a design of laying up any Thing for himself or others after him. I told him, I could not say that of myself, if that had been true of me, you would never have seen my Face—and I think this was true. I was necessitated to ponder in my Youth, to consider of Ways and Means of raising a Subsistence, food and Rayment, and Books and Money to pay for my Education to the Bar. So that I must have sunk into total Contempt and Obscurity, if not perished for Want, if I had not planned for futurity. And it is no Damage to a young Man to learn the Art of living, early, if it is at the Expence of much musing and pondering and Anxiety.

June 27, 1770

JUNE 29. 1770. FRYDAY.

Began my Journey to Falmouth in Casco Bay. Baited my Horse at Martins in Lynn, where I saw T. Fletcher and his Wife, Mr. French &c. Dined at Goodhues in Salem, where I fell in Company with a Stranger, his Name I know not. He made a Genteell Appearance, was in a Chair himself with a Negro Servant. Seemed to have a general Knowledge of American Affairs, said he had been a Merchant in London, had been at Maryland, Phyladelphia, New York &c. One Year more he said would make Americans as quiet as Lambs. They could not do without Great Britain, they could not conquer their Luxury &c.

Oated my Horse and drank baume Tea at Treadwells in Ipswich, where I found Brother Porter and chatted with him 1/2 Hour, then rode to Rowley and lodged at Captn. Jewitts.— Jewitt had rather the House should sit all the Year round, than give up an Atom of Right or Priviledge.—The Governor cant frighten the People, with &c.—

I forgot Yesterday to mention, that I stopped and enquired the Name of a Pond, in Wenham, which I found was Wenham

Pond, and also the Name of a remarkable little Hill at the mouth of the Pond, which resembles a high Loaf of our Country brown Bread, and found that it is called Peters's Hill to this day, from the famous Hugh Peters, who about the Year 1640 or before, preached from the Top of that Hillock, to the People who congregated round the Sides of it, without any Shelter for the Hearers, before any Buildings were erected, for public Worship.

By accidentally taking this new rout, I have avoided Portsmouth and my old Friend the Governor of it. But I must make my Compliments to him, as I return. It is a Duty. He is my Friend And I am his. I should have seen enough of the Pomps and Vanities and Ceremonies of that little World, Portsmouth If I had gone there, but Formalities and Ceremonies are an abomination in my sight. I hate them, in Religion, Government, Science, Life.

Saturday, June 30, 1770

JULY IST. 1770. SUNDAY.

Arose early at Paul Dudley Woodbridge's. A cloudy morning. Took a Walk to the Pasture, to see how my Horse fared. Saw my old Friend and Classmate David Sewall walking in his Garden. My little mare had provided for herself by leaping out of a bare Pasture into a neighbouring Lott of mowing Ground, and had filled herself, with Grass and Water. These are important Materials for History no doubt. My Biographer will scarcely introduce my little Mare, and her Adventures in quest of Feed and Water.

THURSDAY AFTERNOON.

3 O Clock, got into my Desobligeant to go home. 2 or 3 miles out of Town I overtook 2 Men on horseback. They rode sometimes before me, then would fall behind, and seemed a little unsteady. At last one of 'em came up. What is your Name? Why of what Consequence is it what my Name is? Why says he only as we are travelling the Road together, I wanted to know where you came from, and what your Name was. I told him my Name.—Where did you come from? Boston. Where

have you been? To Falmouth. Upon a Frolick I suppose? No upon Business. What Business pray? Business at Court.

Thus far I humoured his Impertinence. Well now says he do you want to know my Name? Yes. My Name is Robert Jordan, I belong to Cape Elizabeth, and am now going round there. My forefathers came over here and settled a great many Years ago.—After a good deal more of this harmless Impertinence, he turned off, and left me.—I baited at Millikins and rode thro Saco Woods, and then rode from Saco Bridge, thro the Woods to Pattens after Night—many sharp, steep Hills, many Rocks, many deep Rutts, and not a Footstep of Man, except in the Road. It was vastly disagreable. Lodged at Pattens.

July 12, 1770

PRAISE FOR A HISTORIAN

To Catharine Macaulay

1770. AUGUST. 9TH. THURSDAY.

Madam

I received from Mr. Gill an Intimation, that a Letter from me would not be disagreable to you, and have been emboldened, by that Means, to run the Venture of giving you this Trouble. I have read with much Admiration, Mrs. Maccaulays History of England &c. It is formed upon the Plan, which I have ever wished to see adopted by Historians. It is calculated to strip off the Gilding and false Lustre from worthless Princes and Nobles, and to bestow the Reward of Virtue, Praise upon the generous and worthy only.

No Charms of Eloquence, can atone for the Want of this exact Historical Morality. And I must be allowed to say, I have never seen an History in which it is more religiously regarded.

It was from this History, as well as from the concurrent Testimony, of all who have come to this Country from England, that I had formed the highest Opinion of the Author as one of the brightest ornaments not only of her Sex but of her Age and Country. I could not therefore, but esteem the Information given me by Mr. Gill, as one of the most agreable and fortunate Occurences of my Life.

Indeed it was rather a Mortification to me to find that a few fugitive Speculations in a News Paper, had excited your Curiosity to enquire after me. The Production, which some Person in England, I know not who, has been pleased to intitle a Dissertation on the cannon and the Feudal Law, was written, at Braintree about Eleven Miles from Boston in the Year 1765, written at Random weekly without any preconceived Plan, printed in the Newspapers, without Correction, and so little noticed or regarded here that the Author never thought it worth his while to give it Either a Title or a signature. And indeed the Editor in London, might with more Propriety have called it The What d ye call it, or as the Critical Reviewers did a flimsy lively Rhapsody than by the Title he has given it.

But it seems it happened to hit the Taste of some one who has given it a longer Duration, than a few Weeks, by printing it in Conjunction with the Letters of the House of Representatives of this Province and by ascribing it to a very venerable, learned Name. I am sorry that Mr. Gridleys Name was affixed to it for many Reasons. The Mistakes, Inaccuracies and Want of Arrangement in it, are utterly unworthy of Mr. Gridlys great and deserved Character for Learning and the general Spirit and Sentiments of it, are by no Means reconcilable to his known Opinions and Principles in Politicks.

It was indeed written by your present Correspondent, who then had formed Designs, which he never has and never will attempt to execute. Oppressed and borne down as he is by the Infirmities of ill Health, and the Calls of a numerous growing Family, whose only Hopes are in his continual Application to the Drudgeries of his Profession, it is almost impossible for him to pursue any Enquiries or to enjoy any Pleasures of the literary Kind.

However, He has been informed that you have in Contemplation an History of the present Reign, or some other History in which the Affairs of America are to have a Share. If this is true it would give him infinite Pleasure—and whether it is or not, if he can by any Means in his Power, by Letters or otherways, contribute any Thing to your Assistance in any of your

Enquiries, or to your Amusement he will always esteem himself very happy in attempting it.

Pray excuse the Trouble of this Letter, and believe me, with great Esteem and Admiration, your most obedient and very huml. servant.

From the Diary: August 19–22, 1770

1770. AUGUST 19. SUNDAY.

Last Fryday went to the Light House with the Committee of both Houses.

Mr. Royal Tyler began to pick chat with me. Mr. Adams, have you ever read Dr. Souths sermon upon the Wisdom of this World? No. I'le lend it to you.—I should be much obliged.—Have you read the Fable of the Bees. Yes, and the Marquis of Hallifax's Character of a Trimmer and Hurds Dialogue upon Sincerity in the Commerce of Life—and Machiavell and Cæsar Borgia. Hard if these are not enough.

Tyler. The Author of the Fable of the Bees understood Human Nature and Mankind, better than any Man that ever lived. I can follow him as he goes along. Every Man in public Life ought to read that Book, to make him jealous and suspicious—&c.

Yesterday He sent the Book, and excellent Sermons they are. Concise and nervous and clear. Strong Ebullitions of the loyal Fanaticism of the Times he lived in, at and after the Restoration, but notwithstanding those Things there is a Degree of Sense and Spirit and Taste in them which will ever render them valuable.

The sermon which Mr. Tyler recommended to my Perusal, is a sermon preached at Westminster Abbey Ap. 30. 1676. from 1. Cor. 3.19. For the Wisdom of this World, is Foolishness with God.—The Dr. undertakes to shew what are those Rules or Principles of Action, upon which the Policy, or Wisdom, in the Text proceeds, and he mentions 4. Rules or Principles. 1. A Man must maintain a constant continued Course of Dissimulation, in the whole Tenor of his Behaviour. 2. That Conscience and Religion ought to lay no Restraint upon Men at

all, when it lies opposite to the Prosecution of their Interest—
or in the Words of Machiavel, "that the Shew of Religion was
helpfull to the Politician, but the Reality of it, hurtfull and pernicious." 3. That a Man ought to make himself, and not the
Public, the chief if not the sole End of all his Actions. 4. That
in shewing Kindness, or doing favours, no Respect at all is to
be had to Friendship, Gratitude, or Sense of Honour; but that
such favours are to be done only to the rich or potent, from
whom a Man may receive a farther Advantage, or to his Enemies from whom he may otherwise fear a Mischief.

1770 AUG. 20. MONDAY.

The first Maxim of worldly Wisdom, constant Dissimulation, may be good or evil as it is interpreted. If it means only a
constant Concealment from others of such of our Sentiments,
Actions, Desires, and Resolutions, as others have not a Right
to know, it is not only lawful but commendable—because
when these are once divulged, our Enemies may avail themselves of the Knowledge of them, to our Damage, Danger and
Confusion. So that some Things which ought to be communicated to some of our Friends, that they may improve them to
our Profit or Honour or Pleasure, should be concealed from
our Enemies, and from indiscreet friends, least they should be
turned to our Loss, Disgrace or Mortification. I am under no
moral or other Obligation to publish to the World, how much
my Expences or my Incomes amount to yearly. There are
Times when and Persons to whom, I am not obliged to tell
what are my Principles and Opinions in Politicks or Religion.

There are Persons whom in my Heart I despize; others I ab-
hor. Yet I am not obliged to inform the one of my Contempt,
nor the other of my Detestation. This Kind of Dissimulation,
which is no more than Concealment, Secrecy, and Reserve, or
in other Words, Prudence and Discretion, is a necessary
Branch of Wisdom, and so far from being immoral and unlawfull, that it is a Duty and a Virtue.

Yet even this must be understood with certain Limitations,
for there are Times, when the Cause of Religion, of Government, of Liberty, the Interest of the present Age and of Posterity, render it a necessary Duty for a Man to make known his

Sentiments and Intentions boldly and publickly. So that it is difficult to establish any certain Rule, to determine what Things a Man may and what he may not lawfully conceal, and when. But it is no doubt clear, that there are many Things which may lawfully be concealed from many Persons at certain Times; and on the other Hand there are Things, which at certain Times it becomes mean and selfish, base, and wicked to conceal from some Persons.

1770. AUGUST 22. WEDNESDAY.

Rode to Cambridge in Company with Coll. Severn Ayers and Mr. Hewitt from Virginia, Mr. Bull and Mr. Trapier from South Carolina, Messrs. Cushing, Hancock, Adams, Thom. Brattle, Dr. Cooper and Wm. Cooper. Mr. Professor Winthrop shewed Us the Colledge, the Hall, Chappell, Phylosophy Room, Apparatus, Library and Musæum. We all dined at Stedmans, and had a very agreable Day. The Virginia Gentlemen are very full, and zealous in the Cause of American Liberty. Coll. Ayers is an intimate Friend of Mr. Patrick Henry, the first Mover of the Virginia Resolves in 1765, and is himself a Gentleman of great fortune, and of great Figure and Influence in the House of Burgesses. Both He and Mr. Hewit were bred at the Virginia Colledge, and appear to be Men of Genius and Learning. Ayers informed me that in the Reign of Charles 2d. an Act was sent over, from England, with an Instruction to the Governor, and he procured the Assembly to pass it granting a Duty of 2s. an Hogshead upon all Tobacco exported from the Colony, to his Majesty forever. This Duty amounts now to a Revenue of £5000 sterling a Year, which is given part to the Governor, part to the Judges &c. to the Amount of about £4000, and what becomes of the other 1000 is unknown. The Consequence of this is that the Governor calls an Assembly when he pleases, and that is only once in two Years.

These Gentlemen are all Valetudinarians and are taking the Northern Tour for their Health.

Draft of an Essay on Juries

At a Time, when the Barriers against Popery, erected by our Ancestors, are suffered to be destroyed, to the hazard even of the Protestant Religion: When the system of the civil Law which has for so many Ages and Centuries, been withstood by the People of England, is permitted to become fashionable: When so many Innovations are introduced, to the Injury of our Constitution of civil Government: it is not surprizing that the great Securities of the People, should be invaded, and their fundamental Rights, drawn into Question. While the People of all the other great Kingdoms in Europe, have been insidiously deprived of their Liberties, it is not unnatural to expect that such as are interested to introduce Arbitrary Government should see with Envy, Detestation and Malice, the People of the British Empire, by their Sagacity and Valour defending theirs, to the present Times.

There is nothing to distinguish the Government of Great Britain, from that of France, or of Spain, but the Part which the People are by the Constitution appointed to take, in the passing and Execution of Laws. Of the Legislature, the People constitute one essential Branch—And while they hold this Power, unlimited, and exercise it frequently, as they ought, no Law can be made and continue long in Force that is inconvenient, hurtful, or disagreable to the Mass of the society. No Wonder then, that attempts are made, to deprive the Freeholders of America and of the County of Middlesex, of this troublesome Power, so dangerous to Tyrants and so disagreable to all who have Vanity enough to call themselves the better Sort.—In the Administration of Justice too, the People have an important Share. Juries are taken by Lot or by Suffrage from the Mass of the People, and no Man can be condemned of Life, or Limb, or Property or Reputation, without the Concurrence of the Voice of the People.

As the Constitution requires, that, the popular Branch of the Legislature, should have an absolute Check so as to put a peremptory Negative upon every Act of the Government, it requires that the common People should have as compleat a Controul, as decisive a Negative, in every Judgment of a Court of Judicature. No Wonder then that the same restless Ambition, of aspiring Minds, which is endeavouring to lessen or destroy the Power of the People in Legislation, should attempt to lessen or destroy it, in the Execution of Lawes. The Rights of Juries and of Elections, were never attacked singly in all the English History. The same Passions which have disliked one have detested the other, and both have always been exploded, mutilated or undermined together.

The british Empire has been much allarmed, of late Years, with Doctrines concerning Juries, their Powers and Duties, which have been said in Printed Papers and Pamphlets to have been delivered from the highest Trybunals of Justice. Whether these Accusations are just or not, it is certain that many Persons are misguided and deluded by them, to such a degree, that we often hear in Conversation Doctrines advanced for Law, which if true, would render Juries a mere Ostentation and Pagentry and the Court absolute Judges of Law and fact. It cannot therefore be an unseasonable Speculation to examine into the real Powers and Duties of Juries, both in Civil and Criminal Cases, and to discover the important Boundary between the Power of the Court and that of the Jury, both in Points of Law and of Fact.

Every intelligent Man will confess that Cases frequently occur, in which it would be very difficult for a Jury to determine the Question of Law. Long Chains of intricate Conveyances; obscure, perplext and embarrassed Clauses in Writings: Researches into remote Antiquity, for Statutes, Records, Histories, judicial Decisions, which are frequently found in foreign Languages, as Latin and French, which may be all necessary to be considered, would confound a common Jury and a decision by them would be no better than a Decision by Lott. And indeed Juries are so sensible of this and of the great Advantages the Judges have to determine such Questions, that, as the Law has given them the Liberty of finding the facts specially and praying the Advice of the Court in the Matter of Law, they very seldom neglect to do it when recommended to them, or when in any doubt of the Law. But it will by no Means follow from thence, that they are under any legal, or moral or divine

Obligation to find a Special Verdict where they themselves are in no doubt of the Law.

The Oath of a Juror in England, is to determine Causes "according to your Evidence"—In this Province "according to Law and the Evidence given you." It will be readily agreed that the Words of the Oath at Home, imply all that is expressed by the Words of the Oath here. And whenever a general Verdict is found, it assuredly determines both the Fact and the Law.

It was never yet disputed, or doubted, that a general Verdict, given *under the Direction of the Court* in Point of Law, was a legal Determination of the Issue. Therefore the Jury have a Power of deciding an Issue upon a general Verdict. And if they have, is it not an Absurdity to suppose that the Law would oblige them to find a Verdict according to the Direction of the Court, against their own Opinion, Judgment and Conscience.

It has already been admitted to be most advisable for the Jury to find a Special Verdict where they are in doubt of the Law. But, this is not often the Case—1000 Cases occur in which the Jury would have no doubt of the Law, to one, in which they would be at a Loss. The general Rules of Law and common Regulations of Society, under which ordinary Transactions arrange themselves, are well enough known to ordinary Jurors. The great Principles of the Constitution, are intimately known, they are sensibly felt by every Briton—it is scarcely extravagant to say, they are drawn in and imbibed with the Nurses Milk and first Air.

Now should the Melancholly Case arise, that the Judges should give their Opinions to the Jury, against one of these fundamental Principles, is a Juror obliged to give his Verdict generally according to this Direction, or even to find the fact specially and submit the Law to the Court. Every Man of any feeling or Conscience will answer, no. It is not only his right but his Duty in that Case to find the Verdict according to his own best Understanding, Judgment and Conscience, tho in Direct opposition to the Direction of the Court.

A religious Case might be put of a Direction against a divine Law.

The English Law obliges no Man to decide a Cause upon Oath against his own Judgment, nor does it oblige any Man to take any Opinion upon Trust, or to pin his faith on the sleve of any mere Man.

February 12, 1771

From the Diary:
April 20, 1771–February 9, 1772

SATURDAY.

Fryday morning by 9 o Clock, arrived at my Office in Boston, and this Afternoon returned to Braintree. Arrived just at Tea time. Drank Tea with my Wife. Since this Hour a Week ago I have led a Life Active enough—have been to Boston twice, to Cambridge twice, to Weymouth once, and attended my office, and the Court too. But I shall be no more perplexed, in this Manner. I shall have no Journeys to make to Cambridge—no general Court to attend—But shall divide my Time between Boston and Braintree, between Law And Husbandry. Farewell Politicks. Every Evening I have been in Town, has been spent till after 9. at my Office. Last Evening I read thro, a Letter from Robt. Morris Barrister at Law and late Secretary to the Supporters of the Bill of Rights, to Sir Richd. Aston, a Judge of the K[ing]'s Bench. A bold, free, open, elegant Letter it is. Annihilation would be the certain Consequence of such a Letter here, where the Domination of our miniature infinitessimal Deities, far exceeds any Thing in England.

This mettlesome Barrister gives us the best Account of the Unanimity of the Kings Bench that I have ever heard or read. According to him, it is not uncommon abilities, Integrity and Temper as Mr. Burrows would perswade us, but sheer fear of Lord M[ansfiel]d, the Scottish Chief which produces this Miracle in the moral and intellectual World—i.e. of 4 Judges, agreeing perfectly in every Rule, order and Judgment for 14 Years together. 4 Men never agreed so perfectly in Sentiment, for so long a Time, before. 4 Clocks never struck together, a thousandth Part of the Time, 4 Minds never thought, reasoned, and judged alike, before for a ten thousandth Part.

April 20, 1771

MAY 2. 1771.

The Tryumphs, and Exultations of Ezekl. Goldthwait and his pert Pupil Price, at the Election of a Register of Deeds, are excessive. They Crow like dunghill Cocks. They are rude and disgusting. Goldthwait says he would try the Chance again for 20 dollars, and he would get it by a Majority of 100 Votes even in this Town. Nay more he says, if he would be Rep and would set up he would be chose Rep. before Adams.—Adams the Lawyer dont succeed in the Interest he makes for People, he is not successfull.—N.B. very true!

Price says to me, if you was to go and make Interest, for me to be Clerk in the Room of Cook, I should get it no doubt.

These are the Insults that I have exposed myself to, by a very small and feeble Exertion for S. Adams to be Register of Deeds. Thus are the Friends of the People after such dangerous Efforts, and such successfull ones too left in the Lurch even by the People themselves. I have acted my sentiments, with the Utmost Frankness, at Hazard of all, and the certain Loss of ten times more than it is in the Power of the People to give me, for the sake of the People, and now I reap nothing but Insult, Ridicule and Contempt for it, even from many of the People themselves. However, I have not hitherto regarded Consequences to myself. I have very chearfully sacrificed my Interest, and my Health and Ease and Pleasure in the service of the People. I have stood by their friends longer than they would stand by them. I have stood by the People much longer than they would stand by themselves. But, I have learn'd Wisdom by Experience. I shall certainly become more retired, and cautious. I shall certainly mind my own Farm, and my own Office.

MAY 3D. 1771. FRYDAY.

Last Evening I went in to take a Pipe with Brother Cranch, and there I found Zeb. Adams. He told me, he heard that I had made two very powerfull Enemies in this Town, and lost two very valuable Clients, Treasurer Gray and Ezek. Goldthwait, and that he heard that Gray had been to me for my Account and paid it off, and determined to have nothing more to do with me. Oh the wretched impotent Malice! They shew their teeth, they are eager to bite, but they have not Strength! I despize their Anger, their Resentment, and their Threats. But, I can tell Mr. Treasurer, that I have it in my Power to tell the World a Tale, which will infallibly unhorse him—whether I am in the House or out. If this Province knew that the public Money had never been counted this twenty Year—and that no Bonds were given last Year, nor for several Years before, there would be so much Uneasiness about it, that Mr. Gray would loose his Election another Year.

It may be said that I have made Enemies by being in the general Court. The Governor, Lieutenant Governor, Gray, Goldthwait, The Gentry at Cambridge, &c. are made my bitter Foes. But there is nothing in this. These People were all my Foes before, but they thought it for their Interest to disguise it. But Now they think themselves at Liberty to speak it out. But there is not one of them but would have done me all the Harm in his Power secretly before.

This Evening Mr. Otis came into my Office, and sat with me most of the Evening—more calm, more solid, decent and cautious than he ever was, even before his late Disorders.—I have this Week had an Opportunity of returning an Obligation, of repaying an old Debt to that Gentleman which has given me great Pleasure. Mr. Otis was one of the 3 Gentlemen, Mr. Gridley and Mr. Thatcher were the other two, who introduced me to Practice in this County. I have this Week strongly recommended 14 Clients from Wrentham and 3 or 4 in Boston, to him, and they have accordingly by my Perswasion engaged him in their Causes, and he has come out to Court And behaved very well, so that I have now introduced him to Practice. This Indulgence to my own gratefull Feelings, was equally my Duty and my Pleasure.

He is a singular Man. It will be amusing to observe his Behaviour, upon his Return to active Life in the Senate, and at the Bar, and the Influence of his Presence upon the public Councils of this Province. I was an Hour with him this Morning at his Office, and there he was off his Guard and Reserve with me. I find his Sentiments are not altered, and his Passions are not eradicated. The fervour of his Spirit is not abated, nor the Irritability of his Nerves lessened.

———————

1771. WEDNESDAY JUNE 5TH.

Rode to the Spring, drank and plunged. Dipped but once. Sky cloudy.

Activity and Industry, care, and Œconomy, are not the Characteristicks of this Family. Green was to set out upon a Journey to Providence to day to get Stores &c. and Stock for Trade, but he lounged and loitered away, hour after Hour till 9 O Clock before he mounted. The Cow, whose Titts strutt with Milk, is unmilked till 9 O Clock. My Horse would stand by the [   ] Hour after Hour if I did not put him out my self, tho I call upon the father and the Sons to put him out.

Looking into a little Closet in my Chamber this Morning I found a pretty Collection of Books, the Preceptor, Douglass's History, Paradise lost, the musical Miscellany in two Volumes, the Life of the Czar, Peter the great &c.

I laid hold of the 2d Volume of the Preceptor, and began to read the Elements of Logick, and considered the four fold Division of the Subject, simple Apprehension, or Perception, Judgment or Intuition, Reasoning, and Method. This little Compendium of Logick, I admired at Colledge. I read it over and over. I recommended it to others, particularly to my Chum David Wyer, and I took the Pains to read a great Part of it to him and with him.

By simple Apprehension or Perception we get Ideas, by Sensation and by Reflection, the Ideas we get are Simple, &c.

Mem.—I hope I shall not forget to purchase these Preceptors, and to make my Sons transcribe this Treatise on Logick entirely with their own Hands, in fair Characters, as soon as they can write, in order to imprint it on their Memories. Nor would it hurt my Daughter to do the same. I have a great Opinion of the Exercise of transcribing, in Youth.

About 11. O Clock arrived, Dr. McKinstry of Taunton and spoke for Lodgings for himself and Co Barrell and his Wife.— It is not you? Is it? says he.—Persons in your Way are subject to a certain weak Muscle and lax Fibre, which occasions

Glooms to plague you. But the Spring will brace you.—I Joy and rejoice at his Arrival. I shall have Opportunity to examine him about this mineral, medicinal Water.

I have spent this day in sauntering about, down in the Pasture to see my Horse, and over the fields in the Neighbourhood. Took my Horse after noon and rode away East, a rugged rocky Road, to take View of the Lands about the Town —and went to the Spring. 30 People have been there to day, they say. The Halt, the Lame, the vapoury, hypochondriac, scrophulous, &c. all resort here. Met Dr. McKinstry at the Spring. We mounted our Horses together, and turned away the Western Road toward Somers to see the Improvements, that I saw Yesterday from the Mountain by the Spring, and returned, to our Lodgings.—The Dr. I find is a very learned Man. He said that the Roman Empire came to its Destruction as soon as the People got set against the Nobles and Commons as they are now in England, and they went on Quarrelling, till one Brutus carried all before him and enslaved em all.—Cæsar, you mean Dr.—No I think it was Brutus, want it? —Thus We see the Dr. is very Book learnt. And when we were drinking Tea, I said, 500 Years hence there would be a great Number of Empires in America, independent of Europe and of each other.—Oh says he I have no Idea that the World will stand so long—not half 500 Years. The World is to conform to the Jewish Calculations, every seventh day was to be a day of Rest, every 7th Year was to be a Jubilee, and the 7th. Thousand Years will be a Thousand Years of Rest and Jubilee—no Wars, no fightings, and there is but about 230 wanting to compleat the 6000 Years. Till that Time, there will be more furious Warrs than ever.

Thus I find I shall have in the Dr. a fund of Entertainment. He is superficial enough, and conceited enough, and enthusiastical enough to entertain.

1771. FRYDAY. JUNE 7TH.

Went to the Spring with the Dr. and drank a Glass and an half i.e. a Jill and an half. My Horse was brought very early— my own Mare I shall leave in a very fine Pasture, with Oats for her twice a Day that she may rest and recruit.

Barrell this Morning at Breakfast entertained Us with an Account of his extravagant Fondness for Fruit. When he lived at New market he could get no fruit but Strawberries, and he used frequently to eat 6 Quarts in a Day. At Boston, in the very hottest of the Weather he breakfasts upon Water Melons —neither Eats nor drinks any Thing else for Breakfast. In the Season of Peaches he buys a Peck, every Morning, and eats more than half of them himself. In short he eats so much fruit in the Season of it that he has very little Inclination to any other Food. He never found any Inconvenience or ill Effect from fruit—enjoys as much Health as any Body. Father Dana is immoderately fond of fruit, and from several other Instances one would conclude it very wholsome.

Rode to Somers, over a very high large Mountain which the People here call Chesnut Hill. It is 5 miles over, very bad Road, very high Land. It is one of a Range of great Mountains, which runs North and South Parallell with Connecticutt River, about 10 miles to the East of it, as another similar Range runs on the Western Side of it. There is a Mountain which they call the bald Mountain which you pass by as you cross Chesnutt hill, much higher from whence you can see the great River, and many of the great Turns upon it, as they say.—Dined at Kibbys, met People going over to the Spring.

In Kibbys Barr Room in a little Shelf within the Barr, I spied 2 Books. I asked what they were. He said every Man his own Lawyer, and Gilberts Law of Evidence. Upon this I asked some Questions of the People there, and they told me that Kibby was a sort of Lawyer among them—that he pleaded some of their home Cases before Justices and Arbitrators &c. Upon this I told Kibby to purchase a Copy of Blackstones Commentaries.

Rode from Kibbys over to Enfield, which lies upon Connecticutt River, oated and drank Tea at Peases—a smart House and Landlord truly, well dressed, with his Ruffles &c., and upon Enquiry I found he was the great Man of the Town— their Representative &c. as well as Tavern Keeper, and just returned from the gen Assembly at Hartford.—Somers and Enfield are upon a Levell, a fine Champaign Country. Suffield lies over the River on the West Side of it.

Rode along the great River to Windsor, and put up at

Bissalls—i.e. in East Windsor, for the Town of Windsor it seems lies on the West Side of the River.

The People in this Part of Connecticutt, make Potash, and raise a great Number of Colts, which they send to the West Indies, and barter away for Rum &c. They trade with Boston and New York but most to New York. They say there is a much greater Demand for Flaxseed of which they raise a great deal, at N. York, than there is at Boston, and they get a better Price for it. Kibby at Somers keeps a Shop, and sells W. India goods and English Trinketts, keeps a Tavern, and petty foggs it.

At Enfield you come into the great Road upon Connecticutt River, which runs back to Springfield, Deerfield, Northampton &c. Northward and down to Windsor and Hartford, Weathersfield and Middleton, Southward.

The Soil as far as I have ridden upon the River if I may judge by the Road is dry and sandy. But the Road is 3/4 of a mile from the River and the intervale Land lies between.

I begin to grow weary of this idle, romantic Jaunt. I believe it would have been as well to have staid in my own Country and amused myself with my farm, and rode to Boston every day. I shall not suddenly take such a Ramble again, merely for my Health. I want to see my Wife, my Children, my Farm, my Horse, Oxen, Cows, Walls, Fences, Workmen, Office, Books, and Clerks. I want to hear the News, and Politicks of the Day. But here I am, at Bissills in Windsor, hearing my Landlord read a Chapter in the Kitchen and go to Prayers with his Family, in the genuine Tone of a Puritan.

1771. SUNDAY, JUNE 9TH.

Feel a little discomposed this Morning. Rested but poorly last night. Anxious about my Return—fearfull of very hot or rainy weather. I have before me an uncomfortable Journey to Casco Bay—little short of 300 miles.

Looking into a little bedroom, in this House Shaylers, I found a few Books, the musical Miscellany, Johnsons Dictionary, the farmers Letters, and the Ninth Volume of Dr. Clarks sermons. This last I took for my Sabbath Day Book, and read the Sermon on the Fundamentals of Christianity, which he says are the Doctrines concerning the Being and Providence of

God, the Necessity of Repentance and Obedience to his Commands, the Certainty of a Life to come, a Resurrection from the dead and a future Judgment.

Read also another Sermon on the Reward of Justice. "There is, says the Dr., a Duty of Justice towards the Public. There is incumbent upon Men the very same Obligation, not to wrong the Community; as there is, not to violate any private Mans Right, or defraud any particular Person of his Property. The only Reason, why Men are not always sufficiently sensible of this; so that many, who are very just in their Dealings between Man and Man, will yet be very fraudulent or rapacious with Regard to the Public; is because in this latter Case, it is not so obviously and immediately apparent upon whom the Injury falls, as it is in the Case of private Wrongs. But so long as the Injury is clear and certain; the Uncertainty of the Persons upon whom the Injury falls in Particular, or the Number of the Persons among whom the damage may chance to be divided, alters not at all the Nature of the Crime itself."

Went to Meeting in the Morning, and tumbled into the first Pew I could find—heard a pretty sensible, Yalensian, Connecticuttensian Preacher. At Meeting I first saw Dr. Eliot Rawson, an old School fellow. He invited me to dine. His House is handsome without, but neither clean nor elegant within, in furniture or any Thing else. His Wife is such another old Puritan as his Cousin, Peter Adams's Wife at Braintree. His Children are dirty, and ill governed. He first took me into his Physick Room, and shewed me a No. of Curiosities which he has collected in the Course of his Practice—first an odd kind of long slender Worm preserved in Spirits. He says he has had between 20 and 30 Patients with such Worms—several Yards long and some of them several Rods. He shewed me some fingers he cutt off and some Wens, and his Physick Drawers And his Machine to pound with his Pestle &c.

His dining Room is crouded with a Bed and a Cradle, &c. &c. We had a picked up Dinner. Went to Meeting with him in the Afternoon, and heard the finest Singing, that ever I heard in my Life, the front and side Galleries were crowded with Rows of Lads and Lasses, who performed all the Parts in the Utmost Perfection. I thought I was wrapped up. A Row of Women all standing up, and playing their Parts with perfect

Skill and Judgment, added a Sweetness and Sprightliness to the whole which absolutely charmed me.—I saw at Meeting this Afternoon Moses Paine, who made a decent Appearance and the Dr. tells me lives by his Trade of a shoemaker comfortably from Day to day.

The more I see of this Town the more I admire it. I regrett extremely that I cant pursue my Tour to New Haven.

The Dr. thinks Hancock vain. Told a Story.—"I was at school with him, and then upon a level with him. My father was richer than his. But I was not long since at his Store and said to Mr. Glover whom I knew, this I think is Mr. Hancock. Mr. H. just asked my Name and nothing more—it was such a Piece of Vanity! There is not the meanest Creature that comes from your Way, but I take Notice of him—and I ought. What tho I am worth a little more than they—I am glad of it, and that I have it that I may give them some of it." I told the Dr. that Mr. H. must have had something upon his Mind—that he was far from being Arrogant—&c.

Drank Tea with Landlady, and her Son Mr. Shaylor, in pretty, western Room. But they are not very sociable. In short, I have been most miserably destitute of Conversation here. The People here all Trade to N. York, and have very little Connection with Boston. After Tea went over to the Drs., and found him very social and very learned. We talked much about History &c. He says, that Boston lost the Trade of this Colony by the severe Laws vs. their old Tenor. But they may easily regain the Trade, for the People here are much disgusted with N. York for their Defection from the N Importation Agreement, and for some frauds and unfair Practises in Trade. He says they have found out that N. York Merchants have wrote home to the Manufacturers in England to make their Goods narrower and of a meaner fabric that they might sell cheaper, and undersell Boston. The Dr. says that Coll. Josa. Quincy quarrells with his Workmen &c. but Norton is a clever Man, he called to see him and was much pleased, &c.

Landlady has an only Son Nat. Shaylor, and she is very fond and very proud of him. He lived with a Merchant—is now 25 or 26 and contents himself still to keep that Merchants Books without any Inclination to set up for himself. Is a great Proficient in Musick. Plays upon the Flute, Fife, Harpsicord, Spinnett

&c. Associates with the Young and the Gay, and is a very fine Connecticutt young Gentleman. Oh the Misery, the Misfortune, the Ruin of being an only Son! I thank my God that I was not, and I devoutly pray, that none of mine may ever be!

1771. THURSDAY JUNE 13TH.

Remarkable, the Change of Thoughts, and feelings, and Reasonings which are occasioned by a Change of Objects. A Man is known by his Company, and evil Communications corrupt good Manners. "Man is a Social Creature and his Passions, his feelings, his Imaginations are contagious." We receive a Tincture of the Characters of those we converse with.

Stopped at Mr. Putnams, and at the Court House, went in and bowed to the Court and shook Hands with the Bar, said How d'ye, and came off. Dined at Coll. Williams's, drank Tea at Munns, with Dr. Cooper and his Lady, Captn. Jona. Freeman and his Lady and Mr. Nat. Barrett and his Lady, who were upon their Return from a Tour to Lancaster.

Rode this day from Worcester to Munns in Company with one Green of Leicester, who was very social, and good Company, an honest, clever Man. By him I learn that Thomas Faxon of Braintree, has removed with his Family, to Leicester, and hired an House near the Meeting House. And I met Joseph Crane to day in Marlborough, going to Rutland. He is about removing his Family there. But I find that People in Rutland, and Leicester and Worcester, &c. are more disposed to emigrate still farther into the Wilderness, than the Inhabitants of the old Towns.

I hear much to day and Yesterday of the Harmony prevailing between the Governor and the House. Cushing is unanimous Commissary, not negatived, and Goldthwait is Truckmaster. Behold how good and pleasant it is, for Brethren to dwell together in Unity. It seems to be forgotten entirely, by what means Hutchinson procured the Government—by his Friendship for Bernard, and by supporting and countenancing all Bernards Measures, and the Commissioners and Army and Navy, and Revenue, and every other Thing we complain of.

I read to day an Address from the Convention of Ministers, and from the Clergy in the northern Part of the County of

Hampshire and from the Town of Almesbury, all conceived in very high Terms, of Respect and Confidence and Affection. Posterity will scarcely find it possible, to form a just Idea of this Gentlemans Character. But if this wretched Journal should ever be read, by my own Family, let them know that there was upon the Scene of Action with Mr. Hutchinson, one determined Enemy to those Principles and that Political System to which alone he owes his own and his Family's late Advancement—one who thinks that his Character and Conduct have been the Cause of laying a Foundation for perpetual Discontent and Uneasiness between Britain and the Colonies, of perpetual Struggles of one Party for Wealth and Power at the Expence of the Liberties of this Country, and of perpetual Contention and Opposition in the other Party to preserve them, and that this Contention will never be fully terminated but by Warrs, and Confusions and Carnage. Cæsar, by destroying the Roman Republic, made himself perpetual Dictator, Hutchinson, by countenancing and supporting a System of Corruption and all Tyranny, has made himself Governor—and the mad Idolatry of the People, always the surest Instruments of their own Servitude, laid prostrate at the Feet of both. With great Anxiety, and Hazard, with continual Application to Business, with loss of Health, Reputation, Profit, and as fair Prospects and Opportunities of Advancement, as others who have greedily embraced them, I have for 10 Years together invariably opposed this System, and its fautors. It has prevailed in some Measure, and the People are now worshipping the Authors and Abetters of it, and despizing, insulting, and abusing, the Opposers of it.—Edward and Alfred

> closed their long Glories with a Sigh to find
> th' unwilling Gratitude of base Mankind.

As I came over Sudbury Causey, I saw a Chaplain of one of the Kings Ships fishing in the River, a thick fat Man, with rosy Cheeks and black Eyes. At Night he came in with his fish. I was in the Yard and he spoke to me, and told me the News. —The Governor gave a very elegant Entertainment to the Gentlemen of the Army and Navy and Revenue, and Mrs. Gambier in the Evening a very elegant Ball—as elegant a cold Collation as perhaps you ever see—all in figures &c. &c. &c.

Read this days Paper. The melodious Harmony, the perfect Concords, the entire Confidence and Affection, that seems to be restored greatly surprizes me. Will it be lasting. I believe there is no Man in so curious a Situation as I am. I am for what I can see, quite left alone, in the World.

Rode with King a D. Sherriff who came out to meet the Judges, into Salem, put up at Goodhues. The Negro that took my Horse soon began to open his Heart.—He did not like the People of Salem, wanted to be sold to Captn. John Dean of Boston. He earned 2 Dollars in a forenoon, and did all he could to give Satisfaction. But his Mistress was cross, and said he did not earn Salt to his Porridge, &c. and would not find him Cloaths &c.

Thus I find Discontents in all Men. The Black thinks his Merit rewarded with Ingratitude, and so does the white. The Black estimates his own Worth, and the Merit of his Services higher than any Body else. So does the White. This flattering, fond Opinion of himself, is found in every Man.

Monday, June 17, 1771

1771. SATURDAY. JUNE 22ND.

Spent this Week at Ipswich in the usual Labours and Drudgery of Attendance upon Court. Boarded at Treadwells. Have had no Time to write.

Landlord and Landlady are some of the grandest People alive. Landlady is the great Grand Daughter of Governor Endicott, and has all the great Notions, of high Family, that you find in Winslows, Hutchinsons, Quincys, Saltonstals, Chandlers, Leonards, Otis's, and as you might find, with more Propriety, in the Winthrops. Yet she is cautious, and modist about discovering of it. She is a new Light—continually canting and whining in a religious Strain. The Governor was uncommonly strict, and devout, eminently so, in his day, and his great grand Daughter hopes to keep up the Honour of the family in hers, and distinguish herself among her Contemporaries as much.— "Terrible Things, Sin causes." Sighs and Groans. "The Pangs of the new Birth." "The death of Christ shews above all things the heignous Nature of sin!" "How awfully Mr. Kent talks about death! How lightly and carelessly. I am sure a Man of his Years who can talk so about Death, must be brought to feel the Pangs of the new Birth here, or made to repent of it forever." "How dreadfull it seems to me to hear him—I, that am so afraid of death, and so concerned lest I ant fit and prepared for it.—What a dreadfull Thing it was, that Mr. Gridley died so— too great, too big, too proud to learn any Thing. Would not let any Minister pray with him. Said he knew more than they could tell him—asked the News and said he was going where he should hear no News," &c.

Thus far Landlady. As to Landlord, he is as happy and as big, as proud, as conceited, as any Nobleman in England. Always calm and good natured, and lazy, but the Contemplation of his farm, and his Sons and his House, and Pasture and Cows, his sound Judgment as he thinks and his great Holiness as well as that of his Wife, keep him as erect in his Thoughts as a Noble or a Prince. Indeed the more I consider of Mankind, the more I see, that every Man, seriously, and in his Conscience believes himself, the wisest, brightest, best, happiest &c. of all Men.

FRYDAY JUNE 28TH. 1771.

At York. Yesterday I spent in Walking, one Way and another, to view the Town. I find that Walking serves me much. It sets my Blood in Motion much more than Riding.

Had some Conversation this Week with Chadburn of Berwick. He says, that Jo. Lee came to him, on the Election day Morning, and said "I know you are a peaceable Man. Why cant you vote for a few Gentlemen who would be agreable to the Governor and then perhaps some Gentlemen may not be negatived who would be agreable to you. Why cant you promote a Coalition?" Chadburn answered, I dont know who would be agreable to the Governor. I have not had a List.— Lee then mentioned Mr. Ropes, Lt. Govr. Oliver, and some of the Judges.—Why cant you choose some of those old Statesmen, who have been long and intimately acquainted with the Policy of the Province? &c.—Thus the Governors Emissaries are busy—instilling, insinuating, their Notions, and Principles, &c.

Had a little Chat this Week with Coll. Sparhawk of Kittery. He says "Now you are come away, they are become peaceable. You kept up a shocking Clamour while you was there."—This he said laughing, but there was rather too much Truth in it, to be made a Jest.—"They do you the Justice to say that no Man ever spoke more freely, than you did, and in Opposition to the rising Sun. But in order to take off from your Virtue, they say there is some private Pique between the Governor and you." —I told him there was none. He had always treated me well personally. If I had been actuated by private Pique, I would not have left the general Court but I would have remained there on Purpose to plague him. I could at least have been a Thorn in his Side—&c. But that I had been fully convinced in my own Mind these 10 Years that he was determined to raise himself and family, at all Hazards, and even on the Ruins of the Province, and that I had uniformly expressed that Opinion these 10 Years.

Sparhawk mentioned the Intrepidity of Sam Adams, a Man he says of great Sensibility, of tender Nerves, and harrased, dependant, in their Power. Yet he had born up against all—it must have penetrated him very deeply, &c.

FRYDAY. JULY 5. 1771.

Cadwallader Ford came to me this Morning, and congratulated me on the Verdict for Freeman.—Sir, says he, I shall think myself forever obliged to you, for the Patriotick manner in which you conducted that Cause. You have obtained great Honour in this County, by that Speech. I never heard a better &c.—All this is from old Cadwallader. Langdon told me, that a Man came running down, when I had done speaking, and said "That Mr. Adams has been making the finest Speech I ever heard in my Life. He's equall to the greatest orator that ever spoke in Greece or Rome."—What an Advantage it is to have the Passions, Prejudices, and Interests of the whole Audience, in a Mans Favour. These will convert plain, common Sense, into profound Wisdom, nay wretched Doggerell into sublime Heroics. This Cause was really, and in truth and without Partiality, or Affectation of Modesty, very indifferently argued by me. But I have often been surprized with Claps and Plauditts, and Hosannas, when I have spoke but indifferently, and as often met with Inattention and Neglect when I have thought I spoke very well.—How vain, and empty is Breath!

Sister Cranch says, she has had an Opportunity of making many Observations, this Year at Commencement. And she has quite altered her Mind about dancing and dancing Schools, and Mr. Cranch seems convinced too, and says it seems, that all such as learn to dance are so taken up with it, that they cant be students. So that if they should live to bring up Billy to Colledge, they would not send him to dancing School—nor the Misses Betsy and Lucy neither.—What a sudden, and entire Conversion is this! That Mrs. C. should change so quick is not so wonderfull, But that his mathematical, metaphysical, mechanical, systematical Head should be turned round so soon, by her Report of what she saw at Cambridge is a little remarkable. However the Exchange is for the better. It is from Vanity to Wisdom—from Foppery to Sobriety and solidity. I never knew a good Dancer good for any Thing else. I have known several Men of Sense and Learning, who could dance, Otis, Sewal, Paine, but none of them shone that Way, and neither of em had the more Sense or Learning, or Virtue for it.

I would not however conclude, peremptorily, against sending Sons or Daughters to dancing, or Fencing, or Musick, but had much rather they should be ignorant of em all than fond of any one of em.

Monday, July 22, 1771

1772. FEBY. 4TH. TUESDAY.

Took a Ride in the Afternoon with my Wife and little Daughter to make a visit to my Brother. But finding him and Sister just gone to visit my Mother we rode down there, and drank Tea, altogether. Chatted about the new Promotions in the Militia, and speculated about the future Officers of this

Company, upon supposition that the old Officers should resign—Billings, Brother, &c. &c.

It is curious to observe the Effect these little Objects of Ambition have upon Mens Minds. The Commission of a Subaltern, in the Militia, will tempt these little Minds, as much as Crowns, and Stars and Garters will greater ones. These are Things that strike upon vulgar, rustic Imaginations, more strongly, than Learning, Eloquence, and Genius, of which common Persons have no Idea.

My Brother seems to relish the Thought of a Commission, and if Rawson and Bass resign, I hope he will have one—under Billings.

————————

1772. FEBY. 9. SUNDAY.

"If I would but go to Hell for an eternal Moment or so, I might be knighted."—Shakespeare.

Shakespeare, that great Master of every Affection of the Heart and every Sentiment of the Mind as well as of all the Powers of Expression, is sometimes fond of a certain pointed Oddity of Language, a certain Quaintness of Style, that is an Imperfection, in his Character. The Motto prefixed to this Paper, may be considered as an Example to illustrate this Observation.

Abstracted from the Point and Conceit in the Style, there is Sentiment enough in these few Words to fill a Volume. It is a striking Representation of that Struggle which I believe always happens, between Virtue and Ambition, when a Man first commences a Courtier. By a Courtier I mean one who applies himself to the Passions and Prejudices, the Follies and Vices of great Men in order to obtain their Smiles, Esteem and Patronage and consequently their favours and Preferments. Human Nature, depraved as it is, has interwoven in its very Frame, a Love of Truth, Sincerity, and Integrity, which must be overcome by Art, Education, and habit, before the Man can become entirely ductile to the Will of a dishonest Master. When such a Master requires of all who seek his favour, an implicit Resignation to his Will and Humour, and these require that he be soothed, flattered and assisted in his Vices, and

Follies, perhaps the blackest Crimes, that Men can commit, the first Thought of this will produce in a Mind not yet entirely debauched, a Soliloqui, something like my Motto—as if he should say—The Minister of State or the Governor would promote my Interest, would advance me to Places of Honour and Profitt, would raise me to Titles and Dignities that will be perpetuated in my family, in a Word would make the Fortune of me and my Posterity forever, if I would but comply with his Desires and become his Instrument to promote his Measures.—But still I dread the Consequences. He requires of me, such Complyances, such horrid Crimes, such a Sacrifice of my Honour, my Conscience, my Friends, my Country, my God, as the Scriptures inform us must be punished with nothing less than Hell Fire, eternal Torment. And this is so unequal a Price to pay for the Honours and Emoluments in the Power of a Minister or Governor, that I cannot prevail upon myself to think of it. The Duration of future Punishment terrifies me. If I could but deceive myself so far as to think Eternity a Moment only, I could comply, and be promoted.

Such as these are probably the Sentiments of a Mind as yet pure, and undifiled in its Morals. And many and severe are the Pangs, and Agonies it must undergo, before it will be brought to yield entirely to Temptation. Notwithstanding this, We see every Day, that our Imaginations are so strong and our Reason so weak, the Charms of Wealth and Power are so enchanting, and the Belief of future Punishments so faint, that Men find Ways to persuade themselves, to believe any Absurdity, to submit to any Prostitution, rather than forego their Wishes and Desires. Their Reason becomes at last an eloquent Advocate on the Side of their Passions, and they bring themselves to believe that black is white, that Vice is Virtue, that Folly is Wisdom and Eternity a Moment.

The Brace of Adams's.

In the Spring of the Year 1771, several Messages passed between the Governor and the House of Representatives, concerning the Words that are always used in Acts of Parliament, and which were used in all the Laws of this Province, till the Administration of Governor Shirley, "in General Court assembled and by the Authority of the same." Governor Shirley in whose Administration those Words were first omitted in Consequence of an Instruction to him, saw and read these Messages in the Newspapers, and enquired of somebody in Company with him at his Seat in Dorchester, who had raised those Words from Oblivion at this Time?—The Gentleman answered, the Boston Seat.—Who are the Boston Seat? says the Governor.—Mr. Cushing, Mr. Hancock, Mr. Adams and Mr. Adams says the Gentleman.—Mr. Cushing I know, quoth Mr. Shirley, and Mr. Hancock I know, but where the Devil this Brace of Adams's came from, I cant conceive.

Q. Is it not a Pity, that a Brace of so obscure a Breed, should be the only ones to defend the Household, when the generous Mastiffs, and best blooded Hounds are all hushed to silence by the Bones and Crumbs, that are thrown to them, and even Cerberus himself is bought off, with a Sop?

The Malice of the Court and its Writers seems to be principally directed against these two Gentlemen. They have been stedfast and immoveable in the Cause of their Country, from the Year 1761, and one of them Mr. Samuel Adams for full 20 Years before. They have always since they were acquainted with each other, concurred in Sentiment that the Liberties of this Country had more to fear from one Man the present Governor Hutchinson than from any other Man, nay than from all other Men in the World. This Sentiment was founded in their Knowledge of his Character, his unbounded Ambition and his unbounded Popularity. This Sentiment they have always freely, tho decently, expressed in their Conversation and Writings, Writings which the Governor well knows and which will be remembered as long as his Character and Administration. It is not therefore at all surprizing that his Indignation and that of all his Creatures should fall upon those Gentlemen. Their Maker has given them Nerves that are delicate, and of Consequence their Feelings are exquisite, and their Constitutions tender, and their Health especially of one of them, very infirm: But as a Compensation for this he has been pleased to bestow upon them Spirits that are unconquerable by all the Art and all the Power of Governor Hutchinson, and his Political Creators and Creatures on both Sides of the Atlantic. That Art and Power which has destroyed a Thatcher, a Mayhew, an Otis, may destroy the Health and the Lives of these Gentlemen, but can never subdue their Principles or their Spirit. They have not the chearing salubrious Prospect of Honours and Emoluments before them, to support them under all the Indignities and Affronts, the Insults and Injuries, the Malice and Slander, that can be thrown upon Men, they have not even the Hope of those Advantages that the suffrages of the People only can bestow, but they have a Sense of Honour and a Love of their Country, the Testimony of a good Conscience, and the Consolation of Phylosophy, if nothing more, which will certainly support them in the Cause of their Country, to their last Gasp of Breath whenever that may happen.

Notes for an Oration on Government

The Origin, the Nature, the Principles and the Ends of Government, in all Ages, the ignorant as well as the enlightened, and in all Nations, the barbarous as well as civilized, have employed the Wits of ingenious Men.

The Magi, the Mufti, the Bramins, and Brachmans, Mandarines, Rabbies, Philosophers, Divines, Schoolmen, Hermits, Legislators, Politicians, Lawyers, have made these the subjects of their Enquiries and Reasonings. There is nothing too absurd, nothing too enthusiastical or superstitious, nothing too wild or whimsical, nothing too prophane or impious, to be found among such Thinkers, upon such Subjects. Any Thing which subtelty could investigate or imagination conceive, would serve for an Hypothesis, to support a System, excepting only what alone can support the System of Truth—Nature, and Experience.

The Science of Government, like all other Sciences, is best pursued by Observation And Experiment—Remark the Phenomina of Nature, and from these deduce the Principles and Ends of Government.

Men are the Objects of this Science, as much as Air, Fire, Earth and Water, are the Objects of Phylosophy, Points, Lines, Surfaces and Solids of Geometry, or the Sun, Moon and Stars of Astronomy. Human Nature therefore and human Life must be carefully observed and studied. Here we should spread before Us a Map of Man—view him in different Soils and Climates, in different Nations and Countries, under different Religions and Customs, in Barbarity and Civility, in a State of Ignorance and enlightened with Knowledge, in Slavery and in freedom, in Infancy and Age.

He will be found, a rational, sensible and social Animal, in all. The Instinct of Nature impells him to Society, and Society causes the Necessity of Government.

Government is nothing more than the combined Force of Society, or the united Power of the Multitude, for the Peace, Order, Safety, Good and Happiness of the People, who compose the Society. There is no King or Queen Bee distinguished from all others, by Size or Figure, or beauty and Variety of Colours, in the human Hive. No Man has yet produced any Revelation from Heaven in his favour, any divine Communication to govern his fellow Men. Nature throws us all into the World equall and alike.

Nor has any Form of Government the Honour of a divine original or Appointment. The Author of Nature has left it wholly in the Choice of the People, to make what mutual Covenants, to erect what Kind of Governments, and to exalt what Persons they please to power and dignities, for their own Ease, Convenience and Happiness.

Government being according to my Definition the collected Strength of all for the general Good of all, Legislators have devised a Great Variety of forms in which this Strength may be arranged.

There are only Three simple Forms of Government.

When the whole Power of the Society is lodged in the Hands of the whole Society, the Government is called a Democracy, or the Rule of the Many.

When the Sovereignty, or Supreme Power is placed in the Hands of a few great, rich, wise Men, the Government is an Aristocracy, or the Rule of the few.

When the absolute Power of the Community is entrusted to the Discretion of a single Person, the Government is called a Monarchy, or the Rule of one, in this Case the whole Legislative and Executive Power is in the Breast of one Man.

There are however two other Kinds of Monarchies. One is when the supreme Power is not in a single Person but in the Laws, the Administration being committed solely to the Prince.

Another Kind is a limited Monarchy, where the Nobles or the Commons or both have a Check upon all the Acts of Legislation of the Prince.

There is an indefinite Variety of other Forms of Government, occasioned by different Combinations of the Powers of Society, and different Intermixtures of these Forms of Government, one with another.

The best Governments of the World have been mixed.

The Republics of Greece, Rome, Carthage, were all mixed Governments. The English, Dutch and Swiss, enjoy the Advantages of mixed Governments at this Day.

Sometimes Kings have courted the People in Opposition to the Nobles. At other Times the Nobles have united with the People in Opposition to Kings. But Kings and Nobles have much oftener combined together, to crush, to humble and to Fleece the People.

But this is an unalterable Truth, that the People can never be enslaved but by their own Tameness, Pusillanimity, Sloth or Corruption.

They may be deceived, and their Symplicity, Ignorance, and Docility render them frequently liable to deception. And of this, the aspiring, designing, ambitious few are very sensible. He is the Statesman qualifyed by Nature to scatter Ruin and Destruction in his Path who by deceiving a Nation can render Despotism desirable in their Eyes and make himself popular in Undoing.

The Preservation of Liberty depends upon the intellectual and moral Character of the People. As long as Knowledge and Virtue are diffused generally among the Body of a Nation, it is impossible they should be enslaved. This can be brought to pass only by debasing their Understandings, or by corrupting their Hearts.

What is the Tendency of the late Innovations? The Severity, the Cruelty of the late Revenue Laws, and the Terrors of the formidable Engine, contrived to execute them, the Court of

Admiralty? Is not the natural and necessary Tendency of these Innovations, to introduce dark Intrigues, Insincerity, Simulation, Bribery and Perjury, among Custom house officers, Merchants, Masters, Mariners and their Servants?

What is the Tendency, what has been the Effect of introducing a standing Army into our Metropolis? Have we not seen horrid Rancour, furious Violence, infernal Cruelty, shocking Impiety and Profanation, and shameless, abandoned Debauchery, running down the Streets like a Stream?

Liberty, under every conceivable Form of Government is always in Danger. It is so even under a simple, or perfect Democracy, more so under a mixed Government, like the Republic of Rome, and still more so under a limited Monarchy.

Ambition is one of the more ungovernable Passions of the human Heart. The Love of Power, is insatiable and uncontroulable.

Even in the simple Democracies of ancient Greece, Jealous as they were of Power, even their Ostracism could not always preserve them from the grasping Desires and Designs, from the overbearing Popularity, of their great Men.

Even Rome, in her wisest and most virtuous Period, from the Expulsion of her Kings to the Overthrow of the Commonwealth, was always in Danger from the Power of some and the Turbulence, Faction and Popularity of others.

There is Danger from all Men. The only Maxim of a free Government, ought to be to trust no Man living, with Power to endanger the public Liberty.

In England, the common Rout to Power has been by making clamorous Professions of Patriotism, in early Life, to secure a great Popularity, and to ride upon that Popularity, into the highest Offices of State, and after they have arrived there, they have been generally found, as little zealous to preserve the Constitution, as their Predecessors whom they have hunted down.

The Earl of Strafford, in early Life, was a mighty Patriot and Anticourtier.

Sir Robert Walpole. Commited to the Tower the Father of Corruption.

Harley also, a great and bold Advocate for the Constitution and Liberties of his Country.

But I need not go to Greece or to Rome, or to Britain for Examples. There are Persons now living in this Province, who for a long Course of their younger Years, professed and were believed to be the Guardian Angells of our civil and Religious Liberties, whose latter Conduct, since they have climbed up by Popularity to Power, has exhibited as great a Contrast to their former Professions and Principles, as ever was seen in a Strafford, an Harley, or a Walpole.

Be upon your Guard then, my Countrymen.

We see, by the Sketches I have given you, that all the great Kingdoms of Europe have once been free. But that they have lost their Liberties, by the Ignorance, the Weakness, the Inconstancy, and Disunion of the People. Let Us guard against these dangers, let us be firm and stable, as wise as Serpents and as harmless as Doves, but as daring and intrepid as Heroes. Let Us cherish the Means of Knowledge—our schools and Colledges—let Us cherish our Militia, and encourage military Discipline and skill.

The English Nation have been more fortunate than France, Spain, or any other—for the Barons, the Grandees, the Nobles, instead of uniting with the Crown, to suppress the People, united with the People, and struggled vs. the Crown, untill they obtained the great Charter, which was but a Restoration and Confirmation of the Laws and Constitution of our Saxon King Edward the Confessor.

Liberty depends upon an exact Ballance, a nice Counterpoise of all the Powers of the state.

When the Popular Power becomes grasping, and eager after Augmentation, or for Amplification, beyond its proper Weight, or Line, it becomes as dangerous as any other. Sweeden is an Example.

The Independency of the Governor, his Salary granted by the Crown, out of a Revenue extorted from this People.

The Refusal of the Governor to consent to any Act for granting a Salary to the Agent, unless chosen by the 3 Branches of the General Court.

The Instruction to the Governor, not to consent to any Tax Bill unless certain Crown Officers are exempted.

The Multiplication of Offices and Officers among Us.

The Revenue, arising from Duties upon Tea, Sugar, Molasses and other Articles, &c.

It is the popular Power, the democraticall Branch of our Constitution that is invaded.

If K, Lords and Commons, can make Laws to bind Us in all Cases whatsoever, The People here will have no Influence, no Check, no Power, no Controul, no Negative.

And the Government we are under, instead of being a mixture of Monarchy, Aristocracy and Democracy, will be a Mixture only of Monarchy and Aristocracy. For the Lords and Commons may be considered equally with Regard to Us as Nobles, as the few, as Aristocratical Grandees, independent of Us the People, uninfluenced by Us, having no fear of Us, nor Love for Us.

Wise and free Nations have made it their Rule, never to vote their Donations of Money to their Kings to enable them to carry on the Affairs of Government, until they had Opportunities to examine the State of the Nation, and to remonstrate against Grievances and demand and obtain the Redress of them. This was the Maxim in France, Spain, Sweeden, Denmark, Poland, while those Nations were free. What Opportunities then shall we in this Province have to demand and obtain the Redress of Grievances, if our Governors and Judges and other Officers and Magistrates are to be supported by the Ministry, without the Gifts of the People.—Consider the Case of Barbadoes and Virginia. Their Governors have been made independent by the imprudent shortsighted Acts of their own Assemblies. What is the Consequence.

Spring 1772

From the Diary:
June 30–December 31, 1772

FALMOUTH, CASCO BAY. JUNE 30TH. 1772. TUESDAY.

My Office at Boston will miss me, this day. It is the last day of Arresting for July Court. What equivalent I shall meet with here is uncertain.

It has been my Fate, to be acquainted, in the Way of my Business, with a Number of very rich Men—Gardiner, Bowdoin, Pitts, Hancock, Rowe, Lee, Sargeant, Hooper, Doane. Hooper, Gardiner, Rowe, Lee, and Doane, have all acquired their Wealth by their own Industry. Bowdoin and Hancock received theirs by Succession, Descent or Devise. Pitts by Marriage. But there is not one of all these, who derives more Pleasure from his Property than I do from mine. My little Farm, and Stock, and Cash, affords me as much Satisfaction, as all their immense Tracts, extensive Navigation, sumptuous Buildings, their vast Sums at Interest, and Stocks in Trade yield to them. The Pleasures of Property, arise from Acquisition more than Possession, from what is to come rather than from what is. These Men feel their Fortunes. They feel the Strength and Importance, which their Riches give them in the World. Their Courage and Spirits are buoyed up, their Imaginations are inflated by them. The rich are seldom remarkable for Modesty, Ingenuity, or Humanity. Their Wealth has rather a Tendency to make them penurious and selfish.

1772. SEPTR. 22.

At Boston. Paid Doctr. Gardiner and took up my last Note to him. I have now got compleatly thro, my Purchase of Deacon Palmer, Coll. Quincy and all my Salt Marsh, being better than 20 Acres, and have paid £250 O.T. towards my House in Boston, and have better than £300 left in my Pockett. At Thirty Seven Years of Age, almost, this is all that my most intense Application to Study and Business has been able to accomplish, an Application, that has more than once been very near costing me my Life, and that has so greatly impaired my Health.

I am now writing in my own House in Queen Street, to which I am pretty well determined to bring my Family, this Fall. If I do, I shall come with a fixed Resolution, to meddle not with public Affairs of Town or Province. I am determined, my own Life, and the Welfare of my whole Family, which is much dearer to me, are too great Sacrifices for me to make. I have served my Country, and her professed Friends, at an immense Expense, to me, of Time, Peace, Health, Money, and Preferment, both of which last have courted my Acceptance, and been inexorably refused, least I should be laid under a Temptation to forsake the Sentiments of the Friends of this Country. These last are such Politicians, as to bestow all their Favours upon their professed and declared Enemies. I will devote myself wholly to my private Business, my Office and my farm, and I hope to lay a Foundation for better Fortune to my Children, and an happier Life than has fallen to my Share.

1772. NOVR. 21.

Next Tuesday I shall remove my Family to Boston, after residing in Braintree about 19 Months. I have recovered a Degree of Health by this Excursion into the Country, tho I am an infirm Man yet. I hope I have profited by Retirement and Reflection!—and learned in what manner to live in Boston! How long I shall be able to stay in the City, I know not; if my Health should again decline, I must return to Braintree and renounce the Town entirely. I hope however to be able to stay there many Years! To this End I must remember Temperance, Exercise and Peace of Mind. Above all Things I must avoid Politicks, Political Clubbs, Town Meetings, General Court, &c. &c. &c.

I must ride frequently to Braintree to inspect my Farm, and when in Boston must spend my Evenings in my Office, or with my Family, and with as little Company as possible.

1772 DECR. 29.

Spent the last Sunday Evening with Dr. Cooper at his House with Justice Quincy and Mr. Wm. Cooper. We were very social and we chatted at large upon Cæsar, Cromwell &c.

Yesterday Parson Howard and his Lady, lately Mrs. Mayhew, drank Tea with Mrs. Adams.

Heard many Anecdotes from a young Gentleman in my Office of Admirall Montagu's Manners. A Coachman, a Jack Tar before the Mast, would be ashamed—nay a Porter, a Shew Black or Chimney Sweeper would be ashamed of the coarse, low, vulgar, Dialect of this Sea Officer, tho a rear Admiral of the Blue, and tho a Second Son of a genteel if not a noble Family in England. An American Freeholder, living in a log House 20 feet Square, without a Chimney in it, is a well bred Man, a polite accomplished Person, a fine Gentleman, in Comparison of this Beast of Prey.

This is not the Language of Prejudice, for I have none against him, but of Truth. His brutal, hoggish Manners are a Disgrace to the Royal Navy, and to the Kings Service.

His Lady is very much disliked they say in general. She is very full of her Remarks at the Assembly and Concert. Can this Lady afford the Jewells and Dress she wears?—Oh that ever my son should come to dance with a Mantua Maker.

As to the Admiral his continual Language is cursing and damning and God damning, "my wifes d——d A——se is so broad that she and I cant sit in a Chariot together"—this is the Nature of the Beast and the common Language of the Man. Admiral Montagu's Conversation by all I can learn of it, is exactly like Otis's when he is both mad and drunk.

The high Commission Court, the Star Chamber Court, the Court of Inquisition, for the Tryal of the Burners of the Gaspee, at Rhode Island, are the present Topick of Conversation. The Governor of that Colony, has communicated to the assembly a Letter from the Earl of Dartmouth. The Colony are in great Distress, and have applied to their Neighbours for Advice, how to evade or to sustain the Shock.

———————

1772 DECR. 31. THURSDAY.
To Mrs. Maccaulay.
Madam

It is so long since I received your obliging Favour, that I am now almost ashamed to acknowledge it. The State of my Health, obliged me to retreat into the Country, where Nineteen Months Relaxation from Care, and rural Exercises, have restored me to such a State, that I have once more ventured into the Town of Boston, and the Business of my Profession.

The Prospect before me, however, is very gloomy. My Country is in deep Distress, and has very little Ground of Hope, that She will soon, if ever get out of it. The System of a mean, and a merciless Administration, is gaining Ground upon our Patriots every Day. The Flower of our Genius, the Ornaments of the Province, have fallen, melancholly Sacrifices, to the heart piercing Anxieties, which the Measures of Administration have occasioned. A Mayhew, a Thatcher, an Otis to name no more, have fallen, the two first by Death and the last by a Misfortune still much worse, Victims to the Enemies of their Country. The Body of the People seem to be worn out, by struggling, and Venality, Servility and Prostitution, eat and spread like a Cancer. Every young rising Genius, in this Country, is in a situation much worse than Hercules is represented to have been in, in the Fable of Prodicus.—Two Ladies are before him: The one, presenting to his View, not the Ascent of Virtue only, tho that is steep and rugged, but a Mountain quite inaccessible, a Path beset with Serpents, and Beasts of Prey, as well as Thorns and Briars, Precipices of Rocks over him, a Gulph yawning beneath, and the Sword of Damocles over his Head.—The other displaying to his View, Pleasures, of every Kind, Honours, such as the World calls by that Name, and showers of Gold and Silver.

If We recollect what a Mass of Corruption human Nature has been in general, since the Fall of Adam, we may easily judge what the Consequence will be.

Our Attention is now engaged by the Vengeance of Despotism that

This Evening at Mr. Cranch's, I found that my constitutional or habitual Infirmities have not entirely forsaken me. Mr. Collins an English Gentleman was there, and in Conversation about the high Commissioned Court, for enquiring after the Burners of the Gaspee at Providence, I found the old Warmth, Heat, Violence, Acrimony, Bitterness, Sharpness of my Temper, and Expression, was not departed. I said there was no more Justice left in Britain than there was in Hell—That I wished for War, and that the whole Bourbon Family was upon the Back of Great Britain—avowed a thoughrough Dissaffection to that Country—wished that any Thing might happen to them, and that as the Clergy prayed of our Enemies in Time of War, that they might be brought to reason or to ruin.

I cannot but reflect upon myself with Severity for these rash, inexperienced, boyish, raw, and aukward Expressions. A Man who has no better Government of his Tongue, no more command of his Temper, is unfit for every Thing, but Childrens Play, and the Company of Boys.

A Character can never be supported, if it can be raised, without a good a great Share of Self Government. Such Flights of Passion, such Starts of Imagination, tho they may strike a few of the fiery and inconsiderate, yet they lower, they sink a Man, with the Wise. They expose him to danger, as well as familiarity, Contempt, and Ridicule.

On the Independence of the Judges No. I

To the PRINTERS.

General Brattle, by his rank, station and character, is intituled to politeness and respect, even when he condescends to harangue in town-meeting, or to write in a news-paper: But the same causes require that his sentiments when erroneous and of dangerous tendency, should be considered, with entire freedom, and the examination be made as public, as the error. He cannot therefore take offence at any gentleman for offering his thoughts to the public, with decency and candor, tho' they may differ from his own.

In this confidence, I have presum'd to publish a few observations, which have occured to me, upon reading his narration of the proceedings of the late town meeting at Cambridge. It is not my intention to remark upon all things in that publication, which I think exceptionable, but only on a few which I think the most so.

The General is pleased to say, "That no man in the province could say whether the salaries granted to the Judges were *durante bene placito*, or *quam diu bene se gesserint*, as the Judges of England have their salaries granted them." "I supposed the latter, tho' these words were not expressed, but necessarily implied." This is said upon the supposition, that salaries are granted by the crown to the judges.

Now, it is not easy to conceive, how the General or any man in the province could be at a loss to say, upon supposition that salaries are granted, whether they are granted in the one way or the other. If salaries are granted by the crown, they must be granted, in such a manner as the crown has power to grant them. Now it is utterly deny'd, that the crown has power to grant them, in any other manner than *durante bene placito*.

The power of the crown to grant salaries to any judges in America is derived solely from the late act of parliament, and that gives no power to grant salaries for life, or during good behaviour. But not to enlarge upon this at present.

The General proceeds. "I was very far from thinking there was any necessity of having quam diu bene se gesserint in their commissions: For they have their commissions now by that tenure, as truly as if said words were in:"

It is the wish of almost all good men, that this was good law. This country would be forever obliged to any gentleman who would prove this point from good authorities, to the conviction of all concerned in the administration of government, here and at home. But I must confess that, my veneration for General Brattle's authority, by no means prevails with me, to give credit to this doctrine. Nor do his reasons in support of it, weigh with me, even so much as his authority. He says, "What right, what estate vests in them, (i.e. the Judges,) in consequence of their nomination and appointment, the common law of England, the Birth-right of every man here, as well as at home, determines, and that is an estate for life, provided they behave well:" I must confess I read these words with surprize and grief. And the more I have reflected upon them the more these sentiments have increased in my mind.

The common law of England is so far from determining, that the Judges have an estate for life in their offices, that it has determined the direct contrary. The proofs of this are innumerable and irresistable. My Ld. Coke in his 4th institute, 74, says, "Before the reign of E. 1. the chief justice of this court, was created by letters patents, and the form thereof (taking one for all) was in these words.

"Rex, &c. Archiepiscopis, Episcopis, Abbatibus, Prioribus, Comitibus, Baronibus, Vice-comitibus, Forestariis, et omnibus aliis fidelibus Regni Angliæ, salutem, cum pro Conservatione nostra, et tranquilitatis Regni nostri, et ad Justitiam universis et singulis de Regno nostro exhibendum constituerimus dilectum et fidelem nostrum Philippum Basset Justiciarium Angliæ *quam diu nobis placuerit* capitalem.—&c.*"

And my Lord Coke says, afterwards in the same page, "King E. 1. being a wise and prudent prince, knowing that cui plus licet quam par est plus vult quam licet (as most of the summi justiciarii did) made three alterations. 1. By limitation of his authority. 2. By changing summus justiciarius to capitalis justiciarius. 3. By a new kind of creation, viz. by writ, lest if he had continued his former manner of creation, he might have had a desire of his former authority, which three do expressly appear by the writ, yet in use, viz. Rex, &c. E.C. militi salutem, sciatis quod constitumus vos justiciarium nostrum capitalem, ad placita coram nobis tenenda, *durante beneplacito nostro* teste, &c." Afterwards in the same page Ld. Coke observes, "it is a rule in law, that ancient offices must be granted in such forms and in such manner, as they have been used to be unless the alteration were by authority of parliament. And continual experience approveth, that for many successions of ages without intermission, they have been, and yet are called by the said writ." His Lordship informs us, also in the same page, that "the rest of the Judges of the King's bench have their offices by letters patent in these words. Rex omnibus ad quos presentes literæ pervenient, salutem, sciatis quod constituimus dilectum et fidelem Johannem Doderidge militem unum justiciariorum ad placita coram nobis tenenda *durante beneplacito, nostro,* teste, &c."

His Lordship says indeed, from Bracton, that "these Judges are called Perpetui by Bracton, because they ought not to be removed without just cause." But the question is not what the Crown ought to do, but what it had legal power to do.

The next reason given by the General in support of his opinion, is that these points of law have been settled and determined by the greatest sages of the law formerly and more lately. This is so entirely without foundation, that the General might both with safety and decency be *challenged*, to produce the name of any one sage of the law ancient or modern, by whom it has been so settled and determined, and the book in which such determination appears. The General adds, "It is so notorious that it becomes the common learning of the law." I believe he may *decently and safely be challenged again*; to produce one Lawyer in this country, who ever before entertained such an opinion, or, heard such a doctrine. I would not be misunderstood; there are respectable Lawyers, who maintain that the Judges here hold their offices during good behaviour; but it is upon other principles, not upon the common law of England. "My Lord chief justice Holt settled it so, not long before the statute of William and Mary, that enacts that the words quam diu bene se gesserint, shall be in the Judges Commissions." And afterwards he says, that "the commissions as he apprehends, were without these words inserted in them, during the reigns of King William, Queen Mary and Queen Ann."

This I presume must have been conjectured from a few words of Lord Holt in the case of Harcourt against Fox, which I think are these. I repeat them from memory, having not the book before me at present. "Our places as judges are so settled, determinable only upon misbehaviour."

Now, from these words I should draw an opposite conclusion from the General, and should think that the influence of that interest in the nation which brought King William to the throne, prevailed upon him to grant the commissions to the Judges, expressly during good behavior. I say, this is the most natural construction, because it is certain, their places were not at that time, viz. 5 Wm. and Mary, determined by an act of parliament to be determinable only upon Misbehavior, and it is as certain, from Lord Coke, and from all history, that they were not so settled by the common law of England.

However, we need not rest upon this reasoning, because we happen to be furnished with the most explicit and decisive evidence, that my conclusion is just, from my Lord Raymond. In the beginning of his second volume of reports, his lordship has given us a list of the chief officers in the law at the time of the death of King William the third 8 March 1701, 2. And he says in these words, that "Sir John Holt, knight, chief justice of the King's bench, holding his office by writ, *though it was quam diu se bene gesserint*, held it to be determined by the demise of the King, notwithstanding the act of 12 & 13 Will. 3d. And therefore the Queen in council gave orders, that he should have a new writ, which he received accordingly, and was sworn before the lord keeper of the great seal the Saturday following, viz. the 14th of March, Chief Justice of Kings Bench."—From this several things appear,

1. That General Brattle is mistaken in apprehending that the Judges commissions were without the clause *quam diu bene se gesserint*, in the reign of King William and Queen Mary, and most probably also in the reign of Queen Ann, because, it is not likely that Lord Holt would have accepted a commission from the Queen during pleasure, when he had before had one from King William during good behaviour. And because if Queen Ann had made such an alteration in the commission, it is most likely Lord Raymond would have taken notice of it. 2. That Lord Holt's opinion was, that by common law he had

not an estate for life in his office, for if he had, it could not expire on the demise of the King. 3. That Lord Holt did not think the clause in the statute of 12 & 13 Wm. 3. to be a declaration of what was common law before, nor in affirmance of what was law before, but a new law and a total alteration of the tenure of the Judges commissions, established by parliament, and not to take place till after the death of the Princess Ann. 4. That in Lord Holt's opinion it was not in the power of the Crown, to alter the tenure of the Judges commissions, and make them a tenure for life determinable only upon misbehaviour, even by inserting, that express clause in them, *quam diu se bene gesserint.*

I have many more things to say upon this subject, which may possibly appear some other time.

Mean while I am, Messi'rs Printers, Your humble Servant,

JOHN ADAMS

Boston Gazette, January 11, 1773

William Brattle Replies to John Adams

To the PRINTERS,   Cambridge, January 18, 1773
As the lines of mens minds are as various as the features of
their faces, they can no more upon every subject think alike
than they can look alike, and yet both be equally honest; consequently they ought respectively to be treated with good
manners, let their stations in life be what they may, by all excepting those who think they have infallibility on their side.
For the publick peace and good order, I should be willing to
be mistaken in my law as John Adams, Esq; in his letter of last
week supposes I am, if the writers upon political controversy
would follow his example in his decent polite writing. As to his
knowledge and learning in the law, I can't expect their imitation, till they have his genius and accomplishments, which I
sincerely believe are rare. It appears to me that Mr. Adams's
sentiments upon the estate that the justices of the superior
court here by virtue of their nomination and appointment
have, namely, that they may be legally displaced, meerly by the
arbitrary will and pleasure of the Governor and Council, are
Tory principles. But as I am convinced to draw the consequence therefrom, that he is one, would be injurious and false,
I hope his sentiments (tho' however mistaken) will not be
improved to his prejudice. I on the other hand have said, and
now declare as my opinion, that the Governor and Council
can no more constitutionally and legally remove any one justice of the superior court, as the commissions now are, unless
there is a fair hearing and trial, and then a judgment that he
hath behaved ill, than they can hang me for writing this my
opinion, and the latter (if it went no further) would not be of
one half the publick mischief and damage as the former,
notwithstanding I am very sensible that this hath been the case
in one or two arbitrary administrations. I recollect but two
since the charter; but these were arbitrary, illegal, unconstitutional measures, and do not determine what the law is, any
more then the arbitrary illegal measures of the Steward Kings
determine that their measures were legal, and ought to be the
rule of his present Majesty's conduct. Arbitrary measures never

did, after people had come to their senses, and I hope never will, determine what the law is.

Further I observe, that supposing a corrupt governor and a corrupt council, whether the words in the commission, are so long as the governor and council please, or during good behaviour, will just come to the same thing, the security as to the public will be just the same, but this is not our unhappy case. I am convinced that nothing would induce his Excellency Governor Hutchinson to nominate, or one member of the council to consent to a nomination in the room of any one justice of the Superiour Court (however disagreeable he might be) till he had after a impartial trial been first adjudged to have behaved ill, and so forfeited his estate by a breach of trust. The first thing Mr. Adams expresses his great surprize at is, that I should be at any loss, or any man in the province should be at a loss for what time the grant is made to the Judges; he says the King can't grant salaries in any other manner than durante bene placito, and that the King's power to grant salaries to any Judges in America, is derived solely from the late act of Parliament, and that gives no power to grant salaries for life or good behaviour, the above assertions without the least color of proof, but Mr. Adams's word for it, I deny. The parliament grants no salaries to the Judges of England, the King settles the salaries and pays his Judges out of the civil list; and I challenge Mr. Adams to show one instance of any Judge who was continued in office, tho' at the same time most disagreeable to the king that his salary was taken from him; to suppose this is frustrating the act of parliament that enacts that their commissions should be during good behaviour; for what if they are during good behaviour, what good will it do them, or what safety will it be to the community if it is in the power of the King to take away their salaries and starve them? Will they not in this case be as dependent upon the Crown as if their commissions were to determine by the will of the King? Again, this act of parliament with respect to the Judges salaries, was made for no other reason than this, that the King might not pay them out of the civil list, but out of another fund, namely, out of the revenue; here the abovementioned act says nothing about durante beneplacito, and therefore if there is a grant made to the Judges, that grant stands upon the same footing with the salaries granted by the King to the Judges in England. Mr. Adams challenges me to produce one lawyer that ever was, or now is, in the country, that entertained such an opinion as I have advanced, namely, that by the common law of England, the Judges commissions are so long as they behave well: He acknowledges there may be respectable lawyers in this country, that hold that the Judges commissions are during good behaviour, though not expressly mentioned in their commission, but it is on other principles. I answer, if they are of that opinion, it must be upon my principles, for there is no statute law about it which extends to the plantations, the canon law nor civil law says nothing about it; and therefore if they are in sentiments with me, they can found their opinion on the common law only; and this I do solemnly declare, the honorable Mr. Read did, who was to every lawyer as highly esteemed for reforming, and correcting the law and the pleadings as Justinian was at Rome. He was my friend, my father, under whose direction I studied the law. I have heard him often and often declare it, as his opinion, and I have living witnesses to prove it; the late Judge Auchmuty was of the same mind. I have asked no gentleman at the bar now on the stage their opinion, and do not know it. But this I know, that it is the opinion of the greatest lawyers who are not at the Bar in the province, that I am right in what I have advanced. Mr. Adams makes a further challenge, and denies that I can produce the name of one of the sages of the law, by whom it hath been settled as I contend for, or in other words, that I am alone in my sentiments. This surprizes me much, that a gentleman of Mr. Adams's learning should be so extreamly mistaken and forgetful: Sir Thomas Powis one of the sages of the law gives his opinion in the words following, "I take it by the common laws and the ancient constitution of the kingdom all officers of courts of justice, and immediately relating to the execution of justice, were in for their lives, only removeable for misbehaviour in their offices: Not only my lords the judges of the courts of Westminster-Hall were anciently as they now are, since the revolution, quam diu se bene gesserint, but all the officers of note in the several courts under them were so, and most of them continue so to this day; as the clerks of the crown in this court and in the chancery, the chief clerk on the civil side in this court, the prothonotaries in the common pleas, the master of the office of pleas in the exchequer, and many others. I think speaking generally they were all in for their lives by the *common law*, and are so to this day.—I shall not enlarge upon this matter, I need not, it being so well known," says Sir Thomas. Sergent Levenz expressly says, that in the time of King Charles the second, S. Archer was made a judge of the common pleas quam diu bene se gesserit. If it never was the common law of England that the judges commissions run during their good behaviour, as Mr. Adams affirms, and there was an act of parliament formerly that they should be during the king's pleasure (which let it be observed Lord Coke never said there was a statute relating to it) unless that statute was repealed, and I challenge Mr. Adams, and so I would my Lord Coke if he was alive, to shew that it was, or even that there ever was such a statute. I quere how it come about that King Charles the second did not conform to said statute, how in the face of an act of parliament or the common law, or both, to give commissions to the judges to continue during good behaviour, and thereby lessen their dependence on him; this can't well be reconciled with the history of his reign. And how come it about that ever since the revolution to George the first time, the commissions were during good behaviour. This I agree with Mr. Adams was the case, and am quite obliged to him for correcting my mistake when in my harrangue I said otherwise. According to Mr. Adams's doctrine, and according to the law, they were ipso facto null and void, because they were directly against law; provided Mr. Adams is right that both common law and statute law formerly obliged the King to give the judges their commission during good pleasure only. But I conceive that King William and Queen Mary that came over to save an almost ruined and undone people, by the tyranny of their predecessors, and their acting directly contrary to the laws of the land, that they should begin their reign by going directly against the law, and thereby violate their coronation oath, this is not credible. What the law was before their reign, was better known, and the law which was often fluctuating by the arbitrary power of some former princes, was put upon a more solid basis since the revolution than it was before. And we are to inquire what the law was formerly by the resolutions, the judgments of court, and the practice since the revolution, and the tenure of the judges commission since the revolution being during good behaviour, to the reign of George the first, and when the act of King William was to take place, and not before, namely, that during good behaviour should be in their commissions, plainly proves what I have advanced to be law, is law, or else great dishonor is reflected upon King William, Queen Mary, and Queen Ann. I am obliged to Mr. Adams for quoting the following passage out of my Lord Coke, which fully justifies my reasoning upon the Judges commissions. The words are these. "It is a rule in law that ancient offices must be granted in such forms and in such manner as they have used to be, unless the alteration was by authority of parliament."

It is manifest to every one that doth not depend upon their memory, that lord chief justice Holt, one of the sages of the law, apprehended that for the Judges commissions being during good behaviour, was upon the rule of the common law. He says after a cause had been argued upon a special verdict; after Sir J. Powes and serjeant Levenz had most positively affirmed, that this was the rule of the common law, not denied by the council on the other side, but rather conceded to: that in giving his opinion upon the whole matter, we all know it, says that great lawyer, and our places as judges are so settled, only determinable by misbehaviour, settled by whom? not by an act that was not to take place till the accession of George the first, not by any statute then existing; where is it? Whoever heard of it? Let it be produced; if not by statute, certainly then by common law. And can any man think that Lord Chief Justice Holt would have taken a commission from King William and Queen Mary, if they had offered him one, supposing it had been contrary to law, or rather if it had not been consonant to law: Or can we suppose that all the judges of the King's bench would have heard the before mentioned gentlemen with respect to the tenure of the judges commissions, without a reproof, or at least without telling them it was not law, if all the judges had not thought it was law; I leave the world to determine.

Mr. Adams says, and says truly, that Sir John Holt, kt. chief justice of the King's bench, holding his office by writ, tho' it was quam diu bene se gesserit; held it to be determined by the demise of the King, and therefore Queen Ann ordered a new writ. And what then? Every civil officers commission holden quam diu bene gesserint, died with the demise of the King, till the act made in the present King's reign. Wherefore there was an act of parliament that all officers should be continued a certain time after the demise of the King, to prevent the total stagnation of justice.

Mr. Adams supposes a material difference between an estate that the judges have as such for life, or so long as they behave well: the following judges his equals at least differ from him. Serjeant Levenz "I take it clear law, that if an office be granted to hold so long as he behaves himself well in the office, that is an estate for life, unless he lose it for misbehaviour; for it hath an annexed condition to be forfeited upon misdemeanor, and this by law is annexed to all offices, they being trusts; and misdemeanors in an office is a breach of trust"; and with his opinion agree the judges of the Kings bench in the case of Harcourt against Fox. J Eyre says, I do not think there is plainly given an estate for life in his office determinable upon his good behaviour: J Gregory says the same: J Dolben says that if any man is to enjoy an office so long as he behaves well in it, no one will doubt but the grantee hath an estate for life in it. My Lord Chief Justice Holt says, I do agree with my brothers in opinion. Upon the whole, using Mr. Adams's own words, *My haranguing in the town meeting in Cambridge hath not received* any sufficient legal answer; and notwithstanding my veneration for Mr. Adams's authority, it by no means prevails with me to give credit to his doctrine: Nor do his reasons in support of it weigh with me even so much as his authority.

W. Brattle

Boston Gazette, January 25, 1773

Reply of the Massachusetts House of Representatives to Governor Hutchinson's First Message

MARTIS, 26 *Die Januarii*, A.D. 1773, *Post-Meridiem*
May it please your Excellency,

Your Excellency's Speech to the General Assembly at the Opening of this Session, has been read with great Attention in this House.

We fully agree with your Excellency, that our own Happiness as well as his Majesty's Service, very much depends upon Peace and Order; and we shall at all Times take such Measures as are consistent with our Constitution and the Rights of the People to promote and maintain them. That the Government at present is in a very disturbed State is apparent! But we cannot ascribe it to the People's having adopted unconstitutional Principles, which seems to be the Cause assigned for it by your Excellency. It appears to us to have been occasioned rather, by the British House of Commons assuming and exercising Power inconsistent with the Freedom of the Constitution to give and grant the Property of the Colonists, and appropriate the same without their Consent.

It is needless for us to enquire what were the Principles that induced the Councils of the Nation to so new and unprecedented a Measure. But when the Parliament by an Act of their own expressly declared, that the King, Lords and Commons of the Nation "have, had, and of Right ought to have full Power and Authority to make Laws and Statutes of sufficient Force and Validity to bind the Colonies and People of America, Subjects of the Crown of Great-Britain, in all Cases whatever," and in Consequence hereof another Revenue Act was made, the Minds of the People were filled with Anxiety, and they were justly alarmed with Apprehensions of the total Extinction of their Liberties.

The Result of the free Enquiries of many Persons into the Right of the Parliament to exercise such a Power over the Colonies, seems in your Excellency's Opinion to be the Cause of what you are pleased to call the present "disturbed State of the Government;" upon which you "may not any longer consistent with your Duty to the King, and your Regard to the Interest of the Province, delay communicating your Sentiments." But that the Principles adopted in Consequence hereof, are unconstitutional, is a Subject of Enquiry. We know of no such Disorders arising therefrom as are mentioned by your Excellency. If Grand Jurors have not on their Oaths found such Offences, as your Excellency with the Advice of his Majesty's Council have *ordered* to be prosecuted, it is to be presumed they have followed the Dictates of good Conscience. They are the constitutional Judges of these Matters, and it is not to be supposed, that moved from corrupt Principles, they have suffered Offenders to escape a Prosecution, and thus supported and encouraged them to go on offending. If any Part of the Authority, shall in an unconstitutional Manner, interpose in any Matter, it will be no wonder if it be brought into Contempt; to the lessening or confounding of that Subordination which is necessary to a well regulated State. Your Excellency's Representation that the Bands of Government are weakened, we humbly conceive to be without good Grounds; though we must own the heavy Burthens unconstitutionally brought upon the People have been and still are universally and very justly complained of as a Grievance.

You are pleased to say, that "when our Predecessors first took Possession of this Plantation or Colony, under a Grant and Charter from the Crown of England, it was their Sense and it was the Sense of the Kingdom, that they were to remain subject to the Supreme Authority of Parliament;" whereby we understand your Excellency to mean in the Sense of the Declaratory Act of Parliament aforementioned, in all Cases whatever. And indeed it is difficult, if possible, to draw a Line of Distinction between the universal Authority of Parliament over the Colonies and no Authority at all. It is therefore necessary for us to enquire how it appears, for your Excellency has not shown it to us, that when or at the Time that our Predecessors took Possession of this Plantation or Colony, under a Grant and Charter from the Crown of England, it was *their Sense*, and the Sense of *the Kingdom*, that they were to remain subject to the Supreme Authority of Parliament. In making this Enquiry, we shall, according to your Excellency's Recommendation, treat the Subject with Calmness and Candor, and also with a due Regard to Truth.

Previous to a direct Consideration of the Charter granted to this Province or Colony, and the better to elucidate the true Sense and Meaning of it, we would take a View of the State of the English North American Continent at the Time when and after Possession was first taken of any Part of it, by the Europeans. It was then possessed by Heathen and Barbarous People, who had nevertheless all that Right to the Soil and Sovereignty in and over the Lands they possessed, which God had originally given to Man. Whether their being Heathen, inferred any Right or Authority to Christian Princes, a Right which had long been assumed by the Pope, to dispose of their Lands to others, we will leave to your Excellency or any one of Understanding and impartial Judgment to consider. It is certain they had in no other Sense forfeited them to any Power in Europe. Should the Doctrine be admitted that the Discovery of Lands owned and possessed by Pagan People, gives to any Christian Prince a Right and Title to the Dominion and Property, still it is invested in the Crown alone. It was an Acquisition of Foreign Territory, not annexed to the Realm of England, and therefore at the absolute Disposal of the Crown. For we take it to be a settled Point, that the King has a constitutional Prerogative to dispose of and alienate any Part of his Territories not annexed to the Realm. In the Exercise of this Prerogative, Queen Elizabeth granted the first American Charter; and claiming a Right by Virtue of Discovery, then supposed to be valid, to the Lands which are now possessed by the Colony of Virginia, she conveyed to Sir Walter Rawleigh, the Property, Dominion and Sovereignty thereof, to be held of the Crown by Homage, and a certain Render, without any Reservation to herself of any Share in the Legislative and Executive Authority. After the Attainder of Sir Walter, King James the First created two Virginia Companies, to be governed each by Laws transmitted to them by his Majesty and not by the Parliament, with Power to establish and cause to be made a Coin to pass current among them; and vested with all Liberties, Franchises and Immunities within any of his other Dominions, to all Intents and Purposes, as if they had been abiding, and born *within the Realm*. A Declaration similar to this is contained in the first

Charter of this Colony, and in those of other American Colonies, which shows that the Colonies were not intended or considered to be within the Realm of England, though within the Allegiance of the English Crown. After this, another Charter was granted by the same King James, to the Treasurer and Company of Virginia, vesting them with full Power and Authority, to make, ordain and establish all Manner of Orders, Laws, Directions, Instructions, Forms and Ceremonies of Government, and Magistracy, fit and necessary, and the same to abrogate, &c. without any Reservation for securing their Subjection to the Parliament and future Laws of England. A third Charter was afterwards granted by the same King to the Treasurer and Company of Virginia, vesting them with Power and Authority to make Laws, with an Addition of this Clause, "so always that the same be not contrary to the Laws and Statutes of this our Realm of England." The same Clause was afterwards copied into the Charter of this and other Colonies, with certain Variations, such as that these Laws should be "consonant to Reason," "not repugnant to the Laws of England," "as nearly as conveniently may be to the Laws, Statutes and Rights of England," &c. These Modes of Expression convey the same Meaning, and serve to show an Intention that the Laws of the Colonies should be as much as possible, conformant in the Spirit of them to the Principles and fundamental Laws of the English Constitution, its Rights and Statutes then in Being, and by no Means to bind the Colonies to a Subjection to the Supreme Authority of the English Parliament. And that this is the true Intention, we think it further evident from this Consideration, that no Acts of any Colony Legislative, are ever brought into Parliament for Inspection there, though the Laws made in some of them, like the Acts of the British Parliament are laid before the King for his Assent or Disallowance.

We have brought the first American Charters into View, and the State of the Country when they were granted, to show that the Right of disposing of the Lands was in the Opinion of those Times vested solely in the Crown—that the several Charters conveyed to the Grantees, who should settle upon the Territories therein granted, all the Powers necessary to constitute them free and distinct States—and that the fundamental Laws of the English Constitution should be the certain and established Rule of Legislation, to which the Laws to be made in the several Colonies were to be as nearly as conveniently might be, comfortable or similar, which was the true Intent and Import of the Words, "not repugnant to the Laws of England," "consonant to Reason," and other variant Expressions in the different Charters. And we would add, that the King in some of the Charters reserves the Right to judge of the Consonance and Similarity of their Laws with the English Constitution to himself, and not to the Parliament; and in Consequence thereof to affirm, or within a limited Time, disallow them.

These Charters, as well as that afterwards granted to Lord Baltimore, and other Charters, are repugnant to the Idea of Parliamentary Authority: And to suppose a Parliamentary Authority over the Colonies under such Charters would necessarily induce that Solecism in Politics *Imperium in Imperio*. And the King's repeatedly exercising the Prerogative of disposing of the American Territory by such Charters, together with the Silence of the Nation, thereupon, is an Evidence that it was an acknowledged Prerogative.

But further to show the Sense of the English Crown and Nation that the American Colonists and our Predecessors in particular, when they first took Possession of this Country by a Grant and Charter, from the Crown did not remain subject to the Supreme Authority of Parliament, we beg leave to observe; that when a Bill was offered by the two Houses of Parliament to King Charles the First, granting to the Subjects of England the free Liberty of Fishing on the Coast of America, he refused his Royal Assent, declaring as a Reason, that "the Colonies were *without the Realm and Jurisdiction of Parliament*."

In like Manner, his Predecessor James the First, had before declared upon a similar Occasion, that "America *was not annexed to the Realm*, and it was not fitting that Parliament should make Laws for those Countries." This Reason was, not secretly, but openly declared in Parliament. If then the Colonies were not annexed to the Realm, at the Time when their Charters were granted, they never could be afterwards, without their own special Consent, which has never since been had, or even asked. If they are not now annexed to the Realm, they are not a Part of the Kingdom, and consequently not subject to the Legislative Authority of the Kingdom. For no Country, by the Common Law was subject to the Laws or to the Parliament, but the Realm of England.

We would, if your Excellency pleases, subjoin an Instance of Conduct in King Charles the Second, singular indeed, but important to our Purpose; who, in 1679, framed an Act for a permanent Revenue for the Support of Virginia, and sent it there by Lord Colpepper, the Governor of that Colony; which was afterwards passed into a Law, and *"Enacted by the King's most excellent Majesty, by and with the Consent of the General Assembly of Virginia."* If the King had judged that Colony to be a Part of the Realm, he would not, nor could he consistently with Magna Charta, have placed himself at the Head of, and joined with any Legislative Body in making a Law to Tax the People there, other than the Lords and Commons of England.

Having taken a View of the several Charters of the first Colony in America, if we look into the old Charter of this Colony, we shall find it to be grounded on the same Principle: That the Right of disposing the Territory granted therein was vested in the Crown, as being that Christian Sovereign who first discovered it, when in the Possession of Heathen; and that it was considered as being not within the Realm, but only within the Fee and Seignory of the King. As therefore it was without the Realm of England, must not the King, if he had designed that the Parliament should have had any Authority over it, have made a special Reservation for that Purpose, which was not done.

Your Excellency says, it appears from the Charter itself, to have been the Sense of our Predecessors who first took Possession of this Plantation or Colony, that they were to remain subject to the Authority of Parliament. You have not been pleased to point out to us how this appears from the Charter, unless it be in the Observation you make on the above-mentioned Clause, viz. "That a favourable Construction has been put upon this Clause, when it has been allowed to intend such Laws of England only as are expressly made to respect us," which you say "is by Charter a Reserve of Power and Authority to Parliament to bind us by such Laws at least as are made expressly to refer to us, and consequently is a Limitation of the Power given to the General Court." But we would still recur to the Charter itself, and ask your Excellency, How this appears from thence to have been the Sense of our Predecessors? Is any Reservation of Power and Authority to Parliament thus to bind us, expressed or implied in the Charter? It is evident, that King Charles the first, the very Prince who granted it, as well as his Predecessor, had no such Idea of the supreme Authority of Parliament over the Colony, from their Declarations before recited. Your Excellency will then allow us further to ask, by what Authority in Reason or Equity the Parliament can enforce a Construction so *unfavourable* to us. *Quod ab anitio injustum est, nullum potest habere juris effectum*, said *Grotius*. Which with Submission to your Excellency may be rendered thus, *Whatever is originally in its Nature wrong, can never be satisfied or made right by Reputation and Use.*

In solemn Agreements subsequent Restrictions ought never to be allowed. The celebrated Author whom your Excellency has quoted, tells us that "neither the one or the other of the interested or contracting Powers hath a Right to interpret at Pleasure." This we mention to show, even upon a Supposition that the Parliament had been a Party to the Contract, the Invalidity of any of its subsequent Acts, to explain any Clause in the Charter; more especially to restrict or make void any Clause granted therein to the General Court. An Agreement ought to be interpreted "in such a Manner as that it may have *its Effect*." But if your Excellency's Interpretation of this Clause is just, "that it is a Reserve of Power and Authority to Parliament to bind us by such Laws as are made expressly to refer to us," it is not only "a Limitation of the Power given to the General Court" to Legislate, but it may whenever the Parliament shall think fit, render it of *no Effect*; for it puts it in the Power of Parliament to bind us by as many Laws as they please, and even to restrain us from making any Laws at all. If your Excellency's Assertions in this and the next succeeding Part of your Speech were well grounded, the Conclusion would be undeniable, that the Charter even in this Clause, "does not confer or reserve any Liberties" worth enjoying "but what would have been enjoyed without it;" saving that within any of his Majesty's Dominions we are to be considered barely as *not Aliens*. You are pleased to say, it cannot "be con-

tended that by the Liberties of free and natural Subjects"
(which are expressly granted in the Charter to all Intents, Purposes and Constructions whatever) "is to be understood an
Exemption from Acts of Parliament because not represented
there; seeing it is provided by the same Charter that such Acts
shall be in Force." If, says an eminent Lawyer, "the King
grants to the Town of D. the same Liberties which London
has, this shall be intended the like Liberties." A Grant of the
Liberties of free and natural Subjects is equivalent to a Grant
of the same Liberties. And the King in the first Charter to this
Colony expressly grants that it "shall be construed, reputed
and adjudged in all Cases most favourably on the Behalf and
for the Benefit and Behoof of the said Governor and Company
and their Successors—any Matter, Cause or Thing whatsoever
to the contrary notwithstanding." It is one of the Liberties of
free and natural Subjects, born and abiding within the Realm,
to be governed as your Excellency observes, "by Laws made
by Persons in whose Elections they from Time to Time have a
Voice." This is an essential Right. For nothing is more evident,
than that any People who are subject to the unlimited Power
of another, must be in a State of abject Slavery. It was easily
and plainly foreseen that the Right of Representation in the
English Parliament could not be exercised by the People of
this Colony. It would be impracticable, if consistent with the
English Constitution. And for this Reason, that this Colony
might have and enjoy all the Liberties and Immunities of free
and natural Subjects within the Realm as stipulated in the
Charter it was necessary, and a Legislative was accordingly
constituted within the Colony; one Branch of which consists
of Representatives chosen by the People, to make all Laws,
Statutes, Ordinances, &c. for the well-ordering and governing
the same, not repugnant to the Laws of England, or, as nearly
as conveniently might be, agreeable to the fundamental Laws
of the English Constitution. We are therefore still at a Loss to
conceive where your Excellency finds it "*provided* in the same
Charter, that such Acts," viz. Acts of Parliament made expressly to refer to us, "shall be in Force" in this Province.
There is nothing to this Purpose expressed in the Charter, or
in our Opinion even implied in it. And surely it would be very
absurd, that a Charter, which is evidently formed upon a

Supposition and Intention, that a Colony is and should be considered as not within the Realm; and declared by the very Prince who granted it, to be not within the Jurisdiction of Parliament, should yet *provide*, that the Laws which the same Parliament should make expressly to refer to that Colony, should be in Force therein. Your Excellency is pleased to ask, "Does it follow that the Government by their (our Ancestors) Removal from one Part of the Dominions to another, loses its Authority over that Part to which they remove; And that they are freed from the Subjection they were under before?" We answer, if that Part of the King's Dominions to which they removed was not then a Part of the Realm, and was never annexed to it, the Parliament lost no Authority over it, having never had such Authority; and the Emigrants were consequently freed from the Subjection they were under before their Removal: The Power and Authority of Parliament being constitutionally confined within the Limits of the Realm and the Nation collectively, of which alone it is the representing and legislative Assembly. Your Excellency further asks, "Will it not rather be said, that by this their voluntary Removal, they have relinquished for a Time at least, one of the Rights of an English Subject, which they might if they pleased have continued to enjoy, and may again enjoy, whenever they return to the Place where it can be exercised?" To which we answer; They never did relinquish the Right to be governed by Laws made by Persons in whose Election they had a Voice. The King stipulated with them that they should have and enjoy all the Liberties of free and natural Subjects born within the Realm, to all Intents, Purposes and Constructions whatsoever; that is, that they should be as free as those who were to abide within the Realm: Consequently he stipulated with them that they should enjoy and exercise this most essential Right, which discriminates Freemen from Vassals, uninterruptedly in its full Sense and Meaning; and they did and ought still to exercise it, without the Necessity of returning, for the Sake of exercising it, to the Nation or State of England.

We cannot help observing, that your Excellency's Manner of Reasoning on this Point, seems to us to render the most valuable Clauses in our Charter unintelligible: As if Persons going from the Realm of England to inhabit in America should hold and exercise there a certain Right of English Subjects; but in order to exercise it in such Manner as to be of any Benefit to them, they must *not inhabit* there, but return to the Place where alone it can be exercised. By such Construction, the Words of the Charter can have no Sense or Meaning. We forbear remarking upon the Absurdity of a Grant to Persons born within the Realm, of the same Liberties which would have belonged to them if they had been born within the Realm.

Your Excellency is disposed to compare this Government to the Variety of Corporations, formed within the Kingdom, with Power to make and execute By-Laws, &c. And because they remain subject to the Supreme Authority of Parliament, to infer that this Colony is also subject to the same Authority. This Reasoning appears to us not just. The Members of those Corporations are Residant within the Kingdom; and Residence subjects them to the Authority of Parliament, in which they are also represented: Whereas the People of this Colony are not Resident within the Realm. The Charter was granted with the express Purpose to induce them to reside without the Realm; consequently they are not represented in Parliament there. But we would ask your Excellency; Are any of the Corporations formed within the Kingdom, vested with the Power of erecting other subordinate Corporations? Of enacting and determining what Crimes shall be Capital? And constituting Courts of Common Law with all their Officers, for the hearing, trying and punishing capital Offenders with Death? These and many other Powers vested in this Government, plainly show that it is to be considered as a Corporation in no other Light, than as every State is a Corporation. Besides, Appeals from the Courts of Law here, are not brought before the House of Lords; which shows that the Peers of the Realm are not the Peers of America: But all such Appeals are brought before the King in Council, which is a further Evidence that we are not within the Realm.

We conceive enough has been said to convince your Excellency, that "when our Predecessors first took Possession of this Plantation or Colony by a Grant and Charter from the Crown of England, it *was not* and never had been the Sense of the Kingdom, that they were to remain subject to the Supreme Authority of Parliament." We will now with your Excellency's

Leave, enquire what *was* the Sense of our Ancestors of this very important Matter.

And as your Excellency has been pleased to tell us, you have not discovered that the Supreme Authority of Parliament has been called in Question even by private and particular Persons, until within seven or eight Years past; except about the Time of the Anarchy and Confusion in England which preceeded the Restoration of King Charles the Second; we beg leave to remind your Excellency of some Parts of your own History of Massachusetts-Bay. Therein we are informed of the Sentiments of "Persons of Influence" after the Restoration, from which the Historian tells us, some Parts of their Conduct, that is of the General Assembly, "may be pretty well accounted for." By the History it appears to have been the Opinion of those Persons of Influence, "that the Subjects of any Prince or State had a natural Right to Remove to any other State or to another Quarter of the World unless the State was weakened or exposed by such Remove; and even in that Case, if they were deprived of the Right of all Mankind, Liberty of Conscience, it would justify a Separation, and *upon their Removal their Subjection determined and ceased.*" That "the Country to which they had removed, was claimed and possessed by independent Princes, whose Right to the Lordship and Sovereignty thereof had been acknowledged by the Kings of England," an Instance of which is quoted in the Margin; "That they themselves had actually purchased for valuable Consideration, not only the Soil but the Dominion, the Lordship and Sovereignty of those Princes;" without which Purchase, "in the Sight of God and Men, they had no Right or Title to what they possessed." That they had received a Charter of Incorporation from the King, from whence arose a new Kind of Subjection, namely, "a voluntary, civil Subjection;" and by this Compact "they were *to be governed by Laws made by themselves.*" Thus it appears to have been the Sentiments of *private* Persons, though Persons, by whose Sentiments the public Conduct was influenced, that their Removal was a justifiable Separation from the Mother State, upon which their Subjection to that State determined and ceased. The Supreme Authority of Parliament, if it had then ever been asserted, must surely have been called in Question, by Men who had advanced such Principles as these.

The first Act of Parliament made expressly to refer to the Colonies, was after the Restoration. In the Reign of King Charles the Second, several such Acts passed. And the same History informs us there was a Difficulty in conforming to them; and the Reason of this Difficulty is explained in a Letter of the General Assembly to their Agent, quoted in the following Words, "They apprehended them to be an Invasion of the Rights, Liberties and Properties of the Subjects of his Majesty in the Colony, *they not being represented in Parliament*, and according to the usual Sayings of the Learned in the Law, the Laws of England were bounded within the four Seas, *and did not reach America*: However as his Majesty had signified his Pleasure that those Acts should be observed in the Massachusetts, they had made Provision by a Law of the Colony, that they should be strictly attended." Which Provision by a Law of their own would have been superfluous, if they had admitted the supreme Authority of Parliament. In short, by the same History it appears that those Acts of Parliament as such were disregarded; and the following Reason is given for it; "It seems to have been a *general* Opinion that Acts of Parliament had no other Force, than what they derived from Acts made by the General Court to establish and confirm them."

But still further to show the Sense of our Ancestors respecting this Matter, we beg Leave to recite some Parts of a Narrative presented to the Lords of Privy Council by Edward Randolph, in the Year 1676, which we find in your Excellency's Collection of Papers lately published. Therein it is declared to be the Sense of the Colony, "that no Law is in Force or Esteem there, but such as are made by the General Court; and therefore it is accounted a Breach of their Privileges, and a Betraying of the Liberties of their Commonwealth, to urge the Observation of the Laws of England." And further, "That no Oath shall be urged or required to be taken by any Person, but such Oath as the General Court hath considered, allowed and required." And further, "there is no Notice taken of the Act of Navigation, Plantation or any other Laws made in England for the Regulation of Trade." "That the Government would make the World believe they are a free State and do act in all Matters accordingly." Again, "These Magistrates ever reserve to themselves a Power to alter, evade and disannul any Law or

Command, not agreeing with their Humour or the absolute Authority of their Government, acknowledging no Superior." And further, "He (the Governor) freely declared to me, that the Laws made by your Majesty and your Parliament, obligeth them in nothing, but what consists with the Interests of that Colony, that the Legislative Power and Authority is and abides in them *solely*." And in the same Mr. Randolph's Letter to the Bishop of London, July 14, 1682, he says, "This *Independency* in Government, claimed and daily practised." And your Excellency being *then* sensible that this was the Sense of our Ancestors, in a Marginal Note in the same Collection of Papers observes, that "this," viz. the Provision made for observing the Acts of Trade, "is very extraordinary, for this Provision was an Act of the Colony declaring the Acts of Trade shall be in Force there." Although Mr. Randolph was very unfriendly to the Colony, yet as his Declarations are concurrent with those recited from your Excellency's History, we think they may be admitted for the Purpose for which they are now brought.

Thus we see, from your Excellency's History and Publications, the Sense our Ancestors had of the Jurisdiction of Parliament under the first Charter. Very different from that which your Excellency *in your Speech* apprehends it to have been.

It appears by Mr. Neal's History of New-England, that the Agents who had been employed by the Colony to transact its Affairs in England at the Time when the present Charter was granted, among other Reasons gave the following for their Acceptance of it, viz. "The General Court has with the King's Approbation as much Power in New-England, as the King and Parliament have in England; they have all English Privileges, and can be touched by *no Law*, and by no Tax but of their own making." This is the earliest Testimony that can be given of the Sense our Predecessors had of the Supreme Authority of Parliament under the present Charter. And it plainly shows, that they, who having been freely conversant with those who framed the Charter, must have well understood the Design and Meaning of it, supposed that the Terms in our Charter "full Power and Authority," intended and were considered as a *sole* and exclusive Power, and that there was no "Reserve in the Charter to the Authority of Parliament, to bind the Colony" by any Acts whatever.

Soon after the Arrival of the Charter, viz. in 1692, your Excellency's History informs us, "the first Act" of this Legislative was a Sort of Magna Charta, asserting and setting forth their general Privileges, and this Clause was among the rest, "No Aid, Tax, Tallage, Assessment, Custom, Loan, Benevolence, or Imposition whatever, shall be laid, assess'd, impos'd or levied on any of their Majesty's Subjects, or their Estates, on any Pretence whatever, but by the Act and Consent of the Governor, Council and Representatives of the People assembled in General Court." And though this Act was disallowed, it serves to show the Sense which the General Assembly contemporary with the granting the Charter had of their sole and exclusive Right to Legislate for the Colony. The History says, "the other Parts of the Act were copied from Magna Charta;" by which we may conclude that the Assembly then construed the Words "not repugnant to the Laws," to mean, conformable to the fundamental Principles of the English Constitution. And it is observable that the Lords of Privy Council, so lately as in the Reign of Queen Anne, when several Laws enacted by the General Assembly, were laid before her Majesty for her Allowance, interpreted the Words in this Charter, "not repugnant to the Laws of England," by the Words "as nearly as conveniently may be agreeable to the Laws and Statutes of England." And her Majesty was pleased to disallow those Acts, not because they were repugnant to any Law or Statute of England, made expressly to refer to the Colony; but because divers Persons, by Virtue thereof, were punished without being tried by their Peers in the ordinary "Courts of Law," and "by the ordinary Rules and known Methods of Justice;" contrary to the express Terms of Magna Charta, which was a Statute in Force at the Time of granting the Charter, and declaratory of the Rights and Liberties of the Subjects within the Realm.

You are pleased to say, that "our Provincial or Local Laws have in numerous Instances had Relation to Acts of Parliament made to respect the Plantations and this Colony in particular." The Authority of the Legislature, says the same Author who is quoted by your Excellency, "does not extend so far as the Fundamentals of the Constitution." "They ought to consider the Fundamental Laws as sacred, if the Nation has not in very express Terms, given them the Power to change them. For the

Constitution of the State ought to be fixed: And since that was
first established by the Nation, which afterwards trusted certain Persons with the Legislative Power, the fundamental Laws
are excepted from their Commission." Now the Fundamentals
of the Constitution of this Province are stipulated in the Charter; the Reasoning therefore in this Case holds equally good.
Much less then ought any Acts or Doings of the General Assembly, however numerous, to neither of which your Excellency has pointed us, which barely relate to Acts of Parliament
made to respect the Plantations in general, or this Colony in
particular, to be taken as an Acknowledgment of this People,
or even of the Assembly, which inadvertently passed those
Acts, that we are subject to the Supreme Authority of Parliament. And with still less Reason are the Decisions in the Executive Courts to determine this Point. If they have adopted that
"as Part of the Rule of Law," which in Fact is not, it must be
imputed to Inattention or Error in Judgment, and cannot
justly be urged as an Alteration or Restriction of the Legislative Authority of the Province.

Before we leave this Part of your Excellency's Speech, we
would observe, that the great Design of our Ancestors, in leaving the Kingdom of England, was to be freed from a Subjection to its spiritual Laws and Courts, and to worship God
according to the Dictates of their Consciences. Your Excellency
in your History observes, that their Design was "to obtain for
themselves and their Posterity the Liberty of worshipping God
in such Manner as appeared to them most agreeable to the
sacred Scriptures." And the General Court themselves declared in 1651, that "seeing just Cause to fear the Persecution of
the then Bishops, and High Commission for not conforming
to the Ceremonies then pressed upon the Consciences of those
under their Power, they thought it their safest Course, to get
to this Outside of the World, out of their View and *beyond
their Reach.*" But if it had been their Sense, that they were still
to be subject to the supreme Authority of Parliament, they
must have known that their Design might and probably would
be frustrated; that the Parliament, especially considering the
Temper of those Times, might make what ecclesiastical Laws
they pleased, expressly to refer to them, and place them in the
same Circumstances with Respect to religious Matters, to be

relieved from which was the Design of their Removal. And we would add, that if your Excellency's Construction of the Clause in our present Charter is just, another Clause therein, which provides for Liberty of Conscience for all Christians except Papists, may be rendered void by an Act of Parliament made to refer to us, requiring a Conformity to the Rites and Mode of Worship in the Church of England or any other.

Thus we have endeavoured to shew the Sense of the People of this Colony under both Charters; and if there have been in any late Instances a Submission to Acts of Parliament, it has been in our Opinion, rather from Inconsideration or a Reluctance at the Idea of contending with the Parent State, than from a Conviction or Acknowledgment of the Supreme Legislative Authority of Parliament.

Your Excellency tells us, "you know of no Line that can be drawn between the Supreme Authority of Parliament and the total Independence of the Colonies." If there be no such Line, the Consequence is, either that the Colonies are the Vassals of the Parliament, or, that they are totally independent. As it cannot be supposed to have been the Intention of the Parties in the Compact, that we should be reduced to a State of Vassallage, the Conclusion is, that it was their Sense, that we were thus Independent. "It is impossible, your Excellency says, that there should be "two independent Legislatures in one and the same State." May we not then further conclude, that it was their Sense that the Colonies were by their Charters made distinct States from the Mother Country? Your Excellency adds, "For although there may be but one Head, the King, yet the two Legislative Bodies will make two Governments as distinct as the Kingdoms of England and Scotland before the Union." Very true, may it please your Excellency; and if they interfere not with each other, what hinders but that being united in one Head and common Sovereign, they may live happily in that Connection and mutually support and protect each other? Notwithstanding all the Terrors which your Excellency has pictured to us as the Affects of a total Independence, there is more Reason to dread the Consequences, of absolute uncontrouled Supreme Power, whether of a Nation or a Monarch; than those of a total Independence. It would be a Misfortune "to know by Experience, the Difference between the Liberties of an English Colonist and those of a Spanish, French and Dutch: And since the British Parliament has passed an Act which is executed even with Rigour, though not voluntarily submitted to, for raising a Revenue and appropriating the same without the Consent of the People who pay it, and have claimed a Power of making such Laws as they please to order and govern us, your Excellency will excuse us in asking, whether you do not think we already experience too much of such a Difference, and have not Reason to fear we shall soon be reduced to a worse Situation than that of the Colonies of France, Spain or Holland.

If your Excellency expects to have the Line of Distinction between the Supreme Authority of Parliament, and the total Independence of the Colonies drawn by us, we would say it would be an arduous Undertaking; and of very great Importance to all the other Colonies: And therefore, could we conceive of such a Line, we should be unwilling to propose it, without their Consent in Congress.

To conclude, These are great and profound Questions. It is the Grief of this House, that by the ill Policy of a late injudicious Administration, America has been driven into the Contemplation of them. And we cannot, but express our Concern, that your Excellency by your Speech has reduced us to the unhappy Alternative, either of appearing by our Silence to acquiesce in your Excellency's Sentiments, or of thus freely discussing this Point.

After all that we have said, we would be far from being understood to have in the least abated that just Sense of Allegiance which we owe to the King of Great-Britain, our rightful Sovereign: And should the People of this Province be left to the free and full Exercise of all the Liberties and Immunities granted to them by Charter, there would be no Danger of an Independance on the Crown. Our Charters reserve great Power to the Crown in its Representative, fully sufficient to balance, analogous to the English Constitution, all the Liberties and Privileges granted to the People. All this your Excellency knows full well—And whoever considers the Power and Influence, in all their Branches, reserved by our Charter to the Crown, will be far from thinking that the Commons of this Province are too Independent.

On the Independence of the Judges No. IV

To the PRINTERS.

One Thing at one Time.   DE WITT.

The question is, in the present state of the controversy, according to my apprehension of it, whether, by the common law of England, the judges of the King's bench and common bench, had estates for life, in their offices, determinable on misbehaviour, and determinable also on the demise of the crown? General Brattle still thinks they had, I, cannot yet find reasons to think so: And as, whether they had, or had not, is the true question between us. I will endeavour to confine myself to it, without wandering.—

Now in order to pursue my enquiry, regularly, it is necessary, to determine with some degree of precision, what is to be understood by the terms "common law"—Out of the Mercian laws, the laws of the West Saxons, and the Danish law, King Edward the confessor extracted one uniform digest of laws, to be observed throughout the whole kingdom, which seems to have been no more than a fresh promulgation of Alfreds code or domebook, with such improvements as the experience of a century and an half had suggested, which is now unhappily lost. This collection is of higher antiquity than memory or history can reach. They have been used time out of mind, or for a time whereof the memory of man runneth not to the contrary. General customs which are the universal rule of the whole kingdom, form the common law in its stricter and more usual signification. This is that law, which determines that there shall be four superior courts of record, the chancery, the king's bench, the common pleas, and the exchequer, among a multitude of other doctrines that are not set down in any written statute or ordinance, but depend merely upon immemorial usage, that is upon common law for their support. Judicial decisions are the principal and most authoritative evidence, that can be given, of the existence of such a custom as shall form a part of the common law. The law, and the opinion of the judge are not always convertible terms, tho' it is a general rule that the decisions of courts of justice are the evidence of what is common law. See 1 Black. Com. 65, 66, 67, 68, 69, 70, 71, 72, 73. I have endeavoured to ascertain what is meant by the common law of England, and the method of determining all questions concerning it from Blackstone. Let us now see what is said upon the same subject by justice Fortescue Aland in the preface to his reports.

Our judges, says he, do not determine according to their Princes or their own arbitrary will and pleasure, but according to the settled and established rules, and ancient customs of the nation, approved for many successions of ages. King Alfred who began to reign in 871, Magnus Juris Anglicani Conditor, the great founder of the laws of England, with the advice of his wise men, collected out of the laws of Ina, Offa, and Æthelbert, such as were the best, and made them to extend equally to the whole nation, and therefore very properly called them, the common law of England, because these laws were now first of all made common to the whole English nation. This jus commune, jus publicum, or Folcright, i.e. the peoples right, set down in one code, was probably the same with the doombook or liber judicialis, which is referred to in all the subsequent laws of the Saxon Kings, and was the book that they determined causes by. And in the next reign, that of Edward the elder, the King commands all his judges to give judgment to all the people of England according to the doom book. And it is from this origin that our common law judges fetch that excellent usage of determining causes, according to the settled and established rules of law, and that they have acted up to this rule above eight hundred years together, and continue to do so to this day. Edward the confessor was afterwards but the restorer of the common law, founded by Alfred, and William the conqueror confirms and proclaims these to be the laws of England, to be kept and observed under grievous penalties, and took an oath to keep them inviolable himself. King Henry the first promised to observe them—King Stephen, King Henry the second and Richard the first confirmed them. King John swore to restore them. King Henry 3d confirmed them. Magna Charta was founded on them. And King Edward the first in parliament confirmed them—page 3, 4, 5, 6, 7, 8, 9, 10.

Now I apprehend General Brattle's opinion to be, that the common law of England, the birthright of every subject, or in

the language of the Saxons, the Folcright, determines, the
judges of the King's bench, and common pleas to have estates
for life in their offices, determinable only on misbehaviour, or
the demise of the Crown. And this I suppose was the meaning
of Sir Thomas Powis, when he said, "I take it, *by the common
law*, and the *ancient constitution of the kingdom*, all officers of
courts of justice, &c. were in for their lives, &c. not only my
lords the judges of the courts in Westminster Hall, were anciently, as they now are since this revolution, quam diu se bene
gesserint."

I have never expressed any disrespect to the character of Sir
Thomas Powis, and I have no disposition, to harbour any: It is
enough for me to say, that these expressions were used by him,
when arguing a cause for his client at the bar, not when he was
determining a cause as a judge; that they were entirely unnecessary for the support of his cause, which was a very good one,
let these expressions be true, or otherwise, i.e. whether the
judges, were anciently, in for their lives, or only at pleasure:
that they depend wholly upon his affirmation, or rather his
opinion, without the colour or pretence of an authority to
support them; and that I really believe them to be untrue. And
I must add, it appears to me, extraordinary, that a gentleman,
educated under that great Gamaliel, Mr. Reed, should ever ad-
duce the simple dictum, of a council at the bar, uttered ar-
guendo, and as an ornament to his discourse too, rather than
any pertinent branch of his reasoning, as evidence of a point
"settled and determined by the greatest sages of the law formerly and more lately." Does Sir Thomas Powis produce, the
doom book itself, in support of his doctrine? That was irrecov-
erably lost for ages before he had a being? Does he produce
any judicial decision ancient or modern, to prove this opinion?
No such thing pretended,—Does he produce, any legal authority, a Hengham, Britton, Fleta, Fortescue, Coke, or any
Antiquarian, Mathew Paris, Dugdale, Lambard, or any other,
or even the single opinion of one historian, to give a colour to
his doctrine? No such matter. Nay I must enquire further, can
general Brattle, draw from any of these sources, a single Iota
to support this opinion? But in order to show for the present
the improbability that any such authority will be found, let us
look a little into history. Mr. Rapin, in his dissertation on the

government of the anglo Saxons, vol. 1. 157. says, "one of the most considerable of the kings prerogatives was the power of appointing the earls, viscounts, *judges* and other officers, civil and military, *very probably, it was in the king's power to change these officers, according to his pleasure,* of which we meet with several instances in history." By this it appears to have been Mr. Rapin's opinion, that very probably, the kings, under the ancient Saxon constitution, had power to change the judges, according to their pleasure. I would not be understood however to lay any great stress, on the opinions of historians, and compilers of antiquities, because it must be confessed, that the Saxon constitution, is involved in much obscurity, and that the monarchical and democratical factions in England, by their opposite endeavors, to make the Saxon constitutions, swear for their respective systems, have much increased the difficulty of determining to the satisfaction of the world, what that constitution in many important particulars, was. Yet Mr. Rapin certainly was not of that monarchical faction, his byass, if he had any, was the other way, and therefore his concession, makes the more in my favour.

Mr. Hume in his "feudal and Anglo Norman government and manners" v.1. quar. 412. says "the business of the court was wholly managed by the chief justiciary, and the Law Barons, who were men appointed by the king, *and wholly at his disposal.*" And since I am now upon Hume, it may be proper to mention the case of Hubert deBurgo, who while he enjoyed his authority, had an entire ascendency over Henry the Third, and was loaded with honours and favours beyond any other subject, and by *an unusual concession* was made chief justiciary of England for life. 2. Hume 162. Upon this I reason thus, if his being made justiciary for life, was an "unusual concession," it could not be, by the immemorial, uninterrupted usage and custom, which is the criterion of common law. And the very next words of Hume shew, how valid and effectual this grant, of the office for life was then esteemed, "yet Henry, says Hume, in a sudden caprice, *threw off* this faithful minister," which implies, that he was discarded and displaced in both his capacities because the summus justiciarius, or chief justiciary, was in those reigns, supream regent of the kingdom, and first minister of state, as well as of the law. And this seems to shew that the grant for life, was void and not binding on the King in the sense of those times, ancient as they were in 1231. This summus justiciarius, is the officer, whose original commission, I gave the public, from lord Coke in my first paper, which was expressly during pleasure. And my lord Coke's account of the change of the chief justice's commission and authority may receive some additional light from lord Gilbert's historical view of the court of exchequer, page 7, towards the latter end of the Norman period; the power of the justiciar was broken, so that the Aula Regis, which was before one great court only distinguished by several offices, and all ambulatory with the King before Magna Charta, was divided into four distinct courts, Chancery, Exchequer, King's Bench, and Common Pleas. The justiciary was laid aside, lest he should get into the throne, as Capet and Pippin, who were justiciars in France, had done there. See also Gilbert's history and practice of the high court of chancery.

Now from the exorbitant powers and authority of these justiciaries arises a proof from the frame of the government and the ballance of the estates that the office in those ages was always considered as dependent on the pleasure of the King, because the jealousy, between the Kings and Nobles, or between the monarchical and aristocratical factions, during the whole Norman period, were incessant and unremitted, and therefore it may be depended on that Kings never would have come into the method, of granting such an office usually for life. For such a grant, if had been made, and been valid, must have cost the grantor his throne, as it made the justiciar, independent of the King, and a much more powerful man than himself—and if during the whole Norman period and quite down to the death of Sir Edward Coke, a course of almost six hundred years, the offices of judges were held during pleasure, what becomes of the title to them for life, which General Brattle sets up, by immemorial, uninterrupted usage or common law?

Sir Thomas Powis, however, has not determined, whether, by the *ancient* constitution of the kingdom, he meant, under the Norman, or the Saxon period; and in order to shew the improbability, that the judges held their offices during good behaviour in either of those periods, I must beg the pardon of

your readers, if I lead them into ages, manners and government, more ancient and barbarous, than any mentioned before.
Our Saxon ancestors, were one of those enterprizing northern
nations, who made inroads upon the provinces of the Roman
empire, and carried with them wherever they went, the customs, maxims and manners of the feudal system: And although
when they intermingled with the ancient Britons, they shook
off some part of the feudal fetters, yet they never disengag'd
themselves from the whole. They retained a vast variety of the
regalia principis, of the feudal system, from whence most
branches of the present prerogatives of our kings are derived.
And among other regalia the creation, and annihilation of
judges, was an important branch. For evidence of this we must
look into the feudal law. It was in consequence of this prerogative, that the courts were usually, held in the aula regis, and
often in the King's presence, who often heard and determined
causes in person, and in those ages the justiciary was only a
substitute or deputy to the king; whose authority ceased entirely in the King's presence. This part of the prerogative, has a
long time ago been divested from the crown, and it has been
determined that, the King has delegated all his authority to his
judges. The power of the King in the Saxon period, over the
judges, was absolute enough however, and they sometimes
treated them with very little ceremony. Alfred himself is said in
the mirror of justices to have hang'd up 44 of his judges in one
year, for misdemeanors.

     To some of these facts and principles, Bracton is a witness.
"Dictum est, says he, de ordinaria, jurisdictene quæ pertinet,
ad regem; consequenter dicendum est de jurisdictione dele-
gata ubi quis est seipso nullam habet authoritatem, sed ab illo
sibi commissam cum ipse qui delegat non sufficiat per se
omnes, causes, sive jurisdictiones terminare et si ipse dom, rex
ad singulus causas terminandas non sufficiat, ut levior fit illi labor, in plures personas, partito onere, eligere debet de regno
suo viros sapientes et timentes deum. Item justiciariorum
quidam sunt capitales generales, perpetui et majores a latere
regis residentes qui omnium aliorum corrigere tenetur, jujurias
et errores, sicut etiam alii perpetui certo loco residentes sicut
in banco. Qui omnes jurisdictionem habere in cipiunt praestito
sacramento. Et quam vis quidam eorum perpetui sunt ut vide-

tur, finitur tamen eorum jurisdictio multis modis. v.g. mortuo eo qui delegavit, &c. *Item cum delegans revocaverit jurisdic-tionem.*" &c. Bracton. chap. 10. Lib. 3.

Serjeant Levenz says, "if any judicial or ministerial office be granted to any man to hold, so long as he behaves himself well in the office, that is an estate for life, unless he loose it for misbehaviour. So was Sir John Waller's case, as to the office of chief baron of the exchequer". To all this I agree, provided it is an office, that by custom, i.e. immemorial usage, or common law, (as that of the chief baron of the exchequer was,) or by an express act of parliament, (as that of clerk of the peace in the case of Harcourt against Fox was) has been granted in that manner, but not otherwise. And therefore these words have no operation at all against me. But the serjeant goes on, "And so was Justice Archer's case in the time of King Charles the second. He was made a Judge of the common pleas quam diu se bene gesserit, and tho' he was displaced as far as they could, yet he continued judge of that court to the time of his death; and his name was used in all the fines and other records of the court:"—General Brattle thinks these words are full in his favour, and he can't reconcile this patent to Judge Archer, with the history of Charles the second's reign &c. We shall presently see, if a way to reconcile it, cannot be discovered: But before I come to this attempt, as it is my desire to lay before the public, every thing I know of, which favours General Brattle's hypothesis, and to assist his argument to the utmost of my power, I will help him to some other authorities, which seem to corroborate, Serjeant Levinz's saying. And the first is Justice Fortescue Aland, Rep. 394. "Justice Archer was removed from the common pleas, but his patent being quam diu se bene gesserit, he refused to surrender his patent, without a scire facias, and continued justice, tho' prohibited to set there. And in his place Sir William Ellis was sworn." The next is, Sir Tho's Ray. 217. "This last vacation Justice Archer was removed from sitting in the court of common pleas, pro quibusdam causis mihi incognitis; but the judge having his patent to be a judge, quam diu se bene gesserit, refused to surrender his patent without a scire facias, and continued justice of that court, tho' prohibited to sit there, and in his place, Sir William Ellis, kt. was sworn."

But will any man from these authorities conclude, that King Charles the second, had power by the common law to grant Judge Archer an estate for life in his office? If he had, how could he be prohibited to sit? How came Justice Ellis to be sworn in his stead? Was not the admission of Ellis, by his brother judges, an acknowledgment of the King's authority?— Will any man conclude, from these authorities, that it had before been the custom time out of mind, for Kings to grant patents to the judges, quam diu se bene gesserint?—If we look into Rushworth 1366, we shall find some part of this mystery unriddled. "After passing these votes against the judges, and transmitting of them unto the house of Peers and their concurring with the house of commons therein, an address was made unto the King shortly after, that his Majesty for the future would not make any judge by patent during pleasure, but that they may hold their places hereafter quam diu se bene gesserint, and his Majesty did readily grant the same, and in his speech to both houses of parliament at the time of giving his royal assent to two bills, one to take away the high commission court, and the other the court of star-chamber, and regulating the power of the council table, he hath this passage—If you consider what I have done this parliament, discontents will not sit in your hearts; for I hope you remember that I have granted that the judges hereafter shall hold their places, quam diu se bene gesserint—And likewise his gracious Majesty King Charles the second observed the same rule and method in granting patents to judges, quam diu se bene gesserint, as appears upon record in the rolls (viz.) to Serjeant Hide, to lord chief justice of the King's bench, Sir Orlando Bridgeman to be lord chief baron, and afterwards to be lord chief justice of the common pleas, to Sir Robert Foster and others; Mr. Serjeant Archer now living (notwithstanding his removal) still enjoys his patent, being quam diu se bene gesserit, and receives a share in the profits of that court, as to fines and other proceedings, by virtue of his said patent, and his name is used in those fines, &c. as a judge of that court." This address was in 1640.

This address of the two houses of parliament, which was in 1640, was made in consequence of a general jealousy conceived of the judges, and the general odium which had fallen upon them, for the opinion they gave in the case of ship money, and other cases, and because there had been not long before changes and removals in the benches; to mention only one, Sir Randolph Crew not shewing so much zeal for the advancement of the loan, as the King was desirous he should, was removed from his place of lord chief justice, and Sir Nicholas Hyde succeeded in his room. See Rushworth, 420. 2. Rush. Append. 266.—And King Charles in 1640 began to believe the discontents of his subjects to be a serious affair, and think it necessary, to do something, to appease them.

But will it do to say, that he had power to give away the prerogative of the crown, that had been established in his ancestors for 800 years, and no man can say how many centuries longer, without an act of parliament? against the express words of Lord Coke, which the General thanks me for quoting. "It is a rule in law that ancient offices must be granted in such forms and in such manner as they have used to be, unless the alteration was by authority of parliament."

As to King Charles the IId, his character is known to have been a man of pleasure and dissipation, who left most kinds of business to his ministers, and particularly in the beginning of his reign, to my Lord Clarendon, who had perhaps a large share in procuring that concession from Charles the Ist, and therefore chose to continue it under the second.

But notwithstanding all this, Charles the IId, soon discovered that by law, his father's concession and his own, had not divested him of the power of removing judges, even those to whom he had given patents, quam diu se bene gesserint, and he actually re-assumed his prerogative, displaced Judge Archer and many others in the latter end of his reign, and so did his successor, see Skinner's reports and Ray. 251. These examples shew that those Kings did not consider these concessions as legally binding on them. They also shew, that the judges in Westminster-Hall were of the same mind, otherwise they would not have admitted the new judges in the room of those displaced; and it seems that even the judges themselves who were then displaced, Judge Archer himself did not venture to demand his place, which he might have done, if he had an estate for life in his office. Nay, it may be affirmed, that the house of Commons themselves, were of the same mind, for in the year 1680, in the reign of Charles the IId, after the removal

of Archer and many other judges, the commons brought in a
bill, to make the office of judge during good behaviour: see 8.
Hume. 143. Now I think they would not have taken this
course, if they had thought Archer had an estate for life in his
office, but would have voted his removal illegal, and would
have impeached the other judges for admitting another in his
room.

Archers "continuing judge," and "receiving fees for fines"
and "his name's being used in the fines," I conjecture are to be
accounted for in this manner. He refused to surrender his
patent, without a scire facias. The King would not have a scire
facias brought, because, that would occasion a solemn hearing,
and much speculation, clamour and heat, which, he chose to
avoid; and as his patent remained unsurrendered and uncan-
celled, and as by law there might be more judges of the common pleas than four, and therefore the appointment of
another judge, might not be a supersedeas to Archer, they
might think it safest to join his name in the fines, and give him
a share in the fees. And no doubt, this might be done in some
instances to keep up the appearance of a claim to the place,
and with a design to provoke the King's servants and friends to
bring a sci. fa. and so occasion an odium on the administrations, and hasten on a revolution.

I have hazarded these conjectures, unnecessarily, for it is incumbent upon General Brattle to shew from good authorities,
for the affirmative side of the issue is with him, that, by common law the judges had estates for life in their offices. In order
to do this, he ought to shew that the King, at common law, i.e.
from time immemorial, granted patents to these judges during
good behaviour, or that he the King had his election to grant
them either durante beneplacito or quam diu se bene gesserit,
as he pleased. Nay, it is incumbent on him to shew that a
patent, without either of these clauses, conveys an estate for
life. None of these things has he done, or can he do.

It was never denied, nor doubted by me that a grant made
in pursuance of immemorial custom, or of an act of parliament, to a man to hold so long as he should behave himself
well, would give him an estate for life. The unanimous judgment of the court in that case of Harcourt against Fox proves
this. But then, in that case an express act of parliament impow-

ered the custos retulorum, to constitute a clerk of the peace for so long time as he should behave himself well. Nor have I any doubt that the patents to the Barons of the exchequer, which are by immemorial usage, quam diu se bene gesserint, convey to them an estate for life: but my difficulty lies here, no custom, no immemorial usage, no act of parliament enabled the King, to grant patents to the judges of Kings bench and common pleas, expressly quam diu se bene gesserint; and there- fore, if Lord Coke's rule is right "that ancient offices must be granted in such forms and in such manner as they have used to be, unless the alteration be by authority of parliament,"—the Kings grant, at common law, to a judge of King's bench or common pleas, of his office for life in terms, or during good behaviour, which is tantamount, would have been void,—void I mean quoad an estate for life or good behaviour, but good as an estate at will, and I conceive when we read that the King cant make a Lord Chancellor for life, but that such a grant would be void, the meaning is, that the habendum for life or good behaviour shall be void; but that this shall not vitiate the other parts of the patents, but that they shall convey such es- tate, and such estate only, as the King had power by custom, or by statute to grant. I don't suppose that the writ to Lord Holt, or the patents to his brothers in the reign of King William were void, but I fear that had the King seen fit to have removed them, by writ, it would have been legally in his power, not- withstanding that clause in their commissions.

JOHN ADAMS

Boston Gazette, February 1, 1773

On the Independence of the Judges No. VII

To the PRINTERS,
In all General Brattle's researches hitherto, aided and assisted as he has been by mine, we have not been able to discover, either that the judges at common law had their commissions quam diu se bene gesserint, or for life, or that the crown had authority to grant them in that manner. Let us now examine

and see, whether estates for life, determinable only on misbehaviour or the demise of the Crown, can be derived to the
Massachusetts Judges from any other source? If they can, they
must be from the Charter, from the nomination and appointment of the Governor with the advice and consent of council,
from the judges commissions, or from the law of the province;
from one, or more, or all these together, they must be derived,
if from any thing. For as the judges of the King's bench and
common bench, are in by the King's grant or by custom or
both, as justices of oyer and terminer, goal delivery, &c. are in
by the King's grant as the clerk of the peace, is said by Lord
Holt in the case of Harcourt against Fox, to be in by the act of
parliament 1 Wm. and Mary, and the officers whose places are
in the gift of the chief justice, are in by the custom, so the Massachusetts Justices are in by one or more or all of the four titles
mentioned above.

And here the first inquiry is, what is meant by an officer's
being in by custom or by statute, &c.? And I suppose the true
answer to be this, He is invested with his powers, is obligated
to his duties, and holds his estate by that custom or statute,
&c. And the next inquiry is, by what are our judges in? that is
by what act, or instrument, are they cloathed with their power,
bound to their duties, and intitled to their estates?

By the Charter, there are no certain powers given them, no
certain duties prescribed to them, nor any certain estate conferred upon them. The Charter impowers the Governor, with
advice and consent of Council, to nominate and appoint them,
that is, to designate the persons; nothing more.

There are three sorts of officers in the charter. Those reserved to the nomination of the King, as the Governor, Lt.
Governor, Secretary, and Judge of Admiralty. And it is not limited how long they shall continue, excepting the first Secretary
Addington, and he is constituted expressly during pleasure;
and the duration of all these officers, has been limited ever
since, expressly by their commissions, to be during pleasure.
The second sort of officers in the charter are those which the
General Court are to name and settle, and the charter expressly says they shall be named and settled annually, so that
their duration is ascertained in the charter. The third sort are
those which the Governor with advice and consent of Council,

is to nominate and appoint—And there are no duties imposed, no powers given, no estates limited to these in the charter. But the power of erecting judicatories, stating the rights and duties, and limiting the estates of all officers, to the council and courts of justice belonging, is given to the General Court, and the charter expressly requires, that all these courts shall be held in the King's name, and that all officers shall take the oaths and subscribe the declarations appointed to be taken and subscribed, instead of the oaths of allegiance and supremacy. And it is in observance of this requisition in the charter, viz. That all courts shall be held in the King's name, that the Judges commissions are in the King's name. The governor and council designate a person, not to be the governor and council's justice, but the King's justice, not of the governor and council's court, but of the King's court. And the law of the province requires that the Justices of the Superiour Court should have a particular species of evidence, of their nomination and appointment, viz. a commission, otherwise as General Brattle says, a nomination and appointment recorded, would be enough. And here I cannot refuse myself the pleasure of observing that the opinion of Mr. Read, concurred with, and I humbly conceive was founded on these principles. Governor Belcher perswaded the council, that upon the appointment of a new governor, it was necessary to renew all civil commissions, and the same thing was proposed in council by his successor: But Mr. Read, who was then a member of the council, brought such arguments against the practice, that the majority of the board refused to consent to it, and it never has been done since. 2. Mass. Hist. 375, 6. This was an important service rendered his country by that great lawyer and upright man, and it was grounded upon the principles I have mentioned. Civil officers are not nominated to be the governor's officers, they don't hold their courts nor commissions in his name, but in the King's, and therefore governors may come and go, as long as the same King reigns, and they continue the same officers. And in conformity to the same principles, upon the demise of the crown, the commissions must be renewed, because the charter requires they should be in the King's name. The words are, "in the name of us, our heirs and successors" and therefore upon the accession of an heir apparent, i.e. after 6 months from his accession, the commissions must be renewed, otherwise they cannot be held in his name, nor the requisition in the charter complied with. I said in 6 months, because the statute of 6 Ann, c. 7 ss. 8. not the statute of the present King's reign (as General Brattle supposes) has provided that no office, place or employment, civil or military, within the kingdoms of Great-Britain or Ireland, dominion of Wales, town of Berwick upon Tweed, Isles of Jersey, Guernsey, Alderney or Sarke, or any of her Majesty's plantations, shall become void, by reason of the demise or death of her Majesty, her heirs or successors, Kings or Queens of this realm; but every person, &c. shall continue in their respective offices, places and employments, for the space of six months next after such demise or death, unless sooner removed and discharged by the next in succession as aforesaid.

But to return, our Judges are not in merely by nomination and appointment of the Governor and Council, because they are not bound to their duties, nor vested with their powers by the charter immediately nor by that nomination and appointment. They are not in, by the grant of the king merely or by their commissions, because their court is not erected, their powers are not derived, their duties are not imposed, and no estate is limitted by that grant. But their commission is nothing more than a particular kind of evidence, required by the province law, to shew their conformity to the charter in holding their court in the king's name, and to shew their nomination and appointment, or the designation of their persons to those offices by the governor and council.

It is the law of the province, which gives them all the powers and imposes upon them all the duties of the courts of king's bench, common pleas, and exchequer; but it does not limit to them any estate, in their offices. If it had said as it ought to have said, that they shall be commissionated quam diu se bene gesserint, they would have been so commissionated, and would have held estates for life in their offices.

Whence then can General Brattle claim for them an estate for life in their offices? No such estate is given them by the charter, by their nomination and appointment, by their commissions, nor by the law of the province.

I cannot agree with General Brattle, that "supposing a corrupt Governor and a corrupt Council, whether the words in the commission are so long as the Governor and Council please, or during good behaviour, will just come to the same thing." Because in the one case a judge may be removed, suddenly and silently, in a Council of seven only; in the other, not without an hearing and tryal, and an opportunity to defend himself before a fuller board, knowing his accuser and the accusation: And this would be a restraint even to corruption itself, for in the most abandoned state of it, there is always some regard shewn to appearances.

It is no part of my plan, in this rencounter with the General, to make my Compliments to his Excellency Governor Hutchinson and the present Council: But I may be permitted, to say that the Governor differs in sentiment, from his Major General, about the power of the Governor and Council. In a note in the second volume of the history of the Massachusetts-Bay, we have these words, "The freedom and independency of the judges of England, is always enumerated among the excellencies of the constitution. The Massachusetts judges are far from independent. In Mr. Belcher's administration, they were peculiarly dependent upon the Governor. Before and since they have been dependent upon the Assembly for their salary granted annually, which sometimes has been delayed, sometimes diminished, and rarely escapes being a subject of debate and altercation. The dependency in Mr. Belcher's time, is attributed to the pusillanimity of the Council, as no appointment can be made without their advice. And we are told too that the emoluments of a Massachusetts Counsellor are very small, and can be but a poor temptation to sacrifice virtue."

All this however has been found in many instances, by experience to be but a poor consolation to the people. Four gentleman, a majority of seven, have since Mr. Belcher's day, been found, under the influence of the same pusillanimity, and for the sake of those emoluments, small as they are, or some other emoluments, have been seen to sacrifice virtue. And it is highly probable men will be composed of the same clay, fifty years hence, as they were forty years ago, and therefore they ought not to be left exposed to the same temptations.

The next thing observable in the General's last publication, is this, "The parliament grants" (says he) "no salaries to the judges of England, the King settles the salaries and pays his judges, out of the civil list." How is it possible this gentleman should make such mistakes? What is the King's civil list? Whence do the monies come to discharge it? Is it a mine of gold? A quarry of precious stones? The King pays the judges! Whence does he get the money? The Crown, without the gift of the people is as poor as any of the subjects. But to dwell no longer upon an error so palpable and gross, let us look into the book. The act of parliament of the 12 and 13 Wm. 3d, expressly enacts, that the judges salaries shall be ascertained and established, meaning no doubt at the sums, which had then usually been allowed them. And another act of parliament was made in the 32d year of George the second, c. 35. augmenting the salaries of the puisne judges five hundred pounds each, and granting and appropriating certain stamp duties to the payment of it—With what colour of truth then can the General say that parliament grants no salaries, but that the King settles the salaries?

Another thing that follows is more remarkable still. "The act of parliament" (says the General, meaning the late act impowering the Crown to appropriate monies, for the administration of justice, in such colonies, where it shall be most needed) "was made for no other reason than this, that the King might not pay them, (i.e. the judges) out of the civil list, but out of another fund, the revenue." The General seems to have in his mind a notion that the King's civil list is, a magazine of gold and silver, and the Crown a spot where diamonds grow. But I repeat it, the Crown has no riches but from the gifts of the people.

The civil list means an enumeration of the King's civil officers and servants, and the sums usually allowed them as salaries, &c. But the money to discharge these sums is every farthing of it granted by parliament. And without the aid of parliament, the Crown could not pay a porter.

Near the beginning of every reign the civil list revenue is granted by parliament. But are the Massachusetts Judges in the King's civil list? No more than the Massachusetts major-general is. If a minister of state, had taken money from the civil list revenue to pay our Judges, would it not have been a misapplication of the public money? Would it not have been peculation? And in virtuous times, would not that minister have been compelled to refund it out of his own pocket? It is true, a minister, who handles the public money, may apply it to purposes for which it was never intended nor appropriated. He may purchase votes and elections with it, and so he may rob the treasury chests of their guineas, and he has as good a right to do one as the other, and to do either, as to apply monies appropriated to the king's civil list, to the payment of salaries to the Massachusetts Judges.

Without the late act of parliament therefore, as the King could not pay our Judges out of the civil list, because the King can do no wrong, he could not pay them at all, unless he had given them presents out of his privy purse. The act must therefore have been made to enable the King to pay them; with what views of policy, I leave to be conjectured by others.

I am very nearly of a mind with the general, that a lawyer who holds the Judges offices here to be during good behaviour, must do it, upon his principles, because I can see none much more solid to ground such an opinion upon. But I believe his principles appear by this time, not to be infallible.

The General solemnly declares, that Mr. Reed, held this opinion, and upon, his principles. Mr. Reed's opinion deserves great veneration, but not implicit faith; and indeed if it was certain that he held it, what resistance could it make against the whole united torrents of law, records and history? However, we see, by the report, the general was pleased to give the public of Lord Holt's words, that it is possible for him to mistake the words and opinions of a sage; and therefore it is possible he may have mistaken Mr. Reed's words as well as his lordships.

I believe the public is weary of my speculations, and the subject of them. I have bestowed more labour upon General Brattle's harangue in town-meeting, and his writings in the news-paper, than was necessary to shew their Imperfection: I have now done with both—and subscribe myself, your's, General Brattle's, and the Public's well-wisher and very humble Servant,

JOHN ADAMS
Boston Gazette, February 22, 1773

Reply of the Massachusetts House of Representatives to Governor Hutchinson's Second Message

MARTIS, 2 *Die Martii*, A.D. 1773, *Post-Meridiem*
May it please your Excellency,

In your Speech at the Opening of the present Session, your Excellency express'd your Displeasure at some late Proceedings of the Town of *Boston*, and other principal Towns in the Province. And in another Speech to both Houses we have your repeated Exceptions at the same Proceedings as being "unwarrantable," and of a dangerous Nature and Tendency; "against which you thought yourself bound to call upon us to join with you in bearing a proper Testimony." This House have not discovered any Principles advanced by the Town of *Boston*, that are unwarrantable by the Constitution; nor does it appear to us that they have "invited every other Town and District in the Province to adopt their Principles." We are fully convinced that it is our Duty to bear our Testimony against "Innovations of a dangerous Nature and Tendency:" but it is clearly our Opinion, that it is the indisputable Right of all or any of his Majesty's Subjects in this Province, regularly and orderly to meet together to state the Grievances they labor under; and to propose and unite in such constitutional Measures as they shall judge necessary or proper to obtain Redress. This Right has been frequently exercised by his Majesty's Subjects within the Realm; and we do not recollect an Instance, since the happy Revolution, when the two Houses of Parliament have been called upon to discountenance or bear their Testimony against it, in a Speech from the Throne.

Your Excellency is pleased to take Notice of some Things which we "alledge" in our Answer to your first Speech: And the Observation you make, we must confess, is as natural and as undeniably true, as any one that could have been made; that "if our Foundation shall fail us *in every Part of it*, the Fabrick we have rais'd upon it, must certainly fall." You think, this Foundation will fail us; but we wish your Excellency had condescended to a Consideration of what we have "adduced in

Support of our Principles." We might then perhaps have had some Things offered for our Conviction, more than bare Affirmations; which, we must beg to be excused if we say, are far from being sufficient, though they came with your Excellency's Authority, for which however we have a due Regard.

Your Excellency says that "as English Subjects and agreeable to the Doctrine of the Feudal Tenure all our Lands are held mediately or immediately of the Crown." We trust your Excellency does not mean to introduce the Feudal System in it's Perfection; which to use the Words of one of our greatest Historians, was "a State of perpetual War, Anarchy and Confusion; calculated solely for Defence against the Assaults of any foreign Power, but in it's Provision for the interior Order and Tranquility of Society extremely defective." "A Constitution so contradictory to all the Principles that govern Mankind, could never be brought about but by foreign Conquest or native Usurpation:" And a very celebrated Writer calls it "that most iniquitous and absurd Form of Government by which human Nature was so shamefully degraded." This System of Iniquity by a strange Kind of Fatility, "though originally form'd for an Encampment and for Military Purposes only, spread over a great Part of Europe:" and to serve the Purposes of Oppression and Tyranny "was adopted by Princes and wrought into their Civil Constitutions;" and aided by the Canon Law, calculated by the Roman Pontiff, to exalt himself above all that is called God, it prevailed to the almost utter Extinction of Knowledge, Virtue, Religion and Liberty from that Part of the Earth. But from the Time of the Reformation, in Proportion as Knowledge, which then darted its Rays upon the benighted World, increas'd and spread among the People, they grew impatient under this heavy Yoke: And the most virtuous and sensible among them, to whose Stedfastness we in this distant Age and Climate are greatly indebted, were determined to get rid of it: And tho' they have in a great Measure subdued it's Power and Influence in England, they have never yet totally eradicated its Principles.

Upon these Principles the King claimed an absolute Right to and a perfect Estate in all the Lands within his Dominions; but how he came by this absolute Right and perfect Estate is a Mystery which we have never seen unravelled, nor is it our

Business or Design at present to enquire. He granted Parts or Parcels of it to his Friends the great Men, and they granted lesser Parcels to their Tenants: All therefore derived their Right and held their Lands, upon these Principles mediately or immediately of the King; which Mr. *Blackstone* however calls "in Reality a meer Fiction of our English Tenures."

By what Right in Nature and Reason the Christian Princes in Europe claimed the Lands of Heathen People, upon a Discovery made by any of their Subjects, is equally mysterious: Such however was the Doctrine universally prevailing when the Lands in *America* were discovered; but as the People of England upon those Principles held all the Lands they possessed by Grants from the King, and the King had never granted the Lands in America *to them*, it is certain they could have no Sort of Claim to them: Upon the Principles advanced, the Lordship and Dominion like that of the Lands in England, was in the King solely: and a Right from thence accrued to him of disposing such Territories under such Tenure and for such Services to be performed, as the King or Lord thought proper. But how the Grantees *became* Subjects of England, that is the Supreme Authority of the Parliament, your Excellency has not explained to us. We conceive that upon the Feudal Principles all Power is in the King; they afford us no Idea *of Parliament*. "The Lord was in early Times the Legislator and Judge over all his Feudatories," says Judge Blackstone. By the Struggles for Liberty in England from the Days of King John to the last happy Revolution, the Constitution has been gradually changing for the better; and upon the more rational Principles that all Men by Nature are in a State of Equality in Respect of Jurisdiction and Dominion, Power in England has been more equally divided. And thus also in America, though we hold our Lands agreeably to the Feudal Principles of the King; yet our Predecessors wisely took Care to enter into Compact with the King that Power here should also be equally divided agreeable to the original fundamental Principles of the English Constitution, declared in Magna Charta, and other Laws and Statutes of England, made to confirm them.

Your Excellency says, "you can by no Means concede to us that it is now or was when the Plantations were first granted the Prerogative of the Kings of England to constitute a Number of new Governments altogether independent of the Sovereign Authority of the English Empire." By the Feudal Principles upon which you say "all the Grants which have been made of America are founded" "the Constitutions of the Emperor have the Force of Law." If our Government be considered as merely Feudatory, we are subject to the King's absolute Will, and there is no Room for the Authority of Parliament, as the Sovereign Authority of the British Empire. Upon these Principles, what could hinder the King's constituting a Number of Independent Governments in America? That King Charles the First did actually set up a Government in this Colony, conceding to it Powers of making and executing Laws, without any Reservation to the English Parliament, of Authority to make future Laws binding therein, is a Fact which your Excellency has not disproved if you have denied it. Nor have you shewn that the Parliament or Nation objected to it, from whence we have inferred that it was an acknowledged Right. And we cannot conceive, why the King has not the same Right to alienate and dispose of Countries acquired by the Discovery of his Subjects, as he has to "restore upon a Treaty of Peace Countries which have been acquired in War," carried on at the Charge of the Nation; or to "sell and deliver up any Part of his Dominions to a foreign Prince or State, against the General Sense of the Nation" which is "an Act of Power" or Prerogative which your Excellency allows. You tell us that "when any new Countries are discovered by English Subjects, according to the general Law and Usage of Nations, *they become Part of the State.*" The Law of Nations is or ought to be founded on the Law of Reason. It was the saying of Sir Edwin Sandis, in the great Case of the Union of the Realm of Scotland with England, which is applicable to our present Purpose, that "there being no Precedent for this Case in the Law, the Law is deficient; and the Law being deficient, Recourse is to be had to Custom; and Custom being insufficient, we must recur to natural Reason," the greatest of all Authorities, which he adds "is the Law of Nations." The Opinions therefore, and Determinations of the greatest Sages and Judges of the Law in the Exchequer Chamber ought not to be considered as decisive or binding in our present Controversy with your Excellency, any further than they are consonant to *natural Reason.* If however we were to recur to such Opinions and Determinations we should find very great Authorities in our Favour, to show that the Statutes of England are not binding on those who are not represented in Parliament there. The Opinion of Lord Coke that Ireland was bound by Statutes of England wherein they *were named*, if compared with his other Writings, appears manifestly to be grounded upon a Supposition, that Ireland had by an Act of their own, in the Reign of King John, consented to be thus bound, and upon any other Supposition, this Opinion would be against *Reason*; for *Consent only* gives human Laws their Force. We beg Leave, upon what your Excellency has observed, of the Colony becoming Part of the State, to subjoin the Opinions of several learned Civilians, as quoted by a very able Lawyer in this Country; "Colonies, says Puffendorf, are settled in different Methods. For either the Colony *continues a Part* of the Common Wealth it was sent out from; or else is obliged to pay a dutiful Regard to the Mother Common Wealth, and to be in Readiness to defend and vindicate its Honor, and so is united by a Sort of unequal Confederacy; or lastly, is *erected into a seperate Common Wealth* and *assumes the same Rights*, with the State it descended from." And King Tullius, as quoted by the same learned Author from Grotius, says "We look upon it to be neither Truth nor Justice that Mother Cities ought of Necessity and *by the Law of Nature to rule over the Colonies.*"

Your Excellency has misinterpreted what we have said, "that no Country by the Common Law, was subject to the Laws or the Parliament but the Realm of England," and are pleased to tell us that we have expressed ourselves "*Incautiously.*" We beg Leave to recite the Words of the Judges of England in the beforementioned Case to our Purpose. "If a King go out of England with a Company of his Servants, Allegiance remaineth among his Subjects and Servants, altho' he be out of his Realm *whereto his Laws are confined.*" We did not mean to say, as your Excellency would suppose, that "the Common Law prescribes Limits to the Extent of the Legislative Power," though we shall always affirm it to be true of the Law of Reason and natural Equity. Your Excellency thinks you have made it appear, that "the Colony of Massachusetts-Bay is holden as feudatory of the Imperial Crown of England;" and therefore you say, "to use the Words of a very great Authority in a Case in *some Respects* analogous to it," being feudatory it necessary follows, that "it is under the Government of the King's Laws." Your Excellency has not named this Authority; but we conceive his Meaning must be, that being Feudatory, it is under the Government of the King's Laws *absolutely*; for as we have before said the Feudal System admits of no Idea of the Authority of Parliament, and this would have been the Case of the Colony but for the Compact with the King in the Charter.

Your Excellency says, that "Persons thus holding *under the Crown* of England remain or *become* Subjects of England;" by which we suppose your Excellency to mean, subject to the Supreme Authority of Parliament "to all Intents and Purposes as fully as if any of the Royal Manors, &c. within the Realm had been granted to them upon the like Tenure." We apprehend with Submission, your Excellency is Mistaken in supposing that our Allegiance is due to the Crown of England. Every Man swears Allegiance for himself to his own King in his Natural Person. "Every Subject is presumed by Law to be Sworn to the King, which is to his Natural Person," says Lord Coke. *Rep. on Calvins Case.* "The Allegiance is due to his Natural Body." And he says "in the Reign of Edward II. the Spencers, the Father and the Son, to cover the Treason hatched in their Hearts, invented this damnable and damned Opinion, that *Homage* and Oath of Allegiance was more by Reason of the King's Crown, that is of his politick Capacity, than by Reason of the Person of the King; upon which Opinion they infer'd execrable and detestable Consequents." The Judges of England, all but one, in the Case of the Union between Scotland and England, declared that "Allegiance followeth the natural Person not the politick;" and "to prove the Allegiance to be tied to the Body natural of the King, and not to the Body politick, the Lord Coke cited the Phrases of diverse Statutes, mentioning our *natural* liege Sovereign."—If then the Homage and Allegiance is not to the Body politick of the King, then it is not to him as the Head or any Part of that Legislative Authority, which your Excellency says "is equally extensive with the Authority of the Crown throughout every Part of the Dominion;" and your Excellency's Observations thereupon must fail. The same Judges mention the Allegiance of a Subject to the Kings of England who is out of the Reach and Extent of the Laws of England; which is perfectly reconcileable with the Principles of our Ancestors quoted before from your Excellency's History, but upon your Excellency's Principles appears to us to be an Absurdity. The Judges, speaking of a Subject, say, "although his Birth was out of the Bounds of the Kingdom of England, and *out of the Reach and Extent of the Laws of England*, yet if it were *within the Allegiance of the King of England, &c.* Normandy, Acquitan, Gascoign, and other Places within the Limits of France, and consequently out of the Realm or Bounds of the Kingdom of England, were in Subjection to the Kings of England. And the Judges say, "*Rex et Regnum* be not so Relatives, as a King can be King but of one Kingdom, which clearly holdeth not but that his Kingly Power extending to divers Nations and Kingdoms, all owe him equal Subjection and are equally born to the Benefit of his Protection, and altho' he is to govern them *by their distinct Laws*, yet any one of the People coming into the other is to have the Benefit of the Laws wheresoever he cometh." So they are not to be deemed Aliens, as your Excellency in your Speech supposes in any of the Dominions; all which accords with the Principles our Ancestors held. "And he is to bear the Burden of Taxes of the *Place where he cometh,* but living in one or for his Livelihood in one, *he is not to be taxed in the other*, because Laws ordain Taxes, Impositions and Charges as a Discipline of Subjection particularized to every particular Nation:" Nothing we think, can be more clear to our Purpose than this Decision, of Judges, perhaps as learned as ever adorned the English Nation; or in Favor of America in her present Controversy with the Mother State.

Your Excellency says, that by our not distinguishing between the Crown of England and the Kings and Queens of England in their personal or natural Capacities, we have been led into a fundamental Error." Upon this very Distinction we have availed ourselves. We have said that our Ancestors considered the Land which they took Possession of in America as out of the Bounds of the Kingdom of England, and out of the Reach and Extent of the Laws of England; and that the King also even in the Act of granting the Charter, considered the Territory as *not within* the Realm; that the King had an absolute

Right in himself to dispose of the Lands, and that this was not disputed by the Nation; nor could the Lands on any solid Grounds be claimed by the Nation, and therefore our Ancestors received the Lands by Grant from the King, and at the same Time compacted with him and promised him Homage and Allegiance, not in his publick or politick but natural Capacity only.—If it be difficult for us to show how the King acquired a Title to this Country in his natural Capacity, or seperate from his Relation to his Subjects, which we confess, yet we conceive it will be equally difficult for your Excellency to show how the Body Politick and Nation of England acquired it. Our Ancestors supposed it was acquired by neither; and therefore they declared, as we have before quoted from your History, that saving their actual Purchase from the Natives, of the Soil, the Dominion, the Lordship, and Sovereignty, they had in the Sight of God and Man, no Right and Title to what they possessed. How much clearer then in natural Reason and Equity must our Title be, who hold Estates dearly purchased at the Expence of our own as well as our Ancestors Labour, and defended by them with Treasure and Blood.

Your Excellency has been pleased to confirm, rather than deny or confute a Piece of History which you say we took from an anonimous Pamphlet, and by which you "fear we have been too easily misled." It may be gathered from your own Declaration and other Authorities besides the anonimous Pamphlet, that the House of Commons took Exception, not at the King's having made an absolute Grant of the Territory, but at the Claim of an exclusive Right to the Fishery on the Banks and Sea-Coast, by Virtue of the Patent. At this you say "the House of Commons was alarmed, and a Bill was brought in for allowing a Fishery." And upon this Occasion your Excellency allows, that "one of the Secretaries of State declared that the Plantations were not annexed to the Crown, and so were not within the Jurisdiction of Parliament." If we should concede to what your Excellency supposes might possibly or "perhaps" be the Case, that the Secretary made this Declaration "as his own Opinion," the Event showed that it was the Opinion of the King too; for it is not to be accounted for upon any other Principle, that he would have denied his Royal Assent to a Bill formed for no other Purpose, but to grant his Subjects in England the Privileges of Fishing on the Sea Coasts in America. The Account published by Sir Ferdinando Gorges himself, of the Proceedings of Parliament *on this Occasion*, your Excellency thinks will remove all Doubt of the Sense of the Nation and of the Patentees of this Patent or Charter in 1620. "This Narrative, you say, has all the Appearance of Truth and Sincerity," which we do not deny: and to us it carries this Conviction with it, that "what was objected" in Parliament was, the exclusive Claim of Fishing only. His imagining that he had satisfied the House after divers Attendances, that the Planting a Colony was of much more Consequence than a *simple disorderly Course of Fishing*, is sufficient for our Conviction. We know that the Nation was at that Time alarmed with Apprehensions of Monopolies; and if the Patent of New-England was presented by the two Houses as a Grievance, it did not show, as your Excellency supposes, "the Sense they then had of their Authority over this new-acquired Territory," but only their Sense of the Grievance of a Monopoly of the Sea.

We are happy to hear your Excellency say, that "our Remarks upon and Construction of the Words *not repugnant to the Laws of England*, are much the same with those of the Council." It serves to confirm us in our Opinion, in what we take to be the most important Matter of Difference between your Excellency and the two Houses. After saying, that the Statute of 7th and 8th of William and Mary favors the Construction of the Words as intending such Laws of England as are made more immediately to respect us, you tell us, that "the Province Agent Mr. Dummer in his much applauded Defence, says that *then* a Law of the Plantations may be said to be repugnant to a Law made in Great-Britain, when it flatly contradicts it so far as the Law made there mentions and relates to the Plantations." This is plain and obvious to common Sense, and therefore cannot be denied. But if your Excellency will read a Page or two further in that excellent Defence, you will see that he mentions this as the Sense of the Phrase, as taken from an Act of Parliament, rather than as the Sense he would chuse himself to put upon it; and he expresly designs to shew, in Vindication of the Charter, that in that Sense of the Words, there never was a Law made in the Plantations repugnant to the Laws of Great-Britain. He gives another Construction much more likely to be the true Intent of the Words; namely, "that the Patentees shall not presume under Colour of their particular Charters to make any Laws *inconsistent with the Great Charter and other Laws of England, by which the Lives, Liberties, and Properties of Englishmen are secured.*" This is the Sense in which our Ancestors understood the Words; and therefore they were unwilling to conform to the Acts of Trade, and disregarded them all till they made Provision to give them Force in the Colony by a Law of their own; saying, that "the Laws of England did not reach America: And those Acts were an Invasion of their Rights, Liberties and Properties," because they were not "represented in Parliament." The Right of being governed only by Laws which were made by Persons in whose Election they had a Voice, they looked upon as the Foundation of English Liberties. By the Compact with the King in the Charter, they were to be as free in America, as they would have been if they had remained within the Realm; and therefore they freely asserted that they "were to be governed by Laws made by themselves and by Officers chosen by themselves." Mr. Dummer says, "It seems reasonable enough to think that the Crown," and he might have added our Ancestors, "intended by this Injunction to provide for all its Subjects, that they might not be oppressed by arbitrary Power— but—being still Subjects, they should be protected by the same mild Laws, and enjoy the same happy Government as if they continued within the Realm". And considering the Words of the Charter in this Light, he looks upon them as designed to be a Fence against Oppression and despotic Power. But the Construction which your Excellency puts upon the Words, reduce us to a State of Vassallage, and exposes us to Oppression and despotic Power, whenever a Parliament shall see fit to make Laws for that Purpose and put them in Execution.

We flatter ourselves that from the large Extracts we have made from your Excellency's History of the Colony, it appears evidently, that under both Charters it hath been the Sense of the People and of the Government that they were not under the Jurisdiction of Parliament. We pray you again to recur to those Quotations and our Observations upon them: And we wish to have your Excellency's judicious Remarks. When we adduced that History to prove that the Sentiments of *private* Persons of Influence, four or five Years after the Restoration, were very different from what your Excellency apprehended them to be when you delivered your Speech, you seem to concede to it by telling us "it was, as you take it, from the *Principles imbibed* in those Times of Anarchy (preceeding the Restoration) that they disputed the Authority of Parliament;" but you add, "the Government would not venture to dispute it." We find in the same History a Quotation from a Letter of Mr. *Stoughton*, dated 17 Years after the Restoration, mentioning "the Country's not taking Notice of the Acts of Navigation *to observe them.*" And it was, as we take it, after that Time, that the Government declared in a Letter to their Agents, that they had not submitted to them; and they ventured to "dispute" the Jurisdiction, asserting that they apprehended the Acts to be an Invasion of the Rights, Liberties, and Properties of the Subjects of his Majesty in the Colony, *they not being represented in Parliament*; and that "the Laws of England *did not reach America.*" It very little avails in Proof that they conceded to the Supreme Authority of Parliament, their telling the Commissioners "that the Act of Navigation had for some Years before been observed here, that they knew not of its being greatly violated, and that such Laws as appeared to be against it were repealed." It may as truly be said now, that the Revenue Acts are observed by some of the People of this Province; but it cannot be said that the Government and People of this Province have conceded that the Parliament had Authority to make such Acts to be observed here. Neither does their Declarations to the Commissioners that such Laws as appeared to be against the Act of Navigation were repealed, prove their Concession of the Authority of Parliament, by any Means so much as their making Provision for giving Force to an Act of Parliament within this Province, by a deliberate and solemn Act or Law of their own, proves the contrary.

You tell us, that "the Government four or five Years before the Charter was vacated more explicitly," that is than by a Conversation with the Commissioners, "acknowledge the Authority of Parliament, and voted that their Governor should take the Oath required of him faithfully to do and perform all Matters and Things enjoined him by the Acts of Trade." But does this, may it please your Excellency, show their explicit Acknowledgment of the Authority of Parliament? Does it not rather show directly the contrary? For, what need could there be for their Vote or Authority to require him to take the Oath already required of him by the Act of Parliament, unless both he and they judged that an Act of Parliament was not of Force sufficient to bind him to take such Oath? We do not deny, but on the contrary are fully persuaded that your Excellency's Principles in Government are still the same with what they appear to be in the History; for you there say, that "the passing the Law plainly shows the wrong Sense they had of the Relation they stood in to England." But we are from hence convinced that your Excellency when you wrote the History was of our Mind in this Respect, that our Ancestors in passing the Law discovered their Opinion that they were without the Jurisdiction of Parliament: For it was upon this Principle alone that they shewed the wrong Sense they had in your Excellency's Opinion, of the Relation they stood in to England.

Your Excellency in your second Speech condescends to point out to us the Acts and Doings of the General Assembly which relates to Acts of Parliament, which you think "demonstrates that they have been acknowledged by the Assembly or submitted to by the People:" Neither of which in our Opinion shows that it was the Sense of the Nation, and our Predecessors when they first took Possession of this Plantation or Colony by a Grant and Charter from the Crown, that they were to remain subject to the Supreme Authority of the English Parliament.

Your Excellency seems chiefly to rely upon our Ancestors, after the Revolution "proclaiming King William and Queen Mary in the Room of King James," and taking the Oaths to them, "the Alteration of the Form of Oaths from Time to Time," and finally "the Establishment of the Form which every one of us has complied with, as the Charter in express Terms requires and makes our Duty." We do not know that it has ever been a Point in Dispute whether the Kings of England were ipso facto Kings in and over this Colony or Province, the Compact was made between King Charles the First, his Heirs and Successors, and the Governor and Company, their Heirs and Successors. It is easy upon this Principle to account for the

Acknowledgment and Submission of King William and Queen Mary as Successors of Charles the First, in the Room of King James. Besides it is to be considered, that the People in the Colony as well as in England had suffered under the TYRANT James, by which he had alike forfeited his Right to reign over both. There had been a Revolution here as well as in England. The Eyes of the People here were upon William and Mary, and the News of their being proclaimed in England was as your Excellency's History tells us, "the most joyful News ever received in New-England." And if they were not proclaimed here "by Virtue of an Act of the Colony," it was, as we think may be concluded from the Tenor of your History, with the general or universal Consent of the People as apparently as if "such Act had passed." It is *Consent alone*, that makes any human Laws binding; and as a learned Author observes, a purely *voluntary* Submission to an Act, because it is highly in our Favor and for our Benefit, is in all Equity and Justice to be deemed as not at all proceeding from the *Right* we include in the Legislators, that they thereby obtain an *Authority* over us, and that ever hereafter we must obey them of *Duty*. We would observe that one of the first Acts of the General Assembly of this Province since the present Charter, was an Act requiring the taking the Oaths mentioned in an Act of Parliament, to which you refer us: For what Purpose was this Act of the Assembly passed, if it was the Sense of the Legislators that the Act of Parliament was in Force in the Province. And at the same Time another Act was made for the Establishment of other Oaths necessary to be taken; both which Acts have the Royal Sanction, and are now in Force. Your Excellency says, that when the Colony applied to King William for a second Charter, they knew the Oath the King had taken, which was to govern them according to the Statutes in Parliament, and (which your Excellency here omits) *the Laws and Customs of the same*. By the Laws and Customs of Parliament, the People of England freely debate and consent to such Statutes as are made by themselves or their chosen Representatives. This is a Law or Custom which all Mankind may justly challenge as their *inherent* Right. According to this Law the King has an undoubted Right to govern us. Your Excellency upon Recollection surely will not infer from hence, that it was the Sense of our Predecessors that there was to remain a Supremacy in the English Parliament, or a full Power and Authority to make Laws binding upon us in all Cases whatever, in that Parliament where we cannot *debate* and *deliberate* upon the Necessity or Expediency of any Law, and consequently without our Consent, and as it may probably happen destructive of the first Law of Society, the Good of the Whole. You tell us that "after the Assumption of all the Powers of Government, by Virtue of the new Charter, an Act passed for the reviving for a limited Time all the local Laws of the Massachusetts-Bay and New-Plymouth respectively, not repugnant to the Laws of England. And at the same Session an Act passed establishing Naval Officers, that all undue Trading contrary to an Act of Parliament—may be prevented." Among the Acts that were then revived we may reasonably suppose was that whereby Provision was made to give Force to this Act of Parliament in the Province. The Establishment therefore of the Naval Officers was to aid the Execution of an Act of Parliament; for the Observance of which within the Colony, the Assembly had before made Provision, after free Debates, with their own Consent and by their own Act.

The Act of Parliament passed in 1741, for putting an End to several unwarrantable Schemes, mentioned by your Excellency, was designed for the general Good, and if the Validity of it was not disputed, it cannot be urged as a Concession of the Supreme Authority, to make Laws binding on us *in all Cases whatever.* But if the Design of it was for the general Benefit of the Province, it was in one Respect at least greatly complained of by the Persons more immediately affected by it; and to remedy the Inconvenience, the Legislative of this Province pass'd an Act, directly militating with it; which is the strongest Evidence, that altho' they may have submitted *sub silentio* to some Acts of Parliament that they conceived might operate for their Benefit, they did not conceive themselves bound by any of its Acts which they judged would operate to the Injury even of Individuals.

Your Excellency has not thought proper to attempt to confute the Reasoning of a learned Writer on the Laws of Nature and Nations, quoted by us on this Occasion, to shew that the Authority of the Legislature does not extend so far as the

Fundamentals of the Constitution. We are unhappy in not having your Remarks upon the Reasoning of that great Man; and until it is confuted, we shall remain of the Opinion, that the Fundamentals of the Constitution being excepted from the Commission of the Legislators, none of the Acts or Doings of the General Assembly, however deliberate and solemn, could avail to change them, if the People have not in very express Terms given them the Power to do it; and that much less ought their Acts and Doings however numerous, which barely refer to Acts of Parliament made expresly to relate to us, to be taken as an Acknowledgment that we are subject to the Supreme Authority of Parliament.

We shall sum up our own Sentiments in the Words of that learned Writer Mr. Hooker, in his Ecclesiastical Policy, as quoted by Mr. Locke, "The lawful Power of making Laws to command whole political Societies of Men, belonging so properly to the same intire Societies, that for any Prince or Potentate of what kind soever, to exercise the same of himself, and not from express Commission immediately and personally received from God, is no better *than mere Tyranny*. Laws therefore they are not which *publick Approbation* hath not made so, for Laws human of what kind soever are available by Consent." "Since Men naturally have no full and perfect Power to command whole politick Multitudes of Men, therefore, utterly without our Consent we could in such Sort be at no Man's Commandment living. And to be commanded we do not consent when that Society whereof we be a Part, hath at any Time before consented." We think your Excellency has not proved, either that the Colony is a Part of the politick Society of England, or that it has ever consented that the Parliament of England or Great-Britain should make Laws binding upon us in all Cases whatever, whether made expresly to refer to us or not.

We cannot help before we conclude, expressing our great Concern, that your Excellency has thus repeatedly, in a Manner insisted upon our free Sentiments on Matters of so delicate a Nature, and weighty Importance. The Question appears to us to be no other, than Whether we are the Subjects of absolute unlimitted Power, or of a free Government formed on the Principles of the English Constitution. If your Excellency's Doctrine be true, the People of this Province hold their Lands of the Crown and People of England, and their Lives, Liberties and Properties are at their Disposal; and that even by Compact and their own Consent. They are subject to the King as the Head *alterius Populi* of another People, in whose Legislative they have no Voice or Interest. They are indeed said to have a Constitution and a Legislative of their own, but your Excellency has explained it into a mere Phantom; limitted, controuled, superceded and nullified at the Will of another. Is this the Constitution which so charmed our Ancestors, that as your Excellency has informed us, they kept a Day of solemn Thanksgiving to Almighty God when they received it? and were they Men of so little Discernment, such Children in Understanding, as to please themselves with the Imagination that they were blessed with the same Rights and Liberties which natural-born Subjects in England enjoyed? when at the same Time they had fully consented to be ruled and ordered by a Legislative a Thousand Leagues distant from them, which cannot be supposed to be sufficiently acquainted with their Circumstances, if concerned for their Interest, and in which they cannot be in any Sense represented.

From the Diary: March 4–December 17, 1773

1773 MARCH 4TH. THURSDAY.

The two last Months have slided away. I have written a tedious Examination of Brattle's absurdities. The Governor and General Court, has been engaged for two Months upon the greatest Question ever yet agitated. I stand amazed at the Governor, for forcing on this Controversy. He will not be thanked for this. His Ruin and Destruction must spring out of it, either from the Ministry and Parliament on one Hand, or from his Countrymen, on the other. He has reduced himself to a most ridiculous State of Distress. He is closetting and soliciting Mr. Bowdoin, Mr. Dennie, Dr. Church &c. &c., and seems in the utmost Agony.

The Original of my Controversy with Brattle is worthy to be comitted to Writing, in these Memorandums.—At the Town Meeting in Cambridge, called to consider of the Judges Salaries, he advanced for Law, that the Judges by this Appointment, would be compleatly independent, for that they held Estates for Life in their offices by common Law and their Nomination and Appointment. And, he said "this I averr to be Law, and I will maintain it, against any Body, I will dispute it, with Mr. Otis, Mr. Adams, Mr. John Adams I mean, and Mr. Josiah Quincy. I would dispute it with them, here in Town Meeting, nay, I will dispute it with them in the Newspapers."

He was so elated with that Applause which this inane Harrangue procured him, from the Enemies of this Country, that in the next Thurdsdays Gazette, he roundly advanced the same Doctrine in Print, and the Thursday after invited any Gentleman to dispute with him upon his Points of Law.

These vain and frothy Harrangues and Scribblings would have had no Effect upon me, if I had not seen that his Ignorant Doctrines were taking Root in the Minds of the People, many of whom were in Appearance, if not in Reality, taking it for granted, that the Judges held their Places during good Behaviour.

Upon this I determined to enter the Lists, and the General was very soon silenced.—Whether from Conviction, or from Policy, or Contempt I know not.

It is thus that little Incidents produce great Events. I have never known a Period, in which the Seeds of great Events have been so plentifully sown as this Winter. A Providence is visible, in that Concurrence of Causes, which produced the Debates and Controversies of this Winter. The Court of Inquisition at Rhode Island, the Judges Salaries, the Massachusetts Bay Town Meetings, General Brattles Folly, all conspired in a remarkable, a wonderfull Manner.

My own Determination had been to decline all Invitations to public Affairs and Enquiries, but Brattles rude, indecent, and unmeaning Challenge of me in Particular, laid me under peculiar Obligations to undeceive the People, and changed my

Resolution. I hope that some good will come out of it.—God knows.

————————————

1773. MARCH 5TH. FRYDAY.
Heard an Oration, at Mr. Hunts Meeting House, by Dr. Benja. Church, in Commemoration of the Massacre in Kings Street, 3 Years ago. That large Church was filled and crouded in every Pew, Seat, Alley, and Gallery, by an Audience of several Thousands of People of all Ages and Characters and of both Sexes.

I have Reason to remember that fatal Night. The Part I took in Defence of Captn. Preston and the Soldiers, procured me Anxiety, and Obloquy enough. It was, however, one of the most gallant, generous, manly and disinterested Actions of my whole Life, and one of the best Pieces of Service I ever rendered my Country. Judgment of Death against those Soldiers would have been as foul a Stain upon this Country as the Executions of the Quakers or Witches, anciently. As the Evidence was, the Verdict of the Jury was exactly right.

This however is no Reason why the Town should not call the Action of that Night a Massacre, nor is it any Argument in favour of the Governor or Minister, who caused them to be sent here. But it is the strongest of Proofs of the Danger of standing Armies.

————————————

1773. MAY 24TH. TUESDAY.
Tomorrow is our General Election. The Plotts, Plans, Schemes, and Machinations of this Evening and Night, will be very numerous. By the Number of Ministerial, Governmental People returned, and by the Secrecy of the Friends of Liberty, relating to the grand discovery of the compleat Evidence of the whole Mystery of Iniquity, I much fear the Elections will go unhappily. For myself, I own I tremble at the Thought of an Election. What will be expected of me? What will be required of me? What Duties and Obligations will result to me, from an Election? What Duties to my God, my King, my Country, my Family, my Friends, myself? What Perplexities, and Intricacies, and Difficulties shall I be exposed to? What

Snares and Temptations will be thrown in my Way? What Self denials and Mortifications shall I be obliged to bear?

If I should be called in the Course of Providence to take a Part in public Life, I shall Act a fearless, intrepid, undaunted Part, at all Hazards—tho it shall be my Endeavour likewise to act a prudent, cautious and considerate Part.

But if I should be excused, by a Non Election, or by the Exertions of Prerogative from engaging in public Business, I shall enjoy a sweet Tranquility, in the Pursuit of my private Business, in the Education of my Children and in a constant Attention to the Preservation of my Health. This last is the most selfish and pleasant System—the first, the more generous, tho arduous and disagreable.

But I was not sent into this World to spend my days in Sports, Diversions and Pleasures.

I was born for Business; for both Activity and Study. I have little Appetite, or Relish for any Thing else.

I must double and redouble my Diligence. I must be more constant to my office and my Pen. Constancy accomplishes more than Rapidity. Continual Attention will do great Things. Frugality, of Time, is the greatest Art as well as Virtue. This Economy will produce Knowledge as well as Wealth.

May 25, 1773

1773. DECR. 17TH.

Last Night 3 Cargoes of Bohea Tea were emptied into the Sea. This Morning a Man of War sails.

This is the most magnificent Movement of all. There is a Dignity, a Majesty, a Sublimity, in this last Effort of the Patriots, that I greatly admire. The People should never rise, without doing something to be remembered—something notable And striking. This Destruction of the Tea is so bold, so daring, so firm, intrepid and inflexible, and it must have so important Consequences, and so lasting, that I cant but consider it as an Epocha in History.

This however is but an Attack upon Property. Another similar Exertion of popular Power, may produce the destruction of Lives. Many Persons wish, that as many dead Carcasses were floating in the Harbour, as there are Chests of Tea:—a much less Number of Lives however would remove the Causes of all our Calamities.

The malicious Pleasure with which Hutchinson the Governor, the Consignees of the Tea, and the officers of the Customs, have stood and looked upon the distresses of the People, and their Struggles to get the Tea back to London, and at last the destruction of it, is amazing. Tis hard to believe Persons so hardened and abandoned.

What Measures will the Ministry take, in Consequence of this?—Will they resent it? will they dare to resent it? will they punish Us? How? By quartering Troops upon Us?—by annulling our Charter?—by laying on more duties? By restraining our Trade? By Sacrifice of Individuals, or how.

The Question is whether the Destruction of this Tea was necessary? I apprehend it was absolutely and indispensably so. —They could not send it back, the Governor, Admiral and Collector and Comptroller would not suffer it. It was in their Power to have saved it—but in no other. It could not get by the Castle, the Men of War &c. Then there was no other Alternative but to destroy it or let it be landed. To let it be landed, would be giving up the Principle of Taxation by Parliamentary Authority, against which the Continent have struggled for 10 years, it was loosing all our labour for 10 years and subjecting ourselves and our Posterity forever to Egyptian Taskmasters—to Burthens, Indignities, to Ignominy, Reproach and Contempt, to Desolation and Oppression, to Poverty and Servitude.

But it will be said it might have been left in the Care of a Committee of the Town, or in Castle William. To this many Objections may be made.

Deacon Palmer and Mr. Is. Smith dined with me, and Mr. Trumble came in. They say, the Tories blame the Consignees, as much as the Whiggs do—and say that the Governor will loose his Place, for not taking the Tea into his Protection before, by Means of the Ships of War, I suppose, and the Troops at the Castle.

I saw him this Morning pass my Window in a Chariot with the Secretary. And by the Marching and Countermarching of Councillors, I suppose they have been framing a Proclamation, offering a Reward to discover the Persons, their Aiders,

Abettors, Counsellors and Consorters, who were concerned in
the Riot last Night.

Spent the Evening with Cushing, Pemberton and Swift at
Wheelwrights. Cushing gave us an Account of Bollans Letters—of the Quantity of Tea the East India Company had on
Hand—40,00000 weight, that is Seven Years Consumption—
two Millions Weight in America.

"THE DYE IS CAST"

To James Warren

Dr Sir   Boston Decr 17 1773
The Dye is cast: The People have passed the River and cutt
away the Bridge: last Night Three Cargoes of Tea, were emptied into the Harbour. This is the grandest, Event, which has
ever yet happened Since, the Controversy, with Britain,
opened!

The Sublimity of it, charms me!

For my own Part, I cannot express my own Sentiments of it,
better than in the Words of Coll Doane to me, last Evening—
Balch Should repeat them—The worst that can happen, I
think, Says he in Consequence of it, will be that the Province
must pay for it. Now, I think the Province, may pay for it, if it
is burn'd as easily as if it is drank—and I think it is a matter of
indifference whether it is drank or drowned. The Province
must pay for it, in Either Case. But there is this Difference. I
believe, it will take them 10 Years to get the Province to pay for
it. If so, we shall Save 10 Years Interest of the Money. Whereas
if it is drank it must be paid for immediately. Thus He—However, He agreed with me that the Province, would never pay
for it. And also in this that the final Ruin, of our Constitution
of Government, and of all American Liberties, would be the
certain Consequence of Suffering it to be landed.

Governor Hutchinson and his Family and Friends will never
have done, with their good services to Great Britain and the
Colonies! But for him, this Tea might have been Saved to
the East India Company. Whereas this Loss if the rest of the

Colonies Should follow our Example, will in the opinion of many Persons bankrupt the Company. However, I dare Say, that the Governors, and Consignees, and Custom House Officers, in the other Colonies will have more Wisdom than ours have had, and take effectual Care that thier Tea shall be sent back to England untouched. If not it will as surely be destroyed there as it has been here.

Threats, Phantoms, Bugbears, by the million, will be invented and propagated among the People upon this occasion. Individuals will be threatened with Suits and Prosecutions. Armies and Navies will be talked of—military Execution—Charters annull'd—Treason—Tryals in England and all that—But—these Terrors, are all but Imaginations. Yet if they should become Realities they had better be Suffered, than the great Principle, of Parliamentary Taxation given up.

The Town of Boston, was never more Still and calm of a Saturday night than it was last Night. All Things were conducted with great order, Decency and *perfect Submission to Government*. No Doubt, we all thought the Administration in better Hands, than it had been.

Please to make Mrs Adams's most respectfull Compliments to Mrs Warren and mine.

I am your Friend,

John Adams

From the Diary: March 6–31, 1774

1774 SUNDAY MARCH 6TH.

Heard Dr. Cooper in the Morning. Paine drank Coffee with me.

Paine is under some Apprehensions of Troops, on Account of the high Proceedings, &c. He says there is a ship in to day, with a Consignment of Tea from some private Merchants at home—&c.

Last Thursday Morning March 3d. died Andrew Oliver Esquire Lieutenant Governor. This is but the second death which has happened among the Conspirators, the original

Conspirators against the Public Liberty, since the Conspiracy was first regularly formed, and begun to be executed, in 1763 or 4. Judge Russell who was one, died in 1766. Nat. Rogers, who was not one of the original's, but came in afterwards, died in 1770.

This Event will have considerable Consequences.—Peter Oliver will be made Lieutenant Governor, Hutchinson will go home, and probably be continued Governor but reside in England, and Peter Oliver will reside here and rule the Province. The Duty on Tea will be repealed. Troops may come, but what becomes of the poor Patriots. They must starve and mourn as usual. The Hutchinsons and Olivers will rule and overbear all Things as usual.

An Event happened, last Fryday that is surprising. At a General Council, which was full as the General Court was then sitting, Hutchinson had the Confidence to Nominate for Justices of the Peace, George Bethune, Nat. Taylor, Ned. Lloyd, Benj. Gridly and Sam Barrett—and informed the Board that they had all promised to take the oath.

The Council had the Pusillanimity to consent by their Silence at least to these Nominations.

Nothing has a more fatal Tendency than such Prostitution of the Council. They tamely, supinely, timorously, acquiesce in the Appointment of Persons to fill every executive Department in the Province, with Tools of the Family who are planning our Destruction.

Neighbour Quincy spent the Evening with me.

SATURDAY. MARCH 12.

There has been and is a Party in the Nation, a very small one indeed, who have pretended to be conscienciously perswaded, that the Pretender has a Right to the Throne. Their Principles of Loyalty, hereditary Right, and passive obedience have led them to this Judgment, and Opinion. And as long as they keep these Opinions to themselves, there is no Remedy against them. But as soon as they express these opinions publicly, and endeavour to make Proselytes, especially if they take any steps to introduce the Pretender, they become offenders, and must suffer the Punishment due to their Crimes. Private Judgment might be alledged in Excuse for many Crimes—a poor Enthusiast [   ] bring himself to believe it lawfull for him to steal from his rich Neighbour, to supply his Necessities, but the Law will not allow of this Plea. The Man must be punished for his Theft.

Ravaillac and Felton probably thought, they were doing their Duty, and nothing more, when they were committing their vile assassinations: But the Liberty of private Conscience, did not exempt them from the most dreadfull Punishment that civil Authority can inflict or human Nature endure.

Hutchinson and Oliver might be brought by their interested Views and Motives, sincerely to think that an Alteration in the Constitution of this Province, and an "Abridgment of what are called English Liberties," would be for the Good of the Province, of America, and of the Nation. In this they deceived themselves, and became the Bubbles of their own Avarice and Ambition. The rest of the World are not thus deceived. They see clearly, that such Innovations will be the Ruin not only of the Colonies, but of the Empire, and therefore think that Examples ought to be made of these great offenders, in Terrorem.

The Enmity of Govr. Bernard, Hutchinson and Oliver, and others to the Constitution of this Province is owing to its being an Obstacle to their Views and Designs of Raising a Revenue by Parliamentary Authority, and making their own Fortunes out of it.

The Constitution of this Province, has enabled the People to resist their Projects, so effectually, that they see they shall never carry them into Execution, while it exists. Their Malice has therefore been directed against it, and their Utmost Efforts been employed to destroy it.

There is so much of a Republican Spirit, among the People, which has been nourished and cherished by their Form of Government, that they never would submit to Tyrants or oppressive Projects.

The same Spirit spreads like a Contagion, into all the other Colonies, into Ireland, and into Great Britain too, from this single Province, of Mass. Bay, that no Pains are too great to be taken, no Hazards too great to be run, for the Destruction of our Charter.

March 12, 1774

1774. THURSDAY MARCH 31.

Let me ask my own Heart, have I patience, and Industry enough to write an History of the Contest between Britain and America? It would be proper to begin at the Treaty of Peace in 1763, or at the Commencement of Govr. Bernards Administration, or at the Accession of George 3d. to the Throne—The Reign, or the Peace.

Would it not be proper, to begin, with those Articles in the Treaty of Peace which relate to America?—The Cession of Canada, Louisiana, and Florida, to the English.

Franklin, Lee, Chatham, Campden, Grenville and Shelburne, Hilsborough, Dartmouth, Whately, Hutchinson, Oliver, J Oliver, Barnard, Paxton, Otis, Thatcher, Adams, Mayhew, Hancock, Cushing, Phillips, Hawley, Warren, with many other Figures would make up the Groope.

THE HUMILIATION OF THE TORIES

To James Warren

Dr Sir   Boston April 9. 1774

It is a great Mortification to me, to be obliged to deny my self the Pleasure of a Visit to my Friends at Plymouth next Week. But so Fate has ordained it.

I am a little Apprehensive too for the State upon this Occasion, for it has heretofore received no small Advantage from our Sage Deliberations, at your Fire side.

I hope Mrs Warren is in fine Health, and Spirits—and that I have not incurred her Displeasure, by making So free with the Skirmish of the sea Deities—one of the most incontestible Evidences of real Genius, which has yet been exhibited—for to take the Clumsy, indigested Conception of another and work it into so elegant, and classicall a Composition, requires Genius equall to that which wrought another most beautifull Poem, out of the little Incident of a Gentlemans clipping a Lock of a Ladys Hair, with a Pair of Scissors.

May a double Portion of her Genius, as well as Virtues,

descend to her Posterity, which united, to the Patriotism &c &c &c of &c &c &c, will make _____. But I am almost in the Strain of Hazelrod.

The Tories were never, Since I was born, in such a state of Humiliation, as at this Moment. Wherever I go, in the Several Counties, I perceive it, more and more.

They are now in absolute Despair of obtaining a Tryumph without Shedding an Abundance of Blood: and they are afraid of the Consequences of this—not that their Humanity starts at it at all.

The Complaisance, the Air of Modesty and Kindness to the Whiggs, the shew of Moderation, the Pains to be thought Friends to Liberty, and all that is amazing. I Admire the Jesuits! The science is so exquisite and there are such immense Advantages in it that it is, if it were not for the Deviltry of it, most ardently to be wish'd. To see them, bowing, Smiling, cringing, and seeming cordially Friendly to persons, whom they openly averred their Malice against 2 Years ago and whom they would gladly butcher now, is provoking, yet diverting.

News We have none. Still—Silent as Midnight. The first Vessells may bring us tidings, which will erect the Crests of the Tories again and depress the Spirits of the Whiggs. For my own Part, I am of the same opinion that I have been for many Years, that there is not Spirit enough on Either side to bring the Question to a compleat Decision—and that We shall oscilate like a Pendulum and fluctuate like the Ocean, for many Years to come, and never obtain a compleat Redress of American Grievances, nor submit to an absolute Establishment of Parliamentary Authority. But be trimming between both as we have been for ten Years past, for more Years to come than you and I shall live. Our Children, may see Revolutions, and be concerned and active in effecting them of which we can form no Conception.

Mrs. Adams is in the Country, unwell. Otherwise she would have written to Mrs. Warren. Believe me and her to be yours and Mrs Warrens real Friends and humb. servants,

John and Abigail Adams

THE MARTYRDOM OF BOSTON

To Abigail Adams

My Dear   Boston May 12. 1774

I am extreamly afflicted with the Relation your Father gave me, of the Return of your Disorder. I fear you have taken some Cold; We have had a most pernicious Air, a great Part of this Spring. I am sure I have Reason to remember it—my Cold is the most obstinate and threatning one, I ever had in my Life: However, I am unwearied in my Endeavours to subdue it, and have the Pleasure to think I have had some Success. I rise at 5, walk 3 Miles, keep the Air all day and walk again in the Afternoon. These Walks have done me more good than any Thing, tho I have been constantly plied with Teas, and your Specific. My own Infirmities, the Account of the Return of yours, and the public News coming alltogether have put my Utmost Phylosophy to the Tryal.

We live my dear Soul, in an Age of Tryal. What will be the Consequence I know not. The Town of Boston, for ought I can see, must suffer Martyrdom: It must expire: And our principal Consolation is, that it dies in a noble Cause. The Cause of Truth, of Virtue, of Liberty and of Humanity: and that it will probably have a glorious Reformation, to greater Wealth, Splendor and Power than ever.

Let me know what is best for us to do. It is expensive keeping a Family here. And there is no Prospect of any Business in my Way in this Town this whole Summer. I dont receive a shilling a Week.

We must contrive as many Ways as we can, to save Expences, for We may have Calls to contribute, very largely in Proportion to our Circumstances, to prevent other very honest, worthy People from suffering for Want, besides our own Loss in Point of Business and Profit.

Dont imagine from all this that I am in the Dumps. Far otherwise. I can truly say, that I have felt more Spirits and Activity, since the Arrival of this News, than I had done before for years. I look upon this, as the last Effort of Lord Norths Despair. And he will as surely be defeated in it, as he was in the Project of the Tea.—I am, with great Anxiety for your Health your   John Adams

THE CONTINENTAL CONGRESS
1774–1775

From the Diary: June 20, 1774

JUNE 20TH. 1774. MONDAY.

At Piemonts in Danvers, bound to Ipswich. There is a new, and a grand Scene open before me—a Congress.

This will be an assembly of the wisest Men upon the Continent, who are Americans in Principle, i.e. against the Taxation of Americans, by Authority of Parliament.

I feel myself unequal to this Business. A more extensive Knowledge of the Realm, the Colonies, and of Commerce, as well as of Law and Policy, is necessary, than I am Master of.

What can be done? Will it be expedient to propose an Annual Congress of Committees? to Petition.—Will it do to petition at all?—to the K? to the L? to the Cs?

What will such Consultations avail? Deliberations alone will not do. We must petition, or recommend to the Assemblies to petition, or—

The Ideas of the People, are as various, as their Faces. One thinks, no more petitions, former having been neglected and despized. Some are for Resolves—Spirited Resolves—and some are for bolder Councils.

I will keep an exact Diary, of my Journey, as well as a Journal of the Proceedings of the Congress.

PREPARING FUTURE POLITICIANS

To James Warren

Dr. Sir   Ipswich June 25. 1774

I am very sorry, I had not the Pleasure of seeing you, after your Return from Salem: as I wanted a great deal of Conversation with you, on several Subjects.

The principal Topick, however was the Enterprise to Phyladelphia. I view, the Assembly that is to be there, as I do, the Court of Ariopagus, the Council of the Amphyctions, a Conclave, a Sanhedrim, A Divan, I know not what. I Suppose you sent me there, to school. I thank you for thinking me, an apt scholar or capable of learning. For my own Part I am at a Loss, totally at a Loss what to do when We get there: but I hope to be there taught.

It is to be a School of Political Prophets I Suppose—a Nursery of American Statesmen. May it thrive, and prosper and flourish and from this Fountain may there issue Streams, which shall gladden all the Cities and Towns in North America, forever.

I am for making of it annual, and for Sending an entire new set every Year, that all the principal Genius's may go to the University in Rotation—that We may have Politicians in Plenty. Our great Complaint is the scarcity of Men fit to govern Such mighty Interests, as are clashing in the present Contest—a scarcity indeed! For who is Sufficient for these Things?

Our Policy must be to improve every opportunity and Means for forming our People, and preparing Leaders for them in the grand March of Politicks. We must make our Children travel.

You and I have too many Cares and Occupations, and therefore We must recommend it to Mrs Warren and her Friend Mrs Adams to teach our Sons the divine Science of the Politicks: And to be frank I suspect they understand it better than we do.

There is one ugly Reflection—Brutus and Cassius were conquered and slain. Hampden died in the Field. Sydney on the Scaffold, Harrington in Goal, &c. This is cold Comfort. Politicks are an ordeal Path, among red hot Ploughshares. Who then would be a Politician for the Pleasure of running about barefoot among them? Yet Somebody must. And I think those, whose Characters, Circumstances, Educations, &c call them ought to follow.

Yet I don't think that one or a few Men are under any moral obligation to Sacrifice themselves and Families, all the Pleasures Profits and Prospects of Life, while others for whose Benefit this is to be done lie idle, enjoying all the Sweets of Society, acumulating Wealth in Abundance, and laying Foundations for oppulent and powerfull Families for many Generations. So I think the arduous Duties of the Times ought to be discharged in Rotation—and I never will engage more in Politicks but upon this System.

I must entreat the Favour of your Sentiments and Mrs. Warrens what is proper, praticable expedient, wise, just, good necessary to be done at Phyladelphia. Pray let me have them in a Letter before I go.

I am your Friend,

John Adams

RICH LAWYERS

To *Abigail Adams*

My Dear   York June 29. 1774

I have a great Deal of Leisure, which I chiefly employ in Scribbling, that my Mind may not stand still or run back like my Fortune.—There is very little Business here, and David Sewall, David Wyer, John Sullivan and James Sullivan and Theophilus Bradbury are the Lawyers who attend the Inferiour Courts and consequently conduct the Causes at the Superiour.

I find that the Country is the Situation to make Estates by the Law. John Sullivan, who is placed at Durham in New Hampshire, is younger, both in Years and Practice than I am; He began with nothing, but is now said to be worth Ten thousand Pounds Lawfull Money, his Brother James allows five or six or perhaps seven thousand Pounds, consisting in Houses and Lands, Notes, Bonds, and Mortgages. He has a fine Stream of Water, with an excellent Corn Mill, Saw Mill, Fulling Mill, Scyth Mill and others, in all six Mills, which are both his Delight and his Profit. As he has earned Cash in his Business at the Bar, he has taken Opportunities, to purchase Farms of his Neighbours, who wanted to sell and move out farther into the Woods, at an Advantageous Rate. And in this Way, has been growing rich, and under the Smiles and Auspices of Governor Wentworth, has been promoted in the civil and military Way, so that he is treated with great Respect in this Neighbourhood.

James Sullivan, Brother of the other, who studied Law under him, without any Accademical Education, (and John was in the same Case,) is fixed at Saco, alias Biddeford in our Province. He began with neither Learning, Books, Estate or any Thing, but his Head and Hands, and is now a very popular Lawyer and growing rich very fast, purchasing great Farms &c., a Justice of the Peace, and Member of the General Court.

David Sewall of this Town never practices out of this County, has no Children, has no Ambition, nor Avarice they say, (however Quære). His Business in this County maintains him very handsomely, and he gets beforehand.

Bradbury at Falmouth, they say, grows rich very fast.

I was first sworn in 1758; My Life has been a continual Scæne of Fatigue, Vexation, Labour and Anxiety. I have four Children. I had a pretty Estate from my Father, I have been assisted by your Father. I have done the greatest Business in the Province. I have had the very richest Clients in the Province: Yet I am Poor in Comparison of others.

This I confess is grievous, and discouraging. I ought however, to be candid enough to acknowledge that I have been imprudent. I have spent an Estate in Books. I have spent a Sum of Money indiscreetly in a Lighter, another in a Pew, and a much greater in an House in Boston. These would have been Indiscretions, if the Impeachment of the Judges, the Boston Port Bill, &c. &c. had never happened; but by the unfortunate Interruption of my Business from these Causes, these Indiscretions become almost fatal to me, to be sure much more detrimental.

John Lowell, at Newbury Port, has built him an House, like the Palace of a Nobleman and lives in great Splendor. His Business is very profitable. In short every Lawyer who has the least Appearance of Abilities makes it do in the Country. In Town, nobody does, or ever can, who Either is not obstinately determined never to have any Connection with Politicks or does not engage on the Side of the Government, the Administration and the Court.

Let us therefore my dear Partner, from that Affection which we feel for our lovely Babes, apply ourselves by every Way, we can, to the Cultivation of our Farm. Let Frugality, And Industry, be our Virtues, if they are not of any others. And above all Cares of this Life let our ardent Anxiety be, to mould the Minds and Manners of our Children. Let us teach them not only to do virtuously but to excell. To excell they must be taught to be steady, active, and industrious.

I am &c. your   John Adams

"I AM DETERMINED TO BE COOL"

To Abigail Adams

York July 1st: 1774

I am so idle, that I have not an easy Moment, without my Pen in my Hand. My Time might have been improved to some Purpose, in mowing Grass, raking Hay, or hoeing Corn, weeding Carrotts, picking or shelling Peas. Much better should I have been employed in schooling my Children, in teaching them to write, cypher, Latin, French, English and Greek.

I sometimes think I must come to this—to be the Foreman upon my own Farm, and the School Master to my own Children. I confess myself to be full of Fears that the Ministry and their Friends and Instruments, will prevail, and crush the Cause and Friends of Liberty. The Minds of that Party are so filled with Prejudices, against me, that they will take all Advantages, and do me all the Damage they can. These Thoughts have their Turns in my Mind, but in general my Hopes are predominant.

In a Tryal of a Cause here to Day, some Facts were mentioned, which are worth writing to you. It was sworn, by Dr. Lyman, Elder Bradbury and others, that there had been a Number of Instances in this Town of fatal Accidents, happening from sudden Noises striking the Ears of Babes and young Children. A Gun was fired near one Child, as likely as any; the Child fell immediately into fits, which impaired his Reason, and is still living an Ideot. Another Child was sitting on a Chamber floor. A Man rapped suddenly and violently on the

Boards which made the floor under the Child [   ]. The Child was so startled, and frightened, that it fell into fits, which never were cured.

This may suggest a Caution to keep Children from sudden Frights and surprizes.

Dr. Gardiner arrived here to day, from Boston, brings us News of a Battle at the Town Meeting, between Whigs and Tories, in which the Whiggs after a Day and an Halfs obstinate Engagement were finally victorious by two to one. He says the Tories are preparing a flaming Protest.

I am determined to be cool, if I can; I have suffered such Torments in my Mind, heretofore, as have almost overpowered my Constitution, without any Advantage: and now I will laugh and be easy if I can, let the Conflict of Parties, terminate as it will—let my own Estate and Interest suffer what it will. Nay whether I stand high or low in the Estimation of the World, so long as I keep a Conscience void of Offence towards God and Man. And thus I am determined by the Will of God, to do, let what will become of me or mine, my Country, or the World.

I shall arouse myself ere long I believe, and exert an Industry, a Frugality, a hard Labour, that will serve my family, if I cant serve my Country. I will not lie down and die in Dispair. If I cannot serve my Children by the Law, I will serve them by Agriculture, by Trade, by some Way, or other. I thank God I have a Head, an Heart and Hands which if once fully exerted alltogether, will succeed in the World as well as those of the mean spirited, low minded, fawning obsequious scoundrells who have long hoped, that my Integrity would be an Obstacle in my Way, and enable them to out strip me in the Race.

But what I want in Comparison of them, of Villany and servility, I will make up in Industry and Capacity. If I dont they shall laugh and triumph.

I will not willingly see Blockheads, whom I have a Right to despise, elevated above me, and insolently triumphing over me. Nor shall Knavery, through any Negligence of mine, get the better of Honesty, nor Ignorance of Knowledge, nor Folly of Wisdom, nor Vice of Virtue.

I must intreat you, my dear Partner in all the Joys and Sorrows, Prosperity and Adversity of my Life, to take a Part with

me in the Struggle. I pray God for your Health—intreat you
to rouse your whole Attention to the Family, the stock, the
Farm, the Dairy. Let every Article of Expence which can possibly be spared be retrench'd. Keep the Hands attentive to their
Business, and [   ] the most prudent Measures of every kind
be adopted and pursued with Alacrity and Spirit.
    I am &c.,   John Adams

MOBS AND TAXATION

To Abigail Adams

                                         Falmouth July. 6. 1774
    Mobs are the trite Topick of Declamation and Invective,
among all the ministerial People, far and near. They are grown
universally learned in the Nature, Tendency and Consequences of them, and very eloquent and pathetic in descanting
upon them. They are Sources of all kinds of Evils, Vices, and
Crimes, they say. They give Rise to Prophaneness, Intemperance, Thefts, Robberies, Murders, and Treason. Cursing,
Swearing, Drunkenness, Gluttony, Leudness, Trespasses,
Maims, are necessarily involved in them and occasioned by
them. Besides, they render the Populace, the Rabble, the scum
of the Earth, insolent, and disorderly, impudent, and abusive.
They give Rise to Lying, Hypocricy, Chicanery, and even Perjury among the People, who are driven to such Artifices, and
Crimes, to conceal themselves and their Companions, from
Prosecutions in Consequence of them.
    This is the Picture drawn by the Tory Pencil: and it must be
granted to be a Likeness; but this is Declamation. What Consequence is to be drawn from this Description? Shall We submit to Parliamentary Taxation, to avoid Mobs? Will not
Parliamentary Taxation if established, occasion Vices, Crimes
and Follies, infinitely more numerous, dangerous, and fatal
to the Community? Will not parliamentary Taxation if established, raise a Revenue, unjustly and wrongfully? If this Revenue is scattered by the Hand of Corruption, among the
public Officers, and Magistrates and Rulers, in the Community,

will it not propagate Vices more numerous, more malignant and pestilential among them. Will it not render Magistrates servile, and fawning to their vicious Superiours? and insolent and Tyrannical to their Inferiours? Is Insolence, Abuse and Impudence more tolerable in a Magistrate than in a subject? Is it not more constantly and extensively, pernicious? And does not the Example of Vice and Folly, in Magistrates descend, and spread downwards among the People?

Besides is not the Insolence of Officers and Soldiers, and Seamen, in the Army and Navy as mischievous as that of Porters, or Sailors in Merchant Service?

Are not Riots raised and made by Armed Men, as bad as those by unarmed? Is not an Assault upon a civil officer, and a Rescue of a Prisoner from lawfull Authority, made by Soldiers with Swords or Bayonets, as bad as if made by Tradesmen with Staves?

Is not the Killing of a Child by R. and the slaughter of half a Dozen Citizens by a Party of Soldiers, as bad as pulling down a House, or drowning a Cargo of Tea? even if both should be allowed to be unlawfull.

Parties may go on declaiming: but it is not easy to say, which Party has excited most Riots, which has published most Libels, which have propagated most Slander, and Defamation.

Verbal Scandal has been propagated in great Abundance by both Parties. But there is this Difference, that one Party have enjoyed almost all public Offices, and therefore their Deffamation has been spread among the People more secretly, more maliciously and more effectually. It has gone with greater Authority, and been scattered by Instruments more industrious. The ministerial News Papers have swarmed with as numerous and as malicious Libels as the antiministerial ones. Fleets Paper, Meins Chronicle, &c. &c. have been as virulent as any that was ever in the Province.

These Bickerings of opposite Parties, and their mutual Reproaches, their Declamations, their Sing Song, their Triumphs and Defyances, their Dismals, and Prophecies, are all Delusion.

We very seldom hear any solid Reasoning. I wish always to discuss the Question, without all Painting, Pathos, Rhetoric, or Flourish of every Kind. And the Question seems to me to be, whether the american Colonies are to be considered, as a distinct Community so far as to have a Right to judge for themselves, when the fundamentals of their Government are destroyed or invaded? Or Whether they are to be considered as a Part of the whole British Empire, the whole English Nation, so far as to be bound in Honour, Conscience or Interest by the general Sense of the whole Nation?

However if this was the Rule, I believe it is very far from the general Sense of the whole Nation that America should be taxed by the british Parliament. If the Sense of all of the Empire, could be fairly and truly collected, it would appear, I believe, that a great Majority would be against taxing us, against or without our Consent. It is very certain that the Sense of Parliament is not the Sense of the Empire, nor a sure Indication of it.

But if all other Parts of the Empire were agreed unanimously in the Propriety and Rectitude of taxing us, this would not bind us. It is a fundamental, inherent, and unalienable Right of the People that they have some Check, Influence, or Controul in their Supream Legislature. If the Right of Taxation is conceded to Parliament, the Americans have no Check, or Influence at all left.—This Reasoning never was nor can be answered.   John Adams

PRIVATE MOBS AND POPULAR COMMOTIONS

To Abigail Adams

My Dear   Falmouth July 7th: 1774

Have you seen a List of the Addressers of the late Governor? There is one abroad, with the Character, Profession or Occupation of each Person against his Name. I have never seen it but Judge Brown says, against the Name of Andrew Fanuil Phillips, is "Nothing," and that Andrew when he first heard of it said, "Better be nothing with one Side, than every Thing with the other."—This was witty and smart, whether Andrew said it, or what is more likely, it was made for him.

A Notion prevails among all Parties that it is politest and genteelest to be on the Side of Administration, that the *better*

Sort, the *Wiser Few*, are on one Side; and that the Multitude, the Vulgar, the Herd, the Rabble, the Mob only are on the other. So difficult it is for the frail feeble Mind of Man to shake itself loose from all Prejudices and Habits. However Andrew, or his Prompter is perfectly Right, in his Judgment, and will finally be proved to be so, that the lowest on the Tory Scale, will make it more for his Interest than the highest on the Whiggish. And as long as a Man Adhers immoveably to his own Interest, and has Understanding or Luck enough to secure and promote it, he will have the Character of a Man of Sense And will be respected by a selfish World. I know of no better Reason for it than this—that most Men are conscious that they aim at their own Interest only, and that if they fail it is owing to short Sight or ill Luck, and therefore cant blame, but secretly applaud, admire and sometimes envy those whose Capacities have proved greater and Fortunes more prosperous.

I am to dine with Mr. Waldo, to day. Betty, as you once said.

I am engaged in a famous Cause: The Cause of King, of Scarborough vs. a Mob, that broke into his House, and rifled his Papers, and terrifyed him, his Wife, Children and Servants in the Night. The Terror, and Distress, the Distraction and Horror of this Family cannot be described by Words or painted upon Canvass. It is enough to move a Statue, to melt an Heart of Stone, to read the Story. A Mind susceptible of the Feelings of Humanity, an Heart which can be touch'd with Sensibility for human Misery and Wretchedness, must reluct, must burn with Resentment and Indignation, at such outragious Injuries. These private Mobs, I do and will detest. If Popular Commotions can be justifyed, in Opposition to Attacks upon the Constitution, it can be only when Fundamentals are invaded, nor then unless for absolute Necessity and with great Caution. But these Tarrings and Featherings, these breaking open Houses by rude and insolent Rabbles, in Resentment for private Wrongs or in pursuance of private Prejudices and Passions, must be discountenanced, cannot be even excused upon any Principle which can be entertained by a good Citizen—a worthy Member of Society.

Dined With Mr. Collector Francis Waldo, Esqr. in Company with Mr. Winthrop, the two Quincys and the two Sullivans. All very social and chearfull—full of Politicks. S. Quincy's Tongue ran as fast as any Bodies. He was clear in it, that the House of Commons had no Right to take Money out of our Pocketts, any more than any foreign State—repeated large Paragraphs from a Publication of Mr. Burke's in 1766, and large Paragraphs from Junius Americanus &c. This is to talk and to shine, before Persons who have no Capacity of judging, and who do not know that he is ignorant of every Rope in the Ship.

I shant be able to get away, till next Week. I am concerned only in 2 or 3 Cases and none of them are come on yet. Such an Eastern Circuit I never made. I shall bring home as much as I brought from home I hope, and not much more, I fear.

I go mourning in my Heart, all the Day long, tho I say nothing. I am melancholly for the Public, and anxious for my Family, as for myself a Frock and Trowsers, an Hoe and Spade, would do for my Remaining Days.

For God Sake make your Children, *hardy, active* and *industrious*, for Strength, Activity and Industry will be their only Resource and Dependance.   John Adams

From the Diary:
August 17–August 23, 1774

1774 AUG. 17. WEDNESDAY AT N HAVEN.

We are told here that New York are now well united and very firm.

This Morning Roger Sherman Esqr., one of the Delegates for Connecticutt, came to see us at the Tavern, Isaac Bears's. He is between 50 and 60—a solid sensible Man. He said he read Mr. Otis's Rights &c. in 1764 and thought that he had conceeded away the Rights of America. He thought the Reverse of the declaratory Act was true, vizt. that the Parliament of G.B. had Authority to make Laws for America in no Case whatever. He would have been very willing the Massachusetts should have rescinded that Part of their Circular Letter, where they allow Parliament to be the Supream Legislative, over the Colonies in any Case.

1774 AUG. 23. TUESDAY.

We went upon the new Dutch Church Steeple and took a View of the City. You have a very fine View of the whole City at once—the Harbour, East River, North River, Long Island, N. Jersey &c. The whole City is upon a Levell—a Flatt. The Houses in general are smaller than in Boston and the City occupies less Ground.

We breakfasted with Mr. Low, a Gentleman of Fortune and in Trade. His Lady is a Beauty. Rich Furniture again, for the Tea Table. Mr. Lott, the Treasurer of the Province, did us the Honour to break fast with us, and politely asked us to dine or to break fast with him—but we were engaged for all the Time we were to stay.

The Conversation turned upon the Constitution of the City; the Mayor and Recorder are appointed by the Governor, the Aldermen and Common Council are annually elected by the People. The Aldermen are the Magistrates of the City and the only ones. They have no Justices of the Peace in the City, so that the Magistracy of the City are all the Creatures of the People. The City cannot tax itself. The Constables, Assessors &c. are chosen annually. They Petition the Assembly every Year to be impowered by Law to assess the City for a certain Sum.

The whole Charge of the Province is annually between 5 and 6000£ York Money. Mr. Cushing says the Charge of the Massachusetts is about 12,000 L.M., which is 16,000 York Currency. The Support of Harvard Colledge, and of Forts and Garrisons and other Things makes the Difference.

About Eleven o Clock Mr. Low, Mr. Curtenius, Mr. Pascall Smith, Mr. Van Shaw and others, a Deputation from the Committee of Correspondence from this City, waited on Us, with an Invitation to dine with them Thursday next which we accepted.

One of the Gentlemen said, he was in England at the Time of a former Non Importation Agreement and it was not much felt among the Merchants or Manufacturers. Another of them replyed the true Cause of that was the German Contract and the Demand from Russia.

Mr. Ebenezer Hazard waited on me with a Letter requesting my assistance in making his Collection of American State

Papers. I recommended him to Mr. S. Adams, and Dr. Samuel Mather. I advised him to publish from Hackluyt, the Voyage of Sebastian Cabot, in this Collection. He thought it good Advice.

Hazard is certainly very capable of the Business he has undertaken—he is a Genius.

Went to the Coffee House, and saw the Virginia Paper. The Spirit of the People is prodigious. Their Resolutions are really grand.

We then went to Mr. Peter Vanbrugh Livingstons where at 3 O Clock we dined, with Scott, McDougal, Phillip Livingston, Mr. Thomas Smith, and a young Gentleman Son of Mr. Peter Livingston.

Smith and young Livingston seem to be modest, decent and sensible Men.

The Way we have been in, of breakfasting, dining, drinking Coffee &c. about the City is very disagreable on some Accounts. Altho it introduces us to the Acquaintance of many respectable People here, yet it hinders us from seeing the Colledge, the Churches, the Printers Offices and Booksellers Shops, and many other Things which we should choose to see.

With all the Opulence and Splendor of this City, there is very little good Breeding to be found. We have been treated with an assiduous Respect. But I have not seen one real Gentleman, one well bred Man since I came to Town. At their Entertainments there is no Conversation that is agreable. There is no Modesty—No Attention to one another. They talk very loud, very fast, and alltogether. If they ask you a Question, before you can utter 3 Words of your Answer, they will break out upon you, again—and talk away.

TRAVELING TO PHILADELPHIA

To Abigail Adams

My Dr.   Prince Town New Jersey Aug. 28th. 1774
    I received your kind Letter, at New York, and it is not easy

for you to imagine the Pleasure it has given me. I have not found a single Opportunity to write since I left Boston, excepting by the Post and I dont choose to write by that Conveyance, for fear of foul Play. But as We are now within forty two Miles of Philadelphia, I hope there to find some private Hand by which I can convey this.

The Particulars of our Journey, I must reserve, to be communicated after my Return. It would take a Volume to describe the whole. It has been upon the whole an Agreable Jaunt, We have had Opportunities to see the World, and to form Acquaintances with the most eminent and famous Men, in the several Colonies we have passed through. We have been treated with unbounded Civility, Complaisance, and Respect.

We Yesterday visited Nassau Hall Colledge, and were politely treated by the Schollars, Tutors, Professors and President, whom We are, this Day to hear preach. Tomorrow We reach the Theatre of Action. God Almighty grant us Wisdom and Virtue sufficient for the high Trust that is devolved upon Us. The Spirit of the People wherever we have been seems to be very favourable. They universally consider our Cause as their own, and express the firmest Resolution, to abide the Determination of the Congress.

I am anxious for our perplexed, distressed Province—hope they will be directed into the right Path. Let me intreat you, my Dear, to make yourself as easy and quiet as possible. Resignation to the Will of Heaven is our only Resource in such dangerous Times. Prudence and Caution should be our Guides. I have the strongest Hopes, that We shall yet see a clearer Sky, and better Times.

Remember my tender Love to my little Nabby. Tell her she must write me a Letter and inclose it in the next you send. I am charmed with your Amusement with our little Johnny. Tell him I am glad to hear he is so good a Boy as to read to his Mamma, for her Entertainment, and to keep himself out of the Company of rude Children. Tell him I hope to hear a good Account of his Accidence and Nomenclature, when I return. Kiss my little Charley and Tommy for me. Tell them I shall be at Home by November, but how much sooner I know not.

Remember me to all enquiring Friends—particularly to Uncle Quincy, your Pappa and Family, and Dr. Tufts and Family. Mr.

Thaxter, I hope, is a good Companion, in your Solitude. Tell him, if he devotes his Soul and Body to his Books, I hope, notwithstanding the Darkness of these Days, he will not find them unprofitable Sacrifices in future.

I have received three very obliging Letters, from Tudor, Trumble, and Hill. They have cheared us, in our Wanderings, and done us much Service.

My Compliments to Mr. Wibirt and Coll. Quincy, when you see them.

Your Account of the Rain refreshed me. I hope our Husbandry is prudently and industriously managed. Frugality must be our Support. Our Expences, in this Journey, will be very great—our only Reward will be the consolatory Reflection that We toil, spend our Time, and tempt Dangers for the public Good—happy indeed, if we do any good!

The Education of our Children is never out of my Mind. Train them to Virtue, habituate them to industry, activity, and Spirit. Make them consider every Vice, as shamefull and unmanly: fire them with Ambition to be usefull—make them disdain to be destitute of any usefull, or ornamental Knowledge or Accomplishment. Fix their Ambition upon great and solid Objects, and their Contempt upon little, frivolous, and useless ones. It is Time, my dear, for you to begin to teach them French. Every Decency, Grace, and Honesty should be inculcated upon them.

I have kept a few Minutes by Way of Journal, which shall be your Entertainment when I come home, but We have had so many Persons and so various Characters to converse with, and so many Objects to view, that I have not been able to be so particular as I could wish.—I am, with the tenderest Affection and Concern, your wandering   John Adams

From the Diary:
August 30–September 5, 1774

1774. AUG. 30. TUESDAY.

Walked a little about Town. Visited the Markett, the State house, the Carpenters Hall where the Congress is to Sit, &c.— then call'd at Mr. Mifflins—a grand, spacious, and elegant House. Here We had much Conversation with Mr. Charles Thompson, who is it seems about marrying a Lady a Relation of Mr. Dickensons with 5000£. st. This Charles Thompson is the Sam. Adams of Phyladelphia—the Life of the Cause of Liberty, they say.

A Friend Collins came to see us and invited us to dine on Thursday.

We returned to our Lodgings and Mr. Lynch, Mr. Gadsden, Mr. Middleton, and young Mr. Rutledge came to visit us. Mr. Linch introduced Mr. Middleton to us. Mr. Middleton was silent and reserved, young Rutledge was high enough. A Promise of the King was mentioned. He started, "I should have no Regard to his Word. His Promises are not worth any Thing," &c. This is a young, smart, spirited Body.

Mr. Blair came to visit us, with another Gentleman. Mr. Smith, an old Gentleman, was introduced to us, by his Son. Another Mr. Smith came in with our Mr. Paine.

The Regularity and Elegance of this City are very striking. It is situated upon a Neck of Land, about two Miles wide between the River De la ware and the River Schuilkill. The Streets are all exactly straight and parrallell to the River. Front Street is near the River, then 2 street, 3d, 4th, 5th, 6th, 7th, 8th, 9th. The cross Streets which intersect these are all equally wide, straight and parallell to each other, and are named from forrest and fruit Trees, Pear Street, Apple Street, Walnut street, Chestnut Street, &c.

Towards the Evening, Mr. Thomas Smith, son of the old Gentleman who made us a Visit who is a Brother of Mr. Smith the Minister of Casco Bay, and Dr. Shippen and his Brother and Mr. Reed, went with Us to the Hospital. We saw, in the lower Rooms under Ground, the Cells of the Lunaticks, a

Number of them, some furious, some merry, some Melancholly, and among the rest John Ingham, whom I once saved
at Taunton Court from being whipped and sold for Horse
stealing. We then went into the Sick Rooms which are very
long, large Walks with rows of Beds on each side, and the lame
and sick upon them—a dreadfull Scene of human Wretchedness. The Weakness and Languor, the Distress and Misery, of
these Objects is truely a Woefull Sight.

Dr. Shippen then carried Us into his Chamber where he
shewed Us a Series of Anatomical Paintings of exquisite Art.
Here was a great Variety of Views of the human Body, whole,
and in Parts. The Dr. entertained us with a very clear, concise
and comprehensive Lecture upon all the Parts of the human
Frame. This Entertainment charmed me. He first shewed us a
Set of Paintings of Bodies entire and alive—then of others with
the Skin taken off, then with the first Coat of Muscles taken
off, then with the second, then with all—the bare bones. Then
he shewed Us paintings of the Insides of a Man, seen before,
all the Muscles of the Belly being taken off. The Heart, Lungs,
Stomach, Gutts.

––––––––––––

1774 AUG. 31. WEDNESDAY.
Breakfasted at Mr. Bayards of Philadelphia, with Mr. Sprout
a presbyterian Minister.

Made a Visit to Governor Ward of Rhode Island at his
Lodgings. There We were introduced to several Gentlemen.

Mr. Dickenson, the Farmer of Pensylvania, came to Mr.
Wards Lodgings to see us, in his Coach and four beautifull
Horses. He was introduced to Us, and very politely said he
was exceedingly glad to have the Pleasure of seeing these Gentlemen, made some Enquiry after the Health of his Brother
and Sister, who are now in Boston. Gave us some Account of
his late ill Health and his present Gout. This was the first Time
of his getting out.

Mr. Dickenson has been Subject to Hectic Complaints. He
is a Shadow—tall, but slender as a Reed—pale as ashes. One
would think at first Sight that he could not live a Month. Yet
upon a more attentive Inspection, he looks as if the Springs of
Life were strong enough to last many Years.

We dined with Mr. Lynch, his Lady and Daughter at their Lodgings, Mrs. McKenzies. And a very agreable Dinner and Afternoon we had notwithstanding the violent Heat. We were all vastly pleased with Mr. Lynch. He is a solid, firm, judicious Man.

He told us that Coll. Washington made the most eloquent Speech at the Virginia Convention that ever was made. Says he, "I will raise 1000 Men, subsist them at my own Expence, and march my self at their Head for the Relief of Boston."

He entertained us with the Scandalous History of Sir Egerton Leigh—the Story of his Wifes Sister, and of his Dodging his Uncle, the Story the Girl swore to before the Lord Mayor, and all that.

There is not says Lynch a greater Rascall among all the Kings Friends. He has great Merit, in this Reign.

Mr. Lynch says they shall export this Year 12,000 Wt. of Indigo and 150,000 Tierces of Rice from S. Carolina. About 300 Ships are employed.

Mrs. Lynch enquired kindly after Mrs. Adams's Health, and Mrs. Smith and family and Mr. Boylstone And Mrs. and Mr. Gill &c.

I find that there is a Tribe of People here, exactly like the Tribe in the Massachusetts, of Hutchinsonian Addressers. There is indeed a Sett in every Colony. We have seen the Revolutions of their Sentiments. Their Opinions have undergone as many Changes as the Moon. At the Time of the Stamp Act, and just before it, they professed to be against the Parliamentary Claim of Right to tax Americans, to be Friends to our Constitutions, our Charter &c. Bernard was privately, secretly endeavouring to procure an Alteration of our Charter. But he concealed his Designs untill his Letters were detected. Hutchinson professed to be a stanch Friend to Liberty, and to our Charter, untill his Letters were detected—a great Number of good People thought him a good Man, and a Sincere Friend to the Congregational Interest in Religion and to our Charter Priviledges. They went on with this machiavilian Dissimulation, untill those Letters were detected—after that they waited untill the Boston Port Bill was passed, and then, thinking the People must submit immediately and that Lord North would carry his whole System triumphantly, they threw off the Mask. Dr. Smith, Mr. Galloway, Mr. Vaughan and others in this Town, are now just where the Hutchinsonian Faction were in the Year 1764, when We were endeavouring to obtain a Repeal of the Stamp Act.

Thursday, September 1, 1774

1774. SATURDAY. SEPTR. 3.

Breakfasted at Dr. Shippens. Dr. Witherspoon was there. Coll. R. H. Lee lodges there. He is a masterly Man.

This Mr. Lee is a Brother of the Sherriff of London, and of Dr. Arthur Lee, and of Mrs. Shippen. They are all sensible, and deep thinkers.

Lee is for making the Repeal of every Revenue Law, the Boston Port Bill, the Bill for altering the Massachusetts Constitution, and the Quebec Bill, and the Removal of all the Troops, the End of the Congress, and an Abstinence from all Dutied Articles the Means—Rum, Mollosses, Sugar, Tea, Wine, Fruits, &c.

He is absolutely certain, that the same Ship which carries home the Resolution will bring back the Redress. If we were to suppose that any Time would intervene, he should be for Exceptions.

He thinks We should inform his Majesty, that We never can be happy, while the Lords Bute, Mansfield and North are his Confidents and Councillors.

He took his Pen and attempted a Calculation of the Numbers of People represented by the Congress which he made about 2200000, and of the Revenue now actually raised which he made 80,000£ st.

He would not allow Ld. North to have great Abilities. He had seen no symptoms of them. His whole Administration had been blunder.

He said the Opposition had been so feeble and incompetent hitherto that it was Time to make vigorous Exertions.

Mrs. Shippen is a religious and a reasoning Lady. She said she had often thought, that the People of Boston could not have behaved through their Tryals, with so much Prudence and firmness at the same Time, if they had not been influenced by a Superiour Power.

Mr. Lee think's that to strike at the Navigation Acts would unite every Man in Britain against us, because the Kingdom could not exist without them, and the Advantages they derive from these Regulations and Restrictions of our Trade, are an ample Compensation for all the Protection they have afforded us, or will afford us.

Dr. Witherspoon enters with great Spirit into the American Cause. He seems as hearty a Friend as any of the Natives—an animated Son of Liberty.

This Forenoon, Mr. Cæsar Rodney, of the lower Counties on Delaware River, two Mr. Tilghmans from Maryland, were introduced to us.

We went with Mr. Wm. Barrell to his Store and drank Punch and eat dryed smoaked Sprats with him, read the Papers and our Letters from Boston.

Dined with Mr. Joseph Reed the Lawyer, with Mrs. Deberdt and Mrs. Reed, Mr. Willing, Mr. Thom. Smith, Mr. De hart, and &c.

Spent the Evening at Mr. Mifflins with Lee and Harrison from Virginia, the two Rutledges, Dr. Witherspoon, Dr. Shippen, Dr. Steptoe, and another Gentleman. An elegant Supper, and We drank Sentiments till 11 O Clock. Lee and Harrison were very high. Lee had dined with Mr. Dickenson, and drank Burgundy the whole Afternoon.

Harrison gave us for a Sentiment "a constitutional Death to the Lords Bute, Mansfield and North." Paine gave us "May the Collision of british Flint and American Steel, produce that Spark of Liberty which shall illumine the latest Posterity." Wisdom to Britain and Firmness to the Colonies, may Britain be wise and America free. The Friends of America throughout the World. Union of the Colonies. Unanimity to the Congress. May the Result of the Congress, answer the Expectations of the People. Union of Britain and the Colonies, on a Constitutional Foundation—and many other such Toasts.

Young Rutledge told me, he studied 3 Years at the Temple. He thinks this a great Distinction. Says he took a Volume of Notes, which J. Quincy transcribed. Says that young Gentlemen ought to travel early, because that freedom and Ease of

Behaviour, which is so necessary, cannot be acquired but in early Life. This Rutledge is young—sprightly but not deep. He has the most indistinct, inarticulate Way of Speaking. Speaks through his nose—a wretched Speaker in Conversation. How he will shine in public I dont yet know. He seems good natured, tho conceited. His Lady is with him in bad Health.

His Brother still maintains the Air of Reserve, Design and Cunning—like Duane, and Galloway, and Bob Auchmuty.

Cæsar Rodney is the oddest looking Man in the World. He is tall—thin and slender as a Reed—pale—his Face is not bigger than a large Apple. Yet there is Sense and Fire, Spirit, Wit and Humour in his Countenance.

He made himself very merry with Ruggles and his pretended Scruples and Timidities, at the last Congress.

Mr. Reed told us, at dinner, that he never saw greater Joy, than he saw in London when the News arrived that the Nonimportation agreement was broke. They were universally shaking Hands and Congratulating each other.

He says that George Haley is the worst Enemy to America that he knew there—swore to him that he would stand by Government in all its Measures, and was allways censuring and cursing America.

1774. SEPTR. 5. MONDAY.

At Ten, The Delegates all met at the City Tavern, and walked to the Carpenters Hall, where they took a View of the Room, and of the Chamber where is an excellent Library. There is also a long Entry, where Gentlemen may walk, and a convenient Chamber opposite to the Library. The General Cry was, that this was a good Room, and the Question was put, whether We were satisfyed with this Room, and it passed in the Affirmative. A very few were for the Negative and they were chiefly from Pensylvania and New York.

Then Mr. Lynch arose, and said there was a Gentleman present who had presided with great Dignity over a very respectable Society, greatly to the Advantage of America, and he therefore proposed that the Hon. Peytoun Randolph Esqr., one of the Delegates from Virginia, and the late Speaker of their House of Burgesses, should be appointed Chairman and he doubted not it would be unanimous.—The Question was put and he was unanimously chosen.

Mr. Randolph then took the Chair, and the Commissions of the Delegates were all produced and read.

Then Mr. Lynch proposed that Mr. Charles Thompson a Gentleman of Family, Fortune, and Character in this City should be appointed Secretary, which was accordingly done without opposition, tho Mr. Duane and Mr. Jay discovered at first an Inclination to seek further.

Mr. Duane then moved that a Committee should be appointed, to prepare Regulations for this Congress. Several Gentlemen objected. I then arose and asked Leave of the President to request of the Gentleman from New York, an Explanation, and that he would point out some particular Regulations which he had in his Mind. He mentioned particularly the Method of voting—whether it should be by Colonies, or by the Poll, or by Interests.

Mr. Henry then arose, and said this was the first general Congress which had ever happened—that no former Congress could be a Precedent—that We should have occasion for more general Congresses, and therefore that a precedent ought to be established now. That it would be great Injustice, if a little Colony should have the same Weight in the Councils of America, as a great one, and therefore he was for a Committee.

Major Sullivan observed that a little Colony had its All at Stake as well as a great one.

This is a Question of great Importance.—If We vote by Colonies, this Method will be liable to great Inequality and Injustice, for 5 small Colonies, with 100,000 People in each may outvote 4 large ones, each of which has 500,000 Inhabitants. If We vote by the Poll, some Colonies have more than their Proportion of Members, and others have less. If We vote by Interests, it will be attended with insuperable Difficulties, to ascertain the true Importance of each Colony.—Is the Weight of a Colony to be ascertained by the Number of Inhabitants merely—or by the Amount of their Trade, the Quantity of their Exports and Imports, or by any compound Ratio of both. This will lead us into such a Field of Controversy as will greatly perplex us. Besides I question whether it is possible to ascertain, at this Time, the Numbers of our People or the

Value of our Trade. It will not do in such a Case, to take each other's Words. It ought to be ascertained by authentic Evidence, from Records.

"A COLLECTION OF THE GREATEST MEN"

To Abigail Adams

My Dear   Phyladelphia Septr. 8. 1774

When or where this Letter will find you, I know not. In what Scenes of Distress and Terror, I cannot foresee.—We have received a confused Account from Boston, of a dreadfull Catastrophy. The Particulars, We have not heard. We are waiting with the Utmost Anxiety and Impatience, for further Intelligence.

The Effect of the News We have both upon the Congress and the Inhabitants of this City, was very great—great indeed! Every Gentleman seems to consider the Bombardment of Boston, as the Bombardment, of the Capital of his own Province. Our Deliberations are grave and serious indeed.

It is a great Affliction to me that I cannot write to you oftener than I do. But there are so many Hindrances, that I cannot.

It would fill Volumes, to give you an Idea of the scenes I behold and the Characters I converse with.

We have so much Business, so much Ceremony, so much Company, so many Visits to recive and return, that I have not Time to write. And the Times are such, as render it imprudent to write freely.

We cannot depart from this Place, untill the Business of the Congress is compleated, and it is the general Disposition to proceed slowly. When I shall be at home I cant say. If there is Distress and Danger in Boston, pray invite our Friends, as many as possible, to take an Assylum with you. Mrs. Cushing and Mrs. Adams if you can.

There is in the Congress a Collection of the greatest Men upon this Continent, in Point of Abilities, Virtues and Fortunes. The Magnanimity, and public Spirit, which I see here, makes me blush for the sordid venal Herd, which I have seen in my own Province. The Addressers, and the new Councillors, are held in universal Contempt and Abhorrence, from one End of the Continent to the other.

Be not under any Concern for me. There is little Danger from any Thing We shall do, at the Congress. There is such a Spirit, thro the Colonies, and the Members of the Congress are such Characters, that no Danger can happen to Us, which will not involve the whole Continent, in Universal Desolation, and in that Case who would wish to live?

Make my Compliments to Mr. Thaxter and Mr. Rice—and to every other of my Friends. My Love to all my dear Children—tell them to be good, and to mind their Books. I shall come home and see them, I hope, the latter End of next Month.

Adieu.   John Adams

P.S. You will judge how Things are like to be in Boston, and whether it will not be best to remove the Office entirely to Braintree. Mr. Hill and Williams, may come up, if they choose, paying for their Board.

THE CONGRESS AND MASSACHUSETTS

To William Tudor

Dear Sir   Philadelphia Septr. 29. 1774

I wish it was in my Power, to write you any Thing for the Relief of your Anxiety, under the Pressure of those Calamities which now distress our beloved Town of Boston and Province of Massachusetts. The Sentiments expressed in your last to me, are Such as would do Honour to the best of Citizens, in the Minds of the Virtuous and worthy of any Age or Country in the worst of Times.

> Dulce et decorum est pro Patria mori.
> Wouldst thou receive thy Countrys loud Applause,
> Lov'd as her Father, as her God ador'd,

> Be thou the bold Asserter of her Cause,
> her Voice in Council, in the Fight her Sword.

You can have no adequate Idea of the Pleasures or of the Difficulties of the Errand I am now upon. The Congress is Such an Assembly as never before came together on a Sudden, in any Part of the World. Here are Fortunes, Abilities, Learning, Eloquence, Acuteness equal to any I ever met with in my Life. Here is a Diversity of Religions, Educations, Manners, Interests, Such as it would Seem almost impossible to unite in any one Plan of Conduct.

Every Question is discussed with a Moderation, and an Acuteness and a minuteness equal to that of Queen Elizabeths privy Council.

This occasions infinite Delays. We are under Obligations of Secrecy in every Thing except the Single Vote which you have Seen approving the Resolutions of the County of Suffolk. What Effect this Vote may have with you is uncertain. What you will do, God knows. You Say you look up to the Congress. It is well you Should: but I hope you will not expect too much from Us.

The Delegates here are not Sufficiently acquainted with our Province and with the Circumstances you are in, to form a Judgment of what Course it is proper for you to take. They Start at the Thought of taking up the old Charter,: They Shudder at the Prospect of Blood. Yet they are unanimously and unalterably against your Submission, to any of the Acts for a Single Moment.

You See by this What they are for—vizt, that you Stand Stock Still, and live without Government, or Law. At least for the present and as long as you can. I have represented to them, wherever I see them, the Utter Impossibility, of four hundred Thousand People existing long without a Legislature or Courts of Justice. They all Seem to acknowledge it: Yet nothing can be as yet accomplished.

We hear, perpetually, the most figurative Panegyricks upon our Wisdom Fortitude and Temperance: The most fervent Exhortations to perseverance. But nothing more is done.

I may venture to tell you, that I believe We Shall agree to

N. Imp. N. Consumption, and Non Exportation, but not to commence so soon as I could wish.

Indeed all this would be insufficient, for our Purpose—a more adequate Support, and Relief to the Massachusetts Should be adopted. But I tremble for fear, We should fail of obtaining it.

There is however a most laudable Zeal, and an excellent Spirit, which every Day increases, especially in this City. The Quakers had a General Meeting here last Sunday, and are deeply affected with the Complexion of the Times. They have recommended it to all their People to renounce Tea, and indeed the People of this City of all Denominations have laid it generally aside Since our Arrival here. They are about setting up Companys of Cadets, voluntarily.—&c. &c. &c.

It is the universal opinion here that the General, Gage, is in the Horrors, and that he means only to act upon the Defensive. How well this opinion is founded you, can judge better than I.

I must beseech you to shew this Letter to no Man, in whom you have not the most perfect Confidence. It may do a great deal of Mischief.

We have had numberless Prejudices to remove here. We have been obliged to act, with great Delicacy and Caution. We have been obliged to keep ourselves out of Sight, and to feel Pulses, and Sound the Depths—to insinuate our Sentiments, Designs and Desires by means of other Persons, Sometimes of one Province and Sometimes of another. A future opportunity I hope, in Conversations will make you acquainted with all. adieu,

John Adams

"THE CONFUSIONS AND DANGERS, WHICH SURROUND YOU"

To Abigail Adams

My Dear   Phyladelphia Septr. 29. 1774
    Sitting down to write to you, is a Scene almost too tender for my State of Nerves. It calls up to my View the anxious, dis-

tress'd State you must be in, amidst the Confusions and Dangers, which surround you. I long to return, and administer all the Consolation in my Power, but when I shall have accomplished all the Business I have to do here, I know not, and if it should be necessary to stay here till Christmas, or longer, in order to effect our Purposes, I am determined patiently to wait.

Patience, Forbearance, Long Suffering, are the Lessons taught here for our Province, and at the same Time absolute and open Resistance to the new Government. I wish I could convince Gentlemen, of the Danger, or Impracticability of this as fully as I believe it myself.

The Art and Address, of Ambassadors from a dozen belligerant Powers of Europe, nay of a Conclave of Cardinals at the Election of a Pope, or of the Princes in Germany at the Choice of an Emperor, would not exceed the Specimens We have seen. —Yet the Congress all profess the same political Principles.

They all profess to consider our Province as suffering in the common Cause, and indeed they seem to feel for Us, as if for themselves. We have had as great Questions to discuss as ever engaged the Attention of Men, and an infinite Multitude of them.

I received a very kind Letter from Deacon Palmer, acquainting me with Mr. Cranch's designs of removing to Braintree, which I approve very much—and wish I had an House for every Family in Boston, and Abilities to provide for them, in the Country.

I submit it to you, my Dear, whether it would not be best to remove all the Books and Papers and Furniture in the Office at Boston up to Braintree. There will be no Business there nor any where, I suppose, and my young Friends can study there better than in Boston at present.

I shall be kill'd with Kindness, in this Place. We go to congress at Nine, and there We stay, most earnestly engaged in Debates upon the most abstruse Misteries of State until three in the Afternoon, then We adjourn, and go to Dinner with some of the Nobles of Pensylvania, at four O Clock and feast upon ten thousand Delicacies, and sitt drinking Madeira, Claret and Burgundy till six or seven, and then go home, fatigued to death with Business, Company, and Care.—Yet I

hold it out, surprizingly. I drink no Cyder, but feast upon Phyladelphia Beer, and Porter. A Gentleman, one Mr. Hare, has
lately set up in this City a Manufactory of Porter, as good as
any that comes from London. I pray We may introduce it into
the Massachusetts. It agrees with me, infinitely better than
Punch, Wine, or Cyder, or any other Spirituous Liquor.—My
Love to my dear Children one by one. My Compliments to
Mr. Thaxter, and Rice and every Body else. Yours most affec-
tionately,   John Adams

VISITING A CATHOLIC CHURCH

To Abigail Adams

My Dear   Phyladelphia Octr. 9. 1774
   I am wearied to Death with the Life I lead. The Business of
the Congress is tedious, beyond Expression. This Assembly is
like no other that ever existed. Every Man in it is a great
Man—an orator, a Critick, a statesman, and therefore every
Man upon every Question must shew his oratory, his Criticism
and his Political Abilities.
   The Consequence of this is, that Business is drawn and spun
out to an immeasurable Length. I believe if it was moved and
seconded that We should come to a Resolution that Three
and two make five We should be entertained with Logick and
Rhetorick, Law, History, Politicks and Mathematicks, con-
cerning the Subject for two whole Days, and then We should
pass the Resolution unanimously in the Affirmative.
   The perpetual Round of feasting too, which we are obliged
to submit to, make the Pilgrimage more tedious to me.
   This Day I went to Dr. Allisons Meeting in the Forenoon
and heard the Dr.—a good Discourse upon the Lords Supper.
This is a Presbyterian Meeting. I confess I am not fond of the
Presbyterian Meetings in this Town. I had rather go to Church.
We have better Sermons, better Prayers, better Speakers,
softer, sweeter Musick, and genteeler Company. And I must
confess, that the Episcopal Church is quite as agreable to my
Taste as the Presbyterian. They are both Slaves to the Domina-

tion of the Priesthood. I like the Congregational Way best—next to that the Independant.

This afternoon, led by Curiosity and good Company I strolled away to Mother Church, or rather Grandmother Church, I mean the Romish Chappell. Heard a good, short, moral Essay upon the Duty of Parents to their Children, founded in justice and Charity, to take care of their Interests temporal and spiritual. This Afternoons Entertainment was to me, most awfull and affecting. The poor Wretches, fingering their Beads, chanting Latin, not a Word of which they understood, their Pater Nosters and Ave Maria's. Their holy Water —their Crossing themselves perpetually—their Bowing to the Name of Jesus, wherever they hear it—their Bowings, and Kneelings, and Genuflections before the Altar. The Dress of the Priest was rich with Lace—his Pulpit was Velvet and Gold. The Altar Piece was very rich—little Images and Crucifixes about—Wax Candles lighted up. But how shall I describe the Picture of our Saviour in a Frame of Marble over the Altar at full Length upon the Cross, in the Agonies, and the Blood dropping and streaming from his Wounds.

The Musick consisting of an organ, and a Choir of singers, went all the Afternoon, excepting sermon Time, and the Assembly chanted—most sweetly and exquisitely.

Here is every Thing which can lay hold of the Eye, Ear, and Imagination. Every Thing which can charm and bewitch the simple and ignorant. I wonder how Luther ever broke the spell.

Adieu.

John Adams

From the Diary: October 11–24, 1774

1774 TUESDAY OCTR. 11.

Dined with Mr. McKean in Markett Street, with Mr. Reed, Rodney, Chace, Johnson, Paca, Dr. Morgan, Mr. R. Penn, &c.

Spent the Evening with Mr. Henry at his Lodgings consulting about a Petition to the King.

Henry said he had no public Education. At fifteen he read

Virgill and Livy, and has not looked into a Latin Book since. His father left him at that Age, and he has been struggling thro Life ever since. He has high Notions. Talks about exalted Minds, &c. He has a horrid Opinion of Galloway, Jay, and the Rutledges. Their System he says would ruin the Cause of America. He is very impatient to see such Fellows, and not be at Liberty to describe them in their true Colours.

————————

1774. MONDAY. OCTR. 24.

In Congress, nibbling and quibbling—as usual.

There is no greater Mortification than to sit with half a dozen Witts, deliberating upon a Petition, Address, or Memorial. These great Witts, these subtle Criticks, these refined Genius's, these learned Lawyers, these wise Statesmen, are so fond of shewing their Parts and Powers, as to make their Consultations very tedius.

Young Ned Rutledge is a perfect Bob o' Lincoln—a Swallow —a Sparrow—a Peacock—excessively vain, excessively weak, and excessively variable and unsteady—jejune, inane, and puerile.

Mr. Dickinson is very modest, delicate, and timid.

Massachusettensis [Daniel Leonard] No. I

To the Inhabitants of the Province of Massachusetts Bay,

MY DEAR COUNTRYMEN,

When a people, by what means soever, are reduced to such a situation, that every thing they hold dear, as men and citizens, is at stake, it is not only excuseable, but even praiseworthy for an individual to offer to the public any thing, that he may think has a tendency to ward off the impending danger; nor should he be restrained from an apprehension that what he may offer will be unpopular, any more than a physician should be restrained from prescribing a salutary medicine, through fear it might be unpalatable to his patient.

The press, when open to all parties and influenced by none, is a salutary engine in a free state, perhaps a necessary one to preserve the freedom of that state; but, when a party has gained the ascendancy so far as to become the licensers of the press, either by an act of government, or by playing off the resentment of the populace against printers and authors, the press itself becomes an engine of oppression or licentiousness, and is as pernicious to society, as otherwise it would be beneficial. It is too true to be denied, that ever since the origin of our controversy with Great Britain, the press, in this town, has been much devoted to the partizans of liberty; they have been indulged in publishing what they pleased, *fas vel nefas*, while little has been published on the part of government. The effect this must have had upon the minds of the people in general is obvious; they must have formed their opinion upon a partial view of the subject, and of course it must have been in some degree erroneous. In short, the changes have been rung so often upon oppression, tyranny and slavery, that, whether sleeping or waking, they are continually vibrating in our ears; and it is now high time to ask ourselves, whether we have not been deluded by sound only.

My dear countrymen, let us divest ourselves of prejudice, take a view of our present wretched situation, contrast it with our former happy one, carefully investigate the cause, and industriously seek some means to escape the evils we now feel, and prevent those that we have reason to expect.

We have been so long advancing to our present state, and by such gradations, that perhaps many of us are insensible of our true state and real danger. Should you be told that acts of high treason are flagrant through the country, that a great part of the province is in actual rebellion, would you believe it true? Should you not deem the person asserting it, an enemy to the province? Nay, should you not spurn him from you with indignation? Be calm, my friends; it is necessary to know the worst of a disease, to enable us to provide an effectual remedy. Are not the bands of society cut asunder, and the sanctions that hold man to man, trampled upon? Can any of us recover a debt, or obtain compensation for an injury, by law? Are not many persons, whom once we respected and revered, driven from their homes and families, and forced to fly to the army for protection, for no other reason but their having accepted commissions under our king? Is not civil government dissolved? Some have been made to believe that nothing short of attempting the life of the king, or fighting his troops, can amount to high treason or rebellion. If, reader, you are one of those, apply to an honest lawyer, (if such an one can be found) and enquire what kind of offence it is for a number of men to assemble armed, and forcibly to obstruct the course of justice, even to prevent the king's courts from being held at their stated terms; for a body of people to seize upon the king's provincial revenue; I mean the monies collected by virtue of grants made by the general court to his majesty for the support of his government, within this province; for a body of men to assemble without being called by authority, and to pass governmental acts; or for a number of people to take the militia out of the hands of the king's representative, or to form a new militia, or to raise men and appoint officers for a public purpose, without the order or permission of the king, or his representative; or for a number of men to take to their arms, and march with a professed design of opposing the king's troops; ask, reader, of such a lawyer, what is the crime, and what the punishment; and if, perchance, thou art one that hast been active in these things, and art not insensibility itself, his answer will harrow up thy soul.

I assure you, my friends, I would not that this conduct should be told beyond the borders of this province; I wish it were consigned to perpetual oblivion; but alas, it is too notorious to be concealed; our news-papers have already published it to the world; we can neither prevent nor conceal it. The shaft is already sped, and the utmost exertion is necessary to prevent the blow. We already feel the effects of anarchy; mutual confidence, affection, and tranquility, those sweetners of human life, are succeeded by distrust, hatred, and wild uproar; the useful arts of agriculture and commerce are neglected for caballing, mobbing this or the other man, because he acts, speaks, or is suspected of thinking different from the prevailing sentiment of the times, in purchasing arms, and forming a militia; O height of madness! with a professed design of opposing Great Britain. I suspect many of us have been induced to join in these measures, or but faintly to oppose them, from an apprehension that Great Britain would not, or could not exert herself sufficiently to subdue America. Let us consider this matter. However closely we may hug ourselves in the opinion, that the parliament has no right to tax or legislate for us, the people of England hold the contrary opinion as firmly. They tell us we are a part of the British empire; that every state, from the nature of government, must have a supreme, uncontrolable power, co-extensive with the empire itself; and that that power is vested in parliament. It is as unpopular to deny this doctrine in Great Britain, as it is to assert it in the colonies; so there is but little probability of serving ourselves at this day by our ingenious distinctions between a right of legislation for one purpose, and not for another. We have bid them defiance; and the longest sword must carry it, unless we change our measures. Mankind are the same, in all parts of the world. The same fondness for dominion that presides in the breast of an American, actuates the breast of an European. If the colonies are not a part of the British empire already, and subject to the supreme authority of the state, Great Britain will make them so. Had we been prudent enough to confine our opposition within certain limits, we might have stood some chance of succeeding once more; but alas, we have passed the Rubicon. It is now universally said and believed, in England, that if this opportunity of reclaiming the colonies, and reducing them to a sense of their duty is lost, they, in truth, will be dismembered from the empire, and become as distinct a state from Great Britain, as Hanover; that is, although they may continue their allegiance to the person of the king, they will own none to the imperial crown of Great Britain, nor yield obedience, to any of her laws, but such as they shall think proper to adopt. Can you indulge the thought one moment, that Great Britain will consent to this? For what has she protected and defended the colonies against the maritime powers of Europe, from their first British settlement to this day? For what did she purchase New-York of the Dutch? For what was she so lavish of her best blood and treasure in the conquest of Canada, and other territories in America? Was it to raise up a rival state, or to enlarge her own empire? Or if the consideration of empire was out of the question, what security can she have of our trade, when once she has lost our obedience? I mention these things, my friends, that you may know how people reason upon the subject in England; and to convince you that you are much deceived, if you imagine that Great Britain will accede to the claims of the colonies, she will as soon conquer as New-England as Ireland or Canada, if either of them revolted; and by arms, if the milder influences of government prove ineffectual. Perhaps you are as fatally mistaken in another respect, I mean, as to the power of Great Britain to conquer. But can any of you, that think soberly upon the matter, be so deluded as to believe that Great Britain, who so lately carried her arms with success to every part of the globe, triumphed over the united powers of France and Spain, and whose fleets give law to the ocean, is unable to conquer us? Should the colonies unite in a war against Great Britain (which by the way is not a supposable case) the colonies south of Pennsylvania would be unable to furnish any men; they have not more than is necessary to govern their numerous slaves, and to defend themselves against the Indians. I will suppose that the northern colonies can furnish as many, and indeed more men than can be used to advantage; but have you arms fit for a campaign? If you have arms, have you military stores, or can you procure them? When this war is proclaimed, all supplies from foreign parts will be cut off. Have you money to maintain the war? Or had you all those things, some others are still wanting, which are absolutely necessary to encounter regular troops, that is discipline, and that subordination, whereby each can command all below him, from a general officer to the lowest subaltern; these you neither have nor can have in such a war. It is well known that the provincials in the late war were never brought to a proper discipline, though they had the example of the regular troops to encourage, and the martial law to enforce it. We all know, notwithstanding the province law for regulating the militia, it was under little more command than what the officers could obtain from treating and humouring the common soldier; what, then, can be expected from such an army as you will bring into the field, if you bring any, each one a politician, puffed up with his own opinion, and feeling himself second to none? Can any of you command ten thousand such men? Can you punish the disobedient? Can all your wisdom direct their strength, courage or activity to any given point? Would not the least disappointment or unfavourable aspect cause a general dereliction of the service? Your new-fangled militia have already given us a *specimen* of their future conduct. In some of their companies, they have already chosen two, in others, three sets of officers, and are as dissatisfied with the last choice as the first. I do not doubt the natural bravery of my countrymen; all men would act the same part in the same situation. Such is the army with which you are to oppose the most powerful nation upon the globe. An experienced officer would rather take his chance with five thousand British troops, than with fifty thousand such militia. I have hitherto confined my observations to the war within the interior parts of the colonies, let us now turn our eyes to our extensive sea coast, and that we find wholly at the mercy of Great Britain; our trade, fishery, navigation, and maritime towns taken from us the very day that war is proclaimed. Inconceivably shocking the scene; if we turn our views to the wilderness, our back settlements a prey to our ancient enemy, the Canadians, whose wounds received from us in the late war, will bleed afresh at the prospect of revenge, and to the numerous tribes of savages, whose tender mercies are cruelties. Thus with the British navy in the front, Canadians and savages in the rear, a regular army in the midst, we must be certain that whenever the sword of civil war is unsheathed, devastation will pass through our land like a whirlwind; our houses be burnt to ashes; our fair possessions laid waste, and he that falls by the sword, will be happy in escaping a more ignominious death.

I have hitherto gone upon a supposition, that all the colonies, from Nova-Scotia to Georgia, would unite in the war against Great Britain; but I believe, if we consider coolly upon the matter, we shall find no reason to expect any assistance out of New-England; if so, there will be no arm stretched out to save us. New England, or perhaps this self-devoted province will fall alone the unpitied victim of its own folly, and furnish the world with one more instance of the fatal consequences of rebellion.

I have as yet said nothing of the difference in sentiment among ourselves. Upon a superficial view we might imagine that this province was nearly unanimous; but the case is far different. A very considerable part of the men of property in this province, are at this day firmly attached to the cause of government; bodies of men, compelling persons to disavow their sentiments, to resign commissions, or to subscribe leagues and covenants, has wrought no change in their sentiments; it has only attached them more closely to government, and caused them to wish more fervently, and to pray more devoutly, for its restoration. These, and thousands beside, if they fight at all, will fight under the banners of loyalty. I can assure you that associations are now forming in several parts of this province, for the support of his majesty's government and mutual defence; and let me tell you, whenever the royal standard shall be set up, there will be such a flocking to it, as will astonish the most obdurate. And now, in God's name, what is it that has brought us to this brink of destruction? Has not the government of Great Britain been as mild and equitable in the colonies, as in any part of her extensive dominions? Has not she been a nursing mother to us, from the days of our infancy to this time? Has she not been indulgent almost to a fault? Might not each one of us at this day have sat quietly under his own vine and fig-tree, and there have been none to make us afraid, were it not for our own folly? Will not posterity be amazed, when they are told that the present distraction took its rise from a three penny duty on tea, and call it a more unaccountable frenzy, and more disgraceful to the annals of America, than that of the witchcraft?

I will attempt in the next paper to retrace the steps and mark the progressions that led us to this state. I promise to do it with fidelity; and if any thing should look like reflecting on individuals or bodies of men, it must be set down to my impartiality, and not to a fondness for censuring.

MASSACHUSETTENSIS.

Massachusetts Gazette; and the Boston
Post-Boy and Advertiser, December 12, 1774

Massachusettensis [Daniel Leonard] No. II

To the Inhabitants of the Province of Massachusetts Bay,

MY DEAR COUNTRYMEN,

I endeavoured last week to convince you of our real danger, not to render you desperate, but to induce you to seek immediately some effectual remedy. Our case is not yet remediless, as we have to deal with a nation not less generous and humane, than powerful and brave; just indeed, but not vindictive.

I shall, in this and successive papers, trace this yet growing distemper through its several stages, from the first rise to the present hour, point out the causes, mark the effects, shew the madness of persevering in our present line of conduct, and recommend what, I have been long convinced, is our only remedy. I confess myself to be one of those, that think our present calamity is in a great measure to be attributed to the bad policy of a popular party in this province; and that their measures for several years past, whatever may have been their intention, have been diametrically opposite to their profession,—the public good; and cannot, at present, but compare their leaders to false guide, that having led a benighted traveller through many mazes and windings in a thick wood, finds himself at length on the brink of a horrid precipice, and, to save himself, seizes fast hold of his follower, to the utmost hazard of plunging both headlong down the steep, and being dashed in pieces together against the rocks below.

In ordinary cases we may talk in the measured language of a courtier; but when such a weight of vengeance is suspended over our heads, by a single thread, as threatens every moment to crush us to atoms, delicacy itself would be ill-timed. I will declare the plain truth whenever I find it, and claim it as a right to canvass popular measures and expose their errors and pernicious tendency, as freely as governmental measures are canvassed, so long as I continue myself within the limits of the law.

At the conclusion of the late war, Great Britain found that though she had humbled her enemies, and greatly enlarged her own empire, that the national debt amounted to almost one hundred and fifty millions, and that the annual expence of keeping her extended dominions in a state of defence, which good policy dictates no less in a time of peace than war, was increased in proportion to the new acquisitions. Heavy taxes and duties were already laid, not only upon the luxuries and conveniences, but even the necessaries of life in Great Britain and Ireland. She knew that the colonies were as much benefitted by the conquests in the late war, as any part of the empire, and indeed more so, as their continental foes were subdued, and they might now extend their settlements not only to Canada, but even to the western ocean.—The greatest opening was given to agriculture, the natural livelihood of the country, that ever was known in the history of the world, and their trade was protected by the British navy. The revenue to the crown, from America, amounted to but little more than the charges of collecting it. She thought it as reasonable that the colonies should bear a part of the national burden, as that they should share in the national benefit. For this purpose the stamp-act was passed. The colonies soon found that the duties imposed by the stamp-act would be grievous, as they were laid upon custom-house papers, law proceedings, conveyancing, and indeed extended to almost all their internal trade and dealings. It was generally believed through the colonies, that this was a tax not only exceeding our proportion, but beyond our utmost ability to pay. This idea, united the colonies generally in opposing it. At first we did not dream of denying the *authority* of parliament to tax us, much less to legislate for us. We had always considered ourselves, as a part of the British empire, and the parliament, as the supreme legislature of the whole. Acts of parliament for regulating our internal polity were familiar. We had paid postage agreeable to act of parliament, for establishing a post-office, duties imposed for regulating trade, and even for raising a revenue to the crown without questioning the right, though we closely adverted to the rate or quantum. We knew that in all those acts of government, the good of the whole had been consulted, and whenever through want of information any thing grievous had been ordained, we were sure of obtaining redress by a proper representation of it. We were happy in our subordination; but in an evil hour, under the influence of some malignant planet, the design was formed of opposing the stamp-act, by a denial of the right of parliament to make it. The love of empire is so predominant in the human breast, that we rarely find an individual content with relinquishing a power that he is able to retain; never a body of men. Some few months after it was known that the stamp-act was passed, some resolves of the house of burgesses in Virginia, denying the right of parliament to tax the colonies, made their appearance. We read them with wonder; they savoured of independence; they flattered the human passions; the reasoning was specious; we wished it conclusive. The transition, to believing it so, was easy; and we, and almost all America, followed their example, in resolving that the parliament had no such right. It now became unpopular to suggest the contrary; his life would be in danger that asserted it. The newspapers were open to but one side of the question, and the inflammatory pieces that issued weekly from the press, worked up the populace to a fit temper to commit the outrages that ensued. A non-importation was agreed upon, which alarmed the merchants and manufacturers in England. It was novel, and the people in England then supposed, that the love of liberty was so powerful in an American merchant, as to stifle his love of gain, and that the agreement would be religiously adhered to. It has been said, that several thousands were expended in England, to foment the disturbances there. However that maybe, opposition to the ministry was then gaining ground, from circumstances, foreign to this. The ministry was changed, and the stamp-act repealed. The repealing statute passed, with difficulty however, through the house of peers, near forty noble lords protested against giving way to such an opposition, and foretold what has since literally come to pass in consequence of it. When the statute was made, imposing duties upon glass, paper, India teas, &c. imported into the colonies, it was said, that this was another instance of taxation, for some of the dutied commodities were necessaries, we had them not within ourselves, were prohibited from importing them from any place except Great Britain, were therefore obliged to import them from Great Britain, and consequently, were obliged to pay the duties. Accordingly newspaper publications, pamphlets, resolves, non-importation agreements, and the whole system of American opposition was again put in motion. We obtained a partial repeal of this statute, which took off the duties from all the articles except teas. This was the lucky moment when to have closed the dispute. We might have made a safe and honorable retreat. We had gained much, perhaps more than we expected. If the parliament had passed an act declaratory of their right to tax us, our assemblies had resolved, ten times, that they had no such right. We could not complain of the three-penny duty on tea as burdensome, for a shilling which had been laid upon it, for the purpose of regulating trade, and therefore was allowed to be constitutional, was taken off; so that we were in fact gainers nine-pence in a pound by the new regulation. If the appropriation of the revenue, arising from this statute was disrelished, it was only our striking off one article of luxury from our manner of living, an article too, which if we may believe the resolves of most of the towns in this province, or rely on its collected wisdom in a resolve of the house of representatives, was to the last degree ruinous to health. It was futile to urge its being a precedent, as a reason for keeping up the ball of contention; for, allowing the supreme legislature ever to want a precedent, they had many for laying duties on commodities imported into the colonies. And beside we had great reason to believe that the remaining part of the statute would be repealed, as soon as the parliament should suppose it could be done with honor to themselves, as the incidental revenue arising from the former regulation, was four fold to the revenue arising from the latter. A claim of the right, could work no injury, so long as there was no grievous exercise of it, especially as we had protested against it, through the whole, and could not be said to have departed from our claims in the least. We might now upon good terms have dropped the dispute, and been happy in the affections of our mother country; but that is yet to come. Party is inseperable from a free state. The several distributions of power, as they are limited by, so they create perpetual dissentions between each other, about their respective boundaries; but the greatest source is the competition of individuals for preferment in the state. Popularity is the ladder by which the partizans usually climb. Accordingly, the struggle is, who shall have the greatest share of it. Each party professes disinterested patriotism, though some cynical writers have ventured to assert, that self-love is the ruling passion of the whole. There were two parties in this province of pretty long standing, known by the name of whig and tory, which at this time were not a little imbittered against each other. Men of abilities and acknowledged probity were on both sides. If the tories were suspected of pursuing their private interest through the medium of court favor, there was equal reason to suspect the whigs of pursuing their private interest by the means of popularity. Indeed some of them owed all their importance to it, and must in a little time have sunk into obscurity, had these turbulent commotions then subsided.

The tories and whigs took different routs, as usual. The tories were for closing the controversy with Great Britain, the whigs for continuing it; the tories were for restoring government in the province, which had become greatly relaxed by these convulsions, to its former tone; the whigs were averse to it; they even refused to revive a temporary riot act, which expired about this time. Perhaps they thought that mobs were a necessary ingredient in their system of opposition. However, the whigs had great advantages in the unequal combat; their scheme flattered the people with the idea of independence; the tories' plan supposed a degree of subordination, which is rather an humiliating idea; besides there is a propensity in men to believe themselves injured and oppressed whenever they are told so. The ferment, raised in their minds in the time of the stamp-act, was not yet allayed, and the leader of the whigs had gained the confidence of the people by their successes in their former struggles, so that they had nothing to do but to keep up the spirit among the people, and they were sure of commanding in this province. It required some pains to prevent their minds settling into that calm, which is ordinarily the effect of a mild government; the whigs were sensible that there was no oppression that could be either seen or felt; if any thing was in reality amiss in government, it was its being too lax. So far was it from the innocent being in danger of suffering, that the most atrocious offenders escaped with impunity. They accordingly applied themselves to work upon the imagination, and to inflame the passions; for this work they possessed great talents; I will do justice to their ingenuity; they were intimately acquainted with the feelings of man, and knew all the avenues to the human heart. Effigies, paintings, and other imagery were exhibited; the fourteenth of August was celebrated annually as a festival in commemoration of a mob's destroying a building, owned by the late Lieutenant Governor, which was supposed to have been erected for a stamp-office; and compelling him to resign his office of stamp-master under liberty tree; annual orations were delivered in the old south meeting house, on the fifth of March, the day when some persons were unfortunately killed by a party of the twenty-ninth regiment; lists of imaginary grievances were continually published; the people were told weekly that the ministry had formed a plan to enslave them; that the duty upon tea was only a prelude to a window tax, hearth tax, land tax, and poll tax; and these were only paving the way for reducing the country to lordships. This last bait was the more easily swallowed, as there seems to be an apprehension of that kind hereditary to the people of New-England; and were conjured by the duty they owed themselves, their country, and their God, by the reverence due to the sacred memory of their ancestors, and all their toils and sufferings in this once inhospitable wilderness, and by their affections for unborn millions, to rouse and exert themselves in the common cause. This perpetual incantation kept the people in continual alarm. We were further stimulated by being told, that the people of England were depraved, the parliament venal, and the ministry corrupt; nor were attempts wanting to traduce Majesty itself. The kingdom of Great Britain was depicted as an ancient structure, once the admiration of the world, now sliding from its base, and rushing to its fall. At the same time we were called upon to mark our own rapid growth, and behold the certain evidence that America was upon the eve of independent empire.

When we consider what effect a well written tragedy or novel has on the human passions, though we know it to be all fictitious, what effect must all this be supposed to have had upon those, that believed these high wrought images to be realities?

The tories have been censured for remissness in not having exerted themselves sufficiently at this period. The truth of the case is this; they saw and shuddered at the gathering storm, but durst not attempt to dispel it, lest it should burst on their own heads. Printers were threatened with the loss of their bread, for publishing freely on the tory side. One Mr. Mein was forced to fly the country for persisting in it.

All our dissenting ministers were not inactive on this occasion. When the clergy engage in a political warfare, religion becomes a most powerful engine, either to support or overthrow the state. What effect must it have had upon the audience to hear the same sentiments and principles, which they had before read in a newspaper, delivered on Sundays from the sacred desk, with a religious awe, and the most solemn appeals to heaven, from lips which they had been taught, from their cradles, to believe could utter nothing but eternal truths? What was it natural to expect from a people bred under a free constitution, jealous of their liberty, credulous, even to a proverb, when told their privileges were in danger, thus wrought upon in the extreme? I answer, outrages disgraceful to humanity itself. What mischief was not an artful man, who had obtained the confidence and guidance of such an enraged multitude, capable of doing? He had only to point out this or the other man, as an enemy of his country; and no character, station, age, or merit could protect the proscribed from their fury. Happy was it for him, if he could secrete his person, and subject his property only to their lawless ravages. By such means, many people naturally brave and humane, have been wrought upon to commit such acts of private mischief and public violence, as will blacken many a page in the history of our country.

I shall next trace the effects of this spirit, which the whigs had thus infused into the body of the people, through the courts of common law, and the general assembly, and mark the ways and means, whereby they availed themselves of it, to the subversion of our charter constitution, antecedent to the late acts of parliament.

MASSACHUSETTENSIS.

Massachusetts Gazette; and the Boston
Post-Boy and Advertiser, December 19, 1774

Massachusettensis [Daniel Leonard] No. III

To the Inhabitants of the Province of Massachusetts Bay,

MY DEAR COUNTRYMEN,

To undertake to convince a person of his error, is the indispensible duty, the certain, though dangerous test of friendship. He that could see his friend persevering in a fatal error, without reminding him of it, and striving to reclaim him, through fear that he might thereby incur his displeasure, would little deserve the sacred name himself. Such delicacy is not only false, but criminal. Were I not fully convinced upon the most mature deliberation, that I am capable of, that the temporal salvation of this province depends upon an entire and speedy change of measures, which must depend upon a change of sentiment, respecting our own conduct, and the justice of the British nation, I never should have obtruded myself on the public. I repeat my promise, to avoid personal reflection, as much as the nature of the task will admit of; but will continue faithfully to expose the wretched policy of the whigs, though I may be obliged to penetrate the arcana, and discover such things as, were there not a necessity for it, I should be infinitely happier in drawing a veil over, or covering with a mantle. Should I be so unfortunate as to incur your displeasure, I shall nevertheless think myself happy, if I can but snatch one of my fellow-subjects as a brand out of the burning.

Perhaps some may imagine that I have represented too many of my countrymen, as well as the leading whigs, in an unjust point of light, by supposing these so wicked as to mislead, or those so little circumspect as to be misled, in matters of the last importance. Whoever has been conversant with the history of man, must know that it abounds with such instances. The same game, and with the same success, has been played in all ages, and all countries.

The bulk of the people are generally but little versed in matters of state. Want of inclination or opportunity to figure in public life, makes them content to rest the affairs of government in the hands, where accident or merit has placed them. Their views and employments are confined to the humbler walks of business or retirement. There is a latent spark however, in their breasts, capable of being kindled into a flame; to do this has always been the employment of the disaffected. They begin by reminding the people of the elevated rank they hold in the universe, as men; that all men by nature are equal; that kings are but the ministers of the people; that their authority is delegated to them by the people for their good, and they have a right to resume it, and place it in other hands, or keep it themselves, whenever it is made use of to oppress them. Doubtless there have been instances where these principles have been inculcated to obtain a redress of real grievances, but they have been much oftener perverted to the worst of purposes. No government, however perfect in theory, is administered in perfection; the frailty of man does not admit of it. A small mistake, in point of policy, often furnishes a pretence to libel government, and persuade the people that their rulers are tyrants, and the whole government a system of oppression. Thus the seeds of sedition are usually sown, and the people are led to sacrifice real liberty to licentiousness, which gradually ripens into rebellion and civil war. And what is still more to be lamented, the generality of the people, who are thus made the dupes of artifice, and the mere stilts of ambition, are sure to be losers in the end. The best they can expect, is to be thrown neglected by, when they are no longer wanted; but they are seldom so happy; if they are subdued, confiscation of estate and ignominious death are their portion; if they conquer, their own army is often turned upon them, to subjugate them to a more tyranical government than that they rebelled against. History is replete with instances of this kind; we can trace them in remote antiquity, we find them in modern times, and have a remarkable one in the very country from which we are derived. It is an universal truth, that he that would excite a rebellion, whatever professions of philanthropy he may make, when he is insinuating and worming himself into the good graces of the people, is at heart as great a tyrant as ever wielded the iron rod of oppression. I shall have occasion hereafter to consider this matter more fully, when I shall endeavour to convince you how little we can gain, and how much we may lose, by this unequal, unnatural, and desperate contest. My present business is, to trace the spirit of opposition to Great Britain through the general court, and the courts of common law. In moderate times, a representative that votes for an unpopular measure, or opposes a popular one, is in danger of losing his election the next year; when party runs high, he is sure to do it. It was the policy of the whigs to have their questions, upon high matters, determined by yea and nay votes, which were published with the representatives' names in the next gazette. This was commonly followed by severe strictures and the most illiberal invectives upon the dissentients; sometimes they were held up as objects of resentment, of contempt at others; the abuse was in proportion to the extravagance of the measure they opposed. This may seem not worth notice, but its consequences were important. The scurrility made its way into the dissentient's town, it furnished his competitor with means to supplant him, and he took care to shun the rock his predecessor had split upon. In this temper of the times, it was enough to know who voted with Cassius and who with Lucius, to determine who was a friend and who an enemy to the country, without once adverting to the question before the house. The loss of a seat in the house was not of so much consequence; but when once he became stigmatized as an enemy to his country, he was exposed to insult; and if his profession or business was such, that his livelihood depended much on the good graces of his fellow citizens, he was in danger of losing his bread, and involving his whole family in ruin.

One particular set of members, in committee, always prepared the resolves and other spirited measures. At first they were canvassed freely, at length would slide through the house without meeting an obstacle. The lips of the dissentients were sealed up; they sat in silence, and beheld with infinite regret the measures they durst not oppose. Many were borne down against their wills, by the violence of the current; upon no other principle can we reconcile their ostensible conduct in the house to their declarations in private circles. The apparent unanimity in the house encouraged the opposition out of doors, and that in its turn strengthened the party in the house. Thus they went on mutually supporting and up-lifting each other. Assemblies and towns resolved alternately; some of them only omitted resolving to snatch the sceptre out of the hands of our sovereign, and to strike the imperial crown from his sacred head.

A master stroke in politics respecting the agent, ought not to be neglected. Each colony has usually an agent residing at the court of Great Britain. These agents are appointed by the three branches of their several assemblies; and indeed there cannot be a provincial agent without such appointment. The whigs soon found that they could not have such services rendered them from a provincial agent, as would answer their purposes. The house therefore refused to join with the other two branches of the general court in the appointment. The house chose an agent for themselves, and the council appointed another. Thus we had two agents for private purposes, and the expence of agency doubled; and with equal reason a third might have been added, as agent for the Governor, and the charges been trebled.

The additional expence was of little consideration, compared with another inconvenience that attended this new mode of agency. The person appointed by the house was the ostensible agent of the province, though in fact he was only the agent of a few individuals that had got the art of managing the house at their pleasure. He knew his continuing in office depended upon them. An office, that yielded several hundred pounds sterling annually, the business of which consisted in little more than attending the levees of the great, and writing letters to America, was worth preserving. Thus he was under a strong temptation to sacrifice the province to a party; and ecchoed back the sentiments of his patrons.

The advices continually received from one of the persons, that was thus appointed agent, had great influence upon the members of the house of more moderate principles. He had pushed his researches deep into nature, and made important discoveries; they thought he had done the same in politics, and did not admire him less as a politician, than as a philosopher. His intelligence as to the disposition of his majesty, the ministry, the parliament and the nation in general, was deemed the most authentic. He advised us to keep up our opposition, to resolve, and re-resolve, to cherish a military spirit, uniformly holding up this idea, that if we continued firm, we had nothing to fear from the government in England. He even proposed some modes of opposition himself. The spirited measures were always ushered into the house with a letter from him. I have been sometimes almost ready to suspect him of being the *primum mobile*, and, that like the man behind the curtain at a puppet-shew, he was playing off the figures here with his own secret wires. If he advised to these measures contrary to his better knowledge, from sinister views, and to serve a private purpose, he has *wilfully* done the province irreparable injury. However, I will do him justice; he enjoined it upon us to refrain from violence, as that would unite the nation against us; and I am rather inclined to think that he was deceived himself, with respect to the measures he recommended, as he has already felt the resentment of that very government, which he told us there was nothing to fear from. This disposition of the house could not have produced such fatal effects, had the other two branches of the legislature retained their constitutional freedom and influence. They might have been a sufficient check.

The councellors depended upon the general assembly for their political existence; the whigs reminded the council of their mortality. If a councellor opposed the violent measures of the whigs with any spirit, he lost his election the next May. The council consisted of twenty-eight. From this principle, near half that number, mostly men of the first families, note and abilities, with every possible attachment to their native country, and as far from temptation as wealth and independence could remove them, were tumbled from their seats in disgrace. Thus the board, which was intended to moderate between the two extremes of prerogative and privilege, lost its weight in the scale, and the political balance of the province was destroyed.

Had the chair been able to retain its own constitutional influence, the loss of the board would have been less felt; but no longer supported by the board, that fell likewise. The Governor by the charter could do little or nothing without the council. If he called upon a military officer to raise the militia, he was answered, they were there already. If he called upon his council for their assistance, they must first enquire into the cause. If he wrote to government at home to strengthen his hands, some officious person procured and sent back his letters.

It was not the person of a Bernard or Hutchinson that made them obnoxious; any other governors would have met with the same fate, had they discharged their duty with equal fidelity; that is, had they strenuously opposed the principles and practices of the whigs; and when they found that the government here could not support itself, wrote home for aid sufficient to do it. And let me tell you, had the intimations in those letters, which you are taught to execrate, been timely attended to, we had now been as happy a people as good government could make us. Gov. Bernard came here recommended by the affections of the province over which he had presided. His abilities are acknowledged. True British honesty and punctuality are traits in his character, too strongly marked to escape the eye of prejudice itself. We know Governor Hutchinson to be amiable and exemplary in private life. His great abilities, integrity and humanity were conspicuous, in the several important departments that he filled, before his appointment to the chair, and reflect honour on his native country. But his abilities and integrity, added to his thorough knowledge of the province, in all its interests and connexions, were insufficient in this case. The constitution itself was gone, though the ancient form remained; the spirit was truly republican. He endeavoured to reclaim us by gentle means. He strove to convince us by arguments, drawn from the first principles of government; our several charters, and the express acknowledgments of our ancestors, that our claims were inconsistent with the subordination due to Great Britain; and if persisted in, might work the destruction of those that we were entitled to. For this he was called an enemy to his country, and set up as a mark for the envenomed arrows of malice and party rage. Had I entertained a doubt about its being the governor, and not the man that was aimed at, the admirable facility with which the newspaper abuse was transferred from Gov. Hutchinson to his humane and benevolent successor, Gen. Gage, almost as soon as he set foot on our shore, would have removed it.

Thus, disaffection to Great Britain being infused into the body of the people, the subtle poison stole through all the veins and arteries, contaminated the blood, and destroyed the very stamina of the constitution. Had not the courts of justice been tainted in the early stages, our government might have expelled the virus, purged off the peccant humors, and recovered its former vigour by its own strength. The judges of the superior court were dependant upon the annual grants of the general court for their support. Their salaries were small, in proportion to the salaries of other officers in the government, of less importance.

They had often petitioned the assembly to enlarge them, without success. They were at this time reminded of their dependance. However, it is but justice to say, that the judges remained unshaken, amid the raging tempests, which is to be attributed rather to their firmness than situation. But the spirit of the times was very apparent in the juries. The grand jurors were elective; and in such places where libels, riots, and insurrections were the most frequent, the high whigs took care to get themselves chosen. The judges pointed out to them the seditious libels on governors, magistrates, and the whole government to no effect. They were enjoined to present riots and insurrections, of which there was ample evidence, with as little success.

It is difficult to account for so many of the first rate whigs being returned to serve on the petit jury at the term next after extraordinary insurrections, without supposing some legerdemain in drawing their names out of the box. It is certain that notwithstanding swarms of the most virulent libels infested the province, and there were so many riots and insurrections, scarce one offender was indicted, and I think not one convicted and punished. Causes of *meum et tuum* were not always exempt from party influence. The mere circumstance of the whigs gaining the ascendancy over the tories, is trifling. Had the whigs divided the province between them, as they once flattered themselves they should be able to do, it would have been of little consequence to the community, had they not cut asunder the very sinews of government, and broke in pieces the ligaments of social life in the attempt. I will mention two instances, which I have selected out of many, of the weakness of our government, as they are recent and unconnected with acts of parliament. One Malcolm, a loyal subject, and as such entitled to protection, the evening before the last winter sessions of the general court, was dragged out of his house, stript, tarred and feathered, and carted several hours in the severest frost of that winter, to the utmost hazard of his life. He was carried to the gallows with an halter about his neck, and in his passage to and from the gallows, was beaten with as cruel stripes as ever were administered by the hands of a savage. The whipping, however, kept up the circulation of his blood, and saved the poor man's life. When they had satiated their malice, they dispersed in good order. This was transacted in the presence of thousands of spectators; some of whom were members of the general court. Malcolm's life was despaired of several days, but he survived and presented a memorial to the general assembly, praying their interposition. The petition was read, and all he obtained was leave to withdraw it. So that he was destitute of protection every hour, until he left the country, as were thousands beside, until the arrival of the king's troops. This originated from a small fracas in the street, wherein Malcolm struck, or threatened to strike a person that insulted him, with a cutlass, and had no connection with the quarrel of the times, unless his sustaining a small post in the customs made it.

The other instance is much stronger than this, as it was totally detached from politics. It had been suspected that infection had been communicated from an hospital, lately erected at Marblehead, for the purpose of innoculating the small-pox, to the town's people. This caused a great insurrection; the insurgents burnt the hospital; not content with that, threatened the proprietors, and many others, some of the first fortunes and characters in the town, with burning their houses over their heads, and continued parading the streets, to the utmost terror of the inhabitants several days. A massacre and general devastation was apprehended. The persons threatened, armed themselves, and petitioned the general assembly, which was then sitting, for assistance, as there was little or no civil authority in the place. A committee was ordered to repair to Marblehead, report the facts, and enquire into the cause. The committee reported the facts nearly as stated in the petition. The report was accepted, and nothing farther done by the assembly. Such demonstrations of the weakness of government induced many persons to join the whigs, to seek from them that protection, which the constitutional authority of the province was unable to afford.

Government at home, early in the day, made an effort to check us in our career, and to enable us to recover from anarchy without her being driven to the necessity of altering our provincial constitution, knowing the predilection that people always have for an ancient form of government. The judges of the superior court had not been staggered, though their feet stood in slippery places, they depended upon the leading whigs for their support. To keep them steady, they were made independent of the grants of the general assembly: but it was not a remedy any way adequate to the disease. The whigs now turned their artillery against them, and it played briskly. The chief justice, for accepting the crown grant, was accused of receiving a royal bribe.

Thus, my friends, those very persons that had made you believe that every attempt to strengthen government and save our charter was an infringement of your privileges, by little and little destroyed your real liberty, subverted your charter constitution, abridged the freedom of the house, annihilated the freedom of the board, and rendered the governor a mere doge of Venice. They engrossed all the power of the province into their own hands. A democracy or republic it has been called, but it does not deserve the name of either; it was, however, a despotism cruelly carried into execution by mobs and riots, and more incompatible with the rights of mankind, than the enormous monarchies of the East. The absolute necessity of the interposition of parliament is apparent. The good policy of the act for regulating the government in this province, will be the subject of some future paper. A particular enquiry into the despotism of the whigs will be deferred for a chapter on congresses. I shall next ask your attention to a transaction, as important in its consequences, and perhaps more so, than any I have yet mentioned; I mean the destruction of the tea, belonging to the East-India company. I am sensible of the difficulty of the task, in combating generally received opinions. It is hard work to eradicate deep-rooted prejudice. But I will persevere. There are hundreds, if not thousands, in the province, that will feel the truth of what I have written, line by line as they read it, and as to those who obstinately shut their eyes against it now, haply the fever of the times may intermit, there may be some lucid interval, when their minds shall be open to truth, before it is too late to serve them; otherwise it will be revealed to them in bitter moments, attended with keen remorse and unutterable anguish.

Magna est veritas et prevalebit.
MASSACHUSETTENSIS.

Massachusetts Gazette; and the Boston
Post-Boy and Advertiser, December 26, 1774

To James Burgh

Sir   Braintree Decr. 28. 1774

I have had the Honour of receiving from you a Present, in two Volumes of Political Disquisitions. The very polite and obliging manner, in which this Present was conveyed to me, demands my gratefull Acknowledgements: But the Present itself is invaluable.

I cannot but think those Disquisitions, the best Service, that a Citizen, could render to his Country, at this great and dangerous Crisis, when the British Empire Seems ripe for Destruction, and tottering on the Brink of a Precipice. If any Thing can possibly open the Eyes of the Nation and excite it to exert itself, it must be such a sight of its Danger, and of the imperceptible Steps, by which it ascended to it.

I have contributed Somewhat to make the Disquisitions more known and attended to in several Parts of America, and they are held in as high Estimation by all my Friends as they are by me, and the more they are read the more eagerly and generally they are sought for.

We have pleased ourselves in America, with Hopes, that the Publication of those Disquisitions, the Exertions of the other Friends of Virtue and Freedom in England, together with the Union of Sentiment and Conduct of America, which appears by the Proceedings of the Congress at Phyladelphia, would have had their full operation and Effect upon the Nation, during this Fall and Winter, while the People were canvassing for Elections, and that in Spight of Bribery, Some alteration in the House of Commons for the better might have been made. But the Sudden Dissolution of Parliament and the impatient Summons for a new Election, have blasted all these Hopes. We now see plainly, that every Trick and Artifice of sharpers, Gamblers and Horse Jockies is to be played off against the cause of Liberty in England and America: and that no Hopes are to be left for Either but in the sword.

We are in this Province sir, at the Brink of a civil War. Our Alva Gage, with his fifteen Mandamous Councillors, are Shutt up in Boston, afraid to Stir, afraid of their own shades, protected with a Dozen Regiments of Regular soldiers, and strong Fortifications, in the Town, but never moving out of it. We have No Council, No House, No Legislature, No Executive. Not a Court of Justice, has sat Since the Month of September. Not a Debt can be recoverd, nor a Trespass rebufed nor a Criminal of any Kind, brought to Punishment.

What the Ministry will do next, is uncertain—inforce the Act for altering our Govt. they cannot. All the Regiments upon the Establishment would not do it. For juries will not serve, nor Represent. Whatever Alva and his Troops may think of it, it has required great Caution and Delicacy in the Conduct of Affairs, to prevent their Destruction. For my own Part I have bent my chief Attention to prevent a Rupture, and to impress my Friends with the Importance of preventing it. Not that I think the Lives of 5 or 10 thousand Men, tho my own should be one of them, would not be very profitably Spent, in obtaining a Restoration of our Liberties. But because I knew, that those Lives would never go unrevenged, and it would be vain ever to hope for a Reconciliation with great Britain afterwards. Britains would not easily forgive the Destruction of their Brethren, I am absolutely certain that New England men never would that of theirs. Nor would any Part of America ever forget or forgive, the destruction of one New England man in this Cause. The Death of 4 or 5 Persons, the most obscure, and inconsiderable that could have been found upon the Continent, on the 5th March 1770 has never yet been forgiven by any Part of America. What then would be the Consequence of a Battle in which, many Thousands must fall of the best Blood, the best Families, Fortunes, Abilities and moral Characters in the Country?

America, never will Submit to the Claims of Parliament and Administration. New England alone has 200,000 fighting Men. And all in a Militia, established by Law, not exact soldiers, but all used to Arms.

Massachuettensis [Daniel Leonard] No. IV

To the Inhabitants of the Province of Massachusetts Bay,

MY DEAR COUNTRYMEN,

Perhaps by this time some of you may enquire who it is, that suffers his pen to run so freely? I will tell you; it is a native of this province, that knew it before many that are now basking in the rays of political sunshine, had a being. He was favored not by whigs or tories, but the people, with such a stand in the community, as that he could distinctly see all the political manœuvres of the province. He saw some with pleasure, others with pain. If he condemns the conduct of the whigs, he does not always approve of the conduct of the tories. He dwells upon the misconduct of the former, because we are indebted to that for bringing us into this wretched state, unless the supineness of the latter, at some periods, and some impolitic efforts to check the whigs in their career, at others, that served like adding fuel to the fire, ought to be added to the account. He is now repaying your favors, if he knows his own heart, from the purest gratitude and the most undissembled patriotism, which will one day be acknowledged. I saw the small seed of sedition, when it was implanted; it was, as a grain of mustard. I have watched the plant until it has become a great tree; the vilest reptiles that crawl upon the earth, are concealed at the root; the foulest birds of the air rest upon its branches. I now would induce you to go to work immediately with axes and hatchets, and cut it down, for a twofold reason; because it is a pest to society, and lest it be felled suddenly by a stronger arm and crush its thousands in the fall.

An apprehension of injustice in the conduct of Great Britain towards us, I have already told you was one source of our misery. Last week I endeavoured to convince you of the necessity of her regulating, or rather establishing some government amongst us. I am now to point out the principles and motives upon which the blockade act was made. The violent attack upon the property of the East-India company, in the destruction of their tea, was the cause of it. In order to form a right judgment of that transaction, it is necessary to go back and view the cause of its being sent here. As the government of England is mixt, so the spirit or genius of the nation is at once monarchial, aristocratical, democratical, martial and commercial. It is difficult to determine which is the most predominant principle, but it is worthy of remark, that, to injure the British nation upon either of these points, is like injuring a Frenchman in the point of honor. Commerce is the great source of national wealth; for this reason it is cherished by all orders of men from the palace to the cottage. In some countries, a merchant is held in contempt by the nobles; in England they respect him. He rises to high honors in the state, often contracts alliances with the first families in the kingdom, and noble blood flows in the veins of his posterity. Trade is founded upon persons or countries mutually supplying each other with their redundances. Thus none are impoverished, all enriched, the asperities of human life worne away, and mankind made happier by it. Husbandry, manufacture and merchandize are its triple support; deprived of either of these, it would cease.

Agriculture is the natural livelihood of a country but thinly inhabited, as arts and manufactures are of a populous one. The high price of labour prevents manufactures being carried on to advantage in the first, scarcity of soil obliges the inhabitants to pursue them in the latter. Upon these, and considerations arising from the fertility and produce of different climates, and such like principles, the grand system of the British trade is founded. The collected wisdom of the nation has always been attentive to this great point of policy, that the national trade might be so balanced and poised, as that each part of her extended dominions might be benefitted, and the whole concentre to the good of the empire. This evinces the necessity of acts for regulating trade.

To prevent one part of the empire being enriched at the expence and to the impoverishing of another, checks, restrictions, and sometimes absolute prohibitions are necessary. These are imposed or taken off as circumstances vary. To carry the acts of trade into execution, many officers are necessary. Thus, we see a number of custom-house officers, so constituted as to be checks and controuls upon each other, and prevent their swerving from their duty, should they be tempted, and a board of commissioners appointed to superintend the whole, like the commissioners of the customs in England. Hence also arises the necessity of courts of admiralty.

The laws and regulations of trade, are esteemed in England, as sacred. An estate made by smuggling or pursuing an illicit trade, is there looked upon as filthy lucre, as monies amassed by gaming, and upon the same principle, because it is obtained at the expence, and often ruin of others. The smuggler not only injures the public, but often ruins the fair trader.

The great extent of sea-coast, many harbours, the variety of islands, the numerous creeks and navigable rivers, afford the greatest opportunity to drive an illicit trade, in these colonies, without detection. This advantage has not been overlooked by the avaricious, and many persons seem to have set the laws of trade at defiance. This accounts for so many new regulations being made, new officers appointed, and ships of war, from time to time, stationed along the continent. The way to Holland and back again is well known, and by much the greatest part of the tea that has been drank in America for several years, has been imported from thence and other places, in direct violation of law. By this the smugglers have amassed great estates, to the prejudice of the fair trader. It was sensibly felt by the East-India company; they were prohibited from exporting their teas to America, and were obliged to sell it at auction in London; the London merchant purchased it, and put a profit upon it when he shipt it for America; the American merchant, in his turn, put a profit upon it, and after him the shopkeeper; so that it came to the consumer's hands, at a very advanced price. Such quantities of tea were annually smuggled that it was scarcely worth while for the American merchant to import tea from England at all. Some of the principal trading towns in America were wholly supplied with this commodity by smuggling; Boston however continued to import it, until advice was received that the parliament had it in contemplation to permit the East-India company to send their teas directly to America. The Boston merchants then sent their orders conditionally to their correspondents in England, to have tea shipt for them in case the East-India company's tea did not come out; one merchant, a great whig, had such an order lying in England for sixty chests, on his own account, when the company's tea was sent. An act of parliament was made to enable the East-India company to send their tea directly to America, and sell it at auction there, not with a view of raising a revenue from the three penny duty, but to put it out of the power of the smugglers to injure them by their infamous trade. We have it from good authority, that the revenue was not the consideration before parliament, and it is reasonable to suppose it; for had that been the point in view, it was only to restore the former regulation, which was then allowed to be constitutional, and the revenue would have been respectable. Had this new regulation taken effect, the people in America would have been great gainers. The wholesale merchant might have been deprived of some of his gains; but the retailer would have supplied himself with this article, directly from the auction, and the consumer reap the benefit, as tea would have been sold under the price that had been usual, by near one half. Thus the country in general would have been great gainers, the East-India company secured in supplying the American market with this article, which they are entitled to by the laws of trade, and smuggling suppressed, at least as to tea. A smuggler and a whig are cousin germans, the offspring of two sisters, avarice and ambition. They had been playing into each others hands a long time. The smuggler received protection from the whig, and he in his turn received support from the smuggler. The illicit trader now demanded protection from his kinsman, and it would have been unnatural in him to have refused it; and beside, an opportunity presented of strengthening his own interest. The consignees were connected with the tories, and that was a further stimulus. Accordingly the press was again set to work, and the old story repeated with addition about monopolies, and many infatuated persons once more wrought up to a proper pitch to carry into execution any violent measures, that their leaders should propose. A bold stroke was resolved upon. The whigs, though they had got the art of managing the people, had too much sense to be ignorant that it was all a mere finesse, not only without, but directly repugnant to law, constitution and government, and could not last always. They determined to put all at hazard, and to be *aut Cæsar aut nullus*. The approaching storm was foreseen, and first ship that arrived with the tea, detained below Castle William. A body meeting was assembled at the old south meeting-house, which has great advantage over a town meeting, as no law has yet ascertained the qualification of the voters; each person present, of whatever age, estate or country, may take the liberty to speak or vote at such an assembly; and that might serve as a screen to the town where it originated, in case of any disastrous consequence. The body meeting consisting of several thousands, being thus assembled, with the leading whigs at its head, in the first place sent for the owner of the tea ship, and required him to bring her to the wharf, upon pain of their displeasure; the ship was accordingly brought up, and the master was obliged to enter at the custom house. He reported the tea, after which twenty days are allowed for landing it and paying the duty.

The next step was to resolve. They resolved that the tea should not be landed nor the duty paid, that it should go home in the same bottom that it came in, &c. &c. This was the same as resolving to destroy it, for as the ship had been compelled to come to the wharf, and was entered at the custom house, it could not, by law, be cleared out, without the duties being first paid, nor could the governor grant a permit for the vessel to pass Castle William, without a certificate from the custom house of such clearance, consistent with his duty. The body accordingly, ordered a military guard to watch the ship every night until further orders. The consignees had been applied to, by the selectmen, to send the tea to England, they answered that they could not; for if they did, it would be forfeited by the acts of trade, and they should be liable to make good the loss to the East India company. Some of the consignees were mobbed, and all were obliged to fly to the castle, and there immure themselves. They petitioned the governor and council to take the property of the East India company under their protection. The council declined being concerned in it. The consignees then offered the body to store the tea under the care of the selectmen or a committee of the town of Boston, and to have no further concern in the matter until they could send to England, and receive further instructions from their principals. This was refused with disdain. The military guard was regularly kept in rotation till the eve of the twentieth day, when the duties must have been paid, the tea landed, or be liable to seizure; then the military guard was withdrawn, or rather omitted being posted, and a number of persons in disguise, forcibly entered the ships, (three being by this time arrived) split open the chests, and emptied all the tea, being of 10,000*l.* sterling value, into the dock, and perfumed the town with its fragrance. Another circumstance ought not to be omitted: the afternoon before the destruction of the tea, the body sent the owner of one of the ships to the governor to demand a pass; he answered, that he would as soon give a pass for that as any other vessel, if he had the proper certificate from the custom house; without which he could not give a pass for any, consistent with his duty. It was known that this would be the answer, when the message was sent, and it was with the utmost difficulty that the body were kept together till the messenger returned. When the report was made, a shout was set up in the galleries and at the door, and the meeting immediately dispersed. The governor had, previous to this, sent a proclamation by the sheriff, commanding the body to disperse; they permitted it to be read, and answered it with a general hiss. These are the facts, as truly and fairly stated, as I am able to state them. The ostensible reason for this conduct, was the tea's being subject to the three-penny duty. Let us take the advocates for this transaction upon their own principle, and admit the duty to be unconstitutional, and see how the argument stands. Here is a cargo of tea subject upon its being entered and landed, to a duty of three-pence per pound, which is paid by the East India company or by their factors, which amounts to the same thing. Unless we purchase the tea, we shall never pay the duty; if we purchase it, we pay the three-pence included in the price: therefore, lest we should purchase it, we have a right to destroy it. A flimsy pretext! and either supposes the people destitute of virtue, or that their purchasing the tea was a matter of no importance to the community; but even this gauze covering is stript off, when we consider that the Boston merchants, and some who were active at the body meeting, were every day importing from England, large quantities of tea subject to the same duty and vending it unmolested; and at this time had orders lying in their correspondent's hands, to send them considerable quantities of tea, in case the East-India company should not send it themselves.

When the news of this transaction arrived in England, and it was considered in what manner almost every other regulation of trade had been evaded by artifice, and when artitice could no longer serve, recourse was had to violence; the British lion was roused. The crown lawyers were called upon for the law; they answered, high treason. Had a Cromwell, whom some amongst us deify and imitate in all his imitable perfections, had the guidance of the national ire, unless compensation had been made to the sufferers immediately upon its being demanded, your proud capital had been levelled with the dust; not content with that, rivers of blood would have been shed to make atonement for the injured honor of the nation. It was debated whether to attaint the principals of treason. We have a gracious king upon the throne; he felt the resentment of a man, softened by the relentings of a parent. The bowels of our mother country yearned towards her refractory, obstinate child.

It was determined to consider the offence in a milder light, and to compel an indemnification for the sufferers, and prevent the like for the future, by such means as would be mild, compared with the insult to the nation, or severe, as our future conduct should be; that was to depend upon us. Accordingly the blockade act was passed, and had an act of justice been done in indemnifying the sufferers, and an act of loyalty in putting a stop to seditious practices, our port had long since been opened. This act has been called unjust, because it involves the innocent in the same predicament with the guilty; but it ought to be considered, that our newspapers had announced to the world, that several thousands attended those body meetings, and it did not appear that there was one dissentient, or any protest entered. I do not know how a person could expect distinction, in such a case, if he neglected to distinguish himself. When the noble lord proposed it in the house of commons, he called upon all the members present, to mention a better method of obtaining justice in this case; scarce one denied the necessity of doing something, but none could mention a more eligible way. Even ministerial opposition was abashed. If any parts of the act strike us, like the severity of a master, let us coolly advert to the aggravated insult, and perhaps we shall wonder at the lenity of a parent. After this transaction, all parties seem to have lain upon their oars, waiting to see what parliament would do. When the blockade act arrived, many and many were desirous of paying for the tea immediately, and some who were guiltless of the crime, offered to contribute to the compensation; but our leading whigs must still rule the roast, and that inauspicious influence that had brought us hitherto, plunged us still deeper in misery. The whigs saw their ruin connected with a compliance with the terms of opening the port, as it would furnish a convincing proof of the wretchedness of their policy in the destruction of the tea, and they might justly have been expected to pay the money demanded themselves, and set themselves industriously to work to prevent it, and engage the other colonies to espouse their cause.

This was a crisis too important and alarming to the province to be neglected by its friends. A number of as respectable persons as any in this province, belonging to Boston, Cambridge, Salem and Marblehead, now came forward, publicly to disavow the proceedings of the whigs, to do justice to the much injured character of Mr. Hutchinson, and to strengthen his influence at the court of Great Britain, where he was going to receive the well deserved plaudit of his sovereign, that he might be able to obtain a repeal or some mitigation of that act, the terms of which they foresaw, the perverseness of the whigs would prevent a compliance with. This was done by several addresses, which were subscribed by upwards of two hundred persons, and would have been by many more, had not the sudden embarkation of Mr. Hutchinson prevented it. The justices of the court of common pleas and general sessions of the peace for the county of Plymouth, sent their address to him in England. There were some of almost all orders of men among these addressers, but they consisted principally of men of property, large family connections, and several were independent in their circumstances, and lived wholly upon the income of their estates. Some indeed might be called partizans; but a very considerable proportion were persons that had of choice kept themselves at a distance from the political vortex; had beheld the competion of the whigs and tories without any emotion, while the community remained safe; had looked down on the political dance in its various mazes and intricacies, and saw one falling, another rising, rather as a matter of amusement;

but when they saw the capital of the province upon the point of being sacrificed by political cunning, it called up all their feelings.

Their motives were truly patriotic. Let us now attend to the ways and means by which the whigs prevented these exertions producing such effects. Previous to this, a new, and until lately, unheard of, mode of opposition had been devised, said to be the invention of the fertile brain of one of our party agents, called a committee of correspondence. This is the foulest, subtlest, and most venemous serpent that ever issued from the eggs of sedition. These committees generally consist of the highest whigs, or at least there is some high whig upon them, that is the ruling spirit of the whole. They are commonly appointed at thin town meetings, or if the meetings happen to be full, the moderate men seldom speak or act at all, when this sort of business comes on. They have been by much too modest. Thus the meeting is often prefaced with, "at a full town meeting," and the several resolves headed with nem. con. with strict truth, when in fact, but a small proportion of the town have had a hand in the matter. It is said that the committee for the town of Boston was appointed for a special purpose, and that their commission long since expired. However that may be, these committees when once established, think themselves amenable to none, they assume a dictatorial style, and have an opportunity under the apparent sanction of their several towns, of clandestinely wreaking private revenge on individuals, by traducing their characters, and holding them up as enemies to their country, wherever they go, as also of misrepresenting facts and propagating sedition through the country. Thus, a man of principle and property, in travelling through the country, would be insulted by persons, whose faces he had never before seen; he would often feel the smart without suspecting the hand that administered the blow. These committees, as they are not known in law, and can derive no authority from thence, lest they should not get their share of power, sometimes engross it all; they frequently erect themselves into a tribunal, where the same persons are at once legislators, accusers, witnesses, judges, and jurors, and the mob the executioners. The accused has no day in court, and the execution of the sentence is the first notice he receives. This is the channel through

which liberty matters have been chiefly conducted the summer
and fall past. This accounts for the same distempers breaking
out in different parts of the province, at one and the same
time, which might be attributed to something supernatural, by
those that were unacquainted with the secret conductors of
the infection. It is chiefly owing to these committees, that so
many respectable persons have been abused, and forced to sign
recantations and resignations; that so many persons, to avoid
such reiterated insults, as are more to be deprecated by a man
of sentiment than death itself, have been obliged to quit their
houses, families, and business, and fly to the army for protec
tion; that husband has been separated from wife, father from
son, brother from brother, the sweet intercourse of conjugal
and natural affection interrupted, and the unfortunate refugee
forced to abandon all the comforts of domestic life. My countrymen, I beg you to pause and reflect on this conduct. Have not
these people, that are thus insulted, as good a right to think
and act for themselves in matters of the last importance, as the
whigs? Are they not as closely connected with the interest of
their country as the whigs? Do not their former lives and conversations appear to have been regulated by principle, as much
as those of the whigs? You must answer, yes. Why, then, do
you suffer them to be cruelly treated for differing in sentiment
from you? Is it consistent with that liberty you profess? Let us
wave the consideration of right and liberty, and see if this conduct can be reconciled to good policy. Do you expect to make
converts by it? Persecution has the same effect in politics, that
it has in religion; it confirms the sectary. Do you wish to silence them, that the inhabitants of the province may appear
unanimous? The maltreatment they receive, for differing from
you, is undeniable evidence that we are not unanimous. It may
not be amiss to consider, that this is a changeable world, and
time's rolling wheel may ere long bring them uppermost; in
that case I am sure you would not wish to have them fraught
with resentment. It is astonishing, my friends, that those who
are in pursuit of liberty, should ever suffer arbitrary power, in
such an hideous form and squalid hue, to get a footing among
them. I appeal to your good sense; I know you have it, and
hope to penetrate to it, before I have finished my publications,
notwithstanding the thick atmosphere that now envelopes it.

But to return from my digression, the committee of correspondence represented the destruction of the tea in their own way; they represented those that addressed Gov. Hutchinson, as persons of no note or property, as mean, base wretches, and seekers that had been sacrificing their country in adulation of him. Whole nations have worshipped the rising, but if this be an instance, it is the only one of people's worshipping the setting sun. By this means the humane and benevolent, in various parts of the continent, were induced to advise us not to comply with the terms for opening our port, and engage to relieve us with their charities, from the distress that must otherwise fall upon the poor. Their charitable intentions ascend to heaven, like incense from the altar, in sweet memorial before the throne of God; but their donations came near proving fatal to the province. It encouraged the whigs to persevere in injustice, and has been the means of seducing many an honest man into the commission of a crime, that he did not suspect himself capable of being guilty of. What I have told you, is not the mere suggestions of a speculatist; there are some mistakes as to numbers, and there may be some as to time and place, partly owing to miscopying, and partly to my not always having had the books and papers necessary to greater accuracy, at hand; but the relation of facts is in substance true, I had almost said, as holy writ. I do not ask you to take the truths of them from an anonymous writer. The evidence of most of them is within your reach; examine for yourselves. I promise that the benefit you will reap therefrom will abundantly pay you, for the trouble of the research; you will find I have faithfully unriddled the whole mystery of our political iniquity. I do not address myself to whigs or tories, but to the whole people. I know you well. You are loyal at heart, friends to good order, and do violence to yourselves in harboring, one moment, disrespectful sentiments towards Great Britain, the land of our forefathers' nativity, and sacred repository of their bones; but you have been most insidiously induced to believe that Great Britain is rapacious, cruel, and vindictive, and envies us the inheritance purchased by the sweat and blood of our ancestors. Could that thick mist, that hovers over the land and involves in it more than Egyptian darkness, be but once dispelled, that you might see our Sovereign, the provident father of all his people, and Great Britain a nursing mother to these colonies, as they really are, long live our gracious king, and happiness to Britain, would resound from one end of the province to the other.

MASSACHUSETTENSIS.

Massachusetts Gazette, and the Boston
Post-Boy and Advertiser, January 2, 1775

Massachusettens [Daniel Leonard] No. V

To the Inhabitants of the Province of Massachusetts Bay,

MY DEAR COUNTRYMEN,

Some of you may perhaps suspect that I have been wantonly scattering firebrands, arrows, and death, to gratify a malicious and revengeful disposition. The truth is this. I had seen many excellent detached pieces, but could see no pen at work to trace our calamity to its source, and point out the many adventitious aids; that conspired to raise it to its present height, though I impatiently expected it, being fully convinced that you wait only to know the true state of facts, to rectify whatever is amiss in the province, without any foreign assistance. Others may be induced to think, that I grudge the industrious poor of Boston their scantlings of charity. I will issue a brief in their favour. The opulent, be their political sentiments what they may, ought to relieve them from their sufferings, and those who, by former donations, have been the innocent cause of protracting their sufferings, are under a tenfold obligation to assist them now; and at the same time to make the most explicit declarations, that they did not intend to promote, nor ever will join in rebellion. Great allowances are to be made for the crossings, windings, and tergiversations of a politician; he is a cunning animal, and as government is said to be founded in opinion, his tricks may be a part of the *arcana imperii*. Had our politicians confined themselves within any reasonable bounds, I never should have molested them; but when I became satisfied, that many innocent, unsuspecting persons were in danger of being seduced to their utter ruin, and the province of Massachusetts Bay in danger of being drenched with blood and carnage, I could restrain my emotions no longer; and having once broke the bands of natural reserve, was determined to probe the sore to the bottom, though I was sure to touch the quick. It is very foreign from my intentions to draw down the vengeance of Great Britain upon the whigs; they are too valuable a part of the community to lose, if they will permit themselves to be saved. I wish nothing worse to the highest of them, than that they may be deprived of their influence, till such time as they shall have changed their sentiments, principles, and measures.

Sedition has already been marked through its zigzag path to the present times. When the statute for regulating the government arrived, a match was put to the train, and the mine, that had been long forming, sprung, and threw the whole province into confusion and anarchy. The occurrencies of the summer and autumn past are so recent and notorious, that a particular detail of them is unnecessary. Suffice it to say, that every barrier that civil government had erected for the security of property, liberty and life, was broken down, and law, constitution and government trampled under foot by the rudest invaders. I shall not dwell upon these harsh notes much longer. I shall yet become an advocate for the leading whigs; much must be allowed to men, in their situation, forcibly actuated by the chagrin of disappointment, the fear of punishment, and the fascination of hope at the same time.

Perhaps the whole story of empire does not furnish another instance of a forcible opposition to government, with so much apparent and little real cause, with such apparent probability without any possibility of success. The stamp-act gave the alarm. The instability of the public councils from the Greenvillian administration to the appointment of the Earl of Hillsborough to the American department, afforded as great a prospect of success, as the heavy duties imposed by the stamp-act, did a colour for the opposition. It was necessary to give the history of this matter in its course, offend who it would, because those acts of government, that are called the greatest grievances, became proper and necessary, through the misconduct of our politicians, and the justice of Great Britain towards us, could not be made apparent without first pointing out that. I intend to consider the acts of the British government, which are held up as the principal grievances, and inquire whether Great Britain is chargeable with injustice in any one of them; but must first ask your attention to the authority of parliament. I suspect many of our politicians are wrong in their first principle, in denying that the constitutional authority of parliament extends to the colonies; if so, it must not be wondered at, that their whole fabric is so ruinous. I shall not travel through all the arguments that have been adduced, for and against this question, but attempt to reduce the substance of them to a narrow compass, after having taken a cursory view of the British constitution.

The security of the people from internal rapacity and violence, and from foreign invasion, is the end and design of government. The simple forms of government are monarchy, aristocracy, and democracy; that is, where the authority of the state is vested in one, a few, or the many. Each of these species of government has advantages peculiar to itself, and would answer the ends of government, were the persons intrusted with the authority of the state, always guided, themselves, by unerring wisdom and public virtue; but rulers are not always exempt from the weakness and depravity which make government necessary to society. Thus monarchy is apt to rush headlong into tyranny, aristocracy to beget faction, and multiplied usurpation, and democracy, to degenerate into tumult, violence, and anarchy. A government formed upon these three principles, in due proportion, is the best calculated to answer the ends of government, and to endure. Such a government is the British constitution, consisting of king, lords and commons, which at once includes the principal excellencies, and excludes the principal defects of the other kinds of government. It is allowed, both by Englishmen and foreigners, to be the most perfect system that the wisdom of ages has produced. The distributions of power are so just, and the proportions so exact, as at once to support and controul each other. An Englishman glories in being subject to, and protected by such a government. The colonies are a part of the British empire. The best writers upon the law of nations tell us, that when a nation takes possession of a distant country, and settles there, that country, though separated from the principal establishment, or mother country, naturally becomes a part of the state, equal with its ancient possessions. Two supreme or independent authorities cannot exist in the same state. It would be what is called *imperium in imperio*, the height of political absurdity. The analogy between the political and human body is great. Two independent authorities in a state would be like two distinct principles of volition and action in the human body, dissenting, opposing, and destroying each other. If, then, we are a part of the British empire, we must be subject to the supreme power of the state, which is vested in the estates of parliament, notwithstanding each of the colonies have legislative and executive powers of their own, delegated, or granted to them for the purposes of regulating their own internal police, which are subordinate to, and must necessarily be subject to the checks, controul, and regulation of the supreme authority.

This doctrine is not new, but the denial of it is. It is beyond a doubt, that it was the sense both of the parent country, and our ancestors, that they were to remain subject to parliament. It is evident from the charter itself; and this authority has been exercised by parliament, from time to time, almost ever since the first settlement of the country, and has been expressly acknowledged by our provincial legislatures. It is not less our interest, than our duty, to continue subject to the authority of parliament, which will be more fully considered hereafter. The principal argument against the authority of parliament, is this; the Americans are entitled to all the privileges of an Englishman; it is the privilege of an Englishman to be exempt from all laws, that he does not consent to in person, or by representative. The Americans are not represented in parliament, and therefore are exempt from acts of parliament, or in other words, not subject to its authority. This appears specious; but leads to such absurdities as demonstrate its fallacy. If the colonies are not subject to the authority of parliament, Great Britain and the colonies must be distinct states, as completely so, as England and Scotland were before the union, or as Great Britain and Hanover are now. The colonies in that case will owe no allegiance to the imperial crown, and perhaps not to the person of the king, as the title to the crown is derived from an act of parliament, made since the settlement of this province, which act respects the imperial crown only. Let us wave this difficulty, and suppose allegiance due from the colonies to the person of the king of Great Britain. He then appears in a new capacity, of king of America, or rather in several new capacities, of king of Massachusetts, king of Rhode-Island, king of Connecticut, &c. &c. For if our connexion with Great Britain by the parliament be dissolved, we shall have none among ourselves, but each colony become as distinct from the others, as England was from Scotland, before the union. Some have supposed that each state, having one and the same person for its king, is a sufficient connection. Were he an absolute monarch, it might be; but in a mixed government, it is no union at all. For as the king must govern each state, by its parliament, those several parliaments would pursue the particular interest of its own state; and however well disposed the king might be to pursue a line of interest, that was common to all, the checks and controul that he would meet with, would render it impossible. If the king of Great Britain has really these new capacities, they ought to be added to his titles; and another difficulty will arise, the prerogatives of these new crowns have never been defined or limited. Is the monarchical part of the several provincial constitutions to be nearer or more remote from absolute monarchy, in an inverted ratio to each one's approaching to, or receding from a republic? But let us suppose the same prerogatives inherent in the several American crowns, as are in the imperial crown of Great Britain, where shall we find the British constitution, that we all agree we are entitled to? We shall seek for it in vain in our provincial assemblies. They are but faint sketches of the estates of parliament. The houses of representatives, or Burgesses, have not all the powers of the house of commons; in the charter governments they have no more than what is expressly granted by their several charters. The first charters granted to this province did not empower the assembly to tax the people at all. Our council boards are as destitute of the constitutional authority of the house of lords, as their several members are of the noble independence, and splendid appendages of peerage. The house of peers is the bulwark of the British constitution, and through successive ages, has withstood the shocks of monarchy, and the sappings of democracy, and the constitution gained strength by the conflict. Thus the supposition of our being independent states, or exempt from the authority of parliament, destroys the very idea of our having a British constitution. The provincial constitutions, considered as subordinate, are generally well adapted to those purposes of government, for which they were intended; that is, to regulate the internal police of the several colonies; but have no principle of stability within themselves; they may support themselves in moderate times, but would be merged by the violence of turbulent ones, and the several colonies become wholly monarchical, or wholly republican, were it not for the checks, controuls, regulations, and supports of the supreme authority of the empire. Thus the argument, that is drawn from their first principle of our being entitled to English liberties, destroys the principle itself, it deprives us of the bill of rights, and all the benefits resulting from the revolution of English laws, and of the British constitution.

Our patriots have been so intent upon building up American rights, that they have overlooked the rights of Great Britain, and our own interest. Instead of proving that we were entitled to privileges, that our fathers know our situation would not admit us to enjoy, they have been arguing away our most essential rights. If there be any grievance, it does not consist in our being subject to the authority of parliament, but in our not having an actual representation in it. Were it possible for the colonies to have an equal representation in parliament, and were refused it upon proper application, I confess I should think it a grievance; but at present it seems to be allowed, by all parties, to be impracticable, considering the colonies are distant from Great Britain a thousand transmarine leagues. If that be the case, the right or privilege, that we complain of being deprived of, is not withheld by Britain, but the first principles of government, and the immutable laws of nature, render it impossible for us to enjoy it. This is apparently the meaning of that celebrated passage in Governor Hutchinson's letter, that rang through the continent, viz: There must be an abridgment of what is called English liberties. He subjoins, that he had never yet seen the projection, whereby a colony, three thousand miles distant from the parent state, might enjoy all the privileges of the parent state, and remain subject to it, or in words to that effect. The obnoxious sentence, taken detached from the letter, appears very unfriendly to the colonies; but considered in connection with the other parts of the letter, is but a necessary result from our situation. Allegiance and protection are reciprocal. It is our highest interest to continue a part of the British empire; and equally our duty to remain subject to the authority of parliament. Our own internal police may generally be regulated by our provincial legislatures, but in national concerns, or where our own assemblies do not answer the ends of government with respect to ourselves, the ordinances or interposition of the great council of the nation is necessary. In this case, the major must rule the minor. After many more centuries shall have rolled away, long after we, who are now bustling upon the stage of life, shall have been received to the bosom of mother earth, and our names are forgotten, the colonies may be so far increased as to have the balance of wealth, numbers and power, in their favour, the good of the empire make it necessary to fix the seat of government here; and some future George, equally the friend of mankind, with him that now sways the British sceptre, may cross the Atlantic, and rule Great Britain, by an American parliament.

MASSACHUSETTENSIS.

Massachusetts Gazette; and the Boston Post-Boy and Advertiser, January 9, 1775

Massachusettensis [Daniel Leonard] No. VI

To the Inhabitants of the Province of Massachusetts Bay,

MY DEAR COUNTRYMEN,

Had a person, some fifteen years ago, undertaken to prove that the colonies were a part of the British empire or dominion, and as such, subject to the authority of the British parliament, he would have acted as ridiculous a part, as to have undertaken to prove a self-evident proposition. Had any person denied it, he would have been called a fool or madman. At this wise period, individuals and bodies of men deny it, notwithstanding in doing it they subvert the fundamentals of

government, deprive us of British liberties, and build up absolute monarchy in the colonies; for our charters suppose regal
authority in the grantor; if that authority be derived from the
British crown, it pre-supposes this territory to have been a part
of the British dominion, and as such subject to the imperial
sovereign; if that authority was vested in the person of the
king, in a different capacity, the British constitution and laws
are out of the question, and the king must be absolute as to us,
as his prerogatives have never been circumscribed. Such must
have been the sovereign authority of the several kings, who
have granted American charters, previous to the several grants;
there is nothing to detract from it, at this time, in those
colonies that are destitute of charters, and the charter governments must severally revert to absolute monarchy, as their
charters may happen to be forfeited by the grantees not fulfilling the conditions of them, as every charter contains an express
or implied condition.

It is curious indeed to trace the denial and oppugnation to
the supreme authority of the state. When the stamp-act was
made, the authority of parliament to impose internal taxes was
denied; but their right to impose external ones, or in other
words, to lay duties upon goods and merchandize was admitted. When the act was made imposing duties upon tea, &c. a
new distinction was set up, that the parliament had a right to
lay duties upon merchandize for the purpose of regulating trade,
but not for the purpose of raising a revenue: that is, the parliament had good right and lawful authority to lay the former
duty of a shilling on the pound, but had none to lay the present duty of three pence. Having got thus far safe, it was only
taking one step more to extricate ourselves entirely from their
fangs, and become independant states, that our patriots most
heroically resolved upon, and flatly denied that parliament had
a right to make any laws whatever, that should be binding
upon the colonies. There is no possible medium between absolute independence, and subjection to the authority of parliament. He must be blind indeed that cannot see our dearest
interest in the latter, notwithstanding many pant after the former. Misguided men! could they once overtake their wish,
they would be convinced of the madness of the pursuit.

My dear countrymen, it is of the last importance that we settle this point clearly in our minds; it will serve as a sure test, certain criterion and invariable standard to distinguish the friends from the enemies of our country, patriotism from sedition, loyalty from rebellion. To deny the supreme authority of the state, is a high misdemeanor, to say no worse of it; to oppose it by force is an overt act of treason, punishable by confiscation of estate, and most ignominious death. The realm of England is an appropriate term for the ancient realm of England, in contradistinction to Wales and other territories, that have been annexed to it. These as they have been severally annexed to the crown, whether by conquest or otherwise, became a part of the empire, and subject to the authority of parliament, whether they send members to parliament or not, and whether they have legislative powers of their own or not.

Thus Ireland, who has perhaps the greatest possible subordinate legislature, and sends no members to the British parliament, is bound by its acts, when expressly named. Guernsey and Jersey are no part of the realm of England, nor are they represented in parliament, but are subject to its authority: and, in the same predicament are the American colonies, and all the other dispersions of the empire. Permit me to request your attention to this subject a little longer; I assure you it is as interesting and important, as it is dry and unentertaining.

Let us now recur to the first charter of this province, and we shall find irresistible evidence, that our being part of the empire, subject to the supreme authority of the state, bound by its laws and entitled to its protection, were the very terms and conditions by which our ancestors held their lands, and settled the province. Our charter, like all other American charters, are under the great seal of England; the grants are made by the king, for his heirs and *successors*; the several tenures to be of the king, his heirs and *successors*; in like manner are the reservations. It is apparent the king acted in his royal capacity, as king of England, which necessarily supposes the territory granted, to be a part of the English dominions, holden of the crown of England.

The charter, after reciting several grants of the territory to sir Henry Roswell and others, proceeds to incorporation in these words: "And for as much as the good and prosperous success of the plantations of the said parts of New England aforesaid, intended by the said sir Henry Roswell and others, to be speedily set upon, cannot but chiefly depend, next under the blessing of almighty God, and the support of our royal authority, upon the good government of the same, to the end that the *affairs of business*, which from time to time shall happen and arise concerning the said lands and the plantations of the same may be the better managed and ordered, we have further hereby, of our especial grace, certain knowledge and mere motion given, granted and confirmed, and for us, our heirs and successors, do give, grant and confirm unto our said trusty and well beloved subjects, sir Henry Roswell, &c. and all such others as shall hereafter be admitted and made free of *the company and society hereafter mentioned*, shall from time to time and at all times, forever hereafter, be by virtue of these presents, *one body corporate, politic in fact and name by the name of the governor and company of the Massachusetts Bay, in New England*; and them by the name of the governor and company of the Massachusetts Bay, in New England, one body politic and corporate in deed, fact and name. We do for us our heirs and successors make, ordain, constitute and confirm by these presents, and that by that name they shall have perpetual succession, and that by that name they and their successors shall be capable and enabled as well *to implead and to be impleaded, and to prosecute, demand and answer and be answered unto all and singular suits, causes, quarrels and actions of what kind or nature soever; and also to have, take, possess, acquire and purchase, any lands, tenements and hereditaments, or any goods or chattels, the same to lease, grant, demise, aleine, bargain, sell and dispose of as our liege people of this our realm of England, or any other corporation or body politic of the same may do.*" I would beg leave to ask one simple question, whether this looks like a distinct state or independent empire? Provision is then made for electing a governor, deputy governor, and eighteen assistants. After which, is this clause: "We do for us, our heirs and successors, give and grant to the said governor and company, and their successors, that the governor or in his absense the deputy governor of the said company, for the time being, and such of the assistants or freemen of the said company as shall be present, or the greater number of them so assembled, whereof the governor or deputy governor and six of the assistants, at the least to be seven, shall have full power and authority to choose, nominate and appoint such and so many others as they shall think fit, and shall be willing to accept the same, to be free of the said company and body, and them into the same to admit and to elect and constitute such officers as they shall think fit and requisite for the ordering, managing and dispatching of the affairs of the said governor and company and their successors, and to make *laws and ordinances for the good and welfare of the said company*, and for the government and ordering of the said lands and plantations, and the people inhabiting and to inhabit the same, as to them from time to time shall be thought meet: *So as such laws and ordinances be not contrary or repugnant to the laws and statutes of this our realm of England*."

Another clause is this, "And for their further encouragement, of our especial grace and favor, we do by these presents, for us, our heirs, and successors, yield and grant to the said governor and company and their successors, and every of them, their factors and assigns, that they and every of them shall be free and quit from all taxes, subsidies and customs in New England for the space of seven years, and from all taxes and impositions for the space of twenty-one years, upon all goods and merchandize, at any time or times hereafter, either upon importation thither, or exportation from thence into our realm of England, or into other of our dominions, by the said governor and company and their successors, their deputies, factors and assigns, &c."

The exemption from taxes for seven years in one case, and twenty one years in the other, plainly indicates that after their expiration, this province would be liable to taxation. Now I would ask by what authority those taxes were to be imposed? It could not be by the governor and company, for no such power was delegated or granted to them; and besides it would have been absurd and nugatory to exempt them from their own taxation, supposing them to have had the power, for they might have exempted themselves. It must therefore be by the king or parliament; it could not be by the king alone, for as king of England, the political capacity in which he granted the charter, he had no such power, exclusive of the lords and commons, consequently it must have been by the parliament. This clause in the charter is as evident a recognition of the authority of the parliament over this province, as if the words, "acts of parliament," had been inserted, as they were in the Pennsylvania charter. There was no session of parliament after the grant of our charter until the year 1640. In 1642 the house of commons passed a resolve, "that for the better advancement of the plantations in New England, and the encouragement of the planters to proceed in their undertaking, their exports and imports should be freed and discharged from all customs, subsidies, taxations and duties until the further order of the house;" which was gratefully received and recorded in the archives of our predecessors. This transaction shews very clearly in what sense our connection with England was then understood. It is true, that in some arbitrary reigns, attempts were made by the servants of the crown to exclude the two houses of parliament, from any share of the authority over the colonies; they also attempted to render the king absolute in England; but the parliament always rescued the colonies, as well as England from such attempts.

I shall recite but one more clause of this charter, which is this, "And further our will and pleasure is, and we do hereby for us, our heirs and successors, ordain, declare and grant to the said governor and company, and their successors, that all and every of the subjects of us, our heirs and successors which shall go to and inhabit within the said land and premises hereby mentioned to be granted, and every of their children which shall happen to be born there, or on the seas in going thither, or returning from thence, shall have and enjoy *all liberties and immunities of free and natural subjects, within any of the dominions* of us, our heirs or successors, to all intents, constructions and purposes whatsoever, as if they and every of them were born within the realm of England." It is upon this, or a similar clause in the charter of William and Mary that our patriots have built up the stupendous fabric of American independence. They argue from it a total exemption from parliamentary authority, because we are not represented in parliament.

I have already shewn that the supposition of our being exempt from the authority of parliament, is pregnant with the grossest absurdities. Let us now consider this clause in connection with the other parts of the charter. It is a rule of law, founded in reason and common sense, to construe each part of an instrument, so as the whole may hang together, and be consistent with itself. If we suppose this clause to exempt us from the authority of parliament, we must throw away all the rest of the charter, for every other part indicates the contrary, as plainly as words can do it; and what is still worse, this clause becomes *felo de se*, and destroys itself; for if we are not annexed to the crown, we are aliens, and no charter, grant, or other act of the crown can naturalize us or entitle us to the liberties and immunities of Englishmen. It can be done only by act of parliament. An alien is one born in a strange country out of the allegiance of the king, and is under many disabilities though residing in the realm; as Wales, Jersey, Guernsey, Ireland, the foreign plantations, &c. were severally annexed to the crown, they became parts of one and the same empire, the natives of which are equally free as though they had been born in that territory which was the ancient realm. As our patriots depend upon this clause, detached from the charter, let us view it in that light. If a person born in England removes to Ireland and settles there, he is then no longer represented in the British parliament, but he and his posterity are, and will ever be subject to the authority of the British parliament. If he removes to Jersey, Guernsey, or any other parts of the British dominions that send no members to parliament, he will still be in the same predicament. So that the inhabitants of the American colonies do in fact enjoy all the liberties and immunities of natural born subjects. We are entitled to no greater privileges than those that are born within the realm; and they can enjoy no other than we do, when they reside out of it. Thus, it is evident that this clause amounts to no more than the royal assurance, that we are a part of the British empire; are not aliens, but natural born subjects; and as such, bound to obey the supreme power of the state, and entitled to protection from it. To avoid prolixity, I shall not remark particularly upon other parts of this charter, but observe in general, that whoever reads it with attention, will meet with irresistible evidence in every part of it, that our being a part of the English dominions, subject to the English crown, and within the jurisdiction of parliament, were the terms upon which our ancestors settled this colony, and the very tenures by which they held their estates.

No lands within the British dominions are perfectly allodial; they are held mediately or immediately of the king, and upon forfeiture, revert to the crown. My dear countrymen, you have many of you been most falsely and wickedly told by our patriots, that Great Britain was meditating a land tax, and seeking to deprive us of our inheritance; but had all the malice and subtilty of men and devils been united, a readier method to effect it could not have been devised, than the late denials of the authority of parliament, and forcible oppositions to its acts. Yet, this has been planned and executed chiefly by persons of desperate fortunes.

MASSACHUSETTENSIS.

*Massachusetts Gazette; and the Boston
Post-Boy and Advertiser*, January 16, 1775

Massachusettensis [Daniel Leonard] No. VII

To the Inhabitants of the Province of Massachusetts Bay,

MY DEAR COUNTRYMEN,

If we carry our researches further back than the emigration of our ancestors, we shall find many things that reflect light upon the object we are in quest of. It is immaterial when America was first discovered or taken possession of by the English. In 1602 one Gosnold landed upon one of the islands, called Elizabeth islands, which were so named in honor of queen Elizabeth, built a fort, and projected a settlement; his men were discouraged, and the project failed. In 1606, king James granted all the continent from 34 to 45 degrees, which he divided into two colonies, viz. the southern or Virginia, to certain merchants at London, the northern or New England, to certain merchants at Plymouth in England. In 1607, some of the patentees of the northern colony began a settlement at Sogadahoc; but the emigrants were disheartened after the trial of one winter, and that attempt failed of success. Thus this territory had not only been granted by the crown for purposes of colonization, which are to enlarge the empire or dominion of the parent state, and to open new sources of national wealth; but actual possession had been taken by the grantees, previous to the emigration of our ancestors, or any grant to them. In 1620, a patent was granted to the adventurers for the northern colony, incorporating them by the name of *the council for the affairs of New Plymouth*. From this company of merchants in England, our ancestors derived their title to this territory. The tract of land called Massachusetts, was purchased of this company, by sir Henry Roswell and associates; their deed bears date March 19th, 1627. In 1628 they obtained a charter of incorporation, which I have already remarked upon. The liberties, privileges and franchises, granted by this charter, do not perhaps exceed those granted to the city of London and other corporations within the realm. The legislative power was very confined; it did not even extend to levying taxes of any kind; that power was however assumed under this charter, which by law worked a forfeiture; and for this among other things, in the reign of Charles the second, the charter was adjudged forfeited, and the franchises seized into the king's hands. This judgment did not affect our ancestors title to their lands, that were not derived originally from the charter, though confirmed by it, but by purchase from the council at Plymouth, who held immediately under the crown. Besides, our ancestors had now reduced what before was a naked right to possession, and by persevering through unequalled toils, hardships and dangers, at the approach of which other emigrants had fainted, rendered New England a very valuable acquisition both to the crown and nation. This was highly meritorious, and ought not to be overlooked in adjusting the present unhappy dispute; but our patriots would deprive us of all the merit, both to the crown and nation, by severing us from both. After the revolution, our ancestors petitioned the parliament to restore the charter. A bill for that purpose passed the house of commons, but went no further. In consequence of another petition, king William and queen Mary granted our present charter, for uniting and incorporating the Massachusetts, New Plymouth, and several other territories into one province. More extensive powers of legislation, than those contained in the first charter, were become necessary, and were granted; and the form of the legislature made to approach nearer to the form of the supreme legislature. The powers of legislation are confined to local or provincial purposes and further restricted by these words, viz. *So as the same be not repugnant or contrary to the laws of this our realm of England.* Our patriots have made many nice distinctions and curious refinements, to evade the force of these words; but after all, it is impossible to reconcile them to the idea of an independent state, as it is to reconcile disability to omnipotence. The provincial power of taxation is also restricted to provincial purposes, and allowed to be exercised over such only as are inhabitants or proprietors within the province. I would observe here, that the granting subordinate powers of legislation, does not abridge or diminish the powers of the higher legislatures; thus we see corporations in England and the several towns in this province vested with greater or lesser powers of legislation, without the parliament, in one case, or the general court in the other, being restrained, from enacting those very laws, that fall within the jurisdiction of the several corporations. Had our present charter been conceived in such equivocal terms, as that it might be construed as restraining the authority of parliament, the uniform usage ever since it passed the seal, would satisfy us that its intent was different. The parliament, in the reign when it was granted, long before and in every reign since, has been making statutes to extend to the colonies, and those statutes have been as uniformly submitted to as authoritative, by the colonies, till within ten or a dozen years. Sometimes acts of parliament have been made, and sometimes have been repealed in consequence of petitions from the colonies. The provincial assemblies often refer to acts of parliament in their own, and have sometimes made acts to aid their execution. It is evident that it was the intention of their majesties, to grant subordinate powers of legislation, without impairing or diminishing the authority of the supreme legislature. Had there been any words in the charter, that precluded that construction, or did the whole taken together contradict it, lawyers would tell us, that the king was deceived in his grant, and the patentees took no estate by it, because the crown can neither alienate a part of the British dominions, nor impair the supreme power of the empire. I have dwelt longer on this subject, than I at first intended, and not by any means done it justice, as to avoid prolix narratives and tedious deduction, I have omitted perhaps more than I have adduced, that evinces the truth of the position, that we are a part of the British dominions, and subject to the authority of parliament. The novelty of the contrary tenets, will appear by extracting a part of a pamphlet, published in 1764, by a Boston gentleman, who was then the oracle of the whigs, and whose profound knowledge in the law and constitution is equalled but by few.

"I also lay it down as one of the first principles from whence I intend to deduce the civil rights of the British colonies, that all of them are subject to, and dependent on Great Britain; and that therefore as over subordinate governments, the parliament of Great Britain has an undoubted power and lawful authority to make acts for the general good, that by naming them, shall and ought to be equally binding, as upon the subjects of Great Britain within the realm. Is there the least difference, as to the consent of the colonists, whether taxes and impositions are laid on their trade, and other property by the crown alone, or by the parliament? As it is agreed on all hands, the crown alone cannot impose them, we should be justifiable in refusing to pay them, *but must and ought to yield obedience to an act of parliament, though erroneous, till repealed.*"

"It is a maxim, that the king can do no wrong; and every good subject is bound to believe his king is not inclined to do any. We are blessed with a prince who has given abundant demonstrations, that in all his actions, he studies the good of his people, and the true glory of his crown, which are inseperable. It would therefore be the highest degree of impudence and disloyalty, to imagine that the king, at the head of his parliament, could have any but the most pure and perfect intentions of justice, goodness and truth, that human nature is capable of. All this I say and believe of the king and parliament, in all their acts; even in that which so nearly affects the interests of the colonists; and that a most perfect and ready obedience is to be yielded to it while it remains in force. The power of parliament is uncontroulable but by themselves, and we must obey. They only can repeal their own acts. There would be an end of all government, if one or a number of subjects, or subordinate provinces should take upon them so far to judge of the justice of an act of parliament, as to refuse obedience to it. If there was nothing else to restrain such a step, prudence ought to do it, for forcibly resisting the parliament and the king's laws is high treason. Therefore let the parliament lay what burdens they please on us, we must, it is our duty to submit and patiently bear them, till they will be pleased to relieve us."

The Pennsylvania Farmer, who took the lead in explaining away the right of parliament to raise a revenue in America, speaking of regulating trade, tells us, that "he who considers these provinces as states distinct from the British empire, has very slender notions of justice, or of their interest; we are but parts of a whole, and therefore there must exist a power somewhere to preside, and preserve the connection in due order. This power is lodged in parliament, and we are as much dependant on Great Britain as a perfectly free people can be on another." He supposes that we are dependant in some considerable degree upon Great Britain; and that that dependance is nevertheless consistent with perfect freedom.

Having settled this point, let us reflect upon the resolves and proceedings of our patriots. We often read resolves denying the authority of parliament, which is the imperial sovereign, gilded over with professions of loyalty to the king, but the golden leaf is too thin to conceal the treason. It either argues profound ignorance or hypocritical cunning.

We find many unsuspecting persons prevailed on openly to oppose the execution of acts of parliament with force and arms. My friends, some of the persons that beguiled you, could have turned to the chapter, page and section, where such insurrections are pronounced rebellion, by the law of the land; and had not their hearts been dead to a sense of justice, and steeled against every feeling of humanity, they would have timely warned you of your danger. Our patriots have sent us in pursuit of a mere *ignis fatuus*, a fascinating glare devoid of substance; and now when we find ourselves bewildered, with scarce one ray of hope to raise our sinking spirits, or stay our fainting souls, they conjure up phantoms more delusive and fleeting, if possible, than that which first led us astray. They tell us, we are a match for Great Britain. The twentieth part of the strength that Great Britain could exert, were it necessary, is more than sufficient to crush this defenceless province to atoms, notwithstanding all the vapouring of the disaffected here and elsewhere. They tell us the army is disaffected to the service. What pains have our wretched politicians not taken to attach them to it? The officers conceive no very favourable opinion of the cause of the whigs, from the obloquy with which their General hath been treated, in return for his humanity, nor from the infamous attempts to seduce the soldiers from his majesty's service. The policy of some of our patriots has been as weak and contemptible, as their motives are sordid and malevolent; for when they found their success, in corrupting the soldiery, did not answer their expectations, they took pains to attach them firmer to the cause they adhered to, by preventing the erecting of barracks for their winter quarters, by which means many contracted diseases, and some lives were lost, from the unwholesome buildings they were obliged to occupy; and, as though some stimulus was still wanting, some provocation to prevent human nature revolting in the hour of battle, they deprived the soldiers of a gratification never denied to the brute creation; straw to lie on. I do not mention this conduct to raise the resentment of the troops; it has had its effect already; and it is proper you should know it; nor should I have blotted paper in relating facts so mortifying to the pride of man, had it not been basely suggested that there would be a defection should the army take the field. Those are matters of small moment, compared to another, which is the cause they are engaged in. It is no longer a struggle between whigs and tories, whether these or those shall occupy posts of honour, or enjoy the emoluments of office, nor is it now whether this or the other act of parliament shall be repealed. The army is sent here to decide a question, intimately connected with the honour and interest of the nation, no less than whether the colonies shall continue a part of, or be for ever dismembered from the British empire. It is a cause in which no honest American can wish our politicians success, though it is devoutly to be wished, that their discomfiture may be effected without recourse being had to the *ultima ratio*—the sword. This, our wretched situation, is but the natural consequence of denying the authority of parliament, and forcibly opposing its acts.

Sometimes we are amused with intimations that Holland,

France or Spain, will make a diversion in our favour. These, equally with the others, are suggestions of despair. These powers have colonies of their own, and might not choose to set a bad example, by encouraging the colonies of any other state to revolt. The Dutch have too much money in the English funds, and are too much attached to their money to espouse our quarrel. The French and Spaniards have not yet forgot the drubbing they received from Great Britain last war; and all three fear to offend that power which our politicians would persuade us to despise.

Lastly, they tell us that the people in England will take our part, and prevent matters from coming to extremity. This is their fort, where, when driven from every other post, they fly for refuge.

Alas, my friends! our congresses have stopped up every avenue that leads to that sanctuary. We hear, by every arrival from England, that it is no longer a ministerial, (if it ever was) but a national cause. My dear countrymen, I deal plainly with you. I never should forgive myself if I did not. Are there not eleven regiments in Boston? A respectable fleet in the harbour? Men of war stationed at every considerable port along the continent? Are there not three ships of the line sent here, notwithstanding the danger of the winter coast, with more than the usual compliment of marines? Have not our congresses, county, provincial, and continental, instead of making advances for an accommodation, bid defiance to Great Britain? *He that runs may read.*

If our politicians will not be pursuaded from running against the thick bosses of the buckler, it is tune for us to leave them to their fate, and provide for the safety of ourselves, our wives, our children, our friends, and our country.

I have many things to add, but most now take my leave, for this week, by submitting to your judgment whether there be not an absolute necessity of immediately protesting against all traitorous resolves, leagues, and associations, of bodies of men, that appear to have acted in a representative capacity. Had our congresses been accidental or spontaneous meetings, the whole blame might have rested upon the individuals that composed them; but as they appear in the character of the people's delegates, is there not the utmost danger of the innocent being confounded with the guilty, unless they take care timely to distinguish themselves?

MASSACHUSETTENSIS.

Massachusetts Gazette; and the Boston Post-Boy and Advertiser, January 23, 1775

Novanglus No. I

To the Inhabitants of the Colony of Massachusetts-Bay

My Friends,

A Writer, under the signature of Massachusettensis, has addressed you, in a series of papers, on the great national subject of the present quarrel between the British administration and the colonies. As I have not in my possession, more than one of his Essays, and that is in the Gazette of December 26, I will take the liberty, in the spirit of candor and decency, to bespeak your attention, upon the same subject.

There may be occasion, to say very severe things, before I shall have finished what I propose, in opposition to this writer, but there ought to be no reviling. *Rem ipsam dic, mitte male loqui*, which may be justly translated, speak out the whole truth boldly, but use no bad language.

It is not very material to enquire, as others have done, who is the author of the speculations in question. If he is a disinterested writer, and has nothing to gain or lose, to hope or fear, for himself, more than other individuals of your community; but engages in this controversy from the purest principles, the noblest motives of benevolence to men, and of love to his country, he ought to have no influence with you, further than truth and justice will support his argument. On the other hand, if he hopes to acquire or preserve a lucrative employment, to screen himself from the just detestation of his countrymen, or whatever other sinister inducement he may have; as far as the truth of facts and the weight of argument, are in his favour, he ought to be heard and regarded.

He tells you "that the temporal salvation of this province depends upon an entire and speedy change of measures, which must depend upon a change of sentiments respecting our own conduct and the justice of the British nation."

The task, of effecting these great changes, this courageous writer, has undertaken in a course of publications in a newspaper. *Nil desperandum* is a good motto, and *Nil admirari*, is another. He is welcome to the first, and I hope will be willing that I should assume the last. The public, if they are not

384

mistaken in their conjecture, have been so long acquainted with this gentleman, and have seen him so often disappointed, that if they were not habituated to strange things, they would wonder at his hopes, at this time to accomplish the most unpromising project of his whole life. In the character of Philanthrop, he attempted to reconcile you, to Mr. Bernard. But the only fruit of his labour was, to expose his client to more general examination, and consequently to more general resentment and aversion. In the character of Philalethes, he essayed to prove Mr. Hutchinson a Patriot, and his letters not only innocent, but meritorious. But the more you read and considered, the more you were convinced of the ambition and avarice, the simulation and dissimulation, the hypocricy and perfidy of that destroying angel.

This illfated and unsuccessful, tho' persevering writer, still hopes to change your sentiments and conduct—by which it is supposed that he means to convince you that the system of colony administration, which has been pursued for these ten or twelve years past, is a wise, righteous and humane plan: that Sir Francis Bernard and Mr. Hutchinson, with their connections, who have been the principal instruments of it, are your best friends;—and that those gentlemen in this province, and in all the other colonies, who have been in opposition to it, are from ignorance, error, or from worse and baser causes, your worst enemies.

This is certainly an inquiry, that is worthy of you: and I promise to accompany this writer, in his ingenious labours to assist you in it. And I earnestly intreat you, as the result of all shall be, to change your sentiments or persevere in them, as the evidence shall appear to you, upon the most dispassionate and impartial consideration, without regard to his opinion or mine.

He promises to avoid personal reflections, but to penetrate the arcana, and expose the wretched policy of the whigs.—The cause of the whigs is not conducted by intrigues at a distant court, but by constant appeals to a sensible and virtuous people; it depends intirely on their good will, and cannot be pursued a single step without their concurrence, to obtain which all designs, measures and means, are constantly published to the collective body. The whigs therefore can have no arcana: But if they had, I dare say they were never so left, as to communicate them to this writer: you will therefore be disappointed if you expect from him any thing which is true, but what has been as publick as records and news-papers could make it.

I, on my part, may perhaps in a course of papers, penetrate arcana too. Shew the wicked policy of the Tories—trace their plan from its first rude sketches to its present compleat draught. Shew that it has been much longer in contemplation, than is generally known—who were the first in it—their views, motives and secret springs of action—and the means they have employed. This will necessarily bring before your eyes many characters, living and dead. From such a research and detail of facts, it will clearly appear, who were the aggressors—and who have acted on the defensive from first to last—who are still struggling, at the expence of their ease, health, peace, wealth and preferment, against the encroachments of the Tories on their country—and who are determined to continue struggling, at much greater hazards still, and like the Prince of Orange resolve never to see its entire subjection to arbitrary power, but rather to die fighting against it, in the last ditch.

It is true as this writer observes, "that the bulk of the people are generally but little versed in matters of state, that they rest the affairs of government where accident has placed them." If this had not been true, the designs of the tories had been many years ago, entirely defeated. It was clearly seen, by a few, more than ten years since, that they were planning and pursuing the very measures, we now see executing. The people were informed of it, and warned of their danger: But they had been accustomed to confide in certain persons, and could never be persuaded to believe, until prophecy, became history. Now they see and feel, that the horrible calamities are come upon them, which were foretold so many years ago, and they now sufficiently execrate the men who have brought these things upon them. Now alas! when perhaps it is too late. If they had withdrawn their confidence from them in season, they would have wholly disarmed them.

The same game, with the same success, has been played in all ages and countries, as Massachusettensis observes. When a favourable conjuncture has presented, some of the most intrigueing and powerful citizens have conceived the design of enslaving their country, and building their own greatness on its ruins. Philip and Alexander, are examples of this in Greece —Caesar in Rome—Charles the fifth in Spain—Lewis the eleventh in France—and ten thousand others.

"There is a latent spark in the breasts of the people capable of being kindled into a flame, and to do this has always been the employment of the disaffected." What is this "latent spark"? The love of Liberty? *a Deo, hominis est indita naturæ.* Human nature itself is evermore an advocate for liberty. There is also in human nature, a resentment of injury, and indignation against wrong. A love of truth and a veneration for virtue.

These amiable passions, are the "latent spark" to which those whom this writer calls the "disaffected" apply. If the people are capable of understanding, seeing and feeling the difference between true and false, right and wrong, virtue and vice, to what better principle can the friends of mankind apply, than to the sense of this difference.

Is it better to apply as, this writer and his friends do, to the basest passions in the human breast, to their fear, their vanity, their avarice, ambition, and every kind of corruption? I appeal to all experience, and to universal history, if it has ever been in the power of popular leaders, uninvested with other authority than what is conferred by the popular suffrage, to persuade a large people, for any length of time together, to think themselves wronged, injured, and oppressed, unless they really were, and saw and felt it to be so.

"They," the popular leaders, "begin by reminding the people of the elevated rank they hold in the universe as men; that all men by nature are equal; that kings are but the ministers of the people; that their authority is delegated to them by the people for their good, and they have a right to resume it, and place it in other hands, or keep it themselves, whenever it is made use of to oppress them. Doubtless there have been instances, when these principles have been inculcated to obtain a redress of real grievances, but they have been much oftener perverted to the worst of purposes."

These are what are called revolution-principles. They are the principles of Aristotle and Plato, of Livy and Cicero, of Sydney, Harrington and Lock.—The principles of nature and eternal reason.—The principles on which the whole government over us, now stands. It is therefore astonishing, if any thing can be so, that writers, who call themselves friends of government, should in this age and country, be so inconsistent with themselves, so indiscreet, so immodest, as to insinuate a doubt concerning them.

Yet we find that these principles stand in the way of Massachusettensis, and all the writers of his class. The Veteran, in his letter to the officers of the army, allows them to be noble, and true, but says the application of them to particular cases is wild and utopian. How they can be in general true, and not applicable to particular cases, I cannot comprehend. I thought their being true in general was because, they were applicable to most particular cases.

Gravity is a principle in nature. Why? because all particular bodies are found to gravitate. How would it sound to say, that bodies in general are heavy; yet to apply this to particular bodies and say, that a guinea, or a ball is heavy, is wild, &c? "Adopted in private life," says the honest amiable Veteran, "they would introduce perpetual discord." This I deny, and I think it plain, that there never was an happy private family where they were not adopted. "In the State perpetual discord." This I deny, and affirm that order, concord and stability in the state, never was or can be preserved without them. "The least failure in the reciprocal duties of worship and obedience in the matrimonial contract would justify a divorce." This is no consequence from those principles. A total departure from the ends and designs of the contract, it is true, as elopement and adultery, would by these principles justify a divorce, but not the least failure, or many smaller failures in the reciprocal duties, &c. "In the political compact, the smallest defect in the prince a revolution." By no means. But a manifest design in the Prince, to annul the contract on his part, will annul it on the part of the people. A settled plan to deprive the people of all the benefits, blessings and ends of the contract, to subvert the fundamentals of the constitution—to deprive them of all share in making and executing laws, will justify a revolution.

The author of a "Friendly Address to all reasonable Americans", discovers his rancour against these principles, in a more explicit manner, and makes no scruples to advance the principles of Hobbs and Filmer, boldly, and to pronounce damnation, *ore rotundo*, on all who do not practice implicit passive obedience, to all established government, of whatever character it may be.

It is not reviling, it is not bad language, it is strictly decent to say, that this angry bigot, this ignorant dogmatist, this foul mouthed scold, deserves no other answer than silent contempt. Massachusettensis and the Veteran, I admire, the first for his art, the last for his honesty.

Massachusettensis, is more discreet than either of the others. Sensible that these principles would be very troublesome to him, yet conscious of their truth, he has neither admitted nor denied them. But we have a right to his opinion of them, before we dispute with him. He finds fault with the application of them. They have been invariably applied in support of the revolution and the present establishment—against the Stuarts, the Charles's and James's,—in support of the reformation and the protestant religion, against the worst tyranny, that the genius of toryism, has ever yet invented, I mean the Romish superstition. Does this writer rank the revolution and present establishment, the reformation and protestant religion among his worst of purposes? What "worse purpose" is there than established tyranny? Were these principles ever inculcated in favour of such tyranny? Have they not always been used against such tyrannies, when the people have had knowledge enough to be apprized of them, and courage to assert them? Do not those who aim at depriving the people of their liberties, always inculcate opposite principles, or discredit these?

"A small mistake in point of policy" says he, "often furnishes a pretence to libel government and perswade the people that their rulers are tyrants, and the whole government, a system of oppression." This is not only untrue, but inconsistent with what he said before. The people are in their nature so gentle, that there never was a government yet, in which thousands of mistakes were not overlooked. The most sensible and jealous people are so little attentive to government, that there are no instances of resistance, until repeated, multiplied oppressions have placed it beyond a doubt, that their rulers had formed settled plans to deprive them of their liberties; not to oppress an individual or a few, but to break down the fences of a free constitution, and deprive the people at large of all share in the government and all the checks by which it is limitted. Even Machiavel himself allows, that not ingratitude to their rulers, but much love is the constant fault of the people.

This writer is equally mistaken, when he says, the people are sure to be loosers in the end. They can hardly be loosers, if unsuccessful: because if they live, they can but be slaves, after an unfortunate effort, and slaves they would have been, if they had not resisted. So that nothing is lost. If they die, they cannot be said to lose, for death is better than slavery. If they succeed, their gains are immense. They preserve their liberties. The instances in antiquity, which this writer alludes to, are not mentioned and therefore cannot be answered, but that in the country from whence we are derived, is the most unfortunate for his purpose, that could have been chosen. The resistance to Charles the first and the case of Cromwell, no doubt he means. But the people of England, and the cause of liberty, truth, virtue and humanity, gained infinite advantages by that resistance. In all human probability, liberty civil and religious, not only in England but in all Europe, would have been lost. Charles would undoubtedly have established the Romish religion and a despotism as wild as any in the world. And as England has been a principal bulwark from that period to this, of civil liberty and the protestant religion in all Europe, if Charles's schemes had succeeded, there is great reason to apprehend that the light of science would have been extinguished, and mankind, drawn back to a state of darkness and misery, like that which prevailed from the fourth to the fourteenth century. It is true and to be lamented that Cromwell did not establish a government as free, as he might and ought; but his government was infinitely more glorious and happy to the people than Charles's. Did not the people gain by the resistance to James the second? Did not the Romans gain by resistance to Tarquin? Without that resistance and the liberty that was restored by it would the great Roman orators, poets and historians, the great teachers of humanity and politeness, the pride of human nature, and the delight and glory of mankind, for seventeen hundred years, ever have existed? Did not the Romans gain by resistance to the Decimvirs? Did not the English gain by resistance to John, when Magna Charta

was obtained? Did not the seven united provinces gain by resistance to Phillip, Alva and Granvell? Did not the Swiss Can-
tens, the Genevans and Grissons, gain by resistance to Albert
and Grisler?

NOVANGLUS

Boston Gazette, January 23, 1775

Massachusettensis [Daniel Leonard] No. VIII

To the Inhabitants of the Province of Massachusetts Bay,

MY DEAR COUNTRYMEN,

As the oppugnation to the king in parliament tends manifestly to independence, and the colonies the would soon arrive at that point, did not Great Britain check them in their career; let us indulge the idea, however extravagant and romantic, and suppose ourselves for ever separated from the parent state. Let us suppose Great Britain sinking under the violence of the shock, and overwhelmed by her ancient hereditary enemies; or what is more probable, opening new sources of national wealth, to supply the deficiency of that which used to flow to her through American channels, and perhaps planting more loyal colonies in the new discovered regions of the south, still retaining her pre-eminence among the nation though regardless of America.

Let us now advert to our own situation. Destitute of British protection, that impervious barrier, behind which, in perfect security, we have increased to a degree almost exceeding the bounds of probability, what other Britain could we look to when in distress? What succedaneum does the world afford to make good the loss? Would not our trade, navigaton, and fishery, which no nation dares violate or invade, when distinguished by British colours, become the sport and prey of the maritime powers of Europe? Would not our maritime towns be exposed to the pillaging of every piratical enterprise? Are the colonies able to maintain a fleet, sufficient to afford one idea of security to such an extensive sea-coast? Before they can defend themselves against foreign invasions, they must unite into one empire; otherwise the jarring interests, and opposite propensities, would render the many headed monster in politics, unwieldly and inactive. Neither the form or seat of government would be readily agreed upon; more difficult still would be to fix upon the person or persons, to be invested with the imperial authority. There is perhaps as great a diversity between the tempers and habits of the inhabitants of this province and the temper and habits of the Carolinians, as there subsists between some different nations; nor need we travel so far; the Rhode-Islanders are as diverse from the people of Connecticut, as these mentioned before. Most of the colonies are rivals to each other in trade. Between others there subsist deep animosities, respecting their boundaries, which have heretofore produced violent altercations, and the sword of civil war has been more than once unsheathed, without bringing these disputes to a decision. It is apparent that so many discordant, heterogeneous particles could not suddenly unite and consolidate into one body. It is most probable, that if they were ever united the union would be effected by some aspiring genius, putting himself at the head of the colonists' army (for we must suppose a very respectable one indeed, before we are severed from Britian) and taking advantage of the enfeebled, bleeding, and distracted state of the colonies, subjugate the whole to the yoke of despotism. Human nature is every where the same; and this has often been the issue of those rebellions, that the rightful prince was unable to subdue. We need not travel through the states of ancient Greece and Rome, or the more modern ones in Europe, to pick up the instances, with which the way is strewed; we have a notable one in our own. So odious and arbitrary was the protectorate of Cromwell, that when death had delivered them from the dread of the tyrant, all parties conspired to restore monarchy; and each one strove to be the foremost in inviting home, and placing upon the imperial throne, their exiled prince, the son of the same Charles, who, not many years before, had been murdered on a scaffold. The republicans themselves now rushed to the opposite extreme, and had Charles 2d. been as ambitious, as some of his predecessors were, he might have established in England a power more arbitrary, than the first Charles ever had in contemplation.

Let us now suppose the colonies united, and moulded into some form of government. Think one moment of the revenue necessary to support this government, and to provide for even the appearance of defence. Conceive yourselves in a manner exhausted by the conflict with Great Britain, now staggering and sinking under the load of your own taxes, and the weight of your own government. Consider further, that to render government operative and salutary, subordination is necessary. This our patriots need not be told of; and when once they had mounted the steed, and found themselves so well seated as to run no risk of being thrown from the saddle, the severity of their discipline to restore subordination, would be in proportion to their former treachery in destroying it. We have already seen specimens of their tyranny, in their inhuman treatment of persons guilty of no crime, except that of differing in sentiment from the whigs. What then must we expect from such scourges of mankind, when supported by imperial power?

To elude the difficulty resulting from our defenceless situation, we are told that the colonies would open a free trade with all the world, and all nations would join in protecting their common mart. A very little reflection will convince us that this is chimerical. American trade, however beneficial to Great Britain, while she can command it, would be but as a drop of the bucket, or the light dust of the balance, to all the commercial states of Europe. Besides, were British fleets and armies no longer destined to our protection, in very short time, France and Spain would recover possession of those territories, that were torn, reluctant and bleeding from them, in the last war, by the superior strength of Britain. Our enemies would again extend their line of fortification, from the northern to the southern shore; and by means of our late settlements stretching themselves to the confines of Canada, and the communications opened from one country to the other, we should be exposed to perpetual incursions from Canadians and savages. But our distress would not end here; for when once these incursions should be supported by the formidable armaments of France and Spain, the whole continent would become their easy prey, and would be parcelled out, Poland like. Recollect the consternation we were thrown into last war, when Fort William Henry was taken by the French. It was apprehended that all New England would be overrun by their conquering arms. It was even proposed, for our own people to burn and lay waste all the country west of Connecticut river, to impede the enemies march, and prevent their ravaging the country east of it. This proposal come from no inconsiderable man. Consider what must *really* have been our fate, unaided by Britain last war.

Great Britain aside, what earthly power could stretch out the compassionate arm to shield us from those powers, that have long beheld us with the sharp, piercing eyes of avidity, and have heretofore bled freely, and expended their millions to obtain us? Do you suppose their lust of empire is satiated? Or do you suppose they would scorn to obtain so glorious a prize by an easy conquest? Or can any be so visionary or impious, as to believe that the Father of the Universe will work miracles in favour of rebellion? And after having, by some unseen arm, and mighty power, destroyed Great Britain for us, will in the same mysterious way defend us against other European powers? Sometimes we are told, that the colonies may put themselves under the protection of some one foreign state; but it ought to be considered, that to do that, we must throw ourselves into their power. We can make them no return for protection, but by trade; and of that they can have no assurance, unless we become subject to their laws. This is evident by our contention with Britain.

Which state would you prefer being annexed to; France, Spain, or Holland? I suppose the latter, as it is a republic. But are you sure, that the other powers of Europe would be idle spectators; content to suffer the Dutch to engross the American colonies, or their trade? And what figure would the Dutch probably make in the unequal contest? Their sword has been long since sheathed in commerce. Those of you that have visited Surinam, and seen a Dutch governor dispensing at discretion his own opinions for law, would not suddenly exchange the English for Dutch government.

I will subjoin some observations from the Farmer's letters. "When the appeal is made to the sword, highly probable it is, that the punishment will exceed the offence, and the calamities attending on war outweigh those preceding it. These considerations of justice and prudence, will always have great influence with good and wise men. To these reflections it remains to be added, and ought forever to be remembered, that resistance in the case of the colonies against their mother country, is extremely different from the resistance of a people against their prince. A nation may change their king, or race of kings, and retaining their ancient form of government, be gainers by changing. Thus Great Britain, under the illustrious house of Brunswick, a house that seems to flourish for the happiness of mankind, has found a felicity unknown in the reigns of the

Stewarts. But if once we are separated from our mother country, what new form of government shall we adopt, or where shall we find another Britain to supply our loss? Torn from the body, to which we are united by religion, laws, affection, relation, language and commerce, we must bleed at every vein. In truth, the prosperity of these provinces is founded in their dependance on Great Britain."

MASSACHUSETTENSIS.

Massachusetts Gazette; and the Boston Post-Boy and Advertiser, January 30, 1775

Novanglus No. II

My Friends,

I have heretofore intimated my intention, of pursuing the Tories, through all their dark intrigues, and wicked machinations; and to shew the rise, and progress of their schemes for enslaving this country. The honour of inventing and contriving these measures, is not their due. They have been but servile copiers of the designs of Andross, Randolph, Dudley, and other champions of their cause towards the close of the last century. These latter worthies accomplished but little: and their plans had been buried with them, for a long course of years, untill in the administration of the late Governor Shirley they were revived, by the persons who are now principally concern'd in carrying them into execution. Shirley, was a crafty, busy, ambitious, intrigueing, enterprizing man; and having mounted, no matter by what means, to the chair of this province, he saw, in a young growing country, vast prospects of ambition opening before his eyes, and he conceived great designs of aggrandizing himself, his family and his friends. Mr. Hutchinson and Mr. Oliver, the two famous Letter writers, were his principal ministers of state—Russell, Paxton, Ruggles, and a few others, were *subordinate* instruments. Among other schemes of this junto, one was to raise a Revenue in America by authority of parliament.

In order to effect their purpose it was necessary to concert measures with the other colonies. Dr. Franklin, who was known to be an active, and very able man, and to have great influence, in the province of Pennsylvania, was in Boston in the year 1754, and Mr. Shirley communicated to him the profound secret, the great design of taxing the colonies by act of parliament. This sagacious gentleman, this eminent philosopher, and distinguished patriot, to his lasting honour, sent the governor an answer in writing with the following remarks upon his scheme. Remarks which would have discouraged any honest man from the pursuit. The remarks are these.

"That the people always bear the burden best, when they have, or think they have, some *share* in the direction.

"That when public measures are generally distasteful to the people, the wheels of government must move more heavily.

"That excluding the people of America from all share in the choice of a grand council for their own defence, and taxing them in parliament, where they have no representative, would probably give extreme dissatisfaction.

"That there was no reason to doubt the willingness of the colonists to contribute for their own defence.

"That the people themselves, whose all was at stake, could better judge of the force necessary for their defence, and of the means for raising money for the purpose, than a British parliament at so great distance.

"That natives of America, would be as likely to consult wisely and faithfully for the safety of their native country, as the Governors sent from Britain, whose object is generally to make fortunes, and then return home, and who might therefore be expected to carry on the war against France, rather in a way, by which themselves were likely to be gainers, than for the greatest advantage of the cause.

"That compelling the colonies to pay money for their own defence, without their consent, would shew a suspicion of their loyalty, or of their regard for their country, or of their common sense, and would be treating them as conquered enemies, and not as free Britons, who hold it for their undoubted right not to be taxed but by their own consent, given through their representatives.

"That parliamentary taxes, once laid on, are often continued, after the necessity for laying them on, ceases; but that if the colonists were trusted to tax themselves, they would remove the burden from the people, as soon as it should become unnecessary for them to bear it any longer.

"That if parliament is to tax the colonies, their assemblies of representatives may be dismissed as useless.

"That taxing the colonies in parliament for their own defence against the French, is not more just, than it would be, to oblige the cinque ports, and other coasts of Britain, to maintain a force against France, and to tax them for this purpose, without allowing them representatives in parliament.

"That the colonists have always been indirectly taxed by the mother country (besides paying the taxes necessarily laid on by their own assemblies) inasmuch as they are obliged to purchase the manufactures of Britain, charged with innumerable heavy taxes; some of which manufactures they could make, and others could purchase cheaper at other markets.

"That the colonists are besides taxed by the mother country, by being obliged to carry great part of their produce to Britain, and accept a lower price, than they might have at other markets. The difference is a tax paid to Britain.

"That the whole wealth of the colonists centers at last in the mother country, which enables her to pay her taxes.

"That the colonies have, at the hazard of their lives and fortunes, extended the dominions, and increased the commerce and riches of the mother country, that therefore the colonists do not deserve to be deprived of the native right of Britons, the right of being taxed only by representatives chosen by themselves.

"That an adequate representation in parliament would probably be acceptable to the colonists and would best unite the views and interests of the whole empire."

The last of these propositions seems not to have been well considered, because an adequate representation in parliament, is totally impracticable: but the others have exhausted the subject. If any one should ask what authority or evidence I have of this anecdote, I refer him to the second volume of political disquisitions, page 276, 7, 8, 9. A book which ought to be in the hands of every American who has learned to read.

Whether the ministry at home or the junto here, were discouraged by these masterly remarks, or by any other cause, the project of taxing the colonies was laid aside, Mr. Shirley was removed from this government, and Mr. Pownal was placed in his stead.

Mr. Pownal seems to have been a friend to liberty and to our constitution, and to have had an aversion to all plots against either, and consequently to have given his confidence to other persons than Hutchinson and Oliver, who, stung with envy, against Mr. Pratt and others, who had the lead in affairs, set themselves, by propagating slanders against the governor, among the people, and especially among the clergy, to raise discontents, and make him uneasy in his seat. Pownal averse to wrangling, and fond of the delights of England, solicited to be recalled, and after some time Mr. Bernard was removed from New Jersey to the chair of this province.

Bernard was the man for the purpose of the junto—educated in the highest principles of monarchy, naturally daring and courageous, skilled enough in law and policy to do mischief, and avaricious to a most infamous degree: needy at the same time, and having a numerous family to provide for—he was an instrument, suitable in every respect, excepting one, for this junto to employ. The exception I mean, was blunt Frankness, very opposite to that cautious cunning, that deep dissimulation, to which they had by long practice disciplined themselves. However, they did not dispair of teaching him this necessary artful quality by degrees, and the event shew'd they were not wholly unsuccessful, in their endeavours to do it.

While the war lasted, these simple provinces were of too much importance in the conduct of it, to be disgusted, by any open attempt against their liberties. The junto therefore, contented themselves with preparing their ground by extending their connections and correspondencies in England, and by conciliating the friendship of the crown officers occasionally here, and insinuating their designs as necessary to be undertaken in some future favourable opportunity, for the good of the empire, as well as of the colonies.

The designs of providence are inscrutable. It affords to bad men, conjunctures favourable for their designs, as well as to good. The conclusion of the peace, was the most critical opportunity, for our junto, that could have presented. A peace founded on the destruction of that system of policy, the most glorious for the nation, that ever was formed, and which was never equalled in the conduct of the English government, except in the interregnum, and perhaps in the reign of Elizabeth; which system however, by its being abruptly broken off, and its chief conductor discarded before it was compleated, proved unfortunate to the nation by leaving it sinking in a bottomless gulph of debt, oppressed and borne down with taxes.

At this lucky time, when the British financier, was driven out of his wits for ways and means, to supply the demands upon

him, Bernard is employed by the junto, to suggest to him the
project of taxing the Colonies by act of parliament.

I don't advance this without evidence. I appeal to a publication made by Sir Francis Bernard himself, the last year, of his
own select letters on the trade and government of America,
and the principles of law and polity applied to the American
colonies. I shall make much use of this pamphlet before I have
done.

In the year 1764, Mr. Bernard transmitted home to different
noblemen and gentlemen four copies of his principles of law
and polity, with a preface, which proves incontestibly, that the
project of new regulating the American colonies were not first
suggested to him by the ministry, but by him to them. The
words of this preface are these. "The present expectation, that
a new regulation of the American governments will soon take
place, probably arises more from the opinion the public has of
the abilities of the present ministry, than from any thing that
has transpired from the cabinet: It cannot be supposed that
their penetration can overlook the necessity of such a regulation, nor their public spirit fail to carry it into execution. But it
may be a question, whether the present is a proper time for
this work; more urgent business may stand before it; some
preparatory steps may be required to precede it; but these will
only serve to postpone. As we may expect that this reformation, like all others, will be opposed by powerful prejudices, it
may not be amiss to reason with them at leisure, and endeavour to take off their force before they become opposed to
government."

These are the words of that arch enemy of North-America,
written in 1764, and then transmitted to four persons, with a
desire that they might be communicated to others.

Upon these words, it is impossible not to observe. First,
That the ministry had never signified to him, any intention of
new regulating the colonies; and therefore, that it was he who
most officiously and impertinently put them upon the pursuit
of this *will with a whisp*, which has led him and them into so
much mire. 2. The artful flattery with which he insinuates
these projects into the minds of the ministry, as matters of absolute necessity, which their great penetration could not fail to

discover, nor their great regard to the public, omit. 3. The importunity with which he urges a speedy accomplishment of his pretended reformation of the governments, and 4. His consciousness that these schemes would be opposed, altho' he affects to expect from powerful prejudices only, that opposition, which all Americans say, has been dictated by sound reason, true policy, and eternal justice. The last thing I shall take notice of is, the artful, yet most false and wicked insinuation, that such new regulations were then generally expected. This is so absolutely false, that excepting Bernard himself, and his junto, scarcely any body on this side the water had any suspicion of it—insomuch that if Bernard had made public, at that time, his preface and principles, as he sent them to the ministry, it is much to be doubted whether he could have lived in this country—certain it is, he would have had no friends in this province out of the junto.

The intention of the junto, was, to procure a revenue to be raised in America by act of parliament. Nothing was further from their designs and wishes, than the drawing or sending this revenue into the exchequer in England to be spent there in discharging the national debt, and lessening the burdens of the poor people there. They were more selfish. They chose to have the fingering of the money themselves. Their design was, that the money should be applied, first in a large salary to the governor. This would gratify Bernard's avarice, and then it would render him and all other governors, not only independent of the people, but still more absolutely a slave to the will of the minister. They intended likewise a salary for the lieutenant governor. This would appease in some degree the knawings of Hutchinson's avidity, in which he was not a whit behind Bernard himself. In the next place, they intended a salary to the judges of common law, as well as admiralty. And thus the whole government, executive and judicial, was to be rendered wholly independent of the people, (and their representatives rendered useless, insignificant and even burthensome) and absolutely dependent upon, and under the direction of the will of the minister of state. They intended further to new model the whole continent of North America, make an entire new division of it, into distinct, though more extensive and less numerous colonies, to sweep away all the charters upon the continent, with the destroying besom of an act of parliament, and reduce all the governments to the plan of the royal governments, with a nobility in each colony, not hereditary indeed, at first, but for life. They did indeed flatter the ministry and people in England, with distant hopes of a revenue from America, at some future period, to be appropriated to national uses there. But this was not to happen in their minds for some time. The governments must be new-moddelled, new regulated, reformed first, and then the governments here would be able and willing to carry into execution any acts of parliament or measures of the ministry, for fleecing the people here, to pay debts, or support pensioners, on the American establishment, or bribe electors, or members of parliament, or any other purpose that a virtuous ministry could desire.

But as ill-luck would have it, the British financier, was as selfish as themselves, and instead of raising money for them, chose to raise it for himself. He put the cart before the horse. He chose to get the revenue into the exchequer, because he had hungry cormorants enough about him in England whose cooings were more troublesome to his ears, than the croaking of the ravens in America. And he thought if America could afford any revenue at all, and he could get it by authority of parliament, he might have it himself, to give to his friends, as well as raise it for the junto here, to spend themselves, or give to theirs. This unfortunate preposterous improvement of Mr. Grenville, upon the plan of the junto, had well nigh ruined the whole.

I will proceed no further without producing my evidence. Indeed to a man who was acquainted with this junto, and had any opportunity to watch their motions, observe their language, and remark their countenances, for these last twelve years, no other evidence is necessary; it was plain to such persons, what this junto was about. But we have evidence enough now under their own hands of the whole of what was said of them by their opposers, through this whole period.

Governor Bernard, in his letter July 11, 1764, says, "that a general reformation of the American governments would become not only a desirable but a necessary measure." What his idea was, of a general reformation of the American governments, is to be learnt from his principles of law and polity,

404 THE CONTINENTAL CONGRESS 1775

which he sent to the ministry in 1764. I shall select a few of
them in his own words; but I wish the whole of them could be
printed in the news-papers, that America might know more
generally the principles and designs and exertions of our junto.

His 29th proposition is, "The rule that a British subject shall
not be bound by laws, or liable to taxes, but what he has consented to, by his representatives, must be confined to the Inhabitants of Great-Britain only; and is not strictly true even
there. 30. The parliament of Great-Britain, as well from its
rights of sovereignty, as from occasional exigences, has a right
to make laws for, and impose taxes upon its subjects in its external dominions, although they are not represented in such
parliament. But 31. Taxes imposed upon the external dominions, ought to be applied to the use of the people, from whom
they are raised. 32. The parliament of Great-Britain has a right
and duty to take care to provide for the defence of the American colonies; especially as such colonies are unable to defend
themselves. 33. The parliament of Great-Britain has a right and
a duty to take care that provision be made for a sufficient support of the American governments. Because 34. The support
of the government is one of the principal conditions upon
which a colony is allowed the power of legislation. Also
because 35. Some of the American colonies have shewn themselves deficient in the support of their several governments,
both as to sufficiency and independency."

His 75th proposition is, "Every American government is capable of having its constitution altered for the better. 76. The
grants of the powers of governments to American colonies by
charters, cannot be understood to be intended for other than
their infant or growing states. 77. They cannot be intended for
their mature state, that is, for perpetuity; because they are in
many things unconstitutional and contrary to the very nature
of a British government. Therefore 78. They must be considered as designed only as temporary means, for settling and
bringing forward the peopling the colonies: which being
effected, the cause of the peculiarity of their constitution
ceases. 79. If the charters can be pleaded against the authority
of parliament, they amount to an alienation of the dominions
of Great Britain, and are, in effect acts of dismembering the
British empire, and will operate as such, if care is not taken to

prevent it. 83. The notion which has heretofore prevailed, that the dividing America into many governments and different modes of government, will be the means to prevent their uniting to revolt, is ill founded; since, if the governments were ever so much consolidated, it will be necessary to have so many distinct states, as to make a union to revolt, impracticable. Whereas 84. The splitting America into many small governments, weakens the governing power, and strengthens that of the people; and thereby makes revolting more probable and more practicable. 85. To prevent revolts in future times (for there is no room to fear them in the present) the most effectual means would be, to make the governments large and respectable, and ballance the powers of them. 86. There is no government in America at present, whose powers are properly ballanced; there not being in any of them, a real and distinct third legislative power mediating between the king and the people, which is the peculiar excellence of the British constitution. 87. The want of such a third legislative power, adds weight to the popular, and lightens the royal scale; so as to destroy the balance between the royal and popular powers. 88. Altho' America is not now (and probably will not be for many years to come) ripe enough for an hereditary nobility; yet it is now capable of a nobility for life. 89. A nobility appointed by the king for life, and made independent, would probably give strength and stability to the American governments, as effectually as an hereditary nobility does to that of Great-Britain. 90. The reformation of the American governments should not be controuled by the present boundaries of the colonies; as they were mostly settled upon partial, occasional, and accidental considerations, without any regard to a whole. 91. To settle the American governments to the greatest possible advantage, it will be necessary to reduce the number of them; in some places to unite and consolidate; in others to seperate and transfer; and in general to divide by natural boundaries, instead of imaginary lines. 92. If there should be but one form of government established for all the North-American provinces, it would greatly facilitate the reformation of them; since, if the mode of government was every where the same, people would be more indifferent under what division they were ranged. 93. No objections ought to arise to the alteration of the boundaries of provinces from proprietors, on account of their property only; since there is no occasion that it should in the least affect the boundaries of properties. 94. The present distinction of one government being more free or more popular than another, tend to embarass and to weaken the whole; and should not be allowed to subsist among people, subject to one king and one law, and all equally fit for one form of government. 95. The American colonies, in general, are, at this time, arrived at that state, which qualifies them to receive the most perfect form of government, which their situation and relation to Great-Britain, make them capable of. 96. The people of North-America, at this time, expect a revisal and reformation of the American governments, and are better disposed to submit to it, than ever they were, or perhaps ever will be again. 97. This is therefore the proper, and critical time to reform the American governments upon a general, constitutional, firm, and durable plan; and if it is not done now, it will probably every day grow more difficult, till at last it becomes impracticable."

My friends, these are the words, the plans, principles, and endeavours of Governor Bernard in the year 1764. That Hutchinson and Oliver, notwithstanding all their disguises which you well remember, were in unison with him in the whole of his measures, can be doubted by no man. It appeared sufficiently in the part they all along acted, notwithstanding their professions. And it appears incontestibly from their detected letters, of which more hereafter.

Now let me ask you—if the parliament of Great-Britain, had all the natural foundations of authority, wisdom, goodness, justice, power, in as great perfection as they ever existed in any body of men since Adam's fall: and if the English nation was the most virtuous, pure and free, that ever was; would not such an unlimited subjection of three millions of people to that parliament, at three thousand miles distance be real slavery? There are but two sorts of men in the world, freemen and slaves. The very definition of a freeman, is one who is bound by no law to which he has not consented. Americans would have no way of giving or withholding their consent to the acts of this parliament, therefore they would not be freemen. But, when luxury, effeminacy and venality are arrived at such a shocking pitch in England, when both electors and elected, are become one mass of corruption, when the nation is oppressed to death with debts and taxes, owing to their own extravagance, and want of wisdom, what would be your condition under such an absolute subjection to parliament? You would not only be slaves—But the most abject sort of slaves to the worst sort of masters! at least this is my opinion. Judge you for yourselves between Massachusettensis and

NOVANGLUS

Boston Gazette, January 30, 1775

Massachusettensis [Daniel Leonard] No. IX

To the Inhabitants of the Province of Massachusetts Bay,

MY DEAR COUNTRYMEN,

When we reflect upon the constitutional connection between Great Britain and the colonies, view the reciprocation of interest, consider that the welfare of Britain, in some measure, and the prosperity of America wholly depends upon that connection; it is astonishing, indeed, almost incredible, that one person should be found on either side of the Atlantic, so base, and destitute of every sentiment of justice, as to attempt to destroy or weaken it. If there are none such, in the name of Almighty God, let me ask, wherefore is rebellion, that implacable fiend to society, suffered to rear its ghastly front among us, blasting, with haggard look, each social joy, and embittering every hour?

Rebellion is the most atrocious offence, that can be perpetrated by man, save those which are committed more immediately against the supreme Governor of the Universe, who is the avenger of his own cause. It dissolves the social band, annihilates the security resulting from law and government; introduces fraud, violence, rapine, murder, sacrilege, and the long train of evils, that riot, uncontrouled, in a state of nature. Allegiance and protection are reciprocal. The subject is bound by the compact to yield obedience to government, and in return, is entitled to protection from it; thus the poor are protected against the rich; the weak against the strong; the individual against the many; and this protection is guaranteed to each member, by the whole community. But when government is laid prostrate, a state of war, of all against all commences; might overcomes right; innocence itself has no security, unless the individual sequesters himself from his fellowmen, inhabits his own cave, and seeks his own prey. This is what is called a state of nature. I once thought it chimerical.

The punishment inflicted upon rebels and traitors, in all states, bears some proportion to the aggravated crime. By our law, the punishment is, "That the offender be drawn to the gallows, and not be carried, or walk; that he be hanged by the neck, and then cut down alive; that his entrails be taken out

and burned while he is yet alive; that his head be cut off; that
his body be divided into four parts; that his head and quarters
be at the king's disposal." The consequences of attainder, are
forfeiture and corruption of blood.

"Forfeiture is two-fold, of real and personal estate; by attainder in high treason a man forfeits to the king all his lands and
tenements of inheritance, whether fee simple, or fee tail; and
all his rights of entry on lands and tenements, which he had at
the time of the offence committed, or at any time afterwards
to be for ever vested in the crown. The forfeiture relates back
to the time of the treason being committed, so as to avoid all
intermediate sales and incumberances; even the dower of the
wife is forfeited. The natural justice of forfeiture, or confiscation of property, for treason, is founded in this consideration,
that he, who has thus violated the fundamental principles
of government, and broken his part of the original contract
between king and people, hath abandoned his connections with
society; hath no longer any right to those advantages, which
before belonged to him purely as a member of the community,
among which social advantages the right of transferring or
transmitting property to others, is one of the chief. Such forfeitures, moreover, whereby his posterity must suffer, as well as
himself, will help to restrain a man, not only by the sense of his
duty and dread of personal punishment, but also by his passions and natural affections; and will influence every dependant and relation he has to keep him from offending." 4 Black.
374. 375.

It is remarkable, however, that this offence, notwithstanding
it is of a crimson color, and the deepest dye, and its just punishment is not confined to the person of the offender, but beggars all his family, is sometimes committed by persons, who are
not conscious of guilt. Sometimes they are ignorant of the law,
and do not foresee the evils they bring upon society; at others,
they are induced to think that their cause is founded in the
eternal principles of justice and truth, that they are only making an appeal to heaven, and may justly expect its decree in
their favour. Doubtless many of the rebels, in the year 1745,
were buoyed up with such sentiments, nevertheless they were
cut down like grass before the scythe of the mower; the gibbet
and scaffold received those that the sword, wearied with

destroying, had spared; and what loyalist shed one pitying tear
over their graves? They were incorrigible rebels, and deserved
their fate. The community is in less danger, when the disaffected attempt to excite a rebellion against the person of the
prince, than when government itself is the object, because in
the former case the questions are few, simple, and their solu-
tions obvious, the fatal consequences more apparent, and the
loyal people more alert to suppress it in embryo; whereas, in
the latter, a hundred rights of the people, inconsistent with
government, and as many grievances, destitute of foundation,
the mere creatures of distempered brains, are pourtrayed in the
liveliest colours, and serve as bugbears to affright from their
duty, or as decoys to allure the ignorant, the credulous and the
unwary, to their destruction. Their suspicions are drowned in
the perpetual roar for liberty and country; and even the professions of allegiance to the person of the king, are improved as
means to subvert his government.

In mentioning high treason in the course of these papers, I
may not always have expressed myself with the precision of a
lawyer; they have a language peculiar to themselves. I have examined their books, and beg leave to lay before you some further extracts, which deserve our attention. "To levy war
against the king, was high treason by the common law, 3 inst. 9.
This is also declared to be high treason by the stat. of 25 Edw.
3. c. 2. and by the law of this province, 8 W. 3 c. 5. Assembling
in warlike array, against a statute, is levying war against the
king, 1 Hale 133. So to destroy any trade generally, 146. Riding
with banners displayed, or forming into companies; or being
furnished with military officers; or armed with military
weapons, as swords, guns, &c. any of these circumstances carries the *speciem belli*, and will support an indictment for high
treason in levying war, 150. An insurrection to raise the price
of servants wages was held to be an overt-act of this species of
treason, because this was done *in defiance of this statute* of
labourers; it was done in defiance of the *king's authority*, 5 Bac.
117 cites 3 inst. 10. Every assembling of a number of men, in a
warlike manner, with a design to redress any *public grievance*,
is likewise an overt-act of this species of treason, because this
being an attempt to do that by *private authority*, which only
ought to be done by the king's authority, is an invasion of the

prerogative, 5 Bac. 117. cites 3 inst. 9. Ha. p. c. 14. Kel. 71. Sid. 358. 1. Hawk. 37. Every assembling of a number of men in a warlike manner, with an intention to reform the government, or the law, is an overt-act of this species of treason, 5 Bac. 117. cites 3 inst. 9. 10. Poph. 122. Kel. 76. 7. 1 Hawk. 37. Levying war may be by taking arms, not only to dethrone the king; but under pretence to reform religion, or the laws, or to remove evil councellors, or other grievances, whether *real* or *pretended*, 4 Black. 81. Foster 211. If any levy war to expulse strangers; to deliver men out of prison; to remove councellors, or against any statute; or any other end, pretending reformation of their own heads, without warrant, this is levying war against the king, because they take upon them royal authority, which is against the king, 3 inst. 9. If three, four, or more, rise to pull down an inclosure, this is a riot; but if they had risen of purpose to alter religion, established within the realm, or laws, or to go from town to town generally, and cast down inclosures, this is a levying of war (though there be no great number of conspirators) within the purview of this statute; because the pretence public and general, and not private in particular, 3 inst. 9. Foster 211. If any, with strength and weapons, invasive and defensive, do hold and defend a castle or fort, against the king and his power, this is levying of war against the king, 3 inst. 10. Foster 219. 1 Hale 149. 296.

It was resolved by all the judges of England in the reign of Henry the 8th, that an insurrection against the statute of labourers, for the enhancing of salaries and wages, was a levying of war against the king, because it was generally against the *king's law*, and the offenders took upon them the reformation thereof, which subject by gathering of power, ought not to do, 3 inst. 10. All risings in order to effect innovations of a *public* and *general* concern, by an armed force, are, in construction of law, high treason within the clause of levying war. For though they are not levelled at the person of the king, they are against his royal majesty. And besides they have a direct tendency to dissolve all the bonds of society, and to destroy all property, and all government too, by numbers and an armed force, Foster 211. In Benstead's case, Cro. car. 593. At a conference of all the justices and barons, it was resolved, that going to Lambeth house, in warlike manner, to surprize the archbishop, who was a privy counsellor (it being with drums and a multitude) to the number of three hundred persons, was treason; upon which Foster, page 212, observes, that if it did appear by the libel, which he says was previously posted up at the exchange, exhorting the apprentices to rise and sack the bishop's house, upon the Monday following, or by the cry of the rabble, at Lambeth house, that the attempt was made on account of measures *the king had taken, or was then taking at the instigation, as they imagined, of the archbishop*, and that the rabble had *deliberately* and upon a *public invitation*, attempted by *numbers* and open force, to take a *severe revenge* upon the *privy counsellor* for the measures the sovereign had taken or was pursuing, the *grounds and reasons* of the resolutions would be sufficiently explained, without taking that *little* circumstance of the *drum* into the case. And he delivers as his opinion, page 208, that no great great stress can be laid on that distinction taken by Ld. C. J. Hale, between an insurrection with, and one without the appearance of an army formed under leaders, and provided with military weapons, and with drums, colours, &c. and says, the *want* of these circumstances weighed nothing with the court in the cases of Damaree and Purchase, but that it was supplied by the *number* of the insurgents. That they were provided with axes, crows, and such like tools, *furor arma ministrat*; and adds, page 208, the true criterion in all these cases, is *quo animo*, did the parties assemble, whether on account of some *private* quarrel, or, page 211 to effect innovations of a *public* and *general* concern, by an armed force. Upon the case of Damaree and Purchase, reported 8 stat. in. 218. to 285. Judge Foster observes, page 215, that "since the meeting houses of protestant dissenters are, by the *toleration act* taken under *protection* of the *law*, the insurrection in the present case, being to pull down all dissenting protestant meetinghouses, was to be considered as a public declaration of the rabble *against that act*, and an attempt to render it *ineffectual* by *numbers* and open force."

If there be a conspiracy to levy war, and afterwards war is levied, the conspiracy is, in every one of the conspirators, an overt act of this species of treason, for there can be no accessary in high treason, 5 Bac. 115. cites 3 inst. 9. 10. 138 Hales P. C. 14. Kel. 19. 1 Hawk. 38. A compassing or conspiracy to levy war is no treason, for there must be a levying of war *in facto*. But if many conspire to levy war, and some of them do levy the same according to the conspiracy, this is high treason in all, for in treason all are principals, and war is levied, 3 inst. 9. Foster 213.

The *painful* task of applying the above rules of law to the several transactions that we have been eye witnesses to, will never be mine. Let me however intreat you, to make the application in your own minds; and those of you that have continued hitherto faithful among the faithless, Abdiel like, to persevere in your integrity; and those of you that have been already ensnared by the accursed wiles of designing men, to cast yourselves immediately upon that mercy, so conspicuous through the British constitution, and which is the brightest jewel in the imperial diadem.

MASSACHUSETTENSIS.

*Massachusetts Gazette; and the
Boston Post-Boy and Advertiser*, February 6, 1775

Novanglus No. III

My Friends,

The history of the Tories, begun in my last, will be inter-rupted for some time: but it shall be reassumed, and minutely related, in some future papers. Massachusettensis, who shall now be pursued, in his own serpentine path, in his first paper, complains, that the press is not free, that a party has gained the ascendency so far as to become the licencers of it; by playing off the resentment of the populace, against printers and au-thors: That the press is become an engine of oppression and licentiousness, much devoted to the partisans of liberty, who have been indulged in publishing what they pleased, *fas vel nefas,* while little has been published on the part of the government.

The art of this writer which appears in all his productions, is very conspicuous in this. It is intended to excite a resentment against the friends of liberty, for tyrannically depriving their antagonists, of so important a branch of freedom, and a com-passion towards the Tories, in the breasts of the people in the other colonies and in Great-Britain, by insinuating that they have not had equal terms. But nothing can be more injurious, nothing farther from the truth. Let us take a retrospective view of the period, since the last peace, and see, whether, they have not uniformly had the press at their service, without the least molestation to authors or printers. Indeed, I believe that the Massachusetts-Spy, if not the Boston Gazette have been open to them as well as to others. The Evening-Post, Massachusetts Gazette and Boston Chronicle, have certainly been always as free for their use as the air. Let us dismiss prejudice and pas-sion, and examine impartially, whether the Tories have not been chargeable with at least as many libels, as much licen-tiousness of the press, as the Whigs? Dr. Mayhew was a Whig of the first magnitude, a clergyman equalled by a very few of any denomination in piety, virtue, genius or learning, whose works will maintain his character, as long as New-England shall be free, integrity esteemed, or wit, spirit, humour, or reason and knowledge admired. How was he treated from the press? Did not the Reverend Tories who were pleased to write against him, the Missionaries of Defamation as well as Bigotry and passive obedience, in their pamphlets, and news papers, bespatter him all over with their filth? With equal falshood and malice charge him with every thing evil? Mr. Otis, was in civil life: and a senator, whose parts, literature, eloquence and integrity, proved him a character in the world, equal to any of the time in which he flourished, of any party in the province. Now be pleased to recollect the Evening-Post. For a long course of years, that gentleman, his friends and connections, of whom the world has and grateful posterity will have a better opinion than Massachusettensis will acknowledge, were pelted with the most infernally malicious, false, and atrocious Libels, that ever issued from any press in Boston. I will mention no other names, lest I give too much offence to the modesty of some, and the envy and rancour of others.

There never was before, in any part of the world, a whole town insulted to their faces, as Boston was, by the Boston Chronicle. Yet the printer was not molested for printing, it was his mad attack upon other printers with his clubs, and upon other gentlemen with his pistols, that was the cause of his flight, or rather the pretence. The truth was, he became too polite to attend his business, his shop was neglected, procurations were coming for more than 2000 sterling, which he had no inclination to pay.

Printers may have been less eager after the productions of the tories than of the whigs, and the reason has been because the latter have been more consonant to the general taste and sense, and consequently more in demand. Notwithstanding this, the former have ever found one press at least devoted to their service, and have used it as licentiously as they could wish. Whether the revenue chest has kept it alive and made it profitable against the general sense, or not, I wot not. Thus much is certain that 200, 3, 4, 5, 600, 800, 1500, sterling a year, has been the constant reward of every scribbler, who has taken up the pen on the side of the ministry, with any reputation, and commissions have been given here for the most wretched productions of dulness itself. Whereas the writers on the side of liberty, have been rewarded only with the consciousness of endeavoring to do good, with the approbation of the virtuous and the malice of men in power.

But this is not the first time, that writers have taken advantage of the times. Massachusettensis knows the critical situation of this province. The danger it is in, without government or law—The army in Boston—The people irritated and exasperated, in such a manner as was never before borne by any people under heaven. Much depends upon their patience at this critical time, and such an example of patience and order, this people have exhibited in a state of nature, under such cruel insults, distresses and provocations, as the history of mankind cannot parallel. In this state of things, protected by an army, the whole junto are now pouring forth the whole torrents of their billingsgate, propagating thousands of the most palpable falshoods, when they knew that the writers on the other side have been restrain'd by their prudence and caution from engaging in a controversy that must excite heats, lest it should have unhappy and tragical consequences.

There is nothing in this world so excellent that it may not be abused. The abuses of the press are notorious. It is much to be desired that writers on all sides would be more careful of truth and decency: but upon the most impartial estimate, the tories will be found to have been the least so, of any party among us.

The honest Veteran, who ought not to be forgotten, in this place, says, "if an inhabitant of Bern or Amsterdam, could read the newspapers, &c. he would be at a loss how to reconcile oppression with such unbounded licence of the press: and would laugh at the charge, as something much more than a paradox, as a palpable contradiction." But with all his taste, and manly spirit, the Veteran is little of a statesman. His ideas of liberty are quite inadequate—his notions of government very superficial. Licence of the press is no proof of liberty. When a people is corrupted, the press may be made an engine to compleat their ruin: and it is now notorious, that the ministry, are daily employing it to encrease and establish corruption, and to pluck up virtue by the roots. Liberty can no more exist without virtue and independence, than the body can live and move without a soul. When these are gone, and the popular branch of the constitution is become dependent on the minister, as it is in England, or cut off, as it is in America, all other forms of the constitution may remain; but if you look for liberty, you will grope in vain, and the freedom of the press, instead of promoting the cause of liberty, will but hasten its destruction, as the best cordials, taken by patients, in some distempers, become the most rancid and corrosive poisons.

This language of the Veteran, however, is like the style of the minister and his scribblers in England, boasting of the unbounded freedom of the press, and assuring the people that all is safe, while that continues: and thus the people are to be cheated with libels in exchange for their liberties.

A stronger proof cannot be wish'd, of the scandalous license of the tory presses, than the swarms of pamphlets and speculations, in New-York and Boston, since last October. "Madness, folly, delusion, delirium, infatuation, frenzy, high treason and rebellion," are charged in every page, upon three millions of as good and loyal, as sensible and virtuous people, as any in the empire: nay upon that congress, which was as full and free a representative, as ever was constituted by any people, chosen universally without solicitation, or the least tincture of corruption: that congress which consisted of governors, counsellors, some of them by mandamus too, judges of supreme courts, speakers of assemblies, planters and merchants of the first fortune and character, and lawyers of the highest class, many of them educated at the temple, call'd to the bar in England, and of abilities and integrity equal to any there.

Massachusettensis, conscious that the people of this continent have the utmost abhorrence of treason and rebellion, labours to avail himself of the magic in these words. But his artifice is vain. The people are not to be intimidated by hard words, from a necessary defence of their liberties. Their attachment to their constitution so dearly purchased by their own and their ancestors blood and treasure, their aversion to the late innovations, their horror of arbitrary power and the Romish religion, are much deeper rooted than their dread of rude sounds and unmannerly language. They dont want the advice of an honest lawyer, if such an one could be found, nor will they be deceived by a dishonest one. They know what offence it is, to assemble, armed and, forceably obstruct the course of justice. They have been many years considering and enquiring, they have been instructed by Massachusettensis and his friends, in the nature of treason, and the consequences of their own principles and actions. They know upon what hinge the whole dispute turns. That the *fundamentals* of the government over them, are disputed, that the minister pretends and had the influence to obtain the voice of the last parliament in his favour, that parliament is the only supream, sovereign, absolute and uncontroulable legislative over all the colonies, that therefore the minister and all his advocates will call resistance, to acts of parliament, by the names of treason and rebellion. But at the same time they know, that in their own opinions, and in the opinions of all the colonies, parliament has no authority over them, excepting to regulate their trade, and this not by any principle of common law, but merely by the consent of the colonies, founded on the obvious necessity of a case, which was never in contemplation of that law, nor provided for by it, that therefore they have as good a right to charge that minister, Massachusettensis and the whole army to which he has fled for protection, with treason and rebellion. For if the parliament has not a legal authority to overturn their constitution, and subject them to such acts as are lately passed, every man, who accepts of any commission and takes any steps to carry those acts into execution, is guilty of overt acts of treason and rebellion against his majesty, his royal crown and dignity, as much as if he should take arms against his troops, or attempt his sacred life. They know that the resistance against the stamp act, which was made through all America, was in the opinion of Massachusettensis, and George Grenville, high treason, and that Brigadier Ruggles, and good Mr. Ogden, pretended at the congress at New-York, to be of the same mind, and have been held in utter contempt and derision by the whole continent, for the same reason, ever since; because in their own opinion, that resistance was a noble stand against tyranny, and the only opposition to it, which could have been effectual. That if the American resistance to the act for destroying your charter, and to the Resolves for arresting persons here and sending them to England for tryal, is treason, the lords and commons, and the whole nation, were traitors at the revolution.

They know that all America is united in sentiment, and in the plan of opposition to the claims of administration and parliament. The junto in Boston, with their little flocks of adherents in the country, are not worth taking into the account; and the army and navy, tho' these are divided among themselves, are no part of America; in order to judge of this union, they begin at the commencement of the dispute, and run thro' the whole course of it. At the time of the Stamp Act, every colony expressed its sentiments by resolves of their assemblies, and every one agreed that parliament had no right to tax the colonies. The house of representatives of the Massachusetts-Bay, then consisted of many persons, who have since figured as friends to government; yet every member of that house concurred most chearfully in the resolves then passed. The congress which met that year at New-York, expressed the same opinion in their resolves. After the paint, paper and tea act was passed, the several assemblies expressed the same sentiments, and when your colony wrote the famous circular letter, notwithstanding all the mandates and threats, and cajolings of the minister and the several governors, and all the crown officers through the continent, the assemblies with one voice ecchoed their entire approbation of that letter, and their applause to your colony for sending it. In the year 1768, when a non importation was suggested and planned by a few gentlemen at a private clubb, in one of our large towns, as soon as it was proposed to the public, did it not spread thro' the whole continent? Was it not regarded, like the laws of the Medes and Persians, in almost all the colonies. When the paint and paper act was repealed, the southern colonies agreed to depart from the association in all things but the dutied articles, but they have kept strictly to their agreement against importing them, so that no tea worth the mentioning, has been imported into any of them from Great-Britain to this day. In the year 1770, when a number of persons were slaughtered in King-Street, such was the brotherly sympathy of all the colonies, such their resentment against an hostile administration; that the innocent blood then spilt, has never been forgotten, nor the murderous minister and governors, who brought the troops here, forgiven, by any part of the continent, and never will be. When a certain masterly statesman, invented a committee of correspondence in Boston, which has provoked so much of the spleen of Massachusettensis, of which much more hereafter;

did not every colony, nay every county, city, hundred and town upon the whole continent, adopt the measure. I had almost said, as if it had been a revelation from above, as the happiest means of cementing the union and acting in concert? What proofs of union have been given since the last March! Look over the resolves of the several colonies, and you will see that one understanding governs, one heart animates the whole body. Assemblies, conventions, congresses, towns, cities, and private clubs and circles, have been actuated by one great, wise, active and noble spirit, one masterly soul, animating one vigorous body.

The congress at Philadelphia, have expressed the same sentiments with the people of New-England, approved of the opposition to the late innovations, unanimously advised us to persevere in it, and assured us that if force is attempted to carry these measures against us, all America ought to support us. Maryland and the Lower Counties on Deleware, have already, to shew to all the world their approbation of the measures of New-England, and their determination to join in them, with a generosity, a wisdom and magnanimity, which ought to make the Tories consider, taken the power of the militia into the hands of the people, without the governor, or minister, and established it, by their own authority, for the defence of the Massachusetts, as well as of themselves. Other colonies are only waiting to see if the necessity of it will become more obvious. Virginia, and the Carolinas, are preparing for military defence, and have been for some time. When we consider the variety of climates, soils, religions, civil governments, commercial interests, &c. which were represented at the congress, and the various occupations, educations, and characters of the gentlemen who composed it, the harmony and unanimity which prevailed in it, can scarcely be parallelled in any assembly that ever met. When we consider, that at the revolution, such mighty questions, as whether the Throne was vacant or not, and whether the Prince of Orange should be king or not, were determined in the Convention Parliament by small majorities of two or three, and four or five only; the great majorities, the almost unanimity with which all great questions have been decided in your house of representatives, and other assemblies, and especially in the Continental Congress, cannot be considered in any other light than as the happiest omens indeed, as providential dispensations in our favour, as well as the clearest demonstrations of the cordial, firm, radical and indissoluble union of the colonies.

The grand aphorism of the policy of the whigs has been to unite the people of America, and divide those of Great-Britain. The reverse of this has been the maxim of the tories, viz. to unite the people of Great-Britain, and divide those of America. All the movements, marches and countermarches of both parties, on both sides of the Atlantic, may be reduced to one or the other of these rules. I have shewn, in opposition to Massachusettensis, that the people of America are united more perfectly than the most sanguine whig could ever have hoped, or than the most timid tory could have fear'd. Let us now examine whether the people of Great-Britain are equally united against us. For if the contending countries were equally united, the prospect of success in the quarrel would depend upon the comparative wisdom, firmness, strength and other advantages of each. And if such a comparison was made, it would not appear to a demonstration that Great Britain could so easily subdue and conquer. It is not so easy a thing for the most powerful state to conquer a country a thousand leagues off. How many year's time, how many millions of money, did it take, with five and thirty-thousand men, to conquer the poor province of Canada? And after all the battles and victories, it never would have submitted without a capitulation, which secured to them their religion and properties.

But we know that the people of Great-Britain are not united against us. We distinguish between the Ministry, the House of Commons, the Officers of the Army, Navy, Excise, Customs, &c. who are dependent on the Ministry, and tempted, if not obliged, to eccho their voices; and the body of the people. We are assured by thousands of letters from persons of good intelligence, by the general strain of publications in public papers, pamphlets, and magazines, and by some larger works written for posterity, that the body of the people are friends to America, and wish us success in our struggles against the claims of parliament and administration. We know that millions in England and Scotland, will think it unrighteous, impolitic and ruinous, to make war upon us, and a minister, tho' he may have a marble heart, will proceed with a diffident, desponding spirit. We know that London and Bristol, the two greatest commercial cities in the empire, have declared themselves in the most decisive manner, in favour of our cause. So explicitly that the former has bound her members under their hands to assist us, and the latter has chosen two known friends of America, one attached to us by principle, birth, and the most ardent affection, the other an able advocate for us on several great occasions. We know that many of the most virtuous and independent of the nobility and gentry are for us, and among them the best Bishop that adorns the bench, as great a Judge as the nation can boast, and the greatest statesman it ever saw. We know that the nation is loaded with debts and taxes by the folly and iniquity of its ministers, and that without the trade of America, it can neither long support its fleet and army, nor pay the interest of its debt.

But we are told that the nation is now united against us, that they hold, they have a right to tax us and legislate for us as firmly as we deny it. That we are a part of the British Empire, that every state must have an uncontroulable power co-extensive with the empire, that there is little probability of serving ourselves by ingenious distinctions between external and internal taxes. If we are not a part of the state, and subject to the supreme authority of parliament, Great-Britain will make us so; that if this opportunity of reclaiming the colonies is lost, they will be dismembered from the empire; and although they may continue their allegiance to the King, they will own none to the imperial crown.

To all this I answer, That the nation is not so united—that they do not so universally hold they have such a right, and my reasons I have given before. That the terms "British Empire" are not the language of the common law, but the language of news papers and political pamphlets. That the dominions of the king of Great-Britain has no uncontroulable power co-extensive with them. I would ask by what law the parliament has authority over America? By the law of GOD in the Old and New Testament, it has none. By the law of nature and nations, it has none. By the common law of England it has none. For the common law, and the authority of parliament founded on it, never extended beyond the four seas. By statute law it has none, for no statute was made before the settlement of the colonies for this purpose; and the declaratory act made in 1766, was made without our consent, by a parliament which had no authority beyond the four seas. What religious, moral or political obligation then are we under, to submit to parliament as a supreme legislative? None at all. When it is said, that if we are not subject to the supreme authority of parliament, Great-Britain will make us so, all other laws and obligations are given up, and recourse is had to the ratio ultima of Lewis the XIVth, and the suprema lex of the king of Sardinia, to the law of brickbats and cannon balls, which can be answer'd only by brickbats and balls.

This language "the imperial crown of Great-Britain", is not the stile of the common law but of court sycophants. It was introduced in allusion to the Roman empire, and intended to insinuate, that the prerogative of the imperial crown of England, was like that of the Roman emperor, after the maxim was established, *quod principi placuit legis habet vigorem*, and so far from including the two houses of parliament in the idea of this imperial crown, it was intended to insinuate that the crown was absolute, and had no need of lords or commons to make or dispense with laws. Yet even these court sycophants when driven to an explanation, never dared to put any other sense upon the words imperial crown, than this, that the crown of England was independent of France, Spain, and all other kings and states in the world.

When he says that the king's dominions must have an uncontroulable power, co-extensive with them, I ask whether they have such a power or not? and utterly deny that they have by any law but that of Lewis the fourteenth, and the king of Sardinia. If they have not, and it is necessary that they should have, it then follows that there is a defect in what he calls the British empire—and how shall this defect be supplied? It cannot be supplied consistently with reason, justice, policy, morality, or humanity, without the consent of the colonies, and some new plan of connection. But if Great-Britain will set all these at defiance, and resort to the ratio ultima, all Europe will pronounce her a tyrant, and America never will submit to her, be the danger of disobedience as great as it will.

But there is no need of any other power than that of

regulating trade, and this the colonies ever have been and will be ready and willing to concede to her. But she will never obtain from America any further concession while she exists.

We are then asked, "for what she protected and defended the colonies against the maritime power of Europe from their first settlement to this day?" I answer for her own interest, because all the profits of our trade centered in her lap. But it ought to be remembered, that her name, not her purse, nor her fleets and armies, ever protected us, untill the last war, and then the minister who conducted that war, informs us, that the annual millions from America enabled her to do it.

We are then asked for what she purchased New-York of the Dutch? I answer she never did. The Dutch never owned it, were never more than trespassers and intruders there, and were finally expelled by conquest. It was ceded it is true by the treaty of Breda, and it is said in some authors, that some other territory in India was ceded to the Dutch in lieu of it. But this was the transaction of the king, not of parliament, and therefore makes nothing to the argument. But admitting for argument sake, (since the cautious Massachusettensis will urge us into the discussion of such questions) what is not a supposeable case, that the nation should be so sunk in sloth, luxury and corruption, as to suffer their minister to persevere in his mad blunders and send fire and sword against us, how shall we defend ourselves? The colonies south of Pennsylvania have no men to spare we are told. But we know better—we know that all those colonies have a back country which is inhabited by an hardy, robust people, many of whom are emigrants from New-England, and habituated like multitudes of New-Englandmen, to carry their fuzees or rifles upon one shoulder to defend themselves against the Indians, while they carry'd their axes, scythes and hoes upon the other to till the ground. Did not those colonies furnish men the last war excepting Maryland. Did not Virginia furnish men, one regiment particularly equal to any regular regiment in the service. Does the soft Massachusettensis imagine that in the unnatural horrid war, he is now supposing their exertions would be less. If he does he is very ill informed of their principles, their present sentiments and temper. But "have you arms and ammunition?" I answer we have; but if we had not, we could make a sufficient quantity of both.

What should hinder? We have many manufacturers of fire-arms
now, whose arms are as good as any in the world. Powder has
been made here, and may be again, and so may salt-petre.
What should hinder? We have all the materials in great abundance, and the process is very simple. But if we neither had
them nor could make them, we could import them. But "the
British navy." Ay there's the rub. But let us consider, since the
prudent Massachusettensis will have these questions debated.
How many ships are taken to blockade Boston harbour? How
many ships can Britain spare to carry on this humane and political war, the object of which is a pepper corn? Let her send
all the ships she has round her island. What if her ill-natur'd
neighbours, France and Spain should strike a blow in their absence? In order to judge what they could all do when they arrived here we should consider what they are all able to do
round the island of Great-Britain. We know that the utmost
vigilance and exertions of them added to all the terrors of san-
guinary laws, are not sufficient to prevent continual smuggling, into their own island. Are there not 50 bays, harbours,
creeks and inlets upon the whole coast of North-America,
where there is one round the island of Great-Britain. Is it to
be supposed then, that the whole British navy could prevent
the importation of arms and ammunition into America, if she
should have occasion for them to defend herself against the
hellish warfare, that is here supposed.

  But what will you do for discipline and subordination? I answer we will have them in as great perfection as the regular
troops. If the provincials were not brought in the last war to a
proper discipline, what was the reason? Because regular generals would not let them fight, which they ardently wished, but
employed them in cutting roads. If they had been allowed to
fight they would have brought the war to a conclusion too
soon. The provincials did submit to martial law, and to the
mutiny and desertion act, the last war, and such an act may be
made here by a legislature which they will obey with much
more alacrity than an act of parliament.

  The new fangled militia, as the specious Massachusettensis
calls it, is such a militia as he never saw. They are commanded
through the province, not by men who procured their commissions from a governor as a reward for making themselves

pimps to his tools, and by discovering a hatred of the people but by gentlemen whose estates, abilities and benevolence have rendered them the delight of the soldiers, and there is an esteem and respect for them visible through the province, which has not been used in the militia. Nor is there that unsteadiness that is charged upon them. In some places, where companies have been split into two or three, it has only served by exciting an emulation between the companies to encrease the martial spirit and skill.

The plausible Massachusettensis may write as he will, but in a land war, this continent might defend itself against all the world. We have men enough, and those men have as good natural understandings and as much natural courage as any other men. If they were wholly ignorant now, they might learn the art of war. But at sea we are defenceless. A navy might burn our sea port towns. What then? If the insinuating Massachusettensis, has ever read any speculations concerning an Agrarian law, and I know he has, he will be satisfied that 350 thousand landholders, will not give up their rights and the constitution by which they hold them, to save fifty thousand inhabitants of maritime towns. Will the minister be nearer his mark after he has burnt a beautiful town and murdered 30,000 innocent people? So far from it, that one such event, would occasion the loss of all the colonies to Great Britain forever. It is not so clear that our trade, fishery and navigation, could be taken from us. Some persons, who understand this subject better than Massachusettensis, with all his sprightly imaginations, are of a different opinion. They think that our trade would be increased. But I will not enlarge upon this subject, because I wish the trade of this continent, may be confined to Great Britain, at least as much of it, as it can do her any good to restrain.

The Canadians and Savages are brought in to thicken the horrors of a picture with which the lively fancy of this writer has terrified him. But although we are sensible that the Quebec act has laid a foundation for a fabrick, which if not seasonably demolished, may be formidable, if not ruinous to the colonies, in future times, yet we know that these times are yet at a distance, at present we hold the power of the Canadians as nothing. But we know their dispositions are not unfriendly to us. The savages will be more likely to be our friends than enemies: but if they should not, we know well enough how to defend ourselves against them.

I ought to apologize for the immoderate length of this paper. But general assertions are only to be confuted by an examination of particulars, which necessarily fills up much space. I will trespass on the readers patience only while I make one observation more upon the art, I had almost said chicanery, of this writer.

He affirms that we are not united in this province, and that associations are forming in several parts of the province. The association he means has been laid before the public, and a very curious piece of ledgerdemain it is. Is there any article in it acknowledging the authority of parliament—the unlimitted authority of parliament? Brigadier Ruggles himself, Massachusettensis himself, could not have signed it if there had, consistent with their known declared opinions. They associate to stand by the king's laws, and this every whig will subscribe. But after all, what a wretched fortune has this association made in the world, the numbers who have signed it, would appear so inconsiderable, that I dare say the Brigadier will never publish to the world their numbers or names. But "has not Great-Britain been a nursing mother to us?" Yes, and we have behaved as nurse children commonly do, been very fond of her, and rewarded her all along tenfold for all her care and expence in our nurture.

But "is not all our distraction owing to parliament's taking off a shilling duty on tea and imposing three pence, and is not this a more unaccountable frenzy, more disgraceful to the annals of America, than the witchcraft."!

Is the three pence upon tea our only grievance? Are we not in this province deprived of the priviledge of paying our governors, judges, &c. Are not trials by jury taken from us! Are we not to be sent to England for tryal! Is not a military government put over us? Is not our constitution demolished to the foundation? Have not the ministry shewn by the Quebec bill, that we have no security against them for our religion any more than our property, if we once submit to the unlimited claims of parliament! This is so gross an attempt to impose on the most ignorant of the people, that it is a shame to answer it.

Obsta principiis—Nip the shoots of arbitrary power in the

bud, is the only maxim which can ever preserve the liberties of any people. When the people give way, their deceivers, betrayers and destroyers press upon them so fast that there is no resisting afterwards. The nature of the encroachment upon the American constitution is such, as to grow every day more and more encroaching. Like a cancer, it eats faster and faster every hour. The revenue creates pensioners, and the pensioners urge for more revenue. The people grow less steady, spirited and virtuous, the seekers more numerous and more corrupt, and every day increases the circles of their dependants and expectants, until virtue, integrity, public spirit, simplicity, frugality, become the objects of ridicule and scorn, and vanity, luxury, foppery, selfishness, meanness, and downright venality, swallow up the whole society.

NOVANGLUS
Boston Gazette, February 6, 1775

Massachusettensis [Daniel Leonard] No. X

To the Inhabitants of the Province of Massachusetts Bay,

MY DEAR COUNTRYMEN,

I offered to your consideration, last week, a few extracts from the law books, to enable those that have been but little conversant with the law of the land, to form a judgment, and determine for themselves, whether any have been so far beguiled and seduced from their allegiance, as to commit the most aggravated offence against society, high treason. The whigs reply, riots and insurrections are frequent in England, the land from which we sprang; we are bone of their bone, and flesh of their flesh.—Granted; but at the same time be it remembered, that in England the executive is commonly able and willing to suppress insurrections, the judiciary to distribute impartial justice, and the legislative power to aid and strengthen the two former if necessary; and whenever these have proved ineffectual to allay intestine commotions, war, with its concomitant horrors, have passed through the land, marking their rout with blood. The bigger part of Britain has at some period or other, within the reach of history, been forfeited to the crown, by the rebellion of its proprietors.

Let us now take a view of American grievances, and try, by the sure touchstone of reason and the constitution, whether there be any act or acts, on the part of the king or parliament, that will justify the whigs even in *foro conscientiæ*, in thus forcibly opposing their government. Will the alteration of the mode of appointing one branch of our provincial legislature furnish so much as an excuse for it, considering that our politicians, by their intrigues and machinations, had rendered the assembly incapable of answering the purpose of government, which is protection, and our charter was become as inefficacious as an old ballad? Or can a plea of justification be founded on the parliament's giving us an exact transcript of English laws for returning jurors, when our own were insufficient to afford compensation to the injured, to suppress seditions, or even to restrain rebellion? It has been heretofore observed, that each member of the community is entitled to protection; for this he pays taxes, for this he relinquishes his natural right of revenging injuries and redressing wrongs, and for this the sword of justice is placed in the hands of the magistrate. It is notorious that the whigs had usurped the power of the province in a great measure, and exercised it by revenging themselves on their opponents, or in compelling them to enlist under their banners. Recollect the frequency of mobs and riots, the invasions and demolitions of dwelling houses and other property, the personal abuse, and frequent necessity of persons abandoning their habitations, the taking sanctuary on board men of war, or at the castle, previous to the regulating bill. Consider that these sufferers were loyal subjects, violators of no law, that many of them were crown officers, and were thus persecuted for no other offence, than that of executing the king's law. Consider futher, that if any of the sufferers sought redress in a court of law, he had the whole whig interest to combat; they gathered like a cloud and hovered like harpies round the seat of justice, until the suitor was either condemned to pay cost to his antagonist, or recovered so small damages, as that they were swallowed up in his own. Consider further, that these riots were not the accidental or spontaneous risings of the populace, but the result of the deliberations and mature councils of the whigs, and were sometimes headed and led to action by their principals. Consider further, that the general assembly lent no aid to the executive power. Weigh these things, my friends, and doubt if you can, whether the act for regulating our government did not flow from the parental tenderness of the British councils, to enable us to recover from anarchy, without Britain being driven to the necessity of inflicting punishment, which is her strange work. Having taken this cursory view of the convulsed state of the province, let us advert to our charter form of government, and we shall find its distributions of power to have been so preposterous, as to render it next to impossible for the province to recover by its own strength. The council was elective annually by the house, liable to the negative of the chair, and the chair restrained from acting, even in the executive department, without the concurrence of the board. The political struggle is often between the governor and the house, and it is a maxim with politicians, that he that is not for us is against us. Accordingly, when party run

high, if a counsellor adhered to the governor, the house refused to elect him the next year; if he adhered to the house,
the governor negatived him; if he trimmed his bark so as to
steer a middle course between Scylla and Charybdis, he was in
danger of suffering more by the neglect of both parties, than
of being wrecked but on one.

In moderate times, this province has been happy under our
charter form of government; but when the political storm
arose, its original defect became apparent. We have sometimes
seen half a dozen sail of tory navigation unable, on an election
day, to pass the bar formed by the flux and reflux of tides at the
entrance of the harbour, and as many whiggish ones stranded
the next morning on Governor's Island. The whigs took the
lead in this game, and therefore I think the blame ought to
rest upon them, though the tables were turned upon them in
the sequel. A slender acquaintance with human nature will inform, experience has evinced, that a body of men thus constituted, are not to be depended upon to act that vigorous,
intrepid and decisive part, which the emergency of the late
times required, and which might have proved the salvation of
the province. In short, the board which was intended to moderate between the governor and the house, or perhaps rather to
support the former, was incapable of doing either by its original constitution. By the regulating act, the members of the
board are appointed by the king in the council, and are not liable even to the suspension of the governor; their commissions
are *durante bene placito*, and they are therefore far from independence. The infant state of the colonies does not admit of a
peerage, nor perhaps of any third branch of legislature wholly
independent. In most of the colonies, the council is appointed
by mandamus, and the members are moreover liable to be suspended by the governor, by which means they are more dependant than those appointed according to the regulating
act; but no inconvenience arises from that mode of appointment. Long experience has evinced its utility. By this statute,
extraordinary powers are devolved upon the chair, to enable
the governor to maintain his authority, and to oppose with
vigor the daring spirit of independance, so manifest in the
whigs. Town meetings are restrained to prevent their passing
traitorous resolves. Had these and many other innovations

contained in this act, been made in moderate times, when due reverence was yielded to the magistrate, and obedience to the law, they might have been called grievances; but we have no reason to think, that had the situation of the province been such that this statute would ever have had an existence—nor have we any reason to doubt, but that it will be repealed, in whole or part, should our present form of government be found by experience to be productive of rapine or oppression. It is impossible that the king, lords or commons could have any sinister views in regulating the government of this province. Sometimes we are told that charters are sacred. However sacred, they are forfeited through negligence or *abuse* of their franchises, in which cases the law judges that the body politic has broken the condition, upon which it was incorporated.

There are many instances of the negligence and abuse, that work the forfeiture of charters, delineated in law books. They also tell us, that all charters may be vacated by act of parliament. Had the form of our provincial legislature been established by act of parliament, that act might have been constitutionally and equitably repealed, when it was found to be incapable of answering the end of its institution. Stronger still is the present case, where the form of government was established by one branch of the legislature only, viz. the king, and all three join in the revocation. This act was however a fatal stroke to the ambitious views of our republican patriots. The monarchial part of the costitution was so guarded by it, as to be no longer vulnerable by their shafts, and all their fancied greatness vanished, like the baseless fabric of a vision. Many that had been long striving to attain a seat at the board, with their faces thitherward, beheld, with infinite regret, their competitors advanced to the honors they aspired to themselves. These disappointed, ambitious, and envious men, instil the poison of disaffection into the minds of the lower classes, and as soon as they are properly impregnated exclaim, *the people* never will submit to it. They now would urge them into certain ruin, to prevent the execution of an act of parliament, designed and calculated to restore peace and harmony to the province, and to recal that happy state, when year rolled round on year, in a contiunal increase of our felicity.

The Quebec bill is another capital grievance, because the

Canadians are tolerated in the enjoyment of their religion, which they were entitled to, by an article of capitulation, when they submitted to the British arms. This toleration is not an exclusion of the protestant religion, which is established in every part of the empire, as firmly as civil polity can establish it. It is a strange kind of reasoning to argue, from the French inhabitants of the conquered province of Quebec being tolerated, in the enjoyment of the Roman Catholic religion, in which they were educated, and in which alone they repose their hope of eternal salvation; that therefore government intends to deprive us of the enjoyment of the protestant religion, in which alone we believe, especially as the political interests of Britain depend upon protestant connexions, and the king's being a protestant himself is an indispensable condition of his wearing the crown. This circumstance however served admirably for a fresh stimulus, and was eagerly grasped by the disaffected of all orders. It added pathos to pulpit oratory. We often see resolves and seditious letters interspersed with *popery* here and there in Italics. If any of the clergy have endeavoured, from this circumstance, to alarm their too credulous audiences, with an apprehension that their religious privileges were in danger, thereby to excite them to take up arms, we must lament the depravity of the best of men; but human nature stands apalled when we reflect upon the aggravated guilt of prostituting our holy religion to the accursed purposes of treason and rebellion. As to our lay politicians, I have long since ceased to wonder at any thing in them; but it may be observed that there is no surer mark of a bad cause, than for its advocates to recur to such pitiful shifts to support it. This instance plainly indicates that their sole dependance is in preventing the passions subsiding, and cool reason resuming its seat. It is a mark of their shrewdness however, for whenever reason shall resume its seat, the political cheat will be detected, stand confest in its native turpitude, and the political knave be branded with marks of infamy, adequate, if possible, to the enormity of his crimes.

MASSACHUSETTENSIS.

*Massachusetts Gazette; and the
Boston Post-Boy and Advertiser*, February 13, 1775

Novanglus No. IV

To the Inhabitants of the Colony of Massachusetts-Bay

My Friends,

Massachusettensis, whose pen can wheedle with the tongue of king Richard the third, in his first paper, threatens you with the vengeance of Great-Britain, and assures you that if she had no authority over you, yet she would support her claims by her fleets and armies, Canadians and Indians. In his next he alters his tone, and sooths you with the generosity, justice and humanity, of the nation.

I shall leave him to shew how a nation can claim an authority which they have not by right, and support it by fire and sword, and yet be generous and just. The nation I believe is not vindictive, but the minister has discovered himself to be so, in a degree that would disgrace a warrior of a savage tribe.

The wily Massachusettensis thinks our present calamity is to be attributed to the bad policy of a popular party, whose measures, whatever their intentions were, have been opposite to their profession, the public good. The present calamity seems to be nothing more nor less, than reviving the plans of Mr. Bernard and the junto, and Mr. Grenville and his friends in 1764. Surely this party, are and have been rather unpopular. The popular party did not write Bernard's letters, who so long ago pressed for the demolition of all the charters upon the continent, and a parliamentary taxation to support government and the administration of justice in America. The popular party did not write Oliver's letters who inforces Bernard's plans, nor Hutchinson's, who pleads with all his eloquence and pathos for parliamentary penalties, ministerial vengeance, and an abridgement of English liberties.

There is not in human nature a more wonderful phænomenon; nor in the whole theory of it, a more intricate speculation; than the *shiftings, turnings, windings* and *evasions* of a guilty conscience. Such is our unalterable moral constitution, that an internal inclination to do wrong, is criminal: and a wicked thought, stains the mind with guilt, and makes it tingle with pain. Hence it comes to pass that the guilty mind, can never bear to think that its guilt is known to God or man, no, nor to itself.

> —Cur tamen hos tu
> Evasisse putes, quos diri conscia facti
> Mens habet attonitos, et surdo verbere cædit
> Occultum quatiente animo tortore flagellum?
> Poena autum vehemens, ac multo sævior illis,
> Quas et Cædicius gravis invenit aut Rhadamanthus,
> Nocte dieque suum gestare in pectore testem,
>   Juv. Sat. 13. 192.

Massachusettensis and his friends the tories, are startled at the calamities they have brought upon their country, and their conscious guilt, their smarting, wounded minds, will not suffer them to confess, even to themselves what they have done. Their silly denials of their own share in it before a people who they know have abundant evidence against them, never fail to remind me of an ancient *fugitive*, whose conscience could not bear the recollection of what he had done. "I know not, am I my brothers keeper"? he replies, with all the apparent simplicity of truth and innocence, to one from whom he was very sensible his guilt could not be hid. The still more absurd and ridiculous attempts of the tories, to throw off the blame of these calamities from themselves to the whigs, remind me of another story which I have read in the old testament. When Joseph's brethren had sold him to the Ishmaelites for twenty pieces of silver, in order to conceal their own avarice, malice, and envy, they dip the coat of many colours in the blood of a Kid, and say that an evil beast had rent him in pieces and devoured him.

However, what the sons of Israel intended for ruin to Joseph, proved the salvation of the family; and I hope and believe that the whigs, will have the magnanimity, like him, to suppress their resentment, and the felicity of saving their ungrateful brothers.

This writer has a faculty of insinuating errors into the mind, almost imperceptibly, he dresses them so in the guise of truth. He says "that the revenue to the crown from America, amounted to but little more than the charges of collecting it," at the close of the last war. I believe it did not amount to so much. The truth is, there was never any pretence of raising a revenue in America before that time, and when the claim was first set up, it gave no alarm, like a warlike expedition against us. True it is that some duties had been laid before by parliament, under pretence of regulating our trade, and by a collusion and combination between the West India planters and the North-American governors, some years before duties had been laid upon molasses, &c. under the same pretence, but in reality merely to advance the value of the estates of the planters in the West India islands, and to put some plunder, under the name of thirds of seisures into the pockets of the governors. But these duties tho' more had been collected in this province than in any other in proportion, were never regularly collected in any of the colonies. So that the idea of an American revenue for one purpose or another had never, at this time, been formed in American minds.

Our writer goes on, "She Great-Britain tho't it as reasonable that the colonies should bear a part of the national burthen, as that they should share in the national benefit."

Upon this subject Americans have a great deal to say. The national debt before the last war was near an hundred millions. Surely America had no share in running into that debt. Where is the reason then that she should pay it? But a small part of the sixty millions spent in the last war, was for her benefit. Did not she bear her full share of the burden of the last war in America? Did not this province pay twelve shillings in the pound in taxes for the support of it: and send a sixth or seventh part of her sons into actual service? And at the conclusion of the war, was she not left half a million sterling in debt? Did not all the rest of New-England exert itself in proportion? What is the reason that the Massachusetts has paid its debt, and the British minister in thirteen years of peace has paid none of his? Much of it might have been paid in this time, had not such extravagance and peculation prevailed as ought to be an eternal warning to America, never to trust such a minister with her money. What is the reason that the great and necessary virtues of simplicity, frugality and œconomy, cannot live in England, Scotland and Ireland, as well as America?

We have much more to say still. Great Britain has confined all our trade to herself. We are willing she should, as far as it can be for the good of the empire. But we say that we ought to be allowed as credit, in the account of public burdens and expences, so much paid in taxes, as we are obliged to sell our commodities to her cheaper than we could get for them at foreign markets. This difference is really a tax upon us, for the good of the empire. We are obliged to take from Great-Britain, commodities that we could purchase cheaper elsewhere. This difference is a tax upon us for the good of the empire. We submit to this chearfully, but insist that we ought to have credit for it, in the account of the expences of the empire, because it is really a tax upon us. Another thing. I will venture a bold assertion. Let Massachusettensis or any other friend of the minister, confute me. The three million Americans, by the tax aforesaid upon what they are obliged to export to Great-Britain only, what they are obliged to import from Great-Britain only, and the quantities of British manufactures which in these climates they are obliged to consume, more than the like number of people in any part of the three kingdoms, ultimately pay more of the taxes and duties that are apparently paid in Great-Britain, than any three million subjects in the three kingdoms. All this may be computed and reduced to stubborn figures, by the minister, if he pleases. We cannot do it. We have not the accounts, records, &c. Now let this account be fairly stated, and I will engage for America, upon any penalty, that she will pay the overplus, if any, in her own constitutional way, provided it is to be applied for national purposes, as paying off the national debt, maintaining the fleet, &c. not to the support of a standing army in time of peace, placemen, pensioners, &c.

Besides, every farthing of expence which has been incurred on pretence of protecting, defending and securing America since the last war, has been worse than thrown away, it has been applied to do mischief. Keeping an army in America has been nothing but a public nuisance.

Furthermore, we see that all the public money that is raised here, and have reason to believe all that will or can be raised, will be applied not for public purposes, national or provincial, but merely to corrupt the sons of America, and create a faction to destroy its interest and happiness.

There is scarcely three sentences together, in all the voluminous productions of this plausible writer which do not convey some error in fact or principle, tinged with a colouring to make it pass for truth. He says "the idea, that the stamps were a tax, not only exceeding our proportion, but beyond our utmost ability to pay, united the colonies generally in opposing it." That we thought it beyond our proportion and ability is true, but it was not this thought which united the colonies in opposing it. When he says that at first we did not dream of denying the authority of parliament to tax us, much less to legislate for us, he discovers plainly either a total inattention to the sentiments of America at that time, or a disregard of what he affirms.

The truth is, the authority of parliament was never generally acknowledged in America. More than a century since, the Massachusetts and Virginia, both protested against even the act of navigation and refused obedience, for this very reason, because they were not represented in parliament and were therefore not bound—and afterwards confirmed it by their own provincial authority. And from that time to this, the general sense of the colonies has been, that the authority of parliament was confined to the regulation of trade, and did not extend to taxation or internal legislation.

In the year 1764, your house of representatives sent home a petition to the king, against the plan of taxing them. Mr. Hutchinson, Oliver and their relations and connections, were then in the legislature, and had great influence there. It was by their influence that the two houses were induced to waive the word rights, and an express denial of the right of parliament to tax us, to the great grief and distress of the friends of liberty in both houses. Mr. Otis and Mr. Thatcher laboured in the committee to obtain an express denial. Mr. Hutchinson expressly said he agreed with them in opinion, that parliament had no right, but tho't it ill policy to express this opinion in the petition. In truth, I will be bold to say, there was not any member of either house, who thought that parliament had such a right at that time. The house of representatives, at that time, gave their approbation to Mr. Otis's Rights of the Colonies, &c. in which it was shewn to be inconsistent with the Right of British Subjects to be taxed, but by our own Representatives. In 1765, our house expressly resolved against the right of parliament to

tax us. The Congress at New York, resolved 3. "That it is in-
separably essential to the freedom of a people, and the undoubted right of Englishmen, that no tax be imposed on
them, but with their own consent given personally, or by their
representatives. 4. That the people of the colonies are not, and
from their local circumstances cannot be represented in the
house of Commons of Great-Britain. 5. That the only representatives of the people of the colonies, are the persons chosen
therein by themselves; and that no taxes ever have been, or can
be constitutionally imposed on them, but by their respective
legislatures." Is it not a striking disregard to truth in the artful
Massachusettensis to say, that at first we did not dream of
denying the right of parliament to tax us? It was the principle
that united the colonies to oppose it, not the quantum of the
tax. Did not Dr. Franklin deny the right in 1754, in his remarks
upon Governor Shirley's scheme, and suppose that all America
would deny it? We had considered ourselves as connected with
Great-Britain, but we never thought parliament the supreme
legislature over us. We never generally supposed it to have any
authority over us, but from necessity, and that necessity we
thought confined to the regulation of trade, and to such
matters as concern'd all the colonies together. We never allowed them any authority in our internal concerns.

This writer says, acts of parliament for regulating our internal polity were familiar. This I deny. So far otherwise that the
hatter's act was never regarded—the act to destroy the Land
Bank Scheme raised a greater ferment in this province, than
the Stamp-Act did, which was appeased only by passing province laws directly in opposition to it. The act against slitting
mills, and tilt-hammers, never was executed here. As to the
postage, it was so useful a regulation, so few persons paid it,
and they found such a benefit by it, that little opposition was
made to it: yet every man who thought about it, call'd it an
usurpation. Duties for regulating trade we paid, because we
thought it just and necessary that they should regulate the
trade which their power protected. As for duties for a revenue,
none were ever laid by parliament for that purpose until 1764,
when, and ever since, its authority to do it has been constantly
denied. Nor is this complaisant writer near the truth, when he
says, "We know that in all those acts of government, the good

of the whole had been consulted." On the contrary, we know that the private interest of provincial governors and West India planters, had been consulted in the duties on foreign molasses, &c. and the private interest of a few Portugal merchants, in obliging us to touch at Falmouth with Fruit, &c. in opposition to the good of the whole, and in many other instances.

The resolves of the House of Burgesses of Virginia, upon the stamp-act, did great honor to that province, and to the eminent patriot Patrick Henry, Esq. who composed them. But these resolves made no alteration in the opinion of the colonies, concerning the right of parliament to make that act. They expressed the universal opinion of the continent at that time, and the alacrity with which every other colony, and the Congress at New-York, adopted the same sentiment in similar resolves, proves the entire union of the colonies in it, and their universal determination to avow and support it.

What follows here, that it became so popular that his life was in danger, who suggested the contrary? And that the Press was open to one side only, are direct misrepresentations and wicked calumnies.

Then we are told, by this sincere writer, that when we obtained a partial repeal of the statute imposing duties on glass, paper and teas, this was the lucky moment, when to have closed the dispute. What? With a Board of Commissioners remaining, the sole end of whose creation was to form and conduct a revenue—with an act of parliament remaining, the professed design of which expressed in the preamble, was to raise a revenue, and appropriate it to the payment of governors and Judges salaries, the duty remaining too upon an article, which must raise a large sum, the consumption of which would constantly increase? Was this a time to retreat? Let me ask this sincere writer a simple question. Does he seriously believe that the designs of imposing other taxes, and of new-moddling our governments, would have been laid aside, by the ministry or by the servants of the crown here? Does he think that Mr. Bernard, Mr. Hutchinson, the Commissioners and others, would have been content then to have desisted: If he really thinks so, he knows little of the human heart, and still less of those gentlemens hearts. It was at this very time that the salary was given to the governor, and an order soliciting for that to the Judges.

Then we are entertained with a great deal of ingenious talk about Whigs and Tories, and at last are told that some of the Whigs owed all their importance to popularity. And what then? Did not as many of the Tories owe their importance to popularity? And did not many more owe all their importance to unpopularity? If it had not been for their taking an active part on the side of the ministry, would not some of the most conspicuous and eminent of them have been unimportant enough? Indeed through the two last administrations to despise and hate the people, and to be despised and hated by them, were the principal recommendations to the favours of government, and all the qualification that was required.

The Tories, says he, were for closing the controversy. That is, they were for contending no more, and it was equally true that they never were for contending at all, but lying at mercy. It was the very end they had aimed at from the beginning. They had now got the Governor's salary out of the revenue—a number of pensions and places, and they knew they could at any time get the judges salaries from the same fountain, and they wanted to get the people reconcil'd and familiarised to this, before they went upon any new projects.

The Whigs were averse to restoring government, they even refused to revive a temporary riot act, which expired about this time. Government had as much vigour then as ever, excepting only in those cases which affected this dispute: The riot act expired in 1770, immediately after the Massacre in King Street. It was not revived and never will be in this colony, nor will any one ever be made in any other, while a standing army is illegally posted here, to butcher the people, whenever a governor, or a magistrate, who may be a tool, shall order it. "Perhaps the Whigs tho't that mobs were a necessary ingredient in their system of opposition." Whether they did or no, it is certain that mobs have been thought a necessary ingredient by the tories in their system of administration, mobs of the worst sort with red coats, fusees and bayonets, and the lives and limbs of the whigs have been in greater danger from these than ever the tories were from others.

"The scheme of the whigs flattered the people with the idea of independence; the tories plan supposed a degree of subordination." This is artful enough as usual, not say jesuitical. The word independence is one of those, which this writer uses as he does treason and rebellion to impose upon the undistinguishing on both sides of the Atlantic. But let us take him to pieces. What does he mean by independence! Does he mean independent of the crown of Great-Britain, and an independent republic in America, or a confederation of independent republics? No doubt he intended the undistinguishing should understand him so. If he did, nothing can be more wicked, or a greater slander on the whigs, because he knows there is not a man in the province among the whigs, nor ever was, who harbours a wish of that sort. Does he mean that the people were flattered with the idea of total independence on parliament? If he does, this is equally malicious and injurious, because he knows that the equity and necessity of parliament's regulating trade has always been acknowledged, our determination to consent and submit to such regulations constantly expressed, and all the acts of trade in fact to this very day, much more submitted to and strictly executed in this province, than any other in America.

There is equal ambiguity, in the words "degree of subordination." The whigs acknowledge a subordination to the king, in as strict and strong a sense as the tories. The whigs acknowledge a voluntary subordination to parliament, as far as the regulation of trade. What degree of subordination then do the tories acknowledge? An absolute dependence upon parliament as their supreme legislative, in all cases whatsoever, in their internal polity as well as taxation? This would be too gross and would loose him all his readers, for there is no body here who will expose his understanding so much as explicitly to adopt such a sentiment. Yet it is such an absolute dependance and submission, that these writers would perswade us to, or else there is no need of changing our sentiments and conduct. Why will not these gentlemen speak out, shew us plainly their opinion that the new government they have fabricated for this province is better than the old, and that all the other measures we complain of are for our and the public good, and exhort us directly to submit to them? The reason is, because they know they should loose their readers.

"The whigs were sensible that there was no oppression that could be seen or felt." The tories have so often said and wrote this to one another, that I sometimes suspect they believe it to be true. But it is quite otherwise. The castle of the province was taken out of their hands and garrisoned by regular soldiers; this they could see, and they thought it indicated an hostile intention and disposition towards them. They continually paid their money to collectors of duties, this they could both see and feel. An host of placemen, whose whole business it was to collect a revenue, were continually rolling before them in their chariots. These they saw. Their governor was no longer paid by themselves according to their charter, but out of the new revenue, in order to render their assemblies useless and indeed contemptible. The judges salaries were threatned every day to be paid in the same unconstitutional manner. The dullest eye-sight could not but see to what all this tended, viz. to prepare the way for greater innovations and oppressions. They knew a minister would never spend his money in this way, if he had not some end to answer by it. Another thing they both saw and felt. Every man, of every character, who by voting, writing, speaking, or otherwise, had favoured the stamp act, the tea act, and every other measure of a minister or governor, who they knew was aiming at the destruction of their form of government, and introducing parliamentary taxation, was uniformly, in some department or other, promoted to some place of honour and profit for ten years together; and on the other hand, every man who favoured the people in their opposition to those innovations, was depressed, degraded and persecuted as far as it was in the power of the government to do it.

This they considered as a systematical means of encouraging every man of abilities to espouse the cause of parliamentary taxation, and the plan of destroying their charter privileges, and to discourage all from exerting themselves, in opposition to them. This they thought a plan to enslave them, for they uniformly think that the destruction of their charter, making the council and judges wholly dependent on the crown, and

the people subject to the unlimited power of parliament as
their supreme legislative, is slavery. They were certainly rightly
told then that the ministry and their governors together had
formed a design to enslave them, and that when once this was
done, they had the highest reason to expect window taxes,
hearth taxes, land taxes and all others. And that these were
only paving the way for reducing the country to lordships.—
Were the people mistaken in these suspicions? Is it not now
certain that Governor Bernard in 1769 had formed a design of
this sort? Read his principles of polity. And that Lt. Governor
Oliver as late as 1768 or 9 inforced the same plan? Read his
letters.

Now if Massachusettensis will be ingenuous, avow this design, shew the people its utility, and that it ought to be done
by parliament, he will act the part of an honest man. But to insinuate that there was no such plan, when he knows there was,
is acting the part of one of the junto.

It is true that the people of this country in general, and of
this province in special, have an hereditary apprehension of
and aversion to lordships temporal and spiritual. Their ancestors fled to this wilderness to avoid them—they suffer'd sufficiently under them in England. And there are few of the
present generation who have not been warned of the danger of
them by their fathers or grandfathers, and injoined to oppose
them. And neither Bernard nor Oliver ever dared to avow
before them, the designs which they had certainly formed to
introduce them. Nor does Massachusettensis dare to avow his
opinion in their favour. I don't mean that such avowal would
expose their persons to danger, but their characters and writings to universal contempt.

When you were told that the people of England were depraved, the parliament venal, and the ministry corrupt, were
you not told most melancholly truths? Will Massachusettensis
deny any of them? Does not every man who comes from England, whig or tory, tell you the same thing? Do they make any
secret of it, or use any delicacy about it? Do they not most of
them avow that corruption is so established there, as to be incurable, and a necessary instrument of government? Is not the
British constitution arrived nearly to that point, where the Roman republic was when Jugurtha left it, and pronounc'd it a

venal city ripe for destruction, if it can only find a purchaser? If Massachusettensis can prove that it is not, he will remove from my mind, one of the heaviest loads which lies upon it.

Who has censured the tories for remissness, I know not. Whoever it was, he did them great injustice. Every one that I know of that character, has been thro' the whole tempestuous period, as indefatigable as human nature will admit, going about seeking whom he might devour, making use of art, flattery, terror, temptation and alurement, in every shape in which human wit could dress it up, in public and private. But all to no purpose. The people have grown more and more weary of them every day, until now the land mourns under them.

Massachusettensis is then seized with a violent fit of anger at the clergy. It is curious to observe the conduct of the Tories towards this sacred body. If a clergyman preaches against the principles of the revolution, and tells the people that upon pain of damnation they must submit to an established government of whatever character, the Tories cry him up as an excellent man, and a wonderful preacher, invite him to their tables, procure him missions from the society, and chaplainships to the navy, and flatter him with the hopes of lawn sleeves. But if a clergyman preaches Christianity, and tells the magistrates that they were not distinguished from their brethren for their private emolument, but for the good of the people, that the people are bound in conscience to obey a good government, but are not bound to submit to one that aims at destroying all the ends of government—Oh Sedition! Treason!

The clergy in all ages and countries, and in this in particular, are disposed enough to be on the side of government, as long as it is tolerable: If they have not been generally in the late administrations on that side, it is demonstration that the late administration has been universally odious.

The clergy of this province are a virtuous, sensible and learned set of men, and they don't take their sermons from news-papers but the bible, unless it be a few who preach passive obedience. These are not generally curious enough to read Hobbs.

It is the duty of the clergy to accommodate their discourses to the times, to preach against such sins as are most prevalent, and recommend such virtues as are most wanted. For example, if exorbitant ambition, and venality are predominant, ought they not to warn their hearers against these vices? If public spirit is much wanted, should they not inculcate this great virtue? If the rights and duties of christian magistrates and subjects are disputed, should they not explain them, shew their nature, ends, limitations and restrictions, how much soever it may move the gall of Massachusettensis?

Let me put a supposition. Justice is a great christian as well as moral duty and virtue, which the clergy ought to inculcate and explain. Suppose a great man of a parish should for seven years together receive 600 sterling a year, for discharging the duties of an important office; but during the whole time, should never do one act or take one step about it. Would not this be great injustice to the public? And ought not the parson of that parish to cry aloud and spare not, and shew such a bold transgressor his sin? Shew that justice was due to the public as well as to an individual, and that cheating the public of four thousand two hundred pounds sterling, is at least as great a sin as taking a chicken from a private hen roost, or perhaps a watch from a fob!

Then we are told that news-papers and preachers have excited outrages disgraceful to humanity. Upon this subject I will venture to say, that there have been outrages in this province which I neither justify, excuse or extenuate; but these were not excited, that I know of, by news-papers or sermons. That however, if we run through the last ten years, and consider all the tumults and outrages that have happened, and at the same time recollect the insults, provocations, and oppressions which this people have endured; we shall find the two characteristicks of this people, religion and humanity, strongly marked on all their proceedings, not a life, nor that I have ever heard, a single limb has been lost thro' the whole. I will take upon me to say, there is not another province on this continent, nor in his majesty's dominions, where the people, under the same indignities, would not have gone greater lengths. Consider the tumults in the three kingdoms, consider the tumults in ancient Rome, in the most virtuous of her periods, and compare them with ours. It is a saying of Machiavel, which no wise man ever contradicted, which has been literally verified in this province that "while the mass of the people is not corrupted, tumults do no hurt." By which he means, that they leave no lasting ill effects behind.

But let us consider the outrages committed by the Tories. Half a dozen men shot dead in an instant, in king street, frequent resistance and affronts to civil officers and magistrates, officers, watchmen, citizens, cut and mangled in a most inhuman manner. Not to mention the shootings for desertion, and the frequent cruel whippings for other faults, cutting and mangling men's bodies before the eyes of citizens, spectacles which ought never to be introduced into populous places. The worst sort of tumults and outrages ever committed in this province, were excited by the tories. But more of this hereafter.

We are then told that the whigs erected a provincial democracy, or republic, in the province. I wish Massachusettensis knew what a democracy, or republic is. But this subject must be considered another time.

NOVANGLUS

Messieurs Printers. Instead of *Cawings* of Cormorants, in a former paper, you have printed *cooings*, too dove-like a word for the birds intended.

Boston Gazette, February 13, 1775

Massachusettensis [Daniel Leonard] No. XI

To the Inhabitants of the Province of Massachusetts Bay,

MY DEAR COUNTRYMEN,

It would be an endless task to remark minutely upon each of the fancied grievances, that swarm and cluster, fill and deform the American chronicles. An adeptness at discovering grievances has lately been one of the principal recommendations to public notice and popular applause. We have had genuises selected for that purpose, called committees upon grievances; a sagacious set they were, and discovered a multitude before it was known, that they themselves were the greatest grievances that the country was infested with. The case is shortly this; the whigs suppose the colonies to be separate or distinct states: having fixed this opinion in their minds, they are at no loss for grievances. Could I agree with them in their first principle, I should acquiesce in many of their deductions; for in that case every act of parliament, extending to the colonies, and every movement of the crown to carry them into execution, would be really grievances, however wise and salutary they might be in themselves, as they would be exertions of a power that we were not constitutionally subject to, and would deserve the name of usurpation and tyranny; but deprived of this their corner stone, the terrible fabric of grievances vanishes, like castles raised by enchantment, and leaves the wondering spectator amazed and confounded at the deception. He suspects himself to have but just awoke from sleep, or recovered from a trance, and that the formidable spectre, that had froze him with horror, was no more than the creature of a vision, or the delusion of a dream.

Upon this point, whether the colonies are distinct states or not, our patriots have rashly tendered Great Britain an issue, against every principle of law and constitution, against reason and common prudence. There is no arbiter between us but the sword; and that the decision of that tribunal will be against us, reason foresees, as plainly as it can discover any event that lies in the womb of futurity. No person, unless actuated by ambition, pride, malice, envy, or a malignant combination of the whole, that verges towards madness, and hurries the man away from himself, would wage war upon such unequal terms. No honest man would engage himself, much less plunge his country into the calamities of a war upon equal terms, without first settling with his conscience, in the retired moment of reflection, the important question respecting the justice of his cause. To do this, we must hear and weigh every thing that is fairly adduced, on either side of the question, with equal attention and care. A disposition to drink in with avidity, what favours our hypothesis, and to reject with disgust whatever contravenes it, is an infallible mark of a narrow, selfish mind. In matters of small moment, such obstinacy is weakness and folly, in important ones, fatal madness. There are many among us, that have devoted themselves to the slavish dominion of prejudice; indeed the more liberal have seldom had an opportunity of bringing the question to a fair examen. The eloquence of the bar, the desk and the senate, the charms of poetry, the expressions of painting, sculpture and statuary have conspired to fix and rivet ideas of independance upon the mind of the colonists. The overwhelming torrent, supplied from so many fountains, rolled on with increasing rapidity and violence, till it became superior to all restraint. It was the reign of passion; the small, still voice of reason was refused audience. I have observed that the press was heretofore open to but one side of the question, which has given offence to a writer in Edes and Gill's paper, under the signature of Novanglus, to whom I have many things to say. I would at present ask him, if the convention of committees for the county of Worcester, in recommending to the inhabitants of that county not to take newspapers, published by two of the printers in this town, and two at New York, have not affected to be licensers of the press? And whether, by proscribing these printers, and endeavouring to deprive them of a livelihood, they have not manifested an illiberal, bigoted, arbitrary, malevolent disposition? And whether, by thus attempting to destroy the liberty of the press, they have not betrayed a consciousness of the badness of their cause?

Our warriors tell us, that the parliament shall be permitted to legislate for the purposes of regulating trade, but the parliament hath most unrighteously asserted, that it "had, hath, and of right ought to have, full power and authority to make laws and statutes of sufficient force and validity to bind the colonies in all cases whatever," that this claim is without any qualification or restriction, is an innovation, and inconsistent with liberty. Let us candidly inquire into these three observations, upon the statute declaratory of the authority of parliament. As to its universality, it is true there are no exceptions expressed, but there is no general rule without exceptions, expressed or implied.

The implied ones in this case are obvious. It is evident that the intent and meaning of this act, was to assert the supremacy of parliament in the colonies, that is, that its constitutional authority to make laws and statutes binding upon the colonies, is, and ever had been as ample, as it is to make laws binding upon the realm. No one that reads the declaratory statute, not even prejudice itself, can suppose that the parliament meant to assert thereby a right or power to deprive the colonists of their lives, to enslave them, or to make any law respecting the colonies, that would not be constitutional, were it made respecting Great Britain. By an act of parliament passed in the year 1650, it was declared concerning the colonies and plantations in America, that they had "ever since the planting thereof been and ought to be subject to such laws, orders and regulations, as are or shall be made by the parliament of England." This declaration though differing in expression, is the same in substance with the other. Our house of representatives, in their dispute with governor Hutchinson, concerning the supremacy of parliament, say, "It is difficult, if possible, to draw a line of distinction between the universal authority of parliament over the colonies, and no authority at all."

The declaratory statute was intended more especially to assert the right of parliament, to make laws and statutes for raising a revenue in America, lest the repeal of the stamp act might be urged as a disclaimer of the right. Let us now inquire whether a power to raise a revenue be not the inherent, unalienable right of the supreme legislative of every well regulated state, where the hereditary revenues of the crown, or established revenues of the state are insufficient of themselves; and whether that power be not necessarily coextensive with the power of legislation, or rather necessarily implied in it.

The end or design of government, as has been already observed, is the security of the people from internal violence and rapacity, and from foreign invasion. The supreme power of a state must necessarily be so extensive and ample as to answer those purposes, otherwise it is constituted in vain, and degenerates into empty parade and mere ostentatious pageantry. These purposes cannot be answered without a power to raise a revenue; for without it neither the laws can be executed, nor the state defended. This revenue ought, in national concerns, to be apportioned throughout the whole empire according to the abilities of the several parts, as the claim of each to protection, is equal; a refusal to yield the former is as unjust as the withholding of the latter. Were any part of an empire exempt from contributing their proportionable part of the revenue, necessary for the whole, such exemption would be manifest injustice to the rest of the empire; as it must of course bear more than its proportion of the public burden, and it would amount to an additional tax. If the proportion of each part was to be determined only by itself in a separate legislature, it would not only involve in it the absurdity of *imperium in imperio*, but the perpetual contention arising from the predominant principle of self-interest in each, without having any common arbiter between them, would render the disjointed, discordant, torn, and dismembered state incapable of collecting or conducting its force and energy for the preservation of the whole, as emergencies might require. A government thus constituted, would contain the seeds of dissolution in its first principles, and must soon destroy itself.

I have already shewn, that by your first charter, this province was to be subject to taxation, after the lapse of twenty-one years, and that the authority of parliament to impose such taxes, was claimed so early as the year 1642.

In the patent for Pennsylvania, which is now in force, there is this clause, "And further our pleasure is, and by these presents, for us, &c. we do covenant and grant to, and with the said William Penn, &c. that we, &c. shall at no time hereafter set or make, or cause to be set, any imposition, custom, or other taxation or rate or contribution whatsoever, in and upon the dwellers, and inhabitants of the aforesaid province, for their lands, tenements, goods or chattels within the said province, or in and upon any goods or merchandise within the said province, to be laden or unladen within the ports or harbours of the said province, unless the same be with the consent of the proprietors, chief governor, or assembly, or *act of parliament*."

These are stubborn facts; they are incapable of being winked out of existence, how much soever, we may be disposed to shut our eyes upon them. They prove, that the claim of a right to raise a revenue in the colonies, exclusive of the grants of their own assemblies, is coeval with the colonies themselves. I shall next shew, that there has been an actual, uninterrupted exercise of that right, by the parliament time immemorial.

MASSACHUSETTENSIS.

Massachusetts Gazette; and the Boston Post-Boy and Advertiser, February 20, 1775

Novanglus No. V

My Friends,

We are at length arrived at the paper, on which I made a few strictures, some weeks ago: these I shall not repeat, but proceed to consider the other part of it.

We are told "It is an universal truth, that he that would excite a rebellion, is at heart, as great a tyrant as ever weilded the iron rod of oppression." Be it so: We are not exciting a rebellion. Opposition, nay open, avowed resistance by arms, against usurpation and lawless violence, is not rebellion by the law of God, or the land. Resistance to lawful authority makes rebellion. Hampden, Russell, Sydney, Somers, Holt, Tillotson, Burnet, Hoadley, &c. were no tyrants nor rebels, altho' some of them were in arms, and the others undoubtedly excited resistance, against the tories. Don't beg the question, Mr. Massachusettensis, and then give yourself airs of triumph. Remember the frank Veteran acknowledges, that "the word rebel is a convertible term."

This writer next attempts to trace the spirit of opposition, through the general court, and the courts of common law. "It was the policy of the whigs, to have their questions upon high matters determined by yea and nay votes, which were published in the gazettes." And ought not great questions to be so determined? In many other assemblies, New-York particularly, they always are. What better way can be devised to discover the true sense of the people? It is extreamly provoking to courtiers, that they can't vote, as the cabinet direct them, against their consciences, the known sense of their constituents, and the obvious good of the community, without being detected. Generally, perhaps universally, no unpopular measure in a free government, particularly the English, ought ever to pass. Why have the people a share in the legislature, but to prevent such measures from passing, I mean such as are disapproved by the people at large? But did not these yea and nay votes, expose the whigs as well as tories to the impartial judgment of the public? If the votes of the former were given for measures

injurious to the community, had not the latter an equal opportunity of improving them to the disadvantage of their adver-
saries in the next election? Besides, were not those few persons
in the house, who generally voted for unpopular measures, near
the governor, in possession of his confidence? Had they not
the absolute disposal in their towns and counties of the favours
of government? Were not all the judges, justices, sheriffs, coro-
ners and military officers in their towns, made upon their recommendation? Did not this give them a prodigious weight
and influence? Had the whigs any such advantage? And does
not the influence of these yea and nay votes, consequently
prove to a demonstration, the unanimity of the people, against
the measures of the court?

As to what is said of "severe strictures, illiberal invectives,
abuse and scurrility, upon the dissentients," there was quite as
much of all these published against the leading whigs. In truth,
the strictures, &c. against the tories were generally nothing
more than hints at the particular place or office, which was
known to be the temptation to vote against the country. That
"the dissentient was in danger of losing his bread and involving his family in ruin" is equally injurious. Not an instance can
be produced, of a member, losing his bread, or injuring his
business, by voting for unpopular measures. On the contrary,
such voters never failed to obtain some lucrative employment,
title or honorary office, as a reward from the court.

If "one set of members in committee, had always prepared
the resolves," &c. which they did not, what would this prove,
but that this set was thought by the house the fittest for the
purpose? Can it ever be otherwise? Will any popular assembly
chuse its worst members for the best services? Will an assembly
of patriots chuse courtiers to prepare votes against the court?
No resolves against the claims of parliament or administration,
or the measures of the governor, (excepting those against the
stamp act, and perhaps the answers to governor Hutchinson's
speeches upon the supremacy of parliament) ever passed
through the house, without meeting an obstacle. The governor had to the last hour of the house's existence, always some
seekers and expectants in the house, who never failed to oppose, and offer the best arguments they could, and were always
patiently heard. That the lips of the dissentients were sealed

up: that they sat in silence, and beheld with regret, measures they dar'd not oppose, are groundless suggestions, and gross reflections upon the honour or courage of those members. The debates of this house were public, and every man who has attended the gallery knows there never was more freedom of debate, in any assembly.

Massachusettensis, in the next place, conducts us to the agent, and tells us "there cannot be a provincial agent without an appointment by the three branches of the assembly. The whigs soon found that they could not have such services rendered them, from a provincial agent as would answer their purposes."

The treatment this province has received, respecting the agency, since Mr. Hutchinson's administration commenced, is a flagrant example of injustice. There is no law, which requires the province to maintain any agent in England, much less is there any reason which necessarily requires, that the three branches should join in the appointment. In ordinary times, indeed, when a harmony prevails among the branches, it is well enough to have an agent constituted by all: But in times when the foundations of the constitution are disputed, and certainly attacked, by one branch or the other, to pretend that the house ought to join the governor in the choice, is a palpable absurdity. It is equivalent to saying that the people shall have no agent at all; that all communication between them and their sovereign shall be cut off; and that there shall be no channel through which complaints and petitions may be conveyed to the royal ear; because a governor will not concur in an agent whose sentiments are not like his; nor will an agent of the governor's appointment be likely to urge accusations against him with any diligence or zeal, if the people have occasion to complain against him.

Every private citizen, much more every representative body, have an undoubted right to petition the king; to convey such petition by any agent, and to pay him for his service. Mr. Bernard, to do him justice, had so much regard to these principles, as to consent to the payment of the people's agents while he staid. But Mr. Hutchinson was scarcely seated in the chair as lieut. governor, before we had intelligence from England, that my lord Hillsborough told Dr. Franklin, he had received a letter from governor Hutchinson, soliciting an instruction against consenting to the salary of the agent. Such an instruction was accordingly soon sent, and no agent for the board or house, has received a farthing for services since that time, although Dr. Franklin and Mr. Bollan have taken much pains, and one of them expended considerable sums of money. There is a meanness in this play that would disgrace a gambler. A manifest fear that the truth should be known to the sovereign or the people. Many persons have thought that the province ought to have dismiss'd all agents from that time, as useless and nugatory, this behaviour amounting to a declaration, that we had no chance or hopes of justice from such a minister.

But this province, at least as meritorious as any, has been long accustomed to indignities and injustice, and to bear both with unparallelled patience. Others, have pursued the same method before and since, but we have never heard that their agents are unpaid. They would scarcely have born it with so much resignation.

It is great assurance to blame the house for this, which was both their right and duty: but a stain in the character of his patron, which will not be soon worn out. Indeed this passage seems to have been bro't in, chiefly for the sake of a stroke or two addressed to the lowest and meanest of the people: I mean the insinuation that the two Agents doubled the *Expence*, which is as groundless as it is contracted; and that the ostensible agent for the province was only agent for a few individuals, that had got the art of wielding the house; and that several hundreds sterling a year, for attending levees and writing letters were worth preserving. We, my friends, know that no members have the art of wielding us or our house, but by concurring in our principles, and assisting us in our designs. Numbers in both houses have turn'd about and expected to wield us round with them; but they have been disappointed, and ever will be. Such apostates have never yet fail'd of our utter contempt, whatever titles, places or pensions they might obtain.

The agent has never ecchoed back, or transmitted to America, any sentiments, which he did not give in substance to governor Shirley twenty years ago; and therefore this insinuation is but another slander. The remainder of what is said of the agency is levell'd at Dr. Franklin, and is but a dull appendix to Wedderburn's ribaldry, having all his malice without any of his wit or spirit. Nero murdered Seneca that he might pull up virtue by the roots, and the same maxim governs the scribblers, and speechifyers, on the side of the minister. It is sufficient to discover that any man has abilities and integrity, a love of virtue and liberty; he must be run down at all events. Witness Pitt and Franklin and too many others.

My design in pursuing this malicious slanderer, concealed as he is under so soft and oily an appearance, through all the doublings of his tedious course, is to vindicate this Colony from his base aspersions; that strangers now among us, and the impartial public, may see the wicked arts which are still employed against us. After the vilest abuse upon the agent of the province and the house that appointed him, we are brought to his Majesty's Council, and are told that "the whigs reminded them of their mortality—if any one opposed the violent measures, he lost his Election next May. Half the whole number mostly men of the first families, note, abilities, attached to their native country, wealthy and independent, were tumbled from their seats in disgrace. Thus the Board lost its weight, and the political balance was destroyed."

It is impossible for any man acquainted with this subject to read this zealous rant, without smiling, until he attends to the wickedness of it, which will provoke his utmost indignation. Let us however consider it soberly.

From the date of our charter, to the time of the Stamp Act, and indeed since that time (notwithstanding the misrepresentations of our charter constitution, as too popular and republican) the council of this province have been generally on the side of the governor and the prerogative. For the truth of this, I appeal to our whole history and experience. The art and power of governors, and especially the negative, have been a stronger motive on the one hand, than the annual election of the two houses on the other. In disputes between the governor and the house, the council have generally adhered to the former, and in many cases have complied with his humour when scarcely any council by mandamus, upon this continent, would have done it.

But in the time of the Stamp Act, it was found productive of many mischiefs and dangers, to have officers of the crown, who were dependent on the ministry, and judges of the superior court whose offices were thought incompatible with a voice in the legislature, members of council.

In May 1765, Lt. Gov. Hutchinson, Sec. Oliver, and Mr. Belcher were officers of the crown, the judges of the superior court, and some other gentlemen who held commissions under the governor, were members of council. Mr. Hutchinson was chief justice and a judge of probate for the first county, as well as lieut. governor, and a counsellor, too many offices for the greatest and best man in the world to hold, too much business for any man to do; besides, that these offices were frequently clashing and interfering with each other. Two other justices of the superior court were councilors, and nearly and closely connected with him by family alliances. One other justice was judge of admiralty during pleasure. Such a jumble of offices, never got together before in any English government. It was found in short, that the famous triumvirate, Bernard, Hutchinson and Oliver, the ever memorable, secret, confidential letter writers, whom I call the junto, had by degrees, and before people were aware of it, erected a tyranny in the province. Bernard had all the executive, and a negative on the legislative; Hutchinson and Oliver, by their popular arts and secret intrigues, had elevated to the board, such a collection of crown officers, and their own relations, as to have too much influence there: and they had three of a family on the superior bench, which is the supreme tribunal in all causes civil and criminal, vested with all the powers of the king's bench, common pleas and exchequer, which gave them power over every act of this court. This junto therefore had the legislative and executive in their controul, and more natural influence over the judicial, than is ever to be trusted in any set of men in the world. The public accordingly found all these springs and wheels in the constitution set in motion to promote submission to the stamp act, and to discountenance resistance to it; and they thought they had a violent presumption, that they would forever be employed to encourage a compliance with all ministerial measures and parliamentary claims, of whatever character they might be.

The designs of the junto, however, were concealed as carefully as possible. Most persons were jealous; few were certain. When the assembly met in May 1766, after the stamp-act was repealed, the whigs flattered themselves with hopes of peace and liberty for the future. Mr. Otis, whose abilities and integrity; whose great exertions and most exemplary sacrifices of his private interest to the public service, had intitled him to all the promotion which the people could bestow, was chosen speaker of the house. Bernard negatived the choice. It can scarcely be conceived by a stranger, what an alarm this manoeuvre gave to the public. It was thought equivalent to a declaration, that altho' the people had been so successful as to obtain a repeal of the stamp-act, yet they must not hope to be quiet long, for parliament, by the declaratory act, had asserted its supreme authority, and new taxations and regulations should be made, if the junto could obtain them: and every man who should dare to oppose such projects, let his powers, or virtues, his family or fortune be what they would, should be surely cut off from all hopes of advancement. The electors thought it high time to be upon their guard. All the foregoing reasons and motives prevailed with the electors; and the crown officers and justices of the superior court, were left out of council in the new choice. Those who were elected in their places were all negatived by Bernard, which was considered as a fresh proof, that the junto still persevered in their designs of obtaining a revenue, to divide among themselves.

The gentlemen elected anew, were of equal fortune and integrity, at least, and not much inferior in abilities to those left out, and indeed, in point of fortune, family, note or abilities, the councils which have been chosen from that time to this, taken on an avarage, have been very little inferior, if any, to those chosen before. Let Massachusettensis descend if he will to every particular gentleman by name through the whole period, and I will make out my assertion.

Every impartial Person, will not only think these reasons a full vindication of the conduct of the two Houses, but that it was their indispensable duty to their country, to act the part they did; and the course of time, which has developed the dark intrigues of the junto, before and since, has confirmed the rectitude and necessity of the measure. Had Bernard's principles of polity been published and known at that time, no member of the house, who should have voted for any one of the persons then left out, if it was known to his constituents, would ever have obtained another election.

By the next step we rise to the chair. "With the board, the chair fell likewise", he says. But what a slander is this? Neither fell: both remained in as much vigour as ever. The junto it is true, and some other gentlemen who were not in their secret, but however had been misled to concur in their measures, were left out of council. But the board had as much authority as ever. The board of 1766 could not have influenced the people to acknowledge the supreme uncontroulable authority of parliament, nor could that of 1765, have done it. So that by the chair, and the boards falling, he means no more, if his meaning has any truth in it, than that the junto fell, the designs of taxing the colonies fell, and the schemes for destroying all the charters on the continent and for erecting Lordships fell. These it must be acknowledged fell very low indeed, in the esteem of the people, and the two houses.

"The Governor," says our wily writer, "could do little or nothing without the Council by the Charter"—"if he call'd upon a military officer to raise the militia, he was answered they were there already," &c. The Council by the Charter, had nothing to do with the militia. The Governor alone had all authority over them. The council therefore are not to blame for their conduct. If the militia refuse obedience to the Captain General, or his subordinate officers, when commanded to assist in carrying into execution the Stamp Act, or in dispersing those who were opposing it, does not this prove the universal sense and resolution of the people not to submit to it? Did not a regular army do more to James the second? If those, over whom the governor had the most absolute authority and decisive influence, refused obedience, does not this shew how deeply rooted in all mens minds was the abhorrence of that unconstitutional power, which was usurping over them? "If he called upon the Council for their assistance, they must first enquire into the cause." An unpardonable crime, no doubt! But is it the duty of a middle branch of legislature, to do as the first shall command them, implicitly, or to judge for themselves? Is it the duty of a privy council, to understand the subject before they give advice, or only to lend their names to any edict, in order to make it less unpopular? It would be a shame to answer such observations as these, if it was not for their wickedness. Our Council, all along, however, did as much as any Council could have done. Was the Mandamus Council at New-York able to do more, to influence the people to a submission to the Stamp act? Was the Chair, the Board, the Septennial House, with the assistance of General Gage and his troops, able to do more, in that city, than our branches did in this province? Not one Iota. Nor could Bernard, his Council, and House, if they had been unanimous, have induced submission. The people would have spurned them all, for they are not to be wheedled out of their liberties by their own Representatives, any more than by strangers. "If he wrote to government at home to strengthen his hands, some officious person procured and sent back his letters." At last it seems to be acknowledged, that the governor did write for a military force, to strengthen government. For what? To enable it to enforce Stamp acts, Tea acts, and other internal regulations, the authority of which, the people were determined never to acknowledge.

But what a pity it was that these worthy gentlemen could not be allowed, from the dearest affection to their native country, to which they had every possible attachment, to go on in profound confidential secrecy, procuring troops to cut our throats, acts of parliament to drain our purses and destroy our charters and assemblies, getting estates and dignities for themselves and their own families, and all the while most devoutly professing to be friends to our charter, enemies to parliamentary taxation, and to all pensions, without being detected? How happy! if they could have annihilated all our charters, and yet have been beloved, nay deified by the people, as friends and advocates for their charters? What masterly politicians! to have made themselves nobles for life, and yet have been thought very sorry that the two houses were deprived of the privilege of choosing the Council? How sagacious, to get large pensions for themselves, and yet be thought to mourn, that pensions and venality were introduced into the country? How sweet and pleasant! to have been the most popular men in the community, for being stanch and zealous dissenters, true-blue calvinists, and able advocates for public virtue and popular government, after they had introduced an American Episcopate, universal corruption among the leading men, and deprived the people of all share in their supreme legislative council? I mention an Episcopate, for altho' I don't know that Gov's. Hutchinson and Oliver ever directly solicited for Bishops, yet they must have seen, that there would have been one effect, very soon, of establishing the unlimitted authority of parliament!

I agree with this writer, that it was not the persons of Bernard, Hutchinson or Oliver, that made them obnoxious; but their principles and practices. And I will agree, that if Chatham, Campden and St. Asaph (I beg pardon for introducing these revered names into such company, and for making a supposition which is absurd) had been here, and prosecuted such schemes, they would have met with contempt and execration from this people. But when he says, "that had the intimations in those letters been attended to, we had now been as happy a people as good government could make us," it is too gross to make us angry. We can do nothing but smile. Have not these intimations been attended to? Have not fleets and armies been sent here, whenever they requested? Have not Governors, Lt. Governors, Secretaries, Judges, Attorney Generals and Solicitor Generals salaries been paid out of the revenue as they solicited? Have not taxes been laid, and continued? Have not English Liberties been abridged as Hutchinson desired? Have not "penalties of another kind" been inflicted, as he desired? Has not our Charter been destroyed, and the Council put into the King's hands, as Bernard requested? In short, almost all the wild mock pranks of this desperate triumverate have been attended to and adopted, and we are now as miserable as Tyranny can well make us. That Bernard came here with the affections of New Jersey, I never heard nor read, but in this writer. His abilities were considerable, or he could not have done such extensive mischief. His true British honesty and punctuality, will be acknowledged by none but such as owe all their importance to flattering him.

That Hutchinson was amiable and exemplary, in some respects, and very unamiable and unexemplary, in others, is a certain truth: otherwise he never would have retained so much popularity on one hand, nor made so pernicious a use of it on the other. His behavior, in several important departments, was with ability and integrity, in cases which did not affect his political system, but he bent all his offices to that. Had he continued stedfast to those principles in religion and government, which in his former life he professed, and which alone had procured him the confidence of the people and all his importance, he would have lived and died, respected and beloved, and have done honor to his native country. But by renouncing these principles and that conduct, which had made him and all his ancestors respectable, his character is now considered by all America, and the best part of the three kingdoms, notwithstanding the countenance he receives from the ministry, as a reproach to the province that gave him birth, as a man who by all his actions aimed at making himself great, at the expence of the liberties of his native country. This gentleman was open to flattery, in so remarkable a degree, that any man who would flatter him was sure of his friendship, and every one who would not, was sure of his enmity. He was credulous, in a ridiculous degree, of every thing that favoured his own plans, and equally incredulous of every thing which made against them. His natural abilities which have been greatly exaggerated by persons whom he had advanced to power, were far from being of the first rate. His industry was prodigious. His knowledge lay chiefly in the laws and politicks and history of this province, in which he had a long experience. Yet with all his advantages, he never was master of the true character of his native country, not even of New England and the Massachusetts Bay. Through the whole troublesome period since the last war, he manifestly mistook the temper, principles, and opinions of this people. He had resolved upon a system, and never could or would see the impracticability of it.

It is very true that all his abilities, virtues, interests and connections, were insufficient; but for what? To prevail on the people to acquiese in the mighty claim of parliamentary authority. The constitution was not gone. The suggestion that it was is a vile slander. It had as much vigor as ever, and even the governor had as much power as ever, excepting in cases which affected that claim. "The spirit" says this writer "was truly republican." It was not so in any one case whatever; any further than the spirit of the British constitution is republican. Even in the grand fundamental dispute, the people arranged themselves under their house of representatives and council, with as much order as ever, and conducted their opposition as much by the constitution as ever. It is true their constitution was employed against the measures of the junto, which created their enmity to it. However I have not such an horror of a republican spirit, which is a spirit of true virtue, and honest independence, I don't mean on the king, but on men in power. This spirit is so far from being incompatible with the British constitution, that it is the greatest glory of it, and the nation has always been most prosperous when it has most prevailed and been most encouraged by the crown. I wish it increased in every part of the world, especially in America; and I think the measures the Tories are now pursuing, will increase it to a degree that will insure us in the end redress of grievances and an happy reconciliation with Great Britain.

"Governor Hutchinson strove to convince us, by the principles of government, our charters and acknowledgments, that our claims were inconsistent with the subordination due to Great Britain," &c. says the writer.

Suffer me to introduce here, a little history. In 1764, when the system of taxing and new moddling the colonies was first apprehended, Lieut. Governor Hutchinson's friends struggled in several successive sessions of the General Court, to get him chosen agent for the province at the court of Great Britain. At this time he declared freely, *that he was of the same sentiment with the people, that Parliament had no Right to tax them; but differed from the country party, only in his opinion of the policy of denying that Right, in their Petitions,* &c. I would not injure him, I was told this by three gentlemen who were of the committee of both houses, to prepare that petition that he made this declaration explicitly before that committee. I have been told by other gentlemen that he made the same declaration to them. It is possible that he might make use of expressions studied for the purpose, which would not strictly bear this construction. But it is certain that they understood him so, and that this was the general opinion of his sentiments until he came to the chair.

The county party saw, that this aspiring genius, aimed at keeping fair with the ministry, by supporting their measures, and with the people, by pretending to be of our principles, and between both to trim himself up to the chair. The only reason why he did not obtain an election at one time, and was excused from the service at another after he had been chosen by a small majority, was because the members knew he would not openly deny the right, and assure his majesty, the parliament, and ministry, that the people never would submit to it. For the same reason he was left out of council. But he continued to cultivate his popularity and to maintain a general opinion among the people, that he denied the right in his private judgment, and this idea preserved most of those who continued their esteem for him.

But upon Bernard's removal, and his taking the chair as lieut. governor, he had no further expectations from the people nor complaisance for their opinions. In one of his first speeches he took care to advance the supreme authority of parliament. This astonished many of his friends. They were heard to say, we have been deceived. We thought he had been abused, but we now find what has been said of him is true. He is determined to join in the designs against this country. After his promotion to the government, finding that the people had little confidence in him, and knowing that he had no interest at home to support him but what he had acquired by joining with Bernard in kicking up a dust, he determined to stroke a bold stroke, and in a formal speech to both houses, became a champion for the unbounded authority of parliament, over the colonies. This he thought would lay the ministry under an obligation to support him in the government, or else to provide for him out of it, not considering that starting that question before that assembly, and calling upon them as he did to dispute with him upon it, was scattering firebrands, arrows and death in sport. The arguments he advanced were inconclusive indeed: but they shall be considered, when I come to the feeble attempt of Massachusettensis to give a colour to the same position.

The house, thus called upon, either to acknowledge the unlimited authority of parliament, or confute his arguments, were bound by their duty to God, their country and posterity, to give him a full and explicit answer. They proved incontestibly that he was out in his facts, inconsistent with himself, and in every principle of his law, he had committed a blunder. Thus the fowler was caught in his own snare: and altho' this country has suffered severe temporary calamities in consequence of this speech, yet I hope they will not be durable: but his ruin was certainly in part owing to it. Nothing ever opened the eyes of the people so much, to his designs, excepting his letters. Thus it is the fate of Massachusettensis, to praise this gentleman, for those things which the wise part of mankind condemn in him as the most insidious and mischievous of actions. If it was out of his power to do us any more injuries, I should wish to forget the part; but as there is reason to fear he is still to continue his malevolent labours against this country, altho' he is out of our sight, he ought not to be out of our minds. This country has every thing to fear, in the present state of the British court, while the lords Bute, Mansfield and North have the principal conduct of affairs, from the deep intrigues of that artful man.

To proceed to his successor, whom Massachusettensis has been pleased to compliment with the epithet of "amiable". I have no inclination to detract from this praise, but have no panegyricks or invectives for any man, much less for any governor, until satisfied of his character and designs. This gentleman's conduct, although he came here to support the systems of his two predecessors, and instructed to throw himself into the arms of their connections, when he has acted himself, and not been teized by others much less amiable and judicious than himself, into measures, which his own inclination would have avoided, has been in general as unexceptionable as could be expected, in his very delicate, intricate and difficult situation.

We are then told "that disaffection to Great-Britain was infused into the body of the people." The leading whigs, have ever, systematically, and upon principle, endeavoured to preserve the people from all disaffection to the king on the one hand, and the body of the people on the other, but to lay the blame where it is justly due on the ministry and their instruments.

We are next conducted into the superiour court, and informed "that the judges were dependant on the annual grants of the general court; that their salaries were small in proportion to the salaries of other officers, of less importance; that they often petitioned the assembly to enlarge them, without success, and were reminded of their dependance; that they remained unshaken amid the raging tempests, which is to be attributed rather to their firmness than situation."

That the salaries were small, must be allowed, but not smaller in proportion than those of other officers. All salaries in this Province have been and are small. It has been the policy of the country to keep them so, not so much from a spirit of parsimony, as an opinion, that the service of the public ought to be an honorary, rather than a lucrative employment; and that the great men ought to be obliged to set examples of simplicity and frugality before the people.

But if we consider things maturely, and make allowance for all circumstances, I think the country may be vindicated. This province during the last war, had such overbearing burdens upon it, that it was necessitated to œconomy in every thing. At the peace she was half a million sterling in debt, nearly. She thought it the best policy to get out of debt before she raised the wages of her servants, and if Great-Britain had thought as wisely, she would not now have had 140 millions to pay, and she would never have thought of taxing America.

Low as the wages were, it was found that whenever a vacancy happened, the place was solicited with much more anxiety and zeal than the kingdom of heaven.

Another cause which had its effect was this. The judges of that court had almost always enjoyed some other office. At the time of the stamp act the chief justice was lieut. governor, which yielded him a profit, and a judge of probate for the county of Suffolk, which yielded him another profit, and a counsellor, which if it was not very profitable, gave him an opportunity of promoting his family and friends to other profitable offices, an opportunity which the country saw he most religiously improved. Another justice of this court was a judge of admiralty, and another was judge of probate for the county of Plymouth. The people thought therefore, that as their time was not wholly taken up by their offices as judges of the superior court, there was no reason why they should be paid as much as if it had been.

Another reason was this: those justices had not been bred to the bar, but taken from merchandize, husbandry and other occupations; had been at no great expence for education or libraries, and therefore the people thought that equity did not demand large salaries.

It must be confessed that another motive had its weight.

The people were growing jealous of the chief justice and two other justices at least, and therefore thought it imprudent to enlarge their salaries, and by that means their influence.

Whether all these arguments were sufficient to vindicate the people for not enlarging their salaries, I shall leave to you, my friends, whose right it is to judge. But that the judges petition'd "often" to the assembly I don't remember. I knew it was suspected by many, and confidently affirmed by some, that judge Russell carried home with him in 1766, a petition to his Majesty, subscribed by himself, and chief justice Hutchinson at least, praying his Majesty to take the payment of the judges into his own hands; and that this petition, together with the solicitations of Governor Bernard, and others, had the success to procure the act of parliament, to enable his Majesty to appropriate the revenue to the support of the administration of justice, &c. from whence a great part of the present calamities of America have flowed.

That the high whigs took *care* to get themselves chosen of the grand juries I don't believe. Nine tenths of the people were high whigs; and therefore it was not easy to get a grand jury without nine whigs in ten, in it. And the matter would not be much mended by the new act of parliament. The sheriff must return the same set of jurors, court after court, or else his juries would be nine tenths of them high whigs still. Indeed the tories are so envenom'd now with malice, envy, revenge and disappointed ambition, that they would be willing, for what I know, to be jurors for life, in order to give verdicts against the whigs. And many of them would readily do it, I doubt not, without any other law or evidence, than what they found in their own breasts. The suggestion of ledgerdemain, in drawing the names of petit jurors out of the box, is scandalous. Human wisdom cannot devise a method of obtaining petit jurors more fairly, and better secured against a possibility of corruption of any kind, than that established by our provincial law. They were drawn by chance out of a box, in open town meeting, to which the tories went, or might have gone, as well as the whigs, and have seen with their own eyes, that nothing unfair ever did or could take place. If the jurors consisted of whigs, it was because the freeholders were whigs, that is honest men. But now, it seems, if Massachusettensis can have his will, the sheriff who will be a person properly qualified for the purpose, is to pick out a tory jury, if he can find one in ten, or one in twenty of that character among the freeholders; and it is no doubt expected, that every news paper that presumes to deny the right of parliament to tax us, or destroy our charter, will be presented as a libel, and every member of a committee of correspondence, or a congress, &c. &c. &c. are to be indicted for rebellion. These would be pleasant times to Massachusettensis and the junto, but they will never live to see them.

"The judges pointed out seditious libels, on governors, magistrates, and the whole government to no effect." They did so. But the jurors thought some of these no libels, but solemn truths. At one time, I have heard that all the newspapers for several years, the Massachusetts Gazette, Evening Post, the Boston Chronicle, Boston-Gazette, and Massachusetts-Spy, were laid before a grand jury at once. The jurors thought there were multitudes of libels written by the tories, and they did not know who they should attack if they presented them; perhaps governor Bernard, lieut. governor Hutchinson, secretary Oliver—possibly the attorney general. They saw so many difficulties they knew not what to do.

As to the riots and insurrections, it is surprizing that this writer should say "scarce one offender was indicted, and I think not one convicted." Were not many indicted, convicted, and punished too in the county of Essex? and Middlesex, and indeed in every other county? But perhaps he will say, he means such as were connected with politicks. Yet this is not true, for a large number in Essex were punished for abusing an informer, and others were indicted and convicted in Boston, for a similar offence. None were indicted for pulling down the stamp office, because this was thought an honorable and glorious action, not a riot. And so it must be said of several other tumults. But was not this the case in royal as well as charter governments? Nor will this inconvenience be remedied by a sheriff's jury, if such an one should ever sit. For if such a jury should convict, the people will never bear the punishment. It is in vain to expect or hope to carry on government, against the universal bent and genius of the people; we may whimper and whine as much as we will, but nature made it impossible, when she made men.

If causes of *meum* and *tuum*, were not always exempt from party influence, the tories will get no credit by an examination into particular cases. Tho' I believe there was no great blame on either party in this respect, where the case was not connected with politicks.

We are then told "the whigs once flattered themselves they should be able to divide the province between them." I suppose he means, that they should be able to get the honorable and lucrative offices of the province into their hands. If this was true they would be chargeable with only designing what the tories have actually done; with this difference, that the whigs would have done it by saving the liberties and the constitution of the province—whereas the tories have done it by the destruction of both. That the whigs have ambition, a desire of profit, and other passions like other men, it would be foolish to deny: But this writer cannot name a set of men in the whole British empire, who have sacrificed their private interest to their nations honour, and the public good, in so remarkable a manner, as the leading whigs have done, in the two last administrations.

As to "cutting asunder the sinews of government and breaking in pieces the ligament of social life," as far as this has been done, I have proved by incontestible evidence from Bernard's, Hutchinson's and Oliver's letters, that the tories have done it, against all the endeavours of the whigs to preserve them from first to last.

The public is then amused with two instances of the weakness of our government, and these are with equal artifice and injustice, insinuated to be chargeable upon the whigs. But the whigs are as innocent of these as the tories. Malcom was injured as much against the inclinations and judgment of the whigs as the tories. But the real injury he received is exaggerated by this writer. The cruelty of his whipping, and the danger of his life, are too highly coloured.

Malcom was such an oddity, as naturally to excite the curiosity and ridicule of the lowest class of people, wherever he went: had been active in battle against the Regulators in North Carolina, who were thought in Boston to be an injured people. A few weeks before, he had made a seizure at Kennebec River, 150 miles from Boston, and by some imprudence had excited the wrath of the people there, in such a degree, that they tar'd and feather'd him over his clothes. He comes to Boston to complain. The news of it was spread in town. It was a critical time, when the passions of the people were warm. Malcom attacked a lad in the street, and cut his head with a cutlass in return for some words from the boy, which I suppose were irritating. The boy run bleeding thro' the street to his relations, of whom he had many. As he passed the street, the people enquired into the cause of his wounds, and a sudden heat arose against Malcom, which neither Whigs nor Tories, tho' both endeavour'd it, could restrain; and produced the injuries of which he justly complained. But such a coincidence of circumstances, might at any time, and in any place, have produced such an effect; and therefore it is no evidence of the weakness of government. Why he petitioned the General Court, unless he was advised to it by the Tories, to make a noise, I know not. That court had nothing to do with it. He might have bro't his action against the trespassers, but never did. He chose to go to England and get £200 a year, which would make his taring the luckiest incident of his life.

The hospital at Marblehead is another instance, no more owing to the politicks of the times, than the burning of the temple at Ephesus. This hospital was newly erected, much against the will of the multitude. The patients were careless, some of them wantonly so, and others were suspected of designing to spread the Small Pox in the town, which was full of people, who had not passed the distemper. It is needless to be particular, but the apprehension became general, the people arose and burnt the hospital. But the whigs are so little blameable for this, that two of the principle whigs in the province, gentlemen highly esteemed and beloved in the town, even by those who burnt the building, were owners of it. The principles and temper of the times had no share in this, any more than in cutting down the market in Boston, or in demolishing mills and dams in some parts of the country, in order to let the Alewives pass up the streams, forty years ago. Such incidents happen in all governments at times. And it is a fresh proof of the weakness of this writer's cause, that he is driven to such wretched shifts to defend it.

Towards the close of this lengthy speculation, Massachusettensis grows more and more splenetical, peevish, angry and absurd.

He tells us, that in order to avoid the necessity of altering our provincial constitution, government at home made the judges independent of the grants of the general assembly. That is, in order to avoid the hazard of taking the fort by storm, they determined to take it by sap. In order to avoid altering our constitution, they changed it in the most essential manner: for surely by our charter the province was to pay the judges as well as the Governor. Taking away this priviledge, and making them receive their pay from the Crown, was destroying the charter so far forth, and making them dependent on the minister. As to their being dependent on the leading whigs, he means they were dependent on the province. And which is fairest to be dependent on, the province, or on the minister? In all this troublesome period, the leading whigs had never hesitated about granting their salaries, nor ever once moved to have them lessened, nor would the house have listened to them if they had. "This was done," he says, "to make them steady." We know that very well. Steady to what? Steady to the plans of Bernard, Hutchinson, Oliver, North, Mansfield and Bute; which the people thought was steadiness to their ruin, and therefore it was found, that a determined spirit of opposition to it, arose in every part of the province like that to the stamp act.

The chief justice it is true was accused by the house of representatives, of receiving a bribe, a ministerial, not a royal bribe. For the king can do no wrong, altho' he may be deceived in his grant. The minister is accountable. The crime of receiving an illegal patent, is not the less for purchasing it, even of the king himself. Many impeachments have been for such offences.

He talks about attempts to strengthen government, and save our charter. With what modesty can he say this, when he knows that the overthrow of our charter was the very object which the junto had been invariably pursuing for a long course of years. Does he think his readers are to be deceived by such gross arts? But he says "the whigs subverted the charter constitution, abridged the freedom of the house, annihilated the freedom of the board, and rendered the governor a doge of

Venice." The freedom of the house was never abridged, the freedom of the board was never lessened. The governor had as much power as ever. The house and board it is true, would do nothing in favour of parliamentary taxation. Their judgments and consciences were against it, and if they ever had done any thing in favour of it, it would have been through fear and not freedom. The governor found he could do nothing in favour of it, excepting to promote in every department in the state, men who hated the people and were hated by them. Eno' of this he did in all conscience, and after filling offices with men who were despised, he wondered that the officers were not revered. "They," the whigs, "engrossed all the power of the province into their own hands." That is, the house and board were whigs, the grand juries and petit juries were whigs, towns were whigs, the clergy were whigs, the agents were whigs, and wherever you found people you found all whigs excepting those who had commissions from the crown or the governor. This is almost true. And it is to the eternal shame of the tories, that they should pursue their ignis fatuus with such ungovernable fury as they have done, after such repeated and multiplied demonstrations, that the whole people were so universally bent against them. But nothing will satisfy them still, but blood and carnage. The destruction of the Whigs, Charters, English Liberties and all, they must and will have, if it costs the blood of tens of thousands of innocent people. This is the benign temper of the Tories.

This influence of the Whigs he calls a democracy or republic, and then a despotism: two ideas incompatible with each other. A democratical despotism is a contradiction in terms.

He then says that "the good policy of the act for regulating the government in this province, will be the subject of some future paper." But that paper is still to come, and I suspect ever will be. I wish to hear him upon it however.

With this he and the junto ought to have begun. Bernard and the rest in 1764 ought to have published his objections to this government, if they had been honest men, and produced their arguments in favour of the alteration: convinced the people of the necessity of it, and proposed some constitutional plan for effecting it. But the same motives which induced them to take another course, will prevail with Massachusettensis to waive the good policy of the act. He will be much more cunningly employed in labouring to terrify women and children with the horrors of a civil war, and the dread of a division among the people. There lies your fort, Massachusettensis. Make the most of it.

NOVANGLUS

Boston Gazette, February 20, 1775

Massachusettensis [Daniel Leonard] No. XII

To the Inhabitants of the Province of Massachusetts Bay,

MY DEAR COUNTRYMEN,

By an act of parliament made in the twenty-fifth year of the reign of Charles 2d. duties are laid upon goods and merchandise of various kinds, exported from the colonies to foreign countries, or carried from one colony to another, payable on exportation. I will recite a part of it, viz: "For so much of the said commodities as shall be laden and put on board such ship or vessel; that is to say, for sugar, white, the hundred weight, five shillings; and brown and Muscovados, the hundred weight, one shilling and six pence; tobacco, the pound, one penny; cotton wool, the pound, one half-penny; for indigo, two-pence; ginger, the hundred weight, one shilling; logwood, the hundred weight, five pounds; fustic, and all other dying wood, the hundred weight, six-pence; cocoa, the pound, one-penny, to be *levied, collected, and paid*, at such places, and to such collectors and other officers, as shall be appointed in the respective plantations, to collect, levy, and receive the same, before the landing thereof, and under such penalties, both to the officers, and upon the goods, as for non-payment of, or *defrauding his majesty of his customs in England*. And for the better *collecting of the several rates and duties imposed by this act*, be it enacted that this whole business shall be ordered and managed, and the several duties hereby imposed shall be caused *to be levied by the commissioners of the customs in England*, by and under the authority of the lord treasurer of England, or commissioners of the treasury."

It is apparent, from the reasoning of this statute, that these duties were imposed for the sole purpose of revenue. There has lately been a most ingenious play upon the words and expressions *tax, revenue, purpose of raising a revenue, sole purpose of raising a revenue, express purpose of raising a revenue*, as though their being inserted in, or left out of a statute, would make any essential difference in the statute. This is mere playing with words; for if, from the whole tenor of the act, it is evident, that the intent of the legislature was to tax, rather than to regulate the trade, by imposing duties on goods and merchandise, it is to all intents and purposes, an instance of taxation, be the form of words, in which the statute is conceived, what it will. That such was the intent of the legislature, in this instance, any one that will take the pains to read it, will be convinced. There have been divers alterations made in this by subsequent statutes, but some of the above taxes remain, and are collected and paid in the colonies to this day. By an act of the 7th. and 8th. of William and Mary, it is enacted, "that every seaman, whatsoever, that shall serve his majesty, or any other person whatever in any of his majesty's ships or vessels, whatsoever, belonging, or to belong to any subjects of England, or any other his majesty's dominions, shall allow, and there shall be paid out of the wages of every such seaman, to grow due for such his service, six-pence per annum for the better support of the said hospital, and to augment the *revenue* thereof." This tax was imposed in the reign of king William 3d. of blessed memory, and is still levied in the colonies. It would require a volume to recite, or minutely to remark upon all the revenue acts that relate to America. We find them in many reigns, imposing new duties, taking off, or reducing old ones, and making provision for their collection, or new appropriations of them. By an act of the 7th. and 8th. of William and Mary, entitled, "an act for preventing frauds and regulating abuses in the plantations." All former acts respecting the plantations are renewed, and all ships and vessels coming into any port here, are liable to the same regulations and restrictions, as ships in the ports in England are liable to; and enacts, "*That the officers for collecting and managing his majesty's revenue, and inspecting the plantation trade in many of the said plantations*, shall have the same powers and authority for visiting and searching of ships, and taking their entries, and for seizing, or securing, or bringing on shore any of the goods prohibited to be imported or exported into or out of any of the said colonies and plantations, *or for which any duties are payable, or ought to be paid by any of the before mentioned acts, as are provided for the officers of the customs in England.*"

The act of the 9th of Queen Ann, for establishing a post-office, gives this reason for its establishment, and for laying taxes thereby imposed on the carriage of letters in Great

Britain and Ireland, the colonies and plantations in North America and the West Indies, and all other her majesty's dominions and territories, "that the business may be done in such manner as may be most beneficial to the people of these kingdoms, and her majesty may be supplied, and the revenue arising by the said office, better improved, settled, and secured to her majesty, her heirs, and successors." The celebrated patriot, Dr. Franklin, was till lately one of the principal collectors of it. The merit in putting the post-office in America upon such a footing as to yield a large revenue to the crown, is principally ascribed to him by the whigs. I would not wish to detract from the real merit of that gentleman, but had a tory been half so assiduous in increasing the America revenue, Novanglus would have wrote parricide at the end of his name. By an act of the sixth of George 2d. a duty is laid on all foreign rum, molasses, syrups, sugars, and paneles, to be *raised, levied, collected, and paid unto, and for the use of his majesty, his heirs, and successors.* The preamble of an act of the fourth of his present majesty declares, "that *it is just and necessary that a revenue in America for defraying the expences of defending, protecting, and securing the same,*" &c. by which act duties are laid upon foreign sugars, coffee, Madeira wine; upon Portugal, Spanish, and all other wine, except French wine, imported from Great Britain; upon silks, bengals, stuffs, calico, linen cloth, cambric, and lawn, imported from particular places.

Thus, my friends, it is evident, that the parliament has been in the actual, uninterrupted use and exercise of the right claimed by them, to raise a revenue in America, from a period more remote than the grant of the present charter, to this day. These revenue acts have never been called unconstitutional till very lately. Both whigs and tories acknowledged them to be constitutional. In 1764, Governor Bernard wrote and transmitted to his friends, his polity alluded to, and in part recited by Novanglus, wherein he asserts the right or authority of the parliament to tax the colonies. Mr. Otis, whose patriotism, sound policy, profound learning, integrity and honour, is mentioned in strong terms by Novanglus, in the self-same year, in a pamphlet which he published to the whole world, asserts the right or authority of parliament to tax the colonies, as roundly as ever Governor Bernard did, which I shall have occasion to take an extract from hereafter. Mr. Otis was at that time the most popular man in the province, and continued his popularity many years afterwards.

Is it not a most astonishing instance of caprice, or infatuation, that a province, torn from its foundations, should be precipitating itself into a war with Great Britain, because the British parliament asserts its right of raising a revenue in America, inasmuch as the claim of that right is as ancient as the colonies themselves; and there is at present no grievous exercise of it? The parliaments refusing to repeal the act is the ostensible foundation of our quarrel. If we ask the whigs whether the pitiful three penny duty upon a luxurious, unwholesome, foreign commodity gives just occasion for the opposition; they tell us it is the precedent they are contending about, insinuating that it is an innovation. But this ground is not tenable; for a total repeal of the tea-act would not serve us upon the score of precedents. They are numerous without this. The whigs have been extremely partial respecting tea. Poor tea has been made the shibboleth of party, while molasses, wine, coffee, indigo, &c. &c. have been unmolested. A person that drinks New England rum, distilled from molasses, subject to a like duty, is equally deserving of a coat of tar and feathers, with him that drinks tea. A coffee drinker is as culpable as either, viewed in a political light. But, say our patriots, if the British parliament may take a penny from us, without our consent, they may a pound, and so on, till they have filched away all our property. This incessant incantation operates like a spell or charm, and checks the efforts of loyalty in many an honest breast. Let us give it its full weight. Do they mean, that if the parliament has a right to raise a revenue of one penny on the colonies, that they must therefore have a *right* to wrest from us all our property? If this be their meaning, I deny their deduction; for the supreme legislature can have no right to tax any part of the empire to a greater amount, than its just and equitable proportion of the necessary, national expence. This is a line drawn by the constitution itself. Do they mean, that if we admit that the parliament may constitutionally raise one penny upon us for the purposes of revenue, they will probably proceed from light to heavy taxes, till their impositions become grievous and intolerable? This amounts to no more than a denial of the right, lest it should be abused. But an argument drawn from the actual abuse of a power, will not conclude to the illegality of such power, much less will an argument drawn from a capability of its being abused. If it would, we might readily argue away all power, that man is entrusted with. I will admit, that a power of taxation is more liable to abuse, than legislation separately considered; and it would give me pleasure to see some other line drawn; some other barrier erected, than what the constitution has already done, if it be possible, whereby the constitutional authority of the supreme legislature, might be preserved entire, and America be guaranteed in every right and exemption, consistent with her subordination and dependance. But this can only be done by parliament. I repeat I am no advocate for a land tax, or any other kind of internal tax, nor do I think we were in any danger of them. I have not been able to discover one symptom of any such intention in the parliament, since the repeal of the stamp-act. Indeed, the principal speakers of the majority, that repealed the stamp-act drew the line for us, between internal and external taxation, and I think we ought, in honour, justice, and good policy, to have acquiesced therein, at least until there was some burdensome exercise of taxation. For there is but little danger from the latter, that is from duties laid upon trade, as any grievous restriction or imposition on American trade, would be sensibly felt by the British; and I think with Dr. Franklin, that "they (the British nation) have a natural and equitable right to some toll or duty upon merchandizes carried through that part of their dominions, viz: the American seas, towards defraying the expence they are at in ships to maintain the safety of that carriage." These were his words in his examination at the bar of the house, in 1765. *Sed tempora mutantur et nos mutamur in illis.* Before we appeal to heaven for the justice of our cause, we ought to determine with ourselves, some other questions, whether America is not obliged in equity to contribute something toward the national defence: whether the present American revenue, amounts to our proportion: and whether we can, with any tolerable grace, accuse Great Britain of *injustice* in imposing the late duties, when our assemblies were previously called upon, and refused to make any provision for themselves. These, with several imaginary grievances,

not yet particularly remarked upon, I shall consider in review-
ing the publications of Novanglus; a performance which,
though not destitute of ingenuity, I read with a mixture of
grief and indignation, as it seems to be calculated to blow up
every spark of animosity, and to kindle such a flame, as must
inevitably consume a great part of this once happy province,
before it can be extinguished.

MASSACHUSETTENSIS.

*Massachusetts Gazette; and the Boston
Post-Boy and Advertiser*, February 27, 1775

Novanglus No. VI

My Friends,

Such events as the resistance to the stamp act, and to the tea act, particularly the destruction of that which was sent by the ministry in the name of the East India Company, have ever been cautiously spoken of by the Whigs, because they knew the delicacy of the subject, and they lived in continual hopes of a speedy restoration of liberty and peace: But we are now thrown into a situation, which would render any further delicacy upon this point criminal.

Be it remembered then, that there are tumults, seditions, popular commotions, insurrections and civil wars, upon just occasions, as well as unjust.

Grotius B. 1. c. 3 §. 1. observes "that some sort of private war, may be lawfully waged. It is not repugnant to the law of nature, for any one to repel injuries by force.

§. 2. "The liberty allowed before is much restrained, since the erection of tribunals: Yet there are some cases wherein that right still subsists; that is, when the way to legal justice is not open; for the law which forbids a man to pursue his right any other way, ought to be understood with this equitable restriction, that one finds judges to whom he need apply," &c.

Sidney's discourses upon government c. 2. §. 24. " 'Tis in vain to seek a government in all points free from a possibility of civil wars, tumults and seditions: that is a blessing denied to this life, and reserved to compleat the felicity of the next. Seditions, tumults, and wars do arise from mistake or from malice; from just occasions or unjust: Seditions proceeding from malice are seldom or never seen in popular governments; for they are hurtful to the people, and none have ever willingly and knowingly hurt themselves. There may be, and often is, malice in those who excite them; but the people is ever deceived, and whatever is thereupon done, ought to be imputed to error, &c. But in absolute monarchies, almost all the troubles that arise proceed from malice; they cannot be reformed, the extinction of them is exceeding difficult, if they have continued

481

long enough to corrupt the people; and those who appear against them seek only to set up themselves or their friends." The mischiefs designed are often dissembled, or denied, till they are past all possibility of being cured by any other way than force: and such as are by necessity driven to use that remedy, know they must perfect their work or perish. He that draws his sword against the prince, say the French, ought to throw away the scabbard; for tho' the design be never so just, yet the authors are sure to be ruined if it miscarry. Peace is seldom made, and never kept, unless the subject retain such a power in his hands, as may oblige the prince to stand to what is agreed; and in time some trick is found to deprive them of that benefit.

"It may seem strange to some that I mention seditions, tumults and wars, upon just occasions; but I can find no reason to retract the term. God intending that men should live justly with one another, does certainly intend that he or they who do no wrong, should suffer none; and the law that forbids injuries, were of no use, if no penalty might be inflicted, on those that will not obey it. If injustice therefore be evil, and injuries be forbidden, they are also to be punished; and the law instituted for their prevention, must necessarily intend the avenging of such as cannot be prevented. The work of the magistracy is to execute this law; the sword of justice is put into their hands to restrain the fury of those within the society who will not be a law to themselves; and the sword of war to protect the people against the violence of foreigners. This is without exception, and would be in vain if it were not. But the magistrate who is to protect the people from injury, may, and is often known, not to have done it: he sometimes renders his office *useless by neglecting to do justice*; sometimes *mischievous by overthrowing it*. This strikes at the root of God's general ordinance, that there should be laws; and the particular ordinances of all societies that appoint such as seem best to them. *The magistrate therefore is comprehended under both, and subject to both, as well as private men.*

"The ways of preventing or punishing injuries are judicial or extrajudicial. Judicial proceedings are of force against those who submit, or may be brought to tryal, but are of no effect against those who resist, and are of such power that they cannot be constrained. It were absurd to cite a man to appear before a tribunal *who can awe the judges, or has armies to defend him*; and impious to think that he who has added treachery to his other crimes, and usurped a power above the law, should be protected by the enormity of his wickedness: Legal proceedings, therefore, are to be used when the delinquent submits to the law; *and all are just; when he will not be kept in order by the legal.*

"The word sedition, is generally applied to all, numerous assemblies, without or against the authority of the magistrate, or of those who assume that power. Athaliah and Jezebel were more ready to cry out treason, than David, &c.

"Tumult is from the disorderly manner of those assemblies, where things can seldom be done regularly; and war is that 'decertatio per vim,' or trial by force, to which men come, when other ways are ineffectual.

"If the laws of God and men, are therefore of no effect, when the magistracy is left at liberty to break them; and if the lusts of those who are too strong for the tribunals of justice, cannot be otherwise restrained than by sedition, tumults and war, those seditions, tumults and wars, are justified by the laws of God and man.

"I will not take upon me to enumerate all the cases in which this may be done, but content myself with three, which have most frequently given occasion for proceedings of this kind. The first is, when one or more men take upon them the power and name of a magistracy, to which they are not justly called. The second, when one or more being justly called, continue in their magistracy longer than the laws by which they are called, do prescribe. And the third, when he or they, who are rightly called, do assume a power, though within the time prescribed, that the law does not give; or turn that which the law does give, to an end different and contrary to that which is intended by it.

"The same course is justly used against a legal magistrate, who takes upon him to exercise a power which the law does not give: for in that respect he is a private man, (Quia,) as Grotius says, (eatenus non habet imperium,) and may be restrained as well as any other, because he is not set up to do what he lists, but what the law appoints for the good of the people; and as he has no other power than what the law allows, so the same law limits and directs the exercise of that which he has."

Puffendorf's law of nature and nations L. 7. c. 8 §. 5 and 6. Barbeyrac's note on §. 6. "When we speak of a tyrant that may lawfully be dethroned, we do not mean by the people, the vile populace or rabble of the country, or the cabal of a small number of factious persons; but the greater and more judicious part of the subjects of all ranks. Besides the tyranny must be so notorious and evidently clear, as to leave no body any room to doubt of it, &c. Now a prince may easily avoid making himself so universally suspected and odious to his subjects: for as Mr. Locke says, in his treatise of civil government c. 18. §. 209. 'It is as impossible for a governor, if he really means the good of the people, and the preservation of them and the laws together, not to make them see and feel it; as it is for the father of a family, not to let his children see he loves and takes care of them.' And therefore the general insurrection of a whole nation does not deserve the name of rebellion. We may see what Mr. Sidney says upon this subject in his discourse concerning government c. 3. §. 36. 'Neither are subjects bound to stay till the prince has entirely finished the chains which he is preparing for them, and has put it out of their power to oppose. 'Tis sufficient that all the advances which he makes are manifestly tending to their oppression, that he is marching boldly on to the ruin of the state.' In such a case, says Mr. Locke admirably well, ubi supra §. 210., 'How can a man any more hinder himself from believing in his own mind, which way things are going, or from casting about to save himself, than he could from believing the captain of the ship he was in, was carrying him and the rest of his company to Algiers, when he found him always steering that course, though cross winds, leaks in his ship, and want of men and provisions, did often force him to turn his course another way for sometime, which he steadily return'd to again, as soon as the winds, weather, and other circumstances would let him.' This chiefly takes place with respect to kings, whose power is limitted by fundamental laws.

" 'If it is objected, that the people being ignorant, and always discontented, to lay the foundation of government in the unsteady opinion and the uncertain humour of the people, is to expose it to certain ruin; the same author will answer you, that on the contrary, people are not so easily got out of their old forms as some are apt to suggest. England, for instance, notwithstanding the many revolutions that have been seen in that kingdom, has always kept to its old legislative of king, lords and commons: and whatever provocations have made the crown to be taken from some of their princes heads, they never carried the people so far as to place it in another line. But 'twill be said, this hypothesis lays a ferment for frequent rebellion. No more, says Mr. Locke, than any other hypothesis. For when the people are made miserable, and find themselves exposed to the ill usage of arbitrary power; cry up their governors as you will for sons of Jupiter, let them be sacred and divine, descended or authorised from heaven; give them out for whom or what you please, the same will happen. The people generally ill treated, and contrary to right, will be ready upon any occasion to ease themselves of a burden that sits heavy upon them. 2. Such revolutions happen not upon every little mismanagement in public affairs. Great mistakes in the ruling part, many wrong and inconvenient laws, and all the slips of human frailty will be borne by the people, without mutiny and murmur. 3. This power in the people of providing for their safety anew by a legislative, when their legislators have acted contrary to their trust, by invading their property, is the best fence against rebellion, and the probablest means to hinder it; for rebellion being an opposition, not the persons, but authority, which is founded only in the constitutions and laws of the government; those whoever they be, *who by force break through, and by force justify the violation of them, are truly and properly rebels.* For when men by entering into society, and civil government, have excluded force, and introduced laws for the preservation of property, peace and unity, among themselves; those who set up force again, in opposition to the laws, do rebellare, that is, do bring back again the state of war, and are properly rebels, as the author shews. In the last place, he demonstrates, that there are also greater inconveniencies in allowing all to those that govern, than in granting something to the people. But it will be said, that ill affected and factious men may spread among the people, and make them believe that the prince or legislative, act contrary to their trust, when they only make use of their due prerogative. To this Mr. Locke answers, that the people however is to judge of all that; because no body can better judge whether his trustee for deputy acts well, and according to the trust reposed in him, than he who deputed him. He might make the like query, (says Mr. LeClark, from whom this extract is taken) and ask, whether the people being oppressed by an authority which they set up, but for their own good, it is just, that those, who are vested with this authority, and of which they are complaining, should themselves be judges of the complaints made against them? The greatest flatterers of kings, dare not say, that the people are obliged to suffer absolutely all their humours, how irregular soever they be; and therefore must confess, that when no regard is had to their complaints, the very foundations of society are destroyed; the prince and people are in a state of war with each other, like two independent states that are doing themselves justice, and acknowledge no person upon earth, who in a sovereign manner, can determine the disputes between them,'" &c.

If there is any thing in these quotations, which is applicable to the destruction of the tea, or any other branch of our subject, it is not my fault: I did not make it.—Surely Grotius, Puffendorf, Barbeyrac, Lock, Sidney, and LeClerk, are writers, of sufficient weight, to put in the scale against the mercenary scriblers in New-York and Boston, who have the unexampled impudence and folly, to call these which are revolution principles in question, and to ground their arguments upon passive obedience as a corner stone. What an opinion must these writers have of the principles of their patrons, the Lords Bute, Mansfield and North, when they hope to recommend themselves by reviving that stupid doctrine, which has been infamous so many years. Dr. Sachevaril himself tells us that his sermons were burnt by the hands of the common hangman, by the order of the king, lords and commons, in order to fix an eternal and indelible brand of infamy on that doctrine.

In the Gazette of January the 2d, Massachusettensis entertains you with an account of his own important self. This is a subject which he has very much at heart, but it is of no consequence to you or me, and therefore little need be said of it: if he had such a stand in the community, that he could have seen all the political manœuvres, it is plain he must have shut his eyes, or he never could have mistaken so grossly, causes for effects, and effects for causes.

He undertakes to point out the principles and motives upon which the Blockade Act was made, which were according to him, the destruction of the East-India Company's Tea. He might have said more properly the Ministerial Tea: for such it was, and the company are no losers: they have received from the public treasury compensation for it.

Then we are amused with a long discourse about the nature of the British government, commerce, agriculture, arts, manufactures, regulations of trade, custom house officers, which as it has no relation to the subject, I shall pass over.

The case is shortly this: The East-India company, by their contract with government, in their charter and statute, are bound, in consideration of their important profitable privileges, to pay to the public treasury, a revenue, annually, of four hundred thousand pounds sterling, so long as they can hold up their Dividends at twelve per cent. and no longer.

The mistaken policy of the ministry, in obstinately persisting in their claim of right to tax America, and refusing to repeal the duty on Tea, with those on glass, paper and paint, had induced all America, except a few merchants in Boston, most of whom were closely connected with the junto, to refuse to import Tea from Great Britain: the consequence of which was a kind of stagnation in the affairs of the company, and an immense accumulation of tea in their stores, which they could not sell. This, among other causes, contributed to affect their credit, and their Dividends were on the point of falling below twelve per cent, and consequently the government was upon the point of losing 400,000 l. sterling a year of revenue. The company solicited the ministry to take off the duty in America: but they adhering to their plan of taxing the colonies and establishing a precedent, framed an act to enable the company to send their tea directly to America. This was admired as a master-piece of policy. It was tho't they would accomplish four great purposes at once: establish their precedent of taxing America; raise a large revenue there by the duties; save the credit of the company; and the 400,000 l. to the government. The company however, were so little pleased with this, that there were great debates among the directors, whether they should risque it, which were finally determined by a majority of one only, and that one the chairman, being unwilling as it is said to interfere in the dispute between the minister and the colonies, and uncertain what the result would be: and this small majority was not obtained, as it is said, until a sufficient intimation was given that the company should not be losers.

When these designs were made known, it appeared, that American politicians were not to be deceived: that their fight was as quick and clear as the minister's, and that they were as steady to their purpose, as he was to his. This was tho't by all the colonies, to be the precise point of time, when it became absolutely necessary to make a stand. If the tea should be landed, it would be sold; if sold the duties would amount to a large sum, which would be instantly applied to increase the friends and advocates for more duties, and to divide the people; and the company would get such a footing, that no opposition afterwards could ever be effectual. And as soon as the duties on tea should be established, they would be ranked among post-office fees, and other precedents, and used as arguments, both of the right and expediency of laying on others, perhaps on all the necessaries, as well as conveniences and luxuries of life. The whole continent was united in the sentiment, that all opposition to parliamentary taxation must be given up forever, if this critical moment was neglected. Accordingly, New-York and Philadelphia determined that the ships should be sent back; and Charlestown, that the tea should be stored and locked up,—this was attended with no danger in that city, because they are fully united in sentiment and affection, and have no *Junto* to perplex them. Boston was under greater difficulties. The Consignees at New York and Philadelphia most readily resigned. The Consignees at Boston, the children, cousins, and most intimate connections of governor Hutchinson, refused. I am very sorry that I cannot stir a single step in develloping the causes of my country's miseries, without stumbling upon this gentleman. But so it is. From the near relation and most intimate connection of the consignees with him, there is great cause of jealousy, if not a violent presumption, that he was at the bottom of all this business, that he had plann'd it, in his confidential letters with Bernard, and both of them joined in suggesting and recommending it to the ministry. Without this supposition, it is difficult to account for the obstinacy with which the Consignees refused to resign, and the governor to let the vessel go. However this might be, Boston is the only place upon the continent, perhaps in the world, which ever breeds a species of misanthropos, who will persist in their schemes for their private interest, with such obstinacy, in opposition to the public good; disoblige all their fellow-citizens for a little pelf, and make themselves odious and infamous, when they might be respected and esteemed. It must be said, however, in vindication of the town, that this breed is spawned chiefly by the Junto. The Consignees would not resign; the custom house refused clearances; governor Hutchinson refused passes by the castle. The question then was, with many, whether the governor, officers, and consignees should be compelled to send the ships hence? An army and navy was at hand, and bloodshed was apprehended. At last, when the continent, as well as the town and province, were waiting the issue of this deliberation with the utmost anxiety, a number of persons, in the night, put them out of suspense, by an oblation to Neptune. I have heard some gentlemen say, "this was a very unjustifiable proceeding"—"that if they had gone at noonday, and in their ordinary habits, and drowned it in the face of the world, it would have been a meritorious, a most glorious action." But to go in the night, and much more in disguise, they tho't very inexcuseable.

"The revenue was not the consideration before parliament," says Massachusettensis. Let who will, believe him. But if it was not, the danger to America was the same. I take no notice of the idea of a monopoly. If it had been only a monopoly, (tho' in this light it would have been a very great grievance) it would not have excited, nor in the opinion of any one justified the step that was taken. It was an attack upon a fundamental principle of the Constitution, and upon that supposition was resisted, after multitudes of petitions to no purpose, and because there was no tribunal in the Constitution, from whence redress could have been obtained.

There is one passage so pretty, that I cannot refuse myself the pleasure of transcribing it. "A smuggler and a whig are cousin germans, the offspring of two sisters, avarice and ambition. They had been playing into each other's hands a long time. The smuggler received protection from the whig, and he in his turn received support from the smuggler. The illicit trader now demanded protection from his kinsman, and it would have been unnatural in him to have refused it; and beside, an opportunity presented of strengthning his own interest."

The wit, and the beauty of the style in this place, seem to have quite inraptured the lively juvenile imagination of this writer. The truth of the fact he never regards, any more than the justice of the sentiment. Some years ago, the smugglers might be pretty equally divided between the whigs and the tories: Since that time, they have almost all married into the tory families, for the sake of dispensations and indulgencies. If I were to let myself into secret history, I could tell very diverting stories of smuggling tories in New-York and Boston,—Massachusettensis is quarrelling with some of his best friends. Let him learn more discretion.

We are then told that "the consignees offered to store the tea, under the care of the selectmen, or a committee of the town." This expedient might have answered, if none of the junto, nor any of their connections had been in Boston. But is it a wonder, that the selectmen declined accepting such a deposit? They supposed they should be answerable, and no body doubted that tories might be found who would not scruple to set fire to the store, in order to make them liable. Besides if the tea was landed, though only to be stored, the duty must be paid, which it was tho't was giving up the point.

Another consideration which had great weight, was, the other colonies were grown jealous of Boston, and tho't it already deficient in point of punctuality, against the dutied articles: and if the tea was once stored, artifices might be used, if not violence, to disperse it abroad: But if through the continual vigilance and activity of the committee and the people, thro' a whole winter, this should be prevented; yet one thing was certain, that the tories would write to the other colonies and to England, thousands of falshoods concerning it, in order to induce the ministry to persevere, and to sow jealousies and create divisions among the colonies.

Our acute logician then undertakes to prove the destruction of the tea unjustifiable, even upon the principle of the whigs, that the duty was unconstitutional. The only argument he uses is this: that "unless we purchase the tea, we shall never pay the duty." This argument is so frivolous, and has been so often confuted and exposed, that if the party had any other, I think they would relinquish this. Where will it carry us? If a duty was laid upon our horses, we may walk; if upon our butchers meat, we may live upon the produce of the dairy; and if that should be taxed, we may subsist as well as our fellow slaves in Ireland, upon Spanish potatoes and cold water. If a thousand pounds was laid upon the birth of every child, if children are not begotten, none will be born; if, upon every marriage, no duties will be paid, if all the young gentlemen and ladies agree to live batchellors and maidens.

In order to form a rational judgment of the quality of this transaction, and determine whether it was good or evil, we must go to the bottom of this great controversy. If parliament has a right to tax us, and legislate for us, in all cases, the destruction of the tea was unjustifiable; but if the people of America are right in their principle, that parliament has no such right, that the act of parliament is null and void, and it is lawful to oppose and resist it, the question then is, whether the destruction was necessary? For every principle of reason, justice and prudence, in such cases, demands that the least mischief shall be done; the least evil among a number shall always be preferr'd.

All men are convinced that it was impracticable to return it, and rendered so by Mr. Hutchinson and the Boston consignees. Whether to have stored it would have answered the end, or been a less mischief than drowning it, I shall leave to the judgment of the public. The other colonies, it seems, have no scruples about it, for we find that whenever tea arrives in any of them, whether from the East India company, or any other quarter, it never fails to share the fate of that in Boston. All men will agree that such steps ought not to be taken, but in cases of absolute necessity, and that such necessity must be very clear. But most people in America now think the destruction of the Boston tea, was absolutely necessary, and therefore right and just. It is very true, they say, if the whole people had been united in sentiment, and equally stable in their resolution, not to buy or drink it, there might have been a reason for preserving it; but the people here were not so virtuous or so happy. The British ministry had plundered the people by illegal taxes, and applied the money in salaries and pensions, by which devices, they had insidiously attached to their party, no inconsiderable number of persons, some of whom were of family, fortune and influence, tho' many of them were of desperate fortunes, each of whom, however, had his circle of friends, connections and dependants, who were determined to drink tea, both as evidence of their servility to administration, and their contempt and hatred of the people. These it was impossible to restrain without violence, perhaps bloodshed, certainly without hazarding more than the tea was worth. To this tribe of the *wicked*, they say, must be added another, perhaps more numerous, of the *weak*; who never could be brought to think of the consequences of their actions, but would gratify their appetites, if they could come at the means. What numbers are there in every community, who have no providence, or prudence in their private affairs, but will go on indulging the present appetite, prejudice, or passion, to the ruin of their estates and families, as well as their own health and characters! How much larger is the number of those who have no foresight for the public, or consideration of the freedom of posterity? Such an abstinence from the tea, as would have avoided the establishment of a precedent, depended on the unanimity of the people, a felicity that was unattainable. Must the wise, the virtuous and worthy part of the community, who constituted a very great majority, surrender their liberty, and involve their posterity in misery in complaisance to a detestable, tho' small party of knaves, and a despicable, tho' more numerous company of fools?

If Boston could have been treated like other places, like New-York and Philadelphia, the tea might have gone home from thence as it did from those cities. That inveterate, desperate junto, to whom we owe all our calamities, were determined to hurt us in this, as in all other cases as much as they could. It is to be hoped they will one day repent and be forgiven, but it is very hard to forgive without repentance. When the news of this event arrived in England, it excited such passions in the minister as nothing could restrain; his resentment was inkindled into revenge, rage, and madness; his veracity was piqued, as his master piece of policy, proved but a bubble: The bantling

was the fruit of a favourite amour, and no wonder that his natural affection was touched when he saw it dispatched before
his eyes. His grief and ingenuity, if he had any, were affected at
the thought that he had misled the East India company, so
much nearer to destruction, and that he had rendered the
breach between the kingdom and the colonies almost irrecon-
cileable: his shame was excited because opposition had gained
a triumph over him, and the three kingdoms were laughing at
him for his obstinacy and his blunders: instead of relieving
the company he had hastened its ruin: instead of establishing
the absolute and unlimited sovereignty of parliament over the
colonies, he had excited a more decisive denial of it, and resistance to it. An election drew nigh and he dreaded the resentment even of the corrupted electors.

In this state of mind bordering on despair, he determines to
strike a bold stroke. Bernard was near and did not fail to embrace the opportunity, to push the old systems of the junto. By
attacking all the colonies together, by the stamp-act, and the
paint and glass act, they had been defeated. The charter constitution of the Massachusetts-Bay, had contributed greatly to
both these defeats. Their representatives were too numerous,
and too frequently elected, to be corrupted: their people had
been used to consider public affairs in their town-meetings:
their councellors were not absolutely at the nod of a minister
or governor, but were once a year equally dependent on the
governor and the two houses. Their grand jurors were elective
by the people, their petit jurors were returned merely by lot.
Bernard and the junto rightly judged that by this constitution
the people had a check, on every branch of power, and therefore as long as it lasted, parliamentary taxations, &c. could
never be inforced.

Bernard, publishes his select letters, and his principles of
polity: his son writes in defence of the Quebec bill: hireling
garretteers were employed to scribble millions of lyes against
us, in pamphlets and news papers: and setters employed in the
coffee houses, to challenge or knock down all the advocates
for the poor Massachusetts. It was now determined, instead of
attacking the colonies together, tho' they had been all equally
opposed to the plans of the ministry, and the claims of parliament, and therefore upon ministerial principles equally guilty,

to handle them one by one; and to begin with Boston and the Massachusetts. The destruction of the tea was a fine event for scribblers and speechifyers to declaim upon; and there was an hereditary hatred of New-England, in the minds of many in England, on account of their non conforming principles. It was likewise thought there was a similar jealousy and animosity in the other colonies against New England; that they would therefore certainly desert her; that she would be intimidated and submit; and then the minister among his own friends, would acquire immortal honour, as the most able, skilfull and undaunted statesman of the age.

The port bill, charter bill, murder bill, Quebec bill, making all together such a frightful system, as would have terrified any people, who did not prefer liberty to life, were all concerted at once: but all this art and violence have not succeeded. This people under great trials and dangers, have discovered great abilities and virtues, and that nothing is so terrible to them as the loss of their liberties. If these arts and violences are persisted in, and still greater concerted, and carried on against them, the world will see that their fortitude, patience and magnanimity will rise in proportion.

"Had Cromwell," says our what I shall call him? "had the guidance of the national ire, your proud capital had been level'd with the dust." Is it any breach of charity to suppose that such an event as this, would have been a gratification to this writer? Can we otherwise account for his indulging himself in a thought so diabolical? Will he set up Cromwell as a model for his deified lords, Bute, Mansfield and North? If he should, there is nothing in the whole history of him so cruel as this. All his conduct in Ireland, as exceptionable as any part of his whole life, affords nothing that can give the least probability to the idea of this writer. The rebellion in Ireland, was most obstinate, and of many years duration; 100,000 protestants had been murdered in a day, in cold blood, by papists, and therefore Cromwell might plead some excuse, that cruel severities were necessary, in order to restore any peace to that kingdom: But all this will not justify him; for as has been observed by an historian, upon his conduct in this instance, "men are not to divest themselves of humanity, and turn themselves into devils, because policy may suggest that they will succeed better as

devils than as men"! But is there any parity or similitude
between a rebellion of a dozen years standing, in which many
battles had been fought, many thousands fallen in war, and
100,000 massacred in a day; and the drowning three cargoes
of tea? To what strains of malevolence, to what flights of diabolical fury, is not tory rage capable of transporting men!

"The whigs saw their ruin connected with a compliance
with the terms of opening the Port."—They saw the ruin of
their country connected in it: But they might have easily voted
a compliance, for they were undoubtedly a vast majority, and
have enjoyed the esteem and affection of their fellow slaves to
their last hours: Several of them could have paid for the Tea,
and never have felt the loss. They knew they must suffer, vastly
more, than the Tea was worth, but they thought they acted for
America and posterity; and that they ought not to take such a
step without the advice of the colonies. They have declared
our cause their own—that they never will submit to a precedent in any part of the united colonies, by which Parliament
may take away Wharves and other lawful estates, or demolish
Charters; for if they do, they have a moral certainty that in the
course of a few years, every right of Americans will be taken
away, and governors and councils, holding at the will of a Minister, will be the only legislatives, in the colonies.

A pompous account of the addressors of Mr. Hutchinson,
then follows. They consisted of his relations, his fellow labourers in the tory vineyard, and persons whom he had raised in
the course of four administrations, Shirley's, Pownal's, Bernard's and his own, to places in the province. Considering the
industry that was used, and the vast number of persons in the
province, who had received commissions under government
upon his recommendation, the small number of subscribers
that was obtained, is among a thousand demonstrations of the
unanimity of this people. If it had been thought worth while
to have procured a remonstrance against him, fifty thousand
subscribers might have been easily found. Several gentlemen of
property were among these addressers, and some of fair character, but their acquaintance and friendships lay among the
junto and, their subalterns entirely: Besides did these addressers approve the policy or justice of any one of the bills,
which were passed the last session of the late parliament? Did

they acknowledge the unlimited authority of parliament? The Middlesex magistrates remonstrated against taxation: But they were flattered with hopes, that Mr. Hutchinson would get the port-bill, &c. repealed, that is, that he would have undone all, which every body but themselves knew he has been doing these fifteen years.

"But these patriotic endeavours, were defeated." By what? "By an invention of the fertile brain of one of our party agents, called a committee of correspondence. *This is the foulest, subtlest and most venemous serpent that ever issued from the eggs of sedition.*"

I should rather call it, the *Ichneumon*, a very industrious, active, and useful animal, which was worshipped in Ægypt as a divinity, because it defended their country from the ravages of the crocodiles. It was the whole occupation of this little creature to destroy those wily and ravenous monsters. It crushed their eggs, wherever they laid them, and with a wonderful address and courage, would leap into their mouths, penetrate their entrails, and never leave until it destroyed them.

If the honor of this invention is due to the gentleman, who is generally understood by the "party agent" of Massachusettensis, it belongs to one, to whom America has erected a statue in her heart, for his integrity, fortitude and perseverance in her cause. That the invention itself is very useful and important, is sufficiently clear, from the unlimited wrath of the tories against it, and from the gall which this writer discharges upon it. Almost all mankind have lost their liberties, thro' ignorance, inattention and disunion. These committees are admirably calculated to diffuse knowledge, to communicate intelligence, and promote unanimity. If the high whigs are generally of such committees, it is because the freeholders who choose them, are such, and therefore prefer their peers. The tories, high or low, if they can make interest enough among the people may get themselves chosen, and promote the great cause of parliamentary revenues, and the other sublime doctrines and misteries of toryism. That these committees think themselves "amenable to none," is false: for there is not a man upon any one of them, who does not acknowledge himself to hold his place, at the pleasure of his constituents, and to be accountable to them, whenever they demand it. If the committee of the town of

Boston, was appointed for a special purpose at first, their commission has been renewed from time to time; they have been frequently thank'd by the town for their vigilance, activity and disinterested labours in the public service. Their doings have been laid before the town and approved of by it. The malice of the tories has several times swelled open their bosoms, and broke out into the most intemperate and illiberal invectives against it: but all in vain. It has only served to shew the impotence of the tories, and increase the importance of the committee.

These committees cannot be too religiously careful of the exact truth of the intelligence they receive or convey; nor too anxious for the rectitude and purity of the measures they propose or adopt: they should be very sure that they do no injury to any man's person, property or character: and they are generally persons of such worth, that I have no doubt of their attention to these rules; and therefore that the reproaches of this writer are mere slanders.

If we recollect how many states have lost their liberties, merely from want of communication with each other, and union among themselves, we shall think that these committees may be intended by providence to accomplish great events. What the eloquence and talents of negociation of Demosthenes himself could not effect, among the states of Greece, might have been effected by so simple a device. Castile, Arragon, Valencia, Majorca, &c. all complained of oppression under Charles the fifth, flew out into transports of rage, and took arms against him. But they never consulted or communicated with each other. They resisted separately, and were separately subdued. Had Don Juan Padilla, or his wife, have been possessed of the genius to invent a committee of correspondence, perhaps the liberties of the Spanish nation might have remained to this hour, without any necessity to have had recourse to arms. Hear the opinion of Dr. Robertson. "While the spirit of disaffection was so general among the Spaniards, and so many causes concurred in precipitating them into such violent measures, in order to obtain the redress of their grievances, it may appear strange that the male-contents in the different kingdoms should have carried on their operations without any mutual concert, or even any intercourse with each other. By uniting their councils and arms, they might have acted both with greater force, and with more effect. The appearance of a national confederacy would have rendered it no less respectable among the people, than formidable to the crown; and the emperor, unable to resist such a combination, must have complied with any terms which the members of it thought fit to prescribe."

That it is owing to those committees that so many persons have been found to recant and resign, and so many others to fly to the army, is a mistake, for the same things would have taken place, if such a committee had never been in being, and such persons would probably have met with much rougher usage. This writer asks, "have not these persons as good a right to think and act for themselves as the whigs?" I answer yes. But if any man, whig or tory shall take it into his head to think for himself, that he has a right to take my property, without my consent, however tender I may be of the right of private judgment and the freedom of thought, this is a point in which I shall be very likely to differ from him, and to think for myself that I have a right to resist him. If any man should think, ever so conscienciously that the roman catholic religion is better than the protestant, or that the French government is preferable to the British constitution in its purity; Protestants and Britons, will not be so tender of that man's conscience as to suffer him to introduce his favourite religion and government. So the well bred gentlemen who are so polite as to think, that the charter constitution of this province, ought to be abolished, and another introduced wholly at the will of a minister or the crown; or that our ecclesiastical constitution is bad, and high church ought to come in, few people will be so tender of these consciences or complaisant to such polite taste, as to suffer the one or the other to be established. There are certain prejudices among the people, so strong, as to be irresistible. Reasoning is vain, and opposition idle. For example, there are certain popular maxims and precepts, call'd the ten commandments. Suppose a number of fine gentlemen, superior to the prejudices of education, should discover that these were made for the common people, and are too illiberal for gentlemen of refined taste to observe, and accordingly should engage in secret confidential correspondences to procure an act of parliament, to abolish the whole decalogue, or to exempt them from all obligation to observe it; if they should succeed, and their letters be detected, such is the force of prejudice, and deep habits among the lower sort of people, that it is much to be questioned, whether those refined genius's would be allowed to enjoy themselves in the latitude of their sentiments. I once knew a man, who had studied Jacob Beckman and other mystic's, until he conscienciously thought the millennium commenced, and all human authority at an end: that the saints only had a right to property; and to take from sinners any thing they wanted. In this persuasion, he very honestly stole a horse. Mankind pitied the poor man's infirmity, but thought it however their duty to confine him that he might steal no more.

The freedom of thinking was never yet extended in any country so far as the utter subversion of all religion and morality; nor as the abolition of the laws and constitution of the country.

But "are not these persons as closely connected with the interest of their country as the whigs?" I answer, they are not: they have found an interest in opposition to that of their country, and are making themselves rich and their families illustrious, by depressing and destroying their country. But "do not their former lives and conversations appear to have been regulated by principles as much as those of the whigs?" A few of them, it must be acknowledged, untill seduced by the bewitching charms of wealth and power, appeared to be men of principle. But taking the Whigs and Tories on an average, the balance of principle, as well as genius, learning, wit and wealth, is infinitely in favour of the former. As to some of these fugitives, they are known to be men of no principles at all in religion, morals or government.

But the "policy" is questioned, and you are asked if you expect to make converts by it? As to the policy or impolicy of it, I have nothing to say: but we don't expect to make converts of most of those persons by any means whatever, as long as they have any hopes that the ministry will place and pension them. The instant these hopes are extinguished, we all know they will be converted of course. Converts from places and pensions are only to be made by places and pensions, all other reasoning is idle; these are the *Penultima Ratio* of the Tories, as field pieces are the *ultima.*

That we are not "unanimous is certain." But there are nineteen on one side to one on the other, through the province. And ninety nine out of an hundred of the remaining twentieth part can be fairly shewn to have some sinister private view, to induce him to profess his opinion.

Then we are threatened high, that "this is a changeable world, and times rolling wheel may e'er long bring them uppermost, and in that case we should not wish to have them fraught with resentment."

To all this we answer, without ceremony, that they always have been uppermost, in every respect, excepting only the esteem and affection of the people; that they always have been fraught with resentment (even their cunning and policy have not restrained them) and we know they always will be.—That they have indulged their resentment and malice, in every instance in which they had power to do it: and we know that their revenge will never have any other limits than their power.

Then this consistent writer, begins to flatter the people, "he appeals to their good sense, he knows they have it." The same people, whom he has so many times represented as mad and foolish.

"I know you are loyal and friends to good order." This is the same people that in the whole course of his writings, he has represented as continuing for ten years together in a continual state of disorder, demolishing the Chair, Board, Supreme Court, and encouraging all sorts of riots, insurrections, treason and rebellion. Such are the shifts to which a man is driven when he aims at carrying a point not at discovering truth.

The people are then told that "they have been insidiously taught to believe that Great Britain is rapacious, cruel and vindictive, and envies us the inheritance purchased by the sweat and blood of our ancestors." The people do not believe this— they will not believe it: On the contrary, they believe if it was not for scandals constantly transmitted from this province by the Tories, the nation would redress our grievances. Nay as little as they reverence the Ministry, they even believe that the Lords North, Mansfield and Bute, would relieve them, and would have done it long ago, if they had known the truth. The moment this is done "long live our gracious king and happiness to Britain," will resound from one end of the province to the other: but it requires a very little foresight to determine, that no other plan of governing the province and the colonies, will ever restore a harmony between the two countries, but desisting from the plan of taxing them and interfering with their internal concerns, and returning to that system of colony administration, which nature dictated, and experience for one hundred and fifty years found useful.

NOVANGLUS

Boston Gazette, February 27, 1775

Massachusettensis [Daniel Leonard] No. XIII

To the Inhabitants of the Province of Massachusetts Bay,

MY DEAR COUNTRYMEN,

Novanglus, and all others, have an indisputable right to publish their sentiments and opinions to the world, provided they conform to truth, decency, and the municipal laws, of the society of which they are members. He has wrote with a professed design of exposing the errors and sophistry which he supposes are frequent in my publications. His design is so far laudable, and I intend to correct them wherever he convinces me there is an instance of either. I have no objection to the minutest disquisition; contradiction and disputation, like the collision of flint and steel, often strike out new light; the bare opinions of either of us, unaccompanied by the grounds and reasons upon which they were formed, must be considered only as propositions made to the reader, for him to adopt, or reject as his own reason may judge, or feelings dictate. A large proportion of the labours of Novanglus consist in denials of my allegations in matters of such public notoriety, as that no reply is necessary. He has alleged many things destitute of foundation; those that affect the main object of our pursuit, but remotely, if at all, I shall pass by without particular remark; others, of a more interesting nature, I shall review minutely. After some general observations upon Massachesettensis, he slides into a most virulent attack upon particular persons, by names, with such incomparable ease, that shews him to be a great proficient in the modern art of detraction and calumny. He accuses the late governor Shirley, governor Hutchinson, the late lieutenant governor Oliver, the late judge Russell, Mr. Paxton, and brigadier Ruggles, of a conspiracy to enslave their country. The charge is high coloured; if it be just, they merit the epithets dealt about so indiscriminately, of enemies to their country. If it be groundless, Novanglus has acted the part of an assassin, in thus attempting to destroy the reputation of the living; and of something worse than an assassin, in entering those hallowed mansions, where the wicked commonly cease from troubling, and the weary are at rest, to disturb the repose of the dead. That the charge is groundless respecting governor Bernard, governor Hutchinson, and the late lieutenant governor, I dare assert, because they have been acquitted of it in such a manner, as every good citizen must acquiesce in. Our house of representatives, acting as the grand inquest of the province, presented them before the king in council, and after a full hearing, they were acquitted with honour, and the several impeachments dismissed, as groundless, vexatious, and scandalous. The accusation of the house was similar to this of Novanglus; the court they chose to institute their suit in, was of competent and high jurisdiction, and its decision final. This is a sufficient answer to the state charges made by this writer, so far as they respect the governors Bernard, Hutchinson and Oliver, whom he accuses as principals; and it is a general rule, that if the principal be innocent, the accessary cannot be guilty. A determination of a constitutional arbiter ought to seal up the lips of even prejudice itself, in silence; otherwise litigation must be endless. This calumniator, nevertheless, has the effrontery to renew the charge in a public news paper, although thereby he arraigns our most gracious Sovereign, and the lords of the privy council, as well as the gentlemen he has named. Not content with wounding the honour of judges, counsellors and governors, with missile weapons, darted from an obscure corner, he now aims a blow at majesty itself. Any one may accuse; but accusation, unsupported by proof, recoils upon the head of the accuser. It is entertaining enough to consider the crimes and misdemeanors alleged, and then examine the evidence he adduces, stript of the false glare he has thrown upon it.

The crimes are these; the persons named by him conspired together to *enslave* their country, in consequence of a plan, the outlines of which have been drawn by sir Edmund Andross and others, and handed down by tradition to the present times. He tells us that governor Shirley, in 1754, communicated the profound secret, the great design of taxing the colonies by act of parliament, to the sagacious gentleman, eminent philosopher, and distinguished patriot, Dr. Franklin. The profound secret is this; after the commencement of hostilities between the English and French colonies in the last war, a convention of committees from several provinces were called by the king, to agree upon some general plan of defence. The principal difficulty they met with was in devising means whereby each colony might be obliged to contribute its pro-portionable part. General Shirley proposed *that application should be made to parliament to impower the committees of the several colonies to tax the whole according to their several propor-tions.* This plan was adopted by the convention, and approved of by the assembly in New York, who passed a resolve in these words: "That the scheme proposed by governor Shirley for the defence of the British colonies in North America, is well con-certed, and that this colony joins therein." This however did not succeed, and he proposed another, viz. for the parliament to assess each one's proportion, and in case of failure to raise it on their part, that it should be done by parliament. This is the profound secret. His assiduity in endeavouring to have some effectual plan of general defence established, is, by the false colouring of this writer, represented as an attempt to aggran-dise himself, family and friends; and that gentleman, under whose administration the several parties in the province were as much united, and the whole province rendered as happy as it ever was, for so long a time together, is called a "crafty, busy, ambitious, intriguing, enterprizing man." This attempt of Gov-ernor Shirley for a parliamentary taxation, is however a cir-cumstance strongly militating with this writer's hypothesis, for the approbation shewn to the Governor's proposal by the con-vention, which consisted of persons from the several colonies, not inferior in point of discernment, integrity, knowledge or patriotism to the members of our late *grand congress,* and the vote of the New York assembly furnishes pretty strong evi-dence that the authority of parliament, even in point of taxa-tion, was not doubted in that day. Even Dr. Franklin, in the letter alluded to, does not deny the right. His objections go to the inexpediency of the measure. He supposes it would create uneasiness in the minds of the colonists should they be thus taxed, unless they were previously allowed to send representa-tives to parliament. If Dr. Franklin really supposes that the parliament has no constitutional right to raise a revenue in America, I must confess myself at a loss to reconcile his con-duct in accepting the office of post-master, and his assiduity in increasing the revenue in that department, to the patriotism predicated of him by Novanglus, especially as this unfortunately happens to be an internal tax. This writer then tells us, that the plan was interrupted by the war, and afterwards by Governor Pownal's administration. That Messieurs Hutchinson and Oliver, stung with envy at Governor Pownal's favourites, propagated slanders respecting him to render him uneasy in his seat. My answer is this, that he that publishes such falsehoods as these in a public newspaper, with an air of seriousness, insults the understanding of the public, more than he injures the individuals he defames. In the next place we are told, that Governor Bernard was the proper man for this purpose, and he was employed by the junto to suggest to the ministry the project of taxing the colonies by act of parliament. Sometimes Governor Bernard is the arch enemy of America, the source of all our troubles, now only a tool in the hands of others. I wish Novanglus's memory had served him better, his tale might have been consistent with itself, however variant from truth. After making these assertions with equal gravity and assurance, he tell us, he does not advance this without evidence. I had been looking out for evidence a long time, and was all attention when it was promised, but my disappointment was equal to the expectation he had raised, when I found the evidence amounted to nothing more than Governor Bernard's letters and principles of law and polity, wherein he asserts the supremacy of parliament over the colonies both as to legislation and taxation. Where this writer got his logic, I do not know. Reduced to a syllogism, his argument stands thus; Governor Bernard, in 1764, wrote and transmitted to England certain letters and principles of law and polity, wherein he asserts the right of parliament to tax the colonies; Messieurs Hutchinson and Oliver were in unison with him in all his measures; therefore Messieurs Hutchinson and Oliver employed Governor Bernard to suggest to the ministry the project of taxing the colonies by act of parliament. The letters and principles are the whole of the evidence, and this is all the appearance of argument contained in his publication. Let us examine the premises. That Governor Bernard asserted the right of parliament to tax the colonies in 1764, is true. So did Mr. Otis, in a pamphlet he published the self-same year, from which I have already taken an extract. In a pamphlet published in 1765, Mr. Otis tells us, "it is certain that the parliament of Great Britain hath a just, clear, equitable and constitutional right, power and authority to bind the colonies by all acts wherein they are named. Every lawyer, nay every Tyro, knows this; no less certain is it that the parliament of Great Britain has a just and *equitable* right, power and authority to impose taxes on the colonies *internal and external, on lands as well as on trade.*" But does it follow from Governor Bernard's transmitting his principles of polity to four persons in England, or from Mr. Otis's publishing to the whole world similar principles, that either the one or the other suggested to the ministry the project of taxing the colonies by act of parliament? Hardly, supposing the transmission and publication had been prior to the resolution of parliament to that purpose; but very unfortunately for our reasoner, they were both subsequent to it, and were the effect and not the cause.

The history of the stamp act is this. At the close of the last war, which was a native of America, and increased the national debt upwards of sixty millions, it was thought by parliament to be but equitable, that an additional revenue should be raised in America, towards defraying the necessary charges of keeping it in a state of defence. A resolve of this nature was passed, and the colonies made acquainted with it through their agents, in 1764, that their assemblies might make the necessary provision if they would. The assemblies neglected doing any thing, and the parliament passed the stamp act. There is not so much as a colourable pretence that any American had a hand in the matter. Had governor Bernard, governor Hutchinson, or the late lieutenant governor been any way instrumental in obtaining the stamp act, it is very strange that not a glimpse of evidence should ever have appeared, especially when we consider that their private correspondence has been published, letters which were written in the full confidence of unsuspecting friendship. The evidence, as Novanglus calls it, is wretchedly deficient as to fixing the charge upon governor Bernard; but, even admitting that governor Bernard suggested to the ministry the design of taxing, there is no kind of evidence to prove that the junto, as this elegant writer calls the others, approved of it, much less that they employed him to do it. But, says he, no one can doubt but that Messieurs Hutchinson and Oliver were in unison with governor Bernard, in all his measures.

This is not a fact, Mr. Hutchinson dissented from him respecting the alteration of our charter, and wrote to his friends in England to prevent it. Whether governor Bernard wrote in favour of the stamp act being repealed or not I cannot say, but I know that governor Hutchinson did, and have reason to think his letters had great weight in turning the scale, which hung doubtful a long time, in favour of the repeal. These facts are known to many in the province, whigs as well as tories, yet such was the infatuation that prevailed, that the mob destroyed his house upon supposition that he was the patron of the stamp act. Even in the letters wrote to the late Mr. Whately, we find him advising to a total repeal of the tea act. It cannot be fairly inferred from persons' intimacy or mutual confidence, that they always approve of each others plans. Messieurs Otis, Cushing, Hancock and Adams were as confidential friends, and made common cause equally with the other gentlemen. May we thence infer, that the three latter hold that the parliament has a just and *equitable right* to impose taxes on the colonies? Or, that "the time may come, when the real interest of the whole may require an act of parliament to annihilate all our charters?" For these also are Mr. Otis's words. Or may we lay it down as a principle to reason from, that these gentlemen never disagree respecting measures? We know they do often, very materially. This writer is unlucky both in his principles and inferences. But where is the evidence respecting brigadier Ruggles, Mr. Paxton, and the late judge Russel? He does not produce even the shadow of a shade. He does not even pretend that they were in unison with governor Bernard in all his measures. In matters of small moment a man may be allowed to amuse with ingenious fiction, but in personal accusation, in matters so interesting both to the individual and to the public, reason and candour require something more than assertion, without proof, declamation without argument, and censure without dignity or moderation: this however, is characteristic of Novanglus. It is the stale trick of the whig writers feloniously to stab the reputation, when their antagonists are invulnerable in their public conduct.

These gentlemen were all of them, and the survivers still continue to be, friends of the English constitution, equally tenacious of the privileges of the people, and of the prerogative of the crown, zealous advocates for the colonies continuing their constitutional dependance upon Great Britain, as they think it no less the interest than the duty of the colonists; averse to tyranny and oppression in all their forms, and always ready to exert themselves for the relief of the oppressed, though they differ materially from the whigs in the mode of obtaining it; they discharged the duties of the several important departments they were called to fill, with equal faithfulness and ability; their public services gained them the confidence of the people, real merit drew after it popularity; their principles, firmness and popularity rendered them obnoxious to certain persons amongst us, who have long been indulging themselves, in hopes of rearing up an American commonwealth, upon the ruin of the British constitution. This republican party is of long standing; they lay however, in a great measure, dormant for several years. The distrust, jealousy and ferment raised by the stamp act, afforded scope for action. At first they wore the garb of hypocrisy, they professed to be friends to the British constitution in general, but claimed some exemptions from their local circumstances; at length threw off their disguise, and now stand confessed to the world in their true characters, American republicans. These republicans knew, that it would be impossible for them to succeed in their darling projects, without first destroying the influence of these adherents to the constitution. Their only method to accomplish it, was by publications charged with falshood and scurrility. Notwithstanding the favorable opportunity the stamp act gave of imposing upon the ignorant and credulous, I have sometimes been amazed, to see with how little hesitation, some slovenly baits were swallowed. Sometimes the adherents to the constitution were called ministerial tools, at others, kings, lords and commons, were the tools of them; for almost every act of parliament that has been made respecting America, in the present reign, we were told was drafted in Boston, or its environs, and only sent to England to run through the forms of parliament. Such stories, however improbable, gained credit; even the fictitious bill for restraining marriages and murdering bastard children, met with some simple enough to think it real. He that readily imbibes such absurdities, may claim affinity with the person mentioned by Mr. Addison, that made it his practice to swallow a chimera every morning for breakfast. To be more serious, I pity the weakness of those that are capable of being thus duped, almost as much as I despise the wretch that would avail himself of it, to destroy private characters and the public tranquility. By such infamous methods, many of the ancient, trusty and skilful pilots, who had steered the community safely in the most perilous times, were driven from the helm, and their places occupied by different persons, some of whom, bankrupts in fortune, business and fame, are now striving to run the ship on the rocks, that they may have an opportunity of plundering the wreck. The gentlemen named by Novanglus, have nevertheless persevered with unshaken constancy and firmness, in their patriotic principles and conduct, through a variety of fortune; and have at present, the mournful consolation of reflecting, that had their admonitions and councils been timely attended to, their country would never have been involved in its present calamity.

MASSACHUSETTENSIS.

Massachusetts Gazette; and the Boston
Post-Boy and Advertiser, March 6, 1775

Novanglus No. VII

To the Inhabitants of the Colony of Massachusetts-Bay

My Friends,

Our rhetorical magician, in his paper of January the 9th continues to *wheedle*. "You want nothing but to know the true state of facts, to rectify whatever is amiss." He becomes an advocate for the poor of Boston! Is for making great allowance for the whigs. "The whigs are too valuable a part of the community to lose. He would not draw down the vengeance of Great Britain. He shall become an advocate for the leading whigs," &c. It is in vain for us to enquire after the *sincerity* or *consistency* of all this. It is agreeable to the precept of Horace. Irritat, mulcet falsis terroribus implet ut magus. And that is all he desires.

After a long discourse, which has nothing in it but what has been answered already, he comes to a great subject indeed, the British constitution; and undertakes to prove that "the authority of parliament extends to the colonies."

Why will not this writer state the question fairly? The whigs allow that from the necessity of a case not provided for by common law, and to supply a defect in the British dominions, which there undoubtedly is, if they are to be governed only by that law, America has all along consented, still consents, and ever will consent, that parliament being the most powerful legislature in the dominions, should regulate the trade of the dominions. This is founding the authority of parliament to regulate our trade, upon *compact* and *consent* of the colonies, not upon any principle of common or statute law, not upon any original principle of the English constitution, not upon the principle that parliament is the supream and sovereign legislature over them in all cases whatsoever.

The question is not therefore, whether the authority of parliament extends to the colonies in any case; for it is admitted by the whigs that it does in that of commerce: But whether it extends in all cases.

We are then detained with a long account of the three simple forms of government; and are told that "the British constitution consisting of king, lords and commons, is formed upon the principles of monarchy, aristocracy and democracy, in due proportion; that it includes the principled excellencies, and excludes the principal defects of the other kinds of government—the most perfect system that the wisdom of ages has produced, and Englishmen glory in being subject to and protected by it."

Then we are told "that the colonies are a part of the British empire". But what are we to understand by this? Some of the colonies, most of them indeed, were settled before the kingdom of Great-Britain was brought into existence. The union of England and Scotland, was made and established by act of parliament in the reign of queen Ann; and it was this union and statute which erected the kingdom of Great-Britain. The colonies were settled long before, in the reigns of the James's and Charles's. What authority over them had Scotland? Scotland, England and the colonies were all under one king before that—the two crowns of England and Scotland, united on the head of James the first, and continued united on that of Charles the first, when our first charter was granted. Our charter being granted by him who was king of both nations, to our ancestors, most of whom were *post nati*, born after the union of the two crowns, and consequently, as was adjudged in Calvin's case, free natural subjects of Scotland, as well as England, had not the king as good a right to have governed the colonies by his Scottish, as by his English parliament, and to have granted our charters under the seal of Scotland, as well as that of England?

But to waive this. If the English parliament were to govern us, where did they get the right, without our consent to take the Scottish parliament, into a participation of the government over us? When this was done, was the American share of the democracy of the constitution consulted? If not, were not the Americans deprived of the benefit of the democratical part of the constitution? And is not the democracy as essential to the English constitution as the monarchy or aristocracy? Should we have been more effectually deprived of the benefit of the British or English constitution, if one or both houses of parliament, or if our house and council had made this union with the two houses of parliament in Scotland, without the king?

If a new constitution was to be formed for the whole British dominions, and a supream legislature coextensive with it, upon the general principles of the English constitution, an equal mixture of monarchy, aristocracy and democracy, let us see what would be necessary. England have six millions of people we will say: America has three. England has five hundred members in the house of commons we will say: America must have two hundred and fifty. Is it possible she should maintain them there, or could they at such a distance know the state, the sense or exigences of their constituents? Ireland too must be incorporated, and send another hundred or two of members. The territory in the East-Indies and West India islands must send members. And after all this, every navigation act, every act of trade must be repealed. America and the East and West Indies and Africa too, must have equal liberty to trade with all the world, that the favoured inhabitants of Great-Britain have now. Will the ministry thank Massachusettensis for becoming an advocate for such an union and incorporation of all the dominions of the king of Great-Britain? Yet without such an union, a legislature which shall be sovereign and supream in all cases whatsoever, and coextensive with the empire, can never be established upon the general principles of the English constitution, which Massachusettensis lays down, viz. an equal mixture of monarchy, aristocracy and democracy. Nay further, in order to comply with this principle, this new government, this mighty Colossus which is to bestride the narrow world, must have an house of lords consisting of Irish, East and West Indian, African, American, as well as English and Scottish noblemen; for the nobility ought to be scattered about all the dominions, as well as the representatives of the commons. If in twenty years more America should have six millions of inhabitants, as there is a boundless territory to fill up, she must have five hundred representatives. Upon these principles, if in forty years, she should have twelve millions, a thousand; and if the inhabitants of the three kingdoms remain as they are, being already full of inhabitants, what will become of your supream legislative? It will be translated, crown and all, to America. This is a sublime system for America. It will flatter those ideas of independency, which the tories impute to them, if they have any such, more than any other plan of independency, that I have ever heard projected.

"The best writers upon the law of nations, tell us, that when a nation takes possession of a distant country and settles there, that country though separated from the principal establishment, or mother country, naturally becomes a part of the state, equal with its ancient possessions". We are not told who these "best writers" are:—I think we ought to be introduced to them. But their meaning may be no more than that it is best they should be incorporated with the ancient establishment, by contract, or by some new law and institution, by which the new country shall have equal right, powers and privileges, as well as equal protection; and be under equal obligations of obedience with the old. Has there been any such contract between Britain and the Colonies? Is America incorporated into the realm? Is it a part of the realm? Is it a part of the kingdom? Has it any share in the legislative of the realm? The constitution requires that every foot of land should be represented, in the third estate, the democratical branch of the constitution. How many millions of acres in America, how many thousands of wealthy landholders, have no representative there?

But let these "best writers" say what they will, there is nothing in the law of nations, which is only the law of right reason, applied to the conduct of nations, that requires that emigrants from a state should continue, or be made a part of the state.

The practice of nations has been different. The Greeks planted colonies, and neither demanded nor pretended any authority over them, but they became distinct independent commonwealths.

The Romans continued their colonies under the jurisdiction of the mother commonwealth—but, nevertheless, she allowed them the priviledges of cities. Indeed that sagacious city seems to have been aware of the difficulties similar to those under which Great Britain is now labouring; she seems to have been sensible of the impossibility of keeping colonies planted at great distances, under the absolute controul of her *senatus consulta*. Harrington tells us, Oceana p. 43. that "the commonwealth of Rome, by planting colonies of its citizens within the bounds of Italy, took the best way of propagating itself, and naturalizing the country; whereas if it had planted such colonies without the bounds of Italy, it would have alienated the citizens, and given a root to liberty abroad, that might have sprung up foreign, or savage and hostile to her; *wherefore it never made any such dispersion of itself, and its strength,* till it was under the yoke of the emperors, who disburdening themselves of the people, as having less apprehension of what they could do abroad than at home, took a contrary course." But these Italian cities, altho' established by decrees of the senate of Rome, to which the colonists was always party, either as a Roman citizen about to emigrate, or as a conquered enemy treating upon terms; were always allow'd all the rights of Roman citizens, and were govern'd by senates of their own. It was the policy of Rome to conciliate her colonies, by allowing them equal liberty with her citizens. Witness the example of the Privernates. This people had been conquered; and complaining of oppressions, revolted. At last they sent ambassadors to Rome to treat of peace. The senate was divided in opinion: Some were for violent, others for lenient measures. In the course of the debate, a senator, whose opinion was for *bringing them to his feet,* proudly asked one of the ambassadors, what punishment he thought his countrymen deserved? *Eam inquit, quam merentur, qui se libertate dignos censent.*—That punishment which those deserve, who think themselves worthy of liberty. Another senator seeing that the *ministerial members* were exasperated with the honest answer, in order to divert their anger, asks another question. What if we remit all punishment? What kind of a peace may we hope for with you? *Si bonam dederitis, inquit, et fidam, et perpetuam; si malam, haud diuturnam.*—If you give us a just peace, it will be faithfully observed, and perpetually: but if a bad one, it will not last long. The *ministerial* senators were all on fire at this answer, cried out, sedition and rebellion: but the wiser majority decreed, "*viri, et liberi, vocem auditam, an credi posse, ullum populum, aut hominem denique, in ea conditione, cujus cum pœniteat, diutius, quam necesse sit, mansurum? ibi pacem esse fidam, ubi voluntarii pacati sint: neque eo loco, ubi servitutem esse velint, fidem sperandam esse.*—"That they had heard the voice of a man and a son of liberty: that it was not natural or credible that any people, or any man, would continue longer than necessity should compel him, in a condition that grieved and displeased him. A faithful peace was to be expected from men whose affections were conciliated—nor was any kind of fidelity to be expected from slaves." The consul exclaimed, *Eos demum, qui nihil præterquam de libertate, cogitent, dignos esse qui Romani fiant.* That they who regarded nothing so much as their Liberty, deserved to be Romans. *Itaque et in senatu causam obtinuere, et ex auctoritate patrum, latum ad populum est, ut privernatibus civitas daretur.*" Therefore the Privernates obtained their cause in the senate, and it was by the authority of those fathers, recommended to the people, that the privileges of a city should be granted them.

The practice of free nations only can be adduced, as precedents of what the law of nature has been thought to dictate upon this subject of colonies. Their practice is different. The senate and people of Rome did not interfere commonly in making laws for their colonies, but left them to be ruled by their governors and senates. Can Massachusettensis produce from the whole history of Rome, or from the Digest, one example of a *Senatus consultum*, or a *Plebiscitum* laying taxes on a colony.

Having mentioned the wisdom of the Romans in not planting colonies out of Italy, and their reasons for it; I cannot help recollecting an observation of Harrington, Oceana, p. 44. "For the colonies in the Indies," says he, "they are yet babes, that cannot live without sucking the breasts of their mother cities; but such as I mistake, if when they come of age, they do not wean themselves: which causes me to wonder at princes that delight to be exhausted that way." This was written 120 years ago: the colonies are now nearer manhood than even Harrington foresaw they would arrive in such a period of time. Is it not astonishing then, that any British minister should ever have considered this subject so little as to believe it possible for him to new moddel all our governments, to tax us by an authority that never taxed us before, and subdue us to an implicit obedience to a legislature, that millions of us scarcely ever tho't any thing about.

I have said that the practice of free governments alone can be quoted with propriety, to shew the sense of nations. But the sense and practice of nations is not enough. Their practice must be reasonable, just and right, or it will not govern Americans.

Absolute monarchies, whatever their practice may be, are nothing to us. For as Harrington observes, "Absolute monarchy, as that of the Turks, neither plants its people at home nor abroad, otherwise than as tenants for life or at will; wherefore its national and provincial government is all one."

I deny therefore that the practice of free nations, or the opinions of the best writers upon the law of nations, will warrant the position of Massachusettensis, that when a nation takes possession of a distant territory, that becomes a part of the state equally with its ancient possessions. The practice of free nations, and the opinions of the best writers, are in general on the contrary.

I agree, that "two supreme and independent authorities cannot exist in the same state," any more than two supream beings in one universe. And therefore I contend, that our provincial legislatures are the only supream authorities in our colonies. Parliament, notwithstanding this, may be allowed an authority supreme and sovereign over the ocean, which may be limited by the banks of the ocean, or the bounds of our charters; our charters give us no authority over the high seas. Parliament has our consent to assume a jurisdiction over them. And here is a line fairly drawn between the rights of Britain and the rights of the colonies, viz. the banks of the ocean, or low water mark. The line of division between common law and civil, or maritime law. If this is not sufficient—if parliament are at a loss for any principle of natural, civil, maritime, moral or common law, on which to ground any authority over the high seas, the Atlantic especially, let the colonies be treated like reasonable creatures, and they will discover great ingenuity and modesty: The acts of trade and navigation might be confirmed by provincial laws, and carried into execution by our own courts and juries, and in this case illicit trade would be cut up by the roots forever. I knew the smuggling tories in New-York and Boston would cry out against this, because it would not only destroy their profitable game of smuggling, but their whole place and pension system. But the whigs, that is a vast majority of the whole continent, would not regard the smuggling tories. In one word, if public principles and motives and arguments, were alone to determine this dispute between the two countries, it might be settled forever, in a few hours; but the everlasting clamours of prejudice, passion and private interest, drown every consideration of that sort, and are precipitating us into a civil war.

"If then we are a part of the British empire, we must be subject to the supreme power of the state, which is vested in the estates in parliament."

Here again we are to be conjured out of our senses by the magic in the words "British empire,"—and "supreme power of the state." But however it may sound, I say we are not a part of the British empire. Because the British government is not an empire. The governments of France, Spain, &c. are not empires, but monarchies, supposed to be governed by fixed fundamental laws, tho' not really. The British government, is still less intitled to the style of an empire: it is a limitted monarchy. If Aristotle, Livy, and Harrington, knew what a republic was, the British constitution is much more like a republic than an empire. They define a republic to be *a government of laws, and not of men*. If this definition is just, the British constitution is nothing more nor less than a republic, in which the king is first magistrate. This office being hereditary, and being possessed of such ample and splendid prerogatives, is no objection to the government's being a republic, as long as it is bound by fixed laws, which the people have a voice in making, and a right to defend. An empire is a despotism, and an emperor a despot, bound by no law or limitation, but his own will: it is a stretch of tyranny beyond absolute monarchy. For altho' the will of an absolute monarch is law, yet his edicts must be registered by parliaments. Even this formality is not necessary in an empire. There the maxim is *quod principi placuit legis, habet vigorem*, even without having that will and pleasure recorded. There are but three empires now in Europe, the German, or Holy Roman, the Russian and the Ottoman.

There is another sense indeed in which the word empire is used, in which it may be applied to the government of Geneva, or any other republic, as well as to monarchy, or despotism. In

this sense it is synonimous with government, rule or dominion. In this sense, we are within the dominion, rule or government of the king of Great-Britain.

The question should be, whether we are a part of the kingdom of Great-Britain: this is the only language, known in English laws. We are not then a part of the British kingdom,
realm or state; and therefore the supreme power of the kingdom, realm or state, is not upon these principles, the supreme
power over us. That "supreme power over America is vested in
the estates in parliament," is an affront to us; for there is not
an acre of American land represented there—there are no
American estates in parliament.

To say that we "must be" subject, seems to betray a consciousness that we are not by any law or upon any principles,
but those of meer power; and an opinion that we ought to be,
or that it is necessary that we should be. But if this should be
admitted, for argument sake only, what is the consequence?
The consequences that may fairly be drawn are these. That
Britain has been imprudent enough to let Colonies be planted,
untill they are become numerous and important, without ever
having wisdom enough to concert a plan for their government, consistent with her own welfare. That now it is necessary to make them submit to the authority of parliament: and
because there is no principle of law or justice, or reason, by
which she can effect it: therefore she will resort to war and
conquest—to the maxim *delenda est Carthago*. These are the
consequences, according to this writers ideas. We think the consequences are, that she has after 150 years, discovered a defect
in her government, which ought to be supply'd by some just
and reasonable means: that is, by the consent of the Colonies;
for metaphysicians and politicians may dispute forever, but
they will never find any other moral principle or foundation of
rule or obedience, than the consent of governors and governed. She has found out that the great machine will not go
any longer without a new wheel. She will make this herself. We
think she is making it of such materials and workmanship as
will tear the whole machine to pieces. We are willing, if she can
convince us of the necessity of such a wheel, to assist with
artists and materials, in making it, so that it may answer the
end: But she says, we shall have no share in it; and if we will

not let her patch it up as she pleases, her Massachusettensis's and other advocates tell us, she will tear it to pieces herself, by cutting our throats. To this kind of reasoning we can only answer, that we will not stand still to be butchered. We will defend our lives as long as providence shall enable us.

"It is beyond doubt, that it was the sense both of the *Parent Country*, and *our Ancestors*, that they were to remain subject to parliament."

This has been often asserted, and as often contradicted, and fully confuted. The confutation, may not, however, have come to every eye which has read this News-Paper.

The public acts of kings and ministers of state, in that age, when our ancestors emigrated, which were not complained of, remonstrated and protested against by the commons, are look'd upon as sufficient proof of the "sense" of the parent country.

The charter to the treasurer and company of Virginia, 23 March 1609, grants ample powers of government, legislative, executive and judicial, and then contains an express covenant "to and with the said treasurer and company, their successors, factors and assigns, that they, and every of them, shall be free from all taxes and impositions forever, upon any goods or merchandizes, at any time or times hereafter, either upon importation thither, or exportation from thence, into our realm of England, or into any other of our realms or dominions."

I agree with this writer that the authority of a supreme legislature, includes the right of taxation. Is not this quotation then an irresistable proof, that it was not the sense of king James or his ministers, or of the ancestors of the Virginians, that they were "to remain subject to parliament as a supreme legislature."

After this, James issued a proclamation, recalling this patent, but this was never regarded—then Charles issued another proclamation, which produced a remonstrance from Virginia, which was answered by a letter from the lords of the privy council, 22d July 1634, containing the royal assurance that "all their estates, trade, freedom, and privileges should be enjoyed by them, in as extensive a manner, as they enjoyed them before those proclamations."

Here is another evidence of the sense of the king and his ministers.

Afterwards parliament sent a squadron of ships to Virginia—the colony rose in open resistance, untill the parliamentary commissioners granted them conditions, that they should enjoy the privileges of Englishmen; that their assembly should transact the affairs of the colony; that they should have a free trade to all places and nations, as the people of England; and 4thly, that "Virginia shall be free from all *taxes*, customs, and impositions whatever, and none shall be imposed on them without consent of their general assembly; and that neither forts nor castles be erected, or garrisons maintained without their consent."

One would think this was evidence enough of the sense both of the parent country, and our ancestors.

After the acts of navigation were passed, Virginia sent agents to England, and a remonstrance against those acts. Charles, in answer, sent a declaration under the privy seal, 19 April 1676, affirming, "that taxes ought not to be laid upon the inhabitants and proprietors of the colony, but by the common consent of the general assembly; except such impositions as the parliament should lay on the commodities imported into England from the colony." And he ordered a charter, under the great seal, to secure this right to the Virginians.

What becomes of the "sense" of the parent country, and our ancestors? For the ancestors of the Virginians, are our ancestors, when we speak of ourselves as Americans. From Virginia let us pass to Maryland. Charles 1st, in 1633, gave a charter to the Baron of Baltimore, containing ample powers of government, and this express covenant, "to and with the said lord Baltimore, his heirs and assigns, that we, our heirs and successors, shall at no time hereafter, set or make, or cause to be set, any imposition, custom, or other taxation, rate, or contribution whatsoever, in and upon the dwellings and inhabitants of the aforesaid province, for their lands, tenements, goods or chattels, within the said province; or to be laden or unladen, within the ports or harbours of the said province."

What then was the "sense" of the parent country, and the ancestors of Maryland? But if by "our ancestors", he confines his idea to New England or this province, let us consider. The first planters of Plymouth were our ancestors in the strictest sense. They had no charter or patent for the land they took possession of, and derived no authority from the English Parliament or Crown, to set up their government. They purchased land of the Indians, and set up a government of their own, on the simple principle of nature, and afterwards purchased a patent for the land of the council at Plymouth, but never purchased any charter for government of the Crown, or the King: and continued to exercise all the powers of government, legislative, executive and judicial, upon the plain ground of an original contract among independent individuals for 68 years, i. e. until their incorporation with Massachusetts by our present charter. The same may be said of the colonies which emigrated to Sea-Brook, New-Haven, and other Parts of Connecticut. They seem to have had no idea of dependence on Parliament, any more than on the Conclave. The Secretary of Connecticut has now in his possession, an original Letter from Charles 2d. to that colony, in which he considers them rather as friendly allies, than as subjects to his English Parliament, and even requests them to pass a law in their assembly, relative to piracy.

The sentiments of your ancestors in the Massachusetts may be learned from almost every ancient paper and record. It would be endless to recite all the passages, in which it appears that they thought themselves exempt from the authority of parliament, not only in the point of taxation, but in all cases whatsoever. Let me mention one. Randolph, one of the predecessors of Massachusettensis, in a representation to Charles 2d, dated 20 September 1676, says, "I went to visit the governor at his house, and among other discourse, I told him, I took notice of several ships that were arrived at Boston, some since my being there, from Spain, France, Streights, Canaries, and other parts of Europe, contrary to your Majesty's laws for encouraging Navigation and regulating the trade of the plantations. He freely declared to me, that the law made by your Majesty and your parliament obligeth them in nothing but what consists with the interest of that colony, that the legislative power is and abides in them solely to act and make laws by virtue of a Charter from your Majesty's royal father." Here is a positive assertion of an exemption from the authority of parliament, even in the case of the Regulation of Trade.

Afterwards in 1677, The General Court passed a law, which

shews the sense of our ancestors in a very strong light. It is in these words. "This court being informed, by letters received this day from our messengers, of his Majesty's expectation that the acts of Trade and Navigation be exactly and punctually observed by this his Majesty's colony, his pleasure therein not having before now been signified unto us, either by express from his Majesty, or any of his ministers of state; It is therefore hereby ordered, and by the authority of this court enacted, that henceforth, all masters of ships, ketches, or other vessels, of greater or lesser burthen, arriving in, or sailing from any of the ports in this jurisdiction, do, without coven, or fraud, yield faithful and constant obedience unto, and observation of, all the said acts of navigation and trade, on penalty of suffering such forfeitures, loss and damage as in the said acts are particularly expressed. And the governor and council, and all officers, commissionated and authorized by them, are hereby ordered and required to see to the strict observation of the said acts." As soon as they had passed this law, they wrote a letter to their agent, in which they acknowledge they had not conformed to the acts of trade; and they say, they "apprehended them to be an invasion of the rights, liberties and properties of the subjects of his Majesty in the colony, they not being represented in parliament, and according to the usual sayings of the learned in the law, *the laws of England were bounded within the four seas, and did not reach America*. However, as his Majesty had signified his pleasure, that these acts should be observed in the Massachusetts, they had made provision by a law of the colony, that they should be strictly attended from time to time, although it greatly discouraged trade, and was a great damage to his Majesty's plantation."

Thus it appears, that the ancient Massachusettensians and Virginians, had precisely the same sense of the authority of parliament, viz. that it had none at all: and the same sense of the necessity, that by the voluntary act of the colonies, their free chearful consent, it should be allowed the power of regulating trade: and this is precisely the idea of the late Congress at Philadelphia, expressed in the fourth proposition in their Bill of Rights.

But this was the sense of the parent country too, at that

time; for K. Charles II. in a letter to the Massachusetts, after this law had been laid before him, has these words, "We are informed that you have lately made *some good provision* for observing the acts of trade and navigation, which is well pleasing unto us." Had he, or his ministers an idea that parliament was the sovereign legislative over the Colony? If he had, would he not have censured this law as an insult to that legislature?

I sincerely hope, we shall see no more such round affirmations, that it was the sense of the parent country and our ancestors, that they were to remain subject to parliament.

So far from thinking themselves subject to parliament, that during the Interregnum, it was their desire and design to have been a free commonwealth, an independent Republic; and after the restoration, it was with the utmost reluctance, that in the course of 16 or 17 years, they were bro't to take the oaths of allegiance: and for some time after this, they insisted upon taking an oath of fidelity to the Country, before that of allegiance to the King.

That "it is evident from the Charter itself," that they were to remain subject to parliament, is very unaccountable, when there is not one word in either Charter concerning parliament.

That the authority of parliament has been exercised almost ever since the settlement of the country, is a mistake; for there is no instance, untill the first Navigation Act, which was in 1660, more than 40 years after the first settlement. This act was never executed or regarded, until 17 years afterwards, and then it was not executed as an act of parliament, but as a law of the colony, to which the king agreed.

"This has been expressly acknowledged by our Provincial Legislatures." There is too much truth in this. It has been twice acknowledged by our House of Representatives, that parliament was the supreme legislative; but this was directly repugnant to a multitude of other votes by which it was denied. This was in conformity to the distinction between taxation and legislation, which has been since found to be a distinction without a difference.

When a great question is first started, there are very few, even of the greatest minds, which suddenly and intuitively comprehend it, in all its consequences.

It is both "our interest and our duty to continue subject to the authority of parliament, as far as the regulation of our trade, if it will be content with that, but no longer."

"If the colonies are not subject to the authority of parliament, Great-Britain and the colonies must be distinct states, as compleatly so as England and Scotland were before the union, or as Great-Britain and Hanover are now:" There is no need of being startled at this consequence. It is very harmless. There is no absurdity at all in it. Distinct states may be united under one king. And those states may be further cemented and united together, by a treaty of commerce. This is the case. We have by our own express consent contracted to observe the navigation act, and by our implied consent, by long usage and uninterrupted acquiescence, have submitted to the other acts of trade, however grievous some of them may be. This may be compared to a treaty of commerce, by which those distinct states are cemented together, in perpetual league and amity. And if any further ratifications of this pact or treaty are necessary, the colonies would readily enter into them, provided their other liberties were inviolate.

That the colonies owe "no allegiance" to any imperial crown, provided such a crown involves in it an house of lords and a house of commons, is certain. Indeed we owe no allegiance to any crown at all. We owe allegiance to the person of his majesty king George the third, whom God preserve. But allegiance is due universally, both from Britons and Americans to the person of the king, not to his crown: to his natural, not his politic capacity: as I will undertake to prove hereafter, from the highest authorities, and most solemn adjudications, which were ever made within any part of the British Dominions.

If his Majesty's title to the crown, is "derived from an act of parliament made since the settlement of these Colonies," it was not made since the date of our charter. Our charter was granted by king William and queen Mary, three years after the revolution. And the oaths of allegiance are established by a law of the province. So that our allegiance to his majesty is not due by virtue of any act of a British parliament, but by our own charter and province laws. It ought to be remembered, that there was a revolution here as well as in England, and that we made an original, express contract with king William, as well as the people of England.

If it follows from thence, that he appears king of the Massachusetts, king of Rhode-Island, king of Connecticut, &c. This is no absurdity at all. He will appear in this light, and does appear so, whether parliament has authority over us or not. He is king of Ireland, I suppose, although parliament is allowed to have authority there. As to giving his Majesty those titles, I have no objection at all: I wish he would be graciously pleased to assume them.

The only proposition, in all this writer's long string of pretended absurdities, which he says follow from the position, that we are distinct states, is this,—That "as the king must govern each state by its parliament, those several parliaments would pursue the particular interest of its own state and however well disposed the king might be to pursue a line of interest that was common to all, the checks and controul that he would meet with, would render it impossible." Every argument ought to be allowed its full weight: and therefore candor obliges me to acknowledge, that here lies all the difficulty that there is in this whole controversy. There has been, from first to last, on both sides of the Atlantic, an idea, an apprehension that it was necessary, there should be some superintending power, to draw together all the wills, and unite all the strength of the subjects in all the dominions, in case of war, and in the case of trade. The necessity of this, in case of trade, has been so apparent, that as has often been said, we have consented that parliament should exercise such a power. In case of war, it has by some been thought necessary. But in fact and experience, it has not been found so. What tho' the proprietary colonies, on account of disputes with the proprietors, did not come in so early to the assistance of the general cause in the last war, as they ought, and perhaps one of them not at all! The inconveniences of this were small, in comparison of the absolute ruin to the liberties of all which must follow the submission to parliament, in all cases, which would be giving up all the popular limitations upon the government. These inconveniences fell chiefly upon New England. She was necessitated to greater exertions. But she had rather suffer these again and again, than others infinitely greater. However this subject has now been so long in contemplation, that it is fully understood now, in all the colonies: so that there is no danger, in case of another war, of any colonies failing of its duty.

But admitting the proposition in its full force, that it is absolutely necessary there should be a supreme power, coextensive with all the dominions, will it follow that parliament as now constituted has a right to assume this supream jurisdiction? By no means.

A union of the colonies might be projected, and an American legislature: or if America has 3,000,000 people, and the whole dominions twelve, she ought to send a quarter part of all the members to the house of commons, and instead of holding parliaments always at Westminster, the haughty members for Great-Britain, must humble themselves, one session in four, to cross the Atlantic, and hold the parliament in America.

There is no avoiding all inconveniences, in human affairs: The greatest possible or conceivable, would arise from ceding to parliament all power over us, without a representation in it: the next greatest, would accrue from any plan that can be devised for a representation there. The least of all would arise from going on as we begun, and fared well for 150 years, by letting parliament regulate trade, and our own assemblies all other matters.

As to "the prerogatives not being defined or limited," it is as much so in the Colonies as in Great Britain, and as well understood, and as cheerfully submitted to in the former as the latter.

But "where is the British constitution, that we all agree we are intitled to?" I answer, if we enjoy, and are intitled to more liberty than the British constitution allows, where is the harm? Or if we enjoy the British constitution in greater purity and perfection than they do in England, as is really the case, whose fault is this? Not ours.

We may find all the blessings "of this constitution in our Provincial Assemblies." Our Houses of Representatives have, and ought to exercise, every power of the house of Commons. The first Charter to this colony, is nothing to the present argument: but it did grant a power of taxing the people—implicitly, tho' not in express terms. It granted all the rights and liberties of Englishmen, which include the power of taxing the people.

"Our Council Boards," in the royal governments, "are destitute of the noble independence and splendid appendages of peerages," most certainly: They are the meerest creatures and tools in the political creation. Dependent every moment for their existence on the tainted breath of a prime minister. But they have the authority of the house of lords, in our little models of the English constitution. And it is this which makes them so great a grievance. The crown has really, two branches of our legislatures in its power. Let an act of parliament pass at home, putting it in the power of the king, to remove any peer from the house of lords at his pleasure, and what will become of the British constitution? It will be overturned from the foundation. Yet we are perpetually insulted, by being told, that making our council by mandamus, brings us nearer to the British constitution. In this province, by charter, the council certainly hold their seats for the year, after being chosen and approved, independant of both the other branches. For their creation, they are equally obliged to both the other branches; so that there is little or no bias in favour of either, if any, it is in favour of the prerogative. In short, it is not easy without an hereditary nobility, to constitute a council more independent, more nearly resembling the House of Lords than the council of this province has ever been by Charter. But perhaps it will be said, that we are to enjoy the British constitution in our supreme legislature, the Parliament, not in our provincial legislatures.

To this I answer, if parliament is to be our supreme legislature, we shall be under a compleat oligarchy or aristocracy, not the British Constitution, which this writer himself defines a mixture of monarchy, aristocracy and democracy. For King, lords and commons, will constitute one great oligarchy, as they will stand related to America, as much as the Decimvirs did in Rome. With this difference for the worse, that our rulers are to be three thousand miles off. The definition of an oligarchy, is a government by a number of grandees, over whom the people have no controul. The states of Holland were once chosen by the people frequently. Then chosen for life. Now they are not chosen by the people at all. When a member dies, his place is filled up not by the people he is to represent, but by the states. Is not this depriving the Hollanders of a free constitution, and subjecting them to an aristocracy, or oligarchy? Will not the government of America be like it? Will not representatives be chosen for them by others, whom they never saw nor heard of? If our provincial constitutions are in any respect imperfect and want alteration, they have capacity enough to discern it, and power enough to effect it, without the interposition of parliament. There never was an American constitution attempted by parliament, before the Quebec Bill and Massachusetts Bill. These are such *samples* of what they may and probably will be, that few Americans are in love with them. However, America will never allow that parliament has any authority to alter their constitution at all. She is wholly penetrated with a sense of the necessity of resisting it, at all hazards. And she would resist it, if the constitution of the Massachusetts had been altered as much for *the better*, as it is for the worse. The question we insist on most, is not whether the alteration is for the better or not, but whether parliament has any right to make any alteration at all. And it is the universal sense of America, that it has none.

We are told that "the provincial constitutions have no principle of stability within themselves". This is so great a mistake, that there is not more order or stability in any government upon the globe, than there ever has been in that of Connecticut. The same may be said of the Massachusetts and Pennsylvania, and indeed of the others, very nearly. "That these constitutions in turbulent times would become wholly monarchial or wholly republican." They must be such times as would have a similar effect upon the constitution at home. But in order to avoid the danger of this, what is to be done. Not give us an English constitution, it seems, but make sure of us at once, by giving us constitutions wholly monarchical, annihilating our houses of representatives first, by taking from them the support of government, &c. and then making the councils and judges wholly dependent on the crown.

That a representation in parliament is impracticable we all agree: but the consequence is, that we must have a representation in our supreme legislatures here. This was the consequence that was drawn by kings, ministers, our ancestors, and the whole nation, more than a century ago, when the colonies were first settled, and continued to be the general sense untill the last peace, and it must be the general sense again soon, or Great-Britain will lose her colonies.

"This is apparently the meaning of that celebrated passage in governor Hutchinsons letter, that rung through the continent, viz. (There must be an abridgment of what is called English liberties.)" But all the art and subtlety of Massachusettensis will never vindicate or excuse that expression. According to this writer, it should have been "there is an abridgment of English liberties and it can't be otherwise." But every candid reader must see that the letter writer had more than that in his *view* and in his *wishes.* In the same letter, a little before, he says, "what marks of resentment the parliament will shew, whether they will be upon the province in general or particular persons, is extremely uncertain; but that they will be placed somewhere is most certain, and I add, *because I think it ought to be so.*" Is it possible to read this without thinking of the port bill, the charter bill, and the resolves for sending persons to England by the statute of H. 8, to be tried! But this is not all. "This is most certainly a crisis," says he. &c. "If no measure shall have been taken to secure this dependence (i. e. the dependence which a colony ought to have upon the parent state) it is all over with us." "The friends of government will be utterly disheartned, and the friends of anarchy will be afraid of nothing, be it ever so extravagant." But this is not all. "I never think of the measures necessary for the peace and good order of the colonies without pain." "There must be an abridgment of what are called English liberties." What could he mean? Any thing less than depriving us of trial by jury? Perhaps he wanted an act of parliament to try persons here for treason by a court of admiralty. Perhaps an act that the province should be governed by a governor and a mandamus council, without an house of representatives. But to put it out of all doubt that his meaning was much worse than Massachusettensis endeavours to make it, he explains himself in a subsequent part of the letter. "I wish," says he, "the good of the colony, *when I wish to see some further restraint of liberty.*" Here it is rendered certain, that he is pleading for a further restraint of liberty, not explaining the restraint, he apprehended the constitution had already laid us under.

My indignation at this letter, has sometimes been softened by compassion. It carries on the face of it, evident marks of *madness*. It was written in such a transport of passions, *ambition*, and *revenge* chiefly, that his reason was manifestly overpowered. The vessel was tost in such a hurricane, that she could not feel her helm. Indeed he seems to have had a confused consciousness of this himself. "Pardon me this excursion," says he, "it really proceeds from the state of mind, into which our perplexed affairs often throws me."

"It is our highest interest to continue a part of the British empire, and equally our duty to remain subject to the authority of parliament," says Massachusettensis.

We are a part of the British dominions, that is of the king of Great-Britain, and it is our interest and duty to continue so. It is equally our interest and duty to continue subject to the authority of parliament, in the regulation of our trade, as long as she shall leave us to govern our internal policy, and to give and grant our own money, and no longer.

This letter concludes with an agreeable flight of fancy. The time may not be so far off, however, as this writer imagines, when the colonies may have the balance of numbers and wealth in her favour. But when that shall happen, if we should attempt to rule her by an American parliament, without an adequate representation in it, she will infallibly resist us by her arms.

NOVANGLUS
Boston Gazette, March 6, 1775

Massachusettensis [Daniel Leonard] No. XIV

To the Inhabitants of the Province of Massachusetts Bay,

MY DEAR COUNTRYMEN,

Our patriotic writers, as they call each other, estimate the services rendered by, and the advantages resulting from the colonies to Britain, at a high rate, but allow but little, if any, merit in her towards the colonies. Novanglus would persuade us that exclusive of her assistance in the last war, we have had but little of her protection, unless it was such as her name alone afforded. Dr. Franklin when before the house of commons, in 1765, denied that the late war was entered into for the defence of the people in America. The Pennsylvania Farmer tells us in his letters, that the war was undertaken solely for the benefit of Great Britain, and that however advantageous the subduing or keeping any of these countries, viz. Canada, Nova-Scotia and the Floridas may be to Great Britain, the acquisition is greatly injurious to these colonies. And that the colonies, as constantly as streams tend to the ocean, have been pouring the fruits of all their labours into their mother's lap. Thus, they would induce us to believe, that we derive little or no advantage from Great Britain, and thence they infer the injustice, rapacity and cruelty of her conduct towards us. I fully agree with them, that the services rendered by the colonies are great and meritorious. The plantations are additions to the empire of inestimable value. The American market for British manufactures, the great nursery for seamen formed by our shipping, the cultvation of deserts, and our rapid population, are increasing and inexhaustible sources of national wealth and strength. I commend these patriots for their estimations of the national advantages accruing from the colonies, as much as I think them deserving of censure for depreciating the advantages and benefits that we derive from Britain. A particular inquiry into the protection afforded us, and the commercial advantages resulting to us from the parent state, will go a great way towards conciliating the affections of those whose minds are at present unduly impressed with different sentiments towards Great Britain. The intestine commotion with which

England was convulsed and torn soon after the emigration of our ancestors, probably prevented that attention being given to them in the earliest stages of this colony, that otherwise would have been given. The principal difficulties that the adventurers met with after the struggle of a few of the first years were over, were the incursions of the French and savages conjointly, or of the latter instigated and supported by the former. Upon a representation of this to England, in the time of the interregnum, Acadia, which was then the principal source of our disquietude, was reduced by an English armament. At the request of this colony, in queen Ann's reign, a fleet of fifteen men of war, besides transports, troops, &c. were sent to assist us in an expedition against Canada; the fleet suffered shipwreck, and the attempt proved abortive. It ought not to be forgot, that the siege of Louisbourg, in 1745, by our own forces, was covered by a British fleet of ten ships, four of 60 guns, one of 50, and five of 40 guns, besides the Vigilant of 64, which was taken during the siege, as she was attempting to throw supplies into the garrison. It is not probable that the expedition would have been undertaken without an expectation of some naval assistance, or that the reduction could have been effected without it. In January, 1754, our assembly, in a message to governor Shirley, prayed him to represent to the king, "that the French had made such extraordinary encroachments, and taken such measures, since the conclusion of the preceding war, as threatened great danger, and perhaps, in time, even the entire destruction of this province, without the interposition of his majesty, notwithstanding any provision we could make to prevent it." "That the French had erected a fort on the isthmus of the peninsula near Bay Vert in Nova Scotia, by means of which they maintained a communication by sea with Canada, St. John's Island and Louisbourg." "That near the mouth of St. John's river, the French had possessed themselves of two forts formerly built by them, one of which was garrisoned by regular troops, and had erected another strong fort at twenty leagues up the river, and that these encroachments might prove fatal not only to the eastern parts of his majesty's territories within this province, but also in time to the whole of this province, and the rest of his majesty's territories on this continent." "That whilst the French held Acadia under the treaty of St. Germain, they so cut off the trade of this province, and galled the inhabitants with incursions into their territories, that OLIVER CROMWELL found it necessary for the safety of New England to make a descent by sea into the river of St. John, and dispossess them of that and all the forts in Acadia. That Acadia was restored to the French by the treaty of Breda it 1667." That this colony felt again the same mischievous effects from their possessing it, insomuch, that after forming several expeditions against it, the inhabitants were obliged in the latter end of the war in queen Ann's reign, to represent to her majesty how destructive the possession of the bay of Fundy and Nova Scotia, by the French, was to this province and the British trade; whereupon the British ministry thought it necessary to fit out a *formal expedition against that province with English troops*, and a considerable armament of our own, under general Nicholson, by which it was again reduced to the subjection of the crown of Great Britain. "That we were then, viz. in 1754, liable to feel more mischievous effects than we had ever yet done, unless his majesty should be graciously pleased to cause them to be removed." They also demonstrated our danger from the encroachments of the French at Crown Point. In April, 1754, the council and house represented, "That it evidently appeared, that the French were so far advanced in the execution of a plan projected more than fifty years since, for the extending their possessions from the mouth of the Mississippi on the south, to Hudson's Bay on the north, for securing the vast body of Indians in that inland country, and for subjecting the whole continent to the crown of France." "That many circumstances gave them great advantages over us, which if not attended to, would soon overbalance our superiority of numbers; and that these advantages could not be removed without his majesty's gracious interposition."

The assembly of Virginia, in an address to the king, represented, "that the endeavours of the French to establish a settlement upon the frontiers, was a high insult offered to his majesty, and if not timely opposed, with vigor and resolution, must be attended with the most fatal consequences," and prayed his majesty to extend his royal beneficence towards them.

The commissioners who met at Albany the same year,

represented, "that it was the evident design of the French to surround the British colonies; to fortify themselves on the back thereof; to take and keep possession of the heads of all the important rivers; to draw over the Indians to their interest, and with the help of such Indians, added to such forces as were then arrived, and might afterwards arrive, or be sent from Europe, to be in a capacity of making a general attack on the several governments; and if at the same time a strong naval force should be sent from France, there was the utmost danger that the whole continent would be subjected to the crown." "That it seemed absolutely necessary that speedy and effectual measures should be taken to secure the colonies from the *slavery* they were threatened with."

We did not pray in vain. Great Britain, ever attentive to the *real grievances* of her colonies, hastened to our relief with maternal speed. She covered our seas with her ships, and sent forth the bravest of her sons to fight our battles. They fought, they bled and conquered with us. Canada, Nova Scotia, the Floridas, and all our American foes were laid at our feet. It was a dear bought victory; the wilds of America were enriched with the blood of the noble and the brave.

The war, which at our request, was thus kindled in America, spread through the four quarters of the globe, and obliged Great Britain to exert her whole force and energy to stop the rapid progress of its devouring flames.

To these instances of actual exertions for our immediate protection and defence, ought to be added, the fleets stationed on our coast and the convoys and security afforded to our trade and fishery, in times of war; and her maintaining in times of peace such a navy and army, as to be always in readiness to give protection as exigencies may require; and her ambassadors residing at foreign courts to watch and give the earliest intelligence of their motions. By such precautions every part of her wide extended empire enjoys as ample security as human power and policy can afford. Those necessary precautions are supported at an immense expense, and the colonies reap the benefit of them equally with the rest of the empire. To these considerations it should likewise be added, that whenever the colonies have exerted themselves in war, though in their own defence, to a greater degree than their proportion with the rest of the empire, they have been reimbursed by parliamentary grants. This was the case, in the last war, with this province.

From this view, which I think is an impartial one, it is evident that Great Britain is not less attentive to our interest than her own; and that her sons that have settled on new and distant plantations are equally dear to her with those that cultivate the ancient domain, and inhabit the mansion house.

                                        MASSACHUSETTENSIS.

Massachusetts Gazette; and the Boston Post-Boy and Advertiser, March 13, 1775

Novanglus No. VIII

To the Inhabitants of the Colony of Massachusetts-Bay

My Friends,

It has been often observed by me, and it cannot be too often repeated, that *Colonization* is *Casus omissus* at common law. There is no such title known in that law. By common law, I mean that system of customs, written and unwritten, which was known and in force in England, in the time of king Richard the first. This continued to be the case, down to the reign of Elizabeth and king James the first. In all that time, the laws of England were confined to the realm, and within the four seas. There was no provision made in this law for governing colonies, beyond the Atlantic, or beyond the four seas, by authority of parliament, no nor for the king to grant charters to subjects to settle in foreign countries. It was the king's prerogative to prohibit the emigration of any of his subjects, by issuing his writ *Ne exeat Regno.* And therefore it was in the king's power to permit his subjects to leave the kingdom. 1 Hawk. P. C. c. 22. § 4. "It is a high crime to disobey the king's lawful commands, or prohibitions,—as not returning from beyond sea, upon the king's letters to that purpose; for which the offenders lands shall be seized 'till he return; and when he does return, he shall be fined,—&c.—or going beyond sea, against the king's will, expressly signified, either by the writ *Ne exeat Regnum,* or under the great or privy seal, or signet, or by proclamation." When a subject left the kingdom, by the king's permission, and if the nation did not remonstrate against it, by the nation's permission too, at least connivance, he carried with him, as a man, all the rights of nature. His allegiance bound him to the king, and intitled him to protection. But how? Not in France: the king of England was not bound to protect him in France, nor in America. Not in the dominions of Lewis, nor of Passachus, or Massachusett. He had a right to protection, and the liberties of England upon his return there, not otherwise. How then do we New Englandmen derive our laws? I say, not from parliament, not from common law, but from the law of nature and the compact made with the king in our charters. Our ancestors were intitled to the common law of England, when they emigrated, that is, to just so much of it as they pleased to adopt, and no more. They were not bound or obliged to submit to it, unless they chose it. By a positive principle of the common law, they were bound, let them be in what part of the world they would, to do nothing against their allegiance to the king. But no kind of provision was ever made by common law, for punishing or trying any man even for treason, committed out of the realm. He must be tried in some county of the realm, by that law, the county whereof the overt-act was done, or he could not be tried at all. Nor was any provision ever made, until the reign of Henry the Eighth, for trying treasons committed abroad, and the acts of that reign were made on purpose to catch Cardinal Pole.

So that our ancestors, when they emigrated, having obtained permission of the king to come here, and being never commanded to return into the realm, had a clear right to have erected in this wilderness a British constitution, or a perfect democracy, or any other form of government they saw fit. They indeed, while they lived, could not have taken arms against the king of England, without violating their allegiance, but their children would not have been born within the king's allegiance, would not have been natural subjects, and consequently not intitled to protection, or bound to the king.

Masachusettensis, Jan. 16, seems possessed of these ideas, and attempts in the most awkward manner, to get rid of them. He is conscious, that America must be a part of the realm, before it can be bound by the authority of parliament; and therefore is obliged to suggest, that we are annexed to the realm, and to endeavour to confuse himself and his readers, by confounding the realm, with the empire and dominions.

But will any man soberly contend, that America was ever annexed to the realm? To what realm? When New-England was settled, there was a realm of England, a realm of Scotland, and a realm of Ireland. To which of these three realms was New England annexed? To the realm of England, it will be said. But by what law? No territory could be annexed to the realm of England, but by an act of parliament. Acts of parliament have been passed to annex Wales, &c. &c. to the realm. But none ever passed to annex America. But if New-England was annexed to the realm of England, how came she annexed to the realm of or kingdom of Great-Britain? The two realms of England and Scotland were by the act of union incorporated into one kingdom by the name of Great-Britain: But there is not one word about America in that act.

Besides, if America was annexed to the realm, or a part of the kingdom, every act of parliament that is made, would extend to it, named or not named. But every body knows that every act of parliament, and every other record, constantly distinguishes between this kingdom, and his Majesty's other dominions. Will it be said that Ireland is annex'd to the realm, or a part of the kingdom of Great-Britain? Ireland is a distinct kingdom or realm by itself, notwithstanding British parliament claims a right of binding it in all cases, and exercises it in some. And even so the Massachusetts is a realm, New-York is a realm, Pennsylvania another realm, to all intents and purposes, as much as Ireland is, or England or Scotland ever were. The king of Great Britain is the sovereign of all these realms.

This writer says, "that in denying that the colonies are annexed to the realm, and subject to the authority of parliament, individuals and bodies of men, subvert the fundamentals of government, deprive us of British liberties, and build up absolute monarchy in the colonies."

This is the first time that I ever heard or read that the colonies are annexed to the realm. It is utterly denied that they are, and that it is possible they should be, without an act of parliament, and acts of the colonies. Such an act of parliament cannot be produced, nor any such law of any one colony. Therefore as this writer builds the whole authority of parliament upon this fact, viz. That the colonies are annexed to the realm; and as it is certain they never were so annexed: the consequence is, that his whole superstructure falls.

When he says, that they subvert the fundamentals of government, he begs the question. We say that the contrary doctrines subvert the fundamentals of government. When he says, that they deprive us of British liberties, he begs the question again: We say that the contrary doctrine deprives us of English Liberties; as to British Liberties, we scarcely know what they are, as the liberties of England and Scotland are not precisely the same to this day. English liberties are but certain rights of nature reserved to the citizen, by the English constitution, which rights cleaved to our ancestors when they crossed the Atlantic, and would have inbred in them, if instead of coming to New-England they had gone to Outaheite, or Patagonia, even altho' they had taken no patent or charter from the king at all. These rights did not adhere to them the less, for their purchasing patents and charters, in which the king expressly stipulates with them, that they and their posterity should for-ever enjoy all those rights and liberties.

The human mind is not naturally the clearest atmosphere; but the clouds and vapours which have been raised in it, by the artifices of temporal and spiritual tyrants, have made it impos-sible to see objects in it distinctly. Scarcely any thing is in-volved in more systematical obscurity, than the rights of our ancestors, when they arrived in America. How, in common sense, came the dominions of king Philip, king Massachusetts, and twenty other sovereign, independent princes here, to be within the allegiance of the king of England, James and Charles? America was no more within the allegiance of those princes, by the common law of England, or by the law of na-ture, than France and Spain were. Discovery, if that was incon-testible could give no title to the English king, by common law, or by the law of nature, to the lands, tenements and here-ditaments of the native Indians here. Our ancestors were sensi-ble of this, and therefore honestly purchased their lands of the natives. They might have bought them to hold allodially, if they would.

But there were two ideas, which confused them, and have continued to confuse their posterity, one derived from the feu-dal, the other from the cannon law. By the former of these sys-tems, the prince, the general, was supposed to be sovereign Lord of all the lands, conquered by the soldiers in his army; and upon this principle, the king of England was considered in law as Sovereign Lord of all the land within the realm. If he had sent an Army here to conquer king Massachusetts, and it had succeeded he would have been sovereign lord of the land here upon these principles; but there was no rule of the common law, that made the discovery of a country by a sub-ject, a title to that country in the prince. But conquest would not have annexed the country to the realm, nor have given

any authority to the parliament. But there was another mist
cast before the eyes of the English nation from another source.
The pope claimed a sovereign propriety in, as well as authority
over the whole earth. As head of the christian church, and
vicar of God, he claimed this authority over all Christendom;
and in the same character he claimed a right to all the countries and possessions of heathens and infidels: a right divine to
exterminate and destroy them at his discretion, in order to
propagate the catholic faith. When king Henry the eighth, and
his parliament, threw off the authority of the pope, stripped
his holiness of his supremacy, and invested it in himself by an
act of parliament, he and his courtiers seemed to think that all
the right of the holy see, were transferred to him: and it was a
union of these two the most impertinent and fantastical ideas
that ever got into an human pericranium, viz. that as feudal
sovereign and supream head of the church together, a king of
England had a right to all the land their subjects could find,
not possessed by any christian state or prince, tho' possessed
by heathen or infidel nations, which seems to have deluded the
nation about the time of the settlement of the colonies. But
none of these ideas gave or inferred any right in parliament,
over the new countries conquered or discovered; and therefore
denying that the colonies are a part of the realm, and that as
such they are subject to parliament, by no means deprives us of
English liberties. Nor does it "build up absolute monarchy in
the colonies." For admitting these notions of the canon and
feudal law to have been in full force, and that the king was absolute in America, when it was settled; yet he had a right to enter into a contract with his subjects, and stipulate that they
should enjoy all the rights and liberties of Englishmen forever,
in consideration of their undertaking to clear the wilderness,
propagate christianity, pay a fifth part of oar, &c. Such a contract as this has been made with all the colonies, royal governments as well as charter ones. For the commissions to the
governors contain the plan of the government, and the contract between the king and subject, in the former, as much as
the charters in the latter.

Indeed this was the reasoning, and upon these feudal and
catholic principles in the time of some of the predecessors of
Massachusettensis.—This was the meaning of Dudley, when

he asked, "Do you think that English liberties will follow you to the ends of the earth?" His meaning was, that English liberties were confined to the realm, and out of that the king was absolute. But this was not true, for an English King had no right to be absolute over Englishmen, out of the realm, any more than in it, and they were released from their allegiance, as soon as he deprived them of their liberties.

But "our charters suppose regal authority in the grantor". True they suppose it, whether there was any or not. "If that authority be derived from the British, (he should have said English) crown, it presupposes this territory to have been a part of the British (he should have said English) dominion, and as such subject to the imperial Sovereign." How can this writer shew this authority to be derived from the English crown, including in the idea of it Lords and Commons? Is there the least colour for such an authority but in the popish and feudal ideas before mentioned? And do these popish and feudal ideas, include parliament? Was parliament, were Lords and Commons parts of the head of the church or was parliament, that is, Lords and Commons, part of the sovereign feudatory? Never. But why was this authority derived from the English, any more than the Scottish or Irish Crown? It is true the land was to be held in socage like the manor of East Greenwich, but this was compact, and it might have been as well to hold, as they held in Glasgow or Dublin.

But says this writer, "if that authority was vested in the person of the king in a different capacity, the British constitution and laws are out of the question, and the king must be absolute as to us, as his prerogatives have never been limitted."— Not the prerogative limited in our charters, when in every one of them all the rights of Englishmen are secured to us! Are not the rights of Englishmen sufficiently known, and are not the prerogatives of the king's among those rights?

As to those colonies which are destitute of charters, the commissions to their governors have ever been considered as equivalent securities both for property, jurisdiction and privileges, with charters; and as to the power of the crown being absolute in those colonies, it is absolute no where. There is no fundamental or other law, that makes a king of England absolute any where, except in conquered countries, and an

attempt to assume such a power, by the fundamental laws, forfeits the princes right even to the limited crown.

As to "the charter governments reverting to absolute monarchy, as their charters may happen to be forfeited, by the
grantees not fulfilling the conditions of them,"—I answer, if
they could be forfeited, and were actually forfeited, the only
consequence would be, that the king would have no power
over them at all: He would not be bound to protect the
people, nor, that I can see, would the people here, who were
born here, be by any principle of common law, bound even to
allegiance to the king. The connection would be broken
between the crown and the natives of the country.

It has been a great dispute whether charters granted within
the realm, can be forfeited at all. It was a question debated
with infinite learning, in the case of the charter of London: it
was adjudged forfeited, in an arbitrary reign: but afterwards,
after the revolution, it was declared in parliament, not forfeited, and by an act of parliament made incapable of forfeiture. The charter of Massachusetts was declared forfeited too.
So were other American charters. The Massachusetts alone,
were tame enough to give it up. But no American charter will
ever be decreed forfeited again, or if any should, the decree
will be regarded no more, than a vote of the lower house of
the robbinhood society. The court of chancery has no authority without the realm; by common law, surely it has none in
America. What! The privileges of millions of Americans depend on the discretion of a lord chancellor? God forbid! The
passivity of this colony in receiving the present charter in lieu
of the first, is in the opinion of some the deepest stain upon its
character. There is less to be said in excuse for it, than the
witchcraft, or hanging the quakers. A vast party in the province
were against it at the time, and thought themselves betrayed
by their agent. It has been a warning to their posterity, and one
principal motive with the people, never to trust any agent with
power to conceed away their privileges again. It may as well be
pretended that the people of Great-Britain can forfeit their
privileges, as the people of this province: if the contract of
state is broken, the people and king of England, must recur to
nature. It is the same in this province. We shall never more

submit to decrees in chancery, or acts of parliament, annihilating charters, or abridging English liberties.

Whether Massachusettensis was born as a politician, in the year 1764, I know not: but he often writes as if he knew nothing of that period. In his attempt to trace the denial of the supreme authority of the parliament, he commits such mistakes, as a man of age at that time ought to blush at. He says, that "when the stamp-act was made the authority of parliament to impose external taxes, or in other words to lay duties upon goods and merchandize was admitted," and that when the tea act was made, "a new distinction was set up, that parliament had a right to lay duties upon merchandize, for the purpose of regulating trade, but not for the purpose of raising a revenue." This is a total misapprehension of the declared opinions of people at those times. The authority of parliament to lay taxes for a revenue, has been always generally denied: and their right to lay duties to regulate trade, has been denied by many, who have ever contended, that trade should be regulated only by prohibitions.

The act of parliament of the 4 G, the third, passed in the year 1764, was the first act of the British parliament that ever was passed, in which the design of raising a revenue, was expressed. Let Massachusettensis name any statute before that in which the word revenue is used, or the thought of raising a revenue, is expressed. This act is intitled, "An act for granting certain duties in the British colonies and plantations in America," &c. The word revenue, in the preamble of this act, instantly ran through the colonies, and rang an alarm, almost as much as if the design of forging chains for the Colonists had been expressed in words. I have now before me, a pamphlet, written and printed in the year 1764 intitled, "The sentiments of a British American," upon this act. How the idea of a revenue, tho' from an acknowledged external tax, was relished in that time, may be read in the frontispiece of that pamphlet—

—Ergo quid refert mea
Cui serviam? clitellas dum portem meas.

Phædrus.

The first objection to this act, which was made in that pamphlet, by its worthy author, OXENBRIDGE THACHER, Esq; who died a Martyr to that anxiety for his country, which the conduct of the Junto gave him, is this, "The first objection is, that a tax is thereby laid on several commodities, to be raised and levied in the plantations, and to be remitted home to England. This is esteemed a grievance inasmuch as the same are laid, without the consent of the representatives of the colonists. It is esteemed an essential British right, that no person shall be subject to any tax; but what in person, or by his representative, he hath a voice in laying." Here is a tax unquestionably external, in the sense in which that word is used in the distinction that is made by some between external and internal taxes, and unquestionably laid in part for the regulation of trade; yet called a grievance, and a violation of an essential British right in the year 1764, by one who was then at the head of the popular branch of our constitution, and as well acquainted with the sense of his constituents, as any man living. And it is indisputable that in those words he wrote, the almost universal sense of this colony.

There are so many egregious errors in point of fact, and respecting the opinions of the people in this writer, that it is difficult to impute to wilful misrepresentation, that I sometimes think he is some smart young gentleman, come up, into life, since this great controversy was opened; if not, he must have conversed wholly with the junto, and they must have deceived him, respecting their own sentiments.

This writer sneers at the distinction between a right to lay the former duty of a shilling on the pound of tea, and the right to lay the three pence. But is there not a real difference between laying a duty to be paid in England upon exportation, and to be paid in America upon importation? Is there not a difference between parliament's laying on duties within their own realm, where they have undoubtedly jurisdiction, and laying them out of their realm, nay laying them on in our realm, where we say they have no jurisdiction? Let them lay on what duties they please in England, we have nothing to say against that.

"Our patriots most heroically resolved to become independent states, and flatly denied that parliament had a right to make any laws what ever that should be binding upon the colonies."

Our scribler more heroically still, is determined to shew the world, that he has courage superior to all regard to modesty, justice or truth. Our patriots have never determined or desired to be independent states, if a voluntary cession of a right to regulate their trade, can make them dependent even on parliament, tho' they are clear in theory, that by the common law, and the English constitution, parliament has no authority over them. None of the patriots of this province, of the present age, have ever denied that parliament has a right from our voluntary cession, to make laws which shall bind the colonies, as far as their commerce extends.

"There is no possible medium between absolute independence and subjection to the authority of parliament." If this is true, it may be depended upon that all North America are as fully convinced of their independence, their absolute independence, as they are of their own existence, and as fully determined to defend it at all hazards, as Great Britain is to defend her independence, against foreign nations. But it is not true. An absolute independence on parliament, in all internal concerns and cases of taxation, is very compatible with an absolute dependence on it in all cases of external commerce.

"He must be blind indeed that cannot see our dearest interest, in the latter (that is, in an "absolute subjection to the authority of parliament") notwithstanding many pant after the former" (that is, absolute independence). The man who is capable of writing, in cool blood, that our interest lies in an absolute subjection to parliament, is capable of writing or saying any thing for the sake of his pension. A legislature that has so often discovered a want of information concerning us, and our country; a legislature interested to lay burdens upon us; a legislature, two branches of which, I mean the Lords and Commons, neither love nor fear us! Every American of fortune and common sense, must look upon his property to be sunk downright one half of its value, the moment such an absolute subjection to parliament is established.

That there are any who pant after "independence," (meaning by this word a new plan of government over all America, unconnected with the crown of England, or meaning by it an exemption from the power of parliament to regulate trade) is as great a slander upon the province as ever was committed to writing. The patriots of this province desire nothing new— they wish only to keep their old privileges. They were for 150 years allowed to tax themselves, and govern their internal concerns, as they tho't best. Parliament governed their trade as they tho't fit. This plan, they wish may continue forever. But it is honestly confessed, rather than become subject to the absolute authority of parliament, in all cases of taxation and internal polity, they will be driven to throw off that of regulating trade.

"To deny the supreme authority of the state, is a high misdemeanor; to oppose it by force, an overt act of treason." True: and therefore Massachusettensis, who denies the king represented by his governor, his majesty's council, by charter, and house of representatives, to be the supreme authority of this province, has been guilty of a high misdemeanour: and those ministers, governors, and their instruments, who have brought a military force here, and employed it against that supreme authority, are guilty of ____ and ought to be punished with ____. I will be more mannerly than Massachusettensis.

"The realm of England is an appropriate term for the ancient realm of England, in contradistinction to Wales and other territories, that have been annexed to it."

There are so many particulars in the case of Wales, analogous to the case of America, that I must beg leave to enlarge upon it.

(*For want of Room we are obliged to deferr the Remainder of this* NOVANGLUS *till our next.*)

Boston Gazette, March 13, 1775

Remainder of the NOVANGLUS *begun in our last.*

Wales was a little portion of the island of Great-Britain, which the Saxons were never able to conquer. The Britons had reserved this tract of land to themselves and subsisted wholly by pasturage, among their mountains. Their princes however, during the Norman period, and untill the reign of king Edward the first, did homage to the crown of England, as their feudal sovereign, in the same manner as the prince of one independant state in Europe frequently did to the sovereign of another. This little principality of shepherds and cowherds, had however maintained their independence, through long and bloody wars against the omnipotence of England, for 800 years. It is needless to enumerate the causes of the war between Lewellyn and Edward the first. It is sufficient to say that the Welch prince refused to go to England to do homage, and Edward obtained a new aid of a fifteenth from his parliament, to march with a strong force into Wales. Edward was joined by David and Roderic, two brothers of Lewellyn, who made a strong party among the Welch themselves, to assist and second the attempts to enslave their native country. The English monarch however, with all these advantages, was afraid to put the valour of his enemies to a tryal, and trusted to *the slow effects of famine* to subdue them. Their pasturage, with such an enemy in their country, could not subsist them, and Lewellyn 19 Nov. 1277 at last submitted; and bound himself to pay a reparation of damages: to do homage to the crown of England, and almost to surrender his independence as a Prince by permitting all the other Barons of Wales, excepting four, to swear fealty to the same crown. But fresh complaints soon arose: The English grew insolent on their bloodless victory, and oppressed the inhabitants—many insults were offered, which at last raised the indignation of the Welch, so that they determined again to take arms, rather than bear any longer the oppression of the haughty victors. The war raged, some time, until Edward summoned all his military tenants, and advanced with an army too powerful for the Welch to resist. Lewellyn was at last surprized, by Edward's General Mortimer, and fighting at a great disadvantage was slain with two thousand of his men. David, who succeeded in the principality, maintained the war for some time, but at last was betrayed to the enemy, sent in Chains to Shrewsbury, brought to a formal trial before the peers of England, and altho' a sovereign prince, ordered by Edward to be hanged, drawn and quartered, as a traitor, for defending by arms the liberties of his native country! All the Welch nobility submitted to the conqueror: The laws of

England, sheriffs, and other ministers of justice, were established in that principality, which had maintained its liberties
and independency, 800 years.

Now Wales was always part of the dominions of England:
"Wales was always feudatory to the kingdom of England." It
was always held of the crown of England, or the kingdom of
England: that is, whoever was king of England, had a right to
homage, &c. from the prince of Wales. But yet Wales was not
parcel of the realm or kingdom, nor bound by the laws of
England. I mention and insist upon this, because it shews, that
altho' the colonies are bound to the crown of England, or in
other words, owe allegiance to whomsoever is king of
England; yet it does not follow that the colonies are parcel of
the realm or kingdom, and bound by its laws. As this is a point
of great importance, I must beg pardon, however unentertaining it may be, to produce my authorities.

Comyns digest. v. 5. page 626. "Wales was always feudatory
to the kingdom of England.

"Held of the crown but not parcel. Per Coke. 1 Roll. 247—
2 Roll. 29. And therefore the kings of Wales did homage, and
swore fealty to H. 2. and John and H. 3.

"And 11 Ed. 1. Upon the conquest of Lewellyn prince or
king of Wales that principality became a part of the dominion
of the realm of England. And by the statute Walliæ 12 Ed. 1. it
was annexed and united to the crown of England, *tanquam
partem corporis ejusdem*, &c.—Yet, if the statute Walliæ, made
at Rutland 12 Ed. 1. was not an act of parliament (as it seems
that it was not) the incorporation made thereby was only an
union *jure feudali, et non jure proprietatis.*"

"Wales before the union with England was governed by its
own proper laws." &c.

By these authorities it appears, that Wales was subject by the
feudal law, to the crown of England, before the conquest of
Lewellyn; but not subject to the laws of England: and indeed
after this conquest, Edward, and his nobles, did not seem to
think it subject to the English parliament, but to the will of the
king as a conqueror of it in war. Accordingly that instrument
which is called *Statutum Walliæ*, and to be found in the appendix to the statutes page 3, altho' it was made by the advice of
the peers, or officers of the army more properly, yet it never

was passed as an act of parliament, but as an edict of the king. It begins not in the style of an act of parliament. *Edwardus dei gratia Rex Angliæ, Dominus Hyberniæ, et Dux Aquitaniæ, omnibus fidelibus suis, &c. in Wallia. Divina providentia, quae in sui dispositione,* says he, *nonfallitur, inter alia dispensationis suæ munera, quibus nos et Regnum nostrum Angliæ decorare dignata est, terram Walliæ, cum incolis suis, prius nobis* jure feudali *subjectam, jam sui gratia,* in proprietatis nostræ dominium, *obstaculis quibuscumque cessantibus, totalliter, et cum integritate convertit,* et coronæ regni prædicti, tanquam partem corporis ejusdem annexuit et univit.

Here is the most certain evidence that Wales was subject to the kings of England by the feudal law before the conquest, tho' not bound by any laws but their own. 2. That the conquest was considered, in that day, as conferring the property as well as jurisdiction of Wales to the English crown. 3. The conquest was considered as annexing and uniting Wales to the English crown, both in point of property and jurisdiction, as a part of one body. Yet notwithstanding all this, parliament was not considered as acquiring any share in the government of Wales by this conquest. If then, it should be admitted that the colonies are all annexed and united to the crown of England, it will not follow that Lords and Commons have any authority over them.

This statutum Walliæ, as well as the whole case and history of that principality, is well worthy of the attention and study of Americans, because it abounds, with evidence, that a country may be subject to the crown of England, without being subject to the Lords and Commons of that realm, which entirely overthrows the whole argument of Governor Hutchinson and of Massachusettensis in support of the supreme authority of parliament, over all the dominions of the imperial crown. "*Nos itaque,*" &c. says King Ed. 1. "*volentes predictam terram,* &c. *sicut et cæteras ditioni nostræ subjectas,* &c. *subdebito regimine gubernari, et incolas seu habitatores terarum illarum, qui alto et basso,* Se submiserunt voluntati nostræ, *et quos sic ad nostram recepimus voluntatem, certis legibus et consuetudinibus,* &c. *tractari Leges, et consuetudines, partum illarum hactenus usitatas coram nobis et proceribus regni nostri secimus necitari, quibus diligenter auditas, et plenus intellectis, quasdam ipsarum*

de concilio procerum predictorum delevimus, quasdampermisi-
mus, et quasdam correximus, et etiam quasdam alias adjungen-
das et statuendas decrevimus, et eas, &c. *observari volumus in*
forma subscripta."

And then goes on to prescribe and establish a whole code of
laws for the principality, in the style of a sole legislator, and
concludes,

Et ideo vobis mandamus, quod premissa de cetero in omnibus
firmiter observetis. Ita tamen quod quotiescunque, et quando-
cunque, et ubicunque, nobis placuerit, possimus predicta statuta
et coram partes singulas declarare, interpretari, addere sive
diminuere, pro nostro libito voluntatis, et prout securitati nostræ
et terræ nostræ predictæ viderimus expedire.

Here is then a conquered people submitting, to a system of
laws framed by the mere will of the conqueror, and agreeing to
be forever governed by his mere will. This absolute monarch
then might afterwards govern this country, with or without
the advice of his English lords and commons.

To shew that Wales was held before the conquest of
Lewellyn, of the king of England, altho' governed by its own
laws, hear lord Coke, 2 Inst. 194, in his commentary on the
statute of Westminster. "At this time viz. in 3. Ed. 1. Lewellyn
was a prince or king of Wales, who held the *same of the king of*
England, as his superior lord, and owed him liege homage and
fealty; and this is proved by our act, viz. that the king of England was *superior dominus,* i. e. sovereign lord of the kingdom or principality of Wales."

Lord Coke in 4 Inst. 239. says "Wales was sometime a realm,
or kingdom (realm from the French word royaume, and both
a regno) and governed *per suas regulas,*" and afterwards, "but
jure feudali, the kingdom of Wales was holden of the *crown of*
England, and thereby as Bracton saith, was *sub potestate regis.*
And so it continued until the 11 year of king E. 1. when he subdued the prince of Wales, rising against him, and executed him
for treason." "The next year, viz. in the 12 year of king E. 1. by
authority of parliament, it is declared thus, speaking in the person of the king (as ancient statutes were wont to do) *divina*
providentia," &c. as in the statute *Walliæ* before recited. But
here is an inaccuracy for the *statutum Walliæ,* was not an act
of parliament, but made by the king with the advice of his

officers of the army, by his sole authority, as the statute itself sufficiently shews. Note, says Lord Coke, "diverse monarchs hold their kingdoms of others *jure feudali*, as the duke of Lombardy, Cicill, Naples, and Bohemia of the empire, Granado, Leons, of Aragon, Navarre, Portugal of Castile. And so others."

After this the Welsh seem to have been fond of the English laws, and desirous of being incorporated into the realm, to be represented in parliament, and enjoy all the rights of Englishmen, as well as to be bound by the English laws. But Kings were so fond of governing this principality by their discretion alone, that they never could obtain these blessings until the reign of Henry the Eighth, and then they only could obtain a statute, which enabled the king to alter their laws at his pleasure. They did indeed obtain in the 15 Ed. 2. a writ, to call 24 members to the parliament at York from south Wales, and twenty four from North Wales, and again in the 20 Ed. 2, the like number of 48 members for Wales, at the parliament of Westminster. But lord Coke tells us "that this wise and warlike nation was long after, the *statutum Walliæ* not satisfied nor contented, and especially, for that they truly and constantly took part with their rightful sovereign and liege lord, king Richard the second; in *revenge whereof they had many severe and invective laws made against them in the reigns of H. 4, H. 5, &c. all which as unjust are repealed and abrogated.* And to say the truth, this nation was never in quiet, until king H. 7, their own countryman obtained the crown. And yet not so really reduced in his time, as in the reign of his son H. 8, in whose time certain just laws, *made at the humble suit of the subjects of Wales,* the principality and dominion of Wales was incorporated and united to the realm of England; and enacted that every one born in Wales, should enjoy the liberties, rights and laws of this realm, as any subjects naturally born within this realm should have and inherit, and that they should have knights of shires, and burgesses of parliament." Yet we see they could not obtain any security for their liberties, for lord Coke tells us, "in the act of 34. H. 8. it was enacted, that the king's most royal majesty should from time to time change, &c. all manner of things in that act rehearsed, as to his most excellent wisdom and discretion should be thought convenient, and also to make laws and ordinances for the commonwealth of his said dominion, of Wales at his majesty's pleasure." But for that, the subjects of the dominion of Wales, &c. had lived in all dutiful subjection to the crown of England, &c. the said branch of the said statute of 34. H. 8. is repealed, and made void by 21 Jac. c. 10.

But if we look into the statute itself of 27. H. 8 c. 26, we shall find the clearest proof that being subject to the imperial crown of England, did not intitle Welchmen to the liberties of England, nor make them subject to the laws of England. "Albeit the dominion, principality and country of Wales *justly and righteously is, and ever hath been incorporated, annexed, united, and subject to and under the imperial crown of this realm, as a very member and joint of the same*; wherefore, the king's most royal majesty of mere droit, and very right, is very head, king, lord and ruler; yet, notwithstanding, because that in the same country, principality and dominion, diverse *rights, usages, laws* and customs be far discrepant from the laws and customs of this realm, &c. Wherefore it is enacted, by king, lords and commons, "that "his" (i. e. the king's) said country or dominion of Wales shall be, stand and continue for ever from henceforth, incorporated, united, and annexed to and with this, his realm of England; and that all and singular person and persons, born or to be born, in the said principality, country, or dominion of Wales, shall have, enjoy, and inherit, all and singular freedoms, liberties, rights, privileges, and laws, within this his realm, and other the king's dominions, as other the king's subjects naturally born within the same have, enjoy, and inherit." § 2. enacts that the laws of England shall be introduced and established in Wales: and that the laws, ordinances and statutes of this realm of England, forever and none other shall be used and practiced, forever thereafter in the said dominion of Wales. The 27th § of this long statute enacts, that commissioners shall enquire into the laws and customs of Wales, and report to the king, who with his privy council, are impowered to establish such of them as they should think proper. § 28 enacts that in all future parliaments *for this realm*, two knights for the shire of Monmouth and one burgess for the town, shall be chosen, and allowed such fees as other knights and burgesses of parliament were allowed. § 29 enacts, that one knight shall be elected for every shire within the country or dominion of Wales, and one burgess for every shire town, to serve in that and every future parliament to be holden for this realm. But by § 36 the king is impowered to revoke, repeal and abrogate that whole act, or any part of it, at any time within three years.

Upon this statute let it be observed 1. That the language of Massachusettensis "imperial crown" is used in it: and Wales is affirmed to have *ever* been annexed, and united to that imperial crown, as a very member and joint: which shews that being annexed to the imperial crown, does not annex a country to the realm, or make it subject to the authority of parliament: because Wales, certainly before the conquest of Lewellyn never was pretended to be so subject, nor afterwards ever pretended to be annexed to the realm, at all, nor subject to the authority of parliament, any otherwise than as the king claimed to be absolute in Wales, and therefore to make laws for it, by his mere will, either with the advice of his proceres, or without. 2. That Wales never was incorporated with the realm of England, until this statute was made, nor subject to any authority of English lords and commons. 3. That the king was so tenacious of his exclusive power over Wales that he would not consent to this statute, without a clause in it, to retain the power in his own hands of giving it what system of law he pleased. 4. That knights and burgesses, i.e. representatives, were considered as *essential* and *fundamental* in the constitution of the new legislature, which was to govern Wales. 5. That since this statute, the distinction between the realm of England and the realm of Wales, has been abolished, and the realm of England, now, and ever since, comprehends both; so that Massachusettensis is mistaken, when he says, that the realm of England is an appropriate term for the ancient realm of England, in contradistinction from Wales, &c. 6. That this union and incorporation was made by the consent, and upon the supplication of the people of Wales, as Lord Coke, and many other authors inform us, so that here was an express contract between the two bodies of people. To these observations, let me add a few questions.

Was there ever any act of parliament, annexing, uniting, and consolidating any one of all the colonies to and with the realm of England or the kingdom of Great-Britain? 2. If such an act of parliament should be made, would it upon any principles of English laws and government, have any validity, without the consent, petition or supplication of the colonies? 3. Can such an union and incorporation, ever be made, upon any principles of English laws and government, without admitting representatives for the colonies in the house of commons, and American lords into the house of peers? 4. Would not representatives in the house of commons, unless they were numerous in proportion to the numbers of people in America, be a snare rather than a blessing? 5. Would Britain ever agree to a proportionable number of American members, and if she would, could America support the expence of them? 6. Could American representatives, possibly know the sense, the exigencies, &c. of their constituents, at such a distance, so perfectly as it is absolutely necessary legislators should know? 7. Could Americans ever come to the knowledge of the behaviour of their members, so as to dismiss the unworthy? 8. Would Americans in general, ever submit to septennial elections? 9. Have we not sufficient evidence, in the general frailty and depravity of human nature, and especially the experience we have had of Massachusettensis and the junto, that a deep, treacherous, plausible, corrupt minister, would be able to seduce our Members to betray us, as fast as we could send them?

To return to Wales: In the statute of 34 and 35 of Henry 8. c. 26. We find a more compleat system of laws and regulations for Wales. But the king is still tenacious of his absolute authority over it. It begins "our sovereign lord the king, of his tender zeal and affection, &c. to his obedient subjects, &c. of Wales, &c. *hath devised and made* divers sundry good and necessary ordinances, which his majesty of his most abundant goodness, *at the humble suit and petition of his said subjects of Wales*, is pleased and contented to be enacted by the assent of the lords spiritual and temporal, and the commons, &c."

Nevertheless, the king would not yet give up his unlimited power over Wales, for by the 119 § of this statute—the king, &c. may at all times hereafter, from time to time, change, add, alter, order, minish and reform all manner of things afore rehearsed, as to his most excellent wisdom and discretion, shall be thought convenient; and also to make laws and ordinances for the common wealth and good quiet of his said dominion

of Wales, and his subjects of the same, from time to time, at his
majesty's pleasure.

And this last section was never repealed, until the 21. Jac. 1.
c. 10 §. 4.

From the conquest of Lewellyn to this statute of James is
near 350 years during all which time, the Welch were very fond
of being incorporated and enjoying the English laws, the English were desirous that they should be; yet the crown would
never suffer it to be compleatly done, because it claimed an
authority to rule it by discretion: It is conceived, therefore that
there cannot be a more compleat and decisive proof of any
thing, than this instance is, that a country may be subject
to the crown of England, the imperial crown; and yet not annexed to the realm, or subject to the authority of parliament.

The word crown, like the word throne, is used in various
figurative senses, sometimes it means the kingly office, the head
of the common wealth, but it does not always mean the political capacity of the king—much less does it include in the idea
of it lords and commons. It may as well be pretended that the
house of commons includes or implies a king. Nay it may as
well be pretended, that the mace includes the three branches
of the legislature.

By the feudal law, a person or a country might be subject to
a king, a feudal sovereign, three several ways.

1. It might be subject to his person, and in this case, it would
continue so subject, let him be where he would, in his dominions or without. 2. To his crown, and in this case subjection
was due, to whatsoever person or family, wore that crown, and
would follow it, whatever revolutions it underwent. 3. To his
crown and realm or state, and in this case it was incorporated,
as one body with the principal kingdom, and if that was bound
by a parliament, diet, or cortes, so was the other.

It is humbly conceived, that the subjection of the colonies
by compact, and law is of the second sort.

Suffer me, my friends, to conclude by making my most respectful compliments to the gentlemen of the regiment of
royal Welch fusileers. In the celebration of their late festival,
they discover'd that they are not insensible of the feelings of a
man for his native country. The most generous minds are the
most exquisitely capable of this sentiment. Let me intreat them

to recollect the history of their brave and intrepid countrymen, who struggled at least 1100 years for liberty. Let them
compare the case of Wales with the case of America, and then
lay their hands upon their hearts and say, whether we can in
justice be bound by all acts of parliament, without being incorporated with the kingdom.

NOVANGLUS

Boston Gazette, March 20, 1775

THE POWER OF SATIRE

To Mercy Otis Warren

Madam   Braintree March 15. 1775
   I thought myself greatly honoured, by your most polite and
agreable Letter of January the thirtieth; and I ought to have
answered it, immediately: but a Variety of Cares and Avocations, at this troublesome Time, which I confess are not a justification of my Negligence, as they were the real Cause of it,
will with your goodness of Disposition be allowed as an Excuse.
   In requesting my opinion, Madam, concerning a Point of
Casuistry, you have done me great Honour, and I should think
myself very happy if I could remove a Scruple from a Mind,
which is so amiable that it ought not to have one upon it. Personal Reflections, when they are artfully resorted to, in order
to divert the Attention from Truth, or from Arguments, which
cannot be answered, are mean and unjustifiable: but We must
give up the Distinction between Virtue and Vice, before We
can pronounce personal Reflections, always unlawfull. Will it
be Said that We must not pronounce Cataline a Conspirator,
and Borgia a Rascall, least we should be guilty of casting personal Reflections? The faithfull Historian delineates Caracters
truly, let the Censure fall where it will. The public is so inter-
rested in public Characters, that they have a Right to know
them, and it becomes the Duty of every good Citizen who
happens to be acquainted with them to communicate his
Knowledge.

There is no other Way of preventing the Mischief, which may be done by ill Men: no other Method of administering the Antidote to the Poison.

Christianity Madam, is so far, from discountenancing the severest Discrimination, between the good and the bad, that it assures us, of the most public and solemn one conceivable, before Angells and Men: and the Practice and Example of Prophetts, and Apostles, is Sufficient to Sanctify Satyr of the Sharpest Kind.

The Truth is, Madam, that, the best Gifts are liable to the worst Uses and Abuses, a Talent at Satyr, is commonly mixed with the choicest Powers of Genius, and it has such irresistable Charms, in the Eyes of the World, that the extravagant Praise, it never fails to extort, is apt to produce extravagant Vanity in the Satirist, and an exuberant Fondness for more Praise, untill it looses that cool Judgment, which alone can justify him.

But the lawfulness of the exercise of this briliant Talent, may be argued from it being a natural one. Nature, which does nothing in vain, bestows no mental Faculties, which are not designed to be cultivated and improved. It may also be inferred from its admirable Utility and Effects. If We look into human Nature, and run through the various Classes of Life, We shall find it is really a dread of Satyr that restrains our Species, from Exorbitances, more than Laws, human moral or divine, indeed the Efficacy of civil Punishments is derived chiefly from the same source. It is not the Pain the Fine, &c that is dreaded so much as the Infamy and Disgrace. So that really the civil Magistrate may be said in a good sense to keep the World in order, by Means of Satyrs, for Goals, Stocks, Whipping Posts and Gallows's are but different Kinds of it. But classical Satyr, such as flows so naturally and easily from the Pen of my excellent Friend had all the Efficacy, and more, in Support of Virtue and in Discountenancing of Vice, without any of the Coarseness and Indelicacy of those other Species of Satyr, the civil and political ones.

If you examine the Life and Actions of your poorest, lowest and most despised Neighbour, or the meanest servant you know, you will find, that there is Some one or more Persons, of whose Esteem and good opinion he is ambitious, and whose Scorn and Derision he dreads perhaps more than any other Evil. And this Desire of Esteem and dread of Scorn is the principle that governs his Life and Actions. Now the Business of satyr is to expose Vice And vicious Men as such to this scorn and to envoke Virtue, in all the Charms which fancy can paint, and by this Means to procure her Lovers and Admirers.

Of all the Genius's which have yet arisen in America, there has been none, Superiour, to one, which now shines, in this happy, this exquisite Faculty. Indeed, altho there are many which have received more industrious Cultivation I know of none, ancient or modern, which has reached the tender, the pathetic, the keen and severe, and at the same time the soft, the Sweet, the amiable, and the pure, in greater Perfection.

I am Madam, with great Respect your Friend,

John Adams

Massachusettensis [Daniel Leonard] No. XV

To the Inhabitants of the Province of Massachusetts Bay,

MY DEAR COUNTRYMEN,

The outlines of British commerce have been heretofore sketched; and the interest of each part, in particular, and of the whole empire conjointly, have been shewn to be the principles by which the grand system is poized and balanced. Whoever will take upon himself the trouble of reading and comparing the several acts of trade, which respect the colonies, will be convinced, that the cherishing their trade, and promoting their interest, have been the objects of parliamentary attention, equally with those of Britain. He will see, that the great council of the empire has ever esteemed our prosperity as inseperable from the British; and if in some instances the colonies have been restricted to the emolument of other parts of the empire, they, in their turn, not excepting England itself, have been also restricted sufficiently to restore the balance, if not to cause a preponderation in our favour.

Permit me to transcribe a page or two from a pamphlet written in England, and lately republished here, wherein this matter is stated with great justice and accuracy.

"The people of England and the American adventurers, being so differently circumstanced, it required no great sagacity to discover, that as there were many commodities which America could supply on better terms than they could be raised in England, so must it be much more for the colonies, advantage to take others from England, than attempt to make them themselves. The American lands were cheap, covered with woods, and abounded with native commodities. The first attention of the settlers was necessarily engaged in cutting down the timber, and clearing the ground for culture; for before they had supplied themselves with provisions, and had hands to spare from agriculture, it was impossible they could set about manufacturing. England, therefore, undertook to supply them with manufactures, and either purchased herself or found markets for the timber the colonists cut down upon their lands, or the fish they caught upon their coasts. It was soon discovered that the tobacco plant was a native of and flourished in Virginia. It had been also planted in England, and was found to delight in the soil. The legislature, however, wisely and equitably considering that England had variety of products, and Virginia had no other to buy her necessaries with, passed an act prohibiting the people of England from planting tobacco, and thereby giving the monopoly of that plant to the colonies. As the inhabitants increased, and the lands became more cultivated, further and new advantages were thrown in the way of the American colonies. All foreign markets, as well as Great-Britian, were open for their timber and provisions, and the British West-India islands were prohibited from purchasing those commodities from any other than them. And since England has found itself in danger of wanting a supply of timber, and it has been judged necessary to confine the export from America to Great-Britain and Ireland, full and ample indemnity has been given to the colonies for the loss of a choice of markets in Europe, by very large bounties paid out of the revenue of Great Britain, upon the importation of American timber. And as a further enouragement and reward to them for clearing their lands, bounties are given upon tar and pitch, which are made from their decayed and useless trees; and the very ashes of their lops and branches are made of value by the late bounty on American pot-ashes. The soil and climate of the northern colonies having been found well adapted to the culture of flax and hemp, bounties, equal to half the first cost of those commodities, have been granted by parliament, payable out of the British revenue, upon their importation into Great Britain. The growth of rice in the southern colonies has been greatly encouraged, by prohibiting the importation of that grain into the British dominions from other parts, and allowing it to be transported from the colonies to the foreign territories in America, and even to the southern parts of Europe. Indigo has been nurtured in those colonies by great parliamentary bounties, which have been long paid upon the importation into Great Britain; and of late are allowed to remain, even when it is carried out again to foreign markets. Silk and wine have also been objects of parliamentary munificence; and will one day probably become considerable American products under that encouragement. In which of these instances, it may be demanded, has the legislature shown itself partial to the people of England and unjust to the colonies? Or wherein have the colonies been injured? We hear much of the restraints under which the trade of the colonies is laid by acts of parliament for the advantage of Great Britain, but the restraints under which the people of Great Britain are laid by acts of parliament for the advantage of the colonies, are carefully kept out of sight; and yet, upon a comparison the one will be found full as grievous as the other. For is it a greater hardship on the colonies, to be confined in some instances to the markets of Great Britain for the sale of their commodities, than it is on the people of Great Britain to be obliged to buy the commodities from them only? If the island colonies are obliged to give the people of Great Britain the preemption of their sugar and coffee, is it not a greater hardship on the people of Great Britain to be restrained from purchasing sugar and coffee from other countries, where they could get those commodities much cheaper than the colonies make them pay for them? Could not our manufactures have indigo much better and cheaper from France and Spain than from Carolina? And yet is there not a duty imposed by acts of parliament on French and Spanish indigo; that it may come to our manufacturers at a dearer rate than Carolina indigo, though a bounty is also given out of *the money* of the people of England to the Carolina planter, to enable him to sell his indigo upon a *par* with the French and Spanish? But the instance which has already been taken notice of, the act which prohibits the culture of the tobacco plant in Great Britain or Ireland, is still more in point, and a more striking proof of the justice and impartiality of the supreme legislature; for what restraints, let me ask, are the colonies laid under, which bear so strong marks of hardship, as the prohibiting the farmers in Great Britain and Ireland from raising upon their own lands, a product which is become almost a necessary of life to them and their families? And this most extraordinary restraint is laid upon them, for the avowed and sole purpose of giving Virginia and Maryland a monopoly of that commodity, and obliging the people of Great Britain and Ireland to buy all the tobacco they consume, from them, at the prices they think fit to sell it for. The annals of no country, that ever planted colonies, can produce such an instance as this of regard and kindness to their colonies, and of restraint upon the inhabitants of the mother country for their advantage. Nor is there any restraint laid upon the inhabitants of the colonies in return, which carries with it so great appearance of hardships, although the people of Great Britain and Ireland have, from their regard and affection to the colonies, submitted to it without a murmur for near a century." For a more particular inquiry, let me recommend the perusal of the pamphlet itself, also another pamphlet lately published, entitled, "the advantages which America derives from her commerce, connection and dependance on Great Britain."

A calculation has lately been made both of the amount of the revenue arising from the duties with which our trade is at present charged, and of the bounties and encouragement paid out of the British revenue upon articles of American produce imported into England, and the latter is found to exceed the former more than four fold. This does not look like a partiality to our disadvantage. However, there is no surer method of determining whether the colonies have been oppressed by the laws of trade and revenue, than by observing their effects.

From what source has the wealth of the colonies flowed? Whence is it derived? Not from agriculture only: exclusive of commerce the colonists would this day have been a poor people, possessed of little more than the necessaries for supporting life; of course their numbers would be few; for population always keeps pace with the ability of maintaining a family; there would have been but little or no resort of strangers here; the arts and sciences would have made but small progress; the inhabitants would rather have degenerated into a state of ignorance and barbarity. Or had Great Britain laid such restrictions upon our trade, as our patriots would induce us to believe, that is, had we been pouring the fruits of all our labour into the lap of our parent and been enriching her by the sweat of our brow, without receiving an equivalent, the patrimony derived from our ancestors must have dwindled from little to less, until their posterity should have suffered a general bankruptcy.

But how different are the effects of our connection with, and subordination to Britain? They are too strongly marked to escape the most careless observer. Our merchants are opulent, and our yeomanry in easier circumstances than the noblesse of some states. Population is so rapid as to double the number of inhabitants in the short period of twenty-five years. Cities are springing up in the depths of the wilderness. Schools, colleges, and even universities are interspersed through the continent; our country abounds with foreign refinements, and flows with exotic luxuries. These are infallible marks not only of opulence but of freedom. The recluse may speculate—the envious repine —the disaffected calumniate— all these may combine to excite fears and jealousies in the minds of the multitude, and keep them in alarm from the beginning to the end of the year; but such evidence as this must for ever carry conviction with it to the minds of the dispassionate and judicious.

Where are the traces of the slavery that our patriots would terrify us with? The effects of slavery are as glaring and obvious in those countries that are cursed with its abode, as the effects of war, pestilence or famine. Our land is not disgraced by the wooden shoes of France, or the uncombed hair of Poland: we have neither racks nor inquisitions, tortures or assassinations: the mildness of our criminal jurisprudence is proverbial, "*a man must have many friends to get hanged in New England.*" Who has been arbitrarily imprisoned, disseized of his freehold, or despoiled of his goods? Each peasant, that is industrious, may acquire an estate, enjoy it in his life time, and at his death, transmit a fair inheritance to his posterity. The protestant religion is established, as far as human laws can establish it. My dear friends, let me ask each one whether he has not enjoyed every blessing, that is in the power of civil government to bestow? And yet the parliament has, from the earliest days of the colonies, claimed the lately controverted right, both of legislation and taxation; and for more than a century has been in the actual exercise of it. There is no grievous exercise of that right at this day, unless the measures taken to prevent our revolting, may be called grievances. Are we, then, to rebel, lest there should be grievances? Are we to take up arms and make war against our parent, lest that parent, contrary to the experience of a century and a half, contrary to her own genius, inclination, affection and interest, should treat us or our posterity as bastards and not as sons, and instead of protecting should *enslave* us? The annals of the world have not yet been deformed with a single instance of so unnatural, so causeless, so wanton, so wicked a rebellion.

There is but a step between you and ruin: and should our patriots succeed in their endeavours to urge you on to take that step, and hostilities actually commence, New England will stand recorded a singular monument of human folly and wickedness. I beg leave to transcribe a little from the Farmer's letters.— "Good Heaven! Shall a total oblivion of former tendernesses and blessings be spread over the minds of a good and wise people by the sordid arts of intriguing men, who covering their selfish projects under pretences of public good, first enrage their countrymen in to a frenzy of passion, and then advance their own influence and interest by gratifying the passion, which they themselves have excited?" When cool dispassionate posterity shall consider the affectionate intercourse, the reciprocal benefits, and the unsuspecting confidence, that have subsisted between these colonies and their parent state, for such a length of time, they will execrate, with the bitterest curses, the infamous memory of those men whose ambition unnecessarily, wantonly, cruelly, first opened the sources of civil discord.

MASSACHUSETTENSIS.

Massachusetts Gazette; and the Boston Post-Boy and Advertiser, March 20, 1775

Massachusettensis [Daniel Leonard] No. XVI

To the Inhabitants of the Province of Massachusetts Bay,

MY DEAR COUNTRYMEN,

Our patriots exclaim, "that humble and reasonable petitions from the representatives of the people have been frequently treated with contempt." This is as virulent a libel upon his majesty's government, as falshood and ingenuity combined could fabricate. Our humble and reasonable petitions have not only been ever graciously received, when the established mode of exhibiting them has been observed, but generally granted. Applications of a different kind, have been treated with neglect, though not always with the contempt they deserved. These either originated in illegal assemblies, and could not be received without implicitly, countenancing such enormities, or contained such matter, and were conceived in such terms, as to be at once an insult to his majesty, and a libel on his government. Instead of being decent remonstrances against real grievances, or prayers for their removal, they were insidious attempts to wrest from the crown, or the supreme legislature, their inherent, unalienable prerogatives or rights.

We have a recent instance of this kind of petition, in the application of the continental congress to the king, which starts with these words: "A standing army has been kept in these colonies ever since the conclusion of the late war, *without the consent of our assemblies.*" This is a denial of the king's authority to station his military forces in such parts of the empire, as his majesty may judge expedient for the common safety. They might with equal propriety have advanced one step further, and denied its being a prerogative of the crown to declare war, or conclude a peace, by which the colonies should be affected, without the consent of our assemblies. Such petitions carry the marks of death in their faces, as they cannot be granted but by surrendering some constitutional right at the same time; and therefore afford grounds for suspicion at least, that they were never intended to be granted, but to irritate and provoke the power petitioned to. It is one thing to remonstrate the inexpediency or inconveniency of a particular act of the prerogative, and another to deny the existence of the prerogative. It is one thing to complain of the inutility or hardship of a particular act of parliament, and quite another to deny the authority of parliament to make any act. Had our patriots confined themselves to the former, they would have acted a part conformable to the character they assumed, and merited the encomiums they arrogate.

There is not one act of parliament that respects us, but would have been repealed, upon the legislators being convinced, that it was oppressive; and scarcely one, but would have shared the same fate, upon a representation of its being generally disgustful to America. But, by adhering to the latter, our politicians have ignorantly or wilfully betrayed their country.

Even when Great Britain has relaxed in her measures, or appeared to recede from her claims, instead of manifestations of gratitude, our politicians have risen in their demands, and sometimes to such a degree of insolence, as to lay the British government under a necessity of persevering in its measures to preserve its honour.

It was my intention, when I began these papers, to have minutely examined the proceedings of the continental congress, as the delegates appear to me to have given their country a deeper wound, than any of predecessors had inflicted, and I pray God it may not prove an incurable one; but am in some measure anticipated by Grotius, Phileareine, and the many pamphlets that have been published; and shall therefore confine my observations to some of its most striking and characteristic features.

A congress or convention of committees from the several colonies, constitutionally appointed by the supreme authority of the state, or by the several provincial legislatures, amenable to, and controulable by the power that convened them, would be salutary in many supposeable cases. Such was the convention of 1754; but a congress otherwise appointed, must be an unlawful assembly, wholly incompatible with the constitution, and dangerous in the extreme, more especially as such assemblies will ever chiefly consist of the most violent partizans. The prince, or sovereign, as some writers call the supreme authority of a state, is sufficiently ample and extensive to provide a remedy for every wrong, in all possible emergencies and contingencies; consequently a power, that is not derived from such authority, springing up in a state, must encroach upon it, and in proportion as the usurpation enlarges itself, the rightful prince must be diminished; indeed, they cannot long subsist together, but must continually militate, till one or the other be destroyed. Had the continental congress consisted of committees from the several houses of assembly, although destitute of the consent of the several governors, they would have had some appearance of authority; but many of them were appointed by other committees, as illegally constituted as themselves. However, at so critical and delicate a juncture, Great Britain being alarmed with an apprehension, that the colonies were aiming at independence on the one hand, and the colonies apprehensive of grievous impositions and exactions from Great Britain on the other; many real patriots imagined, that a congress might be eminently serviceable, as they might prevail on the Bostonians to make restitution to the East India company, might still the commotions in this province, remove any ill founded apprehensions respecting the colonies, and propose some plan for a cordial and permanent reconciliation, which might be adopted by the several assemblies, and make its way through them to the supreme legislature. Placed in this point of light, many good men viewed it with an indulgent eye, and tories, as well as whigs, bade the delegates God speed.

The path of duty was too plain to be overlooked; but unfortunately some of the most influential of the members were the very persons that had been the *wilful* cause of the evils they were expected to remedy. Fishing in troubled waters had long been their business and delight; and they deprecated nothing more than that the storm they had blown up, should subside. They were old in intrigue, and would have figured in a conclave. The subtility, hypocrisy, cunning, and chicanery, habitual to such men, were practised with as much success in this, as they had been before in other popular assemblies.

Some of the members, of the first rate abilities and characters, endeavoured to confine the deliberations and resolves of the congress to the design of its institution, which was "to restore peace, harmony, and mutual confidence," but were obliged to succumb to the intemperate zeal of some, and at length were so circumvented and wrought upon by the artifice and duplicity of others, as to lend the sanction of their names to such measures, as they condemned in their hearts. *Vide* a pamphlet published by one of the delegates, entitled, "A candid examination, &c."

The congress could not be ignorant of what every body else knew, that their appointment was repugnant to, and inconsistent with every idea of government, and therefore wisely determined to destroy it. Their first essay that transpired, and which was matter of no less grief to the friends of our country, than of triumph to its enemies, was the ever memorable resolve approbating and adopting the Suffolk resolves, thereby undertaking to give a continental sanction to a forcible opposition to acts of parliament, shutting up the courts of justice, and thereby abrogating all human laws, seizing the king's provincial revenue, raising forces in opposition to the king's, and all the tumultuary violence, with which this unhappy province had been rent asunder.

This fixed the complexion, and marked the character of the congress. We were, therefore, but little surprized, when it was announced, that as far as was in their power, they had dismembered the colonies from the parent country. This they did by resolving, that "the colonists are entitled to an exclusive power of legislation in their several provincial legislatures." This stands in its full force, and is an absolute denial of the authority of parliament respecting the colonies.

Their subjoining that, "*from necessity* they consent to the *operation* (not the authority) of such acts of the *British* parliament, as *are* (not shall be) *bona fide* restrained to external commerce," is so far from weakening their first principle, that it strengthens it, and is an adoption of the acts of trade. This resolve is a manifest revolt from the British empire. Consistent with it, is their overlooking the supreme legislature, and addressing the inhabitants of Great Britain, in the style of a manifesto, in which they flatter, complain, coax, and threaten alternately; and their prohibiting all commercial intercourse between the two countries: with equal propriety and justice the congress might have declared war against Great Britain; and they intimate that they might justly do it, and actually shall, if the measures already taken prove ineffectual. For in the address to the colonies, after attempting to enrage their countrymen by every colouring and heightening in the power of language, to the utmost pitch of frenzy, they say, "the state of these colonies would certainly justify *other* measures than we have advised; we were inclined to offer *once more* to his *majesty* the petition of his faithful and oppressed subjects in America," and admonish the colonists to "extend their views to *mournful events*, and to be in all respects prepared for every contingency."

This is treating Great Britain as an alien enemy; and if Great Britain be such, it is justifiable by the law of nations. But their attempt to alienate the affections of the inhabitants of the new conquered province of Quebec from his majesty's government, is altogether unjustifiable, even upon that principle. In the truly jesuitical address to the Canadians, the congress endeavour to seduce them from their allegiance, and prevail on them to join the confederacy. After insinuating that they had been tricked, duped, oppressed and enslaved by the Quebec bill, the congress exclaim, why this degrading distinction? "Have not Canadians sense enough to attend to any other public affairs, than gathering stones from one place and piling them up in another? Unhappy people; who are not only injured but *insulted*." "Such a treacherous ingenuity has been exerted, in drawing up the code lately offered you, that every sentence, beginning with a benevolent pretention, concludes with a destructive power; and the substance of the whole divested of its smooth words, is that the *crown* and its ministers shall be as absolute throughout your extended province, as the *despots of Asia or Africa*. We defy you, casting your view upon every side, to discover a single circumstance promising, from any quarter, the faintest hope of liberty to you or your posterity, but from an entire adoption into the union of these colonies." The treachery of the congress in this address is the more flagrant, by the Quebec bill's having been adapted to the genius and manners of the Canadians, formed upon their own petition, and received with every testimonial of gratitude. The public tranquility has been often disturbed by treasonable plots and conspiracies. Great Britain has been repeatedly deluged by the blood of its slaughtered citizens, and shaken to its centre by rebellion. To offer such aggravated insult to British government was reserved for *the grand continental congress*. None but ideots or madmen could suppose such measures had a tendency to restore "union and harmony between Great Britian and the colonies." Nay! The very demands of the congress evince, that that was not in their intention. Instead of confining themselves to those acts, which occasioned the misunderstanding, they demand a repeal of fourteen, and bind the colonies by a law not to trade with Great Britain, until that shall be done. Then, and not before, the colonists are to treat Great Britain as an alien friend, and in no other light is the parent country ever after to be viewed; for the parliament is to surcease enacting laws to respect us forever. These demands are such as cannot be complied with, consistent with either the honor or interest of the empire, and are therefore insuperable obstacles to a union *via* congress.

The delegates erecting themselves into the states general or supreme legislature of all the colonies, from *Nova Scotia* to *Georgia*, does not leave a doubt respecting their aiming, in good earnest, at independency: this they did by enacting laws. Although they recognize the authority of the several provincial legislatures, yet they consider their own authority as paramount or supreme; otherwise they would not have acted decisively, but submitted their plans to the final determination of the assemblies. Sometimes indeed they use the terms request and recommend; at others they speak in the style of authority. Such is the resolve of the 27th of September: "Resolved from and after the first day of December next, there be no importation into British America from Great Britain or Ireland of any goods, wares or merchandize whatsoever, or from any other place of any such goods, wares or merchandize, as shall have been exported from Great Britain or Ireland, and that no such goods, wares or merchandize imported, after the said first day of December next, be used or purchased." October 15, the congress resumed the consideration of the plan for carrying into effect the non-importation, &c. October 20, the plan is compleated, determined upon, and ordered to be subscribed by all the members: they call it an association, but it has all the constituent parts of a law. They begin, "We his majesty's most loyal subjects the delegates of the several colonies of, &c. deputed to *represent them* in a continental congress," and agree for themselves and the inhabitants of the several colonies whom they represent, not to import, export or consume, &c. as also to observe several sumptuary regulations under certain penalties and forfeitures, and that a committee be chosen in every county, city and town, by those who are qualified to vote for representatives in the legislature, to see that the association be observed and kept, and to punish the violators of it; and afterwards, "recommend it to the provincial conventions, and to the committees in the respective colonies to establish such further regulations, as they may think proper, for carrying into execution the association." Here we find the congress enacting laws, that is, establishing, as the representatives of the people, certain rules of conduct to be observed and kept by all the inhabitants of these colonies, under certain pains and penalties, such as masters of vessels being dismissed from their employment; goods to be seized and sold at auction, and the first cost only returned to the proprietor, a different appropriation made of the overplus; persons being stigmatized in the gazette, as enemies to their country, and excluded the benefits of society, &c.

The congress seem to have been apprehensive that some squeamish people might be startled at their assuming the powers of legislation, and therefore, in the former part of their association say, they bind themselves and constituents under the sacred ties of virtue, honor, and love to their country, afterwards establish penalties and forfeitures, and conclude by solemnly binding themselves and constituents under the ties aforesaid, which include them all. This looks like artifice; but they might have spared themselves that trouble; for every law is or ought to be made under the sacred ties of virtue, honor and a love to the country, expressed or implied, though the penal sanction be also necessary. In short, were the colonies distinct states, and the powers of legislation vested in delegates thus appointed, their association would be as good a form of enacting laws as could be devised.

By their assuming the powers of legislation, the congress have not only superseded our provincial legislatures, but have excluded every idea of monarchy; and not content with the havock already made in our constitution, in the plenitude of their power, have appointed another congress to be held in May.

Those, that have attempted to establish new systems, have generally taken care to be consistent with themselves. Let us compare the several parts of the continental proceedings with each other.

The delegates call themselves and constituents "his majesty's most loyal subjects," his majesty's most faithful subjects affirm, that the colonists are entitled "to all the immunities and privileges granted and confirmed to them by royal charters," declare that they "wish not a diminution of the prerogative, nor solicit the grant of any new right of favour," and they "shall always carefully and zealously endeavour to support his royal authority and our connection with Great Britian;" yet deny the king's prerogative to station troops in the colonies, disown him in the capacity in which he granted the provincial charters;

disclaim the authority of the king in parliament; and undertake to enact and execute laws without any authority derived from the crown. This is dissolving all connection between the colonies and the crown, and giving us a new king, altogether incomprehensible, not indeed from the infinity of his attributes, but from a privation of every royal prerogative, and not leaving even a semblance of a connection with Great Britian.

They declare, that the colonists "are entitled to all the rights, liberties and immunities of free and natural born subjects within the realm of England," and "all the benefits secured to the subject by the English constitution," but disclaim all obedience to British government; in other words, they claim the protection, and disclaim the allegiance. They remonstrate as a grievance that "both houses of parliament have resolved that the colonists may be tried in England for offences, alleged to have been committed in America, by virtue of a statute passed in the thirty-fifth year of Henry the eighth"; and yet resolve that they are entitled to the benefit of such English statutes, as existed at the time of their colonization, and are applicable to their several local and other circumstances. They resolve that the colonists are entitled to a free and *exclusive* power of legislation in their several provincial assemblies; yet undertake to legislate in congress.

The immutable laws of nature, the principles of the English constitution, and our several charters are the basis, upon which they pretend to found themselves, and complain more especially of being deprived of trials by juries; but establish ordinances incompatible with either the laws of nature, the English constitution, or our charter; and appoint committees to punish the violaters of them, not only without a jury, but even without a form of trial.

They repeatedly complain of the Roman Catholic religion being established in Canada; and in their address to the Canadians, ask, "If liberty of conscience be offered them *in their religion* by the Quebec bill," and answer, "no: God gave it to you and the temporal powers, with which you have been and are connected, firmly stipulated for your enjoyment of it. If laws, *divine* and *human*, could secure it against the despotic caprices of wicked men, it was secured before."

They say to the people of Great Britain, "place us in the

same situation, that we were in, at the close of the last war, and our harmony will be restored." Yet some of the principal grievances, which are to be redressed, existed long before that era, viz. The king's keeping a standing army in the colonies; judges of admiralty receiving their fees, &c. from the effects condemned by themselves; counsellors holding commissions during pleasure, exercising legislative authority; and the capital grievance of all, the parliament claiming and exercising over the colonies a right both of legislation and taxation. However the wisdom of the grand continental congress may reconcile these seeming inconsistencies.

Had the delegates been appointed to devise means to irritate and enrage the inhabitants of the two countries, against each other, beyond a possibility of reconciliation, to abolish our equal system of jurisprudence, and establish a judicatory as arbitrary, as the Romish inquisition, to perpetuate animosities among ourselves, to reduce thousands from affluence to poverty and indigence, to injure Great Britain, Ireland, the West Indies, and these colonies, to attempt a revolt from the authority of the empire, and finally to draw down upon the colonies the whole vengeance of Great Britain; more promising means to effect the whole could not have been devised than those the congress adopted. Any deviation from their plan would have been treachery to their constituents, and an abuse of the trust and confidence reposed in them. Some idolaters have attributed to the congress the collected wisdom of the continent. It is as near the truth to say, that every particle of disaffection, petulance, ingratitude, and disloyalty, that for ten years past have been scattered through the continent, were united and consolidated in them. Are these thy Gods, O Israel!

MASSACHUSETTENSIS.

Massachusetts Gazette, and the Boston Post-Boy and Advertiser, March 27, 1775

Novanglus No. IX

My Friends,

Massachusettensis, in some of his writings has advanced, that our allegiance is due to the political capacity of the King, and therefore involves in it obedience to the British parliament. Governor Hutchinson in his memorable speech laid down the same position. I have already shewn from the case of Wales, that this position is groundless—and that allegiance was due from the Welch to the King, *jure feodali*, before the conquest of Lewellyn, and after that to the Crown, until it was annexed to the realm, without being subject to acts of parliament any more than to acts of the King, without parliament. I shall hereafter shew from the case of Ireland, that subjection to the Crown implies no obedience to parliament. But before I come to this, I must take notice of a pamphlet, intitled, "A candid Examination of the mutual claims of Great-Britain and the colonies, with a plan of accommodation on constitutional principles." This author, p. 8, says "to him (i. e. the King) in this representative capacity, and as supreme executor of the laws, made by a joint power of him and others, the oaths of allegiance are taken", and afterwards, "Hence these professions (i. e. of allegiance) are not made to him either in his legislative, or executive capacities; but yet it seems they are made to the King. And into this distinction, *which is no where to be found* either in the constitution of the government, in reason or common sense, the ignorant and thoughtless have been deluded ever since the passing of the stamp act, and they have rested satisfied with it without the least examination." And in p. 9, he says, "I do not mean to offend the inventers of this refined distinction, when I ask them 'is this acknowledgment made to the king, in his politick capacity as king of "Great Britain, &c." if so, it includes a promise of obedience to the British laws.'" There is no danger of this gentleman's giving offence to the inventers of this distinction, for they have been many centuries in their graves. This distinction is to be found every where: in the case of Wales, Ireland and elsewhere, as I shall shew most abundantly before I have done. It is to be found in two of the greatest cases and most deliberate and solemn judgments that were ever passed. One of them is Calvin's case, 7 Rep.—which as lord Coke tells us, was as elaborately, substantially and judiciously argued, as he ever heard, or read of any. After it had been argued in the court of king's bench, by learned council, it was adjourned to the exchequer chamber, and there argued again, first by council on both sides and then by the lord chancellor and all the twelve judges of England, and among these were the greatest men, that Westminster hall ever could boast. Ellismore, Bacon, Hide, Hobart, Crook, and Coke, were all among them. And the chancellor and judges were unanimous in resolving. What says the book? 7 rep. 10. "Now seeing the king hath but one person, and several capacities, and one politick capacity for the realm of England, and another for the realm of Scotland, it is necessary to be considered, to which capacity *ligeance* is due. *And it was resolved* that it was due to the *natural person* of the king (which is ever accompanied with the politick capacity, and the politick capacity as it were appropriated to the natural capacity) and it is not due to the politick capacity only, that is, to the crown or kingdom, distinct from his natural capacity." And further on 7 rep. 11. "But it was clearly resolved by all the judges, that presently by the descent his majesty was compleatly and absolutely king," &c. and that coronation was but a royal ornament! 6. "In the reign of Ed. 2d, the Spencers, to cover the treason hatched in their hearts, invented this damnable and damned opinion, that homage and oath of allegiance was more by reason of the king's crown (that is of his politick capacity) than by reason of the person of the king, upon which opinion they inferred execrable and detestible consequences." And afterwards, 12. "Where books and acts of parliament speak of the ligeance of *England*, &c. speaking briefly in a vulgar manner, are to be understood of the ligeance due by the people of England to the King; for no man will affirm that England itself, taking it for the continent thereof, doth owe any ligeance or faith, or that *any faith or ligeance should be due to it*: but it manifestly appeareth, that the ligeance or faith of the subject is *proprium quarto modo* to the King, *omni, soli, et semper*. And oftentimes in the reports of our book cases and in acts of parliament also, the crown or kingdom is taken for the king himself." &c. "Tenure in *capite* is a tenure of the Crown, and is a *seigniorie in grosse*, that is of the person of the King." And afterwards 6. "for special purposes *the law makes him a body politick, immortal and invisible, whereunto our allegiance cannot appertain.*" I beg leave to observe here, that these words in the foregoing adjudication, that "the natural person of the King is ever accompanied with the politick capacity, and the politick capacity as it were appropriated to the natural capacity"; neither imply nor infer allegiance, or subjection to the politick capacity, because in the case of King James the first, his natural person was "accompanied" with three politick capacities at least, as King of England, Scotland and Ireland: yet the allegiance of an Englishman to him did not imply or infer subjection, to his politick capacity as King of Scotland.

Another place in which this distinction is to be found is in Moore's reports, p. 790. "The case of the union of the realm of Scotland with England." And this deliberation, I hope was solemn enough. This distinction was agreed on by commissioners of the English lords and commons in a conference with commissioners of the Scottish parliament, and after many arguments and consultations by the lord chancellor and all the judges, and afterwards adopted by the lords and commons of both nations. "The judges answered with one assent," says the book, "that allegiance and laws were not of equiparation for six causes," the sixth and last of which is, "allegiance followeth the *natural person* not the politick." "If the king go out of England with a company of his servants, allegiance remaineth among his subjects and servants, altho' he be out of his own realm, *whereto his laws are confined*, &c. and to prove the allegiance to be tied to the body natural of the king, not to the body politick, the lord Coke cited the phrases of diverse statutes, &c. And to prove that allegiance extended further than the laws national, they (the judges) shewed that every king of diverse kingdoms, or dukedoms, is to command every people to defend any of his kingdoms, without respect of that nation where he is born; as if the king of Spain be invaded in Portugal, he may levy for defence of Portugal armies out of Spain, Naples, Castie, Millen, Flanders and the like; as a thing incident to the allegiance of all his subjects, to join together in defence of any of his territories, without respect of the extent of the laws of that nation where he was born; whereby it manifestly appeareth, that allegiance followeth the natural person of the king, and is not tied to the body politick respectively in every kingdom." There is one observation, not immediately to the present point, but so connected with our controversy, that it ought not to be overlooked. "For the matter of the great seal the judges shewed that the seal was alterable by the king at his pleasure, and he might make one seal for both kingdoms, for seals, coin, and leagues, are of absolute prerogative of the king without parliament, nor restrained to any assent of the people." "But for further resolution of this point, how far the great seal doth command out of England, they made this distinction, that the great seal was current for remedials which groweth on complaint of the subjects, and thereupon writs are addressed under the great seal of England, which writs are limitted, their precinct to be within the places of the jurisdiction of the court that was to give the redress of the wrong. And therefore writs are not to go into Ireland nor the Isles, nor Wales, nor the counties palatine, because the king's courts here have not power to hold plea of lands, nor things there. But the great seal, hath a power preceptory, to the person, which power extendeth to any place, where the person may be found." Ludlow's case, &c. who "being at Rome, a commandment under the great seal was sent for him to return," &c. "So Bertie's case in Q. Mary's time, and Inglefield's case in Q. Elizabeth's, the privy seal went to command them to return into the realm, and for not coming their lands were seized". &c. But to return to the point, "And as to the objection," says the book, "that none can be born a natural subject of two kingdoms, they denied that absolutely, for altho' locally, he can be born, but in one, yet effectually, the allegiance of the King extending to both, his birthright shall extend to both." And afterwards, "but that his kingly power extendeth to diverse nations and kingdoms, all owe him equal subjection, and are equally born to the benefit of his protection; and altho' he is to govern them by *their distinct laws*, yet any one of the people coming into the other, is to have the benefit of the laws, wheresoever he cometh; but living in one, or for his livelihood in one, he is not to be taxed in the other, because laws ordain taxes, impositions, and charges, as a discipline of subjection particularized to every particular nation."

Another place where this distinction is to be found is in Foster's crown law, p. 184. "There have been writers, who have carried the notion of natural, perpetual, unalienable allegiance, much farther than the subject of this discourse will lead me. They say, very truly, that it is due to the person of the king, &c." "It is undoubtedly due to the person of the king; but in that respect natural allegiance differeth nothing from that we call local. For allegiance considered in every light is alike due to the person of the king; and is paid, and in the nature of things must be constantly paid, to that prince, who for the time being, is in the actual and full possession of the regal dignity."

Indeed allegiance to a sovereign lord, is nothing more than fealty to a subordinate lord, and in neither case, has any relation to, or connection with laws or parliaments, lords or commons. There was a reciprocal confidence between the lord and vassal. The lord was to protect the vassal in the enjoyment of his land. The vassal was to be faithful to his lord, and defend him against his enemies. This obligation on the part of the vassal, was his fealty, *fidelitas*. The oath of fealty, by the feodal law to be taken by the vassal or tenant, is nearly in the very words as the ancient oath of allegiance. But neither fealty, allegiance, or the oath of either implied any thing about laws, parliaments, lords or commons.

The fealty and allegiance of Americans then is undoubtedly due to the person of king George the third, whom God long preserve and prosper. It is due to him, in his natural person, as that natural person is intituled to the crown, the kingly office, the royal dignity of the realm of England. And it becomes due to his natural person, because he is intituled to that office. And because by the charters, and other express and implied contracts made between the Americans and the kings of England, they have bound themselves to fealty and allegiance to the natural person of that prince, who shall rightfully hold the kingly office in England, and no otherwise.

"With us in England," says Blackstone, v. 1. 367. "it becoming a settled principle of tenure, that all lands in the kingdom are holden of the king as their sovereign and lord paramount,

&c. the oath of allegiance was necessarily confined to the Person of the king alone. By an easy analogy, the term of allegiance was soon brought to signify all other engagements, which are due from subjects to their prince, as well as those duties which were simply and merely territorial. And the oath of allegiance, as administered for upwards of six hundred years, contained a promise 'to be true and faithful to the king and his heirs, and truth and faith to bear of life and limb and terrene honour, and not to know, or hear of any ill or damage intended him, without defending him therefrom.'" "But at the revolution, the terms of this oath, being thought perhaps to favour too much the notion of non resistance, the present form was introduced by the convention parliament, which is more general and indeterminate than the former, the subject only promising 'that he will be faithful and bear true allegiance to the king,' without mentioning his heirs, or specifying in the least wherein that allegiance consists."

Thus, I think, that all the authorities in law, coincide, exactly with the observation which I have heretofore made upon the case of Wales, and shew that subjection to a king of England, does not necessarily imply subjection to the crown of England; and that subjection to the crown of England, does not imply subjection to the parliament of England, for allegiance is due to the person of the king, and to that alone, in all three cases, that is, whether we are subject to his parliament and crown, as well as his person, as the people in England are, whether we are subject to his crown and person, without parliament, as the Welch were after the conquest of Lewellyn, and before the union, or as the Irish were after the conquest and before Poyning's law, or whether we are subject to his person alone, as the Scots were to the king of England, after the accession of James 1st, being not at all subject to the parliament or crown of England.

We do not admit any binding authority in the decisions and adjudications of the court of king's bench or common pleas, or the court of chancery over America: but we quote them as the opinions of learned men. In these we find a distinction between a country conquered, and a country discovered. Conquest, they say gives the crown an absolute power: discovery, only gives the subject a right to all the laws of England. They

add, that all the laws of England are in force there. I confess I
don't see the reason of this. There are several cases in books of
law, which may be properly thrown before the public. I am no
more of a lawyer than Massachusettensis, but have taken his
advice, and conversed with many lawyers upon our subject,
some honest, some dishonest, some living, some dead, and am
willing to lay before you what I have learned from all of them.
In Salk. 411. the case of Blankard vs Galdy—"In debt upon a
bond, the defendant prayed oyer of the condition, and pleaded
the stat. E. 6 against buying offices concerning the administration of justice; and averred that this bond was given for the
purchase of the office of provost marshall in Jamaica, and that
it concerned the administration of justice, and *that Jamaica is
part of the revenue and possessions of the crown of England*: The
plantiff replied, that Jamaica is an island *beyond the seas*, which
was conquered from the Indians and Spaniards in Q. Elizabeth's time, and the inhabitants are governed by their own
laws, and not by the laws of England: The defendant rejoined,
that before such conquest, they were governed by their own
laws; but since that, by the laws of England: Shower argued for
the plantiff, that on a judgment in Jamaica, no writ of error lies
here, but only an appeal to the council; *and as they are not represented in our parliament, so they are not bound by our statutes*,
unless specially named. Vid. And. 115. Pemberton contra argued, that *by the conquest of a nation, its liberties, rights and
properties, are quite lost*; that by consequence their laws are lost
too, for the law is but the rule and guard of the other; those
that conquer cannot by their victory lose their laws, and
become subject to others. Vid. Vaugh. 405. That error lies here
upon a judgment in Jamaica, which could not be if they were
not under the same law. Et. per Holt, C. J. and Cur. 1st. *In
case of an uninhabited country, newly found out by English subjects, all laws in force in England are in force there*; so it seemed
to be agreed. 2. Jamaica being conquered, and not pleaded to
be *parcel of the kingdom of England, but part of the possessions
and revenue of the crown of England; the laws of England did
not take place there, until declared so by the conquerer, or his successors*. The isle of Man and Ireland are part of the *possessions* of
the crown of England; yet retain their ancient laws; that in
Davis 36. it is not pretended, that the custom of tanistry was

determined by the conquest of Ireland, but by the new settlement made there after the conquest: that it was impossible the
laws of this nation, by mere conquest without more should
take place in a conquered country; because for a time, there
must want officers without which our laws can have no force;
that if our law did take place, yet they in Jamaica having power
to make new laws, our general laws may be altered by theirs in
particulars; also they held that in case of an infidel country,
their laws by conquest do not entirely cease, but only such as
are against the law of God; and that in such cases where the
laws are rejected or silent, the conquered country shall be governed according to the rule of natural equity. Judgment, pro
Quer.'"

Upon this case I beg leave to make a few observations. 1.
That Shower's reasoning, that we are not bound by statutes
because not represented in parliament, is universal, and therefore his exception "unless specially named," altho' it is taken
from analogy to the case of Ireland, by lord Coke and others,
yet it is not taken from the common law, but is merely arbitrary and groundless, as applied to us. Because if the want
of representation could be supplied, by "expressly naming" a
country, the right of representation might be rendered null
and nugatory. But of this more another time.

2d. That by the opinion of Holt, and the whole court, the
laws of England, common and statute, are in force in a vacant
country, discovered by Englishmen. But America, was not a
vacant country, it was full of inhabitants; our ancestors purchased the land; but if it had been vacant, his lordship has not
shewn us any authority at common law, that the laws of England would have been in force there. On the contrary, by that
law it is clear they did not extend beyond seas, and therefore
could not be binding there, any further than the free will of
the discoverers should make them. The discoverers had a right
by nature, to set up those laws, if they liked them, or any
others, that pleased them better, provided they were not inconsistent with their allegiance to their king. 3d. The court
held that a country must be parcel of the kingdom of England,
before the laws of England could take place there; which seems
to be inconsistent with what is said before, because discovery
of a vacant country does not make it parcel of the kingdom of

England, which shews, that the court, when they said that all laws in *force* in England, are in *force* in the discovered country, meant no more than that the discoverers had a right to all such laws, if they chose to adopt them. 4. The idea of the court, in this case, is exactly conformable to, if not taken from the case of Wales. They consider a conquered country as Ed. 1, and his successors did Wales, as by the conquest annexed to the crown, as an absolute property, possession, or revenue, and therefore to be disposed of at its will. Not intitled to the laws of England, although bound to be govern'd by the king's will, in parliament or out of it, as he pleased. 5. The isle of Man, and Ireland, are considered like Wales, as conquered countries, and part of the possessions (by which the mean property or revenue) of the crown of England, yet have been allowed by the king's will to retain their ancient laws. 6. That the case of America differs totally, from the case of Wales, Ireland, Man, or any other case, which is known at common law or in English history. There is no one precedent in point, in any English records, and therefore it can be determined only by eternal reason, and the law of nature. But yet that the analogy of all these cases of Ireland, Wales, Man, Chester, Durham, Lancaster, &c. clearly concur with the dictates of reason and nature, that Americans are intituled to all the liberties of Englishmen, and that they are not bound by any acts of parliament whatever, by any law known in English records or history, excepting those for the regulation of trade, which they have consented to and acquiesced in. 7. To these let me add, that as the laws of England, and the authority of parliament, were by common law confined to the realm and within the four seas, so was the force of the great seal of England. Salk. 510. "The great seal of England is appropriated to England, and what is done under it has relation to England, and to no other place." So that the king by common law, had no authority to create peers or governments, or any thing out of the realm by his great seal, and therefore our charters and commissions to governors, being under the great seal, gives us no more authority, nor binds us to any other duties, than if they had been given under the privy seal, or without any seal at all. Their binding force, both upon the crown and us, is wholly from compact and the law of nature.

There is another case in which the same sentiments are preserved; it is in 2d. P. Williams, 75. memorandum 9th August, 1722. "It was said by the master of the rolls to have been determined by the lords of the privy council, upon an appeal to the king in council from the foreign plantations, 1st. That if there be a new and uninhabited country, found out by English subjects, *as the law is the birthright of every subject*, so, wherever they go, they carry their laws with them, and therefore such new found country is to be governed by the laws of England; tho' after such country is inhabited by the English, acts of parliament made in England, *without naming the foreign plantations, will not bind them*; for which reason, it has been determined that the statute of frauds and perjuries, which requires three witnesses, and that these should subscribe in the testators presence in the case of a devise of land, does not bind Barbadoes, but that, 2dly. Where the king of England conquers a country, it is a different consideration; *for there the conqueror, by saving the lives of the people conquered, gains a right and property in such people*! In consequence of which he may impose upon them what laws he pleases. But,

3dly. Until such laws, given by the conquering prince, the laws and customs of the conquered country shall hold place; unless where these are contrary to our religion, or enact any thing that is *malum in se*, or are silent; for in all such cases the laws of the conquering country shall prevail."

NOVANGLUS

Boston Gazette, March 27, 1775

Massachusettensis
[Daniel Leonard] No. XVII

To the Inhabitants of the Province of Massachusetts Bay,

MY DEAR COUNTRYMEN,

The advocates for the opposition to parliament often remind us of the rights of the people, repeat the Latin adage *vox populi vox Dei*, and tell us that government in the dernier resort is in the people; they chime away melodiously, and to render their music more ravishing, tell us, that these are *revolution* principles. I hold the rights of the people as sacred, and revere the principles, that have established the succession to the imperial crown of Great Britain, in the line of the illustrious house of Brunswick; but that the difficulty lies in applying them to the cause of the whigs, *hic labor hoc opus est*; for admitting that the collective body of the people, that are subject to the British empire, have an inherent right to change their form of government, or race of kings, it does not follow, that the inhabitants of a single province, or of a number of provinces, or any given part under a majority of the whole empire, have such a right. By admitting that the less may rule or sequester themselves from the greater, we unhinge all government. Novanglus has accused me of traducing the people of this province. I deny the charge. Popular demagogues always call themselves the people, and when their own measures are censured, cry out, the people, the people are abused and insulted. He says, that I once entertained different sentiments from those now advanced. I did not write to exculpate myself. If through ignorance, inadvertence or design, I have heretofore contributed in any degree, to the forming that destructive system of politics that is now in vogue, I was under the greater obligation thus publicly to expose its errors, and point out its pernicious tendency. He suggests, that I write from sordid motives. I despise the imputation. I have written my real sentiments not to serve a party (for, as he justly observes, I have sometimes quarreled with my friends) but to serve the public; nor would I injure my country to inherit all the treasures that

avarice and ambition sigh for. Fully convinced, that our calamities were chiefly created by the leading whigs, and that a
persevering in the same measures that gave rise to our troubles
would complete our ruin, I have written freely. It is painful to
me to give offence to an individual, but I have not spared the
ruinous policy of my brother or my friend; they are both far
advanced. Truth, from its own energy, will finally prevail; but
to have a speedy effect, it must sometimes be accompanied
with severity. The terms whig and tory have been adopted according to the arbitrary use of them in this province, but they
rather ought to be reversed; an American tory is a supporter of
our excellent constitution, and an American whig a subverter
of it.

Novanglus abuses me, for saying, that the whigs aim at
independence. The writer from Hampshire county is my advocate. He frankly asserts the independency of the colonies
without any reserve; and is the only consistent writer I have
met with on that side of the question. For by separating us
from the king as well as the parliament, he is under no necessity of contradicting himself. Novauglus strives to hide the inconsistencies of his hypothesis, under a huge pile of learning.
Surely he is not to learn, that arguments drawn from obsolete
maxims, raked out of the ruins of the feudal system, or from
principles of absolute monarchy, will not conclude to the present constitution of government. When he has finished his
essays, he may expect some particular remarks upon them. I
should not have taken the trouble of writing these letters, had
I not been satisfied that real and permanent good would accrue to this province, and indeed to all the colonies, from a
speedy change of measures. Public justice and generosity are
no less characteristic of the English, than their private honesty
and hospitality. The total repeal of the stamp act, and the partial repeal of the act imposing duties on paper, &c. may convince us that the nation has no disposition to injure us. We are
blessed with a king that reflects honor upon a crown. He is so
far from being avaricious, that he has relinquished a part of his
revenue; and so far from being tyrannical, that he has gener-
ously surrendered part of his prerogative for the sake of freedom. His court is so far from being tinctured with dissipation,
that the palace is rather an academy of the literati, and the

royal pair are as exemplary in every private virtue, as they are exalted in their stations. We have only to cease contending with the supreme legislature, respecting its authority, with the king respecting his prerogatives, and with Great Britain respecting our subordination; to dismiss our illegal committees, disband our forces, despise the thraldom of *arrogant congresses,* and submit to constitutional government, to be happy.

Many appear to consider themselves as *procul a Jove a fulmine procul*; and because we never have experienced any severity from Great Britain, think it impossible that we should. The English nation will bear much from its friends; but whoever has read its history must know, that there is a line that cannot be passed with impunity. It is not the fault of our patriots if that line be not already passed. They have demanded of Great Britain more than she can grant, consistent with honor, her interest, or our own, and are now brandishing the sword of defiance.

Do you expect to conquer in war? War is no longer a simple, but an intricate science, not to be learned from books or two or three campaigns, but from long experience. You need not be told that his majesty's generals, Gage and Haldimand, are possessed of every talent requisite to great commanders, matured by long experience in many parts of the world, and stand high in military fame: that many of the officers have been bred to arms from their infancy, and a large proportion of the army *now* here, have already reaped immortal honors in the iron harvest of the field.—Alas! My friends, you have nothing to oppose to this force, but a militia unused to service, impatient of command, and destitute of resources. Can your officers depend upon the privates, or the privates upon the officers? Your war can be but little more than mere tumultuary rage: and besides, there is an awful disparity between troops that fight the battles of their sovereign, and those that follow the standard of rebellion. These reflections may arrest you in an hour that you think not of, and come too late to serve you. Nothing short of a miracle could gain you one battle; but could you destroy all the British troops that are now here, and burn the men of war that command our coast, it would be but the beginning of sorrow; and yet without a decisive battle, one campaign would ruin you. This province does not produce its necessary provision, when the husbandman can pursue his calling with-out molestation: what then must be your condition, when the demand shall be increased, and the resource in a manner cut off? Figure to yourselves what must be your distress, should your wives and children be driven from such places, as the king's troops shall occupy, into the interior parts of the prov-ince, and they as well as you, be destitute of support. I take no pleasure in painting these scenes of distress. The whigs affect to divert you from them by ridicule; but should war com-mence, you can expect nothing but its severities. Might I hazard an opinion, but few of your leaders ever intended to engage in hostilities, but they may have rendered inevitable what they in-tended for intimidation. Those that unsheath the sword of re-bellion may throw away the scabbard, they cannot be treated with, while in arms; and if they lay them down, they are in no other predicament than conquered rebels. The conquered in other wars do not forfeit the rights of men, nor all the rights of citizens, even their bravery is rewarded by a generous victor; far different is the case of a routed rebel host. My dear coun-trymen, you have before you, at your election, peace or war, happiness or misery. May the God of our forefathers direct you in the way that leads to peace and happiness, before your feet stumble on the dark mountains, before the evil days come, wherein you shall say, we have no pleasure in them.

MASSACHUSETTENSIS.

Massachusetts Gazette; and the Boston Post-Boy and Advertiser, April 3, 1775

Novanglus No. X

My Friends,

Give me leave now to descend from these general matters, to Massachusettensis. He says "Ireland who has perhaps the greatest possible subordinate legislature, and send no members to the British parliament, is bound by its acts, when expressly named." But if we are to consider what ought to be, as well as what is, why should Ireland have the greatest possible subordinate legislature? Is Ireland more numerous and more important to what is called the British empire, than America? Subordinate as the Irish legislature is said to be, and a conquered country as undoubtedly it is, the parliament of Great-Britain, altho' they claim a power to bind Ireland by statutes, have never laid one farthing of a tax upon it. They knew it would occasion resistance if they should. But the authority of parliament to bind Ireland at all, if it has any, is founded upon a different principle entirely from any that takes place in the case of America. It is founded on the consent and compact of the Irish by Poyning's law to be so governed, if it has any foundation at all: and this consent was given and compact made in consequence of a conquest.

In the reign of Henry 2d of England, there were five distinct sovereignties in Ireland, Munster, Leinster, Meath, Ulster and Connaught, besides several small tribes. As the prince of any one of these petty states took the lead in war, he seemed to act, for the time being, as monarch of the island. About the year 1172 Rodoric O'Connor, king of Connaught, was advanced to this pre-eminence. Henry, had long cast a wishful eye upon Ireland, and now partly to divert his subjects from the thoughts of Becket's murder, partly to appease the wrath of the Pope for the same event, and partly to gratify his own ambition, he lays hold of a pretence, that the Irish had taken some natives of England and sold them for slaves, applies to the Pope for license to invade that island. Adrian the 3d, an Englishman by birth, who was then pontiff, and very clearly convinced in his own mind of his right to dispose of kingdoms and empires, was easily perswaded, by the prospect of Peter's pence, to act as emperor of the world, and make an addition to his ghostly jurisdiction of an island which tho' converted to christianity had never acknowledged any subjection to the see of Rome. He issued a bull, premising that Henry had ever shewn an anxious care to enlarge the church, and increase the saints on earth and in Heaven, that his design upon Ireland proceeded from the same pious motives: that his application to the holy see, was a sure earnest of success: that it was a point incontestible, that all christian kingdoms belonged to the patrimony of St. Peter; that it was his duty to sow among them the seeds of the gospel, which might fructify to their eternal salvation; he exhorts Henry to invade Ireland, exterminate the vices of the natives, and oblige them to pay yearly from every house, a penny to the see of Rome: gives him full right and entire authority over the whole island, and commands all to obey him as their sovereign.

Macmorrogh, a licentious scoundrel, who was king of Leinster, had been driven from his kingdom, for his tyranny, by his own subjects, in conjunction with Ororic, king of Meath, who made war upon him for committing a rape upon his queen; applied to Henry for assistance, to restore him, and promised to hold his kingdom in vassallage of the crown of England.

Henry accepted the offer, and engaged in the enterprise. It is unnecessary to recapitulate all the intrigues of Henry, to divide the Irish kingdoms among themselves and set one against another, which are as curious as those of Edward the first, to divide the kingdom of Wales and play Lewellyn's brothers against him, or as those of the ministry, and our junto, to divide the American colonies, who have more sense than to be divided. It is sufficient to say that Henry's expeditions, terminated, altogether by means of those divisions among the Irish, in the total conquest of Ireland, and its annexation forever to the English crown. By the annexation of all Ireland to the English crown, I mean, that all the princes and petty sovereigns in Ireland agreed to become vassals of the English crown. But what was the consequence of this? The same consequence was drawn, by the kings of England in this case, as had been drawn in the case of Wales after the conquest of Lewellyn, viz. that Ireland was become a part of the *property*, *possession* or *revenue* of the English crown, and that its authority over it was absolute, and without controul.

This matter must be traced from step to step. The first monument we find in English records, concerning Ireland, is a mere *rescriptum principis*, intituled *statutum hiberniæ de coheredibus*, 14, Hen. 3d, A. D. 1229. In the old abridgment Tit. Homage, this is said not to be a statute. Vid. Ruffheads statutes at large, V. 1. 15. Mr. Cay very properly observes, that it is not an act of parliament, vid. Barrington's observations on the statutes, p. 34. In this rescript, the king informs certain milites (adventurers probably, in the conquest of Ireland, or their descendents) who had doubts how lands holden by knights service, descending to copartners, within age, should be divided, what is the law and custom in England with regard to this.

But the record itself shews it to be a royal rescript only. *Rex dilecto et fideli suo gerardo sit' mauricii justii' suo Hiberniæ salutem. Quia tales Milites de partibus Hiberniæ nuper, ad nos accedentes nobis ostenderunt, quod, &c. Et a nobis petierunt inde certiorari, qualiter in regno nostro Angliæ, in casu consimili hactenus usitatem sit, &c.* He then goes on and certifies what the law in England was, and then concludes, *Et Ideo vobis mandamus, quod predictas consuetudines in hoc casu, quas in regno nostro Angliæ habemus ut predictum est, in terra nostra Hiberniæ proclamari et firmiter teneri, fac, &c.*

Here again we find the king conducting, exactly as Ed. I, did in Wales, after the conquest of Wales. Ireland had now been *annexed to the English crown* many years, yet parliament was not allowed to have obtained any jurisdiction over it, and Henry ordained laws for it by his sole and absolute authority, as Ed. I did by the statute of Wales. Another incontestible proof, that annexing a country to the crown of England, does not annex it to the realm, or subject it to parliament. But we shall find innumerable proofs of this.

Another incontestable proof of this, is the *ordinatio pro statu Hiberniæ* made 17 Ed. I, 1288.

This is an ordinance made by the king, by advice of his council, for the government of Ireland. "Edward, by the grace of God, king of England, lord of Ireland, &c. to all those who shall see or hear these letters, doth send salutation." He then goes on and ordains many regulations, among which the seventh chapter is "that none of our officers shall receive an original writ pleadable at the common law, but such as be sealed by the great seal of Ireland;" &c. this ordinance concludes "In witness whereof we have caused these our letters patent to be made." Dated at Nottingham 24 Nov. 17 year of our reign.

This law if it was passed in parliament was never considered to have any more binding force, than if it had been made only by the king. By Poyning's law indeed in the reign of H. 7 all precedent English statutes are made to bind in Ireland, and this among the rest, but untill Poyning's law, it had no validity as an act of parliament, and was never executed, but in the English pale, for, notwithstanding all that is said of the total conquest, by H. 2, yet it did not extend much beyond the neighbourhood of Dublin, and the conqueror could not inforce his laws and regulations much further.

There is a note on the roll of 21 Ed. I, in these words, "*Et memorandum quod istud statutum de verbo ad verbum, missum suit in Hyberniam, teste rege apud Kenyngton 14., dic. Augueti anno regni sui vicessimo septimo: et mandatum suit Johanni Wogan, justiciario Hiberniæ, quod prædictim statutum, per Hiberniam, in locis quibus expedire viderit legi, et publice proclamari ac firmiter teneri faciat.*"

"This note most fully proves, that the king by his sole authority, could introduce any English law; and will that authority be lessened by the concurrence of the two houses of parliament? There is also an order of Charles the first, in the third year of his reign, to the treasurers and chancellors of the exchequer both of England and Ireland, by which they are directed to increase the duties upon Irish exports; which shews that it was then imagined, that the king would tax Ireland by his prerogative, without the intervention of parliament." vid. obs. on the statutes, p. 127.

Another instance to shew, that the king by his sole authority, whenever he pleased, made regulations for the government of Ireland, notwithstanding it was annexed and subject to the crown of England, is the *ordinatio facta pro statu terræ Hiberniæ*, in the 31. Ed. I. in the appendix to Ruffhead's statutes, p. 37. This is an extensive code of laws, made for the government of the Irish church and state, by the king alone, without lords or commons. The kings "*volumus et firmiter precipimus*," governs and establishes all, and among other things, he introduces by the 18th chapter the English laws, for the regimen of persons of English extract, settled in Ireland.

The next appearance of Ireland, in the statutes of England, is in the 34. Ed. 3. c. 17. This is no more than a concession of the king to his lords and commons of England, in these words "*item* it is accorded that all the merchants as well aliens as denizens, may come into Ireland, with their merchandizes, and from thence freely to return, with their merchandizes and victuals, without fine or ransom to be taken of them, saving always to the king, his ancient customs and other duties." And by chapter 18. "*Item*, that the people of England, as well religious as other, which have their heritage and possessions in Ireland, may bring their corn, beasts and victuals to the said land of Ireland, and from thence to re-carry their goods and merchandizes into England freely, without impeachment, paying their customs and their devoirs to the king."

All this is no more than an argument between the king and his English subjects, lords and commons, that there should be a free trade between the two islands, and that one of them should be free for strangers. But is no colour of proof that the king could not govern Ireland without his English lords and commons.

The 1. H. 5. c. 8. All Irishmen and Irish clerks, beggars, shall depart this realm before the first day of November, except graduates, serjeants &c. is explained by 1. H. 6. c. 3. which shews what sort of Irishmen only may come to dwell in England. It enacts that all persons born in Ireland shall depart out of the realm of England, except a few, and that Irishmen shall not be principals of any hall, and that Irishmen shall bring testimonials from the lieutenant, or justice of Ireland, that they are of the kings obeysance. By the 8. H. 6. c. 8. "Irishmen resorting into the realm of England, shall put in surety for their good abearing."

Thus I have cursorily mentioned every law made by the king of England, whether in parliament or out of it, for the government of Ireland, from the conquest of it by Henry the 2d, in 1172, down to the reign of Henry the 7th, when an express contract was made between the two kingdoms, that Ireland should for the future be bound by English acts of parliament, in which it should be specially named. This contract was made in 1495, so that upon the whole it appears, beyond dispute, that for more than 300 years, tho' a conquered country, and annexed to the crown of England; yet was so far from being annexed to or parcel of the realm, that the king's power was absolute there, and he might govern it without his English parliament, whose advice concerning it, he was under no obligation to ask or pursue.

The contract I here allude to, is what is called Poyning's law, the history of which is briefly this. Ireland revolted from England, or rather adhered to the partizans of the house of York, and Sir Edward Poyning was sent over about the year 1495, by king Henry the 7th, with very extensive powers, *over the civil as well as military administration.* On his arrival he made severe inquisition about the disaffected, and in particular attacked the earls of Dismond and Kildare. The first stood upon the defensive and eluded the power of the deputy: but Kildare was sent prisoner to England: *not to be executed it seems, nor to be tried upon the statute of H.* 8.—but to be dismissed as he actually was, to his own country, with marks of the king's esteem and favour; Henry judging that, at such a juncture, he should gain more by clemency and indulgence, than by rigour and severity. In this opinion he sent a commissioner to Ireland, with a formal amnesty, in favour of Desmond and all his adherents, whom the tools of his ministers did not fail to call traitors and rebels with as good a grace and as much benevolence, as Massachusettensis discovers.

Let me stop here and enquire, whether lord North has more wisdom than Henry the 7th, or whether he took the hint from the history of Poyning's, of sending General Gage, with his civil and military powers? If he did, he certainly did not imitate Henry, in his blustering menaces, against certain "ringleaders and forerunners."

While Poyning resided in Ireland, he called a parliament, which is famous in history for the acts which it passed in favour of England, and Englishmen settled in Ireland. By these, which are still called Poyning's laws, all the former laws of England, were made to be of force in Ireland, and no bill can be introduced into the Irish parliament, unless it previously receive the sanction of the English privy council; and by a construction if not by the express words of these laws, Ireland is still said to be bound by English statutes in which it is specially named. Here then let Massachusettensis pause and observe the original of the notion that countries might be bound by acts of parliament, if "specially named," tho' without the realm. Let him observe too, that this notion is grounded entirely on the voluntary act, the free consent of the Irish nation, and an act of an Irish parliament, called Poyning's law. Let me ask him, has any colony in America ever made a Poyning's act? Have they ever consented to be bound by acts of parliament, if specially named? Have they ever acquiesced in, or implicitly consented to any acts of parliament, but such as are *bona fide* made for the regulation of trade? This idea of binding countries without the realm, by "specially naming" them, is not an idea taken from the common law. There was no such principle, rule, or maxim, in that law—it must be by statute law then, or none. In the case of Wales and Ireland, it was introduced by solemn compact, and established by statutes, to which the Welch and Irish were parties, and expressly consented. But in the case of America there is no such statute, and therefore Americans are bound by statutes in which they are "named," no more than by those in which they are not.

The principle upon which Ireland is bound by English statutes in which it is named, is this, that being a conquered country, and subject to the mere will of the king, it voluntarily consented to be so bound. This appears in part already, and more fully in 1. Blackstone, 99, 100, &c.—who tells us, "that Ireland is a distinct, tho' a dependent, subordinate kingdom." But how came it dependant and subordinate? He tells us "that king John, in the twelfth year of his reign, after the conquest, went into Ireland, carried over with him many able sages of the law; and there *by his letters patent, in right of the dominion of conquest*, is said to have ordained and established, that Ireland should be governed by the laws of England: which letters patent Sir Edward Coke apprehends to have been there confirmed in parliament." "By the same rule that no laws made in England, between king John's time and Poyning's law, were then binding in Ireland, it follows that no acts of the English parliament, made since the tenth of Henry 7th, do now bind

the people of Ireland, unless specially named or included under
general words. And on the other hand it is equally clear, that
where Ireland is particularly named, or is included under general words, they are bound by such acts of parliament; for it
follows from the very nature and constitution of a dependent
state: dependence being very little else, but an obligation to
conform to the will or law of that superior person or state,
upon which the inferior depends. The original and true ground
of this superiority in the present case, is what we usually call,
tho' somewhat improperly, *the right of conquest*: a right allowed by the law of nations, if not by that of nature; but which
in reason and civil policy can mean nothing more, than that, in
order to put an end to hostilities, *a compact* is either expressly
or tacitly made between the conqueror and conquered, that if
they will acknowledge the *victor* for their *master*, he will treat
them for the future as subjects, and not as enemies."

These are the principles upon which the dependence and
subordination of Ireland are founded. Whether they are just or
not, is not necessary for us to enquire. The Irish nation, have
never been entirely convinced of their justice; have been ever
discontented with them, and ripe and ready to dispute them.
Their reasonings have ever been answered, by the *ratio ultima
et penultima* of the tories, and it requires to this hour, no less
than a standing army of 12000 men to confute them. As little
as the British parliament exercises the right, which it claims of
binding them by statutes, and altho' it never once attempted
or presumed to tax them, and altho' they are so greatly inferior
to Britain in power, and so near in situation.

But thus much is certain, that none of these principles take
place, in the case of America. She never was conquered by
Britain. She never consented to be a state dependent upon, or
subordinate to the British parliament, excepting only in the
regulation of her commerce: and therefore the reasonings
of British writers, upon the case of Ireland, are not applicable
to the case of the colonies, any more than those upon the case
of Wales.

Thus have I rambled after Massachusettensis through Wales
and Ireland: but have not reached my journey's end. I have yet
to travel through Jersey, Guernsey, and I know not where. At
present I shall conclude with one observation. In the history

of Ireland and Wales, though undoubtedly conquered countries, and under the very eye and arm of England, the extreme
difficulty, the utter impractability, of governing a people who
have any sense, spirit, or love of liberty, without incorporating
them into the state, or allowing them some other way, equal
priviledges may be clearly seen. Wales was forever revolting for
a thousand years, untill it obtained that mighty blessing. Ireland, has been frequently revolting, altho' the most essential
power of a supreme legislature, that of imposing taxes has
never been exercised over them, and it cannot now be kept
under, but by force, and it would revolt forever, if parliament
should tax them. What kind of an opinion then must the ministry entertain of America? When her distance is so great, her
territory so extensive, her commerce so important, not a conquered country, but dearly purchased and defended? When
her trade is so essential to the navy, the commerce, the revenue, the very existence of Great-Britain, as an independent
state? They must think America inhabited by three million
fools and cowards.

NOVANGLUS
Boston Gazette, April 3, 1775

Novanglus No. XI

To the Inhabitants of the Colony of Massachusetts-Bay

My Friends,

The cases of Wales and Ireland are not yet exhausted. They
afford such irrefragable proofs, that there is a distinction
between the crown and realm, and that a country may be annexed and subject to the former, and not the latter, that they
ought to be thoroughly studied and understood.

The more these cases, as well as those of Chester, Durham,
Jersey, Guernsey, Calais, Gascoine, Guienne, &c. are examined, the more clearly it will appear, that there is no precedent
in English records, no rule of common law, no provision in the
English constitution, no policy in the English or British government, for the case of the colonies; and therefore that we

derive our laws and government solely from our own compacts with Britain and her kings, and from the great legislature of the universe.

We ought to be cautious of the inaccuracies of the greatest men, for these are apt to lead us astray. Lord Coke, in 7 rep. 21. 6. says "Wales was sometimes a kingdom, as it appeareth by 19 H. 6. fol. 6, and by the act of parliament of 2 H. 5. cap. 6, but while it was a kingdom, the same was holden, and *within the see of the king of England*: and this appeareth by our books, Fleta, lib. 1. E. 3, 14, 8. E. 3, 59, 13. E. 3. Tit. Jurisdict. 10. H. 4, 6. Plow. com, 368. And in this respect, in diverse ancient charters, kings of old time stiled themselves in several manners, as king Edgar, Britanniæ, Basileus, Etheldrus, Totius Albionis Dei providentia Imperator, Edredus magnæ Britanniæ Monarcha, which among many others of like nature I have seen. But by the statute of 12 of Ed. I. *Wales was united and incorporated into England and made parcel of England in possession*; and therefore it is ruled in 7. H. 4. fol. 14. that no protection doth lie, *quia moratur in Wallia*, because Wales is within the realm of England. And where it is recited in the act of 27 H. 8. *that Wales was ever parcel of the realm of England*, it is true in this sense, viz. that before 12 E. I. it was parcel in tenure, and since *it is parcel of the body of the realm*. And whosoever is born within the see of the king of England, though it be in another kingdom, is a natural-born subject, and capable and inheritable of lands in England, as it appeareth in Plow. com. 126. And therefore those that were born in Wales before 12 E. I. while it was only holden of England, were capable and inheritable of lands in England."

Where my lord Coke, or any other sage, shews us the ground on which his opinion stands, we can judge for ourselves, whether the ground is good, and his opinion just. And if we examine by this rule, we shall find in the foregoing words, several palpable inaccuracies of expression. 1. by the 12 E. I. (which is the *Statutum Walliæ* quoted by me before) it is certain, *that Wales was not united and incorporated into England, and made parcel of England*. It was annexed and united to the crown of England only. It was done by the king's sole and absolute authority—not by an act of parliament, but by a mere *constitutio imperatoria*, and neither E. I, nor any of his suc-

cessors, ever would relinquish the right of ruling it, by mere
will and discretion, until the reign of James I. 2d. It is not recited in the 27 H. 8, that Wales was ever parcel of the realm of
England. The words of that statute are, "incorporated, annexed, united and subject to and under the imperial crown of
this realm," which is a decisive proof that a country may be annexed to the one, without being united with the other. And
this appears fully in lord Coke himself, 7 rep. 22, b. "Ireland
originally came to the kings of England by conquest, but who
was the first conqueror thereof hath been a question. I have
seen a charter made by king Edgar, in these words, *Ego
Edgarus Anglorum Basileus, omnium quæ insularum oceani,
quæ Britanniam circumjacent, imperatur et dominus, gratias
ago ipsi Deo omnipotenti regi meo, qui meum imperium sic am-
pliavit et exaltavit super regnum patrum meorum, &c. Mihi
concessit propitia divinitas, cum Anglorum imperis omnia
regna insularum oceani, &c. Cum suis ferocissibus regibus usque
Norvegiam, maximamque partem Hiberniæ, cum sua nobilis-
sima civitate de Dublina, Anglorum regno subjugare, qua-
propter et ego Christi gloriam et laudem in regno meo exaltare,
et ejus servitium amplificare devotus disposui, &c.* Yet for that it
was wholly conquered in the reign of H. 2. The honour of the
conquest of Ireland is attributed to him. That Ireland is a dominion separate and divided from England it is evident by our
books, 20 H. 6, 8.; Sir John Pilkington's case, 32. H. 6, 26.; 20
Eliz. Dyer 360; Plow. com. 360; and 2 r. 3, 12. *Hibernia habet
parliamentum, et saciunt leges, et statuta nostra, non ligant eos,
quia non mittunt milites ad parliamentum* (which is to be
understood unless they be specially named) *sed personæ eorum
sunt subjecti regis, sicut inhabitantes in Calesia, Gasconia et
Guigan.* Wherein it is to be observed, that the Irishman (as to
his subjection) is compared to men born in Calice, Gascoin
and Guian. Concerning their laws, *Ex rotulis patentium de
anno* 11. Regis H. 3, there is a charter which that king made
beginning in these words: *Rex Baronibus, Militibus et omnibus
libere tenentibus L. salutem, satis, ut credimus vestra audivit
discretio, quod quando bonæ memoriæ Johannes quondam rex
Angliæ, pater noster venit in Hiberniam, ipse duxit secum vires
discretos et legis peritos, quorum communi consilio et ad juctan-
tiam Hiberniansium statuit et præcepit leges Anglicanas in*

Hibernia, ita quod leges easdem in scripturas redactas reliquit sub sigillo suo ad scaccarium Dublin. So as now the laws of England became the proper laws of Ireland; and therefore because they have parliaments holden there, whereat they have made diverse particular laws, concerning that dominion, as it appeareth in 20 H. 6, 8, and 20 Eliz. Dyer 360, and for that they retain unto this day diverse of their ancient customs, the book in 20 H. 6, 8, holdeth, that Ireland is governed by laws and customs, separate and diverse from the laws of England. A voyage royal may be made into Ireland. Vid. 11. H. 4. 7. and 7. E. 4. 27. which proveth it a distinct dominion. *And in anno 33. Eliz. it was resolved by all the judges of England in the case of OR URKE an Irishman, who had committed high treason in Ireland, that he by the statute of 33 H. 8. c. 23, might be indicted, arraigned, and tried for the same in England, according to the purview of that statute: the words of which statute be, that all treasons, &c. committed by any person out of the realm of England, shall be from henceforth inquired of, &c. And they all resolved (as afterwards they did also in sir John Perrot's case) that Ireland was out of the realm of England, and that treasons committed there were to be tried within England, by that statute.* In the statute of 4 H. 7, c. 24 of fines, provision is made for them that be out of this land, and it is holden in Plow. com. in Stowell's case 375, that he that is in Ireland is out of this land, and consequently within that proviso. Might not then the like plea be devised as well against any person born in Ireland, as (this is against Calvin a *Postnatus*) in Scotland? For the Irishman is born *extra ligeantia regis, regni sui Angliæ*, &c. which be *verba operativa* in the plea: But all men know, that they are natural born subjects, and capable of, and inheritable to lands in England."

I have been at the pains of transcribing this long passage for the sake of a variety of important observations that may be made upon it. 1. That exuberance of proof that is in it, both that Ireland is annexed to the crown, and that it is not annexed to the realm of England. 2. That the reasoning in the year book, that Ireland has a parliament, and makes laws, and our statutes don't bind them, because they don't send knights to parliament, is universal, and concludes against these statutes binding in which Ireland is specially named, as much as against these in which it is not, and therefore lord Coke's parenthesis, (*which is to be understood unless they be specially named*) is wholly arbitrary and groundless, unless it goes upon the supposition, that the king is absolute in Ireland, it being a conquered country, and so has power to bind it at his pleasure, by an act of parliament, or by an edict: or unless it goes upon the supposition of Blackstone, that there had been an express agreement and consent of the Irish nation to be bound by acts of the English parliament; and in either case it is not applicable even by analogy to America, because that is not a conquered country, and most certainly never consented to be bound by all acts of parliament, in which it should be named. 3. That the *instance, request and consent* of the Irish is stated, as a ground upon which king John and his discreet law-sages, first established the laws of England in Ireland. 4. The resolution of the judges in the cases of Orurke and Perrot, is express that Ireland was *without the realm of England*, and the late resolutions of both houses of parliament and the late opinion of the judges, that Americans may be sent to England upon the same statute to be tried for treason, is also express that America is *out of the realm of England*. So that we see what is to become of us, my friends. When they want to get our money by taxing us, our privileges by annihilating our charters, and to screen those from punishment who shall murder us at their command, then we are told that we are within the realm; but when they want to draw, hang and quarter us, for honestly defending those liberties which God and compact have given and secured to us, oh, then we are clearly *out of the realm*! 5. In Stowell's case it is resolved that Ireland is out of *this land*, that is, the land of England. The consequence is, that it was out of the reach and extent of the *law of the land*, that is the common law. America surely is still further removed from that *land*, and therefore is without the jurisdiction of that law which is called the law of the land in England. I think it must appear by this time, that America is not parcel of the *realm, state, kingdom, government, empire* or *land* of England or Great-Britain, in any sense which can make it subject universally to the supreme legislature of that island.

But for the sake of curiosity, and for the purpose of shewing that the *consent even of a conquered people* has always been carefully conciliated. I beg leave to look over lord Coke's 4. Inst.

p. 12. "After king Henry 2d," says he "had conquered Ireland, he fitted and transcribed this modus (meaning the ancient treatise called *modus tenendi parliamentum*, which was re-hearsed and declared before the conquerer at the time of the conquest, and by him approved for England) into Ireland, in a parchment roll, for the holding of parliaments there, which no doubt H. 2. did by advice of his judges, &c. This *modus*, &c. was anno 6. H. 4. in the custody of Sir Christopher Preston, which roll H. 4. in the same year, *De assensu Johannis Talbot Chevalier*, his lieutenant there, and of his council of Ireland, exemplified," &c.

Here we see the original of a parliament in Ireland, which is assigned as the cause or reason why Ireland is a distant king-dom from England: and in the same, 4. inst. 349. we find more evidence that all this was done at the instance and request of the people in Ireland. Lord Coke says, "H. 2. the father of K. John, did ordain and command, *at the instance of the Irish*, that such laws as he had in England, should be of force and ob-served in Ireland." "Hereby Ireland being of itself a distant dominion, and no part of the kingdom of England, (as it directly appeareth by many authorities in Calvin's case) was to have parliaments holden there, as England, &c." See the re-cord as quoted by lord Coke in the same page, which shews that even this establishment of English laws, was made *De com-muni omnium de Hibernia consensu.*

This whole chapter is well worth attending to, because the records quoted in it shew how careful the ancients were to ob-tain the consent of the governed to all laws, tho' a conquered people and the king absolute. Very unlike the minister of our æra, who is for pulling down and building up the most sacred establishments of laws and government, without the least re-gard to the consent or good will of Americans. There is one observation more of lord Coke that deserves particular notice. "Sometimes the king of England called his nobles of Ireland to come to his parliament of England, &c. and by special words the parliament of England may bind the subjects of Ireland," and cites the record 8. E. 2. and subjoins "an excellent prece-dent to be followed, whensoever any act of parliament shall be made in England, concerning the state of Ireland, &c." By this lord Coke seems to intimate an opinion, that representatives had been and ought to be called from Ireland to the parliament of England, whenever it undertook to govern it by statutes, in which it should be specially named.

After all I believe there is no evidence of any express contract of the Irish nation to be governed by the English parliament, and very little of an implied one; that the notion of binding it by acts in which it is expressly named is meerly arbitrary. And that this nation which has ever had many and great virtues, has been most grievously oppressed:—and it is to this day so greatly injured and oppressed, that I wonder American committees of correspondence and congresses, have not attended more to it than they have. Perhaps in some future time they may. But I am running beyond my line.

We must now turn to Burrows's reports, vol. 2. 834. Rex vs. Cowle. Lord Mansfield has many observations upon the case of Wales, which ought not to be overlooked. Page 850. He says, "Edward 1st. conceived the great design of annexing all other parts of the island of Great Britain to the realm of England. The better to effectuate his idea, as time should offer occasion; he mentioned 'that all parts thereof, not in his own hands or possession, were holden of his crown.' The consequence of this doctrine was, that, by the feudal law, supreme jurisdiction resulted to him, in right of his crown, as sovereign lord, in many cases, which he might lay hold of; and when the said territories should come into his hands and possession, they would come back as parcel of the realm of England, from which (by fiction of law at least) they had been originally severed. This doctrine was literally true as to the counties palatine of Chester and Durham. But (*no matter upon what foundation*) he maintained that the principality of Wales was holden of the imperial crown of England: he treated the prince of Wales as a rebellious vassal; subdued him; and took possession of the principality. Whereupon, on the 4th of December, in the 9th year of his reign, he issued a commission to enquire '*per quas leges et per quas consuetudines, antecessores nostri reges regni consueverant principem Walliæ et barones wallenses Walliæ et pares suos et alios in priores et eorum pares, &c.*' If the principality was feudatory, the conclusion necessarily followed, 'that it was under the government of the king's laws, and the king's courts, in cases proper for them to interpose; though (like counties palatine) they had peculiar laws and customs, *jura regalia*, and complete jurisdiction at home.' There was a writ at the same time issued to all his officers in Wales, 'to give information to the commissioners:' and there were 14 interrogatories specifying the points to be enquired into. The statute of Rutland 12. E. 1. refers to this inquiry. By that statute he does not annex Wales to England, but recites it as a consequence of its coming into his hands. '*Divina providentia terram Walliæ, prius, nobis jure feodali subjectam, jam in proprietatis nostræ dominium convertit, et coronæ regni angliæ, tanquam partem corporis ejusdem annexuit, et univit.*' The 27. H. 8. c. 26. adheres to the same plan, and recites that 'Wales ever hath been incorporated, annexed, united and subject to, and under the imperial crown of this realm, as a very member, and joint of the same.' Edward I. having succeeded as to Wales, maintained likewise that Scotland was holden of the crown of England." This opinion of the court was delivered by lord Mansfield in the year 1759. In conformity to the *system* contained in these words, my lord Mansfield, and my lord North, together with their little friends Bernard and Hutchinson, have "conceived the great design of annexing" all North-America "to the realm of England," and "the better to effectuate this idea, they all maintain, that North-America is holden of the crown."

And (no matter upon what foundation) they all maintained that America is dependent on the imperial crown and parliament of Great Britain: and they are all very eagerly desirous of treating the Americans as rebellious vassals, to subdue them and take possession of their country. And when they do, no doubt America will come back as parcel of the realm of England, from which (by fiction of law at least) or by virtual representation, or by some other dream of a shadow of a shade, they had been originally severed.

But these noblemen and ignoblemen ought to have considered, that Americans understand the laws and the politicks as well as themselves, and that there are 600,000 men in it, between 16 and 60 years of age, and therefore it will be very difficult to chicane them out of their liberties by "fictions of law," and "no matter upon what foundation."

Methinks I hear his lordship upon this occasion, in a soliloquy somewhat like this. "We are now in the midst of a war, which has been conducted with unexampled success and glory. We have conquered a great part, and shall soon compleat the conquest of the French power in America. His majesty is near 70 years of age, and must soon yield to nature. The amiable, virtuous and promising successor, educated under the care of my nearest friends, will be influenced by our advice. We must bring the war to a conclusion, for we have not the martial spirit and abilities of the great commoner: but we shall be obliged to leave upon the nation an immense debt. How shall we manage that? Why, I have seen letters from America, proposing that parliament should bring America to a closer dependence upon it, and representing that if it does not, she will fall a prey to some foreign power, or set up for herself. These hints may be improved, and a vast revenue drawn from that country and the East-Indies, or at least the people here may be flattered and quieted with the hopes of it. It is the duty of a judge to declare law, but under this pretence, many we know have given law or made law, and none in all the records of Westminster hall more than of late. Enough has been already made, if it is wisely improved by others, to overturn this constitution. Upon this occasion I will accommodate my expressions, to such a design upon America and Asia, and will so accommodate both law and fact, that they may hereafter be improved to admirable effect in promoting our design." This is all romance, no doubt, but it has as good a moral as most romances. For 1st. It is an utter mistake that Ed. 1st. conceived the great design of annexing all to England, as one state, under one legislature. He conceived the design of annexing Wales, &c. to his crown. He did not pretend that it was before subject to the crown but to him. "*Nobis jure feodali*" are his words. And when he annexes it to his crown, he does it by an edict of his own, not an act of parliament: and he never did in his whole life allow, that his parliament, that is his lords and commons, had any authority over it, or that he was obliged to take or ask their advice in any one instance concerning the management of it, nor did any of his successors for centuries. It was not Ed. I. but Henry 7. who first conceived the great design of annexing it to the realm, and by him and H. 8. it was done, in part, but never compleated until Jac. I. There is a sense indeed

in which annexing a territory to the crown, is annexing it to
the realm, as putting a crown upon a man's head, is putting it
on the man, but it does not make it part of the man. 2d. His
lordship mentions the statute of Rutland, but this was not an
act of parliament, and therefore could not annex Wales to the
realm if the king had intended it, for it never was in the power
of the king alone to annex a country to the realm. This cannot
be done, but by act of parliament. As to Edward's treating the
prince of Wales as a "rebellious vassal," this was arbitrary, and
is spoken of by all historians as an infamous piece of tyranny.

Ed. I. and H. 8. both considered Wales, as the *property* and
revenue of the crown, not as a part of the realm, and the expressions, "*coronæ regni angliæ, tanquam partem corporis ejesdem*," signified "as part of the same body," that is of the same
"crown," not "realm" or "kingdom"; and the expressions in
27. H. 8. "under the imperial crown of this realm, as a very
member and joint of the same," mean, as a member and joint
of the "imperial crown," not of the realm. For the whole history of the principality, the acts of kings, parliaments, and
people shew, that Wales never was intituled by this annexation
to the laws of England, nor bound to obey them. The case of
Ireland is enough to prove that the crown and realm are not
the same. For Ireland is certainly annexed to the crown of England, and it certainly is not annexed to the realm.

There is one paragraph in the foregoing words of lord
Mansfield, which was quoted by his admirer Governor Hutchinson in his dispute with the house, with a profound compliment. "He did not know a greater authority," &c. But let the
authority be as great as it will, the doctrine will not bear the
test.

"If the principality was feudatory, the conclusion necessarily
follows, that it was under the government of the king's laws."
Ireland is feudatory to the crown of England, but would not
be subject to the king's English laws, without its consent and
compact. An estate may be feudatory to a lord, a country may
be feudatory to a sovereign lord, upon all possible variety of
conditions—it may be only to render homage—it may be to
render a rent, it may be to pay a tribute—if his lordship by
feudatory means, the original notion of feuds, it is true by that
the king the general imperator, was absolute, and the tenant

held his estate only at will, and the subject not only his estate but his person and life at his will. But this notion of feuds had been relaxed in an infinite variety of degrees, in some the estate is held at will, in others for life, in others for years, in others forever, to heirs, &c. in some to be govern'd by prince alone, in some by prince and nobles, and in some by prince, nobles and commons, &c. So that being feudatory, by no means proves that English lords and commons have any share in the government over us. As to counties palatine; these were not only holden of the king and crown, but were exerted by express acts of parliament, and therefore were never exempted from the authority of parliament. The same parliament, which erected the county Palatine, and gave it its *jura regalia*, and compleat jurisdiction, might unmake it, and take away those regalia and jurisdiction. But American governments and constitutions were never erected by parliament, their *regalia* and jurisdiction were not given by parliament, and therefore parliament have no authority to take them away.

But if the colonies are feudatory to the kings of England, and subject to the government of the king's laws, it is only to such laws as are made in their general assemblies, their provincial legislatures.

NOVANGLUS

Boston Gazette, April 10, 1775

Novanglus No. XII

To the Inhabitants of the Colony of Massachusetts-Bay

My Friends,

We now come to Jersey and Guernsey, which Massachusettensis says "are no part of the realm of England, nor are they represented in parliament, but are subject to its authority." A little knowledge of this subject will do us no harm, and as soon as we shall acquire it, we shall be satisfied, how these islands came to be subject to the authority of parliament. It is either upon the principle that the king is absolute there, and has a right to make laws for them by his mere will, and therefore may express his will by an act of parliament or an edict at his pleasure, or it is an usurpation. If it is an usurpation, it ought not to be a precedent for the colonies, but it ought to be reformed, and they ought to be incorporated into the realm, by act of parliament, and their own act. Their situation is no objection to this. Ours is an insurmountable obstacle.

Thus we see that in every instance which can be found, the observation proves to be true, that by the common law, the laws of England, and the authority of parliament and the limits of the realm, were confined within seas. That the kings of England had frequently foreign dominions, some by conquest, some by marriage, and some by descent. But in all those cases the kings were either absolute in those dominions, or bound to govern them according to their own respective laws, and by their own legislative and executive councils. That the laws of England did not extend there, and the English parliament pretended nó jurisdiction there, nor claimed any right to controul the king in his government of those dominions. And from this extensive survey of all the foregoing cases, there results a confirmation of what has been so often said, that there is no provision in the common law, in English precedents, in the English government or constitution, made for the case of the colonies. It is not a conquered, but a discovered country. It came not to the king by descent, but was explored by the settlers. It came not by marriage to the king, but was purchased by the settlers, of the savages. It was not granted by the king of his grace, but was dearly, very dearly earned by the planters, in the labour, blood, and treasure which they expended to subdue it to cultivation. It stands upon no grounds then of law or policy, but what are found in the law of nature, and their express contracts in their charters, and their implied contracts in the commissions to governors and terms of settlement.

The cases of Chester, and Durham, counties palatine within the realm, shall conclude this fatigueing ramble. Chester was an earldom and a county, and in 21 year of king R. 2. A. D. 1397, it was by an act of parliament, erected into a principality, and several castles and towns, were annexed to it, saving to the king the rights of his crown. This was a county palatine, and had *jura regalia*, before this erection of it, into a principality. But the statute which made it a principality, was again repealed, by

1. H. 4. c. 3. and in 1399, by the 1. H. 4. c. 18. Grievous complaints were made to the king in parliament, of murders, manslaughters, robberies, batteries, riots, &c. done by people of the county of Chester, in divers counties of England. For remedy of which it is enacted, that if any person of the county of Chester, commit any murder or felony in any place out of that county, process shall be made against him by the common law, 'till the exigent, in the county where such murder or felony was done: and if he flee into the county of Chester, and be outlawed, and put in exigent for such murder or felony, the same outlawry or exigent, shall be certified to the officers and ministers of the same county of Chester, and the felon shall be taken, his lands and goods within that county shall be seized as forfeit into the hands of the prince, or of him that shall be lord of the same county of Chester, and the king shall have the year and day and waste; and the other lands and goods of such felons, out of said county, shall remain wholly to the king, &c. as forfeit. And a similar provision in case of battery or trespass, &c.

Considering the great seal of England, and the process of the kings contracts did not run into Chester, it was natural that malefactors should take refuge there and escape punishment, and therefore a statute like this, was of indispensible necessity, and afterwards in 1535, another statute was made, 27. H. c. 5. for the making of justices of peace within Chester, &c. Recites the king, considering the manifold robberies, murthers, thefts, trespasses, riots, routs, embraceries, maintenances, oppressions, ruptures of his peace &c. which have been daily done within his county palatine of Chester &c. by reason that common justice hath not been indifferently ministred there, like and in form as it is in other places of this his realm, by reason whereof the said criminals have remained unpunished; for redress whereof, and to the intent that one order of law should be had, the king is impowered to constitute justices of peace, quorum, and goal delivery, in Chester, &c.

By the 32. H. 8. c. 43. another act was made concerning the county palatine of Chester, for shire days.

These three acts soon excited discontent in Chester. They had enjoyed an exemption from the king's English courts, leg-

islative and executive, and they had no representatives in the
English parliament, and therefore they thought it a violation
of their rights, to be subjected even to those three statutes, as
reasonable and absolutely necessary as they appear to have
been: and accordingly we find in 1542.—34. and 35. H. 8. c. 13.
a zealous petition to be represented in parliament, and an act
was made for making of knights and burgesses within the
county and city of Chester. It recites a part of the petition to
the king, from the inhabitants of Chester, shewing, "that the
county palatine, had been excluded from parliament, to have
any knights and burgesses there; by reason whereof, the said
inhabitants have hitherto sustained manifold disherisons, losses
and damages, in lands, goods and bodies, as well as in the good
civil and politick governance and maintenance of the common
wealth, of their said country: and forasmuch as the said inhabitants have always hitherto been bound by the acts and
statutes, made by your highness and progenitors in said court,
(meaning when expressly named, not otherwise,) as far forth
as other counties, cities and boroughs, which have had knights
and burgesses, and yet have had neither knight nor burgess
there, for the said county palatine; the said inhabitants for lack
thereof, have been oftentimes touched and grieved with acts
and statutes, made within the said court, as well derogatory
unto the most ancient *jurisdictions, liberties,* and *privileges* of
your said county palatine, as prejudicial unto the common
weal, quietness, rest and peace of your subjects, &c." For remedy whereof, two knights of the shire and two burgesses for
the city are established.

I have before recited all the acts of parliament, which were
ever made to meddle with Chester, except the 51. H. 3. st. 5. in
1266, which only provides that the justices of Chester, and
other bailiffs, shall be answerable in the exchequer, for wards,
estcheats, and other bailiwicks; yet Chester was never severed
from the crown or realm of England, nor ever expressly exempted from the authority of parliament: yet as they had generally enjoyed an exemption from the exercise of the authority
of parliament, we see how soon they complain of it as grievous, and claim a representation, as a right; and we see how
readily it was granted.—America, on the contrary, is not in the

realm, never was subject to the authority of parliament, by any principle of law, is so far from Great-Britain, that she never can be represented; yet she is to be bound in all cases whatsoever.

The first statute, which appears in which Durham is named, is 27. H. 8. c. 24. §21. Cuthbert bishop of Durham, and his successors, and their temporal chancellor of the county palatine of Durham, are made justices of the peace. The next is 31 Eliz. c. 9. recites, that Durham is, and of long time hath been an ancient county palatine, in which the Queen's writ, hath not, and yet doth not run; enacts that a writ of proclamation upon an exigent, against any person dwelling in the bishoprick, shall run there for the future. And §5. confirms all the other liberties of the bishop and his officers.

And after this, we find no other mention of that bishoprick in any statute until 25 Char. 2. c. 9. This statute recites, "whereas the inhabitants of the county palatine of Durham, have not hitherto had the liberty and priviledge of electing and sending any knights and burgesses to the high court of parliament, altho' the inhabitants of the said county palatine *are liable to all payments, rates, and subsidies, granted by parliament,* equally with the inhabitants of other counties, cities, and burroughs, in this kingdom, who have their knights and burgesses in the parliament, and are therefore *concerned equally with others,* the inhabitants of this kingdom, to have knights and burgesses in the said high court of parliament *of their own election,* to represent the condition of their county, as the inhabitants of other counties, cities, and burroughs of this kingdom have." Enacts two knights for the county, and two burgesses for the city. Here it should be observed, that altho' they acknowledge that they had been *liable* to all *rates,* &c. granted by parliament, yet none had actually been laid upon them before this statute.

Massachusettensis then comes to the first charter of this province, and he tells us, that in it "we shall find irresistable evidence, that our being a part of the empire subject to the supreme authority of the state, bound by its laws, and subject to its protection, was the very terms and conditions by which our ancestors held their lands and settled the province." This is roundly and warmly said: but there is more zeal in it than knowledge. As to our being part of the empire, it could not be the British empire, as it is called, because that was not then in being, but was created seventy or eighty years afterwards. It must be the English empire then, but the nation was not then polite enough to have introduced into the language of the law, or common parlance any such phrase or idea. Rome never introduced the terms Roman empire until the tragedy of her freedom was compleated. Before that, it was only the republic, or the city. In the same manner the realm or the kingdom, or the dominions of the king, were the fashionable style in the age of the first charter. As to being subject to the supreme authority of the state, the prince who granted that charter thought it resided in himself, without any such troublesome tumults as lords and commons; and before the granting that charter, had dissolved his parliament, and determined never to call another, but to govern without. It is not very likely then, that he intended our ancestors should be governed by parliament, or bound by its laws. As to being subject to its protection, we may guess what ideas king and parliament had of that, by the protection they actually afforded to our ancestors. Not one farthing was ever voted or given by the king or his parliament, or any one resolution taken about them. As to holding their lands, surely they did not hold their lands of lords and commons. If they agreed to hold their lands of the king, this did not subject them to English lords and commons, any more than the inhabitants of Scotland holding their lands of the same king, subjected them. But there is not a word about the empire, the supreme authority of the state, being bound by its laws, or obliged for its protection in that whole charter. But "our charter is in the royal style." What then? Is that the parliamentary style? The style is, this "Charles, by the grace of God, king of England, Scotland, France and Ireland, defender of the faith, &c." Now in which capacity did he grant that charter? As king of France, or Ireland, or Scotland, or England? He govern'd England by one parliament, Scotland by another. Which parliament, were we to be governed by? And Ireland by a third, and it might as well be reasoned that America was to be governed by the Irish parliament as by the English. But it was granted "under the great seal of England"—true. But this seal runneth not out of the realm, except to mandatory writs, and when our charter was given, it was never intended to go out of the realm. The charter and the corporation were intended to abide and remain within the realm, and be like other corporations there. But this affair of the seal is a mere piece of imposition.

In Moore's reports in the case of the union of the realm of Scotland with England, it is resolved by the judges that "the seal is alterable by the king at his pleasure, and he might make one seal for both kingdoms (of England and Scotland,) for seals, coin, and leagues are of absolute prerogative to the king, without parliament, nor restrained to any assent of the people", and in determining how far the great seal doth command out of England, they made this distinction. "That the great seal was currant for remedials, which groweth on complaint of the subject, and thereupon writs are addressed under the great seal of England, which writs are limited, their precinct to be within the places of the jurisdiction of the court, that was to give the redress of the wrong. And therefore writs are not to go into Ireland, or the isles, nor Wales, nor the counties palatine, because the king's courts here have not power to hold pleas of lands or things there. But the great seal hath a power preceptory to the person, which power extendeth to any place where the person may be found, &c." This authority plainly shews that the great seal of England, has no more authority out of the realm, except to mandatory or preceptory writs, (and surely the first charter was no preceptory writ) than the privy seal, or the great seal of Scotland, or no seal at all. In truth, the seal and charter were intended to remain within the realm, and be of force to a corporation there; but the moment it was transferred to New England, it lost all its legal force, by the common law of England; and as this translation of it was acquiesced in by all parties, it might well be considered as good evidence of a contract between the parties, and in no other light, but not a whit the better or stronger for being under the great seal of England. But "the grants are made by the king for his heirs and successors." What then? So the Scots held their lands of him who was then king of England, his heirs and successors, and were bound to allegiance to him, his heirs and successors, but it did not follow from thence that the Scots were subject to the English parliament. So the inhabitants of Aquitain, for ten descents, held their lands, and were tied by allegiance to him who was king of England, his heirs and successors, but were under no subjection to English lords and commons.

Heirs and *successors* of the king, are supposed to be the same persons, and are used as synonimous words in the English law. There is no positive, artifical provision made by our laws or the British constitution for revolutions. All our positive laws suppose that the royal office will descend to the eldest branch of the male line, or in default of that to the eldest female, &c. forever, and that the succession will not be broken. It is true that nature, necessity and the great principles of self-preservation, have often over-ruled the succession. But this was done without any positive instruction of law. Therefore the grants being by the king for his heirs and successors, and the tenures being of the king his heirs and successors, and the preservation being to the king his heirs and successors, are so far from proving that we were to be part of an empire as one state subject to the supreme authority of the English or British state, and subject to its protection, that they don't so much as prove that we are annexed to the English crown. And all the subtilty of the writers on the side of the ministry, has never yet proved that America is so much as annexed to the crown, much less to the realm. "It is apparent the king acted in his royal capacity as king of England." This I deny. The laws of England gave him no authority to grant any territory out of the realm. Besides, there is no colour for his thinking that he acted in that capacity, but his using the great seal of England: but if the king is absolute in the affair of the seal, and may make or use any seal that he pleases, his using that seal which had been commonly used in England, is no certain proof that he acted as king of England; for it is plain, he might have used the English seal in the government of Scotland, and in that case it will not be pretended that he would have acted in his royal capacity as king of England. But his acting as king of England "necessarily supposes the territory granted to be a part of the English dominions, and holden of the crown of England." Here is the word "dominions," systematically introduced instead of the word "realm." There was no English dominions but the realm. And I say that America was not any part of the English realm or dominions. And therefore, when the king granted it, he could not act as king of England by the laws of England. As to the "territory being holden of the crown," there is no such thing in nature or art. Lands are holden according to the original notion of feuds of the natural person of the lord. Holding lands, in feudal language, means no more than the relation between lord and tenant. The reciprocal duties of these are all personal. Homage, fealty, &c. and all other services, are personal to the lord; protection, &c. is personal to the tenant. And therefore no homage, fealty, or other services, can ever be rendered to the body politick, the political capacity, which is not corporated, but only a frame in the mind, an idea. No lands here or in England are held of the crown, meaning by it, the political capacity—they are all held of the royal person, the natural person of the king. Holding lands, &c. of the crown, is an impropriety of expression, but it is often used, and when it is, it can have no other sensible meaning than this—that we hold lands of that person, whoever he is, who wears the crown —the law supposes he will be a right, natural heir of the present king forever.

Massachusettensis then produces a quotation from the first charter, to prove several points. It is needless to repeat the whole, but the parts chiefly relied on, are italicised. It makes the company "a body politick in fact and name, &c. and enables it to sue and be sued." Then the writer asks, "whether this looks like a distinct state or independent empire?" I answer no. And that it is plain and uncontroverted, that the first charter was intended only to erect a corporation within the realm, and the governor and company were to reside within the realm, and their general courts were to be held there. Their agents, deputies and servants only were to come to America. And if this had taken place, nobody ever doubted but they would have been subject to parliament. But this intention was not regarded on either side, and the company came over to America, and brought their charter with them. And as soon as they arrived here, they got out of the English realm, dominions, state, empire, call it by what name you will, and out of the legal jurisdiction of parliament. The king might by his writ or proclamation have commanded them to return, but he did not.

NOVANGLUS

Boston Gazette, April 17, 1775

SELECTIONS FROM THE
AUTOBIOGRAPHY

From the Autobiography

JOHN ADAMS

Begun Oct. 5. 1802.

As the Lives of Philosophers, Statesmen or Historians written by them selves have generally been suspected of Vanity, and therefore few People have been able to read them without disgust; there is no reason to expect that any Sketches I may leave of my own Times would be received by the Public with any favour, or read by individuals with much interest. The many great Examples of this practice will not be alledged as a justification, because they were Men of extraordinary Fame, to which I have no pretensions. My Excuse is, that having been the Object of much Misrepresentation, some of my Posterity may probably wish to see in my own hand Writing a proof of the falsehood of that Mass of odious Abuse of my Character, with which News Papers, private Letters and public Pamphlets and Histories have been disgraced for thirty Years. It is not for the Public but for my Children that I commit these Memoirs to writing: and to them and their Posterity I recommend, not the public Course, which the times and the Country in which I was born and the Circumstances which surrounded me compelled me to pursue: but those Moral Sentiments and Sacred Principles, which at all hazards and by every Sacrifice I have endeavoured to preserve through Life.

My Father married Susanna Boylston in October 1734, and on the 19th of October 1735 I was born. As my Parents were both fond of reading, and my father had destined his first born, long before his birth to a public Education I was very early taught to read at home and at a School of Mrs. Belcher the Mother of Deacon Moses Belcher, who lived in the next house on the opposite side of the Road. I shall not consume much paper in relating the Anecdotes of my Youth. I was sent to the public School close by the Stone Church, then kept by Mr. Joseph Cleverly, who died this Year 1802 at the Age of Ninety. Mr. Cleverly was through his whole Life the most indolent Man I ever knew though a tolerable Schollar and a Gentleman. His inattention to his Schollars was such as gave me a disgust to Schools, to books and to study and I spent my time as idle Children do in making and sailing boats and Ships upon the Ponds and Brooks, in making and flying Kites, in driving hoops, playing marbles, playing Quoits, Wrestling, Swimming, Skaiting and above all in shooting, to which Diversion I was addicted to a degree of Ardor which I know not that I ever felt for any other Business, Study or Amusement.

My Enthusiasm for Sports and Inattention to Books, allarmed my Father, and he frequently entered into conversation with me upon the Subject. I told him [   ] love Books and wished he would lay aside the thoughts of sending me to Colledge. What would you do Child? Be a Farmer. A Farmer? Well I will shew you what it is to be a Farmer. You shall go with me to Penny ferry tomorrow Morning and help me get Thatch. I shall be very glad to go Sir.—Accordingly next morning he took me with him, and with great good humour kept me all day with him at Work. At night at home he said Well John are you satisfied with being a Farmer. Though the Labour had been very hard and very muddy I answered I like it very well Sir. Ay but I dont like it so well: so you shall go to School to day. I went but was not so happy as among the Creek Thatch. My School master neglected to put me into Arithmetick longer than I thought was right, and I resented it. I procured me Cockers I believe and applyd myself to it at home alone and went through the whole Course, overtook and passed by all the Schollars at School, without any master. I dared not ask my fathers Assistance because he would have disliked my Inattention to my Latin. In this idle Way I passed on till fourteen and upwards, when I said to my Father very seriously I wished he would take me from School and let me go to work upon the Farm. You know said my father I have set my heart upon your Education at Colledge and why will you not comply with my desire. Sir I dont like my Schoolmaster. He is so negligent and so cross that I never can learn any thing under him. If you will be so good as to perswade Mr. Marsh to take me, I will apply myself to my Studies as closely as my nature will admit, and go to Colledge as soon as I can be prepared. Next Morning the first I heard was John I have perswaded Mr. Marsh to take

you, and you must go to school there to day. This Mr. Marsh
was a Son of our former Minister of that name, who kept a private Boarding School but two doors from my Fathers. To this
School I went, where I was kindly treated, and I began to study
in Earnest. My Father soon observed the relaxation of my Zeal
for my Fowling Piece, and my daily encreasing Attention to
my Books. In a little more than a Year Mr. Marsh pronounced
me fitted for Colledge. On the day appointed at Cambridge
for the Examination of Candidates for Admission I mounted
my horse and called upon Mr. Marsh, who was to go with me.
The Weather was dull and threatened rain. Mr. Marsh said he
was unwell and afraid to go out. I must therefore go alone.
Thunder struck at this unforeseen disappointment, And terrified at the Thought of introducing myself to such great Men
as the President and fellows of a Colledge, I at first resolved to
return home: but foreseeing the Grief of my father and apprehending he would not only be offended with me, but my
Master too whom I sincerely loved, I arroused my self, and
collected Resolution enough to proceed. Although Mr. Marsh
had assured me that he had seen one of the Tutors the last
Week and had said to him, all that was proper for him to say if
he should go to Cambridge; that he was not afraid to trust me
to an Examination and was confident I should acquit my self
well and be honourably admitted; yet I had not the same confidence in my self, and suffered a very melancholly Journey.
Arrived at Cambridge I presented myself according to my directions and underwent the usual Examination by the President Mr. Holyoke and the Tutors Flint, Hancock, Mayhew
and Marsh. Mr. Mayhew into whose Class We were to be admitted, presented me a Passage of English to translate into
Latin. It was long and casting my Eye over it I found several
Words the latin for which did not occur to my memory. Thinking that I must translate it without a dictionary, I was in a great
fright and expected to be turned by, an Event that I dreaded
above all things. Mr. Mayhew went into his Study and bid me
follow him. There Child, said he is a dictionary, there a Gra-
mar, and there Paper, Pen and Ink, and you may take your
own time. This was joyfull news to me and I then thought my
Admission safe. The Latin was soon made, I was declared Admitted and a Theme given me, to write on in the Vacation. I

was as light when I came home as I had been heavy when I
went: my Master was well pleased and my Parents very happy.
I spent the Vacation not very profitably chiefly in reading
Magazines and a British Apollo. I went to Colledge at the End
of it and took the Chamber assigned me and my place in the
Class under Mr. Mayhew. I found some better Schollars than
myself, particularly Lock, Hemmenway and Tisdale. The last
left Colledge before the End of the first Year, and what became
of him I know not. Hemmenway still lives a great divine, and
Lock has been President of Harvard Colledge a Station for
which no Man was better qualified. With these I ever lived in
friendship, without Jealousy or Envy. I soon became intimate
with them, and began to feel a desire to equal them in Science
and Literature. In the Sciences especially Mathematicks, I soon
surpassed them, mainly because, intending to go into the Pulpit, they thought Divinity and the Classicks of more Importance to them. In Litterature I never overtook them.

Here it may be proper to recollect something which makes
an Article of great importance in the Life of every Man. I was
of an amorous disposition and very early from ten or eleven
Years of Age, was very fond of the Society of females. I had my
favorites among the young Women and spent many of my
Evenings in their Company and this disposition although con-
trolled for seven Years after my Entrance into College returned
and engaged me too much till I was married. I shall draw no
Characters nor give any enumeration of my youthfull flames. It
would be considered as no compliment to the dead or the living: This I will say—they were all modest and virtuous Girls
and always maintained this Character through Life. No Virgin
or Matron ever had cause to blush at the sight of me, or to regret her Acquaintance with me. No Father, Brother, Son or
Friend ever had cause of Grief or Resentment for any Intercourse between me and any Daughter, Sister, Mother, or any
other Relation of the female Sex. My Children may be assured
that no illegitimate Brother or Sister exists or ever existed.
These Reflections, to me consolatory beyond all expression, I
am able to make with truth and sincerity and I presume I am
indebted for this blessing to my Education. My Parents held
every Species of Libertinage in such Contempt and horror,
and held up constantly to view such pictures of disgrace, of

baseness and of Ruin, that my natural temperament was always overawed by my Principles and Sense of decorum. This Blessing has been rendered the more prescious to me, as I have seen enough of the Effects of a different practice. Corroding Reflections through Life are the never failing consequence of illicit amours, in old as well as in new Countries. The Happiness of Life depends more upon Innocence in this respect, than upon all the Philosophy of Epicurus, or of Zeno without it. I could write Romances, or Histories as wonderfull as Romances of what I have known or heard in France, Holland and England, and all would serve to confirm what I learned in my Youth in America, that Happiness is lost forever if Innocence is lost, at least untill a Repentance is undergone so severe as to be an overballance to all the gratifications of Licentiousness. Repentance itself cannot restore the Happiness of Innocence, at least in this Life.

I soon perceived a growing Curiosity, a Love of Books and a fondness for Study, which dissipated all my Inclination for Sports, and even for the Society of the Ladies. I read forever, but without much method, and with very little Choice. I got my Lessons regularly and performed my recitations without Censure. Mathematicks and natural Phylosophy attracted the most of my Attention, which I have since regretted, because I was destined to a Course of Life, in which these Sciences have been of little Use, and the Classicks would have been of great Importance. I owe to this however perhaps some degree of Patience of Investigation, which I might not otherwise have obtained. Another Advantage ought not to be omitted. It is too near my heart. My Smattering of Mathematicks enabled me afterwards at Auteuil in France to go, with my eldest Son, through a Course of Geometry, Algebra and several Branches of the Sciences, with a degree of pleasure that amply rewarded me for all my time and pains.

Between the Years 1751 when I entered, and 1754 when I left Colledge a Controversy was carried on between Mr. Bryant the Minister of our Parish and some of his People, partly on Account of his Principles which were called Arminian and partly on Account of his Conduct, which was too gay and light if not immoral. Ecclesiastical Councils were called and sat at my Fathers House. Parties and their Accrimonies arose in the Church and Congregation, and Controversies from the Press between Mr. Bryant, Mr. Niles, Mr. Porter, Mr. Bass, concerning the five Points. I read all these Pamphlets and many other Writings on the same Subject and found myself involved in difficulties beyond my Powers of decision. At the same time, I saw such a Spirit of Dogmatism and Bigotry in Clergy and Laity, that if I should be a Priest I must take my side, and pronounce as positively as any of them, or never get a Parish, or getting it must soon leave it. Very strong doubts arose in my mind, whether I was made for a Pulpit in such times, and I began to think of other Professions. I perceived very clearly, as I thought, that the Study of Theology and the pursuit of it as a Profession would involve me in endless Altercations and make my Life miserable, without any prospect of doing any good to my fellow Men.

The two last years of my Residence at Colledge, produced a Clubb of Students, I never knew the History of the first rise of it, who invited me to become one of them. Their plan was to spend their Evenings together, in reading any new publications, or any Poetry or Dramatic Compositions, that might fall in their Way. I was as often requested to read as any other, especially Tragedies, and it was whispered to me and circulated among others that I had some faculty for public Speaking and that I should make a better Lawyer than Divine. This last Idea was easily understood and embraced by me. My Inclination was soon fixed upon the Law: But my Judgment was not so easily determined. There were many difficulties in the Way. Although my Fathers general Expectation was that I should be a Divine, I knew him to be a Man of so thoughtful and considerate a turn of mind, to be possessed of so much Candor and moderation, that it would not be difficult to remove any objections he might make to my pursuit of Physick or Law or any other reasonable Course. My Mother although a pious Woman I knew had no partiality for the Life of a Clergyman. But I had Uncles and other relations, full of the most illiberal Prejudices against the Law. I had indeed a proper Affection and veneration for them, but as I was under no Obligation of Gratitude to them, which could give them any colour of Authority to prescribe a course of Life to me, I thought little of their Opinions. Other Obstacles more serious than these presented themselves. A Lawyer must have a Fee, for taking me into his Office. I must be boarded and cloathed for several Years: I had no Money; and my Father having three Sons, had done as much for me, in the Expences of my Education as his Estate and Circumstances could justify and as my Reason or my honor would allow me to ask. I therefore gave out that I would take a School, and took my Degree at Colledge undetermined whether I should study Divinity, Law or Physick. In the publick Exercises at Commencement, I was somewhat remarked as a Respondent, and Mr. Maccarty of Worcester who was empowered by the Select Men of that Town to procure them a Latin Master for their Grammar School engaged me to undertake it. About three Weeks after commencement in 1755, when I was not yet twenty Years of Age, a horse was sent me from Worcester and a Man to attend me. We made the journey about Sixty miles in one day and I entered on my Office. For three months I boarded with one Green at the Expence of the Town and by the Arrangement of the Select Men. Here I found Morgans Moral Phylosopher, which I was informed had circulated, with some freedom, in that Town and that the Principles of Deism had made a considerable progress among several Persons, in that and other Towns in the County. Three months after this the Select Men procured Lodgings for me at Dr. Nahum Willards. This Physician had a large Practice, a good reputation for Skill, and a pretty Library. Here were Dr. Cheynes Works, Sydenham and others and Van Sweetens Commentaries on Boerhave. I read a good deal in these Books and entertained many thoughts of Becoming a Physician and a Surgeon: But the Law attracted my Attention more and more, and Attending the Courts of Justice, where I heard Worthington, Hawley, Trowbridge, Putnam and others, I felt myself irresistably impelled to make some Effort to accomplish my Wishes. I made a Visit to Mr. Putnam, and offered myself to him: He received me with politeness and even Kindness, took a few days to consider of it, and then informed me that Mrs. Putnam had consented that I should board in his House, that I should pay no more, than the Town allowed for my Lodgings, and that I should pay him an hundred dollars, when I should find it convenient. I agreed to his proposals without hesitation and immediately took Possession of his Office. His Library at that time was not large: but he had all the most essential Law Books: immediately after I entered with him however he sent to England for a handsome Addition of Law Books and for Lord Bacons Works. I carried with me to Worcester, Lord Bolingbrokes Study and Use of History, and his Patriot King. These I had lent him, and he was so well pleased with them that he Added Bolingbrokes Works to his List, which gave me an Opportunity of reading the Posthumous Works of that Writer in five Volumes. Mr. Burke once asked, who ever read him through? I can answer that I read him through, before the Year 1758 and that I have read him through at least twice since that time: But I confess without much good or harm. His Ideas of the English Constitution are correct and his Political Writings are worth something: but in a great part of them there is more of Faction than of Truth: His Religion is a pompous Folly: and his Abuse of the Christian Religion is as superficial as it is impious. His Style is original and inimitable: it resembles more the oratory of the Ancients, than any Writings or Speeches I ever read in English.

In this Situation I remained, for about two Years Reading Law in the night and keeping School in the day. At Breakfast, Dinner, and Tea, Mr. Putnam was commonly disputing with me upon some question of Religion: He had been intimate with one Peasley Collins, the Son of a Quaker in Boston, who had been to Europe and came back, a Disbeliever of Every Thing: fully satisfied that all Religion was a cheat, a cunning invention of Priests and Politicians: That there would be no future State, any more than there is at present any moral Government. Putnam could not go these whole Lengths with him. Although he would argue to the extent of his Learning and Ingenuity, to destroy or invalidate the Evidences of a future State, and the Principles of natural and revealed Religion, Yet I could plainly perceive that he could not convince himself, that Death was an endless Sleep. Indeed he has sometimes said to me, that he fully believed in a future Existence, and that good Conduct in this Life, would fare better in the next World than its contrary. My Arguments in favor of natural and revealed Religion, and a future State of Rewards and Punishments, were nothing more than the common Arguments and his against them may all be found in Lucretius, together with many more.

At this Time October 1758 the Study of the Law was a dreary Ramble, in comparison of what it is at this day. The Name of Blackstone had not been heard, whose Commentaries together with Sullivans Lectures and Reeves's History of the Law, have smoothed the path of the Student, while the long Career of Lord Mansfield, his many investigations and Decisions, the great Number of modern Reporters in his time and a great Number of Writers on particular Branches of the Science have greatly facilitated the Acquisition of it. I know not whether a sett of the Statutes at large or of the State Tryals was in the Country. I was desirous of seeking the Law as well as I could in its fountains and I obtained as much Knowledge as I could of Bracton, Britton, Fleta and Glanville, but I suffered very much for Want of Books, which determined me to furnish myself, at any Sacrifice, with a proper Library: and Accordingly by degrees I procured the best Library of Law in the State.

Looking about me in the Country, I found the practice of Law was grasped into the hands of Deputy Sheriffs, Pettyfoggers and even Constables, who filled all the Writts upon Bonds, promissory notes and Accounts, received the Fees established for Lawyers and stirred up many unnecessary Suits. I mentioned these Things to some of the Gentlemen in Boston, who disapproved and even resented them very highly. I asked them whether some measures might not be agreed upon at the Bar and sanctioned by the Court, which might remedy the Evil? They thought it not only practicable but highly expedient and proposed Meetings of the Bar to deliberate upon it. A Meeting was called and a great Number of regulations proposed not only for confining the practice of Law to those who were educated to it and sworn to fidelity in it, but to introduce more regularity, Urbanity, Candour and Politeness as well as honor, Equity and Humanity, among the regular Professors. Many of these Meetings were the most delightfull Entertainments, I ever enjoyed. The Spirit that reigned was that of Solid Sense, Generosity, Honor and Integrity: and the Consequences were most happy, for the Courts and the Bar instead of Scenes of Wrangling, Chicanery, Quibbling and ill manners, were soon converted to order, Decency, Truth and Candor. Mr. Pratt was so delighted with these Meetings and their Effects, that when We all waited on him to Dedham in his Way to New York to take his Seat as Chief Justice of that State, when We took leave of him after Dinner, the last Words he said to Us, were, "Brethren above all things forsake not the Assembling of yourselves together."

The next Year after I was sworn, was the memorable Year 1759 when the Conquest of Canada was compleated by the surrender of Montreal to General Amherst. This Event, which was so joyfull to Us and so important to England if she had seen her true Interest, inspired her with a Jealousy, which ultimately lost her thirteen Colonies and made many of Us at the time regret that Canada had ever been conquered. The King sent Instructions to his Custom house officers to carry the Acts of Trade and Navigation into strict Execution. An inferiour Officer of the Customs in Salem whose Name was Cockle petitioned the Justices of the Superiour Court, at their Session in November for the County of Essex, to grant him Writs of Assistants, according to some provisions in one of the Acts of Trade, which had not been executed, to authorize him to break open Ships, Shops, Cellars, Houses &c. to search for prohibited Goods, and merchandizes on which Duties had not been paid. Some Objection was made to this Motion, and Mr. Stephen Sewall, who was then Chief Justice of that Court, and a zealous Friend of Liberty, expressed some doubts of the Legality and Constitutionality of the Writ, and of the Power of the Court to grant it. The Court ordered the question to be argued at Boston, in February term 1761. In the mean time Mr. Sewall died and Mr. Hutchinson then Lt. Governor, a Councillor, and Judge of Probate for the County of Suffolk &c. was appointed in his Stead, Chief Justice. The first Vacancy on that Bench, had been promised, in two former Administrations, to Colonel James Otis of Barnstable. This Event produced a Dissention between Hutchinson and Otis which had Consequences of great moment. In February Mr. James Otis Junr. a Lawyer of Boston, and a Son of Colonel Otis of Barnstable, appeared at the request of the Merchants in Boston, in Opposition to the Writ. This Gentlemans reputation as a Schollar, a Lawyer, a Reasoner, and a Man of Spirit was then very high. Mr. Putnam while I was with him had often said to me, that Otis was by far the most able, manly and commanding Character of his Age at the Bar, and this appeared to me in Boston to be the universal opinion of Judges, Lawyers and the public. Mr. Oxenbridge Thatcher whose amiable manners and pure principles, united to a very easy and musical Eloquence, made him very popular, was united with Otis, and Mr. Gridley alone appeared for Cockle the Petitioner, in Support of his Writ. The Argument continued several days in the Council Chamber, and the question was analized with great Acuteness and all the learning, which could be connected with the Subject. I took a few minutes, in a very careless manner, which by some means fell into the hands of Mr. Minot, who has inserted them in his history. I was much more attentive to the Information and the Eloquence of the Speakers, than to my minutes, and too much allarmed at the prospect that was opened before me, to care much about writing a report of the Controversy. The Views of the English Government towards the Collonies and the Views of the Collonies towards the English Government, from the first of our History to that time, appeared to me to have been directly in Opposition to each other, and were now by the imprudence of Administration, brought to a Collision. England proud of its power and holding Us in Contempt would never give up its pretentions. The Americans devoutly attached to their Liberties, would never submit, at least without an entire devastation of the Country and a general destruction of their Lives. A Contest appeared to me to be opened, to which I could foresee no End, and which would render my Life a Burden and Property, Industry and every Thing insecure. There was no Alternative left, but to take the Side, which appeared to be just, to march intrepidly forward in the right path, to trust in providence for the Protection of Truth and right, and to die with a good Conscience and a decent grace, if that Tryal should become indispensible.

In the Winter of 1764 the Small Pox prevailing in Boston, I went with my Brother into Town and was inocculated under the Direction of Dr. Nathaniel Perkins and Dr. Joseph Warren. This Distemper was very terrible even by Inocculation at that time. My Physicians dreaded it, and prepared me, by a milk Diet and a Course of Mercurial Preparations, till they reduced me very low before they performed the operation. They continued to feed me with Milk and Mercury through the whole Course of it, and salivated me to such a degree, that every tooth in my head became so loose that I believe I could have pulled them all with my Thumb and finger. By such means they conquered the Small Pox, which I had very lightly, but they rendered me incapable with the Aid of another fever at Amsterdam of speaking or eating in my old Age, in short they brought me into the same Situation with my Friend Washington, who attributed his misfortune to cracking of Walnuts in his Youth. I should not have mentioned this, if I had not been reproached with this personal Defect, with so much politeness in the Aurora. Recovered of the Small Pox, I passed the summer of 1764 in Attending Court and pursuing my Studies with some Amusement on my little farm to which I was frequently making Additions, till the Fall when on the 25th of October 1764 I was married to Miss Smith a Daughter of the Reverend Mr. William Smith a Minister of Weymouth, Grand daughter of the Honourable John Quincy Esquire of Braintree, a Connection which has been the Source of all my felicity, Although a Sense of Duty which forced me away from her and my Children for so many Years has produced all the Griefs of my heart and all that I esteem real Afflictions in Life. The Town of Braintree had chosen me, one of the Select Men, Overseers of the Poor and Assessors, which occasioned much Business, of which I had enough before: but I accepted the Choice and attended diligently to the functions of the Office, in which humble as it was I took a great deal of Pleasure.

This Year 1765 was the Epocha of the Stamp Act. . . . I drew up a Petition to the Select Men of Braintree, and procured it to be signed by a Number of the respectable Inhabitants, to call a Meeting of the Town to instruct their Representatives in Relation to the Stamps. The public Attention of the whole

Continent was alarmed, and my Principles and political Connections were well known. . . . I prepared a Draught of Instructions, at home and carried them with me: the cause of the Meeting was explained, at some length and the state and danger of the Country pointed out, a Committee was appointed to prepare Instructions of which I was nominated as one. We retired to Mr. Niles House, my Draught was produced, and unanimously adopted without Amendment, reported to the Town and Accepted without a dissenting Voice. These were published in Drapers Paper, as that Printer first applied to me for a Copy. They were decided and spirited enough. They rung thro the State, and were adopted, in so many Words, As I was informed by the Representatives of that Year, by forty Towns, as Instructions to their Representatives. They were honoured sufficiently, by the Friends of Government with the Epithets of inflammatory &c. I have not seen them now for almost forty Years and remember very little of them. I presume they would now appear a poor trifle: but at that time they Met with such strong feelings in the Readers, that their Effect was astonishing to me and excited some serious Reflections. I thought a Man ought to be very cautious what kinds of fewell he throws into a fire when it is thus glowing in the Community. Although it is a certain Expedient to acquire a momentary Celebrity: Yet it may produce future Evils which may excite serious Repentance. I have seen so many fire brands, thrown into the flames, not only in the worthless and unprincipled Writings of the profligate and impious Thomas Paine and in the French Revolution, but in many others, that I think, every Man ought to take Warning. In the Braintree Instructions however, If I recollect any reprehensible fault in them, it was that they conceeded too much to the Adversary, not to say Enemy. About this time I called upon my Friend Samuel Adams and found him at his Desk. He told me the Town of Boston had employed him to draw Instructions for their Representatives: that he felt an Ambition, which was very apt to mislead a Man, that of doing something extraordinary and he wanted to consult a Friend who might suggest some thoughts to his mind. I read his Instructions and shewed him a Copy of mine. I told him I thought his very well as far as they went, but he had not gone far enough. Upon reading mine he said he was of my Opinion and accordingly took into his, some paragraphs from mine.

On the fourteenth of August this Year, The People in Boston rose, and carried Mr. Oliver who had been appointed Distributor of Stamps, to Liberty Tree where they obliged him to take an Oath, that he would not exercise the office. The Merchants of Boston could not collect their debts, without Courts of Justice. They called a Town Meeting, chose a Committee of thirty Gentlemen to present a Petition to the Governor and Council, to order the Courts of Justice to proceed without Stamped Papers, upon the principle that the Stamp Act was null because unconstitutional. This Principle was so congenial to my Judgment that I would have staked my Life on the question: but had no suspicion that I should have any thing to do with it, before the Council, till a Courier arrived with a Certificate from the Town Clerk that I was elected by the Town, with Mr. Gridley and Mr. Otis, to argue the Point the next morning. With so little preparation and with no time to look into any books for analogous Cases, I went and introduced the Argument but made a very poor figure. Mr. Gridley and Mr. Otis more than supplied all my defects. But the Governor and Council would do nothing. The Court of Common Pleas, however were persuaded to proceed and the Superiour Court postponed and continued the Question till the Act was repealed. At an Inferiour Court in Plymouth, Mr. Paine and I called a Meeting of the Bar, and We laboured so successfully with our Brothers that We brought them all to agree in an Application to the Court to proceed without Stamps, in which We succeeded.

———————

In the Years 1766 and 1767 my Business increased, as my Reputation spread, I got Money and bought Books and Land. I had heard my father say that he never knew a Piece of Land run away or break, and I was too much enamoured with Books, to spend many thoughts upon Speculation on Money. I was often solicited to lend Money and sometimes complied upon Land Security: but I was more intent on my Business than on my Profits, or I should have laid the foundation of a better Estate.

In the Beginning of the Year 1768 My Friends in Boston, were very urgent with me to remove into Town. I was afraid of my health: but they urged so many Reasons and insisted on it so much that being determined at last to hazard the Experiment, I wrote a Letter to the Town of Braintree declining an Election as one of their Select Men, and removed in a Week or two, with my Family into the White House as it was called in Brattle Square, which several of the old People told me was a good omen as Mr. Bollan had lived formerly in the same house for many Years. The Year before this, i.e. in 1767 My Son John Quincy Adams was born on the [   ] day of August, at Braintree, and at the request of his Grandmother Smith christened by the Name of John Quincy on the day of the Death of his Great Grandfather, John Quincy of Mount Wollaston.

In the Course of this Year 1768 My Friend Mr. Jonathan Sewall who was then Attorney General called on me in Brattle Street, and told me he was come to dine with me. This was always an acceptable favour from him, for although We were at Antipodes in Politicks We had never abated in mutual Esteem or cooled in the Warmth of our Friendship. After Dinner Mr. Sewall desired to have some Conversation with me alone and proposed adjourning to the office. Mrs. Adams arose and chose to Adjourn to her Chamber. We were accordingly left alone. Mr. Sewall then said he waited on me at that time at the request of the Governor Mr. Bernard, who had sent for him a few days before and charged him with a Message to me. The Office of Advocate General in the Court of Admiralty was then vacant, and the Governor had made Enquiry of Gentlemen the best qualified to give him information, and particularly of one of great Authority (meaning Lt. Governor and Chief Justice Hutchinson), and although he was not particularly acquainted with me himself the Result of his Inquiries was that in point of Talents, Integrity, Reputation and consequence at the Bar, Mr. Adams was the best entitled to the Office and he had determined Accordingly, to give it to me. It was true he had not Power to give me more than a temporary Appointment, till his Majestys Pleasure should be known: but that he would give immediately all the Appointment in his Power, and would write an immediate Recommendation of me to his Majesty and transmitt it to his Ministers and there was no doubt I should receive the Kings Commission, as soon as an Answer could be returned from England: for there had been no Instance of a refusal to confirm the Appointment of a Governor in such Cases.

Although this Offer was unexpected to me, I was in an instant prepared for an Answer. The Office was lucrative in itself, and a sure introduction to the most profitable Business in the Province: and what was of more consequence still, it was a first Step in the Ladder of Royal Favour and promotion. But I had long weighed this Subject in my own Mind. For seven Years I had been solicited by some of my friends and Relations, as well as others, and Offers had been made me by Persons who had Influence, to apply to the Governor or to the Lieutenant Governor, to procure me a Commission for the Peace. Such an Officer was wanted in the Country where I had lived and it would have been of very considerable Advantage to me. But I had always rejected these proposals, on Account of the unsettled State of the Country, and my Scruples about laying myself under any restraints, or Obligations of Gratitude to the Government for any of their favours. The new Statutes had been passed in Parliament laying Duties on Glass, Paint &c. and a Board of Commissioners of the Revenue was expected, which must excite a great fermentation in the Country, of the Consequences of which I could see no End.

My Answer to Mr. Sewall was very prompt, that I was sensible of the honor done me by the Governor: but must be excused from Accepting his Offer. Mr. Sewall enquired why, what was my Objection. I answered that he knew very well my political Principles, the System I had adopted and the Connections and Friendships I had formed in Consequence of them: He also knew that the British Government, including the King, his Ministers and Parliament, apparently supported by a great Majority of the Nation, were persevereing in a System, wholly inconsistent with all my Ideas of Right, Justice and Policy, and therefore I could not place myself in a Situation in which my Duty and my Inclination would be so much at Variance. To this Mr. Sewall returned that he was instructed by the Governor to say that he knew my political Sentiments very well: but they should be no Objection with him. I should be at full Liberty to entertain my own Opinions, which he did not wish to influence by this office. He had offered it to me, merely because he believed I was the best qualified for it and because he relied on my Integrity. I replied This was going as far in the generosity and Liberality of his sentiments as the Governor could go or as I could desire, if I could Accept the Office: but that I knew it would lay me under restraints and Obligations that I could not submit to and therefore I could not in honor or Conscience Accept it.

Mr. Sewall paused, and then resuming the Subject asked, why are you so quick, and sudden in your determination? You had better take it into consideration, and give me an Answer at some future day. I told him my Answer had been ready because my mind was clear and my determination decided and unalterable. That my Advice would be that Mr. Fitch should be appointed, to whose Views the Office would be perfectly agreable. Mr. Sewall said he should certainly give me time to think of it: I said that time would produce no change and he had better make his report immediately. We parted, and about three Weeks afterwards he came to me again and hoped I had thought more favourably on the Subject: that the Governor had sent for him and told him the public Business suffered and the office must be filled. I told him my Judgment and Inclination and determination were unalterably fixed, and that I had hoped that Mr. Fitch would have been appointed before that time. Mr. Fitch however never was appointed. He acted for the Crown, by the Appointment of the Judge from day to day, but never had any Commission from the Crown or Appointment of the Governor.

This Year 1768 I attended the Superiour Court at Worcester, and the next Week proceeded on to Springfield in the County of Hampshire, where I was accidentally engaged in a Cause between a Negro and his Master, which was argued by me, I know not how, but it seems it was in such a manner as engaged the Attention of Major Hawley, and introduced an Acquaintance which was soon after strengthened into a Friendship, which continued till his Death. During my Absence on this Circuit, a Convention sat in Boston. The Commissioners of the Customs had arrived and an Army Landed. On my Return I found the Town of Boston full of Troops, and as Dr. Byles of punning Memory express'd it, our grievances reddressed. Through the whole succeeding fall and Winter a Regiment was excercised, by Major Small, in Brattle Square directly in Front of my house. The Spirit Stirring Drum, and the Earpiercing fife arroused me and my family early enough every morning, and the Indignation they excited, though somewhat soothed was not allayed by the sweet Songs, Violins and flutes of the serenading Sons of Liberty, under my Windows in the Evening. In this Way and a thousand others I had sufficient Intimations that the hopes and Confidence of the People, were placed on me, as one of their Friends: and I was determined, that as far as depended on me they should not be disappointed: and that if I could render them no positive Assistance, at least I would never take any part against them. My daily Reflections for two Years, at the Sight of those Soldiers before my door were serious enough. Their very Appearance in Boston was a strong proof to me, that the determination in Great Britain to subjugate Us, was too deep and inveterate ever to be altered by Us: For every thing We could do, was misrepresented, and Nothing We could say was credited.

On the other hand, I had read enough in History to be well aware of the Errors to which the public opinions of the People, were liable in times of great heat and danger, as well as of the Extravagances of which the Populace of Cities were capable, when artfully excited to Passion, and even when justly provoked by Oppression. In ecclesiastical Controversies to which I had been a Witness; in the Contest at Woburn and on Marthas Vinyard, and especially in the Tryal of Hopkins and Ward, which I had heard at Worcester, I had learned enough to shew me, in all their dismal Colours, the deceptions to which the People in their passion, are liable, and the totall Suppression of Equity and humanity in the human Breast when thoroughly heated and hardened by Party Spirit.

The danger I was in appeared in full View before me: and I very deliberately, and indeed very solemnly determined, at all Events to adhere to my Principles in favour of my native Country, which indeed was all the Country I knew, or which had been known by my father, Grandfather or Great Grandfather: but on the other hand I never would deceive the People, conceal from them any essential truth, nor especially make myself subservient to any of their Crimes, Follies or Excentricities. These Rules to the Utmost of my capacity and Power, I have invariably and religiously observed to this day 21. Feb. 1805. and I hope I shall obey them till I shall be gathered to the Dust of my Ancestors, a Period which cannot be far off. They have however cost me the torment of a perpetual Vulcano of Slander, pouring on my flesh all my life time.

I was solicited to go to the Town Meetings and harrangue there. This I constantly refused. My Friend Dr. Warren the most frequently urged me to this: My Answer to him always was "That way madness lies." The Symptoms of our great Friend Otis, at that time, suggested to Warren, a sufficient comment on these Words, at which he always smiled and said "it was true." Although I had never attended a Meeting the Town was pleased to choose me upon their Committee to draw up Instructions to their Representatives, this Year 1768 and the next 1769 or in the year 1769 and the Year 1770, I am not certain which two of these Years. The Committee always insisted on my preparing the Draught, which I did and the Instructions were adopted without Alteration by the Town; they will be found in the Boston Gazette for those Years, and although there is nothing extraordinary in them of matter or Style, they will sufficiently shew the sense of the Public at that time.

The Year 1770 was memorable enough, in these little Annals of my Pilgrimage. The Evening of the fifth of March, I spent at Mr. Henderson Inches's House at the South End of Boston, in Company with a Clubb, with whom I had been associated for several Years. About nine O Clock We were allarmed with the ringing of Bells, and supposing it to be the Signal of fire, We snatched our Hats and Cloaks, broke up the Clubb, and went out to assist in quenching the fire or aiding our friends who might be in danger. In the Street We were informed that the British Soldiers had fired on the Inhabitants, killed some and wounded others near the Town house. A Croud of People was flowing down the Street, to the Scene of Action. When We arrived We saw nothing but some field Pieces placed before the south door of the Town house and some Engineers and Grenadiers drawn up to protect them. Mrs. Adams was in Circumstances, and I was apprehensive of the Effect of the Surprise upon her, who was alone, excepting her Maids and a Boy in the House. Having therefore surveyed round the Town house and seeing all quiet, I walked down Boylstons Alley into Brattle Square, where a Company or two of regular Soldiers were drawn up in Front of Dr. Coopers old Church with their Musquets all shouldered and their Bayonetts all fixed. I had no other way to proceed but along the whole front in a very narrow Space which they had left for foot passengers. Pursuing my Way, without taking the least notice of them or they of me, any more than if they had been marble Statues, I went directly home to Cold Lane. My Wife having heard that the Town was still and likely to continue so, had recovered from her first Apprehensions, and We had nothing but our Reflections to interrupt our Repose. These Reflections were to me, disquieting enough. Endeavours had been systematically pursued for many Months, by certain busy Characters, to excite Quarrells, Rencounters and Combats single or compound in the night between the Inhabitants of the lower Class and the Soldiers, and at all risques to inkindle an immortal hatred between them. I suspected that this was the Explosion, which had been intentionally wrought up by designing Men, who knew what they were aiming at better than the Instrument employed. If these poor Tools should be prosecuted for any of their illegal Conduct they must be punished. If the Soldiers in self defence should kill any of them they must be tryed, and if Truth was respected and the Law prevailed must be acquitted. To depend upon the perversion of Law and the Corruption or partiality of Juries, would insensibly disgrace the Jurisprudence of the Country and corrupt the Morals of the People. It would be better for the whole People to rise in their Majesty, and insist on the removal of the Army, and take upon themselves the Consequences, than to excite such Passions between the People and the Soldiers as would expose both to continual prosecution civil or criminal and keep the Town boiling in a continual fermentation. The real and full Intentions of the British Government and Nation were not yet developed: and

We knew not whether the Town would be supported by the Country: whether the Province would be supported by even our neighbouring States of New England; nor whether New England would be supported by the Continent. These were my Meditations in the night. The next Morning I think it was, sitting in my Office, near the Steps of the Town house Stairs, Mr. Forrest came in, who was then called the Irish Infant. I had some Acquaintance with him. With tears streaming from his Eyes, he said I am come with a very solemn Message from a very unfortunate Man, Captain Preston in Prison. He wishes for Council, and can get none. I have waited on Mr. Quincy, who says he will engage if you will give him your Assistance: without it possitively he will not. Even Mr. Auchmuty declines unless you will engage. . . . I had no hesitation in answering that Council ought to be the very last thing that an accused Person should want in a free Country. That the Bar ought in my opinion to be independent and impartial at all Times And in every Circumstance. And that Persons whose Lives were at Stake ought to have the Council they preferred: But he must be sensible this would be as important a Cause as ever was tryed in any Court or Country of the World: and that every Lawyer must hold himself responsible not only to his Country, but to the highest and most infallible of all Trybunals for the Part he should Act. He must therefore expect from me no Art or Address, No Sophistry or Prevarication in such a Cause; nor any thing more than Fact, Evidence and Law would justify. Captain Preston he said requested and desired no more: and that he had such an Opinion, from all he had heard from all Parties of me, that he could chearfully trust his Life with me, upon those Principles. And said Forrest, as God almighty is my Judge I believe him an innocent Man. I replied that must be ascertained by his Tryal, and if he thinks he cannot have a fair Tryal of that Issue without my Assistance, without hesitation he shall have it. Upon this, Forrest offered me a single Guinea as a retaining fee and I readily accepted it. From first to last I never said a Word about fees, in any of those Cases, and I should have said nothing about them here, if Calumnies and Insinuations had not been propagated that I was tempted by great fees and enormous sums of Money. Before or after the Tryal, Preston sent me ten Guineas and at the Tryal of the

Soldiers afterwards Eight Guineas more, which were all the fees I ever received or were offered to me, and I should not have said any thing on the subject to my Clients if they had never offered me any Thing. This was all the pecuniary Reward I ever had for fourteen or fifteen days labour, in the most exhausting and fatiguing Causes I ever tried: for hazarding a Popularity very general and very hardly earned: and for incurring a Clamour and popular Suspicions and prejudices, which are not yet worn out and never will be forgotten as long as History of this Period is read. For the Experience of all my Life has proved to me, that the Memory of Malice is faithfull, and more, it continually adds to its Stock; while that of Kindness and Friendship is not only frail but treacherous. It was immediately bruited abroad that I had engaged for Preston and the Soldiers, and occasioned a great clamour which the Friends of Government delighted to hear, and slyly and secretly fomented with all their Art. The Tryal of the Soldiers was continued for one Term, and in the Mean time an Election came on, for a Representative of Boston. Mr. Otis had resigned: Mr. Bowdoin was chosen in his Stead: at the general Election Mr. Bowdoin was chosen into the Council and Mr. Hutchinson then Governor did not negative him. A Town Meeting was called for the Choice of a Successor to Mr. Bowdoin; Mr. Ruddock a very respectable Justice of the Peace, who had risen to Wealth and Consequence, by a long Course of Industry as a Master Shipwright, was sett up in Opposition to me. Notwithstanding the late Clamour against me, and although Mr. Ruddock was very popular among all the Tradesmen and Mechanicks in Town, I was chosen by a large Majority. I had never been at a Boston Town Meeting, and was not at this, till Messengers were sent to me, to inform me that I was chosen. I went down to Phanuel Hall and in a few Words expressive of my sense of the difficulty and danger of the Times; of the importance of the Trust, and of my own Insufficiency to fulfill the Expectations of the People, I accepted the Choice. Many Congratulations were offered, which I received civilly, but they gave no Joy to me. I considered the Step as a devotion of my family to ruin and myself to death, for I could scarce perceive a possibility that I should ever go through the Thorns and leap all the Precipices before me, and escape with my Life.

At this time I had more Business at the Bar, than any Man in the Province: My health was feeble: I was throwing away as bright prospects any Man ever had before him: and had devoted myself to endless labour and Anxiety if not to infamy and to death, and that for nothing, except, what indeed was and ought to be all in all, a sense of duty. In the Evening I expressed to Mrs. Adams all my Apprehensions: That excellent Lady, who has always encouraged me, burst into a flood of Tears, but said she was very sensible of all the Danger to her and to our Children as well as to me, but she thought I had done as I ought, she was very willing to share in all that was to come and place her trust in Providence.

In the Year 1773 arose a Controversy concerning the Independence of the Judges. The King had granted a Salary to the Judges of our Superiour Court and forbidden them to receive their Salaries as usual from the Grants of the House of Representatives, and the Council and Governor, as had been practiced till this time. This as the Judges Commissions were during pleasure made them entirely dependent on the Crown for Bread as well as office. The Friends of Government were anxious to perswade the People, that their Commissions were during good Behaviour. Brigadier General Brattle, who had been a Practitioner of Law, and was at this time in his Majestys Council, after some time, came out with his name in one of the Gazettes, with a formal Attempt to prove that the Judges held their offices for Life. Perhaps I should not have taken any public Notice of this, if it had not been industriously circulated among the People, that the General had at a Town Meeting in Cambridge the Week before advanced this doctrine And challenged me by name, to dispute the point with him. His Challenge I should have disregarded, but as his Appeal to me was public, if I should remain silent it would be presumed that my Opinion coincided with his. It was of great Importance that the People should form a correct Opinion on this Subject: and therefore I sent to the press a Letter in Answer, which drew me on to the Number of Eight Letters, which may be seen in the Boston Gazette for this Year. The Doctrine and the History of the Independence of Judges was detailed and explained as well as my time, Avocations and Information enabled me: imperfect and unpollished as they were they were well timed. The Minds of all Men were awake and every thing was eagerly read by every one, who could read. These papers Accordingly, contributed to spread correct Opinions concerning the Importance of the Independence of the Judges to Liberty and Safety, and enabled the Convention of Massachusetts in 1779 to adopt them into the Constitution of the Commonwealth, as the State of New York had done before, partially, and as the Constitution of the United States did afterwards in 1787. The Principles developed in these Papers have been very generally, indeed almost universally prevalent among the People of America, from that time, till the Administration of Mr. Jefferson, during which they have been infringed and are now in danger of being lost. In such a Case, as the Ballance in our national Legislature is imperfect and very difficult to be preserved, We shall have no ballance at all of Interests or Passions, and our Lives, Liberties, Reputations and Estates will lie at the mercy of a Majority, and of a tryumphant Party.

It is well known that in June 1774 The General Court at Cambridge appointed Members to meet with others from the other States in Congress on the fifth of August. Mr. Bowdoin, Mr. Cushing, Mr. Samuel Adams, Mr. John Adams and Mr. Robert Treat Paine were appointed. After this Election I went for the tenth and last time on the Eastern Circuit: At York at Dinner with the Court, happening to sit at Table next to Mr. Justice Seward, a Representative of York, but of the unpopular Side, We entered very sociably and pleasantly into conversation, and among other Things he said to me, Mr. Adams you are going to Congress, and great Things are in Agitation. I recommend to you the Doctrine of my former Minister Mr. Moody. Upon an Occasion of some gloomy prospect for the Country, he preached a Sermon from this text "And they know not what to do." After a customary introduction, he raised this Doctrine from his Text, that "in times of great difficulty and danger, when Men know not what to do, it is the Duty of a Person or a People to be very careful that they do not do, they know not what." This oracular Jingle of Words, which seemed, however to contain some good Sense, made Us all very gay. But I thought the venerable Preacher when he had beat the Drum ecclesiastic to animate the Country to undertake the Expedition to Louisbourg in 1745, and had gone himself with it as a Chaplain, had ventured to do he knew not what, as much as I was likely to do in the Expedition to Congress. I told the Deacon that I must trust Providence as Mr. Moody had done, when he did his duty though he could not foresee the Consequences.

To prepare myself as well as I could, for the Storm that was coming on, I removed my Family to Braintree. They could not indeed have remained in Safety in Boston, and when the time arrived Mr. Bowdoin having declined the Appointment Mr. Cushing, Mr. Adams, Mr. Paine and myself, satt out on our Journey together in one Coach. The Anxiety and Expectation of the Country was very great, and all the Gentlemen on the Road assembled from place to place to escort Us all the Way to Philadelphia, especially in Connecticutt, New York, the Jersies and Pensilvania. On the 5th of August Congress assembled in Carpenters Hall. The Day before, I dined with Mr. Lynch a Delegate from South Carolina, who, in conversation on the Unhappy State of Boston and its inhabitants, after some Observations had been made on the Eloquence of Mr. Patrick Henry and Mr. Richard Henry Lee, which had been very loudly celebrated by the Virginians, said that the most eloquent Speech that had ever been made in Virginia or any where else, upon American Affairs had been made by Colonel Washington. This was the first time I had ever heard the Name of Washington, as a Patriot in our present Controversy, I asked who is Colonel Washington and what was his Speech? Colonel Washington he said was the officer who had been famous in the late french War and in the Battle in which Braddock fell. His Speech was that if the Bostonians should be involved in Hostilities with the British Army he would march to their relief at the head of a Thousand Men at his own expence. This Sentence Mr. Lynch said, had more Oratory in it, in his Judgment, than all that he had ever heard or read. We all agreed that it was both sublime, pathetic and beautifull.

The more We conversed with the Gentlemen of the Country, and with the Members of Congress the more We were encouraged to hope for a general Union of the Continent. As the Proceedings of this Congress are in Print, I shall have Occasion to say little of them. A few Observations may not be amiss. After some days of general discussions, two Committees were appointed of twelve members each, one from each State, Georgia not having yet come in. The first Committee was instructed to prepare a Bill of Rights as it was called or a Declaration of the Rights of the Colonies: the second, a List of Infringements or Violations of those Rights. Congress was pleased to appoint me, on the first Committee, as the Member for Massachusetts. It would be endless to attempt even an Abridgment of the Discussions in this Committee, which met regularly every Morning, for many days successively, till it became an Object of Jealousy to all the other Members of Congress. It was indeed very much against my Judgment, that the Committee was so soon appointed, as I wished to hear all the great Topicks handled in Congress at large in the first Place. They were very deliberately considered and debated in the Committee however. The two Points which laboured the most, were 1. Whether We should recur to the Law of Nature, as well as to the British Constitution and our American Charters and Grants. Mr. Galloway and Mr. Duane were for excluding the Law of Nature. I was very strenuous for retaining and insisting on it, as a Resource to which We might be driven, by Parliament much sooner than We were aware. The other great question was what Authority We should conceed to Parliament: whether We should deny the Authority of Parliament in all Cases: whether We should allow any Authority to it, in our internal Affairs: or whether We should allow it to regulate the Trade of the Empire, with or without any restrictions. These discussions spun into great Length, and nothing was decided. After many fruitless Essays, The Committee determined to appoint a Sub committee, to make a draught of a Sett of Articles, that might be laid in Writing before the grand Committee and become the foundation of a more regular debate and final decision. I was appointed on the Subcommittee, in which after going over the ground again, a Sett of Articles were drawn and debated one by one. After several days deliberation, We agreed upon all the Articles excepting one, and that was the Authority of Parliament, which was indeed the Essence of the whole

Controversy. Some were for a flatt denyal of all Authority: others for denying the Power of Taxation only. Some for denying internal but admitting external Taxation. After a multitude of Motions had been made, discussed and negatived, it seems as if We should never agree upon any Thing. Mr. John Rutledge of South Carolina, one of the Committee, addressing himself to me, was pleased to say "Adams We must agree upon Something: You appear to be as familiar with the Subject as any of Us, and I like your Expressions *the necessity of the Case* and *excluding all Ideas of Taxation external and internal.* I have a great Opinion of that same Idea of the Necessity of the Case and I am determined against all taxation for revenue. Come take the Pen and see if you cant produce something that will unite Us." Some others of the Committee seconding Mr. Rutledge, I took a sheet of paper and drew up an Article. When it was read I believe not one of the Committee were fully satisfied with it, but they all soon acknowledged that there was no hope of hitting on any thing, in which We could all agree with more Satisfaction. All therefore agreed to this, and upon this depended the Union of the Colonies. The Sub Committee reported their draught to the grand Committee, and another long debate ensued especially on this Article, and various changes and modifications of it were Attempted, but none adopted. The Articles were then reported to Congress, and debated Paragraph by Paragraph. The difficult Article was again attacked and defended. Congress rejected all Amendments to it, and the general Sense of the Members was that the Article demanded as little as could be demanded, and conceeded as much as could be conceeded with Safety, and certainly as little as would be accepted by Great Britain: and that the Country must take its fate, in consequence of it. When Congress had gone through the Articles, I was appointed to put them into form and report a fair Draught for their final Acceptance. This was done and they were finally accepted.

The Committee of Violations of Rights reported a sett of Articles which were drawn by Mr. John Sullivan of New Hampshire: and These two Declarations, the one of Rights and the other of Violations, which are printed in the Journal of Congress for 1774, were two Years afterwards recapitulated in the Declaration of Independence on the fourth of July 1776. The

Results of the Procedings of Congress for this Year remain in the Journals: and I shall not attempt any Account of the debates, nor of any thing of the share I took in them. I never wrote a Speech beforehand, either at the Bar or in any public Assembly, nor committed one to writing after it was delivered, and it would be idle to attempt a Recollection, of Arguments from day to day, through a whole session, at the distance of thirty Years. The Delegates from Massachusetts, representing the State in most immediate danger, were much visited, not only by the members of Congress but by all the Gentlemen in Phyladelphia and its neighbourhood, as well as Strangers and Occasional Travellers. We took Lodgings all together at the Stone House opposite the City Tavern then held by Mrs. Yard, which was by some Complimented with the Title of Head Quarters, but by Mr. Richard Henry Lee, more decently called Liberty Hall. We were much caressed and feasted by all the principal People, for the Allens, and Penns and others were then with Us, though afterwards some of them cooled and fell off, on the declaration of Independence. We were invited to Visit all the public Buildings and places of resort, and became pretty well acquainted with Men and things in Philadelphia.

There is an Anecdote, which ought not to be omitted, because it had Consequences of some moment, at the time, which have continued to operate for many Years and indeed are not yet worn out, though the cause is forgotten or rather was never generally known. Governor Hopkins and Governor Ward of Rhode Island came to our Lodgings, and said to Us, that President Manning of Rhode Island Colledge and Mr. Bachus of Massachusetts were in Town, and had conversed with some Gentlemen in Philadelphia who wished to communicate to Us a little Business, and wished We would meet them at Six in the Evening at Carpenters Hall. Whether they explained their Affairs more particularly to any of my Colleagues I know not, but I had no Idea of the design. We all went at the hour, and to my great Surprize found the Hall almost full of People, and a great Number of Quakers seated at the long Table with their broad brimmed Beavers on their Heads. We were invited to Seats among them: and informed that they had received Complaints from some Anabaptists and some Friends in Massachusetts against certain Laws of that Province, restrictive of the Liberty of Conscience: and some Instances were mentioned in the General Court and in the Courts of Justice, in which Friends and Baptists had been grievously oppressed. I know not how my Colleagues felt, but I own I was greatly surprized and somewhat indignant, being like my Friend Chase of a temper naturally quick and warm, at seeing our State and her Delegates thus summoned before a self created Trybunal, which was neither legal nor Constitutional.

Israel Pemberton a Quaker of large Property and more intrigue began to speak and said that Congress were here, endeavouring to form a Union of the Colonies: but there were difficulties in the Way, and none of more importance than Liberty of Conscience. The Laws of New England and particularly of Massachusetts, were inconsistent with it, for they not only compelled Men to pay to the Building of Churches and Support of Ministers but to go to some known Religious Assembly on first days &c. and that he and his friends were desirous of engaging Us, to assure them that our State would repeal all those Laws, and place things as they were in Pennsylvania. A Suspicion instantly arose in my Mind, which I have ever believed to have been well founded, that this artfull Jesuit, for I had been before apprized of his Character, was endeavouring to avail himself of this opportunity, to break up the Congress, or at least to withdraw the Quakers and the Governing Part of Pensilvania from Us: for at that time by means of a most unequal Representation, the Quakers had a Majority in their House of Assembly and by Consequence the whole Power of the State in their hands. I arose and spoke in Answer to him. The Substance of what I said was, that We had no Authority to bind our Constituents to any such Proposals: that the Laws of Massachusetts, were the most mild and equitable Establishment of Religion that was known in the World, if indeed they could be called an Establishment: that it would be in vain for Us to enter into any Conferences on such a Subject, for We knew before hand our Constituents would disavow all We could do or say, for the Satisfaction of those who invited Us to this meeting. That the People of Massachusetts were as religious and Consciencious as the People of Pensylvania: that their Consciences dictated to them that it was their duty to support those Laws and therefore the very Liberty of Conscience which Mr. Pemberton invoked, would demand indulgence for the tender Consciences of the People of Massachusetts, and allow them to preserve their Laws. That it might be depended on, this was a Point that could not be carried: that I would not deceive them by insinuating the faintest hope, for I knew they might as well turn the heavenly Bodies out of their annual And diurnal Courses as the People of Massachusetts at the present day from their Meeting House and Sunday Laws.—Pemberton made no Reply but this, Oh! Sir pray dont urge Liberty of Conscience in favour of such Laws!—If I had known the particular complaints, which were to be alledged, and if Pemberton had not broke irregularly into the Midst of Things, it might have been better perhaps to have postponed this declaration. However the Gentlemen proceeded and stated the particular Cases of Oppression, which were alledged in our General and executive Courts. It happened that Mr. Cushing and Mr. Samuel Adams had been present in the General Court, when the Petitions had been under deliberation, and they explained the whole so clearly that every reasonable Man must have been satisfied. Mr. Paine and myself had been concerned at the Bar in every Action in the executive Courts which was complained of, and We explained them all to the entire Satisfaction of impartial Men: and shewed that there had been no Oppression or injustice in any of them. The Quakers were not generally and heartily in our Cause, they were jealous of Independence, they were then suspicious and soon afterwards became assured, that the Massachusetts Delegates and especially John Adams, were Advocates for that Obnoxious Measure, and they conceived prejudices, which were soon increased and artfully inflamed, and are not yet worn out. In some of the late Elections for President, some of the Quakers were heard to say "Friend, thee must know that We dont much affect the Name of Adams." This Sentiment was not however Universal nor General, for I have had Opportunities to know that great Numbers of the Friends in all parts of the Continent, were warmly attached to me, both when I was Vice President and President. I left Congress and Philadelphia in October 1774, with a Reputation, much higher than ever I enjoyed before or since.

Upon our Return to Massachusetts, I found myself elected

by the Town of Braintree into the provincial Congress, and attended that Service as long as it sat. About this time, Drapers Paper in Boston swarmed with Writers, and among an immense quantity of meaner productions appeared a Writer under the Signature of Massachusettensis, suspected but never that I knew ascertained to be written by two of my old Friends Jonathan Sewall and Daniel Leonard. These Papers were well written, abounded with Wit, discovered good Information, and were conducted with a Subtlety of Art and Address, wonderfully calculated to keep Up the Spirits of their Party, to depress ours, to spread intimidation and to make Proselytes among those, whose Principles and Judgment give Way to their fears, and these compose at least one third of Mankind. Week after Week passed away, and these Papers made a very visible impression on many Minds. No Answer appeared, and indeed, some who were capable, were too busy and others too timorous. I began at length to think seriously of the Consequences and began to write, under the Signature of Novanglus, and continued every Week, in the Boston Gazette, till the 19th. of April 1775.

•

Chronology

1735   Born October 30 (October 19, Old Style) in the North
        Precinct of Braintree, Massachusetts, the first child of
        John Adams, a farmer, deacon, and shoemaker, and Susanna
        Boylston Adams. (Father, born 1691, is a great-grandson
        of Henry Adams, who immigrated to Massachusetts from
        Somerset in 1638. Mother, born 1709 in Brookline, is a
        granddaughter of Thomas Boylston, who immigrated to
        Massachusetts from London in 1656. Parents married in
        October 1734.)

1738   Brother Peter Boylston born October 16.

1741–49 Brother Elihu born May 29, 1741. After learning to read at
        home, Adams attends schools kept in Braintree by Mrs.
        Belcher and by Joseph Cleverly. Later describes himself as
        an indifferent student who wished to be a farmer like his
        father, despite his father's intention that he attend Har-
        vard and become a minister.

1750–51 Complaining of the dullness of Cleverly's teaching, Adams
        is sent to Joseph Marsh's school in Braintree, where he
        thrives and dedicates himself to studying Latin, in keeping
        with traditional preparation for college. Begins personal
        library with an edition of Cicero's orations.

1751   Enrolls in Harvard College. Listed fourteenth out of the
        twenty-five entering students in class placement based on
        "dignity of family." Tutored in Latin by the Rev. Joseph
        Mayhew and studies mathematics and natural philosophy,
        including astronomy and meteorology, with Professor
        John Winthrop.

1753   Begins diary on June 8, with detailed records of the
        weather among the earliest entries (will intermittently
        keep diary for the remainder of his life).

1755   Graduates with B.A., and begins to keep school in
        Worcester, Massachusetts, in order to support himself while
        deciding whether to "study Divinity, Law or Physick."
        Lodges at the town's expense (6 shillings a week), with
        Dr. Nathum Willard and avails himself of his medical

library. Writes to his classmate and cousin Nathan Webb: "At Colledge gay, gorgeous, prospects, danc'd before my Eyes, and Hope, sanguine Hope, invigorated my Body, and exhilerated my soul. But now hope has left me, my organ's rust and my Faculty's decay." Decries the "Frigid performances" of local ministers, the disciples of "Frigid John Calvin." Reads Milton, Virgil, Voltaire, and Bolingbroke.

1756   Signs contract on August 21 to read law for two years with Worcester's only attorney, James Putnam, who charges a fee of $100, payable when Adams could "find it convenient." Moves in with Putnam and pursues his studies at night, while continuing to keep school by day.

1758   Attends Harvard commencement July 19 and, after arguing the affirmative side of the question, "An Imperium civile, Hominibus prorsus necessarium, sit" ("Whether civil authority is absolutely necessary for mankind"), receives M.A. Moves back home to Braintree in October despite having received an offer from two of Worcester's leading residents to help establish him as the town's second attorney and its registrar of deeds. Meets on October 25 with prominent Boston lawyer Jeremiah Gridley, who advises him to prepare for admission to the bar of Suffolk County, which at that time includes both Boston and Braintree. (Gridley also advises against early marriage, company keeping, and the study of Greek, "a mere curiosity.") Adams is admitted to the Suffolk bar on November 6, with Gridley serving as his sponsor, and begins practice in the county court of common pleas and before local justices of the peace. Appears for the plaintiff in *Field v. Lambert* seeking damages for trespass, but loses his first case when he submits an improperly worded writ.

1759   In the spring, becomes increasingly attracted to Hannah Quincy, daughter of Colonel Josiah Quincy, a justice of the peace and leading citizen in Braintree, and nearly proposes to her on one occasion when they are alone, before being interrupted by his friend Jonathan Sewall and Quincy's cousin Esther. During the summer visits the Weymouth home of the Rev. William Smith and Elizabeth Quincy Smith, where he meets Abigail Smith (born 1744) and her sisters, but does not come away with a positive first impression, finding them neither "fond, nor frank, nor candid."

1760   Drafts several essays on the appointment of the colony's new chief justice and the evils of licensed houses in his diary, though none of them are known to have been published.

1761   Records argument made by James Otis Jr. on February 24 in the Superior Court of Judicature on writs of assistance, the general search warrants issued to royal customs officials. (In 1817 Adams describes Otis as a "flame of fire" during his argument and asserts: "then and there the child Independence was born.") Father dies on May 25. Adams inherits Braintree property (including the house now known as the John Quincy Adams Birthplace) and, as a freeholder, gains a place in the Braintree town meeting. Admitted to practice in the Superior Court of Judicature, the highest trial and appellate court in Massachusetts.

1762   Begins serving on town committees and traveling circuit of county courts of common pleas. Admitted as barrister in the Superior Court of Judicature. In November his close friend Richard Cranch marries Mary Smith, older sister of Abigail, whom Adams now begins to court.

1763   Publishes first known newspaper contribution in the *Boston Evening Post* on March 3. Signed "Humphrey Ploughjogger," the piece satirizes the political dispute between supporters of the Otis family and the faction led by Governor Francis Bernard and Lieutenant Governor Thomas Hutchinson. Publishes several more "Humphrey Ploughjogger" letters in the *Evening Post* throughout the summer, and responds as "U" in the *Boston Gazette* to his friend Jonathan Sewall, who is writing as "J" in defense of the Bernard-Hutchinson faction. Leaves off regular diary-keeping.

1764   Amid a smallpox outbreak in Boston, Adams is successfully inoculated for the disease on April 13 under the care of Dr. Joseph Warren, who becomes a close friend. Marries Abigail Smith in Weymouth on October 25, then returns with her to the house he had inherited from his father in Braintree.

1765   Joins Sodalitas, a small group of barristers in Boston formed by Jeremiah Gridley to study and discuss the law.

(At the group's February 21 meeting, Adams propounds
Rousseau's *Du contrat social* [1762]; he owns both an edition in French and the first English translation, *A Treatise
on the Social Compact, or the Principles of Politic Law*
[1764].) The Stamp Act, which imposes tax on the paper
used in the colonies for newspapers, almanacs, pamphlets,
broadsides, and legal and commercial documents, is
passed by the House of Commons on February 27, receives royal assent March 22, and is scheduled to take
effect on November 1. Adams is elected surveyor of high-
ways in Braintree in March. Attends sessions of the Plymouth and Bristol courts of common pleas, April–May
and July–August, and travels court circuit in Maine, July.
Daughter Abigail ("Nabby") born July 14. Adams publishes "A Dissertation on the Canon and the Feudal
Law" in four installments in the *Boston Gazette*, August
12–October 21 (later reprinted in the *London Chronicle*
and published in book form in London in 1768). Protests
against the Stamp Act occur throughout the colonies during the summer. In Boston, mobs loot the homes of
Andrew Oliver, a prominent merchant who had been appointed stamp distributor for Massachusetts, on August
14, and of Lieutenant Governor Thomas Hutchinson
(Oliver's brother-in-law) on August 26. (Active opponents of the Stamp Act in Boston will adopt the name
"Sons of Liberty" by the end of the year; among their
leaders is Samuel Adams, a second cousin of John Adams.)
Adams's instructions for the Braintree representatives to
the Massachusetts General Court (legislature) denouncing the Stamp Act are adopted by the town meeting on
September 24; the Braintree instructions are printed in
the *Massachusetts Gazette* on October 10 and adopted by
some forty other towns in the colony. Refusal of lawyers
to use stamped legal paper results in closing of Massachusetts courts. On behalf of the Boston town meeting,
Adams, Jeremiah Gridley, and James Otis Jr. appear before
Governor Bernard on December 20 and argue unsuccessfully for the reopening of the courts. Renews regular
diary-keeping on December 18, observing that "the Year
1765 has been the most remarkable Year of my Life."

1766   Publishes three letters signed "Clarendon" in the *Boston
            Gazette*, January 13, 20, and 27, defending the rights of
            the American colonists under the English constitution.

House of Commons repeals the Stamp Act on February 24. Adams is elected as a selectman in Braintree on March 3. Seeks to improve the practice of the law through his active involvement in the Suffolk County bar association.

1767   Publishes five pseudonymous essays in the *Boston Gazette*, January 5–February 16, in response to series of "Philanthrop" essays written by Jonathan Sewall in defense of Governor Bernard. Son John Quincy born March 4. Chancellor of the Exchequer Charles Townshend proposes imposing duties on lead, glass, paper, tea, and other goods imported into America. Passed by the House of Commons on July 2, the Townshend Acts renew tensions in the colonies; to enforce the acts, Parliament establishes board of custom commissioners headquartered in Boston. Jeremiah Gridley, recently appointed Massachusetts Attorney General, dies on September 10 after having referred many of his clients to Adams, whose law practice flourishes.

1768   Massachusetts House of Representatives (lower chamber of the General Court) adopts petition, written by Samuel Adams, protesting the Townshend Acts. After the protest is circulated to other colonial assemblies, Governor Bernard dissolves the General Court, prompting further popular unrest. Adams declines re-election as Braintree selectman and moves family in April to a rented house in Boston. Writing as "Sui Juris," publishes letter in the *Boston Gazette* on May 23 decrying the creation of an Anglican episcopacy in America. Writes instructions, dated June 17, for the Boston representatives to the General Court protesting the seizure of John Hancock's sloop *Liberty*, and later defends Hancock in admiralty court against smuggling charges (the charges are eventually dropped). Jonathan Sewall, now attorney general of Massachusetts, offers Adams the position of advocate general in the admiralty court; Adams declines, citing his "political Principles" and "Connections and Friendships." The first of five British regiments lands at Boston on October 1 after regular troops are requested by the increasingly harassed customs commissioners. Daughter Susanna born December 28.

1769   Writes instructions, dated May 8, for the Boston representatives to the General Court, protesting the presence of

British troops and the growing power of the admiralty court. Hires Jonathan Williams Austin and William Tudor as clerks to help with his expanding Boston legal practice. After James Otis Jr. is assaulted in a coffee house in September, Adams is engaged as co-counsel in civil case brought by Otis against his assailant, customs commissioner John Robinson.

1770   Begins serving as clerk of the Suffolk bar association on January 3. Daughter Susanna dies on February 4. British soldiers under the command of Captain Thomas Preston open fire on an angry, taunting crowd on March 5, killing five Boston residents. Preston and eight soldiers are indicted for murder, March 13. Parliament repeals most of the Townshend duties in April, retaining only the duty on tea. Adams agrees to lead the defense of Preston and the soldiers charged in the "Boston Massacre." Son Charles born May 29. Elected as a representative to the General Court from Boston on June 7 (serves until April 1771). Defends Captain Preston at trial, October 24–30, by disputing testimony that he had ordered his men to open fire; Preston is acquitted. Argues at the trial of the eight soldiers, November 27–December 5, that the accused had either not fired or had acted in self-defense. The jury convicts two of the defendants of manslaughter and acquits the remaining six (as first-time offenders, each of the convicted men is branded on his hand with a letter "M").

1771   Falls ill in February, suffering from "great anxiety and distress." Moves family back to Braintree in April. Takes mineral springs at Stafford, Connecticut, in late spring in an effort to restore his health. Helps try Otis-Robinson assault case; jury awards his client £2,000 in damages (Otis eventually settles for an apology from Robinson and £112 in costs.) Receives letter, dated July 19, from the English Whig historian Catherine Macaulay praising his essays on the canon and feudal law.

1772   At request of the Braintree town meeting, delivers election-day oration on May 18 on "the civil & religious rights & Priviledges of the People." Moves family back to Boston and maintains a law office there until the outbreak of hostilities. Son Thomas Boylston born September 15.

1773   Publishes articles under his own name in the *Boston Gazette*, January 11–February 22, opposing crown salaries for Superior Court judges, which he believes will compromise judicial independence in the colony and is contrary to the English constitution. Assists the House of Representatives in preparing its replies (January 26 and March 6) to addresses (January 6 and February 16) by Governor Thomas Hutchinson asserting parliamentary supremacy over the colonies. Parliament passes Tea Act on May 10, giving the East India Company a monopoly over the colonial tea trade. On the first day of the new General Court, May 26, Adams is elected by the House of Representatives to the Governor's Council (the upper chamber of the General Court), but his appointment is vetoed by Governor Hutchinson. On June 2 Samuel Adams reads to the House from letters sent by Hutchinson and Andrew Oliver (now lieutenant governor) to a British treasury official in 1767–69; in one letter, Hutchinson wrote that "Abridgement of what are called English Liberties" would be necessary to maintain order in the colony. (The letters were clandestinely obtained in England by Benjamin Franklin, at the time the colonial agent for Pennsylvania, Georgia, New Jersey, and Massachusetts.) Political tensions in the province increase when the House of Representatives adopts resolution charging Hutchinson and Oliver with seeking to subvert the 1691 Massachusetts Charter, petitions the crown for their removal, and makes the letters public. First of three ships carrying East India Company tea arrives in Boston on November 28. Duty is payable upon off-loading, which must by law be accomplished within twenty days of docking, but which Boston mobs prevent. Abigail Adams writes to her friend Mercy Otis Warren, December 5: "The Tea that bainfull weed is arrived. Great and I hope Effectual opposition has been made to the landing of it. . . . The proceedings of our Citizens have been United, Spirited and firm. The Flame is kindled and like Lightening it catches from Soul to Soul." Governor Hutchinson refuses entreaties to allow the ships to depart with their cargo, as happens at several other colonial ports. As the deadline approaches, on December 16, a large crowd boards the ships and dumps 342 chests of tea, worth an estimated £10,000, into the harbor.

1774   In February Adams purchases his father's homestead (now known as the John Adams Birthplace) from his

brother Peter and moves his family to Braintree. Helps
prepare articles of impeachment against Chief Justice
Peter Oliver (brother of Lieutenant Governor Andrew
Oliver, who dies March 3) for accepting a crown salary;
the articles are adopted by the House before proceedings
are stopped by Governor Hutchinson. Drafts report for
General Court on Massachusetts's boundary disputes
with New Hampshire and New York. Parliament responds
to the Boston Tea Party by passing four Coercive Acts.
The Boston Port Bill, which receives royal assent on
March 31, closes port until the East India Company is
compensated for the tea and order is restored. Massachusetts Government Act, signed May 20, abrogates the
1691 royal charter by removing the power to appoint the
Governor's Council from the House of Representatives,
limits town meetings to one annual session for elections,
and gives the governor power to appoint all provincial
judges and sheriffs. Administration of Justice Act, signed
May 20, allows trials of persons accused of committing
capital crimes while enforcing the law or collecting revenue to be removed to Nova Scotia or Britain. Quartering Act, signed June 2, allows the housing of soldiers in
occupied dwellings throughout the colonies. General
Thomas Gage, commander of the British army in North
America, arrives in Boston and replaces Hutchinson as
royal governor. Adams is again elected by the House to
the Governor's Council, but his appointment is vetoed by
Gage on May 25. (Hutchinson sails for London, and what
will be permanent exile, on June 1, the day the Boston
Port Act goes into effect.) On June 7, Gage moves the
legislature to Salem, hoping to reduce the influence of
Boston radicals; the House of Representatives adopts
measure on June 20 calling for a "Meeting of Committees from the several Colonies on this Continent," and
elects as delegates Adams, Samuel Adams, Robert Treat
Paine, Thomas Cushing, and James Bowdoin (who does
not attend). Gage dissolves the General Court on June 25.
During July Adams attends circuit courts in Maine for the
last time. Leaves for Philadelphia on August 10 and travels by way of New York. Widespread mob action and disobedience in Massachusetts prevents Gage from enforcing
laws outside of Boston, and on September 5 he begins to
fortify the town. Congress (later known as the First Continental Congress) opens in Philadelphia on September 5,

attended by delegates from every colony except Georgia; it adopts rule giving each colony a single vote and makes its proceedings secret. Adams signs Declarations and Resolves, adopted on October 14, denouncing the Coercive Acts and enumerating colonial rights. Congress calls for a boycott of British imports after December 1 and for the election of delegates to a second Congress in May 1775. Adams leaves Philadelphia when Congress adjourns on October 28 and returns to Braintree in early November. Attends the first Massachusetts Provincial Congress, held in Cambridge December 5–10, as a member from Braintree. Elected as a delegate to Second Continental Congress along with Samuel Adams, Robert Treat Paine, Thomas Cushing, and John Hancock. First of seventeen "Massachusettensis" essays defending parliamentary rule appears in the *Massachusetts Gazette* on December 12 (series ends on April 3, 1775).

1775   Adams publishes twelve essays signed "Novanglus" in the *Boston Gazette*, January 23–April 17, written in response to "Massachusettensis." (Adams believes "Massachusettensis" is Jonathan Sewall, but will learn late in his life that the essays were written by Daniel Leonard, a former supporter of the colonial cause who had become disaffected by the lawlessness of the Tea Party.) Parliament declares Massachusetts to be in a state of rebellion on February 9. Adams is elected a selectman of Braintree on March 6. Attempt by Gage on April 19 to destroy military supplies stored at Concord leads to fighting at Lexington, Concord, and along the road to Boston in which seventy-three British soldiers and forty-nine Americans are killed. Massachusetts militia begin siege of Boston, and on April 23 the Provincial Congress votes to raise an army of 13,600 men. Adams travels to Philadelphia, where Second Continental Congress meets on May 10. Congress votes on June 14 to form a Continental army. Adams nominates George Washington, a Virginia delegate and colonel in the Virginia militia, to be its commander in chief, and Washington is appointed by a unanimous vote on June 15. Abigail and John Quincy watch Battle of Bunker Hill from Penn's Hill in Braintree, June 17; Adams's friend Dr. Joseph Warren is killed in the fighting while serving with the Massachusetts militia. Adams signs conciliatory Olive Branch Petition to George III, adopted by Congress July 5.

Writes letter to his friend James Warren, a member of the
Massachusetts Provincial Congress, on July 24 expressing
frustration with John Dickinson of Pennsylvania, the leading advocate in Congress of reconciliation with Britain
(letter is intercepted by the British and published in the
Massachusetts Gazette on August 17). Serves on nine committees during session, which adjourns August 1. Travels
to Watertown, Massachusetts, where he begins serving on
the Provincial Council, which functions as both the upper
chamber of the Provincial Congress and as the provincial
executive (will continue as member of the Council until
April 1776). Brother Elihu dies of dysentery on August 11
while serving as an officer in the Massachusetts militia.
Jonathan Sewall sails with his family from Boston for England. George III proclaims colonies in rebellion on August 23. Adams returns to Philadelphia for new session of
Congress, which meets on September 12. Serves on thirteen committees and plays a principal role in establishing
an American navy. Appointed Chief Justice of Massachusetts on October 28, but never serves (resigns in February
1777). Congress adjourns December 9. Adams travels to
Braintree and then to Watertown, where he resumes his
service on the Provincial Council.

1776   *Common Sense*, pamphlet by Thomas Paine denouncing
monarchical rule and advocating an independent American republic, is published anonymously in Philadelphia on
January 10, and sells tens of thousands of copies throughout the colonies. Adams, who is presumed by some to be
the pamphlet's author, praises its "Strength and Brevity,"
but expresses misgivings about its "feeble" understanding
of constitutional government. Returns to Philadelphia on
February 8 for the new session of Congress, during which
he will serve on more than thirty committees. British garrison evacuates Boston on March 17 and sails to Nova
Scotia. Abigail writes to her husband on March 31, asking
him to "Remember the Ladies" in "the new Code of Laws
which I suppose it will be necessary for you to make."
Adams writes essay "Thoughts on Government" in March
and April; circulated first in letters and then as a published
pamphlet, it is widely consulted in the making of new
state constitutions. Introduces resolution, adopted by Congress on May 10, recommending that each of the "United
Colonies" form a government, and drafts preamble,

adopted May 15, calling for royal authority in the colonies to be "totally suppressed." Supports resolution introduced on June 7 by Richard Henry Lee of Virginia declaring that "these United Colonies are, and of right ought to be, free and independent States." Resolution is referred on June 11 to committee composed of Adams, Benjamin Franklin (Pennsylvania), Robert R. Livingston (New York), Thomas Jefferson (Virginia), and Roger Sherman (Connecticut). Jefferson begins drafting declaration of independence. Adams becomes president of the Board of War and Ordnance, created by Congress on June 12 and responsible for raising troops and supplies for the Continental Army. John Dickinson and Adams debate independence resolution on July 1 (Jefferson later describes Adams as "our Colossus on the floor"). Congress votes 12–0 in favor of independence on July 2, with New York abstaining. Declaration of Independence is adopted on July 4. Adams participates in debates in August over proposed Articles of Confederation, drafts model treaty with foreign powers, and drafts instructions for Benjamin Franklin and Silas Deane, the first American commissioners to France (they will later be joined by Arthur Lee). Continental Army suffers major defeat at the Battle of Long Island, August 27. Congress sends Adams, Franklin, and Edward Rutledge to meet with Admiral Lord Richard Howe, the British naval commander in North America, and determine whether Howe is authorized to negotiate peace. Howe refuses to recognize Congress or American independence during conference held on Staten Island on September 11, and Congress does not attempt further negotiations. Adams obtains leave of absence from Congress in October and returns to Braintree in early November.

1777   Leaves Braintree in early January and arrives on February 1 in Baltimore, where Congress had relocated in December 1776. Resumes presidency of the Board of War while serving on twenty-six committees. Congress returns to Philadelphia in March. Adams begins correspondence in May with Thomas Jefferson, who has returned to Virginia. Daughter Elizabeth is stillborn on July 11. Congress leaves Philadelphia and reconvenes in York, Pennsylvania, as British army under General William Howe, brother of Admiral Howe, occupies the city on September 26. After a series of defeats, General John Burgoyne surrenders army of 5,000 men to Americans at Saratoga, New York, on October 17, a victory that bolsters American efforts to secure French aid. Adams obtains leave from Congress on November 7 and returns to Braintree on November 27, intending to resume his law practice. Learns that he has been chosen by Congress to replace Silas Deane and serve as commissioner to France along with Franklin and Arthur Lee. "After much Agitation of mind and a thousand reveries," Adams writes to Henry Laurens, the president of Congress, on December 23 and accepts the commission.

1778   France and the United States sign treaties of alliance and commerce in Paris on February 6; under their terms, France recognizes the independence of the United States and pledges to fight until American independence is won if the treaties lead to war between Britain and France. Adams sails for France with John Quincy on February 15 onboard the American frigate *Boston* and lands in Bordeaux on April 1, after an eventful passage that includes a March 10 encounter with a hostile privateer. Joins Franklin's household in Passy, a suburb of Paris, on April 9, and has his first audience with Louis XVI at Versailles on May 8. War begins between Britain and France on June 14. Congress abolishes three-member diplomatic commission and appoints Franklin as sole minister plenipotentiary to France on September 14.

1779   Adams becomes increasingly concerned with the impact of the bitter controversy involving his predecessor in France, Silas Deane, who had charged fellow commissioner Arthur Lee with disloyalty after Lee had accused him of profiting from French arms shipments to the United States. Sympathetic to Lee, Adams drafts a letter on February 10 and 11 to French foreign minister the Comte de Vergennes, addressing the Deane affair and seeking a private interview without Franklin, who supports Deane. Receives from the Marquis de Lafayette official notice from Congress on February 12 of the revocation of his commission and of Franklin's appointment as sole minister to France, and therefore withholds letter to Vergennes. The notification from Congress neither recalls him nor offers new instructions, simply stating that "In the mean Time we hope you will exercise your whole extensive Abilities on the Subject of our Finances."

Adams writes to Abigail on February 20 of his intention to return home and retire from politics: "I will draw Writs and Deeds, and harangue Jurys and be happy." Leaves Passy with John Quincy on March 8 and travels to Nantes and Lorient. While waiting for passage to the United States, spends time with John Paul Jones and becomes increasingly resentful and suspicious of Franklin. Sails with John Quincy from Lorient on June 17 onboard the French frigate *La Sensible* and arrives in Boston on August 3. Elected as Braintree delegate to the state constitutional convention, August 9. Attends convention in Cambridge in early September, and is appointed to prepare a draft constitution. Congress appoints Adams minister plenipotentiary to negotiate treaties of peace and commerce with Great Britain, September 27. Adams submits his *Report of a Constitution* to the state convention on November 1. (The convention approves his draft with some amendments and after ratification by the voters, the Massachusetts constitution goes into effect on October 25, 1780; it remains today the oldest functioning written constitution in the world.) Adams sails for France on November 15 on *La Sensible* with sons John Quincy and Charles and legation secretary Francis Dana. A series of leaks forces the ship to land on December 8 at El Ferrol, on the northwest coast of Spain. Adams begins overland trip to Paris with his sons and Dana.

1780 Arrives in Paris on February 8. Encounters resistance to his mission from Vergennes, who seeks to control any future peace negotiations. Sends detailed reports to Congress on European affairs and publishes anonymous articles in the weekly *Mercure de France*. Writes to Abigail on May 12: "I must study Politicks and War that my sons may have liberty to study Mathematicks and Philosophy. My sons ought to study Mathematicks and Philosophy, Geography, natural History, Naval Architecture, navigation, Commerce and Agriculture, in order to give their Children a right to study Painting, Poetry, Musick, Architecture, Statuary, Tapestry and Porcelaine." Prepares *Translation of the Memorial to the Sovereigns of Europe*, a condensed and rewritten version of pamphlet by Thomas Pownall, a former royal governor of Massachusetts, on Anglo-American commercial relations; Adams's version is published in French in November 1780 and in English in

January 1781. Writes twelve "Letters from a Distinguished American" in response to essays by the American Loyalist Joseph Galloway (letters are published in London, August–October 1782.) Adams resolves to go to Amsterdam "to try," as Franklin will later report to Congress, "whether something might not be done to render us less dependent on France." Leaves Paris on July 27 and arrives in Amsterdam with John Quincy and Charles on August 10. At the request of Vergennes, Franklin forwards to Congress letters Adams had written to Vergennes criticizing French policy, covering them with a letter, dated August 9, in which he asserts that Adams "has given extreme offense to the court here." Adams learns on September 16 that Congress has commissioned him to raise a loan in the Netherlands. Writes twenty-six letters in response to queries from Hendrik Calkoen, an influential Amsterdam lawyer sympathetic to the American cause (the letters are published in London in 1786 and in the United States in 1789). Seeking to cut off Dutch trade with the United States, Britain declares war on the Netherlands on December 20. Congress appoints Adams to negotiate a treaty of amity and commerce with the Netherlands, December 29.

1781   Arranges for John Quincy, age thirteen, and Charles, ten, to attend lectures at the University of Leyden in addition to their tutorial lessons. Without waiting to be formally received as an envoy, Adams drafts and submits memorial to the States General urging Dutch recognition of American independence and arranges for its publication in Dutch, French, and English. Congress appoints Franklin, Jefferson, John Jay, and Henry Laurens as additional peace negotiators on June 15 and instructs the negotiators to take no action without the "knowledge and concurrence" of the French. (Jefferson declines appointment, while Laurens, having been captured at sea in September 1780, is imprisoned in the Tower of London until December 1781.) Adams visits Paris in July to discuss with Vergennes proposals for Austro-Russian mediation of the American war, and advises against American participation unless all parties recognize the independence of the United States. John Quincy travels to St. Petersburg with Francis Dana, the American minister to Russia (though Catherine the Great withholds official recognition), where he will serve as Dana's secretary and French interpreter from August 1781 to October 1782. Charles leaves the Netherlands for the United States on August 12. Adams is seriously ill with a fever, possibly malarial, in Amsterdam from August to October. General Charles Cornwallis surrenders his army of 7,000 men to Washington at Yorktown, Virginia, on October 19.

1782   Defeat at Yorktown results in the resignation on March 20 of prime minister Lord North and the formation of a new ministry under Lord Rockingham that opens peace negotiations with Franklin in Paris on April 12. States General of the Netherlands recognizes American independence on April 19, and on April 22 Adams presents his diplomatic credentials to Stadholder William V of the Netherlands. Establishes residence at the Hôtel des Etats-Unis at The Hague, the first American legation building in Europe. Contracts with a syndicate of Amsterdam bankers for a loan to the United States of five million guilders on June 11. Signs treaty of amity and commerce with the Netherlands, October 8. Arrives in Paris on October 26 to join Franklin and Jay in negotiations with the British, and agrees with their decision to proceed without consulting the French. Takes leading role in securing recognition of American fishing rights off Canada in preliminary peace treaty, signed on November 30 by Richard Oswald and by Adams, Franklin, Jay, and Henry Laurens.

1783   Attends signing of preliminary Anglo-French and Anglo-Spanish peace treaties at Versailles on January 20. Helps negotiate final peace treaty, resisting British attempts to significantly modify the terms of the preliminary agreement. Travels to the Hague, July–August, and returns with John Quincy. Signs Definitive Treaty of Peace with Franklin, Jay, and British negotiator David Hartley in Paris on September 3. Falls ill with fever, September–October, and recovers in Auteuil outside of Paris. Travels to England in October with John Quincy and spends two months in London before going to Bath in late December.

1784   Learns that American bills of exchange are in danger of default in the Dutch financial markets. Crosses the North Sea with John Quincy during a three-day storm and lands in Zeeland, then travels by foot, iceboat, and farm cart to The Hague, arriving on January 12. Negotiates new loan of two million guilders, March 9, that preserves American credit. Appointed by Congress to serve with Franklin and Jefferson as commissioner to negotiate treaties of amity and commerce with twenty-three European and North African states. Abigail and Nabby sail from Boston, June 20, and arrive in London, July 21, where they are joined by John Quincy on July 30. (Charles and Thomas remain in Massachusetts with Abigail's sister Elizabeth and her husband, the Reverend John Shaw.) Adams returns from the Netherlands on August 7, and the reunited family travels to Paris and settles in Auteuil. Forms closer friendship with Jefferson, who had arrived in Paris with his daughter Martha in early August.

1785   Appointed by Congress on February 24 as the first American minister to Great Britain (continues to serve as minister to the Netherlands and as treaty commissioner). John Quincy leaves France to return to the United States, May 12. Jefferson succeeds Franklin as U.S. minister to France. Adams, Abigail, and Nabby arrive in London, May 26, and Adams has audience with George III, June 1, during which he expresses his desire to restore "the good old nature and the good old humor between people who, though separated by an ocean and under different governments, have the same language, a similar religion, and kindred blood." Latter writes that he "felt more than I did or could express," and describes George III as having listened "with dignity but with apparent emotion." Abigail and Nabby are presented to the King and Queen Charlotte on June 23. Family moves into house on Grosvenor Square that becomes the first American legation in London. Adams signs treaty of amity and commerce with Prussia in London on August 5. Has cordial meeting with Jonathan Sewall, who is living in exile in London. Becomes frustrated by the unwillingness of the British to enter into negotiations for a commercial treaty.

1786   Jefferson arrives in London on March 11 and joins Adams in negotiations with Tripoli; attempt to conclude treaty protecting American shipping from piracy fails because of the inability of the United States to pay the tribute demanded by the sultan's envoy. John Quincy admitted to Harvard College as a junior. Adams and Jefferson make progress in negotiating a commercial treaty with Portugal (agreement is finally concluded in 1791) and spend six days touring English country gardens before Jefferson returns to Paris on April 26. Nabby marries Colonel William Stephens Smith, secretary of the American legation and a former Continental Army officer, on June 12. Visits Braintree in Essex with his family in August, then travels to the Netherlands with Abigail to exchange ratifications of the treaty with Prussia. Witnesses political success of the Dutch Patriot party. Returns to London in September and begins writing treatise on ancient and modern governments.

1787   Somewhat hurriedly (he will later concede), Adams completes a partial manuscript of his historical analysis and publishes it in London in January as the first volume of *A Defence of the Constitutions of Government of the United States of America*. Signs treaty of peace and friendship with Morocco, January 25, that includes payment of tribute as protection against piracy. Grandson William Steuben Smith born in London on April 2. John Quincy graduates from Harvard College. Adams travels to the Netherlands, May–June, and negotiates a third Dutch loan to the United States. Returns to London, where Jefferson's daughter Mary (Polly), and his slave, Sally Hemings, age fourteen, stay with the Adamses, June–July, en route to live with Jefferson in Paris. Adams arranges for the purchase of the Vassall-Borland house in Braintree, Massachusetts, which he will call "Peacefield" and which will later be known as the "Old House," in preparation for his return from Europe. Publishes second volume of *A Defence of the Constitutions of Government of the United States of America* in September. Constitutional Convention ends in Philadelphia on September 17. In October Congress approves Adams's request that he be recalled from his diplomatic missions. Completes third and final volume of *A Defence of the Constitutions of Government of the United States of America* (published in early 1788).

1788   Has farewell audience with George III on February 20. Makes final visit to the Netherlands, where he arranges for a fourth Dutch loan. Sails from Portsmouth with Abigail in late April and arrives in Boston on June 17. After eleven of the thirteen states ratify the Constitution, Congress passes election ordinance on September 13 setting dates for choosing presidential electors and electing a president and vice president. Grandson John Adams

Smith born in New York in early November. Adams is elected to the House of Representatives in the First Federal Congress, but never serves.

1789   Presidential electors meet in their states on February 4 and vote for two candidates in balloting for president. George Washington receives the votes of all sixty-nine electors and is elected president, while Adams receives thrity-four votes and is elected vice president (John Jay receives nine votes, and twenty-six votes are divided among nine other candidates). Travels to New York City, the federal capital, and presides over the Senate for the first time on April 21. Attends Washington's inaugural at Federal Hall on April 30. Takes active role in prolonged Senate debate over the proper title for the president and unsuccessfully advocates variations on "His Highness." Refuses request from Mercy Otis Warren to help her husband James obtain a federal appointment. Abigail arrives in New York on June 24 and moves with Adams to Richmond Hill, a country estate overlooking the Hudson River in lower Manhattan (the house was located near present-day Varick and Charlton Streets). Charles graduates from Harvard College and begins studying law in the New York offices of Alexander Hamilton (later moves to the office of John Laurance). Adams casts first tie-breaking vote in the Senate on July 18, determining that the president does not need the consent of the Senate to remove executive officers who had been confirmed by the Senate. (During his two terms as vice president Adams will cast at least twenty-nine tie-breaking votes.) First session of the First Federal Congress adjourns on September 29.

1790   Presides over the second session of the Senate, January–August; takes less active role in debates while continuing to rule on questions of procedure. Jefferson arrives in New York in March to take up his duties as secretary of state. Adams begins publishing "Discourses on Davila," series of thirty-two essays criticizing unbalanced democracy and the French Revolution that appear in the *Gazette of the United States*, April 28, 1790–April 27, 1791 (although the essays are attributed to "an American Citizen," their authorship is widely known). Son Thomas Boylston graduates from Harvard College. Grandson Thomas Hollis Smith born August 7 in New York. Moves with Abigail to Philadelphia, where the federal capital has been relocated until 1800, and take up residence at Bush Hill, an estate west of the city. Presides over third session of the Senate, December 1790–March 1791.

1791   Elected president of the American Academy of Arts and Sciences in May (serves until 1813). An American edition of Thomas Paine's *Rights of Man* is published in May with an endorsement by Jefferson alluding to "the political heresies which have sprung up among us," a remark widely understood to be a reference to "Discourses of Davila." John Quincy responds by criticizing Paine and Jefferson in series of "Publicola" essays in the Boston *Columbian Centinel*, while other newspapers accuse Adams of supporting monarchy and aristocracy. Grandson Thomas Hollis Smith dies July 8. Jefferson writes to Adams on July 17 and explains that his private note to the printer's brother had been published without his permission. Adams replies on July 29, accepting Jefferson's explanation while denying that he favors "the Introduction of hereditary Monarchy and Aristocracy into this Country." Presides over the Senate during the first session of the Second Congress, October 1791–May 1792. Moves with Abigail from Bush Hill to a smaller house at Fourth and Arch Streets in Philadelphia.

1792   North Precinct of Braintree is incorporated as the town of Quincy in February. Returns to Philadelphia in the fall while Abigail remains in Quincy for health reasons (she will stay in Massachusetts for the remainder of Adams's vice presidency). Presides over the second session of the Senate, November 1792–March 1793. In the electoral balloting on December 5, Washington is reelected with the votes of all 132 electors, and Adams is reelected as vice president with seventy-seven votes, while George Clinton receives fifty electoral votes, Jefferson four, and Aaron Burr one.

1793   Supports Washington's decision to issue proclamation of neutrality, April 22, in the war between the revolutionary French republic and Great Britain. Controversy over relations with France contribute to the emergence of two political parties, with supporters of Jefferson and James Madison, who are sympathetic to France and oppose the financial policies of Secretary of the Treasury Alexander

Hamilton, calling themselves Republicans, and supporters of Hamilton, who favor closer relations with Britain, calling themselves Federalists. Adams presides over the Senate during first session of Third Congress, December 1793–June 1794. Son Thomas Boylston is admitted to the Philadelphia bar. Jefferson resigns as secretary of state, effective December 31.

1794   Washington appoints John Quincy minister resident to the Netherlands, May 30. John Quincy sails for Europe in September with Thomas Boylston as his secretary. Adams presides over the Senate during second session of Third Congress, November 1794–March 1795. John Jay signs treaty in London on November 19 that provides for evacuation of British garrisons from frontier posts in the Northwest (an unfulfilled provision of the 1783 peace treaty) and the establishment of a commission to resolve British claims against American debtors, but which contains few British concessions regarding Anglo-American commerce or neutral maritime rights.

1795   Granddaughter Caroline Amelia Smith born in New York in late January. Adams presides over a special session of the Senate called on June 8 to consider Jay's Treaty. Senate votes 20–10 on June 24 to ratify the treaty after a secret debate. Published on July 1, the treaty is widely attacked for failing to secure American rights, and the controversy further divides Republicans and Federalists. Charles marries Sarah Smith, sister of William Stephens Smith, in New York on August 29. Adams presides over the Senate during the first session of the Fourth Congress, December 1795–May 1796.

1796   Granddaughter Susanna Boylston Adams, first child of Charles and Sarah, born August 8 in New York. Washington makes public his decision not to seek a third term when his farewell address is published on September 19. In the presidential election, Federalists support Adams while Republicans support Jefferson; neither candidate makes any public statements. Adams is embittered by the support for Jefferson given by former friends, including James and Mercy Otis Warren, Benjamin Rush, and Samuel Adams. Returns to Philadelphia for the second session of the Fourth Congress, which begins on December 5. Presidential electors meet on December 7 (the 138 electors are chosen by the voters in seven states, by the legislature in seven states, by the voters and the legislature in one state, and by county delegates appointed by the legislature in one state). Adams receives seventy-one electoral votes and is elected president, Jefferson receives sixty-eight votes and becomes vice president, while Federalist Thomas Pinckney receives fifty-nine votes, Republican Aaron Burr thirty, and forty electoral votes are divided among nine other candidates.

1797   Inaugurated as president on March 4. Retains Washington's cabinet, consisting of Secretary of State Timothy Pickering, Secretary of the Treasury Oliver Wolcott Jr., Secretary of War James McHenry, and Attorney General Charles Lee. Learns that the French Directory has ordered Charles Cotesworth Pinckney, who had been appointed minister to France by Washington in 1796, to leave the country, and that the French navy has increased its seizures of American ships trading with Britain. Moves into the President's House at Sixth and Market Streets. Mother Susanna Boylston Adams dies in Quincy on April 17. Joined in Philadelphia by Abigail on May 10. Addresses special session of Congress on May 16, calling for the strengthening of the navy while announcing that a new diplomatic mission will be sent to France. Nominates Charles Cotesworth Pinckney, John Marshall, and Elbridge Gerry to serve as commissioners to France. Appoints John Quincy minister plenipotentiary to Prussia. Adams and Abigail leave Philadelphia for Quincy on July 19. John Quincy marries Louisa Catherine Johnson in London, July 26. American envoys to France have a brief informal meeting with Talleyrand, the French foreign minister, on October 8, and are then approached by three of Talleyrand's agents, who solicit $240,000 bribe as precondition for further negotiations; the agents also demand that the Americans agree to loan France $12 million and repudiate critical remarks about French policy made by Adams in his address to Congress on May 16. The American commissioners refuse to pay, and describe their reception in dispatches sent to Pickering on October 22 and November 8. Adams delivers his first annual message to Congress on November 22.

1798   Pickering receives coded dispatches from the envoys on March 4, along with an uncoded letter reporting that the

Directory has closed French ports to neutral shipping and made all ships carrying British products subject to capture. After the dispatches are decoded, Adams consults with his cabinet, which divides over whether to seek a declaration of war. Adams sends message to Congress on March 19 announcing failure of the peace mission and requesting the adoption of defensive measures. In response to request from the House of Representatives, Adams submits the dispatches to Congress on April 3, and they are quickly published, with Talleyrand's agents referred to as X, Y, and Z. Revelation of the "XYZ" affair causes popular furor against France. Congress establishes Department of the Navy on May 3, and Adams appoints Benjamin Stoddert as secretary of the navy on May 21. Appoints George Washington as commander of an expanded army on July 2 and, at Washington's request, names Alexander Hamilton as inspector general. Congress passes direct property tax on July 2 and adopts measure on July 9 authorizing the navy and armed merchant vessels to capture armed French ships. Adams signs into law the Alien and Sedition Acts, which extend the period required for naturalization from five to fourteen years; give the president the power to expel or, in time of declared war, to imprison dangerous aliens (no one is expelled under the law, though many French nationals leave voluntarily); and make the publication of "false, scandalous, and malicious writing" attacking the federal government, the president, or the Congress a crime punishable by up to two years in prison. (Ten Republican editors and printers are convicted under the Sedition Act during the Adams administration.) Adams and Abigail leave Philadelphia for Quincy on July 25. *A Selection of the Patriotic Addresses to the President of the United States, together with The President's Answers*, a volume collecting Adams's responses to numerous resolutions and memorials submitted in support of the administration, is published in Boston. Granddaughter Abigail Louisa Smith Adams, second child of Charles and Sarah, born September 8. Adams reluctantly appoints Hamilton as second in command of the army on October 15. Jefferson and Madison secretly draft resolutions attacking the Alien and Sedition Acts as unconstitutional and calling upon the states to resist them. (The Kentucky legislature adopts the Jefferson resolutions in modified form on November 10, and the Virginia legislature adopts the Madison

resolutions on December 24). Adams departs for Phila-
delphia on November 12, while Abigail remains in Quincy.
Limited naval war with France begins in the Caribbean.
Adams delivers his second annual message to Congress
December 8, in which he suggests the possibility of
appointing a new peace mission to France. Appoints
Bushrod Washington, nephew of George Washington, to
the Supreme Court.

1799   Nominates William Vans Murray as special envoy to
France on February 18 and declares that Murray will be
sent only after Talleyrand gives assurances that he will
be properly received; Adams later names Chief Justice
Oliver Ellsworth and William Davie as additional negotiators. Peace overture splits Federalists into pro- and anti-
Adams factions. Adams returns to Quincy in March and
remains there until September 30. Learns that Charles,
who has been drinking heavily for years, has deserted his
family and is bankrupt. Arrives on October 10 in Trenton,
where the government has relocated during a yellow fever
outbreak in Philadelphia. Meets with cabinet to review instructions for the new peace commission, and orders its
departure on October 16 despite the opposition of Pickering, McHenry, and Wolcott. (Adams will later write that
his decision to send the mission was "the most disinterested, prudent, and successful conduct in my whole life.")
Returns to Philadelphia in November and is joined by
Abigail. Delivers third annual message to Congress on
December 3. Federalist caucus in Congress endorses his
reelection. Adams appoints Alfred Moore to the Supreme
Court. George Washington dies on December 14.

1800   Adams refuses to promote Hamilton to commander in
chief of the army, leaving the post unfilled. Demands the
resignation of Secretary of War McHenry on May 5 and
dismisses Secretary of State Pickering on May 12, accusing
them of being subservient to Hamilton. Appoints Samuel
Dexter as secretary of war, John Marshall as secretary of
state, and orders the demobilization of the expanded
"Additional" army created in 1798. Against the advice of
his cabinet, on May 21 Adams pardons John Fries and two
other men sentenced to hang for treason. (Fries had led a
band of armed protestors who forced a federal marshal in
March 1799 to release a group of prisoners jailed for resisting the 1798 federal property tax.) Federalist caucus

again endorses Adams's reelection. Adams visits Washington, D.C., in June, then returns to Quincy. Hamilton meets with leading New England Federalists in June and urges them to support Charles Cotesworth Pinckney, the Federalist vice-presidential candidate, for the presidency over Adams. American envoys in France sign Convention of 1800 on September 30; treaty ends undeclared naval war and suspends 1778 treaty of alliance. Hamilton publishes pamphlet on October 24 describing Adams as unfit for the presidency. Adams arrives in Washington on November 1 and becomes the first occupant of the still unfinished President's House. Delivers fourth annual message to Congress on November 11. Charles dies of liver failure in East Chester, New York, November 30. Presidential electors meet on December 3 (the 138 electors are chosen by the voters in five states, by the legislature in ten states, and by county delegates appointed by the legislature in one state). Jefferson and Aaron Burr each receive seventy-three electoral votes, while Adams receives sixty-five, Charles Cotesworth Pinckney sixty-four, and John Jay one. Official copy of the treaty with France arrives in Washington on December 11. Secretary of the Treasury Wolcott resigns and is replaced by Samuel Dexter, who continues to serve as secretary of war.

1801   Adams appoints John Marshall chief justice of the Supreme Court on January 20 (Marshall continues to serve as secretary of state through the end of the administration). Senate ratifies the treaty with France in amended form on February 3. Adams signs on February 13 a new judiciary act that creates sixteen new circuit court judgeships. House of Representatives elects Jefferson president on February 17 after thirty-six ballots; Burr becomes vice president. Adams nominates, and the Federalist Senate confirms, Federalist circuit court judges. ("Midnight appointments" anger Jefferson and the Republicans, and in 1802 a Republican Congress repeals the judiciary act of 1801 and abolishes the new judgeships.) Adams recalls John Quincy from his position in Prussia. Leaves Washington for Quincy early on the morning of Jefferson's inauguration, March 4. Grandson George Washington Adams, the first child of John Quincy and Louisa Catherine, born April 12 in Berlin.

1802   In April, John Quincy is elected to Massachusetts State Senate. Adams begins writing the first part of his autobiography, "John Adams," on October 5 (completed in June 1805). In November, John Quincy is defeated in a close election as Federalist candidate for Congress.

1803   John Quincy is elected as a U.S. senator from Massachusetts (serves until 1808). Adams loses $13,000 in the failure of the London bank of Bird, Savage, & Bird. To compensate against the losses, John Quincy arranges to buy the Old House and surrounding property in stages. Grandson John Adams 2nd, second child of John Quincy and Louisa Catherine, born July 4 in Boston.

1805   Thomas Boylston marries Ann Harrod of Haverhill, Massachusetts, May 16. Adams resumes his correspondence with Benjamin Rush, which had lapsed amid the partisan contests of the 1790s. Publishes collected edition of *Discourses on Davila*. John Quincy becomes first Boylston Professor of Rhetoric and Oratory at Harvard.

1806   Begins second part of his autobiography, "Travels, and Negotiations" (completed early in 1807.) Granddaughter Abigail Smith Adams, first child of Thomas Boylston and Ann, born July 29 in Quincy.

1807   Commences writing the third part of his autobiography, "Peace," but breaks it off when he begins his controversy with Mercy Otis Warren over her *History of the Rise, Progress and Termination of the American Revolution*, a work highly critical of Adams. Between July 28 and August 19, he writes ten long, angry letters to Warren, who, after six letters of her own, finally ends the exchange by responding that as "an old friend, I pity you, as a Christian I forgive you." Grandson Charles Francis Adams, third child of John Quincy and Louisa Catherine, born August 18 in Boston.

1808   Granddaughter Elizabeth Coombs Adams, second child of Thomas Boylston and Ann, born June 9.

1809   Begins publishing letters of reminiscence in the *Boston Patriot* (his "second autobiography" continues until May 1812.) Publishes four letters in the *Patriot* on British impressment of American seamen that are collected in pamphlet *The Inadmissible Principles, of the King of England's*

Proclamation, of October 16, 1807—Considered. John Quincy appointed minister plenipotentiary to Russia by President James Madison, June 27. Grandson Thomas Boylston Adams Jr., born August 4. John Quincy and his family depart for Russia in August, accompanied by Adams's grandson William Steuben Smith, who serves as John Quincy's secretary.

1811   John Quincy is appointed to the Supreme Court by Madison on February 22; he declines the position. In June, Thomas Boylston is appointed chief justice of the Massachusetts court of common pleas for the Southern Circuit. Granddaughter Frances Foster Adams, fourth child of Thomas Boylston and Ann, born June 22. Granddaughter Louisa Catherine Adams, fourth child of John Quincy and Louisa Catherine, born August 12 in St. Petersburg, Russia. Nabby undergoes mastectomy at the Old House on October 8.

1812   On January 1, through the intercession of Benjamin Rush, Adams resumes his correspondence with Thomas Jefferson; over the next fourteen years he writes 109 letters to Jefferson, who responds with forty-nine. Frances Foster Adams dies March 4. Congress declares war with Great Britain, June 17. Louisa Catherine Adams dies September 15.

1813   Grandson Isaac Hull Adams, fifth child of Thomas Boylston and Ann, born May 26. Nabby dies of cancer at the Old House on August 15.

1814   John Quincy is appointed in January to five-member commission charged with negotiating an Anglo-American peace treaty. Adams begins correspondence with John Taylor of Virginia, whose work *Inquiry into the Principles and Policy of the Government of the United States* is largely a critique of Adams's *Defence.* John Quincy signs peace treaty with Great Britain at Ghent in December.

1815   Madison appoints John Quincy minister plenipotentiary to Great Britain (serves until 1817). Grandson John Quincy Adams, sixth child of Thomas Boylston and Ann, born December 16.

1817   President James Monroe appoints John Quincy secretary of state (serves until 1825). Grandson Joseph Harrod

Adams, seventh child of Thomas Boylston and Ann, born December 16.

1818   Abigail dies of typhoid fever on October 28.

1819   Adams publishes collected edition of *Novanglus and Massachusettensis.*

1820   Attends sessions of the convention called to revise the state constitution as Quincy delegate, and proposes that the Massachusetts bill of rights be changed so as to remove all restrictions on religious freedom.

1822   Gives to the town of Quincy several tracts of granite-bearing land, the profits from which are to be used to build a church and an academy that will eventually house his library.

1823   Brother Peter Boylston dies on June 2 in Braintree. Adams has a granite column erected in the Quincy burial ground with the inscription: "In memory of Henry Adams, who took his flight from the Dragon of persecution in Devonshire, England, and alighted with 8 sons near Mount Wollaston. One of the sons returned to England, and after taking some time to explore the country, four removed to Medfield and the neighboring towns; two to Chelmsford. One only, Joseph, who lies here at his left hand, remained here, who was an original proprietor in the township of Braintree, 1639. This stone and several others have been placed in their yard by a great-grandson from a veneration of the piety, humility, sympathy, prudence, patience, temperance, frugality, industry, and perseverance of his ancestors, in hope of recommending an emulation of their virtues to their posterity."

1824   John Quincy becomes candidate for president. In the election Andrew Jackson receives ninety-nine electoral votes, John Quincy eighty-four, William H. Crawford forty-one, and Henry Clay thirty-seven, forcing the contest into the House of Representatives.

1825   John Quincy is elected President of the United States by the House of Representatives on February 9, receiving the votes of thirteen out of twenty-four state delegations. Adams writes to the president-elect: "this is not an event to excite vanity." Grandson Charles Francis Adams graduates from Harvard in August.

1826   Adams dies at the Old House on the evening of July 4,
              several hours after Jefferson's death at Monticello; among
              his last words are "Thomas Jefferson survives." After ser-
              vice held at the First Congregational Church in Quincy
              on July 7, Adams is buried next to Abigail.

Note on the Texts

This volume prints the texts of seventy-two letters, essays, public messages, and drafts written by John Adams between 1755 and 1775; nineteen selections from his diary for this period; and selected passages from his unfinished autobiography, drafted in 1802 and 1804–5, recalling his life up to 1775. It also includes the text of a newspaper piece by William Brattle published on January 25, 1773, as part of his polemical exchange with Adams regarding the independence of judges in Massachusetts, as well as the texts of the seventeen "Massachusettensis" essays, written by Daniel Leonard and published December 12, 1774–April 3, 1775, that Adams responded to in his twelve "Novanglus" essays, published January 23–April 17, 1775. Although the majority of these documents existed only in autograph manuscript at the time of Adams's death in 1826, many of them were printed during his lifetime. Adams published newspaper essays both under his own name and under a variety of pseudonyms, and some of these essays were then published in pamphlet or book form.

Always keenly aware of his reputation and his place in history, Adams took great care in safeguarding and transporting his papers throughout his many travels, regarding them "as a Sacred Deposit." On December 24, 1818, an eighty-three-year-old Adams wrote to his son John Quincy that he was hard at work searching "after old Papers. Trunks, Boxes, Desks, Drawers, locked up for thirty Years have been broken open because the keys are lost. Nothing stands in my Way. Every Scrap shall be found and preserved for your Affliction or for your good. . . . I shall leave you an inheritance sufficiently tormenting, for example, The huge Pile of family Letters, will make you Alternatly laugh and cry, fret and fume, stamp and scold as they do me." John Quincy Adams eventually entrusted his family's papers to his son, Charles Francis Adams, who edited and published two collections of correspondence, *Letters of Mrs. Adams, the Wife of John Adams* (1840) and *Letters of John Adams, Addressed to His Wife* (2 volumes, 1841), followed by *The Works of John Adams, Second President of the United States: with a Life of the Author, Notes and Illustrations, by his Grandson Charles Francis Adams* (10 volumes, 1850–56), which primarily presented Adams's public writings and official correspondence.

Charles Francis Adams later had a separate fireproof building, the

Stone Library, built on the grounds of the family estate in Quincy, Massachusetts, to house the family archive. On his death in 1886 he left his papers, and those of John Adams and Abigail Adams, and of John Quincy Adams and his wife, Louisa Catherine Adams, to his four sons, one of whom, Charles Francis Adams Jr., later became president of the Massachusetts Historical Society. In 1902 Charles Francis Adams Jr. had the family papers moved from the Stone Library to the Massachusetts Historical Society building in Boston, and in 1905 he created the Adams Manuscript Trust to ensure continued family ownership and control of the papers for the next fifty years. In 1954 the Adams Manuscript Trust entered into an agreement with the Massachusetts Historical Society and Harvard University Press to publish the papers of John Adams, John Quincy Adams, Charles Francis Adams Sr., and their families through the year 1889. The Adams Manuscript Trust was dissolved in 1956 after it transferred ownership of its papers to the Massachusetts Historical Society, which began to identify and photocopy Adams documents in repositories outside of the family archive. Publication of the Adams Family Papers began in 1961 and has proceeded in three series, two of which are still ongoing in respect to John Adams: *Diary and Autobiography of John Adams* (4 volumes; Cambridge: The Belknap Press of Harvard University Press, 1961), supplemented by *The Earliest Diary of John Adams* (Cambridge: The Belknap Press of Harvard University Press, 1966); *Adams Family Correspondence* (9 volumes to date; Cambridge: The Belknap Press of Harvard University Press, 1963–2009); and *Papers of John Adams* (15 volumes to date; Cambridge: The Belknap Press of Harvard University Press, 1977–2010). Documents are transcribed and printed without alteration in their spelling and paragraphing, and with minimal alterations in their capitalization and punctuation, mostly in the substitution of periods for dashes used to end sentences and the omission of dashes in instances where a dash appears following another punctuation mark.

The texts of the selections from the diary printed in this volume, as well as the text of Adams's letter to Catherine Macaulay of August 9, 1770, are taken from *Diary and Autobiography of John Adams*, volumes 1–2 (1961), edited by L. H. Butterfield, with the exception of the diary entry from autumn 1758 that appears on pp. 31.6–32.24, which is taken from *The Earliest Diary of John Adams* (1966), edited by L. H. Butterfield. The texts of the selections from the autobiography included in this volume are taken from *Diary and Autobiography of John Adams*, volume 3 (1961), edited by L. H. Butterfield, and the texts of the letters to Abigail Smith, later Abigail Adams, are taken from *Adams Family Correspondence*, volume 1 (1963), edited by

L. H. Butterfield. The texts of the essays, public messages, drafts, and other letters by John Adams included in this volume, as well as the newspaper piece by William Brattle previously mentioned, are taken from *Papers of John Adams*, volumes 1–2 (1977), edited by Robert J. Taylor. The texts of the "Massachusettensis" essays by Daniel Leonard are taken from *Novanglus, and Massachusettensis; or political essays, published in the years 1774 and 1775, on the principal points of controversy, between Great Britain and her colonies* (Boston: Hews & Goss, 1819).

The present volume prints texts as they appeared in *The Adams Papers* and in *Novanglus, and Massachusettensis*, but with a few alterations in editorial procedure. The bracketed conjectural readings of the editors of *The Adams Papers*, in cases where original manuscripts or printed texts were damaged or difficult to read, are accepted without brackets in this volume when those readings seem to be the only possible ones; but when they do not, or when the editors made no conjecture, the missing word or words are indicated by a bracketed two-em space, i.e., [   ]. In cases where *The Adams Papers* supplied in brackets punctuation, letters, or words that were omitted from the source text by an obvious slip of the pen or printer's error, this volume removes the brackets and accepts the editorial emendation. Similarly, in cases where an obvious slip of the pen or printing error is corrected in *The Adams Papers* by having the correction appear in brackets following the error, this volume removes the brackets and accepts the correction while deleting the error, e.g., at 73.21 "Soils and Manners [Manures]" becomes "Soils and Manures." Bracketed editorial insertions used in *The Adams Papers* to expand abbreviations and contractions or to correct errors of dating in diary entries have been deleted in this volume. In some cases where Adams made changes in a document, the canceled text, if decipherable, was presented in *The Adams Papers* in italic within single angle brackets; this volume omits the canceled material.

This volume presents the texts of the editions chosen as sources here but does not attempt to reproduce features of their typographic design. The texts are printed without alteration except for the changes previously discussed, some changes in headings, and the correction of typographical errors. Spelling, punctuation, and capitalization are often expressive features, and they are not altered, even when inconsistent or irregular. The following is a list of typographical errors corrected, cited by page and line number: 105.34, off,; 112.22, Month of; 119.24, common law; 157.40, govenment,; 243.40, Parliament.; 255.2, were 1231.; 343.13, rspecting; 355.25–26, be side,; 361.13, intercouse; 363.3, provice; 375.21, romoves; 394.16, Britith; 411.2, 37 Every; 411

.24, 10 Foster; 424.5, martime; 429.28, excue; 448.30, whethor; 451.6, pegeantry.; 467.12, necessiated; 473.31, goverment; 474.3, horors; 480.7, extingnished.; 505.24, parliamet; 506.12, aud publication; 533.1, St, Germain,; 563.13, dipassionate; 564.2, causless,; 564.33, petititions; 569.35, Britoin; 570.18, purchased.

Notes

In the notes below, the reference numbers denote page and line of this volume (the line count includes headings). No note is made for material included in the eleventh edition of *Merriam-Webster's Collegiate Dictionary*. In 1822 John Adams donated most of his library to the town of Quincy. In 1893 his books were transferred to the Boston Public Library, where they still reside. A note is provided when reference is made to a title found in the *Catalogue of the John Adams Library in the Public Library of the City of Boston* (Boston, 1917), hereafter cited as the *CJAL*. For further biographical background, references to other studies, and more detailed notes, see *Papers of John Adams*, edited by Robert J. Taylor, et al. (15 vols. to date, Cambridge: Harvard University Press, 1977–2010); *Diary and Autobiography of John Adams*, edited by L. H. Butterfield, et al. (4 vols., Cambridge: Harvard University Press, 1961); *The Earliest Diary of John Adams*, edited by L. H. Butterfield, et al. (Cambridge: Harvard University Press, 1966); *Adams Family Correspondence*, edited by L. H. Butterfield, et al. (9 vols. to date, Cambridge: Harvard University Press, 1963–2009); *Legal Papers of John Adams*, L. Kinvin Wroth and Hiller B. Zobel, editors (3 vols., Cambridge: Harvard University Press, 1965); David McCullough, *John Adams* (New York: Simon & Schuster, 2001).

LAWYER AND PATRIOT, 1755–1774

3.2   *Nathan Webb*] A cousin, childhood friend, and classmate at Harvard (graduating in 1754), Nathan Webb (1734–1760) practiced medicine at Weston, Massachusetts, before his early death.

5.32   Independent Whigg] *The Independent Whig* (1720–1721) was a weekly edited by British radicals John Trenchard and Thomas Gordon that focused its attacks on the pretensions of the established Church of England; widely read in the colonies, fifty-three of its papers were published in book form in 1721 in London and later in America in numerous editions.

6.12   Major Gardiners] Gardiner Chandler (1723–1782) was a member of the leading family of pre-Revolutionary Worcester, with the members of which Adams was friendly.

7.27–28   Putnam . . . the Dr. and his Lady] The party includes: James Putnam (1726–1789), Adams's law teacher in Worcester, with whom, after August 21, Adams boarded while continuing to teach school (Adams was to pay Putnam one hundred dollars when "convenient"); the Rev. Ebenezer Thayer (1734–1792), the minister in Worcester whose services Adams attended; and most probably Dr. and Mrs. Nathan Willard, with whom Adams was then boarding in Worcester.

10.26   *Charles Cushing*] Cushing (1734–1810), was a classmate at Harvard (1755) who studied law and became a merchant trading in Maine; he returned to Boston in 1781, practiced law, and served as a judge of the lower court of common pleas.

11.9–12   Should the whole Frame . . . a falling World.] Quotation from Addison's translation of Horace, *Odes*, III.iii, in the *Spectator*, No. 615, November 3, 1714. Adams could have read Addison's translation in any of several places.

12.20   Dalton] Timothy Dalton (1738–1817) of Newburyport, a classmate at Harvard (1755); he later became a member of the Continental Congress and the U.S. Senate.

12.26   *Orminian*.] Arminian, a believer in universal redemption and thus an anti-Calvinist.

15.19   at the Majors.] Referring to the Chandler family.

17.23   Spencer] A town in central Massachusetts.

20.37   Crawford . . . Harding] Ministers in Worcester.

21.2   Mr. Paines.] Robert Treat Paine (1731–1814), Harvard 1749, was a lawyer and professional rival.

24.13   *Richard Cranch*] Richard Cranch (1726–1811) migrated from England to Massachusetts in 1746 and married Mary Smith, elder sister of Abigail, in 1762; he became Adams's "brother" when John and Abigail wed in 1764. He was a life-long friend and correspondent.

28.30   Mr. Gridleys] Jeremiah Gridley (1702–1767), Harvard 1725, was one of the leading lawyers of Boston and later the attorney general for Massachusetts.

30.1   Co. Litt.] The first volume of *Institutes of the Laws of England* (1628) by Sir Edward Coke (1559–1634) was written as a commentary on the work of Sir Thomas Littleton (1422–1481) and became the standard authority on real property in the English-speaking world.

30.6   Mr. Thatchers] Oxenbridge Thacher (1719–1765), a well-known Boston lawyer who later wrote what Adams called a "pretty little pamphlet" attacking Parliament's Sugar Act of 1764.

30.11   this County is full.] Of lawyers, that is.

30.17   Quincy] Edmund "Ned" Quincy (1733–1768), Harvard 1752, was the son of Josiah Quincy, "the Colonel," and a member of the famous family to which Adams would be related by marriage.

30.19   Mr. Prat, Dana, Kent.]   Benjamin Pratt (1711–1763), Harvard 1737, a leading lawyer of Boston and later chief justice of the province of New York; Richard Dana (1700–1772), Harvard 1718, a Boston lawyer and father of Francis Dana, who became Adams's secretary in Europe; and Benjamin Kent (1708–1788), Harvard 1727, a leading lawyer in Massachusetts and later attorney general of the colony.

32.28   My P. and M.]   Papa and Mamma, or Pater and Mater.

32.30   Peter]   Peter Adams (1738–1823), Adams's younger brother.

32.33   Tully]   Marcus Tullius Cicero.

33.37   H Q or O.]   Hannah Quincy (1736–1826), daughter of Col. Josiah Quincy; Adams almost proposed marriage to her. "O" indicates a fanciful name, possibly Olinda.

35.1–2   Sam Quincy]   Son of Col. Josiah Quincy.

35.5   Easther]   Esther Quincy (1738–1810), daughter of Edmund Quincy and Hannah's first cousin; she married Adams's friend Jonathan Sewall.

35.7–8   Mr. Wibirt]   Rev. Anthony Wibird (1720–1800), minister in Braintree.

35.10   Dr. Marsh]   Joseph Marsh (1710–1761?), Harvard 1728, Braintree schoolmaster who had prepared Adams for Harvard.

35.13   Parson Smith]   Rev. William Smith (1707–1783), Harvard 1725, was the minister at Weymouth; in 1764 he would become Adams's father-in-law.

36.22   Choice of Hercules]   The subject of Hercules's having to choose between the goddess of pleasure and the goddess of virtue became one of the most important symbolic themes of the eighteenth century. Addison wrote an essay on the subject in 1709, Handel composed an oratorio on the theme in 1750, and it was depicted in many paintings and engravings, including the engraving by Simon Gribelin that became the frontispiece to Anthony Ashley Cooper, Lord Shaftesbury's *Characteristics of Men, Manners, Opinions, and Times*, 5th ed., 3 vols. (Birmingham, 1773); in the *CJAL*. In 1776 Adams suggested that this engraving become the Great Seal of the United States.

37.19   Flavels]   John Flavel (1627–1691), an English Presbyterian clergyman and a prolific and popular author.

37.37   Read . . . Story]   Boston lawyers William Reed (sometimes Read); Samuel Swift (1715–1775), Harvard 1735; Samuel Fitch (1724–1799) Yale 1742; William (?) Skinner; and William Story, Suffolk County justice and admiralty registrar.

40.34–35   Oh but a Wit . . . the Mob he meets.]   From Alexander Pope, *The Second Epistle of the Second Book of Horace* (1737).

41.11   a nodding Beam, and pig of Lead]   Also from *the Second Epistle of the Second Book of Horace*: "And then a nodding beam, or pig of lead, / God knows, may hurt the very ablest head."

41.23   Otis]   James Otis Jr. (1725–1783), Harvard 1743, the celebrated lawyer and pamphleteer whose speeches and writings Adams revered.

42.20   Piscataquay]   Portsmouth, New Hampshire, at the mouth of the Piscataqua River.

43.13   P W]   Parson Wibird.

47.16   Parson Smith has no small. . .]   This may have been the first time Adams visited the Smith household, where in 1762 he began wooing Abigail.

47.25   Mr. Maccarty.]   Rev. Thaddeus Maccarty (1721–1784), the minister who engaged Adams to teach school in Worcester.

48.16   Secondat]   The family name of Montesquieu, whose *Spirit of the Laws* (Thomas Nugent translation, 2d edition, London, 1752) Adams had begun to read. The passage referred to here is "Of the Laws of Nature," in bk. I, ch. 2.

50.34–51.2   Parson Robbins . . . Mrs. Apthorps]   Rev. Chandler Robbins (1738–1799), minister of the First Church in Plymouth, Massachusetts; Rev. Moses Taft (1722–1791), Harvard 1751, ordained in Braintree's south parish on August 25, 1752. Cotton Tufts (1734–1815), a Weymouth physician, had married Lucy, daughter of Col. John Quincy, and was thus a uncle by marriage of Abigail Adams; Samuel Niles (1711–1804), the Braintree representative to the General Court; Maj. Ebenezer Miller (1730–1811), a militia officer, selectman, Episcopalian, and, ultimately, Loyalist from Braintree; Rev. Ebenezer Miller (1703–1763) D.D. Oxford 1747, minister for many years of Christ Church, the first Episcopal Church in Braintree; Edmund Quincy (1703–1788), the fourth of his name and brother of "Colonel" Josiah, whose Boston mercantile firm having gone bankrupt, became a farmer in Braintree. Mr. Allins, of a Braintree family; John Borland (1728–1775) had married well and had built a summer home in Braintree in 1751, which Adams would acquire in 1787 and which, much modified, is now called "the Old House" at the Adams National Historical Site; Mrs. Charles W. Apthorp, matriarch of another family that would become Loyalists in the revolution.

51.12   in Skadin]   Often spelled Skadding, a local name for the South Precinct of Braintree where Parson Taft's meeting house was located.

51.21   *Jonathan Sewall*]   Sewall (1728–1796), Harvard 1748, was a lawyer and intimate friend of Adams until they found themselves on opposing sides of the imperial crisis.

55.11–12   *Μηδ' . . . . μικρης.*]   "And do not hate your friend because of a small sin." From the *Golden Verses of Pythagoras*, written by disciples of Pythagoras in the first or second century B.C.

55.18   Cozen Zab]   Rev. Zabdiel Adams (1739–1801), Harvard 1759, Adams's double first cousin, who kept the Latin school in Braintree for three years after he graduated from college.

57.23   Captn. Freeman.]   Jonathan Freeman.

57.24   Dr. Lincoln]   Dr. Bela Lincoln (1734–1773), Harvard 1754, was a physician of Hingham who in 1760 married Hannah Quincy Smith, Abigail's sister.

58.30–31   Parson Potters Affair]   Nathaniel Potter, College of New Jersey 1753, and honorary A.M., Harvard 1758, was minister at Brookline from 1755 until dismissed in June 1759.

59.7   Justice Dyer]   Sir James Dyer (1510–1582) was Speaker of the House of Commons in 1553 and Chief Justice of the Court of Common Pleas from 1559 to his death. Adams knew his *Reports on the Cases of the Reigns of Hen. VIII. Edw. VI. Q. Mary, and Q Eliz.* (London, 1688?), citing it in his debate over the independence of judges in 1773 (see note 223.1).

59.29   Address to the Governor]   This address was adopted by the Massachusetts House of Representatives on December 23, 1760.

60.35   as Dr. Savil does]   Sir George Savile, 1st Marquis of Halifax (1633–1695), a noted English statesman and writer. His book *The Character of a Trimmer* (1688) was perhaps the best-known of his writings.

61.14   Corpus Juris Canonici]   Body of the Canon Law. Adams was reading the edition of the *Corpus Juris Canonici* published in León in 1661.

61.15–16   Yoricks sermons]   *The Sermons of Mr. Yorick* (1760), written by Laurence Sterne, the author of *Tristram Shandy*, very popular in England and America.

61.17   De Wits Maxim]   Johan de Witt (1625–1672) was a famous Dutch statesman and an accomplished mathematician who helped create the modern idea of an annuity; he contributed to the *True Interest and Political Maxims of the Republic of Holland* (1662), a radical republican text. Adams was impressed by De Witt's explanation of how he could accomplish so much amidst the endless multiplicity and variety of business: "by doing one Thing at once," a rule that Adams thought should be applied to the law.

61.19   Lancelots Institutes]   Johannes Paulus Lancelottus (1522–1590), a well known legal scholar of Perugia.

61.28–29   approaching Wedlock]   Quincy was about to be married to Hannah Hill of Boston.

62.6–7   "Nulli Sua . . . alliis aliud."]   "Nothing remains in the same shape; each was at odds with all the others." (Ovid, *Metamorphoses*, 1.17–18).

62.17   Dr. Cheyne]   George Cheyne (1671–1743) was a British physician
and a prolific writer of popular medical works. For a while Adams tried to follow his rigorous dietary regimen.

64.10   De la Motte]   Antoine Houdart de La Motte (1672–1731), a French
poet and critic.

64.12   Mr. Waller]   Edmund Waller (1606–1687), an English poet best
known for his verses in the "cavalier" tradition.

66.28   Aurelia]   Fanciful name for Abigail's elder sister, Mary.

68.1   *Humphrey Ploughjogger*]   These newspaper pieces were the consequence of several years of conflict in Massachusetts politics between the popular supporters of the Otis family and the "court" faction surrounding Gov.
Francis Bernard and Lt. Gov. Thomas Hutchinson. In 1760 James Otis Jr.
had attacked Bernard for naming Lt. Gov. Hutchinson as chief justice in place
of Otis's father, who had twice been promised the post. During the controversy Hutchinson's multiplicity of offices (he was also chief justice of the Superior Court and judge of the Suffolk County Probate Court) became an
issue, as did the Lt. Governor's support for the writs of assistance, general
search warrants used to enforce British customs duties. The younger Otis's
argument in the 1761 case concerning the writs of assistance electrified
Adams. In 1817 he would declare that "then and there was the first scene of
the first Act of Opposition to the arbitrary Claims of Great Britain. Then and
there the child Independence was born." When one of Adams's closest
friends, Jonathan Sewall, writing as "J," became involved in the newspaper
polemics in 1763 on behalf of the Bernard-Hutchinson faction, Adams was
provoked to respond.

68.22   chirch minsturs]   Anglican clergymen who had to go to England
for ordination by a bishop.

68.27   go to Leckshun]   Attend Election Day ceremonies.

69.29   nation]   Short for "damnation," which was used as an adjective
for "great" or "extremely."

71.4   thof]   Dialect for "though."

71.7   Mr. Elliot]   Rev. Jared Eliot (1785–1763), Yale 1706, author of *Essays
upon Field-Husbandry in New England, As It Is or May Be Ordered* (Boston,
1760).

73.15–16   *Huad facile . . . Res angusta Domi,*]   From Juvenal *Satires*,
III.164: "Those people do not easily emerge from obscurity whose abilities
are cramped by narrow means at home."

75.20–28   "a thousand Weight . . . of Lawful Money."]   Quotations
taken from Eliot, *Essays upon Field-Husbandry*, pp. 10–11.

76.32   Præceptor] *The Preceptor: Containing a General Course of Education*, 5th ed., 2 vols. (London, 1764), edited by Robert Dodsley (1703–1764); in the *CJAL*.

76.32–33   Nature delineated] *Nature Delineated* (London, 1743–44), trans. of Noël Antoine Pluche (1688–1764), *La spectacle de la nature* (Paris, 1732–35).

76.33   Chamber's Dictionary]   Much of this account of hemp was taken from Ephraim Chambers (c. 1680–1740), *Cyclopædia: or, an Universal Dictionary of Arts and Sciences* (London, 1728).

76.34   Compleat Body of Husbandry] *A Compleat Body of Husbandry, Containing Rules for Performing, in the Most Profitable Manner, the Whole Business of the Farmer, and Country Gentleman . . . Compiled from the Original Papers of the Late Thomas Hale* (London, 1756, 1758–59).

84.1–2   *fac officium . . . priore.*]   Do what is required as it should be done, but stand well with the abbot.

84.3–4   *fas* and *nefas.*]   By fair means and foul.

86.10   *Zozimus* and *Julian*]   Zosimus (490s–510s), was a Byzantine historian and professed pagan whose *Historia Nova* covered the history of Rome to the time of its conquest by Alaric in 410. Julian (c. 331–363), Flavius Claudius Iulianus, was the last pagan emperor of Rome and a gifted writer of satires and philosophical essays.

88.7   All Men would be Tyrants if they could.]   An epigrammatic phrase made popular by Daniel Defoe and used by Abigail in her famous "Remember the Ladies" letter of 1776, which can be found in the companion to this volume, *John Adams: Revolutionary Writings 1775–1783*, in the note 57.2.

91.4   Mr. Harvey]   James Hervey (1714–1758), a popular eighteenth-century English devotional writer.

91.14–15   Mr. Willard, Mr. Edwards, and Mr. Taylor, and Dr. Whitby]   Noted clerics Samuel Willard (1640–1707), Harvard 1659; Jonathan Edwards (1703–1758), Yale 1720; probably John Taylor (1694–1761); and Daniel Whitby (1638–1726), an English clergyman famous for his anti-Catholic writings. The works of Willard and Taylor are in the *CJAL*.

92.15–16   Dodridge's works]   Philip Doddridge (1702–1751), an English minister noted for his ability to unite nonconformists in common beliefs. His most popular work was *On the Rise and Progress of Religion in the Soul* (London, 1745).

92.16   Sandyman's]   Robert Sandeman (1718–1771), a follower of the independent Presbyterian preacher John Glas and a founder of Glassite churches in New England.

93.7   Hugh Peters] Hugh Peter (1598–1660), English Puritan preacher who briefly came to Massachusetts Bay colony in 1635 but returned to England in 1641 to participate in the Puritan Revolution. With the Restoration of Charles II in 1660, Peter was executed as a regicide.

94.17–18   Bluster and Whackum] Names "J" used for James Otis Jr. and Oxenbridge Thacher.

95.29   Cousin Fleets] Thomas and John Fleet, publishers of the *Boston Evening Post.*

96.1   Smallpox Inoculation] Smallpox was one of the most deadly diseases of the pre-modern world, with estimates of as many as thirty percent of those contracting the disease dying and those surviving often being badly disfigured. Inoculation for smallpox became known in the eighteenth century, but ever since Cotton Mather tried to promote it in Boston in 1721 it had remained controversial in the colony. Until Edward Jenner's discovery of vaccination (inoculation with a milder but immunizing disease, cowpox) in the 1790s, inoculation with the smallpox virus was itself very dangerous, not only to the patient receiving inoculation but to others in the community who had not had the disease. Hence many physicians generally resisted inoculation unless an outbreak of the disease threatened to get out of control.
    Just such an outbreak occurred in Boston early in 1764, and as the disease spread, the town on March 13, 1764 voted to allow anyone and everyone to be inoculated during the next five weeks. By March 30 there had been 699 cases of natural smallpox with 124 deaths, and 4,977 cases of inoculated smallpox with only 46 deaths.
    The preparatory treatment of the body by a milk-and-vegetable diet and purgatives that Adams followed was popularized by Dr. Adam Thomson of Philadelphia, in his *Discourse on the Preparation of the Body for the Small-Pox* (Philadelphia, 1750).

96.8   My Brother] Adams had two younger brothers, Peter Boylston (1738–1823) and Elihu (1741–1775). Probably Peter is referred to here.

96.30   Captn. Cunninghams] James Cunningham (1721–1795) was a glazier and militia officer who in 1741 married Elizabeth Boylston, sister of Adams's mother.

97.15   Deacon Palmer] Joseph Palmer (1716–1788), husband of Richard Cranch's sister.

98.10   Mr. Ayers] Carried letters between Adams and Abigail.

98.13–14   Miss Le Febure] Probably Rebecca, widow of John Lefavour, at whose home Cotton Tufts had been inoculated.

98.27–28   Daughter Betcy] Elizabeth Smith (1750–1815), the younger sister of Abigail.

101.19   Dr. Perkins]   Dr. Nathaniel Perkins.

101.26   Dr. Tufts]   See note 50.34–51.2.

101.33   Dr. Warren]   Joseph Warren (1741–1775), Harvard 1759; physician, orator, and soldier, he became a close friend of Adams before he was killed at the Battle of Bunker Hill.

103.18   Lord And Church]   Dr. Joseph Lord and Dr. Benjamin Church (1734–1776), Harvard 1754, a physician and poet who would later betray the patriot cause.

106.5   Dr. Gelston]   Of Nantucket, at this time resident physician at the inoculating hospital at Castle William in Boston harbor.

112.36   Mrs. Smith.]   Presumably Elizabeth (Storer) Smith (1726–1786), wife of Abigail's uncle, Isaac Smith, a Boston merchant in whose house Abigail was probably staying.

114.1–2   *A Dissertation on the Canon and Feudal Law*]   Published anonymously in the *Boston Gazette* (August 12 and 19, September 30, and October 21, 1765), this essay was Adams's first effort to determine the significance of New England in American history and his initial contribution to the writings of the American Revolution. He had begun writing the essay for the Sodalitas, a private club of Boston lawyers, but decided to expand it when he learned of Parliament's passage of the Stamp Act.

114.5–6   Dr. *Tillotson*]   John Tillotson (1630–1694), Archbishop of Canterbury, was a popular preacher and an advocate of unity among English Protestants. Vols. 1, 3, 7, 10 of his *Works* (1759 ed.) are in the *CJAL*.

118.2   can scarcely read.]   At this point, later printings of the *Dissertation* contained Adams's note: "I always consider the settlement of America with reverence and wonder, as the opening of a grand scene a design in Providence for the illumination of the ignorant and the emancipation of the slavish part of mankind all over the earth."

120.35   Lord Kaim's]   Henry Home, Lord Kames (1692–1782), Scottish judge and philosopher; several of his works are in the *CJAL*.

124.8   "Curse on . . . their country."]   Joseph Addison, *Cato*, IV.iv.

125.23   EBENEZER THAYER]   Col. Ebenezer Thayer Jr. (1721–1794) was Braintree's representative in the General Court and the father of Adams's law clerk Elisha Thayer (1748–1774).

128.29   governor's speech]   Gov. Francis Bernard addressed the General Court on September 15, 1765, defending Parliament's authority to tax the colonies.

128.34   fifth of Novembers]   Pope's Day, commemorating the failed Gunpowder Plot of 1605, which was an attempt by English Catholics to blow up the House of Lords during the opening of Parliament. In Boston this was usually the occasion for an outburst of anti-Catholic demonstrations and battles between Boston's South End and North End mobs.

132.1   one family]   Referring to the clan of Thomas Hutchinson and his brother-in-law Andrew Oliver.

139.18   Mr. Dudleys]   Joseph Dudley, Harvard 1751. He was admitted as an attorney and barrister in the Superior Court in 1762; he died 1767.

139.19   Mr. Adams's]   Samuel Adams (1722–1803), Harvard 1740, Adams's famous cousin and the leader of the popular party in Boston.

139.20–22   Cushing . . . Dr. Parker]   Thomas Cushing (1725–1788), Harvard 1744, a Boston merchant and political moderate who became speaker of the colony's House of Representatives in 1766 and later joined Adams as a delegate to the First and Second Continental Congresses; Samuel Welles, minister and judge; Samuel Pemberton, Boston alderman; Harrison Gray (1711–1794), provincial treasurer and receiver-general; Benjamin Austin; Joseph and Daniel Waldo; Henderson Inches; and Dr. Parker of Boston.

141.9   Major Miller]   Ebenezer Miller (1730–1811), of Braintree; militia officer, selectman, Anglican, and eventual Loyalist.

141.12   Mr. Cleverly]   Joseph Cleverly (1713–1802), Harvard 1733, was Adams's first school master.

141.18   Mr. Lane]   Of London.

141.19   Mr. Dubert]   Dennys De Berdt (1694?–1770), elected in 1765 as Massachusetts agent in London.

141.26   Etter]   Peter Etter.

141.29   at Mr. Lloyds]   In Boston.

141.33   Tom Boylstone]   Thomas Boylston (1721–1798), Boston merchant, a cousin of Adams's mother, and an eventual Loyalist.

142.8   Who is it, that has harrangued]   This refers to the actions of Thomas Hutchinson in his role as chief justice of the Superior Court, especially to what Adams and others thought was the favoritism Hutchinson had shown in cases concerning the appeals of the customs officer, Charles Paxton.

143.30–31   Governor Hopkins of Rhode Island and Mr. Ward]   The Ward-Hopkins controversy in the middle decades of the eighteenth century pitted Stephen Hopkins (1707–1785) and his Providence followers against Samuel Ward (1725–1776) and his Newport supporters for control of the government of the colony.

145.14   Mr. Hewes]   John Hughes, a friend of colonial agent Benjamin Franklin, who had secured the stamp agency in Philadelphia for his friend, almost costing Hughes his life during the ensuing protests against the Stamp Act.

147.1   *"Clarendon" to "William Pym"*] In 1765 a London newspaper printed four letters on the Stamp Act crisis by an author writing under the pseudonym of "William Pym." (The writer mistook the first name of the English parliamentarian and lawyer John Pym [1584–1643].) The British author writing as Pym assumed that the colonists were as dependent on Parliament as the English subjects in the mother county, and since the colonists benefited from the Seven Years' War fought in part on their behalf, they must pay their fair share of the costs of that conflict. If colonists were not bound by the Stamp Act, he wrote, they would be a separate people, an obviously ridiculous notion. Adams responded, writing in the *Boston Gazette* as Edward Hyde, Earl of Clarendon (1609–1674), who tried to reconcile the king and the Parliament; when that effort failed, Clarendon moved to the king's side during the Civil War.

147.16   Mr. Hampden] John Hampden (c. 1595–1643) was an Englishman who died fighting for Parliament in the English Civil War and was widely celebrated in America, as witnessed by the many places named in his honor. Before Adams wrote as "Clarendon," James Otis Jr., writing as "John Hampden," had responded to "William Pym" in a series of eight letters running from December 9, 1765 to January 27, 1766 in the *Boston Gazette.*

147.18–19   Lord Fau'kland] Lucius Cary, 2nd Viscount Falkland (c. 1610–1643) was an English soldier, author, and politician who died fighting for the king in the English Civil War.

148.10   our countryman Speed] Sometimes considered to be the first English historian as distinct from a mere chronicler, John Speed (1552?–1629) wrote *The History of Great Britain under the Conquests of the Romans, Saxons, Danes, and Normans* (London, 1611); Adams's quotation is from pp. 393–94.

150.27–28   two Mr. Boylstones . . . Mr. Hallowel] Nicholas Boylston and Thomas Boylston, wealthy Boston brothers and merchants who eventually become Loyalists; Isaac Smith, Adams's uncle, and John Smith, a Boston brazier; Benjamin Hallowell (1725–1799), comptroller of the customs in Boston, had married Mary Boylston, the sister of Nicholas and Thomas.

150.36   Tantivi.] They ride at full gallop.

152.29   I chose to go into Banishment] Actually Clarendon fled from England to France in 1667 during the reign of Charles II, not James II. As a leader in the king's ministry, he was held responsible for the failures in the Second Anglo-Dutch War of 1665–1667. When he fell out of favor with the king, and the House of Commons began impeachment proceedings against him, he left England and spent the rest of his life in exile. In France he completed his classic multi-volume *History of the Rebellion and Civil Wars in England* (1702–4); vols. two and three of the 1720 edition are in the *CJAL.*

153.15   Conduct of *Barbados*] Since the beginning of January 1766, Adams had been aware that the government of Barbados had submitted to the Stamp Act.

153.24–25   Struggle in *St. Christopher's*] An account of the spirited opposition to the Stamp Act on the island of St. Christopher had been printed in the *Boston Gazette*, December 9, 1765.

155.17–18   your patron and master] This almost certainly alludes to George Grenville, the British minister responsible for the Stamp Act.

157.19–20   Quare, Tomlinson, and Graham] Daniel Quare, William Tomlinson, and George Graham were watch- and clockmakers in early eighteenth-century Britain.

161.30   Hutch's History.] Thomas Hutchinson, *The History of the Colony of Massachusetts-Bay* (Boston, 1764), was the first of three volumes that were eventually published. A modern edition is Thomas Hutchinson, *The History of the Colony and Province of Massachusetts-Bay*, ed. Lawrence S. Mayo, 3 vols. (Cambridge, MA, 1936).

162.23   Who are to be understood . . .] This entry is a draft of an essay that Adams apparently never published, written in response to Jonathan Sewall, who had begun a series of articles over the name "Philanthrop" in the *Boston Evening Post* published from December 1, 1766 through March 2, 1767. In these essays Sewall praised the conduct and virtue of Governor Bernard, declaring that the "better sort" of people supported the governor. "Philanthrop" provoked numerous responses in the press.

163.26   This representative Body] The Massachusetts-Bay General Court was made up of the House of Representatives, the Council, and the governor. The governor was appointed by the Crown while the rest of the General Court was annually elected by those eligible to vote in the colony. Each year the General Court selected twenty-eight of its members to be the Council, with the governor having the authority to veto any of those selected. The Council was both an upper house and a group of executive assistants to the governor. The remaining members of the General Court constituted the House of Representatives.

165.11   except a C—k—e] James Cockle, the Salem customs official whose application for a writ of assistance led to the court case argued by James Otis Jr. in 1761.

167.8–9   a Belief that Subordination is not necessary] This quotation from "Philanthrop" captured the rationale for the English common law of seditious libel, which punished writings that brought public officials into disrepute even when the writings were true. Ever since the famous Zenger trial of 1735 the colonists had fought this common law notion of seditious libel, but only as it pertained to members of the executive. The colonists continued to punish libels against members of their representative assemblies.

167.12–13   Dr. Sewall's Meeting-House] Boston's Old South Church, where Joseph Sewall (1688–1769) was pastor.

170.19   poor distressed Family.] On March 2, 1767, Adams had been re-elected a selectman of Braintree; overseeing the poor was one of his duties. The town relieved selectman of that responsibility in 1786.

171.11   The Case of Cotton and Nye] Rowland Cotton sued Stephen Nye, his political rival in Sandwich, for slander after Nye publicly accused him of forging a General Court committee report. Adams had represented Nye when the case was tried in Barnstable Superior Court on May 14, 1767. The jury found for Cotton and awarded him £7 and costs.

174.35–36   that the Champion] Thomas Bradbury Chandler (1726–1790), an Anglican clergyman in New Jersey, had published in October 1767 *An Appeal to the Public, in Behalf of the Church of England in America*, which called for the establishing of a bishopric in America. Without a bishop, all American candidates for the ministry in the Church of England had to travel to England for ordination. The prospect of such an episcopate in America aroused bitter hostility among dissenters in many of the colonies.

176.1   *Instructions to Boston's Representatives*] On June 10, 1768 customs commissioners seized John Hancock's sloop *Liberty*, which provoked the town of Boston into creating a committee to draft instructions for its representatives. Adams's appointment on this committee was his first participation in Boston's political affairs since he had moved to the town in April 1768. Jonathan Sewall, the advocate general, sued Hancock for £9,000 on smuggling charges in November 1768. Adams defended Hancock in admiralty court and used the case to challenge the legislation that denied the defendant the right to trial by jury. The case ended in March 1769 when Sewall withdrew the charges.

179.4   At Mr. Quincys.] Mount Wollaston Farm on the shore of Quincy Bay, the home of Norton Quincy, Abigail's uncle.

179.7   Stony field Hill] An early name for what is now called President's Hill. Adams later acquired the property and made it part of his homestead.

180.7   Mr. Dickinson the Farmers Brother, and Mr. Reed] Philemon Dickinson, younger brother of John Dickinson, the author of *Letters from a Farmer in Pennsylvania* (1768), the most important and popular pamphlet in the period leading up the Revolution until Thomas Paine's *Common Sense* (1776); Joseph Reed (1741–1785), Princeton 1757. Reed later served as an aide-de-camp to George Washington, but in 1769 was practicing law in New Jersey.

180.20–21   did not see one Person intoxicated] Remarkable, since four-teen toasts were drunk at the event, followed by forty-five more toasts at the dinner, drunk in honor of John Wilkes's *North Briton*, No. 45, which in 1763 had criticized the king, leading to Wilkes's arrest. "No. 45" became a rally-ing cry on both sides of the Atlantic for liberty and freedom of speech.

180.26   at Noices.] Noyes's in Stoughton.

181.3   Mr. Jno. Gill.] John Gill, one of the publishers of the *Boston Gazette*.

181.14   Dr. Peckers] Dr. James Pecker (1724–1794).

181.17   Otis indulged himself . . .] This passage has been cited by histo-rians as possible evidence that the mental breakdown that terminated Otis's public career was not caused solely by the savage beating inflicted on him by customs commissioner John Robinson on September 5, 1769, the day after Adams made this entry.

182.30   funeral of the Child] On February 22, 1770, Christopher Snider, eleven or twelve years old, was shot and killed by Ebenezer Richardson, an employee of the customs service. Richardson had been taunted by a group of boys following a demonstration against a merchant who had violated the agreement to stop importation of most British goods. As early as 1768, in response to the Townshend duties, Boston had taken the lead in non-importation. Adams and his cousin by marriage Josiah Quincy acted as de-fense counsel for Richardson, who was found guilty of murder but was pardoned by the king.

184.30   Brother Porter] Samuel Porter, Harvard 1763, of Salem, was an attorney in the Superior Court who later became a Loyalist.

185.10   my old Friend the Governor of it.] Referring to Adams's Harvard classmate John Wentworth, whose family dominated New Hampshire politics during the generation preceding the Revolution.

185.19   Paul Dudley Woodbridge's.] Tavern in York, Maine.

185.21   my old Friend and Classmate David Sewall] A lawyer who later settled in York, Maine, and held important judicial offices.

186.10   Pattens] A tavern in Arundel, Maine.

186.17   Madam] Catherine Graham Macaulay (1731–1791) was an English political pamphleteer and historian whose *History of England, from the Acces-sion of James I to that of the Brunswick Line* (8 volumes, 1763–1783) was much admired by Whig radicals on both sides of the Atlantic. The five volumes of the third edition are in the *CJAL*.

187.13   the Editor in London] Thomas Hollis, an Englishman who pub-lished Adams's "Dissertation" and promoted radical Whig ideas on both sides of the Atlantic.

188.18   Last Fryday went to the Light House] An expedition of the committee of inspection to Little Brewster, or Beacon Island, in Boston Harbor, where Boston Light stood.

188.10   Mr. Royal Tyler]   Royall Tyler (1724–1771), a prominent merchant and the father of Royall Tyler, the younger, who later unsuccessfully wooed Adams's daughter Abigail.

188.11   Dr. Souths sermon]   Rev. Robert South (1634–1716), an English churchman noted for his sarcastic wit. He collected his sermons in a series entitled *Twelve Sermons Preached upon Several Occasions* (6 vols., 1692–1717). Vol. one of the fifth edition published in 1722 is in the *CJAL.*

188.17   Fable of the Bees]   *Fable of the Bees: or, Private Vices, Public Benefits* by Bernard Mandeville, published in England in 1714. The book, which anticipated much capitalist thinking, became infamous for seeming to justify selfishness and private spending as the source of public prosperity.

190.12   Cushing]   See note 139.20–22.

190.13   Dr. Cooper . . . Mr. Professor Winthrop]   The Rev. Samuel Cooper (1725–1783), Harvard 1743, minister at the liberal Congregationalist Brattle Street Church in Boston, was known for his eloquent sermons in support of the patriot cause; William Cooper, town clerk of Boston, was an active patriot and the older brother of Dr. Cooper; John Winthrop (1714–1779), was the Hollis Professor of Mathematics and Natural Philosophy at Harvard College, and one of Adams's undergraduate instructors.

191.2   At a Time, when . . .]   Recorded in Adams's diary, this essay on the rights of juries appears to have been intended for a newspaper, though no publication has been uncovered.

193.1   Special Verdict]   A jury's finding of a specific fact or facts, leaving the judge to determine the legal effect of the verdict.

195.5   Ezekl. Goldthwait]   Register of deeds for Suffolk County and a man of Tory sympathies, Ezekiel Goldthwait had been elected unanimously to his post for several successive terms. Challenged by Samuels Adams in April 1771, he was reelected 1123 to 467.

197.16–17   Douglass's History]   William Douglass, *A Summary, Historical and Political* 2 vols. (Boston, 1749–51). The 1760 ed. is in the *CJAL.*

197.24–25   my Chum David Wyer]   Wyer, Harvard 1758, practiced law in Falmouth (now Portland), Maine.

200.35–36   Dr. Clarks sermons.]   Samuel Clark (1675–1729), was rector of St. James's, Westminster and a prolific writer on theological subjects.

201.25   his Cousin, Peter Adams's Wife at Braintree.]   Peter Adams was a cousin of Deacon John Adams, Adams's father; his second wife was Elizabeth Rawson.

202.26   their old Tenor.]   Referring to the older paper currency issued by
Massachusetts that had depreciated badly during the first three decades of the
eighteenth century. In 1737 the colony issued a new series of notes called New
Tenor money, but Adams often continued to refer to money in terms of O.T.

204.30–31   closed their long Glories . . . of base Mankind.]   From
Alexander Pope, *The First Epistle of the Second Book of Horace* (1737), lines 13–14.

204.32   Sudbury Causey]   A causeway through the Great Meadows, the
freshwater wetlands formed by the Sudbury and Concord rivers.

205.30   She is a new Light]   New Lights were the most active evangelical
participants in the mid-eighteenth-century Great Awakening, seeking to revive aspects of the traditional Puritan faith by challenging the staid and for-
mulaic practices of those they called Old Lights.

207.30   Langdon]   Timothy Langdon, who had been recommended for
admission to the bar just the day before.

208.12   So that if they should live to bring up Billy]   The Cranches' three
children were William (1769–1855), Harvard 1787, who became chief justice of
the circuit court of the District of Columbia; Elizabeth (1763–1811), who married Rev. Jacob Norton of Weymouth; and Lucy (1767–1846), who married
John Greenleaf.

208.32   to my Brother.]   Adams's youngest brother, Elihu, who lived in
Braintree on property inherited from his father.

211.39   a Mayhew]   Jonathan Mayhew (1720–1766), Harvard 1744, liberal
Congregational minister in Boston who is often considered to have launched
the popular assault on the Crown and the Anglican Church with his *Discourse
concerning Unlimited Submission to the Higher Powers* (Boston, 1750).

215.34   The Earl of Strafford]   Thomas Wentworth, 1st Earl of Strafford
(1593–1641), was an English statesman who initially opposed the arbitrary
policies of James I and Charles I but later became a supporter of the Crown.
When a parliamentary impeachment failed in the House of Lords in 1640,
Strafford was condemned by a parliamentary bill of attainder and executed in
1641. He had become a popular symbol of absolutism.

215.36   Sir Robert Walpole]   Walpole (1676–1745) became a Whig martyr
when he was imprisoned by a Tory government in the Tower of London,
January–July 1712, for alleged misconduct in office. While serving as first lord
of the treasury and leader of the government, 1721–42, Walpole was denounced as "the father of corruption" for his use of patronage and bribery to
maintain power.

215.38   Harley]   Robert Harley, 1st Earl of Oxford (1661–1724), an English
statesman who began as a Whig but later led a Tory ministry under Queen
Anne.

218.28–29   Deacon Palmer]   See note 97.15.

219.1   House in Queen Street]   Queen Street in Boston was that part of present-day Court Street that curved around from present-day Washington Street to Hanover Street.

220.1   Parson Howard]   Rev. Simeon Hayward.

220.4   Admirall Montagu's Manners.]   British naval officer John Montague (1719–1795) had become commander-in-chief of the North American station in 1771. In 1772, in response to the efforts of a local Rhode Island sheriff to arrest the commander of HMS *Gaspee*, which was attempting to enforce the Navigation Acts in Narragansett Bay, Montague threatened to hang as pirates any colonists who tried to rescue "any vessel the King's schooner may take carrying on an illicit trade."

220.27–28   Burners of the Gaspee]   On June 9, 1772, citizens of Providence burned the *Gaspee*, a British revenue schooner, when it went aground in Narragansett Bay. A special royal commission was appointed to investigate the incident but could not gather the names of anyone to punish.

223.1   *On the Independence of the Judges*]   The issue in this exchange between Adams and William Brattle, Harvard 1722, a wealthy landowner, military officer, and senior member of the Council who had previously been a defender of colonial liberties, involved the degree to which English judges had been historically dependent on the Crown. The debate was touched off by the Crown's attempt in 1772 to add the province's superior court judges to the royal civil list, which meant that their salaries would now be paid by the Crown out of the customs revenues rather than by the General Court. This threatened to deprive the colonists of a traditional check on the judiciary.
     At a meeting in December 1772 the town of Cambridge condemned the idea of the Crown paying the salaries of the judges as a violation of the colonists' ancient liberties. At the meeting, however, Major General Brattle unexpectedly defended the Crown's paying of the judges' salaries, and, according to Adams's diary, challenged all patriots, including John Adams by name, to debate him on the subject in the newspapers. Brattle contended that the province's judges in effect possessed their tenure not *durante bene placito* ("as long as it pleases [the prince]"), but rather they held their offices with the same life tenure as the judges in the mother country—*quamdiu bene se gesserint* ("as long as they conduct themselves properly"). Thus the Crown's assumption of their salaries, said Brattle, did not threaten the judges' independence. In 1701 Parliament had passed the Act of Settlement which, among other things, had declared that judges served not at the pleasure of the Crown but during good behavior. Brattle argued that this act did not create a new condition of judicial tenure, but had only reaffirmed the previously existing common law that granted life tenure in judicial offices.
     Adams took up Brattle's challenge, and sought to demonstrate that prior to the Act of Settlement all English judges had not been independent, but had

held their offices at the pleasure of the Crown. The Act of Settlement, he argued, did not reaffirm old law, as Brattle claimed, but created new law that unfortunately had not been extended to the colonies. This meant that the judges of Massachusetts, like the judges in the other colonies, remained totally dependent on the Crown. Adams's lengthy argument with Brattle was only one of many contests over the independence of the judges that were taking place in nearly all the colonies.

223.33   derived solely from the late act of parliament]   The preamble of the Townshend Revenue Act of 1767 stated that revenues raised by the Townshend duties would be used to pay the salaries of judges in those colonies where it would be found necessary.

226.1–2   a few words of Lord Holt]   This passage from the opinion of Chief Justice Sir John Holt (1642–1710) appears in Sir Bartholomew Shower, *Reports of Cases Adjudged in the Court of King's Bench, in the Reign of . . . King William III, with Several Learned Arguments* (London, 1708), 1: 353.

226.18   Lord Raymond.]   Sir Robert Raymond, 1st Baron Raymond, *Reports of Cases Argued and Adjudged in the Courts of King's Bench and Common Pleas, in the Reigns of the late King William, Queen Anne, King George the First, and King George the Second*, 2nd ed., 3 vols. (London, 1765); in the CJAL.

226.25   the act of 12 & 13 Will. 3d.]   The Act of Settlement of 1701.

230.14   Mr. Read]   John Read (1679/80–1749) was the dominant figure in New England law in the early eighteenth century.

230.19–20   the late Judge Auchmuty]   Robert Auchmuty the elder (d. 1750 or 1751), a Scot trained in the Middle Temple who was an admiralty judge for New England from 1733 to 1741.

232.4   the act of King William]   The Act of Settlement of 1701.

234.1–3   *Reply of the Massachusetts House of Representatives to Governor Hutchinson's First Message*]   Massachusetts Governor Thomas Hutchinson (1711–1780) addressed the General Court on January 6, 1773, telling its members that denial of the authority of Parliament over the colony was not possible. Such denials, which were becoming all too frequent, he said, were repugnant to the principles of the constitution. If the people were to benefit from the rights and liberties of the English constitution, then they had to obey the laws enacted by Parliament, the bulwark of their rights and liberties. Hutchinson then invoked the conventional English doctrine of sovereignty—that there must exist in every state one final, supreme, indivisible power, and in the British Empire that power lay in the king in Parliament. He knew of "no Line," he concluded, "that can be drawn between the Supreme Authority of Parliament and the total Independence of the Colonies: it is impossible there should be two independent Legislatures in one and the same State." By posing the alternatives in this stark manner, Hutchinson assumed that no right-thinking colonist would choose independence.

Although not a member of the House of Representatives, Adams was consulted in the drafting of the House's reply that dealt with the constitutional nature of the empire and the colonies' position in it. Following the governor's rebuttal on February 16, the House responded a second time on March 2, with Adams once again being very much involved.

234.24   an Act] The Declaratory Act of 1766, which had accompanied Parliament's repeal of the Stamp Act, stated that Parliament had "full power and authority to make laws and statutes of sufficient force and validity to bind the colonies and people of *America*, subjects of the crown of *Great Britain*, in all cases—whatsoever."

238.32–33   "America *was not annexed to the Realm*] For these assertions by the Stuart kings that colonies were without the realm, Adams was apparently drawing on the 4th ed. of Thomas Pownall, *The Administration of the Colonies* (London, 1768), 48–49.

240.17–18   The celebrated Author whom your Excellency has quoted] Emmerich de Vattel, from his *The Law of Nations, or Principle of the Law of Nature, applied to the Conduct and Affairs of Nations and Sovereigns* (c. 1760).

245.26–27   your Excellency's Collection of Papers lately published.] Hutchinson, *A Collection of Original Papers Relative to the History of the Colony of Massachusetts-Bay* (Boston, 1769), 482, 483, 496, 499, 506, 539, 521.

246.23   Mr. Neal's History of New-England] Daniel Neal, *The History of New England containing an Impartial Account of the Civil and Ecclesiastical Affairs . . . to the Year of our Lord, 1700*, 2 vols. (London, 1720); only the first vol. is in the *CJAL*.

247.36–37   the same Author who is quoted by your Excellency] Vattel.

252.5–6   by justice Fortescue Aland in the preface to his reports] Sir John Fortescue Aland, *Reports of Select Cases in All the Courts of Westminster-Hall* (London, 1748); in the *CJAL*.

253.33   Hengham, Britton, Fleta] Early standard authorities on English law; all in the *CJAL*.

255.7–8   lord Gilbert's historical view of the court of exchequer] Sir Geoffrey Gilbert, *An Historical View of the Court of Exchequer* (London, 1738); in the *CJAL*.

255.16–17   See also Gilbert's history] Sir Geoffrey Gilbert, *The History and Practice of the High Court of Chancery* (London, 1758); in the *CJAL*.

256.25   the mirror of justices] *The Mirror of Justices*, trans. William Hughes (London, 1742).

256.28–257.3   "Dictum est . . . *jurisdictionem.*"]   Adams here strings together a series of excerpts from a section of Henry de Bracton, *Le Legibus et
Consuetudinibus Angliae* (London, 1640). The full passage reads in translation: "We have spoken in the [preceding] of ordinary jurisdiction which belongs to the king. Now we must discuss delegated jurisdiction, where one
having no authority of his own has authority committed to him by another,
since [the king] cannot unaided determine all causes [and] jurisdictions, that
his labour may be lessened, the burden being divided among many, he must
select from his realm wise and God-fearing men in whom there is the truth
of eloquence, who shun avarice which breeds covetousness, and make of
them justices, sheriffs, and other ministers and officials. . . . Some justices
are major, general, permanent and of greater importance, who remain at the
side of the king and whose duty it is to correct the wrongs and errors of all
others. There are also other permanent judges, sitting in a place certain, that
is, in the bench, who determine all pleas for which they have a warrant, all of
whom begin to have jurisdiction after having taken an oath. There are other
justices, travelling from place to place, as from county to county, sometimes
for all pleas, sometimes for certain special pleas, as for assises only and [the
delivery of] gaols, who begin to have authority without an oath, when they
have received the lord king's writ of warrant. There are also justices appointed for certain [named] assises, two or three or several, who are not permanent, and who lose their jurisdiction once they have discharged their
office. Their power is this: once a cause (one or several) is committed to
them, though it is committed simply, their jurisdiction is extended to all
matters necessary to determine the suit, so far as judgment and the execution
of judgment are concerned, and so if there is an incidental or emergent action preliminary to it. [But] they cannot extend their jurisdiction to other
things or other persons, nor take cognisance of things other than those com-
prised in their commission, since the limits of a mandate must be strictly observed. Although some judges are permanent, it is evident that their
jurisdiction may nevertheless be ended in many ways, for example, by the
death of him who delegated, or the death of him to whom the cause was delegated, personally and by name. *And so if the principal revokes the jurisdiction.* . . ." From *Bracton of the Laws and Customs of England*, translated by
Samuel E. Thorne (Cambridge, MA, 1968–1977), II: 306–308.

257.33–34   Sir Tho's Ray. 217.]   Sir Thomas Raymond, *Reports of Special
Cases* (London, 1743); in the *CJAL.*

257.38   a scire facias]   A writ requiring the party against whom it is issued
to appear and show cause why a judicial record should not be enforced or an-
nulled.

258.10   Rushworth 1366]   John Rushworth, ed., *Historical Collections of
Private Passages of State*, 4 part in 7 vols. (London, 1659–1701); later eds. of
vol. 1 are in the *CJAL.*

259.30   see Skinner's reports]   Robert Skinner, *Reports of Cases Adjudged in the Court of King's Bench from the Thirty-Third Year of . . . Charles II to the Ninth Year of William III* (London, 1728); in the *CJAL.*

260.31   either durante beneplacito . . . se bene gesserit] Either at the king's pleasure or during good behavior. See note 223.1.

261.1   custos retulorum] Keeper of the rolls, that is, a justice of the peace charged with custody of court records.

262.33   Addington] Isaac Addington (1645–1715), the first secretary in Massachusetts appointed under the charter of 1691.

269.10–11   one of our greatest Historians] William Robertson, *The History of the Reign of Emperor Charles V* (c. 1762).

269.14–15   "A Constitution so contradictory . . ."] Lord Kames, quoted from Adams's "Dissertation on the Canon and Feudal Law," from which much of this paragraph is drawn.

269.17   a very celebrated Writer] Rousseau, quoted from Adams's "Dissertation."

271.29   Sir Edwin Sandis] Sir Edwin Sandys (1561–1629).

272.13–14   a very able Lawyer in this Country] James Otis Jr., *The Rights of the Colonies Asserted and Proved* (Boston, 1764), quoting Pufendorf and Grotius.

272.30–31   in the beforementioned Case to our Purpose.] That is, *Calvin's Case, or the case of the Union of Scotland and England* (1608), in which Chief Justice Coke held that Scottish subjects born after King James VI of Scotland became James I of England could hold land in England, as well as in Scotland, because both Scots and Englishmen owed allegiance to the same king.

275.24   from an anonimous Pamphlet] Apparently referring to Thomas Pownall, *The Administration of the Colonies*, which the House had cited in its January 26 reply.

276.3   Sir Ferdinando Gorges] Sir Ferdinando Gorges (c. 1568–1647), English author and promoter of exploration of New England. His "Account" appears in his book *A Brief Narration of the Originall Undertakings of the Advancement of Plantations into the Parts of America* (London, 1658).

276.29   Province Agent Mr. Dummer] Jeremiah Dummer (1681–1739), *A Defence of the New-England Charters* (London, 1721).

278.9–10   a Letter of Mr. *Stoughton*] Lt. Gov. William Stoughton's letter of 1677, quoted in Thomas Hutchinson, *History of the Colony and Province of Massachusetts-Bay*, ed. Lawrence S. Mayo, 3 vols. (Cambridge, MA: Harvard University Press, 1936), 1: 270.

281.22   The Act of Parliament passed in 1741] This act put an end to the

Land Bank of the province, which had tended to inflate the currency. The
General Court passed legislation to soften its effects.

281.38   a learned Writer]   Vattel.

282.14   Mr. Hooker]   Richard Hooker (1554?–1600), quoted by Locke,
Two Treatises of Government, Second, ch. 11.

285.3   1773. MARCH 5th. FRYDAY.]   In this entry Adams refers to his
defense of Captain Thomas Preston, the commander of the British soldiers
who fired on the mob in the "Boston Massacre" of March 5, 1770. Although
many Bostonians wanted Preston and his soldiers to have no defense counsel
whatsoever, his co-counsel Josiah Quincy told his father, who had severely
criticized his son for taking the case, that he had undertaken to defend the
soldiers only after leading patriots, including Samuel Adams, John Hancock,
Dr. Joseph Warren, and Samuel Cooper, had urged him to do so. Neither
Adams's nor Quincy's law practice suffered as a consequence of their defending Preston and his men.

285.4   Mr. Hunts Meeting House]   The Old North Church, where John
Hunt was minister.

286.7–8   by the Exertions of Prerogative]   On the first day of the new
General Court on May 26, Adams was elected a member of the Council, but
his election was vetoed by Gov. Hutchinson.

287.31   Deacon Palmer and Mr. Is. Smith]   Joseph Palmer (see note 97.15)
and Isaac Smith Sr. (1719–1787), a Boston merchant and shipowner who was
Abigail's uncle and the father of Rev. Isaac Smith Jr., who spent the war in
England but returned in 1784 and became for a while librarian of Harvard
College.

287.31–2   Mr. Trumble]   John Trumbull (1750–1831), Adams's law clerk.

288.3   Cushing, Pemberton and Swift]   For Cushing, see note 139.20–22;
Samuel Pemberton, alderman of Boston; Samuel Swift (1715–1775), Boston
lawyer and radical leader of the town's North End.

288.4–5   Bollans Letters]   William Bollan, former Massachusetts colonial
agent in London. The Otises had opposed him for being an Anglican, and he
was replaced in 1762. From England he now wrote the Council urging compliance with British regulations.

288.9   *James Warren*]   A farmer and trusted friend and advisor of Adams,
James Warren (1726–1808), Harvard 1745, led the popular party in his home
town of Plymouth. In 1775 he became the president of the Provincial Congress of Massachusetts. He was married to the poet, playwright, and historian
Mercy Otis Warren.

288.18   Coll Doane]   Col. Elisha Doane (c. 1725–1783), wealthy merchant
and long-time client of Adams.

288.19   Balch Should repeat them] Nathaniel Balch (1735–1807?), a Boston hatter and member of the Sons of Liberty, known for his talent for expressing humorous anecdotes and sayings.

288.34   But for him, this Tea might have been Saved] Many Whigs thought that Gov. Hutchinson might have defused the crisis if he had allowed the ship carrying the tea to leave Boston harbor and return to England without unloading its cargo. Instead, Hutchinson stubbornly insisted the tea be unloaded and the duties be paid. Most other royal governors had a weaker sense of duty and thus avoided a similar crisis in their colonies.

291.12–13   an "Abridgment of what are called English Liberties,"] Quoting a statement made by Hutchinson in a January 20, 1769, letter to Thomas Whately. When colonial agent Benjamin Franklin sent the Whately letters to Massachusetts at the end of 1772 (see Chronology for 1772), the revelation of statements like this one effectively destroyed Hutchinson's reputation in the province.

292.27   Skirmish of the sea Deities] A poem by Mrs. Warren that Adams saw into publication in the *Boston Gazette*, March 21, 1774.

294.15   the public News] News of the Boston Port Act by which Parliament ordered the closing of the port of Boston to all trade on June 1, 1774 as punishment for the Tea Party.

THE CONTINENTAL CONGRESS, 1774–1775

299.20   John Sullivan] John Sullivan (1740–1795), Revolutionary major general and statesman who served as a delegate from New Hampshire to the Continental Congress.

300.1   James Sullivan] James Sullivan (1744–1808), lawyer and patriot and younger brother of John Sullivan; he later served as Democratic-Republican governor of Massachusetts.

300.8   David Sewall] See note 185.21.

300.29   John Lowell] John Lowell, Harvard 1760, lawyer and later a federal judge.

302.6   Dr. Gardiner] Dr. Sylvester Gardiner (1707–1786), Boston physician and druggist and one of Adams's earliest clients; he founded Gardiner, Maine.

304.17   Killing of a Child by R.] See note 182.30.

304.31–32   Fleets Paper, Meins Chronicle] Thomas and John Fleet's conservative Boston *Evening Post*, which expired in 1775, and John Mein and John Fleeming's *Boston Chronicle*, which lasted for only three years, 1767–1770.

306.17   Mr. Waldo] Francis Waldo, Harvard 1747, a leading citizen of Falmouth (later Portland), Maine; he later became a Loyalist exile.

306.18–19   Cause of King, of Scarborough vs. a Mob] Richard King, a well-to-do farmer, storekeeper, and timber exporter took the Administration's side during the Stamp Act controversy. On March 13, 1766, a mob of twenty or thirty men attacked his home in Scarborough, Massachusetts (now Maine), terrorized his wife, five children, and servants, smashed furniture and dishes, hacked walls, and destroyed papers. (One of the children was Rufus King, who would become a leading Federalist and a friend of the Adamses.) King sued his persecutors, claiming damages of £2,000; after unsatisfactory verdicts in two trials in 1773 that awarded only £200 in damages, a third trial was held in July 1774 in which Adams became involved as King's counsel. Despite Adams's efforts on his behalf, King was awarded only £60 additional damages.

307.4   a Publication of Mr. Burke's in 1766] Edmund Burke's "A Short Account of the Late Short Administration," a manifesto of the Whig ministry led by Lord Rockingham, which during its brief time in office (July 1765– July 1766) repealed the Stamp Act.

307.5   Junius Americanus] The pen name of Arthur Lee (1740–1792), polemicist and diplomat who earned degrees in both medicine and law in Britain, where he wrote under this pseudonym. As one of the American commissioners in Paris, he later helped negotiate the agreement that brought France into the Revolutionary War on the side of the Americans.

307.25   Roger Sherman] Roger Sherman (1721–1793) would later serve alongside Adams as a member of the committee appointed to draft the Declaration of Independence. Adams would describe him as "an old Puritan, as honest as an angel and as firm in the cause of American Independence as Mount Atlas."

307.33   Circular Letter] The Massachusetts Circular Letter, the House's protest against the Townshend Acts of 1767, was sent to other colonial assemblies in February 1768; it was largely the work of Samuel Adams.

308.28–29   Mr. Low, . . . Mr. Van Shaw] Cornelius Low, Peter T. Curtenius, Pascal Smith, and Peter Van Schaack, all of the New York committee of correspondence; Van Schaack would later refuse to swear allegiance to the new state of New York and be banished to England in 1778.

308.38   Mr. Ebenezer Hazard] A scholar and bookseller who was just beginning his project of collecting documents pertaining to the early history of America, Ebenezer Hazard (1744–1817) has been called America's first historical editor. He eventually published *Historical Collections; Consisting of State Papers . . . Intended as Material for an History of the United States* (Philadelphia, 1792–94) and became postmaster general, 1782–1789.

309.8–9   Their Resolutions are really grand.] Resolutions of the Virginia Convention that had met in Williamsburg August 1–6, 1774 to elect and instruct its delegates to the First Continental Congress.

309.10   Mr. Peter Vanbrugh Livingstons] Peter Van Brugh Livingston (1710–1792), Yale 1731, was a New York merchant and patriot and the brother of Philip and William Livingston.

309.11–12   Scott, McDougal, Phillip Livingston, Mr. Thomas Smith] John Morin Scott (c. 1730–1784), Yale 1746, was a lawyer and polemicist who, along with William Livingston and William Smith in the New York "Triumvirate," supported the Whig Presbyterian cause against the Church of England in the 1750s. He helped organize the New York Sons of Liberty; Alexander McDougall (1732–1786), petty merchant and member of the New York Sons of Liberty. Imprisoned by the New York assembly for a pamphlet published in 1769, he became known as the "Wilkes of America"; Philip Livingston (1716–1778), Yale 1737, merchant and speaker of the New York assembly in 1768, and one of the founders of Kings' College (Columbia). He was a member of the Continental Congress, 1774–1778, and brother of William Livingston and Peter Van Brugh Livingston; Thomas Smith of New York.

310.14   Nassau Hall Colledge] The College of New Jersey, later Princeton.

310.39–40   Uncle Quincy] Norton Quincy (1716–1801), Harvard 1736, Abigail's uncle.

310.40–311.1   Mr. Thaxter] John Thaxter Jr., son of John Thaxter Sr., who was Abigail's uncle by marriage. Thaxter Jr. was Adams's law clerk and a tutor of his sons; in 1779 he accompanied Adams to Europe as his private secretary.

311.5–6   Tudor, Trumble, and Hill.] Law clerks in Adams's office.

312.6   Mr. Mifflins] Thomas Mifflin (1744–1800) was a merchant and politician and a Pennsylvanian delegate to the Continental Congress. John Singleton Copley painted a remarkable portrait of him and his wife Sarah Morris.

312.9   Charles Thompson] Charles Thomson (1729–1824), secretary of the Continental Congress, 1774–1789.

312.12   Collins] Stephen Collins, a Friend, that is, a Quaker, a member of the Society of Friends, and sometimes courier.

312.14–15   Mr. Lynch, Mr. Gadsden, Mr. Middleton, and young Mr. Rutledge] Thomas Lynch Sr. (1727–1776), a South Carolina delegate to the First and Second Continental Congresses; Christopher Gadsden (1724–1805), merchant and radical leader of the mechanics in Charleston and a South Carolina delegate to the First and Second Continental Congresses; Henry Middleton

(1717–1784), South Carolina planter and legislator who served as the second president of the Continental Congress, 1774–1775. He was a moderate who hoped for reconciliation with Britain before resigning from the Congress in February 1776; Edward Rutledge (1749–1800), lawyer from South Carolina and member of the Continental Congress who at first opposed independence but eventually persuaded his delegation to vote for it. He was the younger brother of John Rutledge.

312.21   Mr. Blair]   Rev. Samuel Blair.

312.21–22   Mr. Smith, an old Gentleman]   Samuel Smith, brother of the Rev. Thomas Smith of Maine.

312.22   introduced to us, by his Son.]   Thomas Smith.

312.23   Another Mr. Smith]   John Bayard Smith (1742–1812), a delegate from Pennsylvania.

312.35   Dr. Shippen]   Dr. William Shippen Jr. (1736–1808) studied medicine in London and Edinburgh. He was in charge of a set of anatomical paintings and castings of the human body that the London philanthropist Dr. John Frothergill had given to the newly established Pennsylvania hospital. These paintings and castings were a well-known attraction for Philadelphia tourists, including Adams.

313.22   Mr. Bayards . . . with Mr. Sprout]   John Bayard; James Sproat (1722–1793), Yale 1741, minister of the Second Presbyterian Church of Philadelphia.

313.24   Governor Ward of Rhode Island]   Samuel Ward, governor of Rhode Island for several years in the 1760s and a delegate to the First and Second Continental Congresses. See also note 143.30–31.

314.10–11   the Scandalous History of Sir Egerton Leigh]   The attorney general of South Carolina, Sir Egerton Leigh (1733–1781) fathered a child with Mary Bremar (c. 1754–1777), the younger sister of his wife and a niece of Henry Laurens, who later served as president of the Continental Congress. In December 1772 Egerton forced Bremar to sail to England near the end of her term without a midwife. When she went into labor while the ship was still in harbor, Leigh allegedly intervened to prevent the captain from putting her ashore. Bremar then gave birth on board the vessel, and the child died within days. After arriving in England Mary Bremar made a statement about the affair before the Lord Mayor's Court in London. The scandal served to confirm patriot assumptions about the corrupt and self-serving nature of royal placemen.

315.3   Dr. Smith, Mr. Galloway, Mr. Vaughan]   The Rev. William Smith (1727–1803), Anglican clergyman and educator, and provost of the Philadelphia Academy that became the College of Philadelphia, opposed the various Parliamentary measures of the 1760s and early 1770s but did not sympathize with the move toward independence; Joseph Galloway (1731–1803), who as speaker of the Pennsylvania assembly vainly sought to keep the colonies in the empire, became one of the most famous of the Loyalists; Mr. Vaughn of Philadelphia.

315.9   Dr. Witherspoon] Jonathan Witherspoon (1723–1794), a Presbyterian clergyman who immigrated from Scotland in 1768 to become president of the College of New Jersey (Princeton), also became an active patriot and a member of the Continental Congress in 1776.

315.10   Coll. R.H. Lee] Richard Henry Lee (1732–1794), Virginia legislator, zealous patriot, and member of a famous family of Lees that included his brothers Arthur Lee, Thomas Ludwell Lee, Francis Lightfoot Lee, and William Lee, and his sister Alice Lee Shippen, the wife of Dr. William Shippen Jr. (see note 312.35).

315.11   Sherriff of London] William Lee (1739–1795), Virginia merchant and diplomat who was elected sheriff of London in 1773 and in 1775 elected alderman of London, the only American ever to have held that post.

315.12   Dr. Arthur Lee] See note 307.5.

316.12   Mr. Cæsar Rodney] Cæsar Rodney (1728–1784), speaker of the Delaware legislature and a delegate to the Continental Congress.

316.13   two Mr. Tilghmans from Maryland] Matthew Tilghman (1718–1790), leader of the Maryland delegation to the Continental Congress, and possibly one of his brothers, William or Edward.

316.18   Mr. Joseph Reed] Joseph Reed (1741–1785), lawyer and in 1767 secretary of New Jersey; he later moved to Pennsylvania and in 1774 was appointed a member of the Philadelphia committee of correspondence.

316.21–22   Harrison from Virginia] Benjamin Harrison (1726–1791), planter and statesman who later was elected governor of Virginia. His son, William Henry Harrison, became the ninth President of the United States.

317.7   His Brother] John Rutledge (1739–1800), older brother of Edward Rutledge; he studied law in England and returned to become a distinguished member of the South Carolina legislature and later a delegate to the Continental Congress. Like his brother, he initially sought to hold the empire together. He helped write the new state constitution of South Carolina and later became governor of the state.

317.8   Duane] James Duane (1733–1797) of New York, jurist and delegate to the Continental Congress, where he was unsympathetic to those like Adams who wanted to move faster toward independence.

317.13   Ruggles] Timothy Ruggles (1711–1795), Harvard 1732, lawyer and speaker of the Massachusetts House of Representatives and member of the Stamp Act Congress.

317.19   George Haley] George Hayley was a British merchant who owned a ship in partnership with John Hancock and was known, according to Adams, to be "a ministerial Man."

318.25   Major Sullivan] See note 299.20.

319.9–10   a confused Account from Boston, of a dreadfull Catastrophy.] There were rumors of bloodshed and bombardment in Boston sparked by British General Thomas Gage's removal on September 1, 1774 of powder and weapons from the Quarry Hill arsenal. Thousands of patriot militia in New England began marching toward Boston and only halted when the reports turned out to be false. This massive insurgency anticipated the real bloodshed that occurred six months later, and suggested that the views of a great many ordinary Americans had advanced well beyond those of the more conciliatory members of Congress.

320.11   Mr. Rice] Nathan Rice (1754–1834), Harvard 1773, Adams's law clerk.

320.22   *William Tudor*] One of Adams's law students, William Tudor (1750–1819), Harvard 1769, became a life-long friend and the first judge advocate of the Continental army.

320.31   Dulce et decorum est pro Patria mori.] "It is sweet and becoming to die for one's country." Horace, *Odes*, iii.ii.13.

320.32–321.2   Wouldst thou receive . . . Fight her Sword.] Lines from *The Judgment of Hercules, a Poem. By a Student of Oxford* (Glasgow, 1743), p. 9; this book was by Robert Lowth (1710–1787), professor of poetry at Oxford and later Bishop of London.

321.16   Resolutions of the County of Suffolk] In response to Parliament's Coercive Acts (see Chronology for 1774), Suffolk County in Massachusetts (where Boston is located) on September 9, 1774 adopted a set of radical resolves written by Dr. Joseph Warren, Samuel Adams, and other patriots. The county declared that the Coercive Acts were gross infractions of English rights and that the people of the province owed no obedience to them. Paul Revere carried a copy of the resolves to Philadelphia where the Continental Congress on September 17 endorsed them in a display of American solidarity.

322.15   the General, Gage] Thomas Gage (c. 1720–1787), commander in chief of British forces in North America; per Parliament's Coercive or "Intolerable" Acts of 1774 he replaced Thomas Hutchinson as royal governor of Massachusetts.

324.28   Dr. Allisons Meeting] Francis Allison (1705–1779), provost of the College of Philadelphia and minster of the First Presbyterian Church, on the south side of Market Street between Second and Third Streets.

325.5   the Romish Chappell.]   St. Mary's Roman Catholic Church, built in 1763 on Fourth Street between Spruce and Locust.

325.31   Mr. McKean]   Thomas McKean (1734–1817), lawyer and fervent patriot who represented Delaware in the Congress almost continuously throughout the Revolution. He later moved to Pennsylvania and held important offices in that state.

325.32   Chace, Johnson, Paca, Dr. Morgan, Mr. R. Penn]   Samuel Chase (1741–1811), an ardent revolutionary and Maryland delegate to the Continental Congress who later became an associate justice of the Supreme Court; Thomas Johnson (1732–1819), a Maryland delegate to the Continental Congress who later became the state's first governor; William Paca (1740–1799), elected to the First and Second Continental Congress from Maryland and later the third governor of the state; Dr. John Morgan (1735–1789), a physician who proposed establishing a medical school connected with the College of Philadelphia, and who later became professor of medicine there. He served as chief physician of the Revolutionary army; Richard Penn (1735–1811), grandson of William Penn and lieutenant-governor of Pennsylvania, 1771–1773. He conveyed the Congress's "Olive Branch" petition to the king in 1775.

327.1   *Massachusettensis*]   Beginning in December 1774, Daniel Leonard (1740–1829), writing as "Massachusettensis," launched a series of seventeen essays that would appear in the Boston press over the next four months. Leonard later said that in the aftermath of the Tea Party he had been solicited by several of "the principled gentlemen" in the province "to endeavour to trace the discontents of the people to their source, to point out the criminality and the ruinous tendency of the opposition to the authority of parliament, and to convince the people of the justice of the measures of Administration."
    Leonard, a prosperous lawyer in Taunton, Massachusetts, had been a friend of Adams. In 1769 he had been elected to the House of Representatives and had supported the popular Whig party led by Samuel Adams. Following the Tea Party, however, he turned toward the governor's administration, and in 1774 accepted an appointment as one of the mandamus councilors that the Coercive Acts dictated in place of the elected Council.
    When Adams read the Massachusettensis articles in the Boston newspapers, he thought the author was his good friend, Jonathan Sewall, who some years earlier had gone over to the administration and become attorney general. Indeed, in 1768 Sewall had tried to talk Adams into accepting the position of advocate general of the Court of Admiralty. Adams later recalled that he turned the offer down at once, but since his diary is blank for most of 1768 his immediate reaction to the offer is not known. Although Adams had sparred good-naturedly in the press with his friend Sewall in 1763 and 1766–1767, this time, writing as "Novanglus," he took the challenge much more seriously. Not until a few years before his death in 1826 did Adams come to realize that Massachusettensis was not Sewall but Leonard. Indeed, Leonard's

name did not appear publicly as their author until the Massachusettensis pieces were reprinted in a London edition in 1822.

While the letters of Massachusettensis were reprinted completely in at least a half-dozen newspapers and as a pamphlet in several cities, including New York and London, Adams's Novanglus letters were partially reprinted in only two New England papers.

327.24   *fas vel nefas*]   By fair means and foul.

328.17–18   but their having accepted commissions under our king?]   After Leonard accepted the mandamus appointment to the Council, his neighbors in Taunton made him and his family so uncomfortable that they were forced to move to Boston.

337.15–16   known by the name of whig and tory]   These were party names popular in eighteenth-century England dating back to the Exclusion Crisis of the late seventeenth century. Tories were associated the Crown and the Church of England, while the Whigs saw themselves as the defenders of liberty and Parliament. Since the Tories in England were suspected of supporting the Stuart pretender to the Hanoverian throne, that is, of being Jacobites, they had been excluded from high office since the Hanoverian accession in 1714; and thus "Tory" was often a term of abuse. Many English Whigs believed that George III began bringing Tories back into office in the 1760s.

338.14   the fourteenth of August]   The day in 1765 that mobs threatened Andrew Oliver, the designated stamp agent, hanging him in effigy, destroying his office, and forcing him to resign. Oliver was related to Thomas Hutchinson by marriage and later became lieutenant-governor of the province. Adams recorded his immediate reactions to the events of August 14, 1765 in a diary entry of the following day, in what appears to be a draft for a newspaper letter, though no such publication has been found. It reads as follows:

I hope it will give no offence, to enquire into the Grounds and Reasons of the strange Conduct of Yesterday and last Night, at Boston. Is there any Evidence, that Mr. Oliver ever wrote to the Ministry, or to any Body in England any unfavourable Representations, of the People of this Province? Has he ever placed the Character of the People, their Manners, their Laws, their Principles in Religion or Government, their submission to order and Magistracy, in a false Light?

Is it known that he ever advised the Ministry to lay internal Taxes upon Us? That he ever solicited the office of Distributer of Stamps? or that he has ever done any Thing to injure the People, or to incur their Displeasure, besides barely accepting of that office? If there is no Proof at all of any such Injury done to the People by that Gentleman, has not the blind, undistinguishing Rage of the Rabble done him, irreparable Injustice? To be placed,

only in Pageantry, in the most conspicuous Part of the Town, with such ig-
nominous Devices around him, would be thought severity enough by any
Man of common sensibility: But to be carried thro the Town, in such insolent Tryumph and burned on an Hill, to have his Garden torn in Pieces, his
House broken open, his furniture destroyed and his whole family thrown
into Confusion and Terror, is a very attrocious Violation of the Peace and of
dangerous Tendency and Consequence.

But on the other Hand let us ask a few Questions. Has not his Honour
the Lieutenant Governor discovered to the People in innumerable Instances,
a very ambitious and avaricious Disposition? Has he not grasped four of the
most important offices in the Province into his own Hands? Has not his
Brother in Law Oliver another of the greatest Places in Government? Is not
a Brother of the Secretary, a Judge of the Superiour Court? Has not that
Brother a son in the House? Has not the secretary a son in the House, who
is also a Judge in one of the Counties? Did not that son marry the Daughter
of another of the Judges of the Superiour Court? Has not the Lieutenant
Governor a Brother, a Judge of the Pleas in Boston? and a Namesake and
near Relation who is another Judge? Has not the Lieutenant Governor a near
Relation who is Register of his own Court of Probate, and Deputy Secretary?
Has he not another near Relation who is Clerk of the House of Representatives? Is not this amazing ascendancy of one Family, Foundation sufficient on which to erect a Tyranny? Is it not enough to excite Jealousies
among the People?

Quære further. Has not many a Member of both Houses, laboured to the
Utmost of his Ability, to obtain a Resolution to send home some Petitions
and Remonstrances to the King, Lords and Commons vs. the Impositions
they saw were about to be laid upon Us. Has not the Lieutenant Governor
all along been the very Gentleman who has prevented it, and wiped out every
spirited, if not every sensible Expression out of those Petitions?

Quære further. When the Court was about to chose an Agent, did not the
Governor, Lieutenant Governor, and Secretary, make Use of all their Influence to procure an Election for Mr. Jackson? Was not Mr. Jackson [ ] a secretary to Mr. Greenville? Was not Mr. Greenville, the Author of the late
Measures relative to the Colonies? Was not Mr. Jackson an Agent and a particular Friend of the Governor? Was not all this considering the natural Jealousy of Mankind, enough to excite suspicions among the Vulgar, that all
these Gentlemen were in a Combination, to favour the Measures of the Ministry, at least to prevent any Thing from being done here to discourage the
Minister from his rash, mad, and Dogmatical Proceedings?

Would it not be Prudence then in those Gentlemen at this alarming Conjuncture, and a Condescention that is due to the present Fears and Distresses
of the People, (in some manner consistent with the Dignity of their stations
and Characters,) to remove these Jealousies from the Minds of the People by
giving an easy solution of these Difficulties?

338.20   on the fifth of March]   The date of the Boston Massacre of 1770, which was marked every year by an oration until the commemorations ceased with independence and were replaced by Fourth of July celebrations.

339.15–16   One Mr. Mein was forced to fly the country] John Mein, Tory printer of the *Boston Chronicle*, used his newspaper to attack the Whigs and the nonimportation agreements. On October 28, 1769 he was assaulted by a Boston mob and, fearing for his safety, he sailed a month later for England on a British warship.

342.27–28   who voted with Cassius and who with Lucius] Probably referring to Caius Cassius Longinus, who urged the execution of Lucius Sergius Catilina (that is, Catiline) in the Conspiracy of Catiline.

343.39–40   The advices continually . . . thus appointed agent] Leonard is here referring to Benjamin Franklin, who in 1770 was hired by the Massachusetts House of Representative as its agent in London. In December 1772 Franklin sent to the House letters written by Thomas Hutchinson that created a crisis in England and the North American colonies. On January 29, 1774, Franklin was excoriated and denounced as a thief by Solicitor General Alexander Wedderburn before the Privy Council.

346.36   Causes of *meum et tuum*] Ordinary court cases over ownership of property, over what's mine and what's thine.

347.6   One Malcolm, a loyal subject] John Malcolm, a customs official, was mobbed in January 1774, during which he struck a person with his cane and threatened others with a cutlass. Adams in his "Novanglus" essay of February 20, 1775 wrongly accuses Malcolm of striking a boy with a cutlass. "Massachusettensis" describes Malcolm's punishment.

349.12   *Magna est veritas et prevalebit.*] Truth is mighty, and it shall prevail.

350.2   *James Burgh*] James Burgh (1714–1775) was a British radical Whig whose *Political Disquisitions, or an Enquiry into Public Errors, Defects, and Abuses*, 3 vols. (London, 1774) was very popular among American Whigs; it called for freedom of speech and an expanded suffrage. Volumes one and two are in the *CJAL*.

350.36–37   Our Alva Gage] Comparing General Thomas Gage with the Duke of Alva, the Spanish officer who suppressed the Dutch revolt in the Low Countries in the sixteenth century.

355.37–38   *aut Cæsar aut nullus.*] Either Cæsar or no one, that is, all or nothing.

358.19–20   Accordingly the blockade act was passed] The Boston Port Act, one of the Coercive Acts.

363.31   *arcana imperii.*] state secrets.

375.9   *felo de se*]   Suicidal.

379.7   a pamphlet, published in 1764]   James Otis Jr., *The Rights of the Colonies Asserted and Proved* (Boston, 1774).

380.8   The Pennsylvania Farmer, who took the lead]   John Dickinson, *Letters from a Farmer in Pennsylvania* (Philadelphia, 1768).

380.34   *ignis fatuus*]   Will-o'-the-wisp.

384.35   *Nil desperandum . . . Nil admirari*]   "Fear not" and "Be surprised by nothing."

385.5–6   In the character of Philanthrop]   Jonathan Sewall had written in the press under this pseudonym in 1766–1767. See note 327.1.

385.9   In the character of Philalethes]   Sewall had used this pseudonym in 1773. Adams obviously believed that Sewall was Massachusettensis.

388.8   The Veteran]   Robert Prescott, *A Letter from a Veteran, to the Officers of the Army Encamped at Boston* (New York, 1774).

388.38–39   The author of a "Friendly Address to all reasonable Americans"]   Thomas Bradbury Chandler, *A Friendly Address to All Reasonable Americans* (New York, 1774). Chandler (1726–1790), Yale 1745, was an Anglican minister and passionate Loyalist.

389.1   Hobbs and Filmer]   Thomas Hobbes (1588–1679), English political philosopher whose famous book *Leviathan* argued the need for a strong central authority in order to avoid the evils of discord and civil war; Sir Robert Filmer (1588–1653), English political theorist who defended the divine right of monarchy.

389.2   *ore rotundo*]   Eloquently.

397.9   Andross, Randolph, Dudley]   Edmund Andros (1637–1714), Edward Randolph (1632–1703), and Joseph Dudley (1647–1720), much hated figures in Massachusetts history for their roles in abrogating the original charter in 1684.

397.13   Governor Shirley]   William Shirley (1694–1771) served as governor of Massachusetts from 1741 to 1757.

397.22   Russell, Paxton, Ruggles]   Charles Russell (1739–1780) register of the vice-admiralty court; Charles Paxton (1708–1788), royal custom commissioner and a resolute enforcer of the Navigation Acts; Timothy Ruggles (1711–1795), a delegate to the Stamp Act Congress in 1765 who had refused to sign the Congress's statement of principles.

397.36   The remarks are these.]   What follow are quotations from Franklin's letters to Governor Shirley, written 1754 and published in London in 1766, and excerpted in James Burgh, *Political Disquisitions*.

399.32–33   Mr. Pownal was placed in his stead.]   Thomas Pownall (1722–1805) was royal governor of Massachusetts between 1757 and 1760. See also notes 238.32–33 and 275.24.

399.38   Mr. Pratt]   See note 30.19.

400.3   Mr. Bernard]   Sir Francis Bernard (1712–1799), royal governor of Massachusetts from 1760 to 1769. See also note 68.1.

400.35   its chief conductor]   William Pitt the elder (1708–1778) directed the strategy that won the Seven Years' War against France.

400.38   the British financier]   George Grenville (1712–1770), the minister who was responsible for the Sugar and Stamp Acts.

401.4–5   of his own select letters]   Francis Bernard, *Select Letters on the Trade and Government of America; and the Principles of Law and Polity, Applied to the American Colonies* (London, 1774). The *Letters* were written between 1763 and 1764, and the *Principles* in 1764. In them Bernard laid out plans for remodeling the colonial governments, including proposing that the king appoint a nobility for life to sit in the colonial councils.

409.37   Doubtless many of the rebels, in the year 1745]   Referring to the Jacobite rebellion when Charles Edward Stuart, the Young Pretender (1720–1788), invaded Britain and sought to gain the throne for his father James Stuart. The Jacobites were defeated in the battle of Culloden in 1746, which effectively ended the Stuart threat to the throne.

412.23–24   *furor arma ministrat*]   Rage provides arms.

412.25   *quo animo*]   With what intention.

413.9   Abdiel like]   Extremely faithful and obedient, like the character in Milton's *Paradise Lost*.

415.20   Yet the printer was not molested for printing]   Referring to John Mein, the Tory printer. See note 339.15–16.

418.28   good Mr. Ogden]   Robert Ogden (1716–1787) of New Jersey, one of the delegates to the Stamp Act Congress; he refused to sign the Congress's statement because it denied the authority of Parliament over the colonies.

420.33–34   the revolution.]   That is, the Glorious Revolution of 1688–1689, when James II fled to France and a convention declared William of Orange and his wife Mary their sovereigns.

422.6–7   two known friends of America]   Referring to Henry Cruger (1739–1827), a New York merchant residing in England, and Edmund Burke (1729–1797), the Rockingham Whig who opposed Lord North's colonial policies; both Cruger and Burke were elected to Parliament from Bristol in November 1774 in place of two candidates who had supported North's government.

422.11–12   the best Bishop . . . a Judge . . . the greatest statesman]
Respectively: Jonathan Shipley (1714–1788), Bishop of St. Asaph, who voted
against the Massachusetts Government Act; Charles Pratt, Earl of Camden,
who as Lord Chancellor was noted for his protection of the rights of John
Wilkes; and William Pitt.

423.18   *quod principi placuit legis habet vigorem*]   What pleases the prince
has the strength of law.

427.10–11   The association . . . laid before the public]   A reference to
the association that Timothy Ruggles was trying to form among the Loyalists
in Boston to counteract the Continental Association.

429.25   *foro conscientiæ*]   The tribunal of conscience.

432.40   The Quebec bill]   The Quebec Act, signed on June 22, 1774, established a civil government for Quebec without an elected legislature,
retained French Canadian law in civil matters, granted the Roman Catholic
Church the right to collect tithes, and potentially extended the border
of Quebec to the Mississippi and Ohio rivers. To many Protestant New
Englanders the act suggested a new and frightening model for colonial
administration.

435.3–9   Cur tamen hos tu . . . in pectore testem]   Why should you
think that they have escaped punishment, whom with a mind conscious of
the dreadful deed are held awestruck and cut to pieces with a noiseless whip,
their soul as torturer shaking the hidden lash? Indeed, theirs is a harsh and far
more cruel punishment than those which both severe Caedicius and
Rhadamanthus invent, to carry about in one's heart both night and day one's
own witness (Juvenal, *Satura*, 13:192–198).

440.7   The resolves of the House of Burgesses of Virginia]   A set of resolves, introduced by Patrick Henry and adopted by the Virginia assembly on
May 31, 1765, that declared the right of the colonists to be taxed only by their
elected representatives. False reports published in other colonies, including
Massachusetts, had made the resolves even more radical than they were.

446.38   It is a saying of Machiavel]   The following quote of Niccolo
Machiavelli (1469–1527) is from his *Discourses on Livy* (1512–1517); the phrase
was also cited by Algernon Sidney (1623–1683), the seventeenth-century English republican writer, in his posthumously published *Discourses Concerning
Government* (1698), which is in the *CJAL*.

453.13–14   Hampden, Russell, Sydney, Somers, Holt, Tillotson, Burnet,
Hoadley]   John Hampden (1653–1696), William, Lord Russell (1639–1683)
and Algernon Sidney were arrested in 1683 for their part in a conspiracy
against the Stuarts and Russell and Sidney were executed; John, Lord Somers
(1651–1716) sponsored the Bill of Rights of 1689; Sir John Holt (1642–1710)
was Lord Chief Justice of England and Wales (see also note 226.1–2); John
Tillotson (see also note 114.5–6); Gilbert Burnet (1643–1715) was a participant

in and historian of the Glorious Revolution and, like Benjamin Hoadly (1676–1761), was a prominent Whig bishop whom the colonists often cited.

455.7–8   the agent]   Benjamin Franklin.

457.2   Wedderburn's ribaldry]   Refers to the vicious attack on Franklin by Solicitor General Alexander Wedderburn in the committee room known as the cockpit at Westminster in London on January 29, 1774. See note 343.39–40.

461.6   the Septennial House]   Unlike the English Parliament, many of the colonial assemblies had no limit on how long they might sit, which often became a grievance. New York adopted a septennial act in 1743, which was the same seven-year limit governing the sitting of the House of Commons.

466.14   his successor]   Gen. Thomas Gage succeeded Hutchinson in May 1774 and continued as governor until October 1775.

468.9   judge Russell]   Chambers Russell (1713–1766), long a judge and member of the Massachusetts House of Representatives.

468.15–16   the support of the administration of justice, &c.]   In 1772 the Crown decided to pay the salaries of royal officials in Massachusetts out of the Townshend duties.

468.22   the new act of parliament.]   The Massachusetts Government Act, one of the Coercive Acts, which gave sheriffs appointed by the governor the authority to select jurors.

470.30   Malcom]   See note 347.6.

479.31–32   *Sed tempora mutantur et nos mutamur in illis.*]   Indeed the times change and we change with them.

481.15   Grotius]   Hugo Grotius, *The Rights of War and Peace, in Three Books* (London, 1738), 54; in the *CJAL.*

481.24   Sidney's discourses upon government]   Algernon Sidney, *Discourses Concerning Government* (Edinburgh, 1750), I: 309, 311, 312–14, 316–17; in the *CJAL.* Emphases in quotations are Adams's.

484.3–4   Puffendorf's law . . . and Barbeyrac's note]   Samuel von Pufendorf, *Of the Law of Nature and Nations . . . to Which Are Added All the Large Notes of Mr. Barbeyrac* (London, 1729), 720–21; in the *CJAL.* Jean Barbeyrac (1674–1744) was a French authority on jurisprudence.

486.22   Mr. LeClerk]   Jean Leclerc (1657–1736), Swiss theologian, philosopher, and translator of the works of John Locke. His works are in the *CJAL.*

486.31   Dr. Sachevaril]   Henry Sacheverell (1674–1742), a High Church Anglican clergyman, was impeached by Parliament in 1709 for printing a sermon in which he upheld the doctrine of passive obedience and accused the

Whig ministry of encouraging and protecting Dissenters within the government and the Church of England. In 1710 Sacheverell was convicted and prohibited from preaching for three years.

493.33 his son writes in defence of the Quebec bill] Sir Thomas Bernard, *An Appeal to the Public, Stating and Considering the Objections to the Quebec Bill* (London, 1774).

497.30 Had Don Juan Padilla, or his wife] Don de Padilla and his wife Maria Pacheco were Castilian leaders of the sixteenth-century revolt of the Communeros against Charles I of Spain, better known as Charles V of the Holy Roman Empire.

497.34 Hear the opinion of Dr. Robertson] William Robertson, *The History of the Reign of the Emperor Charles V*, 3 vols. (London, 1769), 2: 185; in the *CJAL*.

505.39–40 a pamphlet published in 1765, Mr. Otis] James Otis Jr., *A Vindication of the British Colonies, against the Aspersions of the Halifax Gentleman* (Boston, 1765).

506.3 Tyro] Novice.

510.13 Irritat, mulcet falsis terroribus implet ut magus.] It angers, soothes, fills with false terrors like a wizard.

513.38 Harrington tells us, Oceana p. 43.] James Harrington, *The Oceana and Other Works. Collected . . . by John Toland*, 3d ed. (London, 1747); in the *CJAL*.

536.5 *Casus omissus*] A case omitted; a matter not addressed.

536.17 *Ne exeat Regno.*] Let him not leave the kingdom.

536.18–19 1 Hawk.] William Hawkins, *A Treatise of Pleas of the Crown*, 4th ed. (London, 1762), in the *CJAL*.

536.33 nor of Passachus, or Massachusett.] Indian chiefs.

537.14 to catch Cardinal Pole.] Reginald Pole (1500–1558), cardinal and Archbishop of Canterbury, who opposed Henry VIII's divorce and his efforts to assume leadership of the church in England.

540.40 This was the meaning of Dudley] Joseph Dudley, governor of Massachusetts from May to December of 1686, was hated because he participated in the voiding of the colony's original charter.

543.30–31 a pamphlet, written and printed in the year 1764] Oxenbridge Thacher, *The Sentiments of a British American* (Boston, 1764).

543.36–37 *Ergo quid refert . . . dum portem meas.*] What difference does it make to me whom I serve, so long as I carry my pack?

548.5   "Wales was always feudatory to the kingdom of England."]   Quoting Sir John Comyns, *A Digest of the Laws of England*, 5:626. This quote is repeated at 548.17–18, followed by three more paragraphs from the same work.

548.19–20   1 Roll. 247-2 Roll. 29]   Henry Rolle, *An Abridgment of the Common Law* (London 1668).

548.25–26   *tanquam partem corporis ejusdem*]   As part of the same body.

548.29   *jure feudali, et non jure proprietatis.*"]   By feudal right, not by right of property, or purchase.

549.2–11   *Edwardus dei gratia Rex Angliæ* . . . annexuit et univit.]   Edward by the grace of God King England, Lord of Ireland and Duke of Aquitaine to all his subjects, etc., in Wales. The divine providence, which is unerring in its government, among other gifts of its dispensation, wherewith it has vouchsafed to distinguish us and our realm of England, has now, all obstacles having been overcome, of its favor wholly and entirely transferred under our dominion the land of Wales, with its inhabitants, heretofore subject to us in feudal right, and has annexed and united the same unto the crown of our realm, as a part of the same body.

549.32–550.4   "*Nos itaque* . . . *in forma subscripta.*"]   "We therefore being desirous that the aforementioned land, etc., like others subject to our power, should be governed with due order, as that the people or inhabitants of those lands who have submitted themselves absolutely to our will, and whom we have so accepted, should be treated under fixed laws and customs, we have caused to be rehearsed before us and the magnates of our realm the laws and customs hitherto in use in those parts, which being carefully heard and fully understood we have, with the advice of the aforementioned magnates, abolished some of them, allowed some and corrected some. We have also commanded certain others to be added and ordained and these, etc., we wish to be observed in the form underwritten."

550.8–13   *Et ideo vobis* . . . *viderimus expedire.*]   We therefore order you that from henceforth you steadfastly observe them completely. In such a way that whenever and as often as it shall be our pleasure, we may declare, interpret, enlarge, or diminish the aforementioned statues and the several parts of them, according to our free will and as to us shall seem expedient for the security of us and our lands aforementioned.

555.36–37   the regiment of royal Welch fusileers.]   The 23rd Regiment of Foot, or Royal Welsh Fusiliers, was deployed in Boston in 1774 to enforce the Coercive Acts.

556.10   *Mercy Otis Warren*]   Poet, dramatist, and historian Warren (1728–1814) was the sister of James Otis Jr. and wife of James Warren. In a January 30, 1775 letter she asked Adams how far was it justifiable for satirist to hold up a criminal character to public derision.

559.19–20   pamphlet written in England . . . republished here]   William Knox, *The Interest of the Merchants and Manufacturers in the Present Contest with the Colonies Stated and Considered* (Boston, 1774), 6–9.

562.9   also another pamphlet lately published]   Henry Barry, *The Advantages Which America Derives from her Commerce, Connexion, and Dependence on Britain* (New York, 1775).

565.11   a recent instance of this kind of petition]   The Continental Congress's Petition to the King of October 26, 1774.

566.12   Grotius, Phileareine]   Presumably pseudonyms of writers in the Massachusetts press.

567.29–30   *Vide* a pamphlet published by one of the delegates]   See *A Candid Examination of the Mutual Claims of Great Britain and the Colonies* (New York, 1775), by the Philadelphia Loyalist, Joseph Galloway.

568.9   "the colonists are entitled to an exclusive power . . . provincial legislatures."]   Quoted from the Declaration and Resolve of the Continental Congress of October 14, 1774, from which Massachusettensis often quotes.

570.11   Such is the resolve of the 27th of September]   An early resolve of the Continental Congress that led to the adoption of the Continental Association on October 20, 1774, which organized the non-importation of British goods and provided for its enforcement by local committees.

575.11–12   Ellismore, Bacon, Hide, Hobart, Crook, and Coke]   Sir Thomas Egerton, Baron Ellesmere (1540–1617); Sir Francis Bacon (1561–1626); Sir Nicholas Hyde (d. 1631); Sir Henry Hobart (d. 1625); Sir John Croke (1553–1620); Sir Edward Coke (1552–1634).

575.39   *proprium quarto . . . et semper.*]   Property in the fourth part to the King, applying to each and all at all times.

576.3   a *seigniorie in grosse*]   A lord without a manor and thus unable to keep a court.

576.17   Moore's reports]   *Cases Collected and Reported . . . per Sir Francis Moore* (London, 1663).

578.4   Foster's crown law]   Sir Michael Foster, *A Report of Some Proceedings on the Commission of Oyer and Terminer . . . and of Other Crown Cases* (London, 1762).

579.30   Poyning's law]   Passed by the Irish parliament in 1494, Poyning's law required all Irish statutes to have the prior approval of the English Crown.

580.8   In Salk. 411.]   William Salkeld, *Reports of Cases Adjudged in the Court of King's Bench from the Revolution to the Tenth Year of Q. Anne*, 3d. ed. (London, 1731); in the *CJAL.*

580.24   Vid. And. 115.]   Probably Sir Edmund Anderson, *Les Reports du treserudite Edmund Anderson . . . Chief Justice del Common-bank* (London, 1664–1665).

580.29   Vid. Vaugh. 405.]   Probably Sir John Vaughn, *The Reports and Arguments of . . . Sir John Vaughn* (London, 1677).

580.40   Davis 36.]   Probably Sir John Davies, *A Report of Cases and Matters in Law, Resolved and Adjudged in the King's Courts in Ireland* (Dublin, 1762, orig. publ. 1615).

583.2   2d. P. Williams]   William Peere Williams, *Reports of Cases Argued and Determined in the High Court of Chancery and of Some Special Cases Adjudged in the Court of King's Bench* (London, 1740).

584.14   *hic labor hoc opus est*]   This is the problem, this is the hard task.

585.15   The writer from Hampshire county]   Joseph Hawley (1723–1788), Yale 1742, radical Whig from western Massachusetts who instead of attending the Continental Congress wrote an agenda for the Congress entitled "Brief Hints."

586.8–9   *procul a Jove a fulmine procul*]   He who is far from Jove is far from the thunderbolt.

586.21   Haldimand]   Frederick Haldimand (1718–1791), Swiss-born British military officer in command of the troops in New York in 1773. General Gage ordered him and his troops to Boston in the wake of the premature militia uprising in September 1774 (see note 319.9–10); he remained in command of the troops while Gage acted as governor of Massachusetts.

590.5–6   *rescriptum principis . . . de coheredibus*]   Rescript of the ruler, entitled a statue of Ireland concerning co-heirs.

590.7–8   Vid. Ruffheads statutes at large, V. I. 15.]   Owen Ruffhead, *The Statutes at Large from Magna Charta to the Union of Great Britain and Ireland*, 18 vols. (London, 1769–1800).

590.8   Mr. Cay]   John Cay and Owen Ruffhead, *The Statutes at Large from Magna Charta to the 13th Year of King George 3d*, 9 vols. (London, 1758–1773).

590.16–25   *Rex dilecto . . . usitatem sit*]   The King to his faithful and beloved Gerard son of Maurice, justiciar [the king's chief political and judicial officer] of Ireland, greeting. Whereas certain knights of the parts of Ireland, lately coming to us, have shown us that, etc. And the said knights have asked to be assured how in a like case it has been used heretofore in our realm of England.

590. 22–25   *Et Ideo vobis . . . teneri, fac*]   And therefore we order you to cause to be proclaimed and firmly kept in our land of Ireland the aforemen-

tioned customs in the case put that be used within our realm of England as aforementioned.

591.17–23   *"Et memorandum . . . teneri faciat."*]   "It is to be remembered that this statute, exactly as it is, was sent to Ireland, attested by the King at Kennington on August 14 in the 22nd year of his reign, and John Wogan, the justiciar of Ireland, was ordered to cause the statute to be read throughout Ireland, in places which he thought proper, and to cause it to be publicly announced and strictly held."

592.1   *"volumus et firmiter precipimus,"*]   "We wish and firmly command."

593.20   *the statute of H.* 8]   This statute, passed during the reign of Henry VIII in 1543, allowed offenses of treason committed outside the realm to be tried in England. Adams is referring sarcastically to England's attempt to try Americans by this ancient statute.

597.9–10   by our books, Fleta]   Citations are from Latin textbook of English called *Fleta* and from Edmund Plowden, *The Commentaries, or Reports of Edmund Plowden . . .* (1741).

597.13–15   king Edgar, Britanniæ . . . Britanniæ Monarcha]   Edgar, King of Britain; Ethelred, Emperor of all Albion by the providence of God; Edred, Monarch of Great Britain.

597.19   *quia moratur in Wallia*]   Because he is delayed in Wales.

598.11–21   *Ego Edgarus . . . devotus disposui, &c.*]   I Edgar, King of the English, emperor and lord of all the islands of the ocean which adjoin Britain, give thanks to the omnipotent God, my King, who so expanded and exalted my kingdom over that of my fathers, etc. His gracious divinity granted me, with the power of the English, the entire rule of the islands of the ocean, etc. Norway with its most savage kings [he has enabled me] to bring under English rule, and the greatest part of Ireland with its most noble city of Dublin, wherefore I have tended to exalt the glory and praise of Christ in my kingdom and devoutly to grow in his service.

598.26–31   *Hibernia habet . . . Gasconia et Guigan.*]   Ireland has a parliament and they make laws; our statutes do not bind them (which is to be understood unless they be specially named) because they do not send knights to parliament, but their persons are the subjects of the king, like the inhabitants of Calais, Gascony, and Aquitane.

598.35–599.2   *Rex Baronibus . . . ad scaccarium Dublin.*]   The King to the barons, knights, and all the free tenants of L., greeting. You have heard sufficiently, we believe, that when John, of good memory, once King of England, our father, came into Ireland he brought with him legally learned men, by whose common counsel, joined to that of the Irish, he established and promoted English laws in Ireland, so that he left under his seal in the Exchequer in Dublin those laws in writing.

599.27–28   *extra ligeantia regis, regni sui Angliæ*]   Outside the King's realm, his realm of England.

601.24–25   *De communi omnium de Hiberniæ consensu.*]   By the common consent of all the Irish.

602.14   Burrows's reports]   Sir James Burrow, comp. *Reports of Cases Adjudged in the Court of King's Bench since the Death of Lord Raymond . . .* , Part 4, 3 vols. (London, 1756–1766); in the *CJAL*.

602.35–37   *'per quas leges . . . et eorum pares, &c.'*]   'Through what laws and through what usages, the preceding kings of our kingdom had been accustomed [to treat] the kings of Wales and the Welsh barons and their equals and others among the first men and their equals, etc.'

603.8–11   *'Divina providentia . . . et univit.'*]   'Divine providence has converted the Land of Wales, once subject to us in feudal right, to our ownership of property and annexed and united it to the crown of the realm of England as part of the body of the same.'

605.13–14   "*coronæ regni angliæ, tanquam partem corporis ejesdem,*"]   "To the crown of the realm of England as part of the same body." Cf. note 548.25–26.

608.8   'till the exigent]   A special writ commanding the recipient to appear in court on pain of being outlawed for nonappearance.

612.5   In Moore's reports]   *Cases Collected and Reported . . . per Sir Francis Moore* (London, 1663), 804. Cf. note 576.17.

612.24   mandatory or preceptory writs]   Writs commanding an action within the power of the individual served.

SELECTIONS FROM THE AUTOBIOGRAPHY

617.3   Begun Oct. 5. 1802]   Prompted by his son John Quincy, Adams somewhat grudgingly began writing the first part of his autobiography in the fall of 1802. He advanced the story only to his admittance to Harvard in 1751 before abandoning the task. He took it up again on November 6, 1804, and over the next seven months he completed Part One, which carries the story to October 1776.

617.26   on the 19th of October 1735]   By the old style calendar; according to the new style Gregorian calendar adopted by Britain in 1752, it was October 30, which Adams usually regarded as his birthday.

618.25–26   I procured me Cockers]   Edward Cocker's *Decimal Arithmetick . . .* 3d. ed. (London, 1703); in *CJAL*.

620.7   particularly Lock, Hemmenway and Tisdale.]   All members of the class of 1755: Rev. Samuel Locke, president of Harvard, 1770–73; Rev. Moses

Hemmenway, minister at Wells, Maine; and William Tisdale, who dropped out after the first year.

621.35–36   Mr. Bryant the Minister of our Parish] Lemuel Briant (1722–1754), Harvard 1739, was the minister of the First or North Church of Braintree, 1745–53. Arminianism was a Calvinist heresy that suggested that good works could help bring about salvation (see also note 12.26). Briant's wife's leaving him did not help his reputation.

623.21   Morgans Moral Phylosopher] Thomas Morgan, *The Moral Philosopher. In a Dialogue between Philalethes a Christian Deist, and Theophanes a Christian Jew*, 3 vols. (London, 1737–1740); in the *CJAL*.

626.3   Mr. Pratt] Benjamin Pratt was appointed chief justice of New York in 1761.

627.15–16   in his history.] George Richards Minot, *Continuation of the History of the Providence of Massachusetts* (Boston, 1798–1803).

630.26–27   Mr. Paine and I called a meeting] Robert Treat Paine (1731–1814), who became a member of the Continental Congress. See note 21.2.

633.17–18   Mr. Fitch should be appointed] Samuel Fitch (1724–1799), Yale 1742; he became a Loyalist.

633.25–26   I told him . . . unalterably fixed] Thomas Hutchinson in his *History of Massachusetts Bay*, ed. Mayo, 3: 213–14, contends that Adams in the early 1760s was at a loss which side to take, and had joined the opposition only after he had become angry with the government when Gov. Bernard refused to appoint him a justice of the peace.

637.7   Mr. Forrest] James Forrest, a native of Ireland and a prosperous Boston merchant who became a Loyalist.

638.3–4   if they had never offered me any Thing] The bill of costs for the trials forwarded to General Gage recorded a total of £126 paid to Adams and his two co-counsels for the defense of Captain Preston and his men.

638.23   Mr. Bowdoin] James Bowdoin (1726–1790), merchant and later the third governor of the state of Massachusetts.

640.27   Mr. Justice Seward] Jonathan Sayward.

640.31–32   my former Minister Mr. Moody.] Samuel Moody, Harvard 1697, eccentric minister at York, Maine.

Index

over, 234–35, 237–43, 249–50, 272–73,
307, 378–79, 418, 465, 504, 516, 536,
538, 544–45, 553, 568; and British
Constitution, 234, 316, 365, 368, 408,
429, 448, 450, 507–8, 510, 527–28,
539, 596; relation to monarch, 277,
279–80, 367, 370, 524–25, 528, 539,
541–42, 548, 572; and representation
in British Parliament, 126, 277, 366,
368, 398–99, 438–39, 504, 512–13, 522,
526, 528–30, 554, 581; taxation of, 126,
138, 141, 151, 239, 250, 278, 287, 291,
297, 303, 305, 307, 314, 329, 334–36,
370, 379–80, 397–99, 401–4, 419,
422, 434, 438, 442–44, 450–52, 459–
61, 464, 469, 473, 475–79, 487–89,
491, 493, 501, 503–7, 519, 543–44,
546, 563, 573, 632, 643
Columbus, Christopher, 53
Commerce, 75, 178, 353–58, 370, 379,
392–95, 422, 424, 426, 436, 438–39,
442, 449, 475–79, 487, 500, 516,
520–26, 530–31, 533–34, 543–46, 559–
62, 568, 570, 582, 494–96, 642
Committees of correspondence, 308,
360, 419, 496–98
Common law, 29, 37, 54, 82, 126, 224–
27, 230–32, 239, 243, 251–52, 254,
260–61, 272, 284, 340, 342, 402, 410,
418, 422–23, 453, 510, 516, 536–37, 539,
542, 545, 581–82, 594, 596, 607
Commonwealth (Puritan), 523, 532
Commonwealths, 121, 272, 513
Comyns, John, 548
Concord, Mass., 172
Congregationalists, 314, 325
Congress. See Continental Congress
Connaught, 588
Connecticut, 69, 180, 183, 199–203,
307, 393, 521, 525, 528, 641
Connecticut River, 199–200, 394
Conscience, freedom of, 129, 134, 244,
248–49, 572, 645–46
Constantine (the Great), 86
Constitution (British), 90, 134, 152, 155–
56, 161, 215–16, 237, 247, 270, 282–83,
306, 367, 370, 388, 413, 418, 444,
498, 530, 537, 541, 545, 565–66, 571,
585–86, 613, 624, 642; and American
Colonies, 234, 316, 365, 368, 408,
429, 448, 450, 507–8, 510, 527–28,

539, 596; democratic spirit of, 511–13;
and elections, 64, 87; and juries, 159–
60, 193, 572; and laws, 156, 159–61,
191, 237–38, 240–41, 368, 370, 379,
448, 450, 545, 571–72; and legislative
branch, 191, 405; and liberty, 157–58,
241, 250, 339, 389–90, 416–17, 526;
republican spirit of, 463–64, 517;
and taxation, 126, 479, 489, 504, 506
Constitution (Massachusetts), 640
Constitution (New York), 640
Constitution (United States), 640
Constitutions, colonial. See Charters,
colonial
Continental Congress: First, 297, 315–
21, 323–26, 350, 417, 420, 522, 565–71,
573, 640–46
Cooper, Myles: A Friendly Address to
All Reasonable Americans, 388–89
Cooper, Samuel, 180, 190, 203, 219,
289, 636
Cooper, William, 190, 219
Cotton, John, 171
Cotton, Roland, 171
Courts, 138, 171–73, 183, 299–300, 328,
468; admiralty, 126–27, 147, 149, 354,
631; of common pleas, 231, 259;
General, 80, 210–11, 219, 240, 245–
48, 262–63, 290, 328, 342–43, 346–
47, 453, 471, 521; role of, 192–93;
superior, 39, 172, 229, 348, 458–59,
466, 639. See also Judges; Juries
Cranch, Elizabeth, 109
Cranch, Lucy, 208
Cranch, Mary Smith, 47–48, 67, 98,
109
Cranch, Richard, 47–48, 67, 98, 195,
208, 221, 323; letter to, 24–26
Crane, Hannah, 111
Crane, Joseph, 203
Crawford, William, 20
Crew, Randolph, 259
Criminal law, 192
Croke, John, 575
Cromwell, Oliver, 7, 60, 93, 153, 219,
358, 390, 393, 494, 533
Crown Point (fort), 533
Cruger, Henry, 422
Culpeper, Thomas, 239
Cunningham, James, 96–97, 101
Curtenius, Peter T., 308

THE LIBRARY OF AMERICA SERIES

The Library of America fosters appreciation and pride in America's literary heritage by publishing, and keeping permanently in print, authoritative editions of America's best and most significant writing. An independent nonprofit organization, it was founded in 1979 with seed money from the National Endowment for the Humanities and the Ford Foundation.

To subscribe to the series or to order individual copies,
please visit www.loa.org or call (800) 964.5778.

This book is set in 10 point Linotron Galliard,
a face designed for photocomposition by Matthew Carter
and based on the sixteenth-century face Granjon. The paper
is acid-free lightweight opaque and meets the requirements
for permanence of the American National Standards Institute.
The binding material is Brillianta, a woven rayon cloth made
by Van Heek-Scholco Textielfabrieken, Holland. Compo-
sition by Dedicated Business Services. Printing by
Malloy Incorporated. Binding by Dekker Book-
binding. Designed by Bruce Campbell.